STRATEGY
FOR
PERSONAL
FINANCE

STRATEGY FOR PERSONAL FINANCE

THIRD EDITION

LARRY R. LANG

THOMAS H. GILLESPIE
University of Wisconsin, Oshkosh

McGRAW-HILL BOOK COMPANY
New York I St. Louis I San Francisco I Auckland I Bogotá I Hamburg
Johannesburg I London I Madrid I Mexico I Montreal I New Delhi I Panama
Paris I São Paulo I Singapore I Sydney I Tokyo I Toronto

STRATEGY
FOR
PERSONAL
FINANCE

1 2 3 4 5 6 7 8 9 0 D O C D O C 8 9 8 7 6 5 4 3

ISBN 0-07-036288-2

This book was set in Trump Medieval by Black Dot, Inc.
The editors were Patricia A. Mitchell and Gail Gavert;
the designer was Nicholas Krenitsky; the production
supervisor was Leroy A. Young. The cartoons were
drawn by Phil Frank; new drawings were done by J & R
Services, Inc.
R. R. Donnelley & Sons Company was printer and
binder.

Library of Congress Cataloging in Publication Data
Lang, Larry R.
    Strategy for personal finance.

    (McGraw-Hill series in finance)
    Includes index.
    1. Finance, Personal.   I. Gillespie, Thomas H.
II. Title.   III. Series.
HG179.L26 1984   332.024   83-19593
ISBN 0-07-036288-2

CONTENTS

TO THE STUDENT

Welcome to the study of personal financial planning; we are pleased you decided to learn about this rewarding, challenging, and exciting subject. Our objective in *Strategy for Personal Finance* is to prepare you to be a life-long personal finance manager. Each of the book's 21 chapters is specifically tailored to improve and develop your financial decision making skills. After reading them, you will be better able to achieve whatever financial goals you establish for yourself. By developing and improving your decision making skills, we believe you can obtain maximum satisfaction from the dollars you will spend to achieve those personal financial goals. Those skills can also help you avoid the major pitfalls and abuses that continue to challenge all consumers. At the same time, you will learn how to develop an insurance plan for safeguarding the financial resources and income that will be an integral part of your overall personal financial plan. In our opinion, studying the materials in *Strategy for Personal Finance* can benefit you in a very measurable dollar-and-cents way throughout your lifetime.

Throughout *Strategy for Personal Finance* we develop a financial decision model that relies on identifying the costs and benefits of each financial product or service alternative. The book will show you how you can discover and analyze the information you need to make sound financial decisions. The examples and materials used in the text draw on currently available financial products and services. If you modify the decision models, they can also be used to judge new products and services as they are introduced.

IT IS YOUR DECISION

The book strives to help you develop a personal financial plan that is "best" for your objectives, needs, and goals. We don't offer one standard financial plan that says, "Here: go do this and your personal finances will be 'well planned'." Everyone of us has far too many unique needs and far too many special situations to make such an all-purpose, standard financial plan desirable. What you can do is use our financial decision model to develop a personal financial plan specifically tailored to your own objectives, needs, and available resources.

PRACTICING YOUR DECISION MAKING SKILLS

To develop and improve your financial decision making skills, we believ
you need practical, realistic examples that illustrate the decision process i
action. Each chapter contains many examples which show how to analyz
the various costs and benefits associated with the different financi
products and services. When an example is less complex, the steps ar
illustrated through one, or two, annotated equations; for more involve
lengthy examples, the associated costs and benefits are developed in
detailed chapter exhibit. Both have been totally integrated into the chapte
material along with explanations of related points and issues. At the end
every chapter, you will have the opportunity to practice those financi
decision skills you learned in that chapter. First, you will have a series
discussion questions which you can utilize to test your comprehension an
retention of the chapter's material. Next, a series of problems provide
practice on the numerical concepts of the chapter. Finally, a detailed cas
study which creates a hypothetical situation requires both your analytica
and reasoning skills in order to find a solution. We believe practice is a
essential step to becoming a good manager of your personal finances. No
only do you need to know what inputs a particular decision model require
you also need some experience to know how those inputs can be tailored t
match different decision situations.

SPECIAL FEATURES OF THIS BOOK

We believe you will find the following features highly useful to your study
personal finance:

First

The chapters cover a broad range of different personal finance topics. W
believe total planning includes all aspects of your personal finances rangin
from the more frequent decisions (where the dollar amount may be smalle
yet the total is large over an extended period) to the less frequent decisior
(where the dollar amount is large, and therefore the consequences of a
inadequate choice would be very costly).

Second

Each chapter opens with a series of summary statements that discuss th
important concepts for that chapter. We encourage you to read them befor
you begin the chapter.

Third

We limit descriptive information to just what we believe is needed t
provide you with a background in that area.

Fourth

Within each chapter, numerical examples are used extensively to illustrat
the decision model that compares the respective costs and benefits. Actua

computations are illustrated either through several annotated equations, or in a chapter exhibit. As you encounter those, carefully review the material to make certain you understand the concepts being presented.

Fifth

Whenever we first introduce you to a new term or concept, we explain it immediately. To dramatize that point, we have placed the term or concept in **boldface** type. To reinforce those points and concepts, they are listed at the end of the chapter. Upon completing the chapter, use that list to test whether you have mastered the major points within the chapter.

Sixth

Practice is the best way to develop and refine your management skills. There are numerous discussion questions, problems, plus a case study at the end of each chapter for you to practice your management skills. We encourage you to use them all to strengthen your understanding of each chapter's financial concepts.

Seventh

For those who are interested, there is a detailed student workbook to let you further practice your money management skills. It includes a crossword, discussion questions, problems, a case study, and a series of sample test questions for each chapter. For much of this material, you can test your own progress because answers to selected parts of those materials are provided at the end of the workbook.

START YOUR MONEY MANAGEMENT CAREER NOW

We think now is the time to begin your money management training. Certainly, the financial rewards and personal satisfaction from being an astute manager are very large. The role is also challenging because the whole field of personal finance is rapidly changing. New products and services continue to be introduced and existing products and services continue to be revised and repackaged to meet the new challenges and needs of individuals. Furthermore, we believe that by expending a reasonable amount of effort you can acquire the necessary skills to become a good personal finance manager. Of course, you need the motivation to begin your money management career. But the very fact you have enrolled in this course suggests you already have that quality. All that remains is for you to turn to page 1, Chapter 1, and begin. We believe you will find studying this text to be interesting, stimulating, and best of all, financially rewarding. Good luck on your management career.

Larry R. Lang
Thomas H. Gillespie

TO THE INSTRUCTOR

Since the second edition of *Strategy for Personal Finance* was published three years ago, there have been sweeping changes in the field of personal finance. Deregulation of financial institutions has caused sizable changes in that area. For the first time, most major institutions have the authority to offer a complete range of personal financial services. At the same time, deregulation has introduced competition to a group of institutions that were previously restrained by a plethora of federal rules and regulations. During these three years, other financial service organizations, such as mutual funds, have been only too willing to develop new products intended to meet the specific financial needs of individuals. In many cases, that entailed repackaging existing financial products into a form that better served consumers. For example, within the life insurance area, universal life insurance has expanded to the point where it is widely available. It provides yet one more alternative that consumers must include in their financial decision process. The housing area has also changed substantially. The question of whether to own or rent must be carefully reexamined because now ownership typically entails greater sacrifice than ever before. New mortgage alternatives have been developed to assist those who decide to purchase their living unit.

Federal income taxes have not been left untouched. Major tax legislation enacted in 1981 and 1982 has made sweeping changes within this area. Consideration of the tax consequences when making many financial decisions continues to be essential. Within the tax area, we have witnessed the development of several new options that permit individuals to defer income taxes while accumulating funds for long-range financial goals. Universal IRAs and salary reduction plans that an increasing number of companies have begun to offer come immediately to mind here. Tax regulations now have begun to encourage the accumulation of financial assets which reverses what seemed to be the previous practice of discouraging their accumulation. We do not claim that this is an exhaustive list of recent developments in personal finance. Rather, it illustrates that personal financial products and services have changed dramatically and that meant that a new edition of *Strategy for Personal Finance* was essential so we could incorporate recent developments.

LIFE-LONG FINANCIAL MANAGERS

Our principal objective in the third edition of *Strategy for Personal Finance*, as in previous editions, continues to be the preparation of students as life-long personal finance managers. As the range of available financial alternatives expands, the importance of that role increases. We continue to use our three-step approach to presenting financial concepts:

> Discuss why a particular finance topic is important to a student.

> Show the student how to develop a financial decision model that incorporates the costs and benefits associated with a particular financial product or service.

> Show students how they can use the above decision model to assist them with their own personal financial decisions.

When preparing the new edition, we incorporated new financial decision models to handle recently introduced financial products and services. We continue our prior practice of providing extensive discussion questions, problems, and case studies so students can practice their financial management skills.

CHANGES IN THE THIRD EDITION

1   The economic data within each chapter has been updated to reflect current conditions in the respective financial products and services.

2   The material on compound rates of return has been revised to better integrate it into Chapter 1. We have added numerous examples to show how those compound rate of return tables are an essential part of developing a total personal financial plan.

3   The personal budgeting material in Chapter 3 has been simplified so that it is easier for students to follow. Now the budget is used to show how the individual's emergency cash reserve has a central role in the operation of that budget. Throughout the book we continue to refer back to Chapter 3 to stress that a personal budget is an important planning tool in the overall financial management process.

4   Materials on federal income taxes were revised to include changes from the Economic Recovery Tax Act of 1981 as well as the Tax Equity and Fiscal Responsibility Act of 1982. In addition, changes in tax regulations continued to be incorporated right up through mid-1983. We reorganized Chapter 6's presentation to improve the students' understanding of this complex topic. We moved the complex topics of income tax planning to the closing sections of the chapter; students now are given a solid foundation in the basics before encountering those planning concepts.

5   The section on housing has been totally revamped to reflect the changes in this area. The discussion of renting versus owning has been strengthened; non-monetary issues are covered in more detail. A new, simplified cost comparison schedule was developed to answer the monetary question: Should I rent or buy? New options for financing the purchase of a housing unit are included. The advantages and disadvantages of each alternative are discussed.

6   Materials on Social Security have been updated and simplified. First, the presentation is now shortened and simplified. Second, all materials have been updated to include changes that resulted from the sweeping 1983 federal legislation that was intended to revive and revamp the system. Third, the materials on the mechanics of indexing prior years' earnings is now in an appendix; now the instructor can decide whether or not to cover that material.

7   Chapter 14 on life insurance has been revised. The major types of life insurance (including universal life) are discussed; the strengths and weaknesses of each type are reviewed. Guidelines have been developed to help students select the right type of insurance. Materials on the "needs approach" to estimating life insurance requirements have been revised. Complete numerical examples show how to use that technique.

8   A numerical procedure for estimating disability insurance needs has been developed for Chapter 15.

9   Chapter 18 on fixed-return investment vehicles discusses investment options, including the new deregulated instruments that financial institutions can now offer. The new variable return investment options are also discussed.

10   Chapter 20 on mutual funds has been completely revised. First, we strengthened and expanded the discussion of the hows and whys of mutual fund operation. The strengths and weaknesses of the major types of funds are discussed. Guidelines have been provided to help students select a suitable fund, or funds.

11   Retirement and estate planning is consolidated into a single chapter. The advantages and restrictions of the currently available tax-deferred retirement options—IRA, Keogh, and salary reduction agreements—are explored. For retirement planning, we developed a worksheet to help estimate the likely sources of future retirement income and how extensively to use the tax-deferred investment options. Estate planning recognizes the sharply lower federal taxes that now apply to all but the largest estates.

PEDAGOGICAL FEATURES
Suitable Courses

This book is designed for use in a one-semester or a one-quarter introductory course such as:

1   Undergraduate personal finance course at both 4-year and 2-year colleges and universities.

2   Undergraduate consumer economics course at 2-year and 4-year colleges and universities.

3   Family management course at 2-year and 4-year colleges and universities.

4   Personal finance course offered as a continuing education or adult education course.

Overall Organization

The 21 chapters are arranged in five major sections. The first section provides background and basic introductory materials to prepare and equip students for their role as life-long financial decision makers. The second section discusses the key points in managing their income. The third analyzes the benefits and costs of large consumer expenditures. Insurance coverage is the central thrust of the fourth section. The fifth discusses the investment alternatives currently available for individuals to build for their financial future. *Strategy for Personal Finance* closes with a chapter on retirement planning and estate planning.

Completing the Chapters

While the material has been organized in what we consider a logical sequence, the chapters can be rearranged to suit a particular instructor's preference. The material within each chapter is self-contained, so one can generally cover any chapter out of sequence. The self-contained feature also means an instructor can drop one or more chapters if desired. Instructors who want to emphasize a particular topic or topics will find the book to be very flexible; time spent emphasizing particular topics in more detail can be recovered by eliminating entire chapters if necessary.

Given the broad topical coverage and the extensive end-of-chapter materials, the text should readily fill the available time in a one-semester or a one-quarter course.

Organization of Individual Chapters

Each time a new term or concept is introduced in a chapter it is shown in **boldface** type, and we immediately explain it or provide an example to illustrate its meaning. Numerical examples are used extensively throughout every chapter of the book to illustrate the benefits and costs of the different personal financial decisions. When the example is fairly short, we use a series of annotated equations to show the steps involved in any computation. On longer, more involved examples, we provide a worksheet in a chapter exhibit to show the computations. In addition, charts, graphs, tables, and cartoons are used wherever possible to convey the different points. We are convinced that good visual displays improve the readability and teachability of the material.

MATERIALS WITHIN EACH CHAPTER

Learning Objectives and Chapter Summaries Each chapter begins with a series of short summaries that outline the major points the student should learn from that chapter. At the end of the chapter, there is a list of key words and phrases that were introduced in the chapter. There is also a chapter summary that reemphasizes the essential points from the chapter through a series of succinct summary statements.

End-of-Chapter Materials The third edition continues and expands on our previous practice of including problems at the end of each chapter. These give students an opportunity to practice their analytical and financial decision making skills. There is also a series of discussion questions covering the material from the chapter. Last, there is a case study which provides the students with a simulated situation where they must analyze a more complex set of the details to arrive at a conclusion. We believe our end-of-chapter materials are the best of any current text.

Student Workbook We have prepared a student workbook to accompany *Strategy for Personal Finance*. The workbook has been extensively revised. We continue the large format that we first used in the second edition so that students can work most of the material directly in the book. We also provide answers to many of the exercises in the workbook so that it is largely self-correcting.

A crossword puzzle leads off each chapter; it is based on the key words and important phrases from that chapter. Next comes a series of discussion questions drawn from the material in the chapter. A separate problem section is next. Some of the problems have partial worksheets, or forms, to help the student through the necessary computations; this can substantially enhance the self-correcting, supporting role the workbook should play. A case study is next. Since it is different from the case in the text, it can be an alternative or a supplement to the text. Finally, there are true and false and multiple-choice questions; answers to these questions are provided. These exercises provide a vehicle for a student to check his or her understanding of the material in the chapter.

We believe the new revised student workbook provides excellent support that can assist students in their understanding of the material. The workbook's heavy emphasis on self-correcting exercises make it suitable in a wide range of classroom situations. It can be used by instructors who spend a considerable amount of class time on the workbook as well as by those who have only limited time to devote to the workbook.

ACKNOWLEDGMENTS

Many people have participated in the preparation of the third edition of *Strategy for Personal Finance*. We would like to express our appreciation to the following reviewers of the manuscript: Brenda Hall, Weber State College; Catherine King, Campbell College; Mary Mennis, University of

Wisconsin, Madison; Nancy Spillman, Los Angeles Trade-Technical College; Paul Asabere, Bentley College; Jeanette Klosterman, Hutchison Community College; and Rick Thompson, Juniata College.

We would like to thank Gail Gavert, Area Editing Supervisor, for her essential service of transforming our draft into a completed book. Thanks to Tom Herzing for his excellent work on all aspects of the manuscript. Thanks also to our excellent cartoonist, Phil Frank. Reviewing Phil's sketches was positively enjoyable. We would also like to express our appreciation for the superb services of our typists, Donna Tritt and Effie Orth; they turned the draft into readable pages. We also very much appreciated the support and assistance of all the individuals at McGraw-Hill who worked on this book.

Larry R. Lang
Thomas H. Gillespie

PART

1

INTRODUCTION

CHAPTER

1

PERSONAL AND FINANCIAL PLANNING

THE need for careful money man-

agement has never been greater. Daily, we are confronted with news stories of price increases, shortages, and other distressing economic information. These factors have produced a situation in which most people find that their income is insufficient for the things they would like to do. In many cases, however, insufficient income is only part of the problem. Poor spending decisions provide the other part. Certainly, anybody offered a pay raise of $1000 or $2000 per year would not turn it down. Yet, many people waste this amount every year because of careless financial planning and unwise buying and investing. You may not be able to get a raise of $1000 this year, but you might be able to save as much by more careful planning.

This chapter will outline a framework for personal financial planning. Each of the topics mentioned here will be discussed in detail in later chapters. The purpose of this chapter is to provide an overview of the book and to make the point that you *must* first set goals for yourself and then make financial decisions to achieve those goals. Without an overall plan, the chances for attaining your goals are poor.

THE PLANNING PROCESS

Planning is the process of setting goals and identifying actions to achieve the goals. Total planning involves an understanding of the interrelationship between short-term and long-term goals. Planning concentrates on how to manage income and expenditures so that the specified goals will be met. The need for coordinating short-term decisions with long-term goals is crucial. For example, many people have as a long-term goal the accumulation of a reasonable amount of money. And, for most people, that goal can be realized only over an extended time period. However, the money needed to achieve the goal must be made available by careful short-term planning.

Exhibit 1-1 depicts the total **financial planning process.** That process is divided into five stages which will each be discussed in the next sections

Stage 1: Identify Your Available Income

The first planning stage is to identify what income you have available. Some potential income sources are wages, salaries, returns on investments, gifts and inheritances. While this step may seem obvious, many people do not take the time to identify the amount and the sources of their income. And you can't do respectable planning without first asking yourself: How much income do I have for my planning process?

Some of your total income will not be available for spending or saving, however, because it goes to pay for unavoidable things such as federal and state income taxes, Social Security contributions, health insurance premiums, and contributions to pension plans. Consequently, your financial plan should be based on your available income.

We define **available income** as *total income minus essential deductions,* such as those just named.

Stage 2: Establish Your Financial Goals

Many people never stop and ask themselves: What do I want from my money? Or, stated another way: What financial goals have I set for myself? Unless you set some goals, it is impossible to measure your progress toward

EXHIBIT 1-1

Total financial planning process.

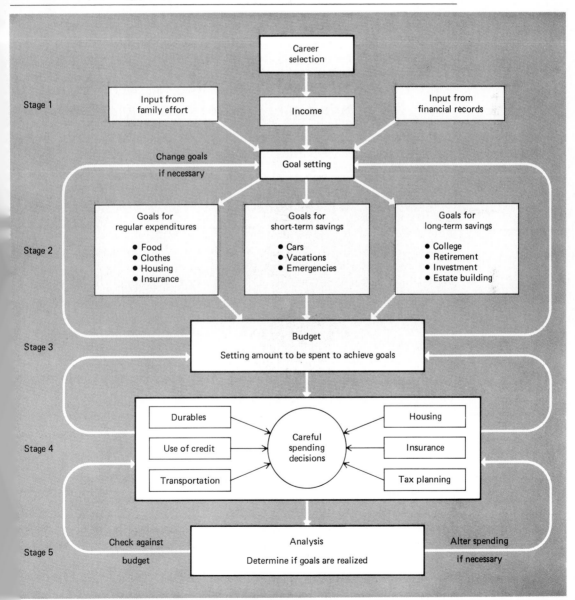

achieving your objectives. In fact, without a detailed set of goals we cannot even estimate what the dollar cost is of attaining each goal. And without a series of dollar estimates, we cannot answer the questions: When can I complete this goal? Given my present financial resources, is a particular goal even attainable? What goals can I reach immediately and what goals will I have to defer?

We do not have some all-inclusive list of recommended financial goals that everyone should strive to emulate. Such a list is not possible, because we each have our own financial objectives, personal values, capabilities, and personal likes and dislikes that shape the set of individual goals we would like to reach. Consequently, you need to develop and specify the financial goals that you want to achieve. Those goals can then become an integral part of your financial planning process.

Setting **financial goals** entails three steps. Short-term goals and long-term goals have one additional step, but we shall wait until a later section of the chapter to discuss it.

The first step is to specify exactly what you want to do. Keep the purpose of that goal narrow, so that you can later judge your progress toward its completion. Typically, you will want to set a number of narrow, specific goals rather than a few broad, generalized goals. Instead of saying, "My goal is to purchase life's necessities," why not say, "My goal is to purchase a new $9000 car in 3 years"?

Your second step in specifying a financial goal is to estimate what you must pay to complete that goal. Typically, you will use the goal's current cost if you expect to complete it within several months. On goals with a more distant completion date, you will likely want to estimate how much inflation will push up the future cost of attaining that goal. That means raising today's cost to cover the future price increase caused by inflation. (We will illustrate how you can do this in a later section of the chapter.) Try to provide a specific, single dollar estimate. It is much easier to do financial planning when you know each goal's dollar amount.

The final step is to set an expected completion date for each of your goals. Ask yourself: When do I want to accomplish this goal? By doing so, you can establish some benchmarks which can be used to judge your progress. Furthermore, setting a completion date encourages you to identify a point at which you will begin taking constructive steps to reach that goal. Even if you later have to extend the completion date, you will at least have begun working toward it.

STRATEGY

There are three steps to establishing a financial goal. Ask yourself:

What do you want to do with this goal?

How many dollars are required to attain this goal?

When do you want to complete this goal?

Stage 3: Use a Budget to Plan Expenditures

When we discuss budgeting in Chapter 3, we will stress that the principal purpose of a **budget** is to serve as a plan of how you want to spend your scarce financial resources. As such, preparing your budget becomes the next step in the total financial plan outlined in Exhibit 1-1. We will use a budget to decide how the financial resources from stage 1 are used to achieve the financial goals outlined in stage 2. Properly done, a good budget can be a systematic planning tool that outlines how you want to use your financial resources to accomplish the financial goals you have established. The budgeting chapter (Chapter 3) will discuss how to develop and use this planning tool.

Stage 4: Careful Spending Decisions

Once you have allocated your available resources among your goals, you still need to decide exactly how the money is to be spent. Careful spending decisions can greatly increase what your resources can accomplish. Returning to our previous automobile goal, a $9000 investment in a new car could prove a good, average, or poor expenditure of your funds. Unless you carefully assess the alternatives and make an informed decision, you will not know which. We will have a lot more to say about how to make careful spending decisions in future chapters.

Stage 5: Review and Analysis

The major purpose of this stage is to check whether your actual spending is proceeding along the lines you established in your budget. If it is not, why

not? It may require corrective changes either in your spending patterns or in your previously established budget. Certainly, given today's highly volatile economic environment, no financial plan should be considered immune from future revisions and modifications. We will discuss the review and analysis stage in more detail in Chapter 3 as part of budgeting.

Saving Is a Part of Planning

Allocating some money to short-term and long-term savings programs is essential for truly successful personal financial management. Begin saving early in your life. For example, if you are twenty-five years old and save $1000 per year, which you invest at 8 percent interest, you will have $259,057 at age sixty-five. If you postpone this annual savings program until you are thirty-five, you will have only $113,283 at sixty-five. The delay of 10 years means that you will have saved $10,000 less. Yet, by the time you reach age sixty-five, that $10,000 not saved earlier means lost interest of $145,774. That is a tremendous sacrifice to make for delaying a regular savings program for only 10 years.

Exhibit 1-2 shows how an investment of $1000 per year will grow, given different rates of interest and periods of investment.

Note how important it is to start saving early and to earn the highest possible interest. The difference in interest earned on only $1000 between rates of 6 and 8 percent might seem insignificant. Yet, over a 40-year period, during which time you invest $1000 per year, the difference between 6 and 8 percent interest amounts to $104,295, certainly a significant amount of money.

COMPOUND RATE-OF-RETURN TABLES

Before we can estimate the required dollar amount for short-term and long-term financial goals, we need to understand the workings of compound interest. If you recall, the earlier section, The Planning Process, pointed out the need to estimate the total dollar cost of achieving each financial goal. But the estimated costs for many short-term goals and most long-term goals involve dollar amounts that occur at some considerable distance in the future. Obviously, then, we will have to restate those future amounts in terms of today's dollars. By doing so, we can include them as part of our current financial plan. A compound rate-of-return table can restate those future amounts for us.

Compound Rate-of-Return Table: Single Lump-Sum Investment

Our discussion of compound rates of return begins with a table that shows the future value of $1 that you invest today and do not add any further investment to in the future. This, then, is a **lump sum investment.** Before we launch into an example, we need to define several terms. We will use year 0 to indicate the present point in time (today). The initial investment of $1 will be made in year 0. Year 1 will be 1 year from today, year 2 will be 2 years from today, and so forth. When we say **compound returns,** we mean all the interest that has been earned is left, or reinvested, in the investment. Furthermore, because the interest is reinvested, the investment pays interest not only on the initial $1 investment, but also on the interest we leave on deposit.

Exhibit 1-3 illustrates the mechanics of compound interest when $1 is invested at a 10 percent rate of interest. In the second year, there are two parts to the 11-cent interest that was earned for the year: 10 cents was earned on the initial investment, and 1 cent was earned on the 10 cents of interest that was reinvested from year 1. Interest in year 3 has three parts: interest on the $1 initial investment, interest on year 1's reinvested interest, and interest on year 2's reinvested interest. From Exhibit 1-3 it is clear that the interest earnings in later years continue to grow because of the reinvestment of the earlier years' interest. In fact, after a few years we will be earning more interest on the reinvested interest than we earn on the original investment.

Exhibit 1-4 is a **compound rate-of-return table** that shows what happens to $1 when it is invested in year 0—today—and the interest is reinvested to compound each year. The exhibit shows the **terminal,** or **final,**

EXHIBIT 1-2

Amounts attained by saving $1000 each year after 10, 20, 30, and 40 years at interest rates of 6 to 12 percent.

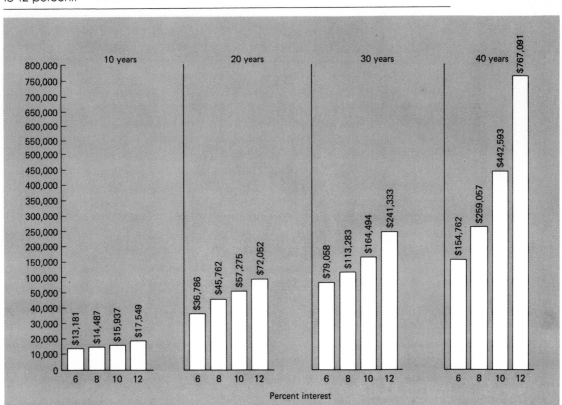

EXHIBIT 1-3

Compound interest on a single $1 invested at 10 percent.

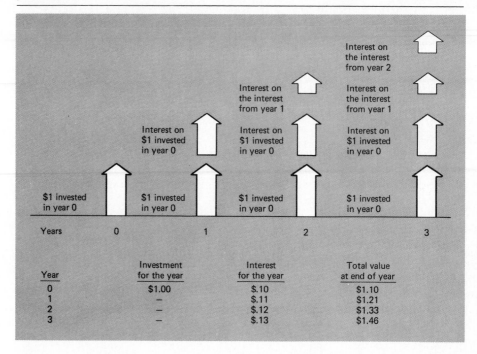

Year	Investment for the year	Interest for the year	Total value at end of year
0	$1.00	$.10	$1.10
1	—	$.11	$1.21
2	—	$.12	$1.33
3	—	$.13	$1.46

value, of $1 invested today when it earns rates of return ranging from 4 to 15 percent for periods ranging from 1 to 40 years. While the terminal values in the table represent the compound growth of $1 invested initially, these values can be used to calculate the terminal value of any amount of money invested. For example, the terminal value of a $500 investment is exactly 500 times the terminal value shown for $1. You can also calculate the terminal value of $1 for rates of return between the rates shown in the table, e.g., rates such as 4⅜, 5½, or 6¾ percent. To illustrate this calculation, assume you want to know the terminal value of $1 invested at 6¾ percent for 12 years.

$$\text{Interest rate}$$

$$\frac{\text{Terminal value of \$1}}{\text{compounded 12 years}} = \frac{6\%}{\$2.01} \quad \frac{6\frac{3}{4}\%}{?} \quad \frac{7\%}{\$2.25}$$

$$\$2.19 \qquad = \$2.01 \qquad + \frac{3}{4} \times (\$2.25 - \$2.01)$$

Terminal value at = Terminal value + ¾ × ⎡Terminal value at⎤
6¾%, 12 years   at 6%, 12 years   ⎣7%   6%   ⎦

Terminal Value of an Investment Exhibit 1-4 can be used to find the terminal value of an investment made today (a lump-sum investment). Assume we invest $525 as a lump sum today at 6 percent compounded

EXHIBIT 1-4

Value of $1 at various rates of compound interest.

INVESTMENT PERIOD IN YEARS	4%	5%	6%	7%	8%	9%	10%	11%	12%	13%	14%	15%
1	1.04	1.05	1.06	1.07	1.08	1.09	1.10	1.11	1.12	1.13	1.14	1.15
2	1.08	1.10	1.12	1.15	1.17	1.19	1.21	1.23	1.25	1.28	1.30	1.32
3	1.13	1.16	1.19	1.23	1.26	1.30	1.33	1.37	1.41	1.44	1.48	1.52
4	1.17	1.22	1.26	1.31	1.36	1.41	1.46	1.52	1.57	1.63	1.69	1.75
5	1.22	1.28	1.34	1.40	1.47	1.54	1.61	1.69	1.76	1.84	1.93	2.01
6	1.27	1.34	1.42	1.50	1.59	1.68	1.77	1.87	1.97	2.08	2.20	2.31
7	1.32	1.41	1.50	1.61	1.71	1.83	1.95	2.08	2.21	2.35	2.50	2.66
8	1.37	1.48	1.59	1.72	1.85	1.99	2.14	2.31	2.48	2.66	2.85	3.06
9	1.42	1.55	1.69	1.84	2.00	2.17	2.36	2.56	2.77	3.00	3.25	3.52
10	1.48	1.63	1.79	1.97	2.16	2.37	2.59	2.84	3.11	3.40	3.71	4.05
11	1.54	1.71	1.90	2.11	2.33	2.58	2.85	3.15	3.48	3.84	4.23	4.65
12	1.60	1.80	2.01	2.25	2.52	2.81	3.14	3.50	3.90	4.34	4.82	5.35
13	1.67	1.89	2.13	2.41	2.72	3.07	3.45	3.88	4.36	4.90	5.49	6.15
14	1.73	1.98	2.26	2.58	2.94	3.34	3.80	4.31	4.89	5.54	6.26	7.08
15	1.80	2.08	2.40	2.76	3.17	3.64	4.18	4.79	5.47	6.25	7.14	8.14
16	1.87	2.18	2.54	2.95	3.43	3.97	4.60	5.31	6.13	7.07	8.14	9.36
17	1.95	2.29	2.69	3.16	3.70	4.33	5.05	5.90	6.87	7.99	9.28	10.76
18	2.03	2.41	2.85	3.38	4.00	4.72	5.56	6.54	7.69	9.02	10.58	12.38
19	2.11	2.53	3.03	3.62	4.32	5.14	6.12	7.26	8.61	10.20	12.06	14.23
20	2.19	2.65	3.21	3.87	4.66	5.60	6.73	8.06	9.65	11.52	13.74	16.37
25	2.67	3.39	4.29	5.43	6.85	8.62	10.83	13.59	17.00	21.23	26.46	32.92
30	3.24	4.32	5.74	7.61	10.06	13.27	17.45	22.89	29.96	39.12	50.95	66.21
35	3.95	5.52	7.69	10.68	14.79	20.41	28.10	38.57	52.80	72.07	98.10	133.18
40	4.80	7.04	10.29	14.97	21.72	31.41	45.26	65.00	93.05	132.78	188.88	267.86

annually. We want to know the terminal value of that investment after 5 years. Going to the 6 percent column and looking down that column to the investment period, 5 years, we find that the $1 will be worth $1.34. The $525 investment will be:

$703.50   = $525   × 1.34

Terminal value = Initial   × Factor from
at 6 percent   investment   Exhibit 1-4:
for 5 years   5 years at 6 percent

The figures are approximate since the values in Exhibit 1-4 have been rounded to two decimal places.

STRATEGY

Use Exhibit 1-4 when you want to estimate the terminal value for a single lump-sum investment that has remained invested for a specified time period.

Compound Rate-of-Return Table: Equal Annual Investments

The second rate-of-return table shows what happens when $1 is invested each year. We assume that the first $1 is invested at the end of year 1, the second $1 at the end of year 2, the third $1 at the end of year 3, and so forth. Again, it is compound interest, so all interest earned remains in the investment. That means all interest earned on the annual $1 investments plus interest earned on the prior years' interest will be reinvested in the account.

Exhibit 1-5 shows the results of compounding when $1 is invested each year at a 10 percent rate of interest. Notice that there is no interest in year 1. That is because the $1 investment was not made until the end of that year, so it earns nothing. If we analyze year 3, we note that the 21 cents of interest has three parts: 10 cents on the $1 invested for year 2, 10 cents on the $1 invested for year 1, and 1 cent from the 10 cents of interest that was reinvested in year 2.

The compound rate-of-return table in Exhibit 1-6 shows what happens when $1 is invested at the end of each year (an **equal-sized annual investment**) and interest is left to compound each year. The exhibit shows the terminal value of investing $1 each year for periods from 1 to 40 years and at rates of return ranging from 4 to 15 percent. The basis of this table is the following: $1 invested at the end of the first year. One year later (the end of the second year), the investment grows by an amount equal to the yearly interest on that dollar, and yet another dollar is then added to the original investment. The total amount invested thus far earns interest during the third year; another dollar is added to the investment at the end of the third year, and so on.

The main difference between Exhibits 1-4 and 1-6 can best be illustrated with an example. If we had a $100 lump sum to invest once at the beginning of a specified period, we would use Exhibit 1-4 to determine the terminal value at the end of the period. On the other hand, if we were going to invest $100 at the end of each year over a specified period, we would use Exhibit 1-6 to determine the terminal value of the yearly investments.

Since Exhibit 1-6 was constructed assuming $1 invested per year, it is easy to use the values in the table to calculate terminal values for any amount invested annually. Likewise, Exhibit 1-6 can be modified for fractional percentage rates of return by dividing the difference between the two nearest whole percentage returns in exactly the same way as was illustrated for Exhibit 1-4. For example, let's find the factor for 5½ percent for 5 years.

Terminal value of $1 per year compounded for 5 years	5%	Interest rate 5½%	6%
	= $5.53	?	$5.64

EXHIBIT 1-5

Compound interest on $1 invested each year at 10 percent.

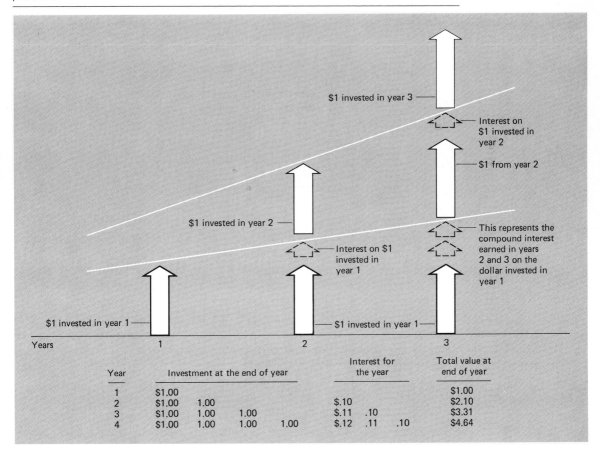

Year	Investment at the end of year				Interest for the year			Total value at end of year
1	$1.00							$1.00
2	$1.00	1.00			$.10			$2.10
3	$1.00	1.00	1.00		$.11	.10		$3.31
4	$1.00	1.00	1.00	1.00	$.12	.11	.10	$4.64

$$\$5.59 \qquad = \$5.53 \qquad + \tfrac{1}{2} \times (\$5.64 - \$5.53)$$

| Terminal value at | = | Terminal value | + | $\tfrac{1}{2}$ | × | ⎡ Terminal value at ⎤ |
| 5½%, 5 years | | at 5%, 5 years | | | | ⎣ 6%   5% ⎦ |

Future Value of an Annual Investment We can use Exhibit 1-6 to find the future value of a particular annual investment. Assume we plan to invest $100 at the end of every year for the next 5 years. The investment's rate of return is 8 percent. Going to the 8 percent column and finding the line representing an investment period of 5 years, we discover that the $1 invested per year for 5 years at 8 percent would be worth $5.87. Thus, our $100 annual investment is worth:

$$\$587 \qquad = \$100 \qquad \times 5.87$$

Future value	=	Annual	×	Factor from
of the		investment		Exhibit 1-6, 5 years
investment		for 5 years		at 8 percent

STRATEGY

Use Exhibit 1-6 when you want to estimate the terminal value of equal-sized investments made for a specified time period.

Compound Rate-of-Return Table: Equal Monthly Investments

Our final compound rate-of-return table modifies the table in Exhibit 1-6 by assuming **equal-sized monthly investments** rather than annual investments. Each investment will be made at the end of the month beginning with month 1 (one month from today). We assume that interest is earned monthly on the balance in the investment. Furthermore, all interest earnings are reinvested, so they earn additional interest.

The compound rate-of-return table in Exhibit 1-7 shows the end value, or terminal value, of investing $1 at the end of each month for periods from ½ to 5 years with rates of return ranging from 4 to 16 percent. The basis of this table is this: $1 is invested at the end of the first month, $1 at the end of the second month, $1 at the end of the third month, and so forth. Each month, 1/12 of the annual interest rate is earned on the total amount invested. And all interest earned remains in the investment to earn additional interest.

Since the amount in Exhibit 1-7 is for $1, the table is easily modified for other amounts. Investing $24 per month gives a terminal value that is exactly 24 times the value shown in Exhibit 1-7 for $1. Likewise, we can compute the value where the interest rate is between the values shown in Exhibit 1-7. Suppose we want the terminal value of investing $1 at 9½ percent for 4 years. To find it, we obtain the value for 8 percent and add to it ¾ of the difference between 8 and 10 percent (because 9½ percent is three-fourths of the distance from 8 to 10 percent). The computations are on page 16.

EXHIBIT 1-6

Compound value of $1 invested at the end of each year at varying rates of interest.

INVESTMENT PERIOD IN YEARS	4%	5%	6%	7%	8%	9%	10%	11%	12%	13%	14%	15%
1	1.00	1.00	1.00	1.00	1.00	1.00	1.00	1.00	1.00	1.00	1.00	1.00
2	2.04	2.05	2.06	2.07	2.08	2.09	2.10	2.11	2.12	2.13	2.14	2.15
3	3.12	3.15	3.18	3.22	3.25	3.28	3.31	3.34	3.37	3.41	3.44	3.47
4	4.25	4.31	4.38	4.44	4.51	4.57	4.64	4.71	4.78	4.85	4.92	4.99
5	5.42	5.53	5.64	5.75	5.87	5.99	6.11	6.23	6.35	6.48	6.61	6.74
6	6.63	6.80	6.98	7.15	7.34	7.52	7.72	7.91	8.12	8.32	8.54	8.75
7	7.90	8.14	8.39	8.65	8.92	9.20	9.49	9.78	10.09	10.41	10.73	11.07
8	9.21	9.55	9.90	10.26	10.64	11.03	11.44	11.86	12.30	12.76	13.23	13.73
9	10.58	11.03	11.49	11.98	12.49	13.02	13.58	14.16	14.78	15.42	16.09	16.79
10	12.00	12.58	13.18	13.82	14.49	15.19	15.94	16.72	17.55	18.42	19.34	20.30
11	13.49	14.21	14.97	15.78	16.65	17.56	18.53	19.56	20.66	21.81	23.04	24.35
12	15.03	15.92	16.87	17.89	18.98	20.14	21.38	22.71	24.13	25.65	27.27	29.00
13	16.63	17.71	18.88	20.14	21.50	22.95	24.52	26.21	28.03	29.99	32.09	34.35
14	18.29	19.60	21.02	22.55	24.22	26.02	27.98	30.10	32.39	34.88	37.58	40.51
15	20.02	21.58	23.28	25.13	27.15	29.36	31.77	34.41	37.28	40.42	43.84	47.58
16	21.83	23.66	25.67	27.89	30.32	33.00	35.95	39.19	42.75	46.67	50.98	55.72
17	23.70	25.84	28.21	30.84	33.75	36.97	40.55	44.50	48.88	53.74	59.12	65.08
18	25.65	28.13	30.91	34.00	37.45	41.30	45.60	50.40	55.75	61.73	68.39	75.84
19	27.67	30.54	33.76	37.38	41.45	46.02	51.16	56.94	63.44	70.75	78.97	88.21
20	29.78	33.07	36.79	41.00	45.76	51.16	57.28	64.20	72.05	80.95	91.03	102.44
25	41.65	47.73	54.86	63.25	73.11	84.70	98.35	114.41	133.33	155.62	181.87	212.79
30	56.08	66.44	79.06	94.46	113.28	136.31	164.49	199.02	241.33	293.20	356.79	434.75
35	73.65	90.32	111.43	138.24	172.32	215.71	271.02	341.59	431.66	546.68	693.57	881.17
40	95.03	120.80	154.76	199.64	259.06	337.88	442.59	581.83	767.09	1013.70	1342.03	1779.09

$$\begin{array}{llll}
\text{Terminal value} & = \text{Terminal value} \times & \text{Fraction of} & \times \text{Difference} \\
\text{at } 9\tfrac{1}{2}\%, 4 \text{ years} & \text{at } 8\%, & \text{distance from} & \text{between} \\
& 4 \text{ years} & 8\% \text{ to } 10\% & 10\% \text{ and } 8\%
\end{array}$$

$$\$58.129 \qquad = \$56.350 \qquad + \left\{ \left[\frac{9\tfrac{1}{2}\% - 8\%}{10\% - 8\%} \right] \times \left[\$58.722 - \$56.350 \right] \right\}$$

Future Value of Monthly Investment Exhibit 1-7 can also be used to find the future value of a particular monthly investment. Assume we plan to invest $15 at the end of each month during the next 3 years. During that time, we expect to earn 12 percent on our investment. From the 12 percent column of Exhibit 1-7, we see that $1 per month for 3 years amounts to $43.077. Our $15 monthly investment is worth

$$\begin{array}{lll}
\$646.16 & = \$15 & \times 43.077 \\
\Uparrow & \Uparrow & \Uparrow \\
\text{Future value of} & = \text{Monthly investment} \times & \text{Factor from Exhibit 1-7,} \\
\text{investment} & \text{during 3 years} & \text{3 years at 12\%}
\end{array}$$

STRATEGY

Use Exhibit 1-7 when estimating the end value from making equal-sized investments each month for a specified time period.

We can now summarize the differences among the three compound rate-of-return tables shown in Exhibits 1-4, 1-6, and 1-7. If we had a $100 lump sum to invest once, we would use Exhibit 1-4. But if we planned to invest $100 each year for a specified period, Exhibit 1-6 would be used. On the other hand, if we planned to invest $100 each month for a specified period, Exhibit 1-7 would be the one to use.

Now that we have discussed compound rate-of-return tables, let us go back to financial goals and the financial planning process to see how these

EXHIBIT 1-7

Compound value of $1 invested at the end of each month at varying rates of interest.

TIME PERIOD IN YEARS	ANNUAL INTEREST RATES						
	4%	6%	8%	10%	12%	14%	16%
½	6.050	6.076	6.101	6.126	6.152	6.178	6.204
1	12.222	12.336	12.450	12.566	12.683	12.801	12.920
1½	18.519	18.786	19.057	19.333	19.615	19.901	20.193
2	24.943	25.432	25.933	26.447	26.973	27.513	28.066
3	38.182	39.336	40.536	41.782	43.077	44.423	45.822
4	51.960	54.098	56.350	58.722	61.223	63.858	66.636
5	66.299	69.770	73.477	77.437	81.670	86.195	91.036

tables can be used in planning. One of the things we will illustrate is how you can use Exhibits 1-4, 1-6, and 1-7 to estimate the current dollar requirements of your short-term and long-term financial goals.

SHORT-TERM FINANCIAL GOALS

A **short-term financial goal** is any goal that we expect to achieve within the next 5 years. The 5-year cutoff is a bit arbitrary, since there is no hard-and-fast rule on when short-term goals end and long-term goals begin. But we have found 5 years to be a reasonable dividing line. Several examples of short-term financial goals will give you a better idea of what we are discussing:

To buy an automobile: You will need $5000 and your present auto to trade in for a new one in 3 years.

To pay property taxes: You will need $1200 to pay property taxes on your house in 12 months.

To buy an appliance: You will need $900 to purchase a new refrigerator in 6 months.

To take a vacation: You will need $4000 to cover expenses of a European junket in 2 years.

All these goals have the three essential features discussed in the earlier planning section: Each statement specifies the purpose, the planned completion date, and the estimated cost of each goal.

Implementing Short-Term Goals   Since most short-term goals will not actually be completed until some point in the future, the required dollar amount can be accumulated systematically during that time. And, because the amount is likely to be large, most people will want to accumulate the money through regular monthly savings. During the time the required money is being accumulated, it should be invested so that it will earn interest. That means the money for most future goals will come from two sources. Part of it will be the money you store up, and the balance will be interest that is earned while the money is invested. The amount of interest that will be earned on each dollar depends on the length of time the money is invested and the rate of interest it earns.

We already have an estimate of the time the money will be invested. Recall that we said the third step in specifying a financial goal is to set the estimated date of completion. From that completion date we know how many months or years we have to accumulate the necessary money. Estimating the rate of interest the invested money will likely earn is the fourth step needed to specify a short-term financial goal. When we talk about investments later in the book, we will show you how to estimate this rate of interest. But, for now, we will give you the rate of interest in the examples we use and in the problems at the end of the chapter.

Required Saving for Short-Term Goals   Ultimately, you will want to be able to include each short-term goal as part of your regular budget. To do so, you need to convert each short-term goal to a required monthly savings amount. Let's examine several examples to show how Exhibit 1-7 can be used in this step in financial planning.

Emergency Savings   Suppose one of our short-term financial goals is to accumulate $50 per month over the next 2 years to provide an emergency reserve. During those 2 years, the money is expected to earn 8 percent interest. We want to know what balance we will have in the reserve after those 2 years. Using Exhibit 1-7, we can compute:

$1296.65   = $50   × 25.933

⇧   ⇧   ⇧

Total balance = Planned   × Factor from
in emergency   monthly   Exhibit 1-7, 2
reserve   investment years at 8%

Automobile Purchase   Suppose our short-term financial goal is to accumulate $5400 in 4 years so that we can trade an existing car for a new one. During those 4 years, we expect the money will earn 10 percent interest. Here, we know what the terminal value must be—$5400—but we need to decide how much we must invest each month during the 4-year period (48 months) to achieve our $5400 objective. Simply dividing 5400 by 48 to arrive at $112.50 per month is not correct. We ignore any interest we could earn while accumulating the money. To include it, we use Exhibit 1-7. It shows us that investing $1 each month for 4 years at 10 percent will generate $58.722. We don't want $58.722, but if we take our desired $5400 and divide it by $58.722, we can estimate how many dollars we should invest each month. The required monthly investment needed to accumulate $5400 over the 4 years is:

$91.96   = $5400   ÷ 58.722

⇧   ⇧   ⇧

Required monthly = Desired   ÷ Factor
investment   dollar   from Exhibit
                   balance   1-7, 4 years
                               at 10%

Therefore, if we invest $91.96 each month at 10 percent interest, we will have $5400 in 4 years. Of the total amount, we will have invested $4414.08 ($91.96 × 48), with the remaining $985.92 coming from interest earnings.

Need more practice? What is the required monthly investment to accumulate $2500 in 3 years if the money earns 8 percent interest during that time? Your answer should be $61.67.

Short-Term Investment   Suppose someone wants you to invest in a proposal that promises to pay you $3381 in 4 years, if you invest $60 each month during those years. Here we know the final value ($3381) and the monthly investment ($60), but we would like to know what rate of return the investment provides. Again, Exhibit 1-7 can give us the answer because it shows what happens to $1 per month at various rates of return. To use Exhibit 1-7, we need to know how well each of our original dollars has done. We compute this by dividing the final value by the original monthly investment:

56.35	= $3,381	÷ $60
⇧	⇧	⇧
Investment factor	= Final value of investment	÷ Monthly investment

We can now answer the question: If I had invested $1 per month for 4 years and its terminal value was $56.35, how well did I do? To use Exhibit 1-7, we read across the columns at 4 years until we come closest to the 56.35 factor we computed above. This occurs at 8 percent. So our investment provides an 8 percent return.

LONG-TERM FINANCIAL GOALS

We define a **long-term financial goal** as one that we do not plan to complete until more than 5 years from now. Unfortunately, all too many people will tell you that they never include long-term goals in their financial plans because they never plan that far ahead. Or they may claim that so many things can happen during the years before the goal is reached that distant planning does not make sense. Others will say that future costs are likely to change, so it does little good to plan for those costs today.

Quite to the contrary, we think planning for long-term goals does make sense. First, the dollar amount needed to achieve many long-term

WE WERE TRYING TO DECIDE OUR LONG-TERM GOALS, AND BEFORE WE WERE DONE, THE SUBJECT HAD CHANGED TO OUR HEALTH INSURANCE COVERAGE....

goals is very large. Without advance planning, most people will never have the money to complete these goals. Second, because long-term goals will not be achieved until some rather distant point in the future, you can earn a considerable amount of interest while you are accumulating the necessary money. But to do so, you must start the required investment *today.* Finally, most people are prone to procrastinate when it comes to beginning to work toward long-term goals. By including these goals as part of your financial plan, you are far more likely to follow through on them.

Here are several examples of what we mean by long-term financial goals.

Homeownership   The cost of an average single-family house now exceeds $80,000, which certainly qualifies as a large dollar amount. Given that sizable cost, making a down payment of 10 percent—$8,000—presents a major savings task for most people. Accumulating that amount of money will likely require a systematic savings plan over a number of years.

College Education Fund   One financial goal for a family with young children might be to provide a college education for each child. Whether they plan to cover all, or only a part of, those college costs, the total amount required is likely to be high. While the exact time available to accumulate the money depends on the child's current age, for most families this period will be quite lengthy. And during the accumulation period, the money can earn considerable interest.

Retirement Fund   While many people have difficulty thinking about retirement early in their work career, today's financial environment makes it imperative to begin accumulating a retirement fund. Regardless of your employer's pension plan, you will probably have to provide part of your retirement income. That means you should start building your retirement fund early in your working life. An early start reduces your contributions because the money can be invested longer. So you will have more interest earnings to push up your fund balance.

Implementing Long-Term Goals   While you are accumulating money for your long-term financial goals, it should be invested so that it earns interest. Interest obviously helps you because the larger the interest component, the smaller your required contributions. And the interest you earn should be sizable because the money will typically be invested for a lengthy period, given the distant completion date for most long-term goals. The exact amount of interest depends on the length of time the money will be invested and the rate of interest it will earn while it is invested. The money for a long-term goal should come from two sources: (1) the dollars that you invest and (2) the interest that is earned on the money you have invested.

Long-term financial goals require that you specify the three previously discussed initial steps:

What you want to do

What it will cost to do it

When you want to do it

In addition, we add a fourth step: What rate of interest will the money likely earn while you are accumulating it? As the section on short-term goals pointed out, we will discuss investments later in the book so that you can answer the rate-of-return question for yourself. For now, all the examples and problems will provide the rate of return you should use. Once you have completed the four steps, you can address the question: What annual amount will an individual have to save to achieve a particular long-term goal?

Required Lump-Sum Investments for Long-Term Goals   Since the completion date for long-term goals is a considerable distance in the future, we will use annual compounding to estimate the future value of a given lump-sum investment. In this first section, we will show how Exhibit 1-4 can be used to plan these long-term goals. Recall that this exhibit assumes a single, one-time investment where all interest earned on the investment is reinvested to earn additional interest. Let us work through several examples to show some of the ways Exhibit 1-4 can be used.

College Fund   Assume we plan to make a one-time $1500 investment for a college education fund. We expect the fund to earn 11 percent during the 12 years it remains in the investment. We want to know how large the fund will be after 12 years. Using Exhibit 1-4, we can compute:

$5250	= $1500	× 3.50
⬆	⬆	⬆
Terminal value of college fund	= Initial investment	× Factor from Exhibit 1-4, 11% for 12 years

Down Payment for House   Our goal is to accumulate $7000 to use as a down payment for a single-family house. We want to make a single lump-sum investment that will earn 8 percent during the 9 years it remains in the investment. Since Exhibit 1-4 gives the results from investing $1, we can use it to answer the question: How many dollars must we invest to achieve a given goal? Since $1 invested at 8 percent for 9 years grows to $2, we can use that $2 factor to compute how many dollars we should start with to have $7000 after 9 years. Using Exhibit 1-4, we would have:

$3500	= $7000	÷ 2
⬆	⬆	⬆
Required lump sum investment	= Desired terminal value	÷ Interest factor from Exhibit 1-4, 8% for 9 years

Long-Term Investment Opportunity   Suppose we had a chance to invest $1000 today in return for $2840 in 10 years. Our question is: What rate of return does the investment provide? Again, Exhibit 1-4 can answer this question because it shows what happens to each dollar we invest. First, we begin by computing how each of our original dollars performed:

$$2.84 \quad = \$2840 \quad \div \$1000$$

⬆ ⬆ ⬆

Interest = Terminal value ÷ Initial
factor   of investment   investment

If $1 has grown to $2.84 in 10 years, we can go to Exhibit 1-4 to see what return that suggests. We read across the line for 10 years until we find the interest factor closest to $2.84. We see that the investment promises an 11 percent rate of return.

Required Annual Savings for Long-Term Goals   Given the distant completion point for long-term goals, we will compute the annual investment needed to accumulate the money for a long-term goal. If necessary, we can divide the annual investment by 12 to give approximate monthly amounts. This section shows how you can use Exhibit 1-6 to plan your long-term financial goals. Recall that that exhibit assumes an equal investment at the end of each year. All interest earned on those annual investments remains in the account to earn additional interest. Several examples will demonstrate some of the ways you can use Exhibit 1-6.

Retirement Fund   Assume that for the next 12 years we plan to deposit $800 each year in a retirement fund. All invested amounts will earn 9 percent interest. We can use Exhibit 1-6 to estimate the value of the retirement fund after 12 years:

$$\$16,112 \quad = \$800 \quad \times 20.14$$

⬆ ⬆ ⬆

Terminal value = Annual   + Factor from Exhibit
of retirement   investment   1-6, 9% for
fund   12 years

For the moment, we ignore any income taxes that may have to be paid on the fund's interest earnings.

Down Payment on Condominium   Suppose that, over the next 7 years, we want to accumulate sufficient money to make a $4600 down payment on a condominium. We plan to make equal investments at the end of each of the 7 years. All amounts invested will earn 9 percent interest. We want to know the amount we must invest each year to accumulate $4600 in 7 years. With a little modification, Exhibit 1-6 can answer that question for us. We know it tells us what happens when we invest $1 each year at 9 percent for 7 years. So, if we divide the $4600 we want by the terminal value from investing $1 each year—it is $9.20—we can compute how many dollars we must invest each year. The required annual investment is:

$$\$500 \quad = \$4600 \quad \div 9.20$$

⬆ ⬆ ⬆

Required   = Desired   ÷ Factor from Exhibit
annual   terminal   1-6, 9%
investment   value   for 7 years

IRA Account A local financial institution has promised that if you deposit $1500 each year in its Individual Retirement Account (IRA), your balance in 20 years will be $96,300. Our question is, What rate of return does the IRA account provide? If we know the terminal value for each dollar invested, Exhibit 1-6 can tell us what rate of return those dollars will earn. Our first task is to compute how well each invested dollar will perform. That computation is:

$$64.2 \quad = \$96,300 \quad \div \$1,500$$

⬆	⬆	⬆
Interest factor	Terminal value of IRA account	Required annual investments

Since the deposits are for 20 years, we go to Exhibit 1-6 to see what it means to have each invested dollar worth 64.2. Reading across the 20-year line, we find that an interest factor of 64.2 suggests the IRA will earn an 11 percent rate of return.

COORDINATING LONG-TERM AND SHORT-TERM GOALS

We have already demonstrated the first step needed to coordinate short-term and long-term goals: estimating the dollar amount needed to achieve each financial goal. The second step is to rank all your financial goals in descending order of importance. We don't have a master list that claims to show you which goals you should rank first, second, and so on. That ranking should be based on your values and your future plans. It should reflect what you want to use your scarce financial resources for and when you want to complete the various goals.

Once you have done the ranking, you can compare the monthly and annual costs of the different goals with the financial resources you currently have available. Don't be surprised if your list of goals is much larger than your pool of available resources. Frankly, we would be surprised if it weren't. All it means is that you will defer some of those goals to the future, owing to a lack of current resources. You might want to go back and reexamine the priority of your ranking to make certain it reflects your sense of what is important. But we think you will benefit from estimating the dollar cost for each of the goals and ranking them in order of their significance to you. Your financial plan now provides a much clearer idea of what you can currently do. And it forces you to ask: Which goals are most important right now? By bringing the cost of the various financial goals together, you should have a more realistic picture of what is possible and what must be deferred.

ESTIMATING THE IMPACT OF INFLATION

While Exhibit 1-4 was constructed primarily to show what happens when $1 is invested and all interest earned is reinvested, it can also tell you the impact of inflation on future prices. An example will show how it can do so.

Assume that the price of a $1 gumbat (don't worry about what it is) will rise 10 percent per year for the next 3 years. That means that in one year, the price will be $1.10, the $1 original price plus a 10 percent increase. At the end of the second year, the price will rise to $1.21. If you go back to Exhibit 1-4 and look down the 10 percent column, you will see that $1 invested at 10 percent becomes $1.10 after 1 year, $1.21 after 2 years, and $1.33 after 3 years. Does this look familiar? It is identical to our previous 10 percent investment example.

Now let us move to a real-world example. Assume a particular color television set currently costs $600. During the next 3 years, we expect that the price will rise 9 percent each year owing to inflation. We want to estimate the money you will need to buy a similar television set in 3 years. Using Exhibit 1-4, we would have:

$$\$780 \quad = \$600 \quad \times 1.30$$

| Expected price in 3 years | = | Current price of television | × | Factor from Exhibit 1-4, 3 years at 9% |

Do you want more practice? What will today's $10,000 automobile cost in 5 years if inflation pushes up the price 8 percent each year? Your answer should be $14,700.

Later in the book, we will discuss inflation and financial planning in more detail. At that time, we will make further use of Exhibit 1-4 to show more about the impact of inflation.

SUMMARY

1   Financial planning includes both short-term and long-term considerations.

2   Total financial planning involves five stages: (*a*) Identify available income, (*b*) establish financial goals, (*c*) use a budget to allocate income, (*d*) make careful spending decisions, and (*e*) analyze and review results.

3   Establishing financial goals requires three steps. You must decide:

What you want to do

What it will cost to do it

When you want to do it

4   Saving is an integral part of every financial plan.

5   Compound rate-of-return tables provide the final, or terminal, value from investing $1 in one of the following three ways:

As a single lump sum

At the end of each year

At the end of each month

6   Short-term financial goals involve an objective that will be completed within 5 years.

7   Calculating short-term financial goals requires one added step beyond the three outlined in point 3: What rate of return will the money earn while it is accumulated?

8   A compound rate-of-return table can be used to estimate the required monthly saving for a short-term goal.

9   Long-term financial goals require an estimate of the rate of return the money will earn while it accumulates, in addition to the three steps outlined in point 3.

10   Compound rate-of-return tables can be used to estimate the lump-sum investment or the annual investment required to achieve a long-term goal.

11   A compound rate-of-return table can be used to estimate the impact of inflation on the future price of an item.

REVIEW YOUR UNDERSTANDING OF

Financial planning process	Equal-sized annual investment
Available income	Equal-sized monthly investment
Financial goals	Terminal, or final, value
Budget	Short-term financial goals
Compound return	Long-term financial goals
Compound rate-of-return tables	
Lump-sum investment	

DISCUSSION QUESTIONS

1   What are the five stages of the total financial planning process?

2   Briefly describe the objective or role for each of the five stages in the total financial planning process.

3   What are the three steps required to establish a financial goal? What additional step do short-term and long-term financial goals add? Why?

4   If Ronald Retire wants to accumulate a large retirement fund, should he be most concerned with earning a high interest rate for a short savings period or earning a moderate interest rate for an extended savings period? (*Hint:* Review Exhibit 1-2 *carefully.*)

5   What are the major differences among the compound rate-of-return tables in Exhibit 1-4, 1-6, and 1-7?

6   Give several examples of short-term financial goals that include the four essential steps for each goal.

7   Assume Sam Shorterm's goal is to accumulate $2000 to purchase new furniture in 2 years. Will Sam have to provide the entire $2000? If not, why not?

8   When retirement, a likely long-term goal, is far in the future, why is it important to start thinking about it today?

9   What dollar amounts or rates of return can a compound rate-of-return table estimate for short-term financial goals?

10   Describe the different ways a lump-sum compound rate-of-return table can be used to estimate dollar amounts or rates of return for long-term financial goals. What amounts and returns can a compound rate-of-return table with equal annual investments estimate for long-term goals?

11   How can a compound rate-of-return table help estimate the impact of inflation on prices? Why is it necessary to incorporate inflation into financial planning?

PROBLEMS

1-1   What amount will we have if we save $40 at the end of each month for 3 years and earn 11 percent on that money?

1-2   Sue Sun wants to have $5000 in 5 years to purchase a sailboat. If she can earn 9 percent on her investments, how much should she invest each month?

1-3   Phyllis Planner decides to invest $900 at the end of each year for the next 30 years to accumulate a retirement fund.

   a If she earns 10 percent on her investment, how large will her fund be in 30 years?

   b Out of that total balance, what amount must she contribute?

   c What amount will come from interest?

1-4   Clyde Condo needs $7820 for a down payment on a condominium in 7 years. How much should Clyde contribute each year if he can earn 9 percent on his investment?

1-5   Loretta Lucky recently won $20,000 in a state lottery contest. She wants to know how many dollars she should invest in a lump sum today at 10 percent so that she will have a $28,000 retirement fund in 20 years.

1-6   Assume Ned Nearterm and Len Longterm each want to accumulate a retirement fund. Details are:

	TIME TO RETIREMENT	DESIRED FUND BALANCE	RATE OF RETURN EARNED	REQUIRED ANNUAL INVESTMENT
Ned	10 years	$10,000	10 percent	___?___
Len	30 years	$30,000	10 percent	___?___

   a What annual investment will each one have to make?
   b Despite the fact that both Ned and Len are trying to accumulate $10,000 every 10 years, Len's annual contribution is much lower. Why is this so? (*Hint:* Carefully consider the amount of interest each fund will earn.)

1-7   Two banks have advertised Individual Retirement Accounts (IRAs) with the following details:

BANK	PLANNED ANNUAL INVESTMENT	PROMISED RATE OF RETURN	PERIOD INVESTMENTS WILL BE MADE	FINAL BALANCE IN IRA ACCOUNT
Small-Town	$1,200	6 percent	20 years	___?___
Aggressive	$1,200	12 percent	20 years	___?___

   a What balance will be in each IRA account after 20 years?
   b How much would you lose by staying with the Small-Town Bank?

1-8   Fast Phil, a local investment sales agent, is currently selling an investment that promises that if you invest $1000 each year for 8 years, you will have $12,300 at the end. What rate of return does Phil's investment promise?

1-9   If inflation continues to increase the price of automobiles 8 percent per year, what will today's $9000 auto cost in 5 years?

1-10   If you could earn 8 percent interest, what would you have to save to have $5000 in 5 years if:

   a   Investments are made monthly?

   b   Investments are made each year?

   c   Why is the monthly amount (Part **a**) less than one-twelfth the annual amount (Part **b**)?

1-11   If you invest $1000 each year for 7 years and earn 8¼ percent interest, how much will you have in 7 years?

1-12   If you invest $100 each month for 3 years and earn 9½ percent interest, how much will the investment be worth at the end?

CASE PROBLEM

Newlyweds Jerry and Pam Hoss are trying to set long-term and short-term goals for themselves. The would like to purchase a new car in 3 years and they estimate that today's $9000 car will increase in cost 6 percent a year. In saving for the car, they estimate that they can earn 8 percent on the monthly deposits they make to a savings account.

Pam and Jerry would also like to buy a house, but they feel it would take at least 5 years to accumulate the down payment, which is estimated at $10,000. Money which is earmarked for the down payment should earn 7 percent annually. They also plan to make monthly deposits in a savings account to achieve this goal.

Also, a coworker recently told Jerry about a mutual fund which has earned an average annual return of 10 percent for the past few years. Jerry thinks this might be a good way to start a college fund for the children they expect to have. They think that they can invest $1000 annually over the next 18 years.

1   How much will the $9000 car cost in 3 years, assuming the 6 percent inflation?

2   Assuming the Hosses can earn 8 percent on their investments, how much will they have to invest monthly to buy the car in 3 years?

3   How much must they invest monthly at 7 percent to accumulate the down payment?

4   If they invest $1000 annually for 18 years at 10 percent, how much will they have at the end of the time period?

CHAPTER

2

FINANCIAL AND PERSONAL RECORDS

**AFTER COMPLETING THIS CHAPTER
YOU WILL HAVE LEARNED**

The major types of *financial records* and *personal documents* everyone needs for good financial planning

How to prepare a personal *income statement*

What your personal *balance sheet* can show you

How to prepare a personal *property inventory*

What you should have in your *tax record file*

What *homeownership records* you should maintain

How your *insurance policy record* can alert you to upcoming insurance renewals

That your *investment record* can track how well your investments are performing, as well as summarize any income and gains needed for tax purposes

Where and for how long you should *store* your *personal records* and *documents*

FROM the day you are born, when a

birth certificate officially attests to your existence, to the day you die, when a death certificate is official evidence that you are no longer alive, documents and records are an important part of your life. Once you start taking responsibility for yourself, there are checking accounts to balance, insurance policies to renew, mortgage or rent payments to record, and tax returns that must be prepared every year.

Records are neither difficult nor time-consuming to maintain. Surprisingly, the organized record keeper spends less time on personal paperwork than the person who does everything on the backs of envelopes and matchbook covers.

The most difficult part of good record keeping is setting up the records. After that, the process is relatively mechanical. This chapter will help you develop a good personal record system by showing you a set of records designed to provide the information most people need. The chapter will also acquaint you with the most important documents you will need to be aware of.

SETTING UP YOUR RECORDS AND DOCUMENTS

The major types of records which most people should have are outlined in Exhibit 2-1. The first two items, the income statement and the balance sheet, are primarily for planning rather than record keeping. These records show how you spent and saved your money in the previous year. They should help you in deciding how you would like to spend and save your money in the following year. Because these records are used for planning, they are perhaps more important than records used only for keeping data. Also described in the exhibit are documents that people typically save. The proper safeguarding of these and many other documents is discussed later in this chapter.

The Income Statement

An **income statement** is important because it summarizes the income you have available to take care of your needs and desires. It actually is a listing of both your income and your expenses. Often, by reviewing your past expenses, you can better plan your future expenses and, if necessary, alter your life-style to fit your level of income.

The mechanics of completing a personal income statement, as shown in Exhibit 2-2, are reasonably straightforward. Your checkbook, bills, and memory should enable you to adequately complete the income statement. Remember, an income statement is for your benefit only; it is not an official document. Accuracy to the penny is not as important as filling out the form and recognizing how much money you spend and the sources of that money.

Even if you don't have complete records of all your expenses, or if some categories do not apply to you, it is still important to complete an income

EXHIBIT 2-1

Summary of important working records and personal documents.

Records

1   Income statement. This is a summary of income and expenses for a selected time period.

2   Balance sheet. This is a listing in dollars of the things you own (assets) and the amounts of money you owe to others (liabilities). The difference between assets and liabilities is your financial or net worth.

3   Personal inventory. This is a list of personal possessions; each item listed should show date of purchase and original cost.

4   Tax records. Adequate records consist of income data, a list of deductions accumulated during the year, and copies of your tax returns.

5   Homeownership records. These record what investments you made in your house—additions, repairs, improvements—and how much you spent for each.

6   Insurance records. These records list the dates that payments must be made on each of your insurance policies.

7   Investment records. A record of all purchases and sales of stocks, bonds, and other investments should be retained.

Documents

1   Birth certificate. Official copies of birth certificates for all family members should be kept in a safe place. Your certificate is issued by the county where you were born and is easy and inexpensive to obtain.

2   Marriage license. This will be needed only infrequently, such as when a widow is applying for survivors' benefits from the Social Security program.

3   Insurance policies. Copies of all life insurance, homeowners insurance, automobile insurance, and disability income insurance should be retained.

4   Wills. A will specifies exactly how a person's property will be distributed after death. In the absence of a will, a person's property will be distributed in accordance with state law, which may not be according to the wishes of the individual.

5   Letter of last instructions. Accompanying the will there should be a letter providing a listing of financial records. The letter would contain, for example, a statement of the location and number for (a) bank accounts, (b) life insurance policies, (c) certificates of automobile ownership, (d) deeds to real estate, (e) prior income tax returns, (f) canceled checks, (g) stock accounts, (h) mutual funds, and (i) other insurance policies. The letter may also give special instructions about the type of funeral service you want.

6   Military separation papers. If you have been released from military service, you should safeguard the official discharge notice. It is important if you apply for any benefits payable to veterans.

EXHIBIT 2-2

Personal income statement for 19XX,
Frank and Mary Swanson.

Income

Husband's salary	$16,000	
Wife's salary	14,000	
Dividends and interest	400	
(1) Total income		$30,400

Taxes

Federal income taxes	$ 3,565	
State income taxes	1,300	
Social Security contributions	2,010	
(2) Total taxes		$ 6,875
(3) Available income: line 1 − line 2		$23,525

Expenses

Food		$ 3,500
Housing		
Rent or mortgage	$ 3,900	
Real estate taxes	−	
Utilities	1,200	
Insurance, homeowners	80	
		$ 5,180
Clothing		$ 960
Transportation		
Gas, oil, maintenance	$ 1,290	
Insurance, repairs, license	750	
		$ 2,040
Vacation and entertainment		$ 1,420
Life insurance		$ 250
Medical		
Doctor, dentist, medicine	$ 400	
Health insurance	800	
		$ 1,200
Personal		$ 900
Child care		$ 2,600
Loan payments		
Auto	$ 2,400	
Furniture	1,200	
		$ 3,600
(4) Total expenses		$21,650
Amount remaining: line 3 − line 4		$ 1,875

statement. Only by making yourself sit down and reconstruct *how* you spent your money will it be possible for you to decide how you *would like* to spend it. When you complete your income statement, you will probably be in for a big surprise—the large amount of income that you cannot account for. This fact alone should illustrate the need for a budgeting system. By specifying how you want to spend your money, you will be able to make far better use of your income than you do when your expenses are totally unplanned.

Most of the items on the income statement are self-explanatory. The statement in the exhibit may not exactly fit your circumstances; however, minor modifications should make it work reasonably well.

STRATEGY

We recommend that you prepare an income statement at the end of each year. You can then use it to help budget your next year's income.

Analyzing Your Expenditures The value of an income statement is in the helpful information it provides. A quick glance at the statement shows that certain expenditures must be made and are therefore *essential* expenditures, while others do not have to be made and are considered *discretionary* expenditures. Let's examine the Swansons' income statement and see which expenditures are essential and which are discretionary.

Essential Expenditures Most of the Swansons' expenses are essential. Examples are the $3900 for rent and the $1200 for utilities—heat, electricity, and telephone. Other expenditures, such as transportation, will likely combine the essential and the discretionary. Certainly, the travel expenses of commuting to work are essential, as is the cost of a shopping trip to purchase food. However, the costs of traveling to a show, dinner out, or a weekend trip will most likely fall into the discretionary category.

Discretionary Expenditures The vacation and entertainment expenditures of $1420 are an example of a true discretionary expenditure for the Swansons. This item could be eliminated without creating undue hardship. Life may not be as much fun without discretionary expenditures, but they are not essential to living. For most people who try to reduce their total expenditures to match their available income, reductions in discretionary expenditures are the place to begin cutting down.

The Balance Sheet

The next document you will need for analyzing your financial situation is a **balance sheet.** This lists the things you own (your **assets**) and deducts the amounts you owe to others (your **liabilities**). There are two types of assets: liquid and other assets. *Liquid assets* are cash or items which can be easily converted into cash. Examples are savings accounts and checking accounts. *Other assets* are items which you may not be able to readily convert to cash without suffering a loss. An automobile is a good example of an asset which is not liquid. *Liabilities* include bills and loans. Your **net worth** is the difference between your assets and liabilities.

Exhibit 2-3 shows a sample balance sheet for the Swansons. A balance sheet is always prepared for a given point in time—e.g., December 31, 19XX—and details all your assets and liabilities on that date. A balance sheet is extremely important because it neatly summarizes the level of your net worth—a good measure of your current financial position. Without understanding your situation, it is impossible to develop short-range, intermediate-range, or long-range financial plans. Making judgments about what changes you want to make in your plans during the next year becomes much easier when you have this information.

Analysis of Current Position A balance sheet can be used to analyze your present financial position. For example, the Swansons might conclude, after

EXHIBIT 2-3

Balance sheet for 19XX, Frank and Mary Swanson.

Assets		
Liquid assets		
Cash		
Checking account	$ 320	
Savings account	530	
Mutual fund, money market	2,800	$ 3,650
Life insurance, cash value		$ 950
Investments		
Common stock*	$2,100	
Mutual funds*	2,650	$ 4,750
(1) Total liquid assets		$ 9,350
Other assets		
Automobile*	$4,600	
Furniture and appliances	4,250	
Personal (jewelry, clothing, etc.)	2,000	
(2) Total other assets		$10,850
(3) Total assets: line 1 + line 2		$20,200
Liabilities		
Current bills		
Credit cards†	$ 150	
Charge accounts†	75	$ 225
Consumer loans		
Automobile†	$4,100	
Appliances†	1,150	$ 5,250
(4) Total liabilities		$ 5,475
Net worth: line 3 − line 4		$14,725

*The value shown represents the current market value of the asset.
†Represents the unpaid balance.

IT STARTED OUT TEN YEARS AGO
AS A FOLDER FULL OF IMPORTANT PAPERS
AND JUST GREW!

analyzing their balance sheet in Exhibit 2-3, that their cash balance ($3650) is too low. One short-term goal for the next year might be to raise their balance by $500. By comparing your liquid assets with your liabilities, you can get an idea of what flexibility or safety coverage you have; that is, should your income cease temporarily, could you continue the payments on your liabilities? If so, for how long?

Comparison with Prior Years   Once you have prepared balance sheets for several years, you can compare them to see whether you are making progress toward your goals. For example, the Swansons could compare their net worth from their prior years' balance sheets with this year's $14,725 balance to see whether it has increased.

Projected Future Balance Sheet   A balance sheet can also be used to project what financial position you would like to have in 5 to 10 years. If you draw up such a balance sheet, you can better answer the question: Are the projections realistic? While it may be difficult to project that far in the future, doing so can give you an idea of what you may have to do to achieve your long-term financial goals.

Personal Property Inventory

Many people are unaware of the amount they have invested in furniture, china, jewelry, and clothes. In the "Other assets" category may be very valuable items like gun collections, cameras, or stereo equipment. If you came home some night to discover that fire had destroyed your house or apartment or that burglars had cleaned you out, could you itemize all your belongings for the insurance company? Most people would have difficulty doing so unless they had some systematic record of what they own. The more accurate your records are, the more likely it is that you will be able to collect the fair value of your possessions in the event of fire or theft.

Your **personal property inventory** should include a description of each item, its condition, the value when you acquired it, and the date you acquired it. If the item is of special value, such as an antique or a painting, it should be appraised to verify its worth. An appraisal is simply an expert's opinion of an item's value. Insurance companies will accept appraisals from independent appraisers when settling insurance claims. If you have appraisals made, they should become a part of your records.

The inventory can be maintained on loose-leaf pages, as is shown in Exhibit 2-4, or on index cards so that additions and deletions can be made easily. Periodically—say, once a year—the inventory should be updated.

Tax Records

Your taxes will be both lower and simpler to calculate if you have kept accurate and systematic records of certain expenses during the year. These kinds of expenses are called *deductions* and they reduce the amount of taxes you will have to pay. We will discuss them in detail and how they reduce taxable income when we get to Chapter 6. Meanwhile, we merely want to stress that to get the benefit of these deductions, you should be sure to set up your records for the following categories: (1) income, (2) taxes paid, (3) interest payments, (4) contributions, (5) medical expenses, and (6) miscellaneous deductions.

An easy way to develop good tax records is to have a file folder, an accordion file, or just a large manila folder marked "Taxes." When you have a receipt, bill, or statement relating to income taxes, drop it in your **tax file.** Likewise, when you travel or attend some conference, the cost of which is tax-deductible (more on this later), write a note to yourself that includes all monetary details and put it in your file.

EXHIBIT 2-4

Sample personal property inventory.

Room: Living Room		Date of Inventory: Oct. 14, 19XX	
DESCRIPTION	CONDITION	PURCHASE PRICE	PURCHASE DATE
Sofa	Excellent	$1475	Feb. 1978
Easy chair	Good	700	Mar. 1977
Table lamps (2)	Excellent	150	Apr. 1975
Oriental rug (appraised by J. Smith, Aug. 1980)	Very good	1500	Aug. 1971
Stereo	Excellent	1500	Mar. 1982

After we talk about taxes in Chapter 6, you will understand more clearly what things you should include in the file and why they should be there. A good tax file can save you countless hours when preparing your tax returns. Most important, it will also help you reduce the amount of taxes you pay.

STRATEGY

Keep a separate file where you can store all tax-related receipts, bills, statements, and special reminder notes.

When you calculate your taxes and complete your tax forms, you should make duplicate copies of the tax forms and keep the copies in your tax file. You should also keep worksheets and the receipts for all the expenses used as deductions in figuring out how much tax you owe.

We recommend that you keep copies of your tax returns for at least 4 years after the date the return was due. For example, on April 15, 1984, you can dispose of the tax return for calendar year 1979: it has been 4 years since you filed that return on April 15, 1980. The reason we suggest 4 years rather than the more traditional 3 years is that you may need those prior years' returns to complete this year's tax return if you use income averaging: we will discuss income averaging in Chapter 6.

Homeownership Records

Perhaps the most important homeownership record you possess is the deed, a legal document specifying that you are the owner of the house. You should also maintain records of any amounts you spent to improve your house, such as adding another room or building a garage. Now let's look at each of these records in more detail.

The Deed A deed is the legal document which is proof of property ownership. It is an extremely valuable document because you cannot transfer property without it. In many localities, it is difficult and often expensive to replace a deed. Therefore, it should be not only kept but kept in a very safe place.

Other Ownership Records Ownership documents which should be protected include the survey that defines the boundaries of your property and your title insurance policies. Title insurance protects your ownership in a property against any claims that may arise because of improper recording of deeds or similar mistakes. Finally, if you have house blueprints, they should be saved; they can be useful if you plan to remodel the house at a future time.

Income Taxes When You Sell If you sell your house for more than you originally paid for it, you may have to pay income taxes on the gain (the difference between the sale price and the purchase price). We say "may" because, if you buy another house, you may be able to defer, or put off, paying any tax. You may also be able to add the amounts you spent to improve the house to your original purchase price. Such expenditures lower your gain and therefore reduce any tax you might otherwise have to pay.

Home Improvement or Maintenance? The tax authorities make a distinction between the money you spend to improve your house and the money you spend to maintain it during the time you own it. As we just noted, expenditures for **home improvements** can be added to the home's original purchase price. **Home maintenance** expenditures cannot be added. When you add improvements that increase the home's value, you reduce your overall gain and thus the amount on which you may have to pay taxes. In other words, the potential gain is:

$$\begin{array}{l} \text{Potential} \\ \text{gain} \end{array} = \begin{array}{l} \text{Sale price} \\ \text{of home} \end{array} - \left[\begin{array}{l} \text{Home's original} \\ \text{purchase price} \end{array} + \begin{array}{l} \text{Cost of} \\ \text{improvements} \end{array} \right]$$

Improvements increase the value of your home or lengthen its useful life. Examples include such changes as adding a new room, putting up a fence, installing new wiring or plumbing, putting on a new roof, and paving the driveway.

Maintenance or repair expenditures merely keep your home in good condition. Examples include such things as painting the interior or exterior of the house, repairing a window, patching plaster, or fixing a broken section of your sidewalk.

Since you may own a house for 10, 20, or even more years, it is essential that you keep accurate records of the improvements you make. Exhibit 2-5 gives a sample form that you might want to use. All entries on the form should be backed up with receipts, canceled checks, and other records for each improvement. An accurate and complete record of home improvements can save you time and taxes.

Insurance Record

In later chapters, we shall discuss how to plan your insurance coverage and give guidelines for purchasing your desired coverage. A good starting point

EXHIBIT 2-5

Record of home improvements to 210 Easy Street.

DATE	ITEM	AMOUNT	TOTAL COST OF PROPERTY
	Balance		$47,500
10/17/80	Driveway	$2820	50,320
5/11/82	Trees	300	50,620
12/15/83	Paneled basement	970	51,590
.	.	.	.
.	.	.	.
.	.	.	.

for your insurance plan is an **insurance policy record** showing your various policies. Typically, your record should show items covered, policy number, insurance company, dollar coverage, premium due date or dates, and the premium amounts. Exhibit 2-6 shows one such record.

By referring to your insurance checklist periodically, you will be prepared for the premium notices from the insurance company when they are due to be paid. This list will be a big help in setting a monthly budget. Equally important, it will give you enough advance warning to allow you to make any changes in the coverage well before the premium due date.

Investment Records

If you invest in common stocks, bonds, or mutual funds, you need to keep a record on each separate investment. Exhibit 2-7 is a sample **investment**

EXHIBIT 2-6

Insurance policy record.

INSURANCE COVERAGE	POLICY NUMBER	COMPANY	AMOUNT OF INSURANCE PROTECTION	DUE DATE	PREMIUM
Life	283728	You Bet Your Life	$10,000	June 20	$125
	396278	Last Gamble Life	15,000	July 8	162
Auto	12876243	Fidelity	100/300/25* 100 Ded	Aug. 20	175
Homeowners	4728316	Friendship Mutual HO-3†	52,000	Jan. 15	157
Health	114732	Blue Cross-Blue Shield		Nov. 1	635

*Refers to liability limits (see Chapter 16 for a complete discussion).
†Refers to the type of homeowners policy (also discussed in Chapter 16).

EXHIBIT 2-7

Record of your investments.

LINE DESCRIPTION	Investments		
	LAST DITCH MUTUAL FUND	HIGH FLYER COMMON STOCK	STOIC BOND
1. Purchase date	5/1/1981	3/6/1983	7/10/1982
2. Original purchase price	$1500	$2000	$3000
3. Market value, January 19XX	$2000	$2500	$3000
4. Interest or dividends during 19XX	$ 120	$ 50	$ 360
5. Market price, December 19XX	$2200	$2400	$3000
6. Change in value of investment during past year: line 5 − line 3	$ 200	−$100	0
7. Rate of return during 19XX (line 4 + line 6) divided by line 3	16%	−2%	12%

record that includes details on the original purchase, returns during the year, and rate of return on each investment during the year. There are two major reasons for keeping an investment record. First and foremost, you should be following how well your investments are doing; that is, you should be reviewing the rate of return to see whether it meets your expectations. Second, the tax authorities will want to share in your good fortune: The interest and dividends you receive will have to be included on your annual tax return. Furthermore, any gain on the sale of the investment (when your selling price exceeds your purchase price) must be included on your tax return. And, to make the system fair, when you sell an investment at a loss (when your selling price is less than your purchase price), you can deduct this loss on your tax return. Chapter 6 will discuss these income tax implications in considerable detail.

Maintaining and Safeguarding Your Records

The average person's financial and personal records are too important to be kept in a shoe box. After all, organized record keeping is the start of successful financial planning. Get yourself a supply of manila folders and a small file cabinet, and you have a start on efficiently maintaining your records.

Exhibit 2-8 summarizes most of the important papers a person may accumulate and indicates the proper storage for them. Also indicated is the length of time the records should be maintained under normal circumstances.

A Safe-Deposit Box

Some of the records and papers which you accumulate should be guarded more carefully than others. They may be very costly or even impossible to

EXHIBIT 2-8

Where to keep your important documents.

| ITEM | TIME PERIOD THAT RECORD SHOULD BE HELD | SAFE-DEPOSIT BOX | Filed at Home | | ON YOUR PERSON |
			CURRENT FILE	PERMANENT FILE	
Adoption papers	Permanent	X			
Auto registration	Until renewed				X*
Auto title	Until sale of auto	X			
Bank statements	Prior 3 years		X		
Birth certificate	Permanent	X†		X‡	
Bonds: savings & others	Until sold	X			
Canceled checks	Prior 3 years		X§	X	
Citizenship papers	Permanent	X			
Contracts, installment	6 years after paid	X			
Driver's license	Until renewed				X
Guarantees, warranties	While covered item is owned			X	
Health records	Permanent			X	
Insurance policies	Until new policy is issued			X	
Marriage and divorce papers	Permanent	X			
Military papers	Permanent	X			
Personal inventory	Permanent	X			
Real estate deeds	Until real estate is sold	X			
Receipts, important	6 years after paid			X	
Social Security card	Permanent	X			X¶

THE CABINET YOU'VE BEEN STORING OUR PERSONAL PAPERS IN ALSO HAPPENS TO BE OUR TRASH COMPACTOR.

replace. You can obtain adequate protection by renting a **safe-deposit box,** a small fireproof storage box within a bank's vault. It may usually be rented from a commercial bank, a savings and loan association, or a mutual savings bank. The cost depends on the size of the box. But a typical fee for a small box is $10 to $30.

Opening a safe-deposit box requires two keys; one key is held by the person renting it and the other is retained by the bank. The bank does not have a master key to fit the customer's lock nor can it open a box unless the customer is present. Likewise, the customer cannot open the box unless the bank's representative is present.

EXHIBIT 2-8 (Continued)

ITEM	TIME PERIOD THAT RECORD SHOULD BE HELD	SAFE-DEPOSIT BOX	Filed at Home		ON YOUR PERSON
			CURRENT FILE	PERMANENT FILE	
Stock certificates	Until sold	X			
Tax returns	Prior 4 years			X	
Will and letter of last instruction	Permanent	X†		X‡	

*Should be retained in car.
†Original.
‡Duplicate.

§Prior year's checks.
¶Top portion.

SUMMARY

1 You should prepare an income statement summarizing your income and expenditures each year.

2 Prepare an annual balance sheet to show your assets (the things you own), your liabilities (what you owe others), and your net worth (assets minus liabilities).

3 An inventory of personal property should be updated annually to assure that you will be reimbursed fairly in the event that an item is destroyed by fire or is stolen.

4 Keep a separate tax file for each year where you can file all receipts, reminders to yourself, canceled checks, worksheets, and copies of your tax returns.

5 Homeownership records, including the deed, title, and recorded details on your insurance and home improvements, must be safeguarded. They can be useful for tax purposes as well.

6 Insurance records should show the essential details for each insurance policy: items covered, insurance company, dollar amount of coverage, premium amount, and due date.

7 Your investment record summarizes how well your investments, such as common stock, bonds, and mutual funds, have performed during the past year. It should also show what income or gains you must include on your tax return.

8 Personal record keeping can be made easier by buying a file cabinet and a good supply of manila folders.

9 Personal records and documents that would be difficult or costly to replace should be stored in a safe-deposit box.

REVIEW YOUR UNDERSTANDING OF

Income statement	Homeownership records
Balance sheet	Deed
Assets	Home improvements
Liabilities	Home maintenance
Net worth	Insurance policy record
Personal property inventory	Investment records
Tax file	Safe-deposit box

DISCUSSION QUESTIONS

1 What information does an income statement summarize? How can you use it to assist you in your financial planning?

2 What information does a balance sheet show? How can you use it in your financial planning?

3 What information should a personal property inventory include? What are the uses for this inventory?

4 What types of items would you keep in your personal tax file? How can such a file assist you when you prepare your tax return?

5 What legal document provides proof of your property ownership? Where should it be stored? Why?

6 What difference or differences distinguish a home improvement expenditure from a maintenance expenditure? Give several examples of each type.

7 What are the reasons for having an insurance policy record? How can it help you in your financial planning?

8 What information should your investment record contain? Name two ways in which the record can assist your financial plans.

9 What features make a safe-deposit box secure and reasonably free of manipulation by unauthorized people? Where can you find such a box? What types of records would you store there?

PROBLEMS

2-1 Charlie Closecount needs some help to finish an income statement for the past year. So far, Charlie has summarized the following information for that year in this way:

Wages	$14,000	Medical expenses	$ 340
Checking account	300	Personal expenses	210
Taxes	2,300	Miscellaneous expenses	100
Rent and utilities	3,660	Travel and entertainment	1,690
Unpaid loan balance	1,100	Clothing	600
Auto expenses	2,000	Insurance premiums	400
Credit card balance	200	Loan payments	600
		Food	1,500

Please prepare an income statement for Charlie.

2-2 Wayne and Wendy Worth want to prepare a balance sheet for the end of the year. Their balances and details for the year are:

Checking account	$ 300	House	$62,000*
Unpaid bills	800	Mortgage	40,000†
Automobile	6,500*	Mutual fund, common stock	3,400*
Mutual fund,		Personal property	4,300
money market account	1,500	Auto loan	5,200†

*Current market value.
†Present unpaid balance.

Can you help the Worths with the balance sheet?

2-3 To do this problem, you must have completed problem 2-2. Please show how the following two items would impact on the Worths' balance sheet:

a The Worths use $1000 from their money-market mutual fund to repay $1000 of their present automobile loan.

b The Worths borrow $9000 to purchase a new $9000 automobile.

2-4 Dennis Disorganized is reviewing the possible gain on the recent sale of his house. Details from the 3 years he owned the house include:

Original purchase price	$40,000	Painting exterior and interior at time of purchase	$ 3,000
Cost of adding new bedroom	6,000	Sale price	58,000
Remodeling kitchen	5,000	Replacing two broken sections of sidewalk	300

a Which of the above items will qualify as home improvements?

b Using the improvements you have listed in part **a**, figure Dennis's potential gain on the sale.

2-5 Summarized below are Connie Comparison's balance sheets for the past 3 years.

YEAR	12/31/81	12/31/82	12/31/83
Assets			
Cash	$ 300	$ 300	$ 300
Money-market mutual fund	4,300	2,000	400
Automobile	500	9,500	12,900
Personal property	2,000	4,000	6,000
Total	$7,100	$15,800	$19,600
Liabilities			
Current bills	$ 300	$ 800	$ 1,800
Auto loan	0	8,000	12,000
Cash loans		2,500	3,500
Total	$ 300	$11,300	$17,300
Net Worth	$6,800	$ 4,500	$ 2,300

a What has happened to Connie's net worth during the 3 years?

b What has caused the change in her net worth?

c Might you suggest any changes for Connie's personal finances?

CASE PROBLEM

Gloria Schultz is planning to start her junior year in college this September. Her first 2 years were spent at a community college and she lived at home. She was able to pay her tuition from the money she made working part-time at the school bookstore. She will spend her junior and senior years at the main campus of the state university. Consequently, she must pay room and board, as well as tuition. Gloria has applied for financial aid, and as part of the application she must complete a balance sheet and an income statement showing her family's financial situation

Her father has provided her with the following information, but because he is extremely busy, he has asked her to complete the two statements. He earned $26,000 last year as a roller in a steel mill. Out of this income, he paid $1820 in Social Security, $1550 in federal taxes, and $850 in state taxes. The Schultzes own a house for which they paid $61,000 about 3 years ago. (Current market value is $72,500.) The mortgage has a remaining balance of $48,200. The estimated living costs of the Schultzes are:

1 Food $350 per month

2 Mortgage   500 per month

3 Real estate taxes   900 annually

4 Utilities   90 per month

5 Health care   600 annually

6 Clothes   100 per month

7 Entertainment   720 annually

8 Car payments   165 per month

9 Car operation   60 per month

10 Insurance, life   420 annually
   and home

11 Miscellaneous   200 per month

In addition to their home, the Schultzes have a money-market mutual fund with a balance of $1100 and $250 in their checking account. They have two cars: one is an 11-year-old compact worth $300, and the other is a 3-year-old station wagon with a book value of $5600. The balance due on the car loan is $4300. Other bills outstanding are $750 on their MasterCard and a dentist's bill, not covered by health insurance, for $120. Their personal assets are currently worth $12,000.

1   Complete an income statement for the Schultzes.

2   Complete a balance sheet for the Schultzes.

PART
2
DEVELOPING AND MANAGING YOUR INCOME

CHAPTER

3

PERSONAL BUDGETING

**AFTER COMPLETING THIS CHAPTER
YOU WILL HAVE LEARNED**

What the *four major steps* to the *budgeting process* are

How to *estimate* your *available income*

How to *define* your *major budget categories*

How to *develop* dollar estimates for each *budget expenditure category*

What the *purpose* of a *budget summary sheet* is

Why *short-term and long-term financial goals* are included on the budget summary sheet

How your *emergency cash reserve* can balance out *differences between actual income and actual expenditures*

Why you should complete *a quarterly review and analysis* of your *budget summary sheet*

What *dollar balance* you should hold in your *emergency cash reserve*

PRAY TELL — WHAT LUCKY BUSINESS GETS PAID THIS MONTH?

TRYING to get the most out of your

income without budgeting is like trying to drive to an unfamiliar place without a road map. The trip may turn out to be successful, but then again, it may not. A budget is the road map that can guide you to where you want to go; it can direct you in making expenditures which will help you meet your goals, such as having money for a down payment on a house, for a winter vacation, for a new car, or for any other major purchase.

A budget does not tell you how to use your money. You are the one who makes that decision. How you spend your money is a very personal value judgment; *you* decide the benefits you get from your spending. No matter what your values or your life-style, a budget can assist you in obtaining the maximum satisfaction from your income.

A good budgeting system, with appropriate budget categories, requires little clerical effort and provides a lot of information. The budget system we will develop contains only one repetitive clerical step. Typically, it will require only 1 to 3 hours of work each month to maintain it.

BUDGETING: THE PRELIMINARIES

A budget system will work smoothly if you pay attention to some planning details. The **budgeting process**, illustrated in Exhibit 3-1, consists of four distinct steps:

1   Estimating available income

2   Defining major expenditure categories and setting spending levels

3   Using the budget summary sheet to list actual income and expenditures

4   Periodically reviewing and analyzing your budgeting system to make sure that it is still appropriate for your changing circumstances

You cannot formulate a successful budgeting program without first completing the basic preparations. These preliminary steps are (1) estimating available income and (2) defining expenditure categories and setting spending levels. Step 1, figuring total income, is relatively easy for most people. Step 2 is the most difficult part of the budgeting process. Here, you must evaluate past information on your spending to decide how you would like to use your income in the future. The only ongoing clerical work occurs in steps 3 and 4. In step 3, you enter your income and summary expenses on the summary sheet at the end of each month. Finally, you compare your expected and actual results to see whether you should make some changes. The benefits of budgeting far outweigh the small clerical effort required to keep the records up to date, once you have set up the system.

EXHIBIT 3-1

CHAPTER 3

51

PERSONAL
BUDGETING

The budgeting process.

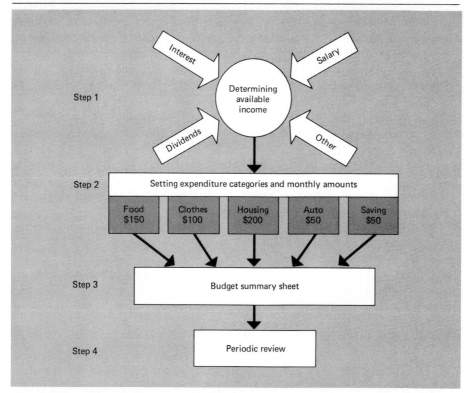

Step 1: Estimating Available Income

Let's say you are hired for a job, which you accept with the understanding that your salary (that is, your earnings) will be $2200 per month. There is no doubt about it; your earnings for the month are $2200. But when you get your pay, you find considerably less than that! Is your boss cheating you? Not at all!

What you get paid is your **take-home pay**. The difference between your earnings and your take-home pay is caused by **deductions** from your salary. Some of those deductions you agreed to when you took the job; these are voluntary deductions. But some of the deductions are the opposite: you *must* agree to them. These nonvoluntary deductions result from certain policies in the city or community and state where you live and the company you work for.

Voluntary deductions represent contributions from your earnings to things such as a bond-a-month plan, a stock-purchase plan, a savings plan, and the like. They all represent income that would become available to you should you decide or need to discontinue these kinds of savings and investments.

Nonvoluntary deductions represent taxes on your earnings—regular federal income taxes, state income taxes, and local income taxes—which your employer is required by law to deduct from your earnings and send to various government units on your behalf. Also included among your nonvoluntary deductions are payments to Social Security and any deductions for pension plans and medical insurance premiums.

Your **available income** is the total amount of money you have available if you need it. You use it to budget or plan with, because it is what you currently have. The largest component in available income is usually your salary. An imaginary couple, Sam and Samantha Jones, will help us illustrate the steps needed to compute available income. Exhibit 3-2 shows how that process starts with the couple's monthly gross pay.

In addition to salary, available income includes all interest and dividends received on savings accounts, bonds, common stocks, and mutual funds. The exhibit therefore summarizes the interest and dividends the Joneses expect to receive. Since those payments do not arrive each month, we took the total for the year and divided by 12 to convert to monthly amounts. If you expect to receive a bonus or a commission check and are reasonably certain of that amount, you should also include it in available income. Exhibit 3-2 shows that Samantha Jones expects to receive an $1800 bonus ($150 monthly) this year.

Nonvoluntary deductions should now be subtracted from the income items to compute available income. The middle section of Exhibit 3-2 lists Sam and Samantha Jones's nonvoluntary deductions. After deducting these items, they find that their combined monthly available income is $1875.

EXHIBIT 3-2

Estimating regular available income: Sam and Samantha Jones.

	SAM	SAMANTHA	TOTAL
Monthly gross pay	$1200	$1000	$2200
Interest	15*	15*	30
Dividends	10*	10*	20
Bonus		150	150
Less: Nonvoluntary deductions			
Federal income tax	$ 108	$ 104	$ 212
State income tax	43	41	84
Social Security	80	77	157
Pension	12	23	35
Medical insurance	17	20	37
Total available income	$ 965	$ 910	$1875
Less: Voluntary deductions			
Credit union	$ 70		$ 70
Stock-purchase plan		$ 85	85
Total take-home income	$ 895	$ 825	$1720

*Total amount for the year was divided by 12 for monthly amount; this amount was then split between Sam and Samantha Jones.

This is the income that Sam and Samantha should use to establish their budget, since it represents their available resources.

STRATEGY

As the starting point for your budget, figure your available income thus:

$$\text{Available income} = \text{Gross pay} + \text{Interest earnings} + \text{Dividend payments} + \text{Bonus and commissions} - \text{Nonvoluntary deductions}$$

Step 2: Defining the Major Expenditure Categories

How detailed do you want your budget to be? It can be a very simple statement with a few major **expenditure categories,** such as food, rent, and clothing. Or it can be far more elaborate, containing detailed breakdowns of each of the major categories. *A word of caution:* A lot of detail will provide a great deal of information, but it will take you more time and make the budget more work. Too little detail will make your budget easy to prepare, but it won't enable you to analyze your expenditures very well.

STRATEGY

Most people will find that a budget with eight to ten major expenditure categories will be sufficient. No more than 25 or 30 subcategories should be enough to summarize all normal expenditures.

Regular and Occasional Expenses   Many budgeting systems categorize expenses as either fixed or variable. However, this is somewhat unrealistic since very few expenses are fixed amounts. Even food expenses vary somewhat. Therefore the terms *regular* and *occasional expenses* more accurately describe the breakdown of normal expenditures. **Regular expenses** are the costs of everyday living: food, housing, transportation, entertainment, regular savings, and monthly payments on installment debt, such as auto loans.

   Occasional expenses are bills for insurance and major purchases that may occur only once or twice a year. Make sure that these expenses are considered in your budget. An amount of money sufficient to cover the annual totals for these occasional expenses should be included as a major expense each month.

STRATEGY

Your budget should include an amount to be put aside monthly to meet large bills when they come due. By planning in this way, you are effectively converting occasional expenses to regular expenses.

The Budget Period   You should budget your expenses for a full one-year period. Although many of your bills must be paid monthly, you will also have a number of bills, such as insurance premiums, which are paid only once each year or, at the most, several times during the year. If you view your expenses shortsightedly only on a monthly basis, you will most likely overlook these annual or perhaps quarterly payments until they come due. But if you keep an eye on your expenses more broadly over a full year, then you will know they will eventually come due for payment during the year. If you budget properly, you will have the entire amount available when you need to make the payment.

Once you have decided to prepare an annual budget, you need to decide on your **budget period**. In other words, you must determine whether to break your income and various expenses into monthly or weekly amounts. We strongly recommend the monthly option. It provides you with sufficient detail to plan expenditures, yet does not require undue clerical effort. It also gives you enough information for later analysis and review to see whether your actual expenditures parallel your plans. Most people find that maintaining a weekly budget is so time-consuming that they quickly lose interest and abandon it.

Deciding How to Spend Your Money: Expense Categories The next step in budgeting is deciding and setting amounts for each expense category. Everybody has a limited income and must decide how that income should be spent. How much for food? Clothes? Housing? Transportation? Recreation? Savings? You must answer these questions in order to develop a workable budget. How you divide your income will depend on what you think is most important. Remember, what you spend your income on is entirely your own concern and no one else's, so long as your spending is within your income.

Now is the time to examine three techniques that can help you estimate how many dollars you want to allocate to each expense category. **Expense Estimates: Past Spending** One way to plan your future spending for each expense category is to analyze how you spent your money in the past year. To do so, you will have to summarize your actual expenditures in that year. Sam and Samantha Jones have summarized their actual expenditures during the past year in Exhibit 3-3. When you look at the exhibit, you will notice that we did two things to hold down the size of the summary. First, the exhibit shows only the first seven of the Jones's expense categories. When we develop their budget summary sheet in Exhibit 3-5, you will see all their expense categories. We do, however, sum all those categories to give the "Grand total" line at the bottom of Exhibit 3-3. Second, we include the monthly expense details for only 3 months. But here also, we summed all 12 months to give the annual total. We divided that total by 12 to compute monthly averages. Keep in mind that a summary like Exhibit 3-3 is *not* a budget. It is a historical record of how one family spent available funds during a certain year. But now Sam and Samantha can use these monthly averages to help plan what they wish to spend in each category. This plan becomes their budget because it shows how they want to spend their available income.

Expense Estimates: Your Checkbook Unless you have kept reasonably detailed records, you probably will find it rather difficult to compile an expenditure summary like Exhibit 3-3. As an alternative, you may be able to

HELEN.. IT'S TIME WE FACE THE FACTS....OUR ENTERTAINMENT ELEMENT IS WAY OUT OF LINE WITH OUR INCOME.

make a rough estimate of your expenditures by reviewing your checkbook record during the last 3 to 6 months. This method, of course, assumes you use checks for most of your payments. By reviewing to whom you wrote checks and the amounts during those 3 to 6 months, you should have an idea of how you spent your money. These estimates should help you make dollar estimates of your planned expenditures for the next year. Don't try to estimate everything to the last penny—to the nearest $20 or $30 is fine.

EXHIBIT 3-3

Record for spending in 19XX: Sam and Samantha Jones.

EXPENSE	JAN.	FEB.	MAR.	QUARTER	TOTAL	AVERAGE
Food	$ 280	$ 265	$ 250	$ 795	$ 3,120	$ 260
Housing:						
Mortgage or rent	525	525	525	1,575	6,300	525
Real estate taxes	450	—	—	450	900	75
Utilities	140	130	165	435	1,380	115
Homeowners insurance	—	—	168	168	168	14
Maintenance	—	65	—	65	528	44
Total housing	$1,115	$ 720	$ 858	$2,693	$ 9,276	$ 773
Clothing	$ 30	$ 115	$ 20	$ 165	$ 1,080	$ 90
.	.	.	.	.	.	.
.	.	.	.	.	.	.
.	.	.	.	.	.	.
Grand total	$1,635	$1,455	$1,608	$4,698	$19,524	$1,627

Note: All amounts rounded to nearest dollar.

Expense Estimates: Use a Trial Period Let us suppose your records are such that you cannot summarize last year's spending. Furthermore, your checkbook record may not be too good, either. What should you do? First and foremost, don't give up the idea of a budget. Instead, make a rough estimate of how much you would like to spend in each expense category. Once you do that, you can record your actual expenditures for the next several months (we will show you how this is done in step 3.) Now you can go back and revise those previous rough estimates. Don't be surprised if you must make some sizable revisions. The important thing is that you have started the process of planning *how* you want to spend your available income. Even with those revisions, you have begun the process of controlling your finances rather than their controlling you: That makes the whole effort worthwhile.

Determining Your Short-Term and Long-Term Financial Goals Recall that, in Chapter 1, we discussed the importance of incorporating short-term and long-term goals in any overall financial plan. We also illustrated how the future cost of those two types of goals can be converted into a current monthly or annual dollar cost. In that discussion, we pointed out that those current dollar costs will become part of your budget. Let's see how and why they do so.

The second section of your budget should summarize the dollar amounts that must be saved each month for your future short-term and long-term goals. Those monthly amounts will allow you to accumulate the money needed for those goals. Since Chapter 1 illustrated the computations for monthly savings, we will just review it briefly here. Sam and Samantha Jones will provide our example. Assume that they have the following goals:

To save $3000 for a sailboat in 4 years

To save $12,900 in 13 years to cover part of the college expense of their child, Linda

The Joneses estimate they can earn 8 percent interest while accumulating the necessary money. Exhibit 3-4 summarizes the monthly saving needed to achieve their two goals. The footnotes to that exhibit review how the monthly amounts were computed. We should also point out that the $50 required monthly savings for the college fund is only a rough approximation. We merely computed the required annual savings (by using Exhibit 1-6) and divided by 12. But that is close enough for budgeting purposes.

By including the required monthly dollar amounts for short-term and long-term goals in your budget, you can see whether they are realistic given your available income. For the Joneses, that means asking whether they can save the approximate $121 needed each month to reach the two goals they have set. If not, this would be the time to reevaluate their other spending plans, or the goals themselves, to see what changes they must make. They are now in a position to develop alternatives if necessary.

Including the monthly amount needed to reach a goal as part of the budget greatly improves the chance the goal will actually be achieved.

Without planning for the required monthly saving, it will likely never be completed. Having the amount as part of the budget means that you will have a record of whether you are actually doing what you planned to do. The budget summary sheet, which is the topic of a later section, will show you when you fall behind in your savings plans.

STRATEGY

Compute the required monthly dollar savings for each short-term and long-term financial goal and include it in your budget.

Determining How to Meet Payments Due on Loans When we discussed planning expenditures for the different expense categories, we intentionally ignored payments on consumer loans. Our reasons for separating the payments are several. To begin, the required monthly payment on those loans is fixed; even if you wanted to spend less on the payment, you could not do so. Lenders will normally take more, but never less, than what you promised to pay. Second, at any point in time you should know exactly how many months remain until a loan is fully repaid. Should you finish making those payments midway through the budget year, you would just drop that monthly payment from your budget for the rest of the year. Finally, showing loan payments separately highlights the fixed contractual nature of those monthly amounts. In the next section, on the budget summary sheet, we will show how Sam and Samantha Jones would show their $110 monthly auto-loan payment.

Step 3: The Budget Summary Sheet

A **budget summary sheet** is designed to highlight three things. First, it shows what you planned to do: your budgeted income and budgeted expenditures. Second, it lists what your actual income and actual expenditures were during the budget period. Last, for each income item and expenditure, it spotlights those times when the actual amount was different

EXHIBIT 3-4

Short-term and long-term financial goals for Sam and Samantha Jones.

(A) GOAL	(B) AMOUNT REQUIRED	(C) WHEN NEEDED	Value of $1 Invested		Required Monthly Savings	
			(D) MONTHLY (EXHIBIT 1-7)	(E) ANNUALLY (EXHIBIT 1-6)	(F) SHORT-TERM [(B) ÷ (D)]	(G) LONG-TERM [(B) ÷ (E) ÷ 12]
Sailboat	$ 4,000	4 years	$56.35		$70.98*	
College fund	12,900	13 years		$21.50		$50.00†

Monthly savings = Amount required ÷ Value of $1 per period ÷ Conversion to monthly, if needed

*$70.98 = $ 4000 ÷ $56.35 (Exhibit 1-7)
†$50.00 = $12,900 ÷ $21.50 (Exhibit 1-6) ÷ 12

from the budgeted amount. We define each difference as either a surplus or a deficit.

Typically, the top section of your summary sheet shows what portion of your available income you budgeted for each month of the year. You will have developed this in step 1 of the budget process. On Exhibit 3-5, we have entered the $1875 of available income that we developed for Sam and Samantha Jones in Exhibit 3-2. A normal budget sheet would also show your actual available income for each month of the year. When *actual* income exceeds *budgeted* income, we consider that favorable and define the difference as a **surplus**. Conversely, a **deficit** occurs when actual income is less than budgeted income. To distinguish between the two on a budget summary, deficits are enclosed in parentheses; surpluses are shown without extra marking. To keep Exhibit 3-5 to a manageable size, we show only 3 months of actual income, together with the applicable deficit or surplus, for Sam and Samantha Jones. (This exhibit is on pages 60–61.)

The middle section of the budget summary sheet shows all the expense categories you have set for your budget. Step 2 of the budgeting process discussed how you can specify these categories. The budget summary sheet shows the amount you budgeted, or planned, for each expense category. For Sam and Samantha Jones, the budgeted amounts in Exhibit 3-5 were developed using their prior year's expenditures from Exhibit 3-3. For each month of the year, the budget summary sheet shows the actual expenditure for each expense category. Surpluses are still considered favorable, but we reverse the position of budgeted and actual expenditures. When actual spending is less than budgeted spending, we say there is a surplus. A deficit occurs when actual spending exceeds what is budgeted. Deficits continue to be distinguished by enclosing them in parentheses. Exhibit 3-5 shows the actual expenditures of Sam and Samantha Jones for the first 3 months of the year. In each expenditure category, actual expenditures are compared with budgeted amounts to compute a surplus or deficit.

Next, the budget summary sheet shows what monthly savings are needed to achieve your short-term and long-term financial goals. Depending on personal preference, each goal can have a separate line. Or the dollar amounts for all the goals can be totaled on a single line. As a procedural step, the reasons for which should become clear in a minute, we force actual savings and budgeted savings to be identical. Consequently, no surplus or deficit appears. The net effect is that we force any difference between actual expenditures and budgeted expenditures into the balancing account at the bottom of the summary sheet: "Emergency cash reserve." Let's go over several examples to show how that happens.

Assume we had budgeted $1200 for expenses and $300 as the necessary saving for our short-term and long-term goals. This month, actual spending for our expenses totaled $1300. By holding the saving for short- and long-term goals at $300, we must draw $100 from our emergency cash reserve to meet the $100 overspending. Suppose that in the next month, actual spending for our expenses was $1150. Again we place $300 in savings for short- and long-term goals. But now we can add $50 back to our cash reserve, because we underspent our budget by $50.

Later in the chapter, we will talk more about the emergency cash reserve. The budgeted required monthly savings for the Jones's short-term and long-term financial goals were developed in Exhibit 3-4. They have been transferred directly to Exhibit 3-5. Notice that the Jones's actual savings were forced to equal their budgeted savings.

Next, the budget summary shows any loan payments you must make. While the summary sheet has a surplus and deficit column, we would not expect any entries there because actual loan payments should equal budgeted amounts. As expected, the Jones's actual loan payment in Exhibit 3-5 equaled what they had budgeted.

If our only concern were the budgeted or planned amounts, our summary sheet would now be complete. The combined total of our budgeted expenditures should equal our budgeted available income. Stated in a more detailed form:

$$\begin{array}{ll} \text{Budgeted} & \text{Budgeted} & \text{Monthly savings} & \text{Required} \\ \text{available} = \text{expense} + \text{for short-term and} + \text{loan} \\ \text{income} & \text{amounts} & \text{long-term goals} & \text{payments} \end{array}$$

But actual amounts you expend each month will not always equal your budgeted amounts. In some months, actual income will exceed or fall short of budgeted income. Even more frequently, actual expenditures will exceed or fall short of budgeted expenditures. What we need is an emergency cash reserve that we can use to cover those months when actual expenditures exceed actual income. Of course, in months when actual income exceeds actual expenditures, we should deposit those extra dollars back into the emergency reserve.

The final section of the budget summary sheet shows deductions and additions to the emergency cash reserve. Several examples will demonstrate how the reserve operates. Assume actual income was $1500 while actual expenditures totaled $1600 during the same month. For that month, we would draw $100 from emergency cash reserve. We use parentheses for that amount, entering ($100), to show it is a decrease. Now suppose actual income was $1550 while all the monthly expenditures totaled $1500. In that month, we would add $50 to our emergency reserve. Later in the chapter, we shall develop guidelines to help you decide how many dollars you should have in your emergency cash reserve.

Exhibit 3-5 illustrates the activity in Sam and Samantha Jones's emergency reserve during the first 3 months of the year. In January, they added $247 to their reserve. But they drew money out of it during the other 2 months.

Monthly Recording: Actual Income and Expenditures   Each month, you will need to record, or "post," your actual income and expenditures to your budget summary sheet. Typically, you can obtain the needed information on your income from two sources: first, the attached stub or listing that comes with your paycheck, and second, the deposits in your checking account. Likewise, by reviewing your canceled checks, you should be able to identify what you spent in each expense category and any loan payments. Another potential source for this information is the monthly statement on each of your credit card accounts, assuming you have one or more cards. A

EXHIBIT 3-5

Budget summary sheet for Sam and Samantha Jones.

	BUDGETED AMOUNT	January ACTUAL	January SURPLUS (DEFICIT)	February ACTUAL	February SURPLUS (DEFICIT)
Available income	$1875	$2075	$200	$1830	$ (45)
Expenses					
Food	263	273	(10)	248	15
Housing					
Mortgage or rent	525	525	—	525	—
Real estate taxes	75	450	(375)	—	75
Utilities	120	160	(40)	130	(10)
Homeowners insurance	14	—	14	—	14
Maintenance	44	—	44	—	44
Clothing	90	15	75	135	(45)
Medical expenses	26	—	26	30	(4)
Automobile					
Gas, oil, maintenance	110	80	30	230	(120)
Repairs, insurance, other	53	—	53	45	8
Contributions	60	40	20	75	(15)
Life insurance	32	—	32	—	32
Personal	38	20	18	60	(22)
Entertainment and travel	124	14	110	60	(64)
Miscellaneous	70	20	50	80	(10)
Total expense	$1644	$1597	$ 47	$1618	$ 26
Monthly savings					
Short-term goals	$ 71	$ 71	—	$ 71	—
Long-term goals	50	50	—	50	—
Total savings	$121	$ 121	—	$ 121	—
Loan payments					
Auto	$ 110	$ 110	—	$ 110	—
Expenses, savings, and loan payments	$1875	$1828		$1849	
Emergency cash reserve:					
Deposits (withdrawals)	$ 0	$ 247		$ (19)	

third source is the amounts you paid in cash. To keep track of these, jot down the dollar amounts and their purposes in a notebook during the month. By adding up these amounts at month's end, you can transfer the total to your summary sheet. Where possible, we favor using checks for most payments because doing so makes the month's recording much easier.

March		Quarterly Summary		
ACTUAL	SURPLUS (DEFICIT)	BUDGETED AMOUNT	ACTUAL	SURPLUS (DEFICIT)
$1740	$(135)	$5625	$5645	$ 20
288	(25)	789	809	(20)
525	—	1575	1575	—
—	75	225	450	(225)
170	(50)	360	460	(100)
168	(154)	42	168	(126)
—	44	132	—	132
35	55	270	185	85
12	14	78	42	36
80	30	330	390	(60)
80	(27)	159	125	34
40	20	180	155	25
105	(73)	96	105	(9)
5	33	114	85	29
34	90	372	108	264
15	55	210	115	95
$1557	$ 87	$4932	$4772	$ 160
$ 71	—	$ 213	$ 213	—
50	—	150	150	—
$ 121	—	$ 363	$ 363	—
$ 110	—	$ 330	$ 330	—
$1788		$5625	$5465	$160
$ (48)		$ 0	$ 180	$180

Each check provides a record of how you spent a certain amount of your money.

The best time to post actual amounts to your summary sheet is right when you are paying your bills for the month. Unless your budget is very detailed or your records are poor, you can usually complete the recording step in 30 to 60 minutes. You should also have time enough to compute the surpluses and deficits—budgeted versus actual—for each item.

Sam and Samantha Jones have posted their actual income and expenditures in Exhibit 3-5 for the first 3 months of the year. They also computed the surpluses and deficits for those months.

Step 4: Review and Analysis of the Budget Summary Sheet

The initial purpose of a budget is to help you plan your expenditures. Once that is done, you will want to review how well your financial plan is doing. This **review and analysis period** involves comparing the actual results with your planned results on your budget summary sheet in order to judge your progress. If the two amounts are significantly different, you may want to analyze the surpluses and deficits to see what caused the gap. We intentionally said, "You *may* want to analyze the difference." A difference of a few dollars probably does not merit further work. Later, we will give some examples to help you decide whether a difference is significant.

Review and Analysis Period   While the budget summary sheet shows monthly surpluses and deficits, we favor a 3-month, or quarterly, review. To make that review easier, the budget summary sheet should have a set of three columns to summarize, for those 3 months, the budgeted amounts, the actual amounts, and the surpluses or deficits when the budgeted and actual items are different. The Jones's budget summary sheet in Exhibit 3-5 has these columns.

Analysis of Budget Surpluses and Deficits.   In the analysis step, we want to determine why actual amounts differ significantly from budgeted

amounts. Our rule of thumb is that a surplus or deficit should be analyzed when it exceeds 5 to 10 percent of what you budgeted for that expenditure. Consequently, a $5 surplus or deficit on an item that is budgeted at $100 probably is not worth analyzing. But a $25 surplus or deficit on that $100 budgeted item probably warrants an analysis to see why it occurred.

Once you have decided why a particular surplus or deficit occurred, you need to ask: "Do I need to take corrective action?" Many surpluses or deficits will require little, if any, action. Take expenses like property taxes and auto insurance. Typically, you make only one or two payments on these items each year. So a large deficit is expected during the quarter that payment was made: The bill covered 6 months while the budgeted amount covered only 3 months. As long as it appears that the total bill for the year will be in line with what you budgeted, no action is needed. During those quarters when you made no payment, these expense categories will likely have a sizable surplus. No corrective action is needed here either. Expenditures for utilities are another place where sizable deficits and surpluses may occur. Variations in the temperature between seasons may readily explain a surplus or deficit. Northern-tier states will likely have deficits during the winter months and surpluses during the summer. Southern-tier states will have the opposite pattern.

When corrective action is necessary, several choices are open to you. First, you might decide to keep the budgeted amount unchanged from your original budget plan. This means that you will have to revise your future spending so that it parallels your budget plan. Raise your spending if you are running a surplus—probably easy to do. Or lower your spending if you are running a deficit—probably a much more difficult step. Second, you may decide to revise the amount you budgeted in your original plan. Recognize, however, that you will probably have to change some other expenditures at the same time. If you just raise planned expenditures but have no change in income, you will likely have a continuing draw on your emergency cash reserve.

The quarterly summary columns for Sam and Samantha Jones in Exhibit 3-5 give us some examples to practice on. The small $20 surplus in available income is not significant, so no further analysis is needed. Likewise, the small $20 deficit in food is not large enough to be a concern. The sizable deficit in real estate taxes warrants an analysis. It appears that one-half, $450, of the budgeted annual tax bill ($900 = 12 months × $75 budgeted) was paid this quarter. That caused the deficit. No corrective action seems necessary because the actual expenditure for the whole year should be in line with the budgeted amount. The fact that Sam and Samantha Jones live in northern Michigan explains the substantial deficit in utility expenses. Now drop down to the clothing category where they had a significant ($85) surplus. From the limited information we have, actual spending apparently fell short of that budget in 2 of the 3 months. The Joneses might want to ask themselves: Do we really expect to spend an average of $90 monthly on clothing? If they answer yes, then they should leave the category as is. If they answer no, they may want to lower the original budgeted amount. As the last example, we see a $60 deficit for the gas, oil, and maintenance category under the automobile heading. The Joneses should ask: Is the $100 budgeted for this category adequate? Yes? Then leave it unchanged. No? Then revise it upward. Should they decide to raise it, they will have to lower some other budgeted amounts if budgeted expenditures are to equal budgeted income.

STRATEGY

By analyzing the significant surpluses and deficits in your budget each quarter (each 3 months), you can adjust your actual spending so that it matches your planned spending.

Planning Your Budget for Next Year A completed full-year budget summary sheet like the one shown in Exhibit 3-5 should help you plan next year's expenditures. Since it already summarizes your spending for last year, an expenditure summary like the one in Exhibit 3-3 is no longer necessary. Once you have budgeted for a year, developing your budget for the next year is relatively easy.

Emergency Cash Reserve

Everyone should have an **emergency cash reserve** that can be used to meet unexpected expenditures. As we've said before, there will be times when major expenses for car repairs, home maintenance, or medical problems arise that were not planned. If they are large, they probably cannot be paid from current income. But an emergency cash reserve can handle them. Even with a good budget, there will be months when actual expenditures exceed that month's available income. Again, an emergency cash reserve can provide the dollars to cover those months. Later, when actual income exceeds expenditures, you can repay the cash reserve. The reserve can also assist when you are changing jobs or are temporarily unemployed.

How large should the emergency cash reserve be? At a minimum, it should equal 2 to 3 months of your available monthly income. If your present employment is secure, that should be enough. However, if there is a considerable likelihood that your present employment may be terminated through a layoff, a reserve of 6 months' available income is recommended. Or if you change jobs frequently and there are gaps between them, a cash reserve of 6 months' income is also advised.

STRATEGY

Your emergency cash reserve should equal at least 2 to 3 months of your budgeted available income. Raise that amount to 6 months if your job is insecure or if you switch jobs frequently, with some unemployment between them.

Do Not Make Your Budget a Straitjacket or a Bad Dream

If your budget becomes too detailed and demanding, you will quickly lose interest in the process. First, don't break your expenses into so many categories that you need several pages to list them. Second, your expenses should include a "Miscellaneous" category, where the money does not have to be accounted for each month. As a general guide, we suggest that category be not more than 10 percent of monthly income. Third, when recording your actual expenditures each month, do not worry about accounting for each penny. Round each item off to the nearest $1, $5, or $10. Finally, do not make your quarterly review and analysis an exercise in self-punishment. Before deciding your budget is a disaster, take a close look to see whether you have set your budgeted expenditures unrealistically low. If you view a budget as a positive planning tool that can help you do the things you want to do, you are far more likely to stick with it. And the benefits to you will be sizable.

SUMMARY

1   A budget can help you plan how you spend your income.

2   The budget process has four steps:

a   You estimate available income.

b   You define major expenditure categories and set spending levels.

c   You use a budget summary sheet to accumulate actual income and expenditures.

d   You periodically review and analyze your progress on the budget.

3   Available income includes all sources, such as salary, interest, dividends, bonuses, and commissions.

4   For most people, a monthly budget is most appropriate.

5   Planned expenditures for the next year can be based on spending during the prior year, on spending during the past 3 or 6 months, or on a trial amount that you will revise after several months.

6   A budget summary sheet highlights your budgeted income and expenditures, your actual income and expenditures, and the difference between actual and budgeted amounts—surpluses and deficits.

7   Each month you should record your total actual income and expenditures on your budget summary sheet.

8   The actual and planned income and expenditures on a budget summary sheet should be reviewed every 3 months. Significant surpluses and deficits should be analyzed to decide whether corrective action is required.

9   An emergency cash reserve can cover the shortfalls when actual expenditures exceed actual income. Likewise, when income exceeds expenditures, the excess can be deposited in that cash reserve.

REVIEW YOUR UNDERSTANDING OF

Budgeting process	Voluntary deduction
Take-home pay	Nonvoluntary deduction
Deductions	Available income

Expenditure categories
   Regular expenses
   Occasional expenses
   Budget period
Budget summary sheet

Surplus
Deficit
Review and analysis period
Emergency cash reserve

DISCUSSION QUESTIONS

1   What is the principal purpose of the four preliminary steps in the budget process?

2   How would you compute your monthly available income? What role does it have in a person's budget?

3   What are the advantages and disadvantages of using a limited number of expenditure categories in a budget? What are the advantages and disadvantages of a large number of categories?

4   What time period do most people use in their budgets? Why is that period generally chosen?

5   Why are the monthly savings for short-term and long-term goals included in a budget? How can short-term goals be converted to monthly amounts? How about monthly amounts for long-term goals?

6   What information would you expect to find on a budget summary sheet? What is the principal purpose of that summary sheet?

7   How often should a person typically record, or post, his or her actual income and expenditures on a budget summary sheet? What sources or records might be used to provide the necessary information?

8   Why is there a section entitled "Emergency cash reserve" on a budget summary? How does it operate? Give an example of a time when that reserve would decline (money is withdrawn). Give an example of a time when the reserve would increase.

9   What is the meaning of having a surplus in the available income section of the budget summary sheet? A deficit? What has happened when an expenditure category shows a surplus on the summary sheet? A deficit?

10   Give several examples of expenditure categories where we might have a surplus or deficit on the budget summary sheet for several months, yet decide that no corrective action is required.

11   Assume Oliver Overspend budgeted $100 for entertainment during each of the first 3 months of the year. Yet his actual spending was $1200.

    a   To stay within his budget, how much can he spend during the rest of the year?

    b   What options does Oliver have to correct his expenditure overrun?

PROBLEMS

3-1   Agnes Twine wants your help to estimate the monthly available income she should use for her budget. Details on her income include:

Voluntary deductions (monthly)	$ 150
Gross monthly salary	$1400
Annual interest income	$ 288

Nonvoluntary deductions (monthly) $ 360
Annual bonus from employer $1080

What is Agnes's monthly available income?

3-2   Ed and Edna Endpoint have detailed the following short-term and long-term financial goals:

GOAL	AMOUNT	DATE WANTED	MONTHLY SAVINGS
Auto	$6000	3 years	___?___
Condominium down payment	$7000	8 years	___?___

During the accumulation period, the Endpoints expect they can earn 10 percent on any invested money. What monthly savings will they have to set aside to achieve their goals?

3-3   Shown below is a portion of Fred and Francine Freshstart's budget summary sheet:

CATEGORY	BUDGETED	**April** ACTUAL	**April** SURPLUS (DEFICIT)	**May** ACTUAL	**May** SURPLUS (DEFICIT)	**June** ACTUAL	**June** SURPLUS (DEFICIT)
Income	$1045	$1005	$(40)	$1000		$1140	
Rent	220	220	—	220		220	
Utilities	80	90	(10)	60		30	
Renters insurance	7	—	7	—		84	
Clothing	30	20	10	70		—	
.	.	.	.	.		.	
.	.	.	.	.		.	
.	.	.	.	.		.	
Short-term goals	80	80	—	80		80	
Loan payments	175	175	—	175		175	
Total expenditures	1045	1000	45	1100		1200	
Emergency cash	—	5					

a Complete the surpluses and deficits for this budget summary sheet.

b If the Freshstarts had $2000 in their emergency cash reserve on April 1, what is the balance at the end of June? (Assume that the only withdrawals and deposits are those shown in their budget summary sheet.)

3-4   Carl and Jan Tryzinski need your help to complete the review and analysis of their budget summary sheet. The quarterly totals for some expenditure categories are these:

CATEGORY	Quarterly Summary		SURPLUS (DEFICIT)
	BUDGETED	ACTUAL	
Rent	$660	$660	_____
Utilities	240	300	_____
Renters insurance	21	0	_____
Clothing	90	30	_____
Entertainment	300	1200	_____

a Complete the surplus (deficit) column for this quarterly summary.

b Analyze the surpluses and deficits and write an explanation for the major ones.

c What corrective actions, if any, do you suggest?

3-5   The following table summarizes the totals in the quarterly summary for Steve and Sally Spendit's budget summary sheet.

CATEGORY	Quarterly Summary		SURPLUS (DEFICIT)
	BUDGETED	ACTUAL	
Available income	$4200	$3800	_____
Total expense categories	3220	3645	_____
Total short-term and long-term goals	650	650	_____
Loan payments	330	330	_____
Emergency cash reserve	—	—	

a Compute the surpluses and deficits needed to complete this summary.

b Briefly describe what happened during the quarter in the Spendits' category for:

    Available income   Loan payments

    Expenses   Emergency cash reserve

    Short-term and long-term goals

c What has likely happened to the balance in the Spendits' emergency cash reserve? Why?

d What corrective action, if any, would you recommend for Steve and Sally? Why?

CASE PROBLEM

Gloria Gonzalez recently graduated from college and started work as a management trainee for a large manufacturing firm. She is single, but she plans to be married next June (a year hence) when her fiancé, Jamie, graduates from college, although he plans to continue on to graduate school.

Her salary is $1575 per month, and after deductions for Social Security, federal and state taxes, and health insurance, her take-home pay is $1160. She plans to share an apartment this year with a college friend. The monthly rent will be $210 each, including utilities. By cooking most meals herself, she thinks she can keep her food bill under $140 per month. Her other major expenses will include (all amounts are for the year unless noted otherwise):

Operating auto (monthly)	$ 120	Entertainment	$ 540
Life insurance premium	312	Contributions	360
Auto insurance	240	Renters insurance	96
Personal	240	Miscellaneous (monthly)	50
Clothing	1020		

At present, Gloria is making monthly car payments of $170 and will continue to make them for 22 more months. During the next 18 months, she would like to save $2500 so that she and Jamie can travel after their marriage. Over that same 18-month period, Gloria also wants to save $2000 to buy some furniture for an apartment. She expects to earn an 8 percent return.

Using this information, Gloria would like to complete a budget for the next year. When compiling it, she knows that she should consider her regular expenses, her loan payments, and her short-term financial goals. But she is uncertain how to proceed.

1   Can you prepare the budget Gloria needs?

2   Will Gloria be able to achieve the spending plans she has currently set for herself?

3   Does she have much latitude in spending options? That is, can her actual spending vary significantly from her plans and still allow her to complete her goals?

4   If your answer to part **3** was no, why?

5   If Gloria for some reason had to reduce her spending below the amounts listed above, which categories would likely be easiest to reduce? Which would be very difficult to reduce?

6   If Gloria should decide not to save for the travel fund and the furniture purchase, what other option or options would she have? Are there any advantages to saving for these two items?

**AFTER COMPLETING THIS CHAPTER
YOU WILL HAVE LEARNED**

What *inflation* can do to the future price of an item

How to determine what the *real rate of return* is on an investment and under what conditions saving for a financial goal may no longer be justified

Why *inflation* can make the *option of borrowing* the money to buy an item immediately more attractive

How to *compare* the *cost of borrowing* the money to purchase an item immediately to the *cost of waiting* while you save the necessary money to buy the item later

Why a *sizable percentage of the second income* in a two-income household will probably be needed to pay the various *taxes* and *work related expenses* on that income

How to *compute* the amount of *spendable income* that a second income will provide

What the *fringe benefits* that a second income provides may be *worth*

What a *warranty* is all about, and the differences between a *full warranty* and a *limited warranty*

What *caveat emptor* means and what *consumer protection legislation* attempts to accomplish

What strategy can help you obtain *satisfaction* when you have a *defective product* or receive *inadequate service*

CHAPTER
4
ISSUES IN CONSUMER DECISIONS

UNTIL some 25 or 30 years ago, peo-

ple who felt they were being treated unfairly, socially or economically, merely murmured privately about dissatisfaction and injustice. Since then, such people have formed themselves into groups to let their feelings be known more forcefully and to effect social and economic change.

During the 1960s and 1970s, consumer groups lobbied hard for the passage of legislation that would improve the position of the consumer. In many cases they were quite successful. An example of that new legislation includes the "cooling off" period, which allows a consumer to change his or her mind about an agreement to purchase merchandise sold door-to-door. An impressive example of the success of consumer group effort is the *manufacturer's recall*. At one time, if you were one of many new car owners having the same problem caused by a defect in the design or manufacture of your car and you complained to the auto manufacturer, the manufacturer would have said to you "Tough!" or "Too bad!" and you were stuck. That's no longer the case. The manufacturer is now required to announce a recall, asking owners to bring in cars for repairs or adjustments. And there are numerous other examples of legislation and court decisions that changed situations that were formerly lopsided—benefiting the businesses at the expense of the consumers.

We will then look at something that no consumer organization and no amount of consumer force or legislation can change—inflation. In fact, the recent, extremely high level of inflation has negated many former axioms of consumer decision making. For example, when inflation was at an annual rate of 1 to 3 percent, it could be argued conclusively that an individual should save to pay cash for an automobile rather than buy immediately and borrow the money to finance the purchase. When inflation exceeds 10 percent annually, this advice needs to be examined carefully.

We will then analyze several major consumer issues in this chapter. These analyses should equip you better to understand the business environment in which you are operating and enable you to make sounder life-style and purchasing decisions.

INFLATION: THE ULTIMATE RIP-OFF

Imagine yourself paying over $50,000 for a new car. It must be a Mercedes Benz or a BMW. Unfortunately not; it's only a VW Rabbit or a Honda Civic; that's what today's $7,500 car would cost in 20 years if inflation were to rise 10 percent each year. A Mercedes, which currently costs $33,000, would cost a breathtaking $220,000 in 20 years. Even more staggering is what will happen to the price of the average house. A typical $85,000 home today will cost over $570,000 in just 20 years if inflation runs 10 percent annually.

Exhibit 4-1 shows how the price of a $7,500 automobile will increase when the inflation rate is 5 or 10 percent per year. We didn't want to take the exhibit beyond 20 years because the result would be difficult to compre-

EXHIBIT 4-1

Future cost of today's $7,500 car if inflation is 5 or
10 percent per year.

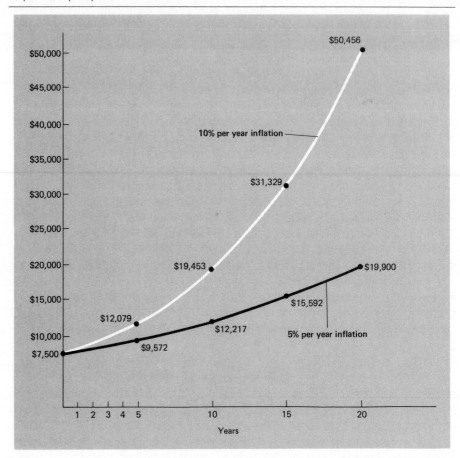

hend. At 10 percent inflation, the $7,500 car will cost $339,444 in 40 years!
Let's examine some of the issues implied by these drastic increases in cost
over time. Among them is the estimated inflation rate.

Issue: When Does Saving No Longer Make Sense?

When inflation rates exceed the interest you earn on an investment, it is
hard to justify continuing a savings plan. Let us see why by using the
examples in Exhibit 4-2. Assume that you face the following two options:

> Use the $1000 you have in the bank to purchase a new widget (that's
> economists' jargon for some piece of merchandise).

> Invest the $1000 for 1 year, during which time you will earn 10 percent
> interest; purchase a widget after 1 year.

Investing the $1000 at a **nominal** (promised) **rate of return** of 10 percent will
provide $1100 in 1 year. But the key to your real return is what that $1100

will buy. Finding your **real rate of return** centers on what will happen to prices during that 1 year of investment. Exhibit 4-2 illustrates four different situations. In case A, we assume zero inflation. That means today's $1000 widget will still cost $1000 next year. Your real return after inflation is the same 10 percent that the investment promised: You earned $100 on the investment and you get to keep the whole amount because the widget costs the same $1000 as it did 1 year ago.

But suppose inflation is 5 percent, as in case B; the widget will cost $1050 in 1 year. Now you have to spend $50 of your $100 return (10 percent of $1000) just to buy the widget; that $50 is lost to inflation. In effect, you will have earned only $50 on your $1000 investment, as is shown in column 5. Your real return is only 5 percent because you earned $50 on a $1000 investment. Or an easier way to compute the real return is:

$$\text{Real rate of return} = \text{Nominal or promised} - \text{Inflation rate}$$
$$\text{rate of return}$$

What happens when inflation rises to 10 percent (as in case C)? First, the widget's cost rises to $1100 by the end of the year. You will have to spend your entire $100 return just to buy the widget; that leaves you nothing. We summarize this in column 5. Now your real return after inflation is zero (0 percent). Sure, you will still have earned 10 percent on the $1000, but all of it will go to offset the year's 10 percent rise in prices. With 15 percent inflation, the picture is even more grim. Not only does inflation take your entire $100 return, but it also takes $50 from your original investment. Just to buy the widget requires $1150 (case D) at the end of 1 year. Losing $50 on your original $1000 investment means you earned a negative 5 percent return. That is hardly the foundation on which you can build castles of wealth.

Before deciding to save now in order to buy later, you need to answer the question, "What will be my real return on this investment?" During the late 1970s and early 1980s, federal and state regulations held the rates of return on many investments for small savers below inflation rates. That restriction condemned many small savers to a solid string of negative

EXHIBIT 4-2

Real rate of return on a $1000 investment earning 10 percent interest annually.

CASE	Investment		INFLATION RATE (3)	WIDGET PRICE IN 1 YEAR (4)	REAL DOLLAR RETURN: (2) − (4) (5)	REAL RATE OF RETURN: (1) − (3) (6)
	NOMINAL RETURN (1)	VALUE IN 1 YEAR (2)				
A	10%	$1100	0%	$1000	$100	10%
B	10	1100	5	1050	50	5
C	10	1100	10	1100	0	0
D	10	1100	15	1150	$−50	−5

returns, certainly not the kind of thing that encourages more savings. But, as later sections of the book will discuss, relief has finally arrived. Increasingly, many of those rates of return are being deregulated; these deregulated returns on investments should exceed the inflation rate. Positive real rates of return should once more become the rule, not the exception.

STRATEGY

Carefully review what your real rate of return will likely be on a particular investment. If it is positive, regular investing makes sense. If it is negative, then regular investing is highly questionable.

Saving Is Still Important Despite the dismal results of the late 1970s, we believe a regular savings program is still important. Historically, real returns over extended periods have been positive. For that reason, we believe it is essential to develop a regular investment program for most of your medium- to long-term financial goals. As interest rates are deregulated, real returns should again match their positive long-run historical pattern.

Issue: Is Borrowing Money Smart?

While inflation tends to reduce the attractiveness of saving or investing for some future purchase, it does the exact opposite for borrowing money. In fact, under certain conditions, inflation can reduce the cost of borrowing to a very low or negative amount. Before deciding whether or not to borrow, you need to know the **net cost of the loan.** Let us use the series of examples in Exhibit 4-3 to illustrate this point. First, recognize that it costs money to borrow $1000. Lenders are like anyone else who rents out something; they expect to be paid rent (interest) for their loan of that item. We will assume that the lender charges 12 percent interest; if you should borrow $1000, you would be expected to pay $1120 when you repay the loan in 1 year. Assume that you are faced with two options:

> Borrow $1000 for 1 year at 12 percent interest and immediately purchase a $1000 widget (our old friend from the last example).

EXHIBIT 4-3

Cost of borrowing $1000 to purchase an item
immediately versus waiting 1 year to purchase it.

CASE	Borrowing Option		INFLATION RATE (3)	WIDGET COST IN 1 YEAR (4)	NET COST TO BORROW (2) − (4) (5)	NET COST OF LOAN (1) − (3) (6)
	COST TO BORROW (1)	COST TO REPAY LOAN (2)				
A	12%	$1120	8%	$1080	$40	4%
B	12	1120	12	1120	0	0
C	12	1120	16	1160	−40	−4

Wait 1 year and purchase that widget when you have the money. (We ignore any interest you might earn while accumulating the money.)

We will explore three examples: (1) case A assumes 8 percent inflation, (2) case B assumes 12 percent inflation, and (3) case C assumes 16 percent inflation.

Under all three scenarios, the 12 percent $1000 loan will cost you $1120 when you repay it in 1 year. But the key to the loan's true cost is what the $1120 will actually purchase when it is time to repay the loan. If inflation has pushed up prices during that year, paying $1120 will be less of a sacrifice than it was when you took out the loan. Let us use case A to illustrate. With 8 percent inflation, today's $1000 widget will cost you $1080 next year. Borrowing $1000 to purchase the widget immediately therefore costs you only $40. Granted, you paid $120 to borrow that money. But delaying the purchase for 1 year would have cost you an additional $80. So your net cost to borrow is $40, or 4 percent; these calculations are shown in columns 5 and 6 of Exhibit 4-3, respectively.

What happens at higher inflation rates? Clearly, the price of the widget will rise more rapidly, so it will cost you more next year. That makes borrowing the money now more attractive, as you can avoid those future price increases. How much more attractive? Well, at 12 percent inflation (case B in Exhibit 4-3), the net cost of borrowing drops to zero. Both the borrow-to-buy-now and the wait-to-buy options cost the same $1120. The cost of borrowing, column 5 and 6, is now zero. But what happens when inflation exceeds the loan's interest rate? Then the net cost to borrow becomes negative. Case C of Exhibit 4-3 shows a negative $40 as the net cost to borrow. Or, looking at the real cost in another way, you actually save $40 by borrowing. The loan's net cost is a negative 4 percent. Would individuals want to borrow under these circumstances? Yes! Lenders would be besieged with potential borrowers. In fact, few lenders would even exist in this case.

But before you rush out to borrow as much as possible so you can cash in on the savings, several observations are in order. No doubt people who had taken out loans at 6 or 7 percent benefited handsomely when inflation rose to 10 percent. But lenders, like savers, are not totally naive. The interest rates lenders charge on new loans clearly exceed current inflation rates. When inflation reached 10 to 12 percent in the early 1980s, loan rates of 16 percent and more were not uncommon. These high interest charges reduce, if not remove, the inflationary advantage of borrowing to beat future price increases. When you could borrow at 10 percent interest while prices were expected to rise 10 to 12 percent, borrowing offered a definite advantage. But as interest rates rose to 14 percent and more, that advantage disappeared. Now the net cost to borrow is positive. Once more, you must decide whether it is worthwhile to pay the cost of borrowing to obtain the immediate use of the purchased item. We will explore this issue further in Chapter 7.

Buy Now versus Buy Later   The decision to buy now rather than later entails a trade-off between two costs. Exhibit 4-4 will illustrate this process.

EXHIBIT 4-4

Cost of buying now versus buying later.

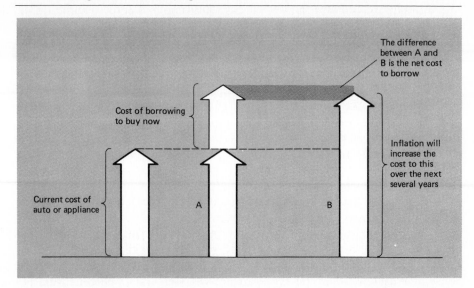

If you buy now, you purchase at the current price; mark that fact up as an advantage. But if you must borrow the money to make your purchase, you must pay interest on your loan. Mark that down as a disadvantage. Column A of Exhibit 4-4 shows the combination of purchasing at today's price and the cost of the interest on the loan.

Column B of Exhibit 4-4 shows the option of waiting to purchase the item. The cost of this option depends on how much prices will rise during the coming year. If inflation is moderate, the price of the item will increase relatively little. Consequently, the cost will be small. However, if inflation is high, the item's price will rise sharply. That makes the cost of waiting substantial.

Historically, the cost of waiting—option B in Exhibit 4-4—has been less than the cost of borrowing to buy the item immediately (option A). Granted, during several periods in the 1970s, the reverse was true. But borrowing costs have risen to reflect the higher inflation rates; that increase effectively reverses borrowing's favorable cost spread. Currently, there is a net cost to borrow. So your decision to borrow or not to borrow centers on whether the advantage of having the item early (by buying now) will offset your added cost. We will discuss this dilemma more fully in Chapter 7.

STRATEGY

The cost of borrowing generally exceeds the future expected inflation rate. Consequently, borrowing now solely to beat future price increases is usually not justified.

Inflation Rates All the calcualtions we've made are based on **estimated inflation rates**. To make decisions between buying today and buying later, you must make some estimate of what will happen to prices. You can either make your own estimates or use estimates from government agencies, banks, and economic forecasters. Newspapers, magazines, and national television news programs regularly carry reports that discuss the outlook for inflation. If you watch for these, you should very quickly get a pretty good idea of what the "experts" think will happen to prices. These predictions on inflation rates are probably as good as any for use in making financial decisions.

THE TWO-INCOME HOUSEHOLD

Both husband and wife in more than half the households in the United States have incomes from jobs, and there are indications that this percentage will continue to increase. This trend contrasts sharply with the late 1940s and early 1950s, when fewer than 25 percent of American households had incomes from both spouses.

At one time, the main reason for **two-income households** was financial —they needed more income to pay increasing bills and to fulfill greater needs and wants. While the financial incentive of two incomes is still strong, for many couples it has been joined by a greatly expanded list of motivating forces. That list includes such things as both people wanting to pursue active work careers, improved self-esteem, bolstered self-confidence, and emotional independence.

Throughout our discussion, we will refer to the two wage-earners as the *principal* wage-earner and the *second* wage-earner. Our principal earner may be either the husband or the wife, and the term does not necessarily imply the person who earns the highest salary. The second earner is simply the person who has some degree of choice about working or not working outside the home.

Should Both Partners Work? Monetary Considerations

Although the desire for extra money is not the sole factor in deciding whether both partners will work, for most couples it still is an important part of the decision. Unfortunately, many people never make an effort to determine how much money that second salary really adds to the household's available income. Some couples consider only the gross amount of

the second income, without realizing that some of it is taken by income taxes and that some of it must pay for work-related expenses, such as transportation to work, lunches, and work clothes. At the opposite extreme, some couples entirely ignore the second income in their plans and consider it merely as extra money or pin money.

We believe a position between these extremes is best. Couples should carefully compute just how much of the second salary is really available as spendable income; that second salary, together with the first salary, should be part of their total financial plan. And a couple should not be totally dependent on every penny of the second income.

Impact of Taxes   Higher incomes mean higher income taxes; it doesn't matter whether an individual or a household of two wage-earners is making the higher income. Later, in Chapter 6, we'll see in detail how federal income taxes are structured and how the higher a couple's income, the higher their tax rate and the greater the **impact of taxes.** For example, a couple with only a principal wage-earner having an income of $22,000 might have a tax rate of 19 percent on a dollar of income. But if the second wage-earner went to work, raising the partners' total income to $31,000, that extra income could easily boost their tax rate to 26 percent on every dollar of income.

The second wage-earner also pays Social Security taxes on his or her salary; the current rate is 6.7 percent. Those tax payments entitle the second wage-earner to some additional benefits beyond what he or she would receive just for being the spouse of the principal wage-earner. Some people argue quite convincingly, however, that the added tax payments far exceed the added benefits. But Social Security taxes are mandatory, so you have no choice. And, since most states also have a personal income tax, they take an additional amount from that second salary.

The net effect of all these tax bites is that taxes consume a sizable portion of that second salary before the couple ever gets any income to spend.

Exhibit 4-5 summarizes the combined impact of federal and state income taxes and Social Security taxes on the second wage-earner's salary. The percentages in the exhibit show what portion of the second salary remains after federal and state taxes are taken out of it. To illustrate, assume the principal wage-earner's salary is $15,000, while the second salary is $10,000. There are two people in the household: husband and wife. Based on Exhibit 4-5, the percentage of the second salary that remains after taxes is approximately:

$6,900   = $10,000 × 69%

⬆   ⬆   ⬆

Remaining   Second   Percentage
portion of   = salary   × remaining after taxes
second salary   (Exhibit 4-5)

Had there been four family members, they would have retained $7,100.

EXHIBIT 4-5

Approximate percentage of second salary
remaining after deducting federal, state, and
Social Security taxes, 1983.

GROST EARNINGS OF SECOND WAGE-EARNER	NUMBER IN FAMILY	Gross Earnings of Prinicipal Wage-Earner			
		$10,000	$15,000	$20,000	$25,000
$ 5,000	2	74%	71%	67%	63%
	4	76	73	69	64
$10,000	2	73	69	65	60
	4	74	71	67	62
$15,000	2	71	67	63	58
	4	73	69	64	60
$20,000	2	69	65	60	56
	4	70	67	62	57
$25,000	2	67	62	58	54
	4	68	64	60	56

Table was constructed using the following assumptions:
a Federal income taxes: couple filed jointly; 2 or 4 exemptions were claimed at
$1000 each; couple used zero bracket amount.
b State income taxes were set equal to 23% of the federal income taxes.
c Social Security taxes were set at 6.7%.
d All percentages were rounded.

Constructing Exhibit 4-5 necessarily entails a number of assumptions. The purpose of the exhibit is only to give you some general idea of how income taxes affect the second salary.

Determining Work-Related Expenses for the Second Salary In addition to taxes, a considerable portion of the second salary must also be spent for **work-related expenses.**

Exhibit 4-6 is a worksheet that begins with the amount of second-salary income that is left after all taxes have been deducted. The exhibit lists the general categories of work-related expenses, which we'll discuss as we explain the worksheet.

Line 1 shows the gross salary, and line 2 shows the percentage remaining after taxes; multiplying the two gives the after-tax income shown on line 3. The categories of work-related expenses are detailed on lines 4 (a) through 4 (g). Some of these expenses stem directly from the duties and responsibilities of the second job: commuting expenses, extra clothing, dues, memberships, lunches, journal subscriptions, and continuing education. Other expenses arise because the second wage-earner is no longer available to perform some services about the home: child care, additional food expenses, housecleaning, and maintenance services.

Child Care Services Where child care is necessary, its costs can vary widely depending on the number of children, their ages, and the type of care desired. Typically, there is considerable latitude in the kinds of child care. For example, the cost of sending a preschool child to a day care center will likely be lowest; sending the child to someone else's house for babysitting will probably be more costly; and having someone come to your house to care for your child will be more expensive still. Furthermore, child care costs will vary substantially depending on where you live; they are lower in rural areas and higher in cities. If you need child care services, you will have to obtain local estimates for the type of care you prefer.

Commuting Expenses For those who can use public transportation to travel to work, this cost estimate should be straightforward. If you must drive your car to work, Chapter 9 can help you estimate the cost for each mile when you own and operate a car. Once you know those operating costs, it is easy to estimate monthly commuting expenses based on the miles driven.

Clothing When estimating clothing expenses, you should take particular care to include only the *added* clothing costs directly attributed to the new

EXHIBIT 4-6

Estimating the income from the second wage-earner's salary after deducting work-related expenses.

LINE	DESCRIPTION	AMOUNT	
1	Gross salary of second wage-earner		$_____
2	Percentage of salary remaining after taxes*		_____%
3	After-tax income: Line 1 × line 2		$_____
4	Less work-related expenses		
	a Child care	$_____	
	b Commuting expenses	$_____	
	c Clothing: expenditures over and above regular wardrobe	$_____	
	d Dues, special memberships, other expenses as an employee	$_____	
	e Food: additional convenience items and meals out	$_____	
	f Housecleaning and maintenance services	$_____	
	g Lunches	$_____	
	h Total work-related expenses	$_____	$_____
5	Available income after deducting work-related items: Line 3 − line 4(h)		$_____
6	Percentage of gross income remaining as available income: Line 5 ÷ line 1		_____%

*Obtained from Exhibit 4-5 on the basis of the respective salaries of the two wage-earners.

employment. A certain amount of clothing expenditures is to be expected, regardless of whether you work or not; including these normal costs understates what the second salary actually provides.

Dues, Memberships, Other Expenses as an Employee   Included in this group would be memberships in professional associations, unions, and other trade groups. In addition, it would include any special expenses, such as magazine and newspaper subscriptions, attendance at professional conferences, and work supplies, that you incur as an employee.

Food   When both partners work, monthly food costs may rise because they may rely more on convenience foods at home, including food items where some or all of the preparation has been done by the manufacturer. Frozen dinners, prepared mixes, and canned or frozen main courses and desserts are some examples. Food costs may also rise if more meals must be eaten in restaurants. When estimating this work-related cost, include only those added food costs that arise solely because the second person works. For example, if you already ate out every day before the second wage-earner started work, it would be incorrect to claim the cost of eating out was due to the second income.

Housecleaning and Maintenance Services   When both individuals work outside the home, there generally is less time and energy for performing regular cleaning and maintenance jobs for the house or apartment. Should you decide that the second job necessitates your hiring cleaning or maintenance services, the cost must be included as a work-related cost.

Workday Meals   The added cost of eating meals away from home during working hours should be included as a work-related expense. Again, the cost should be only the difference in cost between eating meals at home and eating them at work, whether they are brown-bag or restaurant meals. For example, if you usually make a lunch of soup and a sandwich for $1.50 when at home but, now that you work, you find that lunch costs you $4.50, your work-related meal cost is $4.50 − $1.50, or $3 each day.

Estimating Available Income   Line 4 (*h*) of Exhibit 4-6 is the total of all the work-related expenses. This line is deducted from line 3, after-tax income, and the result is line 5, which shows what income you actually have available from that second salary. Do not be surprised if this final amount is but a ghost of its former self: your gross income. With federal income taxes claiming 25 percent or more, state taxes claiming approximately 6 percent, Social Security taxes taking 7 percent, and work-related expenses taking another 20 percent, the 100 percent gross income you began with is devastated! You can therefore easily see why only one-third of the gross income you began with at line 1 may be left over at line 5 as available, spendable income. Your calculation will also point out why tax relief has become the rallying point for many disgruntled two-income households.

If the second income is rather small, such as the low income of a beginning salary, the available dollars on line 5 will likely be very few. But there are several additional points to consider before immediately dismissing the second salary as not worthwhile. First, the beginning position may pay a low income, but you may have an opportunity to switch to higher-paying positions once you have some work experience. Or, the second job may offer other economic benefits that should be given weight in your decision. This is the topic of our next section.

Those "Other" Economic Benefits

In addition to the income of a second job, there are also the fringe benefits you receive as an employee, which you should consider in evaluating the second job. **Fringe benefits** include such things as health, dental, disability, and life insurance; retirement plans; company savings plans; common-stock purchase plans; and profit-sharing or bonus plans. These added benefits can substantially improve the economic attractiveness of having a second income. First, those benefits cover the costs of services that would be expensive if you had to pay for them: premiums on health and dental insurance, coverage for income continuation in the event of your disability, and premiums for life insurance protection. Second, in most cases the costs of these benefits are not included in your annual income, so you do not have to pay income or Social Security taxes on them. Even though you may eventually have to pay taxes on some of these benefits—retirement, savings plans, stock plans—the tax bite can often be deferred, or put off, for a few years. The net effect is that the economic benefit of that second income may be substantially greater than what we estimated as available income on line 5 of Exhibit 4-6.

Now the major problem: estimating the value for those "other" economic benefits. Several things make the problem a bit complex. First, there is no set package of fringe benefits that comes with any job. Some jobs offer few, if any, benefits, while others provide a long list. Second, we cannot give even a rough estimate of what a certain fringe benefit might be worth. That is, the value of particular fringe items vary widely: premiums on a poor health-insurance program may be worth less than $100 a year, whereas premiums on a good one exceed $1500. Last, your situation can heavily influence the value of a particular fringe benefit. For example, if the principal wage-earner already has excellent health insurance coverage from his or her job, the added health insurance of the second wage-earner may duplicate existing coverage and be worth very little. Yet the same health insurance may be highly valuable if the principal wage-earner has little or no health coverage.

Valuing the "Other" Benefits Offered   Exhibit 4-7 summarizes the major fringe benefits that are likely to be offered by the second job. Each benefit will be discussed briefly in the next section. It is not our goal at this point to try to assign a dollar value to each benefit. To do that, we would need considerably more background information for each topical area; the discussion of insurance (Chapters 12 through 16), investments (Chapters 17 through 20), and retirement (Chapter 21) will give you that background. Now we will point out the broad issues without going into great detail.

Health Insurance   The value of this fringe benefit will be determined by what it would cost to buy the same health-insurance coverage as a private purchaser. If the principal wage-earner already has health insurance that

EXHIBIT 4-7

CHAPTER 4

83

ISSUES IN
CONSUMER
DECISIONS

Valuing the fringe benefits provided by the
second wage-earner's job.

LINE	DESCRIPTION	AMOUNT	
1	Available income from line 5 of Exhibit 4-6		$_____
2	Estimated value of each fringe benefit:		
	a Health insurance	$_____	
	b Dental insurance	$_____	
	c Income continuation in the event of disability	$_____	
	d Life insurance coverage	$_____	
	e Employer-sponsored savings plans, common stock purchase plans, profit-sharing, and bonus plans	$_____	
	f Total	$_____	$_____
3	Estimated economic value of the second wage-earner's job: Line 1 plus line 2(f)		$_____

covers the members of the household, the value would likely be less; that portion of the insurance coverage that merely duplicates the coverage under the principal earner's health policy provides no additional value.

Dental Insurance Again, the primary value determinant is going to be the cost of purchasing similar dental insurance as an individual. Duplication is far less likely, since dental insurance is less common than health insurance.

Income Continuation in the Event of Disability One way to estimate the value of this fringe benefit is to consider the amount it would cost to purchase the same income-continuation protection from a private insurance company. There will be no problem with duplication, because the income continuation applies strictly to the earnings of the second wage-earner.

Life Insurance The best way to value the life insurance fringe benefit is to determine what you would pay to purchase the same dollar amount of coverage from a private insurance company. Duplicating the principal wage-earner's coverage is not a problem because the life insurance covers only the second wage-earner.

Company-Sponsored Savings Plans, Common-Stock Purchase Plans, and Profit-Sharing and Bonus Plans The range of available benefits is very broad and diverse. Your overall goal here should be to identify what added payment or benefit you would receive that would not be there if you did not have the second job. That is, what additional economic benefit is the employer providing through these different fringe benefits? Frequently, these company-sponsored plans are one of the most difficult fringes on which to place a dollar value.

Retirement Benefits One difficulty with estimating the value of retirement benefits is that payments will typically take place in the distant future. Nevertheless, they certainly have a value, since the second wage-earner is building up a potential retirement income. At this point, we simply say that the retirement benefit definitely has value, but we will wait until Chapter 21 before trying to judge the extent of that value.

Special Financial Planning Needs of Two-Income Households

A detailed personal financial plan is just as important to a two-income household as it is when there is only one income. In fact, we argue that it probably is more important. First, total annual income in a two-income household usually entails managing larger and probably more extensive expenditures. Second, that increased income frequently broadens the range of financial alternatives and options. Third, the fringe benefits of both jobs may overlap and therefore require special analysis and management to avoid unnecessary duplication. Last, the higher income may lull some people into thinking their income is so large that they can just skip planning how to spend the money. Rare is the income that permits such an approach.

Most of the personal financial planning topics we discuss throughout the book apply equally to one- and two-income households.

We now ease our way into the sometimes volatile area of consumer protection with a discussion of warranties and guarantees.

WARRANTIES AND GUARANTEES

On the one hand, manufacturers use advertising to help sell their products, and we know that, to one degree or another, the advertising isn't entirely truthful in all cases. On the other hand, manufacturers do try to back up their claims, or at least to give consumers some reassurance that they are responsible for these claims. When consumers plop down their hard-earned money for a product, they also get a written assurance that the product will do what it is supposed to do, at least for a specified period after purchase, or else the manufacturer will repair it, or replace it, or do something else, depending on the written assurance, to satisfy the customer.

The written assurance is called either a **warranty** or a **guarantee.** The terms are used interchangeably, and there is no difference between them.

Improving the Warranty Mess

Many warranties were once not much more than a marketing gimmick. But now the **Federal Trade Commission** (FTC) has the power under federal law to get manufacturers to state specifically what their warranties cover and to back these warranties up with satisfaction for consumers.

Disclosure Warranties must be stated clearly and concisely, telling the consumer exactly what is covered. Warranties can neither hedge nor contain misleading or fraudulent statements. They must disclose:

1   Exactly what is covered

2   Who is covered

3   The name and address of the warrantor

4   How to file a claim

5   How to file a complaint

6   The coverage period

Coverage under Warranties   The amount of protection offered by the warranty is determined by the type of warranty. The two major types are the "full" coverage warranty and the "limited" warranty. Often a product may be covered by a combination of both types of warranties. Automobiles, for example, have certain parts covered by a full warranty, while other components have only limited coverage. In addition, all products are covered by "implied" warranties.

Full Warranty   A **full warranty** guarantees that the defective product will be repaired during the warranty period at no charge and within a reasonable time. If the defect cannot be corrected, the manufacturer must replace the item or give you a pro rata refund.

Limited Warranty   Any warranty that does not meet the conditions of a full warranty must be clearly labeled as a **limited warranty.** The warranty must specify the parts that are covered and the length of the coverage. Any exclusions must also be disclosed.

Implied Warranty   Even if a product is not covered by a full or a limited warranty, it will be covered under the doctrine of **implied warranty.** This simply means that the product will perform as the manufacturer claims. For example, a stepladder may not have a written warranty. But if you use it in a normal manner and it collapses, you will likely have a claim against the manufacturer.

Adjustment Procedure   Should a manufacturer offering a full warranty be unable or unwilling to repair a product after a reasonable number of attempts, the buyer can request a free replacement or a *pro rata* cash refund. A pro rata refund means that the warrantor can deduct a reasonable allowance to cover the wear on the unit up to the time it became defective.

If the warranty has an informal settlement procedure, its details must be clearly stated. For example, the informal procedure may require that the store that sold the product be given several opportunities to correct the problem. Or it may specify that the unit must be returned to the manufacturer's factory for corrective service work.

Where there is no procedure stated in the warranty, or where there was a procedure which the buyer followed without a satisfactory settlement, the buyer can sue. If the buyer wins, the manufacturer must pay attorney's fees.

Consumer's Responsibility   Implied in every warranty is the buyer's responsibility for maintaining the product and not abusing it. When a product is defective, the buyer must give the warrantor an opportunity to repair it or correct the problem. Also implied in the warranty is the buyer's responsibility for reading the warranty and understanding its conditions. For example, if the warranty states that the manufacturer's responsibility ceases if the product is used in certain ways, the manufacturer will not be liable if the buyer is unaware of the restriction because of not having read the warranty.

What the FTC Cannot Do   The FTC will not press the buyer's complaint against the manufacturer. That is still the buyer's responsibility. Nor does the FTC prosecute manufacturers that fail to meet their warranty responsibility. The buyer must do that through the court system.

Evaluating a Warranty   Exhibit 4-8 provides a checklist to help evaluate a warranty. A large number of "no" responses suggests a warranty that is restrictive and that offers limited coverage.

EXHIBIT 4-8

Checklist to help you judge the effectiveness of
a warranty.

	YES	NO
What Is Covered		
Does the warranty give full coverage?	____	____
Is there a single warranty?	____	____
If there are several, is the coverage on different parts (full or limited) specified?	____	____
Is that coverage reasonable?	____	____
If the warranty is limited, do the exclusions and limitations seem reasonable?	____	____
Are the costs of both parts and labor covered?	____	____
Is the total repair charge covered?	____	____
Who Is Covered		
Does the warranty cover subsequent owners?	____	____
Does the coverage remain in force when the unit is moved?	____	____
Is there a special registration requirement (e.g., card to be mailed in)?	____	____
Duration of Coverage		
Length of full coverage?	____	____
Length of limited coverage?	____	____
Is coverage equal to that of competing brands?	____	____
How Adjustments Are Made		
Is the adjustment procedure clear?	____	____
If the unit must be returned to the manufacturer, does the manufacturer pay the shipping cost?	____	____
Are there local service facilities?	____	____
Is the adjustment procedure reasonable and feasible?	____	____
The Adjustment Procedure		
Is there an informal settlement procedure?	____	____
Is the procedure explained?	____	____
Does it appear fair?	____	____
Is it feasible?	____	____
If there are other legal remedies, are they explained?	____	____

Compare warranty coverage by various manufacturers of similar items to judge the relative merits of each warranty. Downgrade any brand with heavily restrictive or limited coverage.

Action on Warranty Claims   When you have a warranty claim, the first step is to discuss your problem with the contact person noted in the warranty, typically the dealer who sold the product or the nearest service shop authorized by the manufacturer to repair its products. When presenting your claim, describe what the problem is, what has been done, and what you expect the contact person to do. Even if that person does not give you satisfaction the first time, you should return the unit until this source has been thoroughly exhausted.

CONSUMER PROTECTION

For many centuries, whenever there was any problem in an exchange between buyer and seller, it was resolved according to the business doctrine of **caveat emptor**, a Latin term meaning "Let the buyer beware." And, for centuries, because the buyer had to beware, the seller surely had the edge in any exchange situation.

Literally interpreted, "Let the buyer beware" essentially means that the buyer is responsible for examining a product for possible defects and shortcomings before making the purchase. Under this doctrine, should the product prove defective or perform inadequately, the buyer typically has little recourse against the seller. But the increased complexity of products and services has pointed up weaknesses in this doctrine. First, the average consumer cannot be expected to have the wide array of technical and engineering skills needed to judge complex products. Second, today's consumers are involved in a tremendous number of purchase decisions every year. It is not possible for them to fully evaluate and analyze each decision.

Consumers have become much more vocal and have taken a more active role in pushing new consumer legislation. More consumers are becoming more aware that they really do have a choice when selecting products and services. That is, they do not have to accept everything the seller offers. Further, they realize that a product or service can be reasonably trouble-free if the manufacturer or service firm makes a concerted effort. This consumer awareness has fostered legislation that specifies certain minimum quality and performance standards and establishes avenues of redress for the purchaser should the product be faulty.

To no small degree, the sellers' attitude of "the consumer be damned" indirectly encouraged additional consumer legislation. When a product proved faulty, their defense was "caveat emptor." When customers complained, their complaints seldom got any results. Yet, sellers continued to advertise that this year's product was vastly better than last year's. "Buy this and your every problem, need, and desire will be fulfilled." Advertising that made false claims and products that failed to fulfill such claims left a trail of irate buyers who demanded increased consumer legislation.

Consumer Protection Legislation

Most consumer legislation has taken two decidedly different tacks in order to achieve increased protection. One approach has placed specific limits and controls on certain business practices. The other approach requires that a consumer be provided with sufficient information to evaluate a product or service.

Limits and Controls on Business Practices Essentially, this kind of legislation assumes that consumers are not in a position to judge business practices and therefore that rules and regulations are needed to protect them. The thrust of this legislation has been to set minimum product quality and health standards. It has also established safety standards for products, as well as the guidelines for eliminating fraudulent and deceptive practices.

Sufficient Consumer Information Much of the recent consumer legislation has been directed toward requiring that consumers be provided with sufficient information to enable them to know what they are buying. Given this information, consumers can make an educated decision.

Unfortunately, a basic premise of this legislation is that consumers have the necessary skills and training to use the information. Present evidence suggests that many consumers are just not adequately prepared to use the information because it is quite technical. Clearly, greater educational efforts should be made to train consumers on how to use the new disclosures effectively.

Recovering Your Losses: When, Where, How

A thorough analysis before buying a product or service will minimize, although not eliminate, the possibility of your having problems after you buy it. Even with a well-executed advance plan, you may encounter a product that should be returned or a service that is not totally acceptable. Consequently, you will need an action plan that will correct the particular problem or recover the loss you have suffered.

Compiling an Effective Complaint   To be effective, a complaint should be complete in every detail; leave nothing to your listener's or reader's imagination. Be sure to stick only to the facts that pertain to your complaint.

The first step is to furnish purchase details: receipt, company's billing, guarantee, and any other relevant records.

Next, document your complaint with details on why you are dissatisfied and what you have done to try to correct the problem. Describe what you have received from the product or service and why it does not measure up to what you expected. Include copies of invoices for any corrective repairs made thus far. Be very sure to make your complaint immediately when you detect a problem. Many people wait weeks or months and thus reduce their chances of recovery.

Finally, describe exactly what corrective action you want: repair of the product, rework of the service, or replacement of the product. *Important*: Keep copies of all letters you write. Send *copies* of supporting documents (invoices, receipts, guarantees) so that you can keep the originals in your file.

If there is no response within a week or two, follow up on your complaint with another letter. Much of the recent warranty legislation sets a definite time limit for the manufacturer to resolve a customer's complaint; failure to do so within the specified period can make the customer eligible for a refund. These time limits should help, because the manufacturer has an added incentive to take prompt action on your complaint.

Obtaining Satisfaction: The Selling Store or Service Firm   Customers have one major thing in their favor in any complaint action: Most stores or service firms do not want dissatisfied customers. Consequently, most will try to correct the problem. The initial starting point is to take your documented complaint to the store or service firm where you made the purchase. Whenever possible, try to do this at a time when the staff is not very busy. You are then more likely to find a supervisor on duty. If the clerk cannot help, discuss the matter with the department manager. If you are still unsuccessful, arrange for a conference with the store manager. Whenever you present your complaint to the next higher level, remember that the interviewer has not been in on your previous discussions. Therefore, present your complete case to each person you meet with.

Better Business Bureau   Most major cities have a **better business bureau**. While the bureau has a host of responsibilities, you are primarily concerned with its role in consumer complaints.

Traditionally, the bureau's role has been that of an independent third party which informally tries to help the consumer and the business firm reach an agreeable solution. It does not negotiate a settlement. Rather, it simply tries to bring the customer and the business firm to an agreement. The bureau's recommendations are not binding on either party.

However, a number of better business bureaus have established formal hearing procedures or arbitration boards to hear consumer complaints and determine their solution. The decision to accept arbitration is strictly voluntary for the consumer and the business firm. But if both agree to arbitration, the board's findings are binding and can be legally enforced.

Some bureaus provide the service without charge, while others require a fee ranging from $20 upward. Typically, those without a fee have nonpaid volunteers serving on the arbitration boards. Those charging a fee rely on paid professional arbitrators.

Manufacturer   If the local store has been unable to resolve your problem, you should contact the manufacturer. Most manufacturers have factory representatives who visit the various retail stores, especially those handling large, expensive items—major appliances, furniture, and automobiles. If there is such a representative, ask your local store to arrange an appointment to discuss your problem. Or write directly to the manufacturer's central office. (Check your warranty information for the address or ask the local librarian to help you locate the firm's headquarters.) Direct your complaint to the customer relations office if one is named on your warranty. Otherwise, send the letter to the president. If you have not received a reply within several weeks, send off a copy of your complaint with a new letter, saying that you received no reply to your first letter. Remember to keep copies of all correspondence for your file.

Legal Action: When?   Legal action has to be considered one of the last steps in the complaint process. In most cases, it will be the last resort when all other approaches have been used.

Small Claims Court   Most states have **small claims courts** (courts set up to handle disputes involving small amounts of money) that can provide a possible avenue of recourse if you have been unsuccessful in your other appeals. This route has several distinct advantages over initiating action through a regular trial court. The proceedings are informal, so you can often present your own case without the need for legal counsel. This approach helps to keep the cost low. In most states, you obtain speedy action on your complaint—a far cry from the 1- to 5-year wait that prevails in the regular court system. Most small claims courts will not handle cases that involve more than $500, although a few have higher ceilings. Since most consumer complaints are typically small, this is not a serious constraint.

STRATEGY

If you have been unsuccessful in the other avenues of redress, you should consider action in a small claims court.

Regular Court Action Initiating action through the regular court system should be considered a last-resort measure. Often the amount involved does not warrant the high cost of such action. Furthermore, the entire process can be extremely time-consuming. Given the sizable time commitments and the need for legal counsel, the effort may not be worthwhile.

SUMMARY

1   The high inflation rates of the late 1970s and early 1980s have added a new dimension that must be considered in your personal financial decisions.

2   To justify a regular investment program, your real rate of return—nominal (promised) rate of return less expected inflation rate—should be positive.

3   Two changes have eliminated most of the negative real rates of return that individuals experienced during the late 1970s and early 1980s:

    a   Rates of return on certain investments for small investors have increased.

    b   Rates of inflation declined in early 1983 (when this book was written).

4   Since the cost of borrowing nearly always exceeds the rate of inflation, there is a net positive cost to borrowing. Consequently, borrowing to buy now solely to avoid future price increases is generally not warranted. One exception to this generalization may be the purchase of a house. We discuss that purpose in Chapter 11.

5   The percentage of two-income households in the United States continues to grow. Financial considerations are not the sole motivation for that growth.

6   The available income remaining after deducting taxes and work-related expenses is frequently only a small fraction of the gross income of a household's second salary. The fringe benefits that accompany a second job should also be considered when deciding whether both partners should work.

7   Two-income households are likely to have special financial planning needs due to their higher discretionary income, wider range of viable financial options, and potential overlaps in the fringe benefits of the two wage-earners.

8   A good warranty or guarantee should correct the problems, mistakes, and design shortcomings that are directly attributable to the manufacturer.

9   All sections of the warranty relating to a major purchase should be read and carefully analyzed before deciding to buy the item.

10   Consumer protection legislation has taken two distinct approaches:

    a   Regulation and limitation of certain business practices

    b   Provision of sufficient information so that the consumer can make an informed decision.

11   An effectively presented consumer complaint should offer sufficient detail to allow the reader or listener to understand the facts of the case.

12   The better business bureau can help consumers obtain satisfaction in a complaint against a local retail store or service firm.

13   Legal action to resolve a consumer complaint should be considered a last resort.

REVIEW YOUR UNDERSTANDING OF

Nominal rate of return	Federal Trade Commission (FTC)
Real rate of return	Warranty or guarantee
Net cost of loan	Full warranty
Estimated inflation rate	Limited warranty
Two-income household	Implied warranty
Impact of taxes	Caveat emptor
Work-related expenses	Better business bureau
Fringe benefits	Small claims court

DISCUSSION QUESTIONS

1   Under what conditions do high inflation rates make savings a losing proposition? When deciding whether saving is justified, what rate of return would be most important? Why?

2   Len Buyit claims, "It is best to borrow money to buy the item now because you avoid the higher price of buying the item later." Do you agree? Under what conditions is Len correct?

3   Would you expect that the cost of borrowing (the loan rate) would normally be greater than, or less than, the expected inflation rate? Why?

4   What factors have caused the recent growth in the number of two-income households? Do you think that growth will continue? Why or why not?

5   Gordon and Janet Heath have a combined household income of $20,000: they each earn $10,000. Are they likely to have more than one-half the second salary as available income? Why or why not?

6   What are the major work-related expenses that should be deducted when computing available income from a second salary? Which ones are easiest to estimate? Which are the most difficult?

7   Should the fringe benefits that the second wage-earner's job provides be considered when deciding the financial merits of taking that job? Why? Why can the dollar value of these benefits be rather difficult to estimate in some circumstances?

8   Does the Federal Trade Commission's role relieve the consumer of all responsibility for warranty problems? Why or why not?

9   What deficiencies do you see in the axiom of caveat emptor? Does it provide true consumer protection? Should caveat emptor be completely replaced? Why or why not?

10   What key points should be included when initiating a complaint about a defective product or inadequate service? Why is it important to have complete details in the complaint?

11   How do better business bureaus help resolve consumer complaints? How does their arbitration service differ from their traditional role?

12   What advantages does a small claims court have over the regular court system for resolving consumer complaints? Why must the regular court system be considered a last resort for consumer complaints?

PROBLEMS

4-1   Shirley Shortsighted is about to reinvest $1000 that she currently has available. She has that money because the investment she made 1 year ago has now matured and returned her original $1000 investment. In addition, it paid her 12 percent interest during the year she had the money invested. For that year, inflation averaged 8 percent. One of Shirley's major concerns is that now 1-year investments are offering only 10 percent interest. During the next year, inflation is expected to average 5 percent.

a How many dollars did Shirley really earn on last year's investment after adjusting for inflation? What real rate of return did she earn?

b If she invests $1000 in a new investment, how many dollars will she earn after considering inflation (assume it will be 5 percent)? What real return will she likely earn?

c Which investment is really the better one? Why?

4-2   Borris Broomfeld is trying to decide between the following two options:

Borrow $10,000 to immediately purchase a new Sluggo sport sedan; the loan would be repaid at the end of 2 years.

Wait 2 years and buy the car for cash; thus, he would not have to borrow any of the money.

Borris believes his present car will operate for 2 more years, should he decide on the second option. Borris is concerned that car prices will probably rise 8 percent annually over the next 2 years. A helpful lender has said that Borris would pay $2950 of interest on the proposed $10,000 auto loan.

a What will a new Sluggo sedan likely cost in 2 years? (*Hint*: Exhibit 1-4 will help.) How much does Borris save by buying now?

b Do the savings that were computed in question **a** justify "buying now to beat the price increase"? Why?

c What would you recommend?

4-3   Allan and Monica North are discussing whether she should accept the transfer her company has offered; it requires moving but raises her salary from $10,000 to $15,000. The Norths expect that Allan could duplicate his present $15,000 position in the new area. Assume Allan is the principal wage-earner. The Norths have no children.

a What percentage of her present salary does Monica have after paying income and Social Security taxes?

b What percentage of the new salary will she have after paying taxes?

c How much of her $5000 raise will Monica actually have after taxes? Roughly, what percentage of the $5000 will she have after taxes? Why is it rather limited?

4-4   Gus and Sue Stein want to estimate how much of his $15,000 salary would be available if both of them worked. Currently, Sue is the principal wage-earner with a $20,000 annual salary. The Steins have estimated the added weekly expenses related to Gus's working:

Meals eaten out: $30	Lunches: $15
Commuting expenses: $20	Clothing: $10

a What is Gus's approximate after-tax salary?

b How much of Gus's $15,000 salary is available? What percentage of his initial gross salary do the Steins have?

c What additional monetary factors should they consider in their decision on Gus's salary?

CASE PROBLEM

Jack and Sharon Levin have been having a continuing problem with their 6-month-old Speed Frog clothes dryer. Despite four trips to the service department of the store where they bought the dryer, they are still dissatisfied with the unit's performance. When the two-position temperature control is set on "Cool," the unit takes 2 hours to dry the clothes. On the "Hot" setting, however, the dryer scorches them in 20 minutes or less. During their latest complaint trip, the service person told them that nothing else could be done since their problem was "the nature of the beast." Finding the unit no better than before, the Levins have arranged a meeting with the dealer's service manager.

1 Assuming the service manager was not directly involved in the earlier complaint trips, how should the Levins prepare for the meeting?

2 If the Levins do not obtain satisfaction from the service manager, what is the next avenue of appeal? How would they initiate a complaint? What should their complaint contain?

3 Assuming the Levins are not satisfied with the corrective action in (**2**), what is their next appeal route? What is involved in filing a complaint with this group? What should their complaint contain?

CHAPTER

5

FINANCIAL SERVICES: USING THEM EFFECTIVELY

**AFTER COMPLETING THIS CHAPTER
YOU WILL HAVE LEARNED**

The different types of *payment accounts*, their features, and their costs

The advantages of a *personal payment account*

How to determine which type of *checking account* best meets your needs

How to determine which *endorsement* would be most appropriate in a given situation

The purpose of a *certified check*—how and when to use it

What a *stop-payment order* is and when it might be necessary to use one

How to reconcile your *checking, NOW,* or *share draft* account

What services a *remote electronic terminal* can provide

The difference between a *cashier's check* and a *money order*

What *traveler's checks* are, what services they provide, and what they cost

WELL, IT'S NOT **MY** IDEA OF MAKING THE BEST USE OF THE BANK'S SERVICES..

ALL kinds of financial institutions

regularly blast you with advertisements. On TV and radio, in the newspapers, and from the sides of buses, each financial institution proclaims that it is a one-stop personal finance center. Although many different kinds of institutions make this claim, commercial banks currently come closest to fulfilling it. They provide a range of personal financial services, including several kinds of checking accounts, a variety of savings plans, numerous borrowing options, financial counseling, and many other personal financial services. But mutual savings banks, savings and loan associations, and credit unions—all commonly called "nonbanks" as opposed to commercial banks—have expanded their services to the point where they are serious contenders as one-stop personal finance centers.

There are several reasons why you should understand what financial services are available to you and how to use them. First, effective management of your personal financial affairs has become sufficiently complex that the use of these services is almost essential.

Second, although the current range of services is large, it is likely to expand even more as competition among financial institutions increases.

Third, the cost of these services varies so widely that it is worth the effort to investigate thoroughly what is available. For example, a heavily used checking account can easily cost $75 per year at one bank, while a competing institution may provide the same checking service absolutely free.

Finally, the proper use of these services can be a tremendous convenience and assistance to your overall personal financial plan.

INSTITUTIONS THAT OFFER FINANCIAL SERVICES

Before we analyze the different financial services, we need to discuss the businesses that offer those services. We will begin by defining what we mean by a financial institution. For our purposes, it is any business that specializes in providing financial services to its customers. And those services typically entail the transfer of money between the customer and the financial institution or between the customer and some other individual or business. While a number of specialized businesses match this description, we will concentrate on commercial banks, savings and loan associations, mutual savings banks, and credit unions.

Commercial Bank   **Commercial banks** have operated in the United States for several hundred years. Their financial services include supplying a place to save money and borrow money, providing a checking account you can use to pay your bills, and some other more specialized financial services. At present, they come closest to being the one-stop center that meets the complete financial service needs of individuals.

Savings and Loan Association Compared with commercial banks, **savings and loan associations** (S&Ls) are much more recent arrivals. While S&Ls have been in operation since the mid-1800s, their emergence as major financial institutions has been fairly recent. Originally, their principal purpose was to assist the members of the S&L to obtain loans to purchase houses. When people deposited money in the S&L, they became members. By pooling the monies from the members, the S&L was able to reloan it to other members who needed money to purchase homes.

S&Ls are still heavily involved in lending money to potential home-owners. But many have expanded their offerings so they can provide their customers with a more complete range of financial services.

Mutual Savings Bank The main purpose of **mutual savings banks** (MSBs) is to pool the savings from individuals and reloan the money to others for the purchase of homes and other items. Initially, MSBs limited their lending activities nearly exclusively to home purchases. But that purpose continues to change as many MSBs push to provide more than just a place where individuals can save money and borrow money to buy a house. Most will now lend money to buy automobiles, furniture, and to pay for other major items and services. Also, most offer a payment account similar to a checking account that customers can use to pay their bills. Many MSBs now provide a complete package of financial services for the individual.

Many people may never have heard of MSBs; nearly all of them are located in the New England and Mid-Atlantic states. Unless you live in that region, you probably have never encountered an MSB. If you live in one of the states with MSBs, you are much less likely to encounter an S&L; they are far less common in areas where MSBs are located.

Credit Union A **credit union** is composed of a group of members who share some common bond. These individuals may work for the same employer, go to the same church, belong to a particular union, or live in a particular neighborhood. Only members can use the financial services of the credit union. The accounts in which members place their money are called **share accounts**, since each person shares in the ownership of the credit union. In addition to enjoying a savings service, members can borrow money from the credit union. Once, loans tended to be fairly small and usually had to be repaid within a fairly short time. Now, some credit unions offer larger loans and longer repayment schedules. Some credit unions offer a payment account (a share draft account) similar to a checking account that members can use to pay their bills. Credit unions of the future will continue to expand their service offerings so that they can provide a more complete package of financial services for their members.

PAYMENT ACCOUNTS

Let's first tackle some terminology. Then, having defined our terms, as Aristotle would have us do before any discussion, we will be prepared to begin.

When we talk about a *checking account*, we are really talking about a form of payment account. Simply, a **payment account** is an arrangement with a financial institution; the institution agrees to accept a person's money, keep a record of it, and pay it out in amounts and to recipients as specified in a written order by the person whose money it is. This is more familiarly known to most of us as a checking account.

For a considerable length of time, checking accounts have been the primary payment account used by individuals. But, during the past 5 years, the range has changed dramatically. Now, consumers have two additional payment account choices: negotiable orders of withdrawal accounts and share draft accounts.

Checking Account With a **checking account**, you write a payment order—the check—which instructs the bank to pay the amount specified on the check to the individual or business—the payee—to whom you make the payment. When the check is presented or delivered to your bank by the person or business whose name you wrote on the check or by the payee's bank, your bank pays out the money. It then deducts that amount from the balance in your checking account. Owing to a federal prohibition that has been in force since 1933, the bank cannot pay interest on the balance in your checking account.

Negotiable Order of Withdrawal (NOW) Account With a NOW account, you write a payment order—a **negotiable order of withdrawal**—against your savings account. With a traditional savings account, an individual could deposit money in the account, earn interest on the balance of the account, and withdraw money from the account. But that withdrawal had to be made in person. For example, John Swift (the owner of the savings account) could *not* write and give a withdrawal order to his landlord that instructed his financial institution to take $200 from his savings account and pay it to the landlord. Withdrawal orders on those savings accounts were nonnegotiable; they could not be given to an individual or a business as payment for a bill. The negotiable order of withdrawal—a NOW draft—changed that. With it, John can give a $200 NOW draft to his landlord. When it is presented to the bank, MSB, or S&L where John has his savings account, the institution will pay out the money.

The negotiable order is essentially the same as a check; in fact, the two look so much alike that it is hard to tell them apart. The main difference is that the money is taken out of a savings account rather than a checking account.

Since NOW drafts are drawn against a savings account, the bank, S&L or MSB can pay interest on the account; but it is not required to do so. While there is no minimum rate, the current (1983) maximum rate on NOW accounts is 5¼ percent.

Super NOW Accounts During 1983, financial institutions started offering a new deregulated NOW account, commonly referred to as the Super NOW account. Its major distinguishing feature is that there is no limit on what interest rate the account can pay. A financial institution can offer any rate it chooses. But to qualify for that unrestricted interest rate, your initial deposit to open the account must be at least $2500. Then, should your account balance drop below $2500, your interest rate reverts to the traditional NOW account rate (5¼ percent in 1983). And financial institutions can add their own restrictions. Unfortunately, many institutions have done exactly that. First, some have set their minimum balance at $5000 or more. Second, even with the substantial $2500 minimum balance, some institutions assess user fees on the account: perhaps a $6 monthly fee coupled with a $.20 fee for each check written. Needless to say, those hefty fees could easily offset most of the interest the account would earn each month. Finally, the rate offered by some institutions has been only slightly higher than the 5¼ percent paid on traditional NOW accounts, certainly not high enough to justify tying up $2500 or more.

Our comments are based on the very short time that these accounts have been offered. Perhaps some of the Super NOW accounts which currently have very high user fees or poor rates of return will improve after they have been on the market longer. But, for now, it is essential that you carefully review the terms and conditions on any Super NOW account you consider.

Share Draft Account   Credit unions have pioneered the **share draft account** as their answer to the checking account of commercial banks. Since you must be a member of a credit union to use its services, the account in which you deposit your savings is called a share account because the members of a credit union share its ownership. The payment order you write against your share account is called a share draft. When the person or business you write the share draft to presents the draft to the credit union, the amount is deducted from your share account.

Generally, most credit unions can offer a share draft account that pays interest. But they are not required to offer these accounts. Nor are they required to pay a specified rate of interest on the account. They are free to set their rate at whatever level they want to pay. Since 1982, there has been no maximum interest rate.

Similarities and Differences between Payment Accounts   Exhibit 5-1 summarizes what we consider to be the major similarities and differences among the three payment accounts.

Benefits of a Payment Account

Most adults have a payment account, such as a checking account, which they use extensively in their daily financial transactions. These accounts offer a number of benefits. First of all, you can pay your monthly bills by mailing a personal check. Thus, you do not have to travel around town carrying large sums of cash and waiting in line to pay those bills. Also, checks are as good as cash in paying for most purchases at stores. A further benefit is the record of payments that your checkbook, NOW draftbook, or share draftbook provides. Since you will be recording the amount and payee in your checkbook or draftbook each time you write a check, NOW, or share draft, you will have a good summary of your major expenditures. Your checkbook or draftbook can be very helpful when summarizing the monthly expenses for your budget worksheet. It can also aid your search for those expenses that qualify as deductible for income tax purposes. (We shall discuss what expenses qualify in Chapter 6.) Finally, the canceled check or draft that the financial institution returns to you after it pays out the money is proof that you paid a particular bill.

PRINCIPAL TYPES OF PAYMENT ACCOUNTS

Currently, commercial banks (and to a lesser extent MSBs, S&Ls, and credit unions) offer several types of payment accounts. They differ mainly with respect to how much they cost and the range of services they provide. Exhibit 5-2 (page 103) summarizes the main features and service charges for the major payment accounts.

EXHIBIT 5-1

Similarities and differences among major payment accounts: checking account, NOW and Super NOW accounts, and share draft account.

ACCOUNT	OFFERED BY	PRINCIPAL SIMILARITIES	MAJOR DIFFERENCES
Checking account	Commercial banks and some MSBs	Used to pay individuals or businesses Readily accepted, with identification, as payment	Interest cannot be paid on account balance Offered by nearly all commercial banks Offered throughout the country
NOW and Super NOW accounts	Commercial banks, MSBs, and S&Ls	Used to pay individuals or businesses Readily accepted, with identification, as payment	Institution can pay interest on balance in NOW account Owing to recency of enabling legislation, not all banks, MSBs, and S&Ls offer NOW accounts
Share draft account	Credit unions	Used to pay individuals or businesses Readily accepted, with identification, as payment	Interest can be paid on share draft account To date, share draft accounts not offered by some credit unions.

I REALIZE THE PICTURE ON THE CHECK IS A RUBBER PLANTATION BUT THE CHECK IS QUITE GOOD.

Minimum Savings Balance

Some commercial banks give a free checking account to a customer who also maintains a stipulated minimum balance in a regular savings account. This is called a **minimum savings balance** account. NOW and Super NOW accounts at banks, MSBs, and S&Ls are similar except that the customer has only one account—the savings account against which the NOW drafts and Super NOW drafts are written. By maintaining the specified minimum dollar amount in this account, all service charges for the drafts are eliminated. A credit union member with a share draft account also has only one account—the share account on which the drafts are written. If the customer maintains the necessary minimum cash balance in this account, there are no service charges on the drafts. Most financial institutions charge a flat monthly fee of $5 to $10 for any month when your savings account balance drops below the required minimum; during that month, your checking, NOW, or Super NOW account is certainly not free.

The principal advantage of a minimum savings balance account is that the customer has free checking, yet still earns regular interest on the minimum savings balance. The major disadvantage is the reduced flexibility because of the dollars that must be kept in savings to meet the minimum balance. For most people, this would not be a serious restriction.

A distinct advantage of the NOW, the Super NOW, and the share draft accounts is that you do earn interest not only on the minimum savings balance, but also on any working balance over and above the minimum you keep in the account. To illustrate: Suppose a customer was considering opening a payment account that required a $300 minimum balance, and also suppose that the customer intended to keep $380 in the account at all times. If the customer opened a savings account and a checking account at a commercial bank, $300 would go into the savings account to fulfill the minimum savings balance requirement and the checking account would be free. But the customer would keep the $80 as a working balance in the checking account. In the savings account, the customer's $300 would earn the following interest each year:

$$\$15.75 = \$300 \times 5\tfrac{1}{4}\%$$

$$\underset{\substack{\text{Interest} \\ \text{earned}}}{\triangle} = \underset{\substack{\text{Savings} \\ \text{balance}}}{\triangle} \times \underset{\substack{\text{Rate of} \\ \text{interest}}}{\triangle}$$

The $80 working balance in the checking account earns nothing—checking accounts are non–interest-paying accounts. With a NOW or share draft account, the entire $380 would be in a savings account or share account paying 5¼ percent interest; annual interest would be at least:

$$\$19.95 = \$380 \times 5\tfrac{1}{4}\%$$

$$\underset{\substack{\text{Annual} \\ \text{interest}}}{\triangle} = \underset{\substack{\text{Savings} \\ \text{balance}}}{\triangle} \times \underset{\substack{\text{Rate of} \\ \text{interest}}}{\triangle}$$

And the higher the expected working balance in the payment account, the greater the advantage to the NOW, the Super NOW, or the share draft account.

Overall, we would rank a NOW account or a share draft account among the best of the payment accounts in Exhibit 5-2. Both kinds of accounts eliminate any non–interest-bearing balance; the entire dollar balance is held in an interest-earning savings or share account. *One word of caution*: A few MSBs, S&Ls, and credit unions pay only a token 2 or 3 percent interest on their share draft and NOW accounts. For most people, that eliminates any advantage these accounts offer.

For those who have sufficient funds to meet the sizable minimum balance requirements, a Super NOW account *should* be an attractive alternative. We emphasize "should" because some Super NOW accounts have restrictions and fees that cancel most of their added benefits. But it may well be that competition will improve the less attractive accounts.

STRATEGY

Before selecting a Super NOW account, carefully consider its fees as well as its interest rate. A traditional NOW account, combined with a money market deposit account (Chapter 18) or a money market mutual fund (Chapter 20), may be a better overall combination.

We would rate a minimum savings balance combined with a free checking account at a commercial bank as a good payment alternative, but not as good as either a NOW or a share draft account. It has the highly desirable feature that a customer receives free checking when the required dollar balance is maintained in a savings account. But its shortfall is that any balance in the checking account earns no interest.

Unconditional Free Checking

The advantages of **unconditional free checking** are that it does not require any minimum balance and you pay nothing for the account. This is without a doubt the best kind of payment account—if you can get it. Most banks have stopped issuing them.

Minimum Checking Balance

As the name suggests, if the customer keeps a **minimum checking balance** specified by the bank in his or her checking account, all service charges for the account are eliminated. Some banks compute that minimum by averaging the daily balance during the period. Others use the lowest balance during the period. The following example will quickly demonstrate why using the lowest balance during that period is the more costly method.

Suppose an account requires a $300 minimum balance. Under the average daily balance method, the balance could drop below $300 for several days as long as there were enough days when the balance was above $300 to offset that shortfall. Under the lowest balance technique, just one day with the account balance below $300, even if there were 29 days with the balance

CHAPTER 5

103

FINANCIAL
SERVICES: USING
THEM EFFECTIVELY

EXHIBIT 5-2

Major types of payment accounts.

TYPE OF ACCOUNT	MINIMUM BALANCE YOU MUST MAINTAIN	ACCOUNT AVAILABLE AS	SERVICE FEES AND SPECIAL FEATURES
Minimum savings balance	$100 to $2000 in NOW, SD, or SAV; $2500 to $5000 in SP-NOW	NOW SD CHK SP-NOW	No fee if minimum balance is maintained; interest paid on NOW, SD but not CHK; SP-NOW requires at least $2500 balance; no interest ceiling on rates paid on SP-NOW
Unconditional fee checking	None	NOW SD CHK	No fees; interest paid on NOW and SD
Minimum checking balance	$100 to $1000 in CHK	CHK	No fee if minimum balance is maintained
Activity	None	NOW CHK	Fee is $.10 to $.25 per check plus $1 to $10 monthly; interest on NOW
Package checking	None	CHK	Fee of $5 to $15 monthly; may include safe deposit box, traveler's checks, credit card, preferred loan rate, accident insurance, and possibly more

Account legend:
CHK   Checking
SP-NOW Super Negotiable Order Of Withdrawal
SAV   Savings
NOW   Negotiable Order of Withdrawal
SD   Share draft

well over $300, would mean that the account would be charged a service fee. That service charge takes one of two forms. Either there is a flat monthly charge of $5 to $10, or the customer pays a clearing fee for each check plus a set monthly fee.

Although minimum balance checking accounts are frequently touted as "free checking," they nevertheless do entail an implicit cost. That cost is the interest that could have been earned on the money that is tied up as the minimum balance in the checking account where it earns nothing. Thus, returning to our example, the customer could have deposited the $300 minimum balance in a savings account earning 5¼ percent annually. Had that been done, the annual interest would be:

$$\$15.75 \ = \ \$300 \qquad\qquad \times\ 5\tfrac14\%$$

$$\underset{\substack{\text{Annual} \\ \text{interest}}}{\Big\Uparrow} = \underset{\substack{\text{Required minimum} \\ \text{balance}}}{\Big\Uparrow} \times \underset{\substack{\text{Rate of interest} \\ \text{on savings}}}{\Big\Uparrow}$$

In effect, the cost of this free checking account is $15.75—the lost interest on the minimum balance. Of course, the lower the required minimum balance, the closer the cost of the account approaches truly free checking.

For people who are able to maintain the necessary minimum balance, this account is generally less expensive than an activity account (defined in the next section). For someone who writes numerous checks each month, minimum balance checking is considerably less costly than the costs of an activity account.

Activity Account

The cost of an **activity account** is determined by two things: a fixed monthly charge called a **monthly maintenance charge** and a **check-clearing fee** for each check charged against the account. Thus, the more active the account and the more checks written, the greater the total service charge.

An example is the best way to illustrate how to determine the annual cost of an activity account. Assume a customer expects to write an average of 25 checks monthly. Also assume that the service charges on the account are 15 cents per check, with a $3.25 monthly maintenance fee. The monthly cost for the checking account is:

$$\$7.00 \ = \ (25\ \text{checks} \quad \times\ 15\ \text{cents}) \qquad +\ \$3.25$$

$$\underset{\substack{\text{Monthly} \\ \text{cost}}}{\Big\Uparrow} = \underset{\substack{\text{Number} \\ \text{of checks} \\ \text{each month}}}{\Big\Uparrow} \times \underset{\substack{\text{Check-} \\ \text{clearing fee}}}{\Big\Uparrow} + \underset{\substack{\text{Monthly} \\ \text{maintenance} \\ \text{fee}}}{\Big\Uparrow}$$

For the entire year, the cost of the checking account would be $84 (12 months at $7 per month).

Because the cost of an activity account can be substantial, we rank it far down the list of alternatives in Exhibit 5-2. Even the interst received on a

NOW account does little to reduce the sizable costs when the institution charges for the activity in the NOW account.

Package Account

The **package account** provides a number of banking services, including unlimited free checking, covering overdrafts on the checking account (the bank automatically lends money to cover a check if there isn't enough money in the account), traveler's checks, money orders, bank credit card, safe-deposit box, and lower finance charges on certain loans (typically ½ to 1 percent below the prevailing rate).

The best way to evaluate a package account is to estimate the value of each service in the package. If the total annual value of all the individual services exceeds the annual fee, the package represents good value. Consider an example: Assume the package costs $60 annually ($5 monthly) and provides free checking, free traveler's checks, a free safe-deposit box, and a perferred lending rate ½ percent below the bank's regular loan rates. Assume we investigate and find it will cost $30 annually to obtain a competing checking account. Next, we find it will cost $10 to obtain a safe-deposit box. If we normally purchase $500 of traveler's checks annually, we would pay:

$$\$5 \qquad = \$1 \qquad \times 5 \text{ packets}$$

$$\underset{\substack{\text{Annual cost} \\ \text{of traveler's} \\ \text{checks}}}{\Uparrow} = \underset{\substack{\text{Usual service} \\ \text{fee for } \$100 \\ \text{of traveler's} \\ \text{checks}}}{\Uparrow} \times \underset{\substack{\text{Number of } \$100 \text{ packets} \\ \text{of traveler's checks:} \\ \$500 \div \$100}}{\Uparrow}$$

Be aware, however, that many S&Ls and MSBs supply traveler's checks free to their customers; thus, the value of the traveler's check service would be eliminated from the package plan. Furthermore, the preferred lending rate is valuable to you only if (1) you plan to borrow money during the year, and (2) the annual finance charge (more on this in Chapters 7 and 8) is less than the annual finance charge you would have to pay other lenders for the same loan.

Without yet considering the value of the perferred lending rate, the total value of services up to this point is:

$$\$45 \qquad = \$30 \qquad + \$10 \qquad + \$5$$

$$\underset{\substack{\text{Total value} \\ \text{of service}}}{\Uparrow} = \underset{\substack{\text{Service charge} \\ \text{for comparable} \\ \text{checking account}}}{\Uparrow} + \underset{\substack{\text{Rent on safe-} \\ \text{deposit box}}}{\Uparrow} + \underset{\substack{\text{Service fee} \\ \text{to purchase} \\ \text{traveler's checks}}}{\Uparrow}$$

Therefore, unless the preferred lending rate is worth at least $15 annually, you would do better by purchasing the services separately rather than through a package account.

Package checking accounts are probably best suited to people who not only use their checking accounts heavily, but also use the extra services frequently.

SELECTING YOUR PAYMENT ACCOUNT

When selecting a payment account, two of the major considerations should be:

1   Annual service cost on the account, based on how much you expect to use it

2   Range of personal financial services that are available from the institution offering the account

Annual Service Cost

The first step in comparing the costs of competing payment accounts is to ask the commercial banks in your area for complete details on the accounts they offer. You should also talk to the S&Ls and credit unions and, if you live in the eastern part of the United States, see your savings banks for the details on the NOW or checking accounts that these nonbanks offer. To make a valid cost comparison, you will need details on:

1   *Minimum balance.* Are you required to hold a specified dollar balance in a savings or checking account?

2   *Clearing fee.* Are you charged a fee for each check or draft charged against your account?

3   *Maintenance fee.* Is there a monthly fee for processing and handling your account?

4   *Printing charge.* Is there a charge for printing your personalized checks or drafts?

5   *Fees on transfers.* Is there a charge when you transfer money from your savings to your checking account?

6   *Other fees.* Does the institution charge any additional fees to provide a payment account?

Once you have the cost data from each institution, estimate the annual cost of the checking account based on your anticipated usage of the account. The previous discussion of the major payment accounts will provide you with necessary guidelines to make this estimate.

Range of Services Provided

When evaluating where to open your payment account, you should also consider what additional financial services the bank, S&L, MSB, or credit union offers. For example, it is a definite advantage if the institution provides loans for buying such things as automobiles and furniture and for other major personal needs. Likewise, it is an advantage if the institution makes home mortgage loans to its customers. A very desirable payment account service is called **automatic overdraft**; this simply means that if you don't have enough money in your account to cover a check, the bank won't "bounce" it but, instead, will automatically put the money in your account as a loan. (This service is quite important; we'll discuss it further after the next several pages.) You may also reap a benefit if the institution provides some of the sundry financial services: safe-deposit boxes, traveler's checks, one of the major credit cards, and personal financial counseling.

OPENING A PAYMENT ACCOUNT

Opening a payment account—checking, NOW, or share draft—is a relatively simple procedure. Most institutions require that you answer several questions on what is called a signature card and, as you might well imagine, that you write your signature on the signature card. This signature is essential because the bank uses it to verify that the signature on a check or draft drawn against your account is indeed yours, and therefore that the check should be paid as written. And, of course, you will have to make an initial deposit to open the account.

Some banks do not charge for the printed personalized checks if only your name is printed on them. If you also want your address and telephone number printed on the check, you will have to pay the printing charge. The checks or drafts themselves can range from a single color with no design to bright multicolored checks with a scenic landscape in the background. Typically, the more involved the design and color, the more expensive the check. Likewise, the cover (or book) in which you carry the checks or drafts, as well as the record for listing the amounts and payees when you write the checks or drafts, are also available in many colors, designs, and materials. You may select what you like, but be sure you know the extra charge for exotic designs and covers and consider whether the cost is worth the result.

Most personal checks come prenumbered. With this convenience, you do not have to assign a number each time you write a check. The greatest benefit of prenumbering is that it helps to minimize or eliminate the error of not recording a check in your checkbook.

USING YOUR ACCOUNT

Using a checking account is reasonably easy and straightforward. However, you should know several things that can make the procedure work more smoothly and efficiently.

Exhibit 5-3 illustrates a sample check and explains its key points. Let's discuss each of these points on that sample check:

a   *Current date.* This is the date on which you write the check. Contrary to what some people think, a check dated on a Sunday or holiday is as valid as a check dated on any other day. Most banks will not, however, accept a check that has been dated ahead of the current date; this is called **postdating** a check. Thus, on June 10, the bank would not accept a check dated June 13.

EXHIBIT 5-3

Key features on your personal check.

Phil Fast	No. 517
1456 Deadend	
Leadpoint, USA 98765	

(a) _____ 19 ____

Pay to the
Order of _____ (b) _____ $ ____ (c) ____

_____ (d) _____ Dollars

Last National Bank
Leadpoint, USA 98765

(e)

Memo _____ (f) _____   ■0123■■0098■■11 ■ 56■■1133311■517

(g)

b   *The name of the person or organization*—the payee—you want to receive your money.

c   *The dollar amount of the check in numerals* is shown on this line.

d   *Write the dollar-and-cent amount of the check in words* on this line. If there is a difference between the amounts on line (c) and line (d), the bank will pay the written amount (d).

e   *Your signature on the check* on this line, using the same signature you placed on the signature card when you opened the account.

f   *Memo.* This is where you can describe what you are paying for with the check. The bank does nothing with this information. But it can be useful for your own records. You should get in the habit of filling in the memo line.

g   *Magnetic ink character recognition* (MICR) *numbers.* These numbers identify the financial institution where you have your account, the identification number for your account, and the number of the check being written (517 in the example). These numbers allow your check to be sorted and processed by machines.

Recording Checks and Deposits

Whenever you write a check or make a deposit, you should promptly enter the amount in the record portion of the checkbook. Exhibit 5-4 illustrates a typical checkbook record and the recording of a check and a deposit. While this record seems like an obvious thing to make, it is amazing how many people fail to keep the record part of their checkbooks up to date. People who keep poor checkbook records are the ones who usually receive a bank notice informing them that their account is overdrawn; that is, they have written checks for more money than there is in the account. Another possible consequence of failing to record the amount of the check immediately is

EXHIBIT 5-4

An example of how to record a deposit and a
check in the checkbook record.

CHECK NUMBER	DATE	CHECK ISSUED TO	AMOUNT OF CHECK	DEPOSIT	BALANCE
					$ 54.00
	5/15	Deposit		$200	254.00
517	5/15	Sunken Swamp Estates	$200.25		53.75

that you may not remember it correctly when you record it later. The result is anguish when you attempt to compare the current balance shown in your checkbook record with the current dollar balance that your account should have according to the monthly statement sent to you by the bank.

Making a Deposit

Nearly all payment accounts provide you with personalized deposit slips for making deposits; frequently, they will be included as part of your packet of personalized checks. At the bottom of each slip will be a series of MICR numbers similar to those shown on the check in Exhibit 5-3. There are two parts to that series of numbers. One part is the code number of the financial institution where you keep your payment account. The other part is the identification number for your account.

Promptly deposit any checks you receive. If you hold a check for a long time, it may become difficult or complicated to deposit. Before you can deposit the check in your account or ask the financial institution to convert it into cash, you must sign (endorse) it on the reverse side. When the person or business—the payee—to whom the check is made out endorses it on the reverse side, it indicates that the payee is ready to deposit or cash the check.

Although the traditional place for an endorsement is on the extreme left end of the reverse side, the endorsement can go anywhere as long as it does not alter or obscure the check's essential information. Three basic endorsements are illustrated in Exhibit 5-5.

Blank Endorsement   A **blank endorsement** (top of Exhibit 5-5) converts the check to a bearer instrument. That means that the check can be cashed by any person who holds it. For that reason, you should not endorse a check in blank until the moment you are about to deposit it or cash it. For a similar reason, a check should not be endorsed in blank if it is to be mailed to the bank. Anyone anywhere, from the moment that the check is mailed until it is supposed to be deposited in your account, can cash the blank endorsed check.

Restrictive Endorsement   A **restrictive endorsement**, as the name implies, restricts the use of an endorsed check, and the restriction is written as

EXHIBIT 5-5

Types of endorsement.

Blank endorsements

Grazelda H. Procrostirator

*Ralph and
Becky Smith*

Restrictive endorsements

*For Deposit Only
Fred Bear*

*For deposit to the
account of Wiloms
Schultz*

Special endorsements

*Pay to the order of
Jack Winter
Sally Jones*

*Pay to the order of
Fast National Savings
and Joan Association
Bjorn Anderson*

part of the endorsement. For example, the money from the two checks
shown in the middle of Exhibit 5-5 could be deposited only in the account of
Fred Bear, as shown in the endorsement on the left, or that of Wiloms
Schultz, as shown on the right. Because of this restriction, this type of
endorsement is recommended whenever you endorse a check and deposit it
by mail.

Special Endorsement   A **special endorsement** is used when the payee
wants to limit the right to cash the check to one person. For example,
assume Sally Jones is the payee on a check and she wants to endorse that
check to Jack Winter so that only he can cash it. The endorsements
illustrated at the bottom of Exhibit 5-5 will assure that. At this point, only
Jack Winter can cash the check; he will have to endorse it below Sally's
signature when he cashes it. But until he endorses it, the check remains
unnegotiable. By specially endorsing a check to the order of your bank,
credit union, or S&L, this technique can also be used for a mail deposit.
Bjorn Anderson has done this in the example on the right at the bottom of
Exhibit 5-5.

Special Features

Most checking accounts have several special features which you should know about because you may need to use them.

Certified Check   A **certified check** is a check drawn on a regular checking account, but the bank has certified that the account has sufficient funds to pay the amount when the check is presented. In most cases where the amount of the check is sizable, the payee will require this added assurance. To ensure there will be sufficient funds, the bank immediately reduces the account balance when the check is certified. This check is easily identified because the word "certified" is stamped across it and it is initialed by one of the bank's officers. Though some banks provide the service free, many charge a fee somewhere between $3 and $10. The cashed check is generally retained by the bank. Should the drawer need a copy, the bank will provide one.

Stopping Payment   There are times when you may decide that you want to prevent payment on a particular check. As long as the check has not yet been presented to your bank for payment, you can do so by having a **stop-payment order** placed on the check. Your order to stop payment begins with filling out a form giving check number, date, payee, and amount. The completed form is then circulated to the bank's tellers to alert them to the check. Most banks require 1 or 2 days after the order is accepted before it becomes effective. As a temporary measure, most banks accept a verbal order over the telephone.

Generally, all banks charge a fee—$5 to $20—for stopping payment on a check. Nearly all stop-payment orders contain a clause exempting the bank from liability should the check be cashed by oversight or error. In effect, the bank does not guarantee performance; it merely promises to make its best effort to avoid paying the check.

A bank will not accept a stop-payment order on a certified check.

Overdrawing the Account

If you write a check for more money than you have in your account, the bank has two choices.

The bank may simply refuse to cash any check that would overdraw (the amount on the check exceeds the dollar balance in the account) the account. That check would be returned to the business or person who deposited it with a note that your account does not have sufficient funds. Your check has "bounced." The depositor is not going to waste any time in contacting you about the bounced check.

The bank's other choice is to cash the check even though your account lacks the necessary funds. The bank will, however, request that you immediately deposit the necessary money in the account. Obviously, banks are not enthusiastic about this alternative because they are forced to make a temporary loan to the check writer. To show their displeasure, they charge the account holder a penalty for the overdraft. Depending on the bank, the penalty is usually between $5 and $20.

Some overdrafts are intentional; the check writer knew when writing the check that there was not enough money in the account to cover the check. But many overdrafts arise because you made a numerical error in your checkbook record. Accurate and prompt record keeping should lessen the possibility of accidentally overdrawing your account.

Automatic Overdraft   Overdrafts occur less frequently today because many banks have adopted an **automatic overdraft** system. That is, you can overdraw your account up to an approved limit. The bank will honor your check, and you will not be charged a penalty for the overdraft. Instead of a penalty, you pay a finance charge based on the amount of the overdraft and the length of time that amount has been overdrawn.

STRATEGY

When possible, your checking account should have an automatic overdraft. Even if you do not plan to use it, the automatic overdraft can cover those times when an error causes an overdraft.

RECONCILING YOUR CHECKING, NOW, OR SHARE DRAFT ACCOUNT

Reconciling a checking, NOW, or share draft account simply means comparing the dollar balance you show in the account according to the record in your checkbook (Exhibit 5-4) with the dollar balance the bank, MSB, S&L, or credit union shows you have in the account. The procedure is known as **bank reconciliation**. Each month, the financial institution where you have your account will send a statement (there is an example in Exhibit 5-6 if you look ahead) that summarizes all checks charged against your account, all deposits made to the account, any service fees or other charges against your account, and the dollar balance that was in the account on the day the statement was prepared. In addition, the institution generally sends back all the canceled checks that have been charged against your account. If the two balances agree, there is no problem because you and the institution agree on what your balance was at that particular time. If they do not agree, you will have to take some additional steps to identify the items that caused the difference between the two balances.

There are three things you accomplish by reconciling your checking account.

First, you test the accuracy of the bank's records as well as those in your checkbook.

Second, you have the opportunity to correct your records for any service fee, finance charge, or interest that has been recorded during the period.

And third, by deducting the service fee or finance charge and any required corrections from the balance in your records, plus adding any interest the account earned, you will have an adjusted balance that accurately shows how much you have in your account.

While, logically, it may make more sense to reconcile your account for the entire month from the first to the last day of each month, the institution doesn't make it that easy. The problem is that closing dates on bank statements rarely coincide with the last day of the month. Because banks cannot possibly prepare and mail all their statements on the last day of the month, an account's closing date normally depends on the first letter of the customer's last name. However, the exact closing date of the bank's statement is not critical because you can reconcile all activity in the account since the closing date of the previous statement, thus covering a 1-month period, although not a calendar month.

To reconcile your account, you must identify five items: the balance according to the bank statement, the balance according to your checkbook, any service charges or interest, outstanding checks (checks that you have written but have not been cashed by the bank), and any deposits in transit (deposits you have made but the bank has not yet added to your account).

In Exhibits 5-6 and 5-7, we have reproduced the essential records needed to reconcile a checking account. Exhibit 5-6 includes the items that would normally be in Fred Bear's monthly bank statement: a statement of the account together with the canceled checks that have been charged against the account. Exhibit 5-7 illustrates a selected page out of Fred Bear's checkbook. Our example spans the period of April 10 through May 10. While many people's statements would have more checks than our example, the steps are identical whether you are reconciling an account with few checks or one with an enormous number of checks.

Balance According to the Bank's Statement   The balance according to the bank statement is shown as the last entry on the statement. In addition, most statements summarize the month's activity (balance at the beginning of the month, total deposits during the month, total checks paid during the month, service charges and interest at the end of the month, and closing balance) at the top or bottom of the statement. According to the bank, Bear's balance is $170.60 in Exhibit 5-6. Again, we point out that we are not reconciling as of the end of the month, but rather as of the end of the period that the statement covers—May 10.

EXHIBIT 5-6

The monthly bank statement.

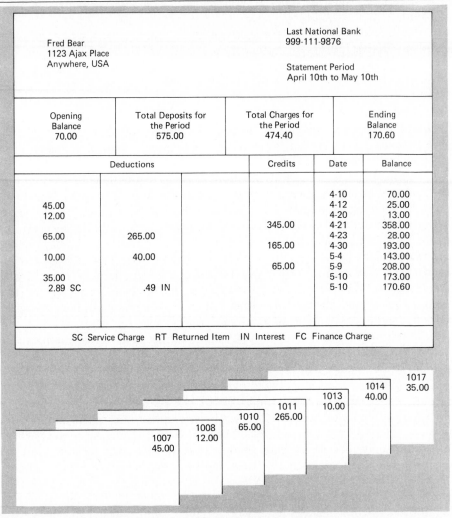

Fred Bear			Last National Bank 999-111-9876	
1123 Ajax Place				
Anywhere, USA			Statement Period April 10th to May 10th	

Opening Balance 70.00	Total Deposits for the Period 575.00	Total Charges for the Period 474.40	Ending Balance 170.60

Deductions			Credits	Date	Balance
				4-10	70.00
45.00				4-12	25.00
12.00				4-20	13.00
			345.00	4-21	358.00
65.00	265.00			4-23	28.00
			165.00	4-30	193.00
10.00	40.00			5-4	143.00
			65.00	5-9	208.00
35.00				5-10	173.00
2.89 SC	.49 IN			5-10	170.60

SC Service Charge   RT Returned Item   IN Interest   FC Finance Charge

1017 35.00

1014 40.00

1013 10.00

1011 265.00

1010 65.00

1008 12.00

1007 45.00

Balance According to the Checkbook   The balance according to your checkbook should be the balance the checkbook shows as of the closing date on the bank statement. In our example, the checkbook balance was $78 on May 10 (Exhibit 5-7). But there still are several steps we have to take to determine whether the checkbook balance and the bank statement balance agree.

Service Charges and Interest   Service charges are any fees that are charged against the payment account. Examples include the finance charge for using the automatic overdraft provision, the cost of printing checks, and the fee for a stop-payment order. The service charge is indicated at the bottom of Exhibit 5-6 with the letters "SC"; it is $2.89. Deduct this charge from your checkbook to update it.

NOW accounts and share draft accounts may also pay interest on the average account balance for the month. Interest earnings in Exhibit 5-6 are indicated by the letters "IN" at the bottom of the exhibit; it is 49 cents. Add that amount to the checkbook to update it.

List of Outstanding Checks The initial step in making a complete **outstanding check list** is to compare the amount and payee on each canceled check returned with the bank statement with the same check as recorded in your checkbook record. Not only does this test the accuracy of your checkbook record; it also highlights any check which may have been cashed for an amount different from what the drawer intended. As you make the comparison, place a small mark (√) on the checkbook record next to any check that has been returned. Checks without a mark are still outstanding; that is, these are checks which you have deducted from your checking account balance but which have not yet cleared the bank and therefore have not been deducted from the balance on the bank statement. The list of outstanding checks for Exhibit 5-7 include: #1009—$15, #1012—$60, #1015—$35, and #1016—$20. The total amount of the outstanding checks is $130.

Canceled Checks May Not Be Returned Some new checkbooks now contain *two* copies of each check, share draft, or NOW draft. The first is the traditional check form we are all accustomed to; the second is a duplicate, a copy made by carbonless paper whenever you write a check. These duplicates are clearly marked, so it is impossible for someone who steals or finds your checkbook to cash them.

EXHIBIT 5-7

Checkbook Details.

CHECK NUMBER	DATE	CHECK ISSUED TO	CHECK AMOUNT	DEPOSIT AMOUNT	BALANCE
1007	4/9	Ace Plumbing Supply	$ 45.00 ✔		$ 25.00
1008	4/11	Valley Telephone	12.00 ✔		13.00
	4/19	Deposit		$345.00	358.00
1009	4/19	Ralph Smith	15.00		343.00
1010	4/20	Electric and Gas Co.	65.00 ✔		278.00
1011	4/21	First Savings and Loan	265.00 ✔		13.00
	4/28	Deposit		165.00	178.00
1012	4/29	John Waldo, M.D.	60.00		118.00
1013	4/31	Swift Drugs	10.00 ✔		108.00
1014	5/2	Shopper's Market	40.00 ✔		68.00
1015	5/4	Central TV Repair	35.00		33.00
1016	5/8	Douglas Dog Hospital	20.00		13.00
	5/8	Deposit		65.00	78.00
1017	5/9	Cash	35.00 ✔		43.00
	5/10	Deposit		35.00	78.00
1018	5/11	Sully Oil Company	25.00		53.00
1019	5/15	Jones Nursery	6.00		47.00

When the payee presents the original check to the bank, S&L, MSB, or credit union, it is charged against your account in the regular fashion. However, since you automatically have a copy of each of your checks, the financial institution no longer returns the canceled checks charged against your account to you. Instead, it sends you a monthly statement which has a detailed listing showing, by check number, the dollar amounts that have been charged against your account. The financial institution will make a copy of a check or draft if you need one.

To generate your list of outstanding checks, you simply take the list of cashed checks or drafts provided by the financial institution and compare it with the record supplied by your duplicate copies. When you encounter a check or draft that has been cashed, you place a small mark (√) in your record. All checks or drafts without the (√) mark are still outstanding.

Deposit in Transit   A **deposit in transit** is a deposit that you have recorded in your checkbook but that has not yet been credited to your account by the bank and is not shown on the bank statement. To determine whether there are any such items, compare the deposits for the month according to your checkbook with deposits according to the bank statement. Comparing the deposits in Exhibit 5-7 with those in Exhibit 5-6, we can see that the $35 deposit of May 10 was not credited on the bank statement. Therefore, the deposit in transit is $35.

The Reconciliation

At this point we have the information necessary to reconcile Fred Bear's checking account. The actual computations necessary to reconcile the account are illustrated in Exhibit 5-8.

Essentially, we are adjusting the two different balances to reflect the account's true cash balance. We do that in two parts.

First, let's work with the bank statement. The deposit in transit must be added to the bank balance because that deposit will soon arrive at the bank. Likewise, the outstanding checks must be deducted because they represent future claims that will ultimately be cashed by the bank. Adding the in-transit deposit and deducting the total amount of the outstanding checks from the balance on the bank statement gives your **adjusted cash balance according to the bank**.

The second part of the reconciliation process uses the checkbook record. First, deduct all service charges from the balance in your checkbook record. Second, add interest that the account earned during the month to your checkbook balance. These two steps give you the **adjusted cash balance according to your checkbook**.

If everything is in order, the two adjusted balances—line 5 and line 8 in Exhibit 5-8—should be equal. If the two are not equal, there is an error somewhere: in the arithmetic, your checkbook, or the bank statement. The checklist at the bottom of this exhibit should help you locate the error. If the mistake is in your checkbook, you should make the necessary adjustments to correct it. Should the error be the bank's, contact the accounting department at the bank and request a correction.

EXHIBIT 5-8

CHAPTER 5

117

FINANCIAL
SERVICES: USING
THEM EFFECTIVELY

Checking account reconciliation.

LINE	DESCRIPTION	AMOUNT
	Per Bank Statement	
1	Balance per bank statement	$170.60
2	Add: Deposits in transit	35.00
3	Subtotal	$205.60
4	Less: Outstanding checks	130.00
5	Adjusted cash balance per bank	$ 75.60
	Per Checkbook	
6	Balance per checkbook	$ 78.00
7	Less: Service charges	2.89
	Add: Interest earned	.49
8	Adjusted cash balance per checkbook	$ 75.60

Checklist

1 If line 5 equals line 8, you are done. If not, proceed to steps 2 through 6.

2 If line 5 is greater than line 8:
  a Recheck your list of outstanding checks.

3 If line 8 is greater than line 5:
  a Recheck your list of outstanding checks.
  b Check your deposits in transit.
  c Review bank statements for additional bank charges.

4 If line 8 and line 5 still do not agree:
  a Test the addition and subtraction in your checkbook.
  b Recompare the amounts on the returned checks to the amount recorded in the checkbook.

5 If line 5 and 8 still do not agree:
  a Compare the dollar amount that you wrote on each check with the dollar amount that the bank coded in magnetic ink (MICR) at the bottom of that check.

6 If the two lines still do not agree:
  a Take a short break; you are probably overlooking an obvious error.

OTHER PAYMENT METHODS

In addition to the standard payment accounts shown in Exhibit 5-2, financial institutions offer several other ways to make a payment. Currently, most are considered as supplements to a checking account, rather than replacements for it.

Remote Electronic Terminals

The **remote electronic terminal** (RET) is designed to be operated by the customer without any assistance from the financial institution. By locating

RETs in shopping centers, large commercial buildings, and small drive-up facilities, and on the outside of commercial banks, MSB, or S&L buildings, customers are able to carry out financial transactions 24 hours a day, 7 days a week. Through a typical RET, a customer can make a deposit, transfer money between savings and checking accounts, make a payment on a loan, and withdraw cash. Most terminals, however, restrict the amount of cash that can be withdrawn at one time. RETs have a number of safeguards to prevent an unauthorized withdrawal of funds or tampering with an account. Typically, they require the user to have a plastic ID card and a multiple-digit "secret" ID number agreed upon by the user and the bank.

Let's assume that you lose your card and someone finds it and tries to use it to withdraw cash from a RET. The finder inserts your card into the terminal and takes some wild guesses at your secret identification number. After a couple of guesses, the machine retains the identification card (the RET "swallows" it) and locks up your account from any further use. To recover your card and reactivate the account, you must visit the institution's main office.

STRATEGY

Other things being equal, select an institution that has a network of remote electronic terminals.

Cashier's Check

The drawer on a **cashier's check** is an authorized officer of the financial institution itself. Because the check is backed by the promise of the financial institution, it is readily accepted in any transaction. You can't write cashier's checks, but you can purchase them in any amount from most financial institutions: commercial banks, S&Ls, MSBs, and credit unions. You simply pay the institution the face amount of the check plus a service charge for the check. Some institutions provide the checks free of charge if the customer has an account with them. Others charge a nominal fee for the service. Since the check is made out to a specific payee, these checks are a convenient and safe way to make mail payments.

The check is not returned to the purchaser once it has been cashed; instead, it is retained by the selling institution. The purchaser does, however, receive a duplicate copy of the check. The selling institution can furnish a copy of the cashed check if necessary.

Money Order

Money orders are issued by a wide range of organizations, including the United States Post Office and some financial service firms. When the money order is cashed or deposited, the orgnization that issued the money order makes the payment. Because the issuers are large, well-known enterprises, the payee is reasonably confident of being paid. Consequently, money orders are readily accepted in most transactions. Since they are payable to a specific payee, they are also a safe, convenient way of making mail payments.

When you purchase it, a money order is always made out for a specific dollar amount, but the payee section is frequently left blank for you to fill in. A typical fee ranges from 75 cents to $5.

As proof of purchase, the buyer retains a duplicate copy or a stub from the money order. The cashed money order itself is returned to the issuing organization. Should the buyer have a question about when and where a money order was cashed, the issuing organization can provide that information from its records.

Traveler's Check

Traveler's checks are a special kind of payment order, designed to meet the cash needs of people who are away from home. These checks are superior to personal checks because they are issued by large commercial banks (both in the United States and in foreign countries) and specialized financial service companies. With this backing, they are readily accepted at hotels, motels, restaurants, airlines, major department stores, and other businesses serving the needs of travelers. This acceptability extends throughout the United States and abroad. To give the purchaser added safety assurance, all institutions that sell traveler's checks promise to replace any checks that are lost or stolen.

When you buy a traveler's check, you pay the face amount of the check as well as a small service charge for the check. Thus, in a way, a traveler's check is like a cashier's check. The checks are available in denominations ranging from $10 to $1000 per check. While the service fee usually runs $1 per $100 worth of checks, some financial institutions provide traveler's checks at no charge.

Since these checks have no time limit, many people hold unused checks rather than cash them in. The issuing company actively encourages doing so because it has use of the purchaser's money as long as a check remains outstanding. But good financial practice suggests you hold the check no longer than 70 days. If you do not need the checks within that period, you can earn more by having the money in a savings account than it will cost to buy new checks (at $1 per $100) when you need them. For example, assume you had $300 worth of traveler's checks that you did not expect to use for 6 months. Deposited in a savings account that paid 5½ percent, the money would earn:

$$\$8.25 \; = \$300 \qquad \times 5\tfrac{1}{2}\% \quad \times 6 \text{ months/12 months}$$

| Interest earned | = Deposited in savings account | × Rate of interest | × Fraction of year money is on deposit |

That is considerably more than the $3 it would cost to repurchase the traveler's checks if you needed them again in 6 months.

STRATEGY

Check the financial institutions in your area to see whether any of them offer free traveler's checks. And cash all unused traveler's checks unless you expect to use them within 70 days.

SUMMARY

1   Financial institutions have made a considerable effort to identify themselves as one-stop personal finance centers.

2   While checking accounts are still the most widely used type of payment account, NOW accounts and share draft accounts are increasingly popular.

3   NOW accounts and share draft accounts combine the best features offered by savings and checking:

   a   The interest of a savings account
   b   The convenience of a checking account

4   A payment account:

   a   Eliminates the need to carry large sums of cash
   b   Provides a ready and safe method of making mail payments
   c   Provides canceled checks that are valid payment receipts

5   The five major types of payment accounts are:

   a   Minimum savings balance

   b   Unconditional free checking

   c   Minimum checking balance

   d   Activity

   e   Package account

6   Two criteria should be considered when evaluating checking alternatives:

a Annual service cost

b Range of services

7   Most checks are personalized, which means that the account holder's name, address, and account number are printed on them.

8   A check should not be endorsed in blank until the moment it is to be cashed.

9   A restrictive endorsement or special endorsement is best to use when depositing an endorsed check by mail.

10   Many payment accounts now provide an automatic overdraft that allows the customer to overdraw the account up to a fixed dollar limit.

11   You can prevent payment on a check you have written by placing a stop-payment order on that check.

12   Your checking account is reconciled when the adjusted cash balance from the bank statement equals the adjusted balance from your checkbook.

13   Remote electronic terminals (RETs) provide added checking account convenience by allowing deposits, payments, transfers, and cash withdrawals 24 hours a day, 7 days a week.

14   Traveler's checks are a convenient and safe way to carry money and make payments when you are away from home.

REVIEW YOUR UNDERSTANDING OF

Commercial bank	Restrictive endorsement
Savings and loan association (S&L)	Special endorsement
Mutual savings bank (MSB)	Certified check
Credit union	Stop-payment order
Checking account	Automatic overdraft
Negotiable order of withdrawal (NOW) account	Bank reconciliation
Share draft account	Outstanding check list
Payment accounts	Deposit in transit
Minimum savings balance	Adjusted cash balance according
Unconditional free checking	to the bank
Minimum checking balance	Adjusted cash balance according
Activity account	to your checkbook
Package account	Remote electronic terminal (RET)
Monthly maintenance charge	Cashier's check
Check-clearing fee	Money order
Postdating	Traveler's check
Blank endorsement	

DISCUSSION QUESTIONS

1   Are commercial banks the only financial institutions that provide the necessary financial services that qualify them to be described as a one-stop personal finance centers? What services should a one-stop personal financial center give its customers? Are there any other financial institutions in your area that could qualify as one-stop centers?

2 What are the principal similarities and differences among traditional checking accounts, NOW accounts, and share draft accounts? Are there any advantages to a NOW account or a share draft account? Can a traditional checking account provide the same service? Why or why not?

3 Michelle Repinski is undecided between two checking account alternatives:

a She can maintain a $300 minimum balance in a 5 percent NOW account at Second Federal Savings and Loan. With that balance, there are no fees on checking services.

b She can maintain a $300 minimum in a 5 percent savings account at Last Ditch National Bank. The bank will then provide a service-free checking account.

What are the strengths of each account? Does either account offer a decided advantage? Why or why not?

4 How would you respond to the following advertisement: "Totally free checking when you maintain a $300 minimum balance in your checking account?"

5 Why is it difficult to analyze the cost of a package checking account? Who would benefit most with this account? Least?

6 What is the principal difference between a restrictive endorsement and a blank endorsement? Under what conditions would each be most appropriate?

7 Don Smith has devised a simplified recording system for his checking account. He never records any checks; instead, he waits until the bank sends an overdraft notice. At that time, he deposits $500 in the account. That $500 may be enough to cover the account for several weeks or more. His account has an automatic overdraft, so he is not as-sessed the regular $5 overdraft penalty. But the bank charges an 18 percent annual finance charge on the outstanding overdraft balance.

What are the strengths and weaknesses of Don's system? Would you recommend any changes? What improvements do your revisions promise?

8 How does a certified check differ from a regular personal check? Why would a bank refuse to accept a stop-payment order on a certified check?

9 Does a stop-payment order eliminate the possibility of a check's being cashed? Can you give several examples of where such an order would be used?

10 How is a deposit which is recorded in your checkbook, but not on the bank statement, handled in a reconciliation? In a reconciliation, how do you treat checks which have been written and entered in the checkbook, but have not been cashed?

11 After completing his reconciliation, Dick Smith found that his adjusted cash balance according to the bank was $35.10, while the adjusted cash balance in his checkbook was $17.10. What would you recommend? Why?

12 Why are banks and financial service companies willing to offer traveler's checks with no set expiration date? If the seller of the traveler's check receives most of the $1 per $100 commission, how does the issuer of the traveler's check make a profit?

13 Assume that a sales contract states: "Payment must be made with either a certified check or a cashier's check. A personal check is not acceptable." Why might the contract make that distinction? Can you give several situations where a seller might require payment with a certified or cashier's check?

14 What benefits does a remote electronic terminal offer to a customer? How does the terminal benefit the financial institution that installed it?

PROBLEMS

5-1 Sharon Swift is considering the following options for her personal checks:

OPTION	FEE
a Personalized with name, but not pre-numbered	Free from the bank
b Personalized with name and address, and prenumbered	$1.00 per 100 checks
c Personalized with name, address, and scenic landscape, and prenumbered	$2.50 per 100 checks
d Personalized "totally"—name, address, reproduction of famous art work, and prenumbered	$4.50 per 100 checks

Sharon expects to write about 30 checks a month during the year.

a What is the cost of each option?

b In addition to cost, are there other advantages or disadvantages Sharon should consider in her decision?

c What would you recommend? Why?

5-2 Nicholas and Kathy O'Brien are evaluating three checking alternatives:

Thrifty Check—No minimum balance; 50 cents monthly mainte-nance fee; 10 cents for each check written.

250 Econo—Minimum balance of $250 in checking account, and there are no service fees; minimum is based on average of daily balances.

Minimum Savings Checking—Bank provides a service-free checking account when customer maintains a $500 balance in a 4½ percent savings account; transfers from savings to checking account are not automatic. (*Hint:* The interest earnings on this savings account are 1½ percent less than on their current credit union account. The O'Briens currently have their 6 percent savings account at a credit union.)

a If the O'Briens anticipate writing five checks per month, what is the annual cost of each checking alternative? Which would you recommend?

b Had the O'Briens expected to write 20 checks per month, would your recommendation be the same?

5-3 Susan Weber is reconciling her checking account as of August 27. At this point, she has determined:

The balance according to checkbook on August 27 is $56.10.

Check numbers 513 for $75.00, 517 for $13.50, 523 for $37.75, 524 for $6.50, and 527 for $17.25 have been recorded in her checkbook but were not deducted on the August bank statement, nor were they returned with it.

The bank statement shows a $1.35 deduction for finance charges during August. There were no other charges.

The balance according to the bank statement on August 27 is $205.00.

The bank statement shows that the account earned 25 cents in interest during the month.

a What is the total of Susan's outstanding checks?

b What is the adjusted cash balance for the bank? What is the adjusted cash balance for the checkbook?

c Will Susan need to make any adjustment to her checkbook to complete the reconciliation?

5-4 Ralph DiCassa is considering the following two options:

Cash the $500 of traveler's checks he currently has. Deposit the proceeds in a 5 percent savings account. Purchase new traveler's checks in 180 days.

Retain the $500 of traveler's checks, thereby avoiding the $1 fee per $100 of new checks.

a What is the cost of each option? Which would you recommend?

b If Ralph planned to use the checks within 30 days, would your advice be the same as you gave in part **a?**

c At what length of holding period (number of days) are the costs of the two options equal? (*Hint:* Compute the daily holding cost.)

5-5 Last Ditch National Bank has offered Fred Fewpays the following three payment options:

PAYMENT OPTION	ACTIVITY ACCOUNT	CASHIER'S CHECKS	NOW ACCOUNT
Required minimum balance	None	None	$1,000
Charge per check	$0.20	$0.40	None
Monthly maintenance fee	$2.00	None	None
Interest on account	None	None	5%

Fred expects to write approximately five checks per month. To meet the NOW account's $1000 minimum balance, he will draw the money from an investment that currently pays 8 percent interest.

a What is the annual cost of each payment option?

b Which account would you recommend?

5-6 Manda Moreorless is confused by two competing offers she has for a payment account. One local bank offers a free checking account (no interest paid) when the person maintains a $500 balance in a 5 percent savings account. A local S&L combines the two into a 5 percent NOW account that requires a $500 minimum balance. Based on her experience of the past 2 years, Manda expects to keep a working balance—over and above the required minimum—of $200 in her payment account.

a Is there any difference in cost between the two accounts? If so, how much?

b Assume that some individuals and businesses to which Manda writes checks are slow in cashing them. Should that influence Manda's decision? Why?

CASE PROBLEM

Phil Fast has recently opened a personal checking account. Being new to the checking account world, he is having more than a few problems with his monthly reconciliation. To date, his reconciliation consists of:

Balance from bank statement $142.50

Balance from checkbook $121.00

The fact that the two do not agree disturbs him, but he is unclear about how to proceed. His checkbook, bank statement, and returned checks are shown below and on p. 126 so that you can help Phil solve his problem.

CHECK NUMBER	DATE	CHECK ISSUED TO	CHECK AMOUNT	DEPOSIT AMOUNT	BALANCE 51.00
1511	10/7	Central Food Mart	$ 10.00		$ 41.00
1512	10/14	Leadpoint Public Service	40.00		1.00
	10/14	Deposit		$320.00	321.00
1514	10/15	Ajax Retail Service	155.00		166.00
1515	10/15	Quick Charge, Inc.	25.00		141.00
1516	10/15	Ralph Smith, M.D.	10.00		131.00
1517	10/15	Red Dot Insurance	40.00		91.00
1518	10/18	Central Food Mart	15.00		76.00
	10/21	Deposit		90.00	166.00
1519	10/25	Fred's Auto Repairs	37.00		129.00
1520	10/30	Tony's Clothes	25.00		104.00
1521	10/30	Cash	12.00		92.00
1522	11/2	Central Food Mart	16.00		76.00
	11/4	Deposit		45.00	121.00
1523	11/6	Western Beverage Spot	13.50		107.50

1   Why is the balance per bank statement, $142.50, different from the balance in Phil's checkbook, $121.00?

2   What information is needed before the account can be reconciled?

3   Using this information, compile a list of outstanding checks. Why is this needed?

4   Are there any deposits in transit?

5   Complete the reconciliation of Phil's account.

6   What corrections, if any, should Phil make in his checkbook?

Phil Fast
1456 Deadend
Leadpoint, USA 98765

Last National Bank
Leadpoint, USA 98765

Statement Period: October 5 to November 5

Beginning Balance	Total Deposit	Total Charges	Ending Balance
51.00	410.00	318.50	142.50

Charges			Credits	Date	Balance
				10-6	51.00
10.00				10-11	41.00
			320.00	10-15	361.00
40.00	60.00	155.00		10-17	106.00
25.00				10-20	81.00
			90.00	10-22	171.00
15.00				10-24	156.00
12.00				11-4	144.00
SC 2.45	IN .95			11-5	142.50

SC Service Charge	FC Finance Charge	DM Debit Memo	IN Interest

1521
$12.00

1518
$15.00

1515
$25.00

1514
$155.00

1513
$60.00

1512
$40.00

1511
$10.00

Phil Fast

Pay to the
Order of *Food Mart*

Oct 7, 19 *83*

$ *10 00/100*

Ten _____ *00/100* Dollars

Last National Bank
Leadpoint, USA 98765

Phil Fast

Memo *Food*

CHAPTER

6

HOW TO "MANAGE" YOUR INCOME TAXES

**AFTER COMPLETING THIS CHAPTER
YOU WILL HAVE LEARNED**

The major *components* and *computations* in the income tax process

How to compute *gross income*

What the major *adjustments to gross income* are

The *zero bracket amount*—what it means and how to use it

The most common *itemized deductions*

How to treat your *medical and dental expenses* when figuring your taxes

What *deductions* you are allowed from a casualty or theft loss

The five *eligibility tests* to decide whether a person qualifies as a dependent

What *taxable income* is

How to compute the *amount of taxes* you must pay

What *income averaging* is all about and how to determine whether you are eligible for income averaging

What *tax credits* are

The qualifications for the *child* and *disabled dependent care* credit

When it is necessary to prepare an estimate of your taxes and file an *estimated tax declaration*

How to avoid the *penalty for underpayment* of tax

How *marginal tax rates* are determined and how they are used in tax computations

How to survive an *audit* by the Internal Revenue Service

"AS certain as death and taxes."

If you haven't come across that saying before, we're sure you will see it and hear it again. And we're sure you will think of it the first time you recognize how much of your income you have to pay out in taxes, especially in income taxes. Current estimates are that the average individual works from January to May of each year to earn the money necessary to pay his or her taxes for that year. Although we don't like to think about either of these two certainties, we must face them. One certainty we must experience regularly every year; the other we must experience only once, and after having done so, we don't have to experience the regular one (or anything else) anymore.

Income taxes are a levy that must be paid on income. And you pay those taxes on your income to the federal government, to your state government, and (in many places) also to your local and city government. However, the largest tax bite is taken by the federal government. With the tax rates for many people reaching 30 percent or more, the federal government even takes a sizable portion of the income of those in the middle-income ranks. Therefore, it is more than reasonable that you pay only the amount of taxes the law requires you to pay and no more. In other words, you should learn how to use every available legal means to minimize your taxes. Unfortunately, learning how to do that is not very easy. Current tax laws are written in language that is verbose, vague, confusing, tortuous, and seemingly contradictory.

It is essential that you have at least a working knowledge of taxes for several reasons. First, taxes can drastically alter the financial implications of a particular decision. Second, treating a tax item improperly can cost you hundreds of dollars in unnecessary taxes. And third, because some of the tax advice that suddenly appears around tax time is not highly reliable, you should learn to manage your tax matters yourself.

We won't try to teach you what you should know about income taxes by working through a complete set of tax forms, line by line. That's the "cookbook" approach, and that's what gets some people in trouble when they prepare their tax forms. Change the "recipe" a little bit or vary one of the "ingredients" in the recipe, and people don't know what to do.

We will try to teach you about income taxes by stressing the basic concepts underlying each major point in preparing tax forms and carrying out tax calculations. By understanding the basic concepts, you should be able to handle variations or divergencies from them. We will present major concepts and not get bogged down in the details surrounding each one. When we think you should know the details and have more complete information, we will refer you to one of the tax reference guides listed at the end of the chapter.

Our discussion will concentrate almost exclusively on federal income taxes. The features and provisions for state and local income taxes tend to vary so widely that it would be nearly impossible to discuss them adequately in a few pages.

Avoiding, Not Evading, Taxes

While it is not possible to prove it, we believe that a sizable number of people overpay their income taxes, either through oversight, confusion, error, or timidity. This is an extremely poor way to use your money. You can spend your money more wisely by **avoiding taxes**. And when we say *avoiding* taxes, we don't mean evading taxes. There is a considerable difference between the two. **Evading taxes** is deliberately failing to pay taxes, understating income, or cheating in any way for the purpose of lowering taxes. All such processes are illegal, and we certainly are not recommending evasion as a tax strategy.

Taxpayers do, however, have every right to reduce their taxes as much as allowed by the tax regulations. In fact, the Supreme Court has affirmed that it is a taxpayer's right to avoid taxes. Too often, people are hesitant to reduce their taxes as much as allowed because they are afraid the Internal Revenue Service (IRS) may question them about the reduction. Our recommendation is direct and simple: If you feel you are eligible to reduce your taxes in a particular way, do it. You may have to explain it but you won't have to go to jail. Very few taxpayers ever draw a criminal penalty; the ones who do have intentionally and willfully attempted to evade taxes.

BASIC INCOME TAX STRUCTURE

We will discuss income taxes in this chapter in a pattern that pretty much follows the basic income tax structure shown in Exhibit 6-1. This exhibit shows the steps in figuring out taxes payable by (1) starting with the total of all the various sources of income that must be accounted for, (2) subtracting the amounts you are allowed to deduct (which are really reductions) from that total income, and thus (3) finding the total amount of income on which you have to pay taxes.

Before we proceed to discuss the tax structure shown in Exhibit 6-1, let's first explain and define some of the concepts represented in the boxes. We will start at the top and work our way down.

Gross income is the total of all income dollars that, according to the tax regulations and rules, you must include when computing your taxes. Examples of amounts you would have to include are such things as wages you earn, interest on your savings account, and the profits you receive from your ownership of a business.

Adjustments to gross income are special items you are allowed to deduct from your gross income. Later, we will discuss the individual adjustments in more detail.

Itemized deductions are a select group of expenses which you can deduct from adjusted gross income. The net effect is that they further reduce the income on which you must pay income taxes. Examples of expenses or payments you can deduct include interest on the money you borrow, state income taxes you pay, and contributions to a charity.

The **zero bracket amount** is a set dollar total that you can substitute for the total of your itemized deductions. Your choice between the two would be whichever dollar amount is larger: the zero bracket amount or total itemized deductions. People whose itemized deductions are small will elect

EXHIBIT 6-1

Basic income tax structure.

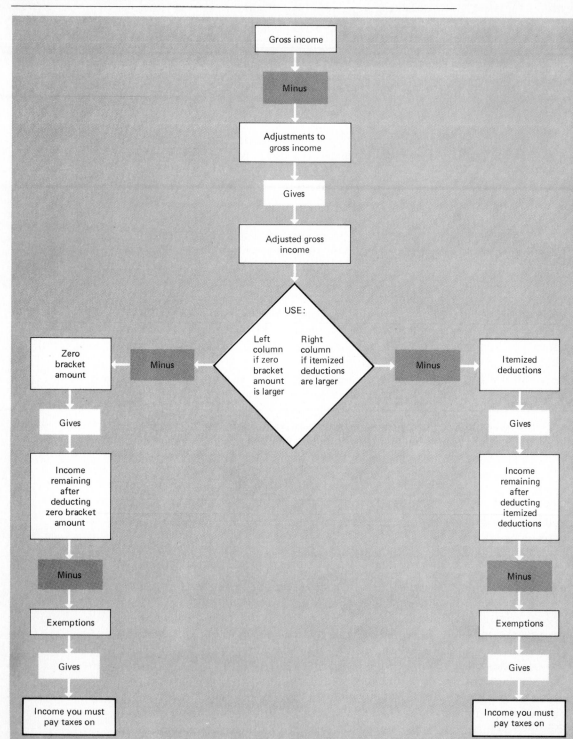

to deduct the zero bracket amount; you can elect the zero bracket amount regardless of how small your itemized deductions are. People with extensive itemized deductions will want to deduct their total itemized deductions rather than their zero bracket amount. The actual dollar amount of your zero bracket amount depends upon your marital status.

An **exemption** allows you to deduct a set dollar amount from your income. To do so, you must establish the fact that someone qualifies as your dependent. In effect, you are allowed to exclude, or exempt, part of your income from taxes by deducting the dollar amount from the income on which you must pay taxes. At this point, it is sufficient to know that the major qualifications for determining whether someone qualifies as your dependent center on the percentage of their living expenses you pay and their relationship to you.

When computing your taxes, it's always nice to be able to reduce (legally) the amount of income on which you must pay taxes. Therefore, you should be especially keen about the boxes that follow those "Minus" boxes: both "Adjustments to gross income" and either "Zero bracket amount" or "Itemized deductions" and "Exemptions." We will explain all these things further as we proceed through this chapter.

GROSS INCOME

Exhibit 6-2 summarizes the sources of income you must include in your gross income. While most of the sources of income shown in that exhibit are relatively straightforward, the treatment of capital gains and losses is more involved and, alas, we must discuss it in some detail.

Capital Gains and Losses

Perhaps you own one or more of the following:

Common stock, which means you are a partial owner of a company

Corporate bonds, which means you loaned money to a company

Municipal bonds, which means you loaned money to a state or city

Treasury securities, which means you loaned money to the United States Treasury

Real estate, which means you own property such as a building, a house, or land[1]

If you do, you own assets which can produce income from a capital gain if you sell the asset at a price that exceeds the purchase price, or a loss if you sell it at a price lower than the purchase price. While a loss is not good news, it is not all bad news; including that negative amount in gross income reduces your income from other sources.

If you owned any of these assets for a year or less, the income gained or

---

[1]Your personal residence receives special tax treatment. We shall wait until Chap. 11 to discuss that topic.

lost when you sold each of them is classified as a **short-term capital gain or loss** for tax purposes. If you owned them for longer than a year, the gain or loss from the sale is classified as a **long-term capital gain or loss**.

These are called "capital gains or losses" because they arise from the sale of assets—whether they be common stock, bonds, or real estate—in which you have invested your capital (your money).

Short-Term Gains and Losses

For tax purposes, the income from short-term gains and losses is treated much the same as income from regular wages or salary. The entire short-term gain is included as part of gross income. Likewise, a short-term loss is deducted from the income from other sources to give total gross income.

Before we proceed with an example, we need to define two terms: net purchase price and net sale price.

Net Purchase Price   An asset's **net purchase price** includes the initial price of the item plus all commissions or fees paid at the time of purchase. For example, assume you bought 100 shares of common stock with a purchase price of $1000 and paid a $60 fee to the broker who handled the transaction for you. Your net purchase price is

$1060   = $1000   + $60

⬆   ⬆   ⬆

Net purchase   =   Purchase   +   Broker's fee
price   price   for purchase

The net purchase price on real estate would include these two items. It

---

EXHIBIT 6-2

Items that must be included in gross income.

Alimony received by taxpayer	Lottery winnings
Capital gains and losses	Partnership income
Commissions	Payments from Individual Retirement
Contest winnings	Accounts and Keogh Plans
Dividends over $100 ($200 on joint return)	Pensions
Gambling winnings but only to the extent they exceed losses*	Profits from business operations
	Salaries
Interest on savings and certificates of deposit (CDs) (see note below)	Tips
	U.S. savings bond interest
	Wages
Interest on corporate and U.S. treasury bonds and notes (see note below)	

*If gambling losses were $500 and winnings were $600, only the $100 excess of winnings would be included. If the opposite were true—winnings were $500 and losses were $600— none of the winnings would be included. But *none* of the $600 loss could be deducted.
   Note: Beginning in 1985, you may be allowed to exclude up to 15 percent of your net interest income. But there are rules and requirements, so consult a tax reference book.

would also include the taxpayer's cost of any additions or improvements made while owning the real estate.

Net Sale Price   The **net sale price** equals the total sale price less any commissions or fees paid at the time of sale. To illustrate, assume you sold those 100 shares of common stock we used in the previous example for $1200 and paid a broker a $72 fee to complete the sale. The net sale price is:

$$\$1128 \quad = \$1200 \quad - \$72$$

$$\underset{\substack{\text{Net sale} \\ \text{price}}}{\triangle} = \underset{\substack{\text{Total sale} \\ \text{price}}}{\triangle} - \underset{\substack{\text{Broker's fee} \\ \text{on sale}}}{\triangle}$$

Computing the Short-Term Gain or Loss   Now several examples will illustrate how short-term gains and losses are computed and how those gains or losses are handled for tax purposes: Exhibit 6-3 summarizes the computations. Assume Sue Monks sold the 100 shares of XQ common stock she purchased 11 months ago. The top line of Exhibit 6-3 summarizes the other details. All her $1000 loss is deductible from income for tax purposes because it is a short-term loss. However, that also works in reverse. When she sold her Zug corporate bonds (second line in the exhibit), she had to include all the $400 short-term gain in her income for tax purposes.

Long-Term Gains and Losses

Let's take long-term gains and losses one at a time: gains first. The principal distinction of a long-term gain is that only 40 percent of the amount of any long-term gain must be included as taxable income. That is very attractive, especially to taxpayers with high tax rates. Several examples will illustrate the computation of long-term gains and losses. Again, Exhibit 6-3 will summarize the details for our examples. Assume that Fred Holt sold the Slug common stock he purchased 2 years ago. The third line of Exhibit 6-3 shows the details. Because it is a long-term gain, Fred pays tax only on $120 (40 percent) of the $300 gain.

Now that we have shown you how a long-term gain is taxed, we should explain how the actual tax computation is made. To begin, the entire gain is included in gross income. But 60 percent of the gain can be deducted as an

EXHIBIT 6-3

Computation of short-term and long-term gains and losses.

CAPITAL ASSET	ASSET HELD FOR	SHORT-TERM (ST) OR LONG-TERM (LT)	NET PURCHASE PRICE	NET SALES PRICE	GAIN (LOSS)	GAIN THAT IS TAXED	LOSS THAT CAN BE DEDUCTED
XQ Stock	11 months	ST	$3000	$2000	($1000)	—	($1000)
Zug Bonds	10 months	ST	1700	2100	400	$400	—
Slug Stock	2 years	LT	4675	4975	300	120	—
QT Bonds	27 months	LT	2750	1550	(1200)	—	(600)

adjustment to gross income. The net effect is that you have to pay income taxes on only the 40 percent that remains as part of gross income.

With a long-term loss, the taxpayer can deduct only 50 percent of that loss from other sources of income: wages, interest, dividends. Assume that Sue English recently sold the QT corporate bonds she has held for 27 months: the fourth line in Exhibit 6-3 summarizes the details of that sale. Sue can deduct only $600 (50 percent) of the $1200 long-term loss on that sale.

Again, the actual treatment on a tax return is different. First, the entire loss—it is negative—is subtracted from income. But then the loss is reduced by 50 percent as an adjustment to gross income. The net effect is that 50 percent of the loss is, in fact, deducted; that is exactly the same dollar amount that we computed in our example.

Limits When Deducting Capital Losses During any one year, a taxpayer cannot deduct more than $3000 of capital losses. That $3000 of losses can be short-term, long-term, or some combination of the two. When losses exceed $3000, the excess over $3000 is carried forward to be deducted in future years. Of course, any future deduction is also limited to $3000 per year. Assume Len Loser had $5000 of short-term capital losses this past year. He would deduct $3000 of that loss on this year's tax return. He then will deduct the $2000 that remains on next year's return. Let us change the loss situation to one where a taxpayer had $14,000 of long-term losses. Only one-half of a long-term loss can be deducted, so only $7000 of those losses are deductible. Again, $3000 would be deducted this year. The remaining $4000 is carried forward: $3000 will be deducted next year, with the remaining $1000 deducted the following year.

Combinations of Short-Term and Long-Term Gains and Losses The general guidelines and basic principles we just presented still apply when you have both a short-term gain or loss and a long-term gain or loss in the same year. Computing the short-term loss and the long-term gain is done the same way as was illustrated. But determining how that loss and gain are to be included in gross income is governed by a reasonably complex set of rules. So, if you have both a short-term gain or loss and a long-term gain or loss, you will need to consult a tax reference book.

Sources of Income that Can Be Excluded from Gross Income

Exhibit 6-4 summarizes the sources of income you do not have to include in your gross income. Most of the sources of income shown in the exhibit are relatively straightforward. We shall discuss several of these items later in the book.

Adjustments to Gross Income

Adjustments to gross income are a select group of expenses and expenditures which you can deduct from gross income. If, during the year, you incurred an expense or made an expenditure that qualifies as an adjustment to gross income, you are allowed to deduct that amount, regardless of whether you elect to use the zero bracket amount or the total of your

EXHIBIT 6-4

CHAPTER 6

135

HOW TO
"MANAGE" YOUR
INCOME TAXES

Sources of income that need not be included in
gross income.

Annuity payments: the portion that represents your original cost	Life insurance payments
Child support payments	Scholarship and fellowship awards
Disability benefits: but there are upper limits on how much can be excluded	Social Security benefits for disability or survivors; retirement benefits for some higher income taxpayers may be partially taxable
Gifts and inheritances	Common stock dividends and stock splits (discussed in Chapter 19)
Health and accident insurance payments for expenses of illnesses and accidents	Unemployment benefits, but part may have to be included in gross income if taxpayer's gross income exceeds $20,000
Interest on bonds issued by states and cities	Welfare benefits
Insurance payments for damages to your automobile, your house, or your personal belongings	Workers' compensation

itemized deductions. Our discussion concentrates on the major adjustments
to gross income permitted in 1983.

Contributions to Retirement Plans

Self-employed persons and certain people who are not covered by a regular
pension plan where they work can establish their own retirement plans if
they meet certain qualifications. Money placed in a retirement plan is called
a **contribution** in order to distinguish it from a required payment. That is,
most taxpayers have free choice as to whether they want to contribute to
this type of pension plan. The principal advantage is that contributions to
the plan are "sheltered" from income taxes until the money is withdrawn
from the plan.

There are limits on the amount you can contribute each year. And the
taxes are only deferred. The entire amount of each retirement payment is
subject to income tax in the future.

Pension Plan for the Self-Employed (Keogh) An individual's maximum contribution to a **self-employed pension plan (Keogh)** is the lesser of
$30,000 or 25 percent of the income from the self-employment. Of course, a
self-employed individual can decide to contribute less than the maximum
amount. For example, if your income from self-employment was $8000,
your maximum pension contribution would be:

$2000	= $8000	× 25%
⬆	⬆	⬆
Maximum pension contribution	= Income from self-employment	× Maximum contribution rate

It is not necessary that your only source of income be self-employment. You may have income from another job at the same time and still contribute up to 25 percent of your income from self-employment to a retirement plan.

Individual Retirement Account (IRA)   Every taxpayer who works for an employer (and most people do) can establish an **Individual Retirement Account** (IRA). The contribution for a year is limited to $2000 or the taxpayer's earnings, whichever is less. Or, when the IRA is set up jointly with a nonworking spouse, the maximum contribution rises to $2250. Furthermore, even a person who worked part-time and earned $3000 for the year can contribute up to $2000 to an IRA account. A taxpayer can, of course, always contribute less than the allowed maximum.

STRATEGY

Carefully investigate whether you qualify to contribute to either a Keogh or an IRA pension plan. The reduction in the taxes that you would otherwise have to pay may make such an investment extremely attractive.

Moving Expenses

If you accept a new job or are transferred to a new location with your present job, all or part of the **moving expenses** may be deducted from gross income as an adjustment to gross income. To be eligible for this deduction, you must meet two qualifications.

First, the move must be 35 miles or more. That distance computation is illustrated by the following example:

Distance from old residence to new job location	65 miles
Less distance from old residence to old job location	13 miles
Equals mileage difference	52 miles

In this example, your previous job was 13 miles from your old residence and the new job is 65 miles from that old residence. That 52-mile difference satisfies the first requirement.

The second qualification is that you must be employed full-time at the new job location at least 39 weeks during the 12 months following the move. Those 39 weeks do not have to be either consecutive or with the same employer, but they must be in the same locality.

If you meet these two qualifications, you should know what moving expenses can be included as adjustments.

Traveling Expenses   All costs incurred for transportation (public transportation or the expenses of your car), meals, and lodging on the trip to the new job location can be deducted as a moving expense.

Moving Costs   You can include the costs of packing, crating, and transporting possessions, and in-transit storage for up to 30 days, the costs of

insuring your possessions in transit and of shipping an automobile, and charges for disconnecting and reconnecting household appliances.

House-Hunting Trips   The costs incurred on house-hunting or apartment-search trips (meals, lodging, and transportation) can be deducted. There is no set limit on the number of trips allowed, and a trip does not have to be successful to qualify.

Temporary Living Costs   If you do not have a permanent residence at the new job location, you are allowed to deduct the costs for meals and temporary lodging. This deduction is limited to meals and lodging costs incurred for any 30 consecutive days after you obtain employment.

Expenses of Selling, Purchasing, or Leaving a Residence   You can deduct the expenses of selling your old house and transferring ownership to the buyer. Likewise, the expenses of purchasing a new house and transferring ownership to your name can be deducted. When the move involves a house or apartment rental, you can include the expense of settling the rental agreement—the lease—on your previous house or apartment as well as the cost of acquiring a lease on a new house or apartment.

Employer Reimbursements   When an employer reimburses an employee for the partial or total costs of the moving expense, the amount of reimbursement is included in the employee's gross income. The employee then includes all the moving-related expenses as an adjustment to gross income and deducts those expenses to compute adjusted gross income in the normal manner.

Alimony

The alimony or maintenance a person pays to a spouse or a former spouse can be included as an adjustment to gross income. Typically, alimony or maintenance payments arise when a taxpayer is divorced or separated from his or her spouse.

Child support payments made by a taxpayer *cannot* be deducted as an adjustment to gross income. But, by making those payments, the taxpayer may be able to show that the child is a dependent. That would allow the taxpayer to deduct a set dollar amount as an exemption.

Disability Income Payments

The income payments you receive while you are disabled and unable to work must be included in gross income just as is regular income. But you may be able to deduct a portion, or all, of those payments from gross income, and thereby avoid paying any tax on part, or all, of any disability income. You should consult a tax reference book to learn the qualifications and limitations.

Employee Business Expenses

In general, employees can deduct those business-related expenses incurred while performing their jobs and for which they were not reimbursed by their employers. Typical deductible **employee business expenses** include transportation costs, meals and lodging while away from home, automobile expenses, and certain entertainment expenses. On automobile expenses, you have a choice. You can deduct your actual out-of-pocket expenses for owning and operating your automobile when used for business. Or you can deduct a set amount per mile. As this is written, the amount is 20 cents for each mile driven on business-related trips.

Two-Earner Married-Couple Deduction

Two working spouses, filing jointly, generally pay more taxes than they would if they each filed a tax return as a single person. This added tax has frequently been labeled the "marriage tax penalty." Part of the penalty arises because the zero bracket amount for a married couple is $3400. But each single person receives a zero bracket amount of $2300, so two single returns have a total allowance of $4600. Further, the tax rates are structured in such a way that they also contribute to the marriage tax penalty. To lessen the penalty, the Economic Recovery Tax Act of 1981 created a special adjustment to gross income for married working couples: the **two-earner married-couple deduction**.

The act allows a two-earner family to deduct 10 percent of the lower-paid spouse's income. However, the maximum credit is limited to $3000. A couple can take the deduction regardless of whether they use the zero bracket amount or itemize their deductions. To illustrate the two-earner married couple deduction, assume that, for 1983, Alice Weber earned $14,000 while her spouse, George, earned $13,000. The Webers' deduction is:

$$\$1,300 \quad = \quad \$13,000 \quad \times \quad 10\%$$

$\Uparrow$		$\Uparrow$		$\Uparrow$
Two-earner married-couple deduction	=	Income: Lower-paid spouse	×	Allowed deduction rate

The Webers would reduce their combined income by the $1300, thus lowering the amount of tax they must pay.

DEDUCTIONS FROM ADJUSTED GROSS INCOME: ZERO BRACKET AMOUNT OR TOTAL ITEMIZED DEDUCTIONS

When we first mentioned the basic tax structure and presented a sketch of that structure in Exhibit 6-1, we briefly discussed the zero bracket amount and itemized deductions. At that point, we indicated that the two items are substitutes. That is, the taxpayer is allowed to deduct whichever amount is larger: the zero bracket amount or the total of all itemized deductions.

Zero Bracket Amount

Currently, the maximum zero bracket amount (for 1982) that taxpayers are allowed is:

$3400 for married taxpayers who are filing a single, combined tax return (filing jointly)

$2300 for unmarried taxpayers

$1700 for each person of a married couple that elects to file two returns

The zero bracket amount is fixed; it does not increase with income. A high-income taxpayer receives the same zero bracket amount as a low-income taxpayer. Thus, if a single taxpayer's income of $12,000 should double to $24,000, the zero bracket amount would remain at $2300.

The dollar limits on the zero bracket amount do, however, change quite frequently. So check a standard tax reference book for the current amount.

A point of information on how the term "zero bracket amount" evolved: A few years ago, tax regulations used the term "standard deduction" to describe the above flat dollar deductions. Zero bracket amount has now replaced the standard deduction term. Essentially, they both refer to the same thing.

Itemized Deductions

Now that we know something about the zero bracket amount, we need to examine its substitute: itemized deductions. These are a special group of expenses that you can deduct from adjusted gross income instead of the zero bracket amount.

Interest and Finance Charges The **interest and finance charges** you pay on home mortgages, consumer loans, credit cards, charge accounts, and most other loans and forms of credit are deductible expenses. Many lenders indicate to borrowers the total amount of interest or finance charges paid during the year on their January or December billing. If you are uncertain about the total interest or finance charge paid during the entire year, ask the lender.

Taxes In general, the following **taxes** can be included as an itemized deduction:

Real property taxes (state, local, and foreign)—Examples are the taxes you had to pay on your house or on land you own.

Personal property taxes (state and local)—Examples are required taxes on your car, household furnishings, or other personal property.

Income taxes (state, local, and foreign)—Examples are the state taxes you pay on your income for the year and the city income taxes you pay because you live in a particular city.

Sales and use taxes (state and local)—An example would be the state sales tax you are required to pay when buying a car, a boat, or other items.

The United States Treasury has developed tables that estimate state and local sales and use taxes for taxpayers. But the tables are strictly optional. Taxpayers can always use their own records to compute state and local sales and use taxes. The only requirement is that they must provide proof of the deduction if asked to do so.

STRATEGY

When using the optional sales and use tax tables, you are allowed to add the taxes on expensive items, such as cars, boats, etc. If your actual sales tax payments exceed those shown in the table and you can prove that they do, use the larger amount.

Contributions A taxpayer can deduct **contributions** to most religious, charitable, educational, and other philanthropic organizations. Examples include contributions to (1) churches, synagogues, or other religious organizations; (2) Community Chest, United Fund, and many similar organizations, and (3) colleges, universities, and most educational organizations. A contribution made to a political subdivision of a state or of the United States qualifies if it is exclusively for public purposes. If you are unsure whether contributions to an organization are deductible, ask the organization if it has been approved by the U.S. Treasury Department, or check the Treasury's list of approved organizations. Contributions to the following do not qualify as deductions: lobbying organizations, many fraternal groups, professional groups, social clubs, chambers of commerce, civic leagues, and gifts to needy individuals.

Contributions are deductible in the year in which you made the payment or donated the property. You should obtain receipts from the charitable organization for cash donations or pay by check so you have the canceled check as a receipt. If you made a cash contribution, by all means include it even if you do not have a receipt. The worst thing that could happen is that you would have difficulty supporting that contribution should your return be questioned. However, most IRS auditors will accept unsupported cash contributions if the amounts seem reasonable.

Donations of property—books, craft items, clothes, furniture, food items, securities, and real estate—are also deductible. In most cases, the allowable amount for the deduction is the fair market value of the property when it was donated. The *fair market value* is the price that property would sell for in the open market between a regular buyer and seller. Special rules apply, however, when the donated property has increased in value so much that its fair market value exceeds your cost on the item.

The value of donated personal services is not deductible. But if you incur expenses such as postage, phone, stationery, and office supplies while donating personal services, they are deductible. In addition, when you use your automobile to travel to the charitable organization's office, or as part of volunteer work, you can include a set amount for each mile you traveled; as this is written, the amount is set at 9 cents per mile.

Medical and Dental Expenses In general, deductible **medical and dental expenses** include professional services (doctor, dentist, nurse, etc.), medical equipment, prescription drugs, laboratory tests, medical treatment, hospital services, and premiums for health-insurance policies. Transportation expenses to and from the doctor's office or hospital are also deductible —either the actual cost of commercial transportation or a set amount per mile for your own auto can be deducted. As this is written, the amount is 9 cents per mile.

There are, however, restrictions and special calculations to determine how much of the actual expenses are allowable as deductions.

First, the expense must have been paid in the current tax year and it must be for yourself, your spouse, or for a person who qualifies as your dependent. We will discuss those dependent qualifications later in the chapter (they are illustrated in Exhibit 6-8).

Second, you cannot include any medical or dental expense for which you have been reimbursed by insurance or for which you have received other compensation.

Third, only medical expenses in excess of 5 percent of your adjusted gross income are deductible.

Exhibit 6-5 provides an example of how to calculate a medical deduction. Assume the Jones family incurred the following medical expenses during the year: premium on medical insurance, $750; unreimbursed medical and dental expenses, $1150, and unreimbursed prescription drug expenses, $200. The Jones's combined adjusted gross income was $12,500.

EXHIBIT 6-5

Computation of medical deductions the Joneses can include as an itemized deduction.

Medical and dental expenses	$1150
Prescription drugs	200
Health-insurance premium	750
Subtotal	$2100
Less: 5% of adjusted gross income:	
$12,500 × 5%	625
Allowable deduction	$1475

Education Expense   Taxpayers can deduct an **education expense** provided that three conditions are met:

First, the taxpayer is currently employed or self-employed.

Second, the taxpayer already meets the minimum education requirements of his or her present employment. That is, if a job requires an employee to have a certain minimum level of education and the taxpayer pursues an education program to meet that minimum level, the cost is not deductible.

Third, the education program must (1) maintain or improve the skills required for the person's present position, or (2) be required by the individual's employer, or (3) be required by present laws and regulations in order for the person to keep his or her present status, salary, or employment.

The fact that the person eventually obtains a college degree does not void the deduction as long as all three of the above qualifications are satisfied. Likewise, if the person qualifies for and receives a job promotion during the education program, the deduction will be allowed as long as the job duties remain similar.

Deductible education expenses include course fees, tuition, books, supplies, transportation costs from the job to the course, travel expenses to a school away from home, and living expenses incurred at a school away from home. Courses that qualify as education expenses can be at the basic, intermediate, or advanced level. And they can be taken at a university, a vocational school, or an adult education program, or by correspondence.

Job Search Expenses   If you are currently, or have recently been, employed in a particular trade, profession, or occupation, the expenses of searching for new employment in that same career field can be included as an itemized deduction. **Job search expenses** are deductible whether the search is successful or not. Typical deductible job search expenses include the cost of preparing and printing résumés, employment agency fees, telephone calls, and travel expenses for interviews. These items are not deductible, however, when the taxpayer is applying for a position in an area other than the present career field. Nor can they be deducted when the taxpayer is seeking employment for the first time or when the expenses are paid by the employer.

Casualty and Theft Losses   According to tax rules and regulations, a **casualty** or **theft loss** is any damage or loss of property due to an event that is sudden, unexpected, or unusual in nature. An example will illustrate what is needed. If Grazelda Bushbacker was in her car at the corner of Third and Walnut while waiting for the stop signal to turn green and Borris Bumbler crashed his car into hers, then the necessary qualifications have been met: sudden and unexpected damage. On the other hand, if Grazelda never washed her car and it became a rusty, undrivable hulk in 2 years, her loss is not deductible as a casualty loss. The loss due to the rusting process was gradual, not sudden, and Grazelda's actions, or lack thereof, had a role in ultimate loss. Typical events that would be covered are losses caused by fire, storms, flood, earthquake, other natural catastrophies, riots, vandalism, and accidents. Examples of losses that would not qualify are diseases of trees and plants, termite damage, insect damage, and prolonged drought.

Two restrictions seriously limit the deductibility of casualty losses. To begin, the first $100 of each casualty loss cannot be deducted—a minor restriction. Second, only that portion of the casualty that exceeds 10 percent of the taxpayer's adjusted gross income can be deducted—a nearly prohibitive restriction. This final restriction means that you can deduct only that portion of casualty loss that exceeds 10 percent of your income.

Let us use an example to demonstrate why most people cannot qualify for a casualty or theft deduction. Assume that Borris Bumbler's car accident, discussed above, caused $1200 damage to his new car; unfortunately, he had no insurance. His adjusted gross income is $13,000. The 10 percent of adjusted gross income hurdle means that Borris can deduct only that part of the casualty loss that exceeds $1300 (10 percent of his income); in terms of our example, Borris can deduct nothing. Had Borris's accident caused $2500 of damage, how much could he deduct? Exhibit 6-6 summarizes the amount of his possible deduction. From our example, it is clear that most people are rarely able to deduct their casualty and theft losses. Unless those losses are extremely large, they will not exceed the 10 percent hurdle.

Miscellaneous Deductions   Because the list of miscellaneous deductions is extensive, we give only the more frequently used ones in Exhibit 6-7. For a complete list, consult one of the tax reference books listed at the end of this chapter.

Should You Itemize Deductions?

Before we can answer the question "Should you itemize deductions?" we need a brief explanation. Up to this point, when we said "itemized deductions," we meant that special group of expenses and payments that a taxpayer is allowed to deduct from adjusted gross income. But in the jargon of taxes, the statement "to itemize deductions" means listing or detailing all the items that qualify as itemized deductions. So, when you itemize your deductions, you will list the items you can claim as itemized deductions.

To detemine whether to itemize your deductions, itemize them.

EXHIBIT 6-6

Computing the portion of a casualty loss that can be included as an itemized deduction.

Amount of casualty loss		$2500
Less: $100 exclusion on all losses	$ 100	
10% of adjusted gross income:		
10% × $13,000	$1300	$1400
Amount deductible as casualty loss		$1100

Simply make a rough list of deductible items that quickly come to mind and estimate the amount of each itemized deduction. Add the amounts.

If the total is larger than your zero bracket amount, you should itemize, and the next step is to do so very thoroughly and carefully.

If the total is just under your zero bracket amount, you should also make a detailed list of your itemized deductions. This second, more careful list will most likely put your itemized deductions total over the zero bracket amount.

If your rough estimate of itemized deductions is much less than your zero bracket amount, you might still itemize more carefully and thoroughly. It's a good exercise and review of how well you handle your personal finances, although the exercise will most likely not produce a large saving in the amount of taxes you must pay.

STRATEGY

Rather than accept some generalization, compute your itemized deductions. If the total exceeds your zero bracket amount, use itemized deductions on your tax return.

EXHIBIT 6-7

Miscellaneous expenses that qualify as itemized deductions.

Appraisal fee	Periodicals and books used in business or profession
Specialized clothing	
Dues—union, professional societies, trade associations	Safe-deposit box rental
	Tax preparation fees
Investment counsel fee	Tools used in profession

EXEMPTION

An **exemption** is a flat dollar amount that a taxpayer can deduct from his or her income. Since that reduces the amount of income that is subject to taxes, the taxpayer pays less taxes. The net effect of allowing exemptions is that income equal to the dollar amount of the exemption is exempt from taxes. Currently, the amount for each exemption is $1000.

To complete the tax return, the taxpayer must determine how many exemptions he or she can claim. Every person who files a tax form is allowed at least one exemption for himself or herself. Taxpayers who are sixty-five or more years of age may claim another exemption. The taxpayer who is blind is allowed an additional exemption. Thus, a single, blind, sixty-eight-year old taxpayer is entitled to three exemptions.

Married couples who file a single tax return that combines their incomes and deductions—a joint return—are allowed two exemptions. Similarly, they may claim additional exemptions for age (sixty-five or over) and blindness.

In addition, a taxpayer can claim an exemption for every person who qualifies as a dependent. Unlike taxpayers, dependents cannot qualify for the extra exemptions for age and blindness.

To qualify as your dependent, the person you claim as a dependent must meet the tests outlined in Exhibit 6-8. There must be a *yes* response to at least one part of each test. Most of the tests are self-explanatory, but several need additional comment. First, Exhibit 6-9 summarizes those relatives who would meet the "relative test" specified in Question 1 of Test 1. Second, a complication arises when the person receives support from several people, as shown in Test 2, Question 2. The entire group must provide more than 50 percent of the person's support. The taxpayer in the group who claims the dependent must provide more than 10 percent of the person's *total support*. Also, everyone who provides more than 10 percent of the person's support must agree on who will claim the dependent. By "support," we mean the entire range of living expenses an individual would normally incur. Examples include such costs as lodging, food, clothing, medical and dental care, recreation, entertainment, and education expenses. For the questions in Test 3, gross income includes the same sources of income as were discussed early in this chapter.

Whether you have decided to use the zero bracket amount or to itemize your deductions has no impact on this deduction; you are entitled to the exemption deduction—number of exemptions x $1000—regardless of what other deductions you have.

STRATEGY

Since each additional exemption reduces adjusted gross income by $1000, carefully consider every possible exemption.

FILING STATUS

There are four major **filing statuses** that are available when filing taxes: single, married–joint return, married–separate returns, and head of household.

EXHIBIT 6-8

Five tests that must be met before you can
claim a person as your dependent.

	YES	NO
TEST 1: Relationship of Member of Household		
1 Is the person one of the relatives listed in Exhibit 6-9?	( )	( )
or		
2 Did the person reside in your home, and was the person a household member during the entire year?	( )	( )
TEST 2: Support Test		
1 Did you pay more than half of the person's support?	( )	( )
or		
2 If the person received support from several people:		
a Did combined support from these people exceed 50 percent of the person's total support?		
b Did you provide more than 10 percent of the person's total support?	( )	( )
c Has everyone who provided more than 10 percent of the person's support agreed to your claiming the dependent?	( )	( )
TEST 3: Gross Income Test		
1 Was the dependent's gross income less than $1000?	( )	( )
or		
2 Is the dependent your child and under nineteen or a full-time student? (If yes, the $1000 gross income test does not apply.)	( )	( )
TEST 4: Citizenship or Resident Test		
1 Is the dependent a U.S. citizen or a resident of the United States, Canada, or Mexico?	( )	( )
TEST 5: Joint Return Test		
1 If married, does the dependent file a separate, rather than a joint, return?	( )	( )

Single Taxpayers who are not married on December 31 of the year for which they are filing taxes are considered single for the entire preceding year. As a **single taxpayer**, the person would use the tax rates established for singles.

Married—Joint Return If two people are married on December 31 or before, they are considered to have been married for the entire preceding year. A joint return means that the couple elects to file a single tax return that combines all the tax-related items from both persons: sources of income, adjustments to gross income, itemized deductions or zero bracket amount, and exemptions. The tax rates for **married—joint return** are the lowest of the four groups. For most married couples, filing a joint return usually minimizes the taxes they must pay.

EXHIBIT 6-9

CHAPTER 6

147

HOW TO
"MANAGE" YOUR
INCOME TAXES

The following relatives qualify as dependents.

Child, stepchild, or adopted child	Brother-in-law or sister-in-law
Grandchild	Stepbrother or stepsister
Parent, grandparent, or stepparent	Niece or nephew if related by blood
Aunt or uncle if related by blood	Foster child who resided in taxpayer's
Son-in-law or daughter-in-law	home the entire year as a member of
Father-in-law or mother-in-law	taxpayer's family
Brother or sister	

Married—Separate Returns   Even if they qualify for a joint return, a married couple has the option of filing a **married—separate return** for each person. Only in special circumstances may it be advantageous for a couple to file separate returns.

Head of Household   The **head of household** is a special category for taxpayers who maintain a home for one or both parents or one of the qualifying relatives in Exhibit 6-9. A "home" can be an apartment, a single-family house, a condominium, or a mobile home. To qualify, you must meet three tests:

First, you must be unmarried on December 31 of the year for which you are filing the tax return. Certain married persons who are legally separated or live apart from their spouses can also qualify.

Second, you must pay more than one-half the cost of maintaining the home. For all relatives other than parents, both you and the relative must live in the residence you are maintaining.

Third, you must qualify to claim the relative or parent as a dependent, as outlined in the tests in Exhibit 6-8.

TREATMENT OF THE ZERO BRACKET AMOUNT AND ITEMIZED DEDUCTIONS UNDER PRESENT TAX REGULATIONS

In this section we want to explain the very special way that the zero bracket amount and itemized deductions are treated by the present tax regulations. Our discussions up to this point have emphasized that a taxpayer, regardless of income, is entitled to the zero bracket amount. And, if the total of a taxpayer's itemized deductions is larger, the taxpayer can substitute itemized deductions in place of the zero bracket amount. We are not going to change in any way this part of our previous discussion. What we will modify are the computations taxpayers actually make once they decide on the zero bracket amount or the itemized deductions.

Given the way the tax regulations have been designed, you do *not* really subtract the zero bracket amount when computing your taxes. This is contrary to our statements up to this point, because we talked about deducting the zero bracket amount *or* itemized deductions, whichever was larger. What we are now saying is that you do not have to subtract the zero bracket amount, because the tax rate schedules have been designed so that they automatically incorporate the zero bracket amount. The major reason for eliminating your having to deduct the zero bracket amount was to simplify the computation of your taxes and to reduce the possibility of your making a mistake.

An immediate question is: If, as a taxpayer, I do not actually subtract the zero bracket amount, do I receive the benefits—lowered taxes—that the zero bracket amount provides? The answer is a *definite* yes. The tax rates have been adjusted so that they already incorporate the zero bracket amount. That means that when you use those rates, you will receive the full benefit the zero bracket amount.

Excess Itemized Deductions

Up to this point we have concentrated on taxpayers who elect to use the zero bracket amount. What about those taxpayers who elect to use their itemized deductions? Their first task is to figure their **excess itemized deductions**, which we define as the dollar amount by which your total itemized deductions exceed your zero bracket amount. Another example is the best way to illustrate how to handle itemized deductions.

Assume that Vince Green is single and has an adjusted gross income of $13,900. His itemized deductions total $3300, so he will want to use that amount rather than the $2300 zero bracket amount. Recall that the tax rates already allow for the zero bracket amount: $2300 in our example. In effect, the tax rates have already given Vince credit for $2300. So he is allowed to deduct only the $1000 of itemized deductions that *exceeds* his zero bracket amount: his excess itemized deductions.

Vince's excess itemized deductions are:

$1000	= $3300	− $2300
⬆	⬆	⬆
Excess itemized deductions	= Total itemized deductions	− Zero bracket amount for single person

BASIC INCOME TAX STRUCTURE: REVISED

Most of the basic tax structure shown in Exhibit 6-10 is quite similar to the one in Exhibit 6-1. But several new features have been added. First, additional detail is included to show examples of what you would include in gross income. Likewise, there are now examples of the major adjustments to gross income. Second, the treatment of deductions from adjusted gross income is consistent with the preceding discussion. The zero bracket amount is not deducted if the taxpayer elects to use it. Likewise, when a taxpayer elects to use itemized deductions because they are larger, only the excess itemized deductions are deducted. Next, the total exemption deduction for which the taxpayer is eligible is subtracted.

We have a new term that needs to be defined: **taxable income**—the income on which your taxes are based. If you elect to use the zero bracket amount:

$$\text{Taxable income} = \text{Gross income} - \text{Adjustments to gross income} - \text{Exemption deduction}$$

EXHIBIT 6-10

What to consider when starting your tax report.

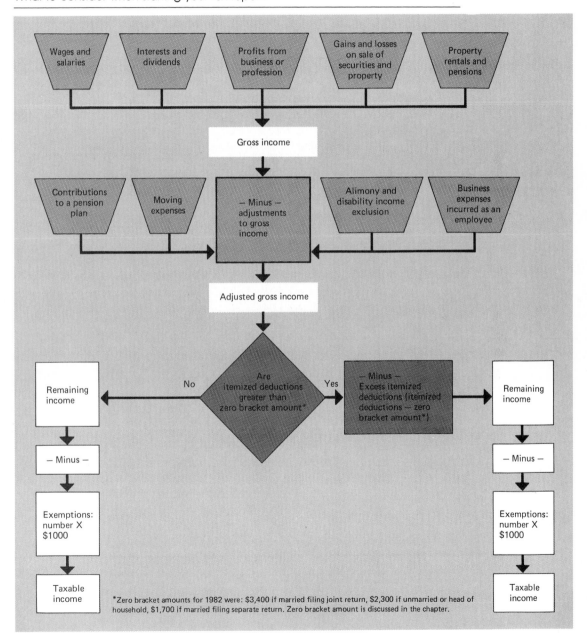

*Zero bracket amounts for 1982 were: $3,400 if married filing joint return, $2,300 if unmarried or head of household, $1,700 if married filing separate return. Zero bracket amount is discussed in the chapter.

Because the tax rates already provide for the zero bracket amount, it is not deducted from gross income.

An example is the easiest way to demonstrate the computation of taxable income. Assume that the tax details for Chester Hunt, who is single, include: $13,600 gross income, no adjustments to gross income, $600 in itemized deductions, and one exemption (himself). Chester's taxable income is:

$$\$12,600 = \$13,600 - \$0 \qquad\qquad - \$1,000$$

$$\underset{\text{income}}{\text{Taxable}} = \underset{\text{income}}{\text{Gross}} - \underset{\text{gross income}}{\text{Adjustments to}} - \underset{\text{deduction}}{\text{Exemption}}$$

Chester would not deduct any part of the $600 of itemized deductions because he would use the zero bracket amount.

If the taxpayer uses itemized deductions because they exceed the zero bracket amount, taxable income equals:

$$\underset{\text{income}}{\text{Taxable}} = \underset{\text{income}}{\text{Gross}} - \underset{\text{gross income}}{\text{Adjustments to}} - \underset{\text{deductions}}{\text{Excess itemized}} - \underset{\text{deduction}}{\text{Exemption}}$$

The additional required step is to subtract *excess itemized deductions*. Recall, we deduct only the excess of itemized deductions over the zero bracket amount because the tax rates already incorporate the zero bracket amount.

Let us use an example to test your understanding of taxable income. Suppose the tax details for John and Ann Swift are: $26,500 gross income, $500 adjustment to gross income, $4,400 of itemized deductions, and two exemptions (themselves). As a married couple, the Swifts' excess itemized deductions are $1,000. Their taxable income is:

$$\$23,000 = \$26,500 - \$500 \qquad - \$1,000 \qquad - \$2,000$$

$$\underset{\text{income}}{\text{Taxable}} = \underset{\text{income}}{\text{Gross}} - \underset{\text{gross income}}{\text{Adjustment to}} - \underset{\text{deductions}}{\text{Excess itemized}} - \underset{\text{deduction}}{\text{Exemption}}$$

PRINCIPAL METHODS OF COMPUTING THE AMOUNT OF TAXES

The three most frequently used methods for computing the taxes you must pay are: using the tax table, using the tax rate schedules, and income averaging. Since each of the methods has some special features, we will explain them individually.

Tax Table

The **tax table** has been designed to eliminate all computations by the taxpayer. With this table, the taxpayer merely finds where his or her taxable income fits in the table and looks up how much tax must be paid. To illustrate how the table works, we have reproduced a small section of the tax table in Exhibit 6-11. Actually, the complete table covers all incomes from

$1,700 to $50,000. Clearly, by covering that range of incomes, the tax table is what most people use to compute the taxes they owe.

To show how the tax table would be used, assume that Carol Chin is single and has a taxable income of $13,730. Reading across the line "$13,700 to $13,750" to the column for "Single," we find the tax to be $1,829. Need another example? Ed and Ann Comb plan to file a joint return with their combined taxable income of $13,960. Their tax will be $1,502.

By reading across any of the lines in the tax table, you can readily see which group pays the highest tax. For a given amount of taxable income, married couples filing a joint return pay the lowest tax. Next comes those who qualify as head of household. Single individuals pay the next highest tax. And capturing the top tax category is a married couple who file separate returns.

Tax Rate Schedules

Taxpayers whose taxable income exceeds the upper limits of the tax table (currently $50,000) must calculate their own income taxes. To do that, they use a series of **tax rate schedules** similar to those shown in Exhibit 6-12. To keep this exhibit to a manageable size, we have reproduced only a portion of each tax schedule. There is a separate tax rate schedule for each filing status. A portion of the rate schedule for single taxpayers is shown in the top section of Exhibit 6-12; part of the second rate schedule, for heads of household, is shown in the middle section; and the rate schedule for married couples filing a joint return appears in the bottom section. The final rate schedule—for married couples who file separate returns—is not shown in Exhibit 6-12.

Like the previously discussed tax table, the tax rate schedule already includes an allowance for the zero bracket amount. Consequently, taxpayers

EXHIBIT 6-11

Section from the tax table.

Range of Taxable Income		Tax According to Status			
OVER	BUT NOT OVER	SINGLE	MARRIED-JOINT	MARRIED-SEPARATE	HEAD OF HOUSEHOLD
$13,500	$13,550	$1,787	$1,425	$2,147	$1,720
13,550	13,600	1,798	1,434	2,160	1,729
13,600	13,650	1,808	1,442	2,173	1,739
13,650	13,700	1,819	1,451	2,186	1,748
13,700	13,750	1,829	1,459	2,198	1,758
13,750	13,800	1,840	1,468	2,212	1,767
13,800	13,850	1,850	1,476	2,225	1,777
13,850	13,900	1,861	1,485	2,238	1,786
13,900	13,950	1,871	1,493	2,251	1,796
13,950	14,000	1,882	1,502	2,264	1,805

Note: Tax amounts are based on proposed 1983 rates.

EXHIBIT 6-12

Tax rate schedules for single taxpayers, heads of household, and married taxpayers filing a joint return. (*Note:* Tax amounts are based on *proposed* 1983 tax rates.)

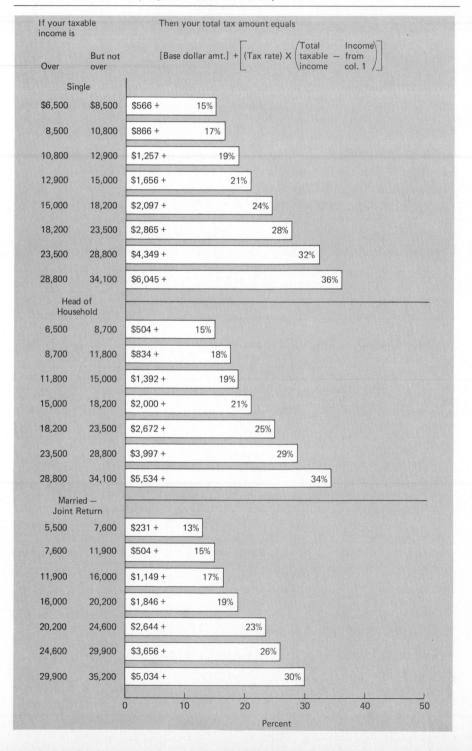

If your taxable income is		Then your total tax amount equals
Over	**But not over**	[Base dollar amt.] + [(Tax rate) X (Total taxable income − Income from col. 1)]

Single

Over	But not over	Base dollar amt.	Tax rate
$6,500	$8,500	$566 +	15%
8,500	10,800	$866 +	17%
10,800	12,900	$1,257 +	19%
12,900	15,000	$1,656 +	21%
15,000	18,200	$2,097 +	24%
18,200	23,500	$2,865 +	28%
23,500	28,800	$4,349 +	32%
28,800	34,100	$6,045 +	36%

Head of Household

Over	But not over	Base dollar amt.	Tax rate
6,500	8,700	$504 +	15%
8,700	11,800	$834 +	18%
11,800	15,000	$1,392 +	19%
15,000	18,200	$2,000 +	21%
18,200	23,500	$2,672 +	25%
23,500	28,800	$3,997 +	29%
28,800	34,100	$5,534 +	34%

Married — Joint Return

Over	But not over	Base dollar amt.	Tax rate
5,500	7,600	$231 +	13%
7,600	11,900	$504 +	15%
11,900	16,000	$1,149 +	17%
16,000	20,200	$1,846 +	19%
20,200	24,600	$2,644 +	23%
24,600	29,900	$3,656 +	26%
29,900	35,200	$5,034 +	30%

0   10   20   30   40   50

Percent

do not have to deduct that amount. Likewise, the schedule uses taxable income just as the tax table does. But unlike the tax table, the tax rate schedule requires that you calculate the amount of the taxes you owe.

An example will illustrate how a tax rate schedule is used. Chantile Bourge has a taxable income of $25,500 and she qualifies as a head of household. Her total tax will be:

$$\$4,577 = \$3,997 \quad + [29\% \quad \times (\$25,500 - \$23,500)]$$

Total tax	Base amount = of tax on $23,500	Tax rate: + income of $23,500 to $28,800	Taxable × income	Income from − first column: Exhibit 6-12

There are two parts to the total tax amount. The first amount is the tax on the lower income amount for that particular income bracket; that is $23,500 in our example. The second amount is the tax on the income that is over and above the minimum amount for that income bracket. Need more practice? What will be the total tax for a married couple filing a joint return if the couple's taxable income is $32,000? You should find that their total tax is $5664.

Tax Table Versus Tax Rate Schedule Will your taxes be the same regardless of which one you use? The answer is yes. If you compute the taxes using a tax table (assuming the income is covered by the table), that amount should be nearly identical to the taxes you calculate if you use the tax rate schedule.

Except for a small difference due to the construction of the tax tables, the taxes on a particular income will be the same regardless of whether a tax table or a tax rate schedule is used. At this point you may wonder: Why use a tax rate schedule when the tax table is easier? It is necessary that we use tax rate schedules throughout the rest of the chapter because we did not reproduce the entire table; that would have taken 9 to 12 pages! But using the tax rate schedule is not a serious problem because we can readily substitute it for the tax table.

Income Averaging

As Exhibit 6-12 demonstrates, tax rates are much higher for the higher-income brackets; when your income is high, you pay a larger amount of tax on each dollar of income. This has special significance for anyone who has a highly volatile income pattern: high income for 1 or 2 years followed by low income for several years. Without income averaging, a person with a volatile income stream would pay more taxes than would another person who received the identical total income but received it in a relatively steady stream each year.

An example will illustrate the tax implications of a volatile income pattern. Exhibit 6-13 shows the taxable income for Tom Lee (column 2) and Tim Lee (column 4) during the past 5 years. Tom's income has been quite variable from year to year, while Tim's income has been very steady. Over the 5 years shown, however, both had the same total income. The income taxes Tom would have paid as a single person, ignoring any income averaging, are shown in column 3. The income taxes Tim would have paid as a single person are shown in column 5. Despite having identical total incomes during the 5 years, Tom's total tax would be $11,927, while Tim's would be only $10,485. Clearly, if no other treatment were available, Tom's volatile income stream would force him to pay more taxes.

As a means of handling a highly volatile income stream, taxpayers can use the technique of **income averaging**; that is, they can average their incomes over a 5-year period. Their taxes are then based on the average annual income. The net effect is to lower taxes by smoothing out the income over the 5-year period. Taxpayers will be most likely to use income averaging during any year in which their income has risen sharply. There is no limit to how often you may use income averaging, but you must meet some qualifications to be eligible. Taxpayers who have recently graduated from school or have recently begun work frequently cannot use income averaging: the rules seriously restrict its use by these two groups. Any one of the tax reference books listed at the end of the chapter will discuss the qualifications for income averaging and also show the necessary computations.

STRATEGY

If your income has risen sharply during the year, carefully consider whether you qualify for the benefits of income averaging.

EXHIBIT 6-13

Comparison of the income taxes on a volatile income stream with taxes on the same total income received evenly each year.

| | Tom Lee | | Tim Lee | |
DESCRIPTION	TAXABLE INCOME	INCOME TAXES* (EXHIBIT 6-12)	TAXABLE INCOME	INCOME TAXES* (EXHIBIT 6-12)
Current year	$23,500	$4,349	$15,000	$ 2,097
1 year ago	15,000	2,097	15,000	2,097
2 years ago	6,500	566	15,000	2,097
3 years ago	6,500	566	15,000	2,097
4 years ago	23,500	4,349	15,000	2,097
Total income for the 5 years	$75,000		$75,000	
Average income (Total ÷ 5)	$15,000		$15,000	
Total taxes for the 5 years		$11,927		$10,485

*Income taxes were computed using the "Single" tax rate schedule in Exhibit 6-12. Income averaging was not used.

TAX CREDITS

A **tax credit** is a specified amount that is deducted directly from the taxes you must pay. It has several advantages.

First, you qualify for most credits regardless of whether you use the zero bracket amount or itemize your deductions.

Second, because each dollar of a tax credit reduces your taxes by a full dollar, tax credits can provide a sizable benefit.

Child and Disabled Dependent Care Credit

Taxpayers can deduct a **child and disabled dependent care** tax credit ranging from 20 to 30 percent of the cost of certain household and care expenses for a child (under fifteen) or a disabled dependent. If your adjusted gross income is $10,000 or less, you can take the full 30 percent. For each $2,000 that your adjusted gross income exceeds $10,000, the credit drops 1 percent. Thus, at an adjusted gross income of $12,500, the credit drops to 28 percent. At $20,000, the credit drops to 25 percent. For any adjusted gross income above $28,000, the credit is 20 percent. To be eligible for this tax credit:

You must be employed (full- or part-time) during the time you incurred the expenses.

You must maintain a household for the child or disabled dependent.

If married, you and your spouse must both work unless one of you is a full-time student or incapacitated.

Deductible expenses include child care expenses outside your house (day care, nursery school, at a baby-sitter's house), cost of having someone (like a nurse, a baby-sitter, or a caretaker) care for your dependent in your home, and the cost of domestic services (cleaning, washing, cooking) for your house. Payments to relatives can generally qualify for child or dependent care.

Maximum allowable expenses for the tax credit are limited to $2400 per year for one dependent and $4800 for two or more dependents. Thus the maximum credit for one dependent, if your adjusted gross income is $10,000 or less, is:

$$\$720 \quad = \$2400 \quad \times 30\%$$

$$\underset{\substack{\text{Maximum} \\ \text{tax credit}}}{\Uparrow} = \underset{\substack{\text{Maximum} \\ \text{expenses}}}{\Uparrow} \times \underset{\substack{\text{Rate for dependent} \\ \text{and child care credit}}}{\Uparrow}$$

For two or more dependents, the maximum tax credit is:

$$\$1440 = \$4800 \times 30\%$$

Residential Energy Credit

To encourage energy conservation and the switch to alternative energy sources, the government allows taxpayers to claim part of the cost of things that help to conserve energy as a **residential energy credit**. Since your taxes are reduced by the amount of the credit, the net cost of the energy-saving item declines by a similar amount. Consult one of the tax reference books listed at the end of the chapter for complete details on what expenditures qualify and how you compute the credit.

PAYMENT OF TAXES

Individuals pay their income taxes through a combination of three methods: payroll withholding, tax estimates, or directly with their tax returns.

Payroll Withholding

Most people pay their taxes through **tax withholding** from their salary. That is, the employer withholds from the employee's pay an estimated amount of tax for each pay period and forwards it to the United States Treasury. The amount estimated and withheld as taxes is based on information you write on Form W-4, which every employee files with an employer. The W-4 form lists filing status, number of exemptions, and any special withholding instructions. With the appropriate instruction, you can have additional tax withheld or you can claim a special allowance to reduce the amount of the tax withheld. File a new W-4 superseding a previous form at any time.

Overwithholding: A Good Savings Plan? Unfortunately, too many people intentionally understate their exemptions on the W-4. Consequently, more tax will be withheld than is required. People take this means to assure themselves a refund when they file their tax returns. While it may force them to save, they receive no interest on those excessive withholdings.

STRATEGY

Do you need a forced savings plan? We recommend a payroll deduction. The amount is automatically deposited in a savings account: it forces you to save but does something the United States Treasury doesn't do with your withholdings—it pays interest on every dollar in the account.

Estimated Taxes

The federal government does not withhold taxes from everyone's earnings. For example, taxes are not withheld for self-employed people. And those people who earn substantial income over and above their regular wages will typically find that enough taxes are not being withheld. To deal with this problem, there is another method of paying taxes. Taxpayers estimate what their income will be for the year and compute the amount of taxes they will probably owe. During the year, they make **estimated tax payments** in four equal quarterly installments: April 15, June 15, September 15, and January 15 of the next year.

Despite some rather specific rules as to who must file an estimated tax form, there is no specific penalty for not filing one. However, failure to file may subject you to a penalty for underpayment of taxes—our topic for the next section.

UNDERPAYMENT OF TAXES

Taxpayers who do not pay their taxes in sufficient and regular payments throughout the year may be assessed a penalty for **underpayment of taxes**. A clear case of this would be where a taxpayer has $4000 of taxes withheld during the year, yet the total taxes due for the year are $8000. If a taxpayer's total taxes paid during the year through withholding or estimated tax payments are less than 80 percent of the taxes owed for that year, a penalty may be assessed. We say "may be assessed" because, as the next section describes, you may be able to avoid the penalty. Exhibit 6-14 illustrates several possible underpayment penalty situations.

Avoiding the Underpayment Penalty   A taxpayer may be able to use one of four special exceptions to avoid the penalty for underpayment of taxes. Probably the most frequently used exception is the following: *If the taxes you paid during the current year (estimated plus withholding) equal or exceed the total income taxes you paid last year (estimated plus withholding plus taxes paid directly with your tax return), you can avoid the penalty.*

The other three exceptions are rather involved and less frequently used, so we will leave their explanation to one of the tax reference books cited at the end of the chapter.

FILING THE TAX RETURN

For most taxpayers, April 15 is the last day to settle their tax accounts. As long as your tax return is postmarked before or on April 15, you have filed the return on time. Some post offices even go so far as to say open late on April 15 to postmark last-minute tax returns.

STRATEGY

If you expect a refund, file your tax return as soon after December 31 as possible. If you owe taxes, wait until the last minute to file.

Taxpayers, however, may not want to wait until the last minute to file if they are going to be assessed a penalty for underpayment of tax. Since that

EXHIBIT 6-14

Examples of possible penalties for underpayment of income taxes.

INDIVIDUAL	TOTAL TAXES OWED	Taxes paid through:		POSSIBLE PENALTY
		WITHHOLDING	ESTIMATES	
Sam Swift	$2000	$1700	0	No
Tamie Wonder	$2500	$1500	$ 400	Yes
Jan and Tom Ace	$3200	$1000	$1000	Yes

penalty increases with the lateness of payment, the best option may be to file as soon as possible to minimize that penalty.

Time Extension

By filing the appropriate form, a taxpayer can obtain an automatic 60-day extension that postpones the date on which the tax form is due—from April 15 to June 15. The extension does not change the date on which the taxes must be paid; that remains April 15. You must *estimate* your tax and pay that when you file for the extension. Then, when you calculate your actual tax, any shortfall must be paid. For those needing still more time, an additional extension of 2 to 4 months can be requested.

MAKING IT EASIER

Many people do little, if anything, about their taxes during the year. Then, a few days before April 15, they start dealing with their taxes in several long, miserable night sessions. We can't transform tax time into a period of joy. We do, however, feel that some advanced work and planning can remove much of the drudgery from tax preparation.

Keep Records

One major problem is that many people don't keep records during the year. Consequently, they must reconstruct everything at the time they prepare their returns. That means they will most likely overlook some important items. A far better method is to set up a tax file at the beginning of the year. That way, tax-related material, whether it be an invoice, a check, a receipt, or a special note reminding you of some item, can easily be dropped in the file throughout the year.

Think Taxes

While you certainly do not have to think taxes continuously, you should consider the tax implications of your financial actions and decisions. For example, when making a charitable contribution, note it in the memo space on the check. Then pay it with a check rather than cash. When you have a special tax situation, such as donating property or searching for a new job, write out the details and put them in the tax file.

Use Reference Books

A good tax reference book is essential to help answer your tax questions and guide your tax preparation. Any of the tax reference books (there are many such publications) listed at the end of this chapter will be helpful. The examples and explanations in these books can vastly simplify the whole process of preparing and calculating taxes. Moreover, the cost of the book can be included as a miscellaneous itemized deduction.

Consider Timing

There are several advantages to preparing your tax return long before the April 15 deadline. For one thing, you have time to get answers on question-

THEY'RE NICE CLUBS.. BUT LIKE I SAID..
THEY'RE ONLY DEDUCTIBLE AS TOOLS WHEN
YOU'RE A PROFESSIONAL GOLFER!

able items. Also, should you be missing an item in your records, you have time to obtain a duplicate. And, like preparing for exams, it is simply much easier and a lot less frustrating to work on taxes in several short sessions rather than in a single crash session.

MARGINAL TAX RATE

When people talk or write about a tax rate, they generally mean a marginal tax rate. Throughout the book, we will be using marginal tax rates. So let's discuss the subject now. A **marginal tax rate** is the percentage of your last dollar of taxable income you paid in taxes. Let us see what that means.

Assume Ralph Smith is single, with a taxable income of $14,500. According to the top portion of Exhibit 6-15, his marginal tax rate is 21 percent. That is, he paid 21 cents in taxes on that last dollar of income that took him from $14,499 to $14,500. If Ralph should earn $1 more so that his income increased to $14,501, he would pay 21 cents of the last dollar of income. What if Ralph's salary should rise to $17,000? That would place him in a different income bracket, and the base amount of his tax would change. But, as the center part of Exhibit 6-15 shows, the tax rate on his last dollar of income is 24 percent, the marginal tax rate for that particular income bracket. This tax rate will be the one that he is most concerned about. If his income increases or decreases slightly, the 24 percent tax rate shows how his taxes will be affected. Likewise, if his taxable income is $21,000 (bottom part of Exhibit 6-15), the marginal tax rate is 28 percent. Again his central concern is the 28 percent marginal tax rate because any changes in income around that $21,000 will have a tax rate of 28 percent.

IMPACT OF TAXES ON FINANCIAL DECISIONS

Income taxes can have a major impact on many personal financial decisions. Unfortunately, some people fail to consider the effects of taxes when making their financial decisions. As a consequence, they don't make the best possible decisions. Of course, it would be equally inappropriate to go to the opposite extreme, making taxes the central issue in every decision. We think a compromise between the two extremes is probably best for most people.

Timing of Financial Decisions   Income taxes can alter the timing of an individual's financial decisions. For example, assume John Fountin, a car salesperson, earns $20,000 in salary and commissions during a normal year. But this year has been extremely good, so his salary and commissions will total $40,000. John also owns some common stock whose price has risen sharply since he bought it. If he sold the stock now, he would make a $10,000 short-term capital gain on it. That would boost his total income for the year to $50,000. Because John's income is already higher than usual, his marginal tax rate is also much higher. He might want to defer selling the stock. Should his salary and commissions drop next year, he could sell the stock at that time.

On the other hand, if the stock's price has declined sharply, he may

EXHIBIT 6-15

Marginal tax rates: what they are and why they are used. (*Note*: Tax amounts are based on *proposed* 1983 tax rates.)

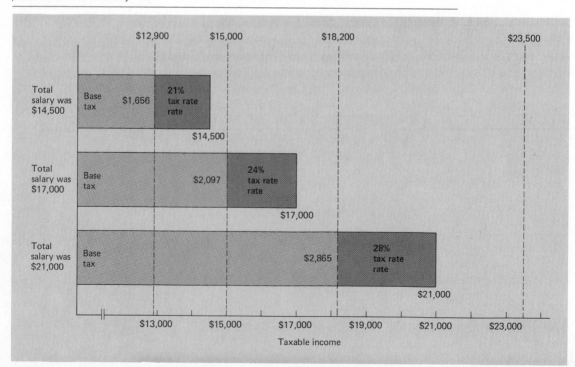

want to sell it this year. Assume that instead of a $10,000 gain, the stock's price was such that he had a $3,000 short-term loss. That loss would be deducted from his $40,000 of commissions and salary, so his total income would drop to $37,000. Since the marginal tax rate on this year's salary and commissions is high, lowering his gross income with the stock loss would substantially reduce the taxes he would have to pay.

STRATEGY

If possible, consider shifting your deductible expenses and losses to years when you have unusually high income; conversely, move increased income and gains to low-income years.

Tax-Exempt Income   Income taxes can make certain types of income very attractive. For example, the interest paid on many of the bonds issued by states, cities, and agencies of states and cities does not have to be included in your gross income. Therefore you do not have to pay federal income taxes on the interest. That exemption can make those bonds a very desirable investment for taxpayers with high marginal tax rates. To illustrate, suppose Juan Lopez has a 50 percent marginal tax rate. If he receives $100 of interest income from an investment that is fully taxable, he will have to pay:

$$\underset{\substack{\text{Amount} \\ \text{of taxes}}}{\$50} = \underset{\substack{\text{Marginal} \\ \text{tax rate}}}{50\%} \times \underset{\substack{\text{Taxable interest} \\ \text{income}}}{\$100}$$

After paying the tax, he will get to keep only $50. Had that $100 of interest been from a tax-exempt bond investment, he would retain the full $100 because he would pay no tax on that income. In fact, Juan would willingly accept much less interest on the tax-exempt investment, as little as $50.01, because $50.01 in nontaxable income is more than the $50.00 he can keep after paying 50 percent taxes on $100 of taxable income.

Deferring Income Taxes   One input to some financial decisions is whether or not income taxes can be deferred until a later period. A good example of deferring tax payments is a pension plan. We briefly discussed pension plans earlier in this chapter and will cover them more fully in Chapter 21. Meanwhile a short example will demonstrate the advantage of deferring tax payments.

Assume a taxpayer—40 percent marginal tax rate—receives $100 of interest income on a particular investment. If it were regular income and therefore had to be included in taxable income, the taxpayer would keep only:

$$\underset{\substack{\text{Interest income} \\ \text{after taxes}}}{\$60} = \underset{\substack{\text{Total interest} \\ \text{income}}}{\$100} - \underset{\substack{\text{Interest} \\ \text{income}}}{(\$100} \times \underset{\substack{\text{Marginal} \\ \text{tax rate}}}{40\%)}$$

Thus the taxpayer would have only $60 to reinvest after paying taxes. If the taxes on the $100 of interest could be deferred, the entire $100 could be reinvested. Of course, the taxes will likely have to be paid at some point in the future since they are merely deferred. But deferring them benefits the taxpayer in two ways:

1   Taxpayer will earn future income on the entire $100 because no taxes had to be paid.

2   Taxpayer's marginal tax rate may be less at the time the taxes are paid.

Deductible Expense: A Possible Tax Saving   Earlier in the chapter, we discussed the expenses that you can include as itemized deductions. We also illustrated how itemized deductions can reduce your taxable income and therefore the amount of taxes you must pay. Now we would like to show how income taxes may lower the net cost of a deductible expense. Recall from our discussion of marginal tax rate (the middle section of Exhibit 6-15) that a single person with taxable income of $17,000 had a 24 percent marginal tax rate. Of every additional dollar of income, 24 cents must be paid in taxes. The converse is also true. For example, let's assume that your salary was $17,001, and for some reason it was reduced to $17,000. The loss to you in taxable income is $1, but the actual loss of spendable income is only 76 cents—remember that 24 cents of that last dollar would have been paid as income taxes. To compute the loss of spendable income, we have:

$$\underset{\substack{\text{Spendable} \\ \text{income lost}}}{\underbrace{76 \text{ cents}}} = \underset{\substack{\text{Taxable} \\ \text{income lost}}}{\underbrace{\$1}} \times \underset{\substack{\text{Total} \\ \text{portion}}}{\underbrace{(100\%}} - \underset{\substack{\text{Marginal} \\ \text{tax rate}}}{\underbrace{24\%)}}$$

We can now show how an expense that qualifies as a deduction from income works in much the same way as in the previous discussion about losing $1 of taxable income. Because a deductible expense reduces the amount of income subject to taxes, it really represents a reduction in income. To confirm this point, assume that Susan Rouft is considering giving $100 to her favorite charity; this gift may be taken as an itemized deduction. Before the contribution, her taxable income is $17,100. By giving that $100, she lowers her taxes:

$$\underset{\substack{\text{Tax} \\ \text{reduction}}}{\underbrace{\$24}} = \underset{\substack{\text{Reduction in} \\ \text{taxable income}}}{\underbrace{\$100}} \times \underset{\substack{\text{Marginal} \\ \text{tax rate}}}{\underbrace{24\%}}$$

Because she now pays $24 less taxes, that contribution really cost her only:

$76 \qquad = \$100 \qquad - \$24$

$$\underset{\begin{array}{c}\text{Net cost of}\\\text{contribution}\end{array}}{\triangle} = \underset{\text{Contribution}}{\triangle} - \underset{\begin{array}{c}\text{Reduction}\\\text{in taxes}\end{array}}{\triangle}$$

Rather than use two steps to compute the net cost of a deductible expense (like the above contribution), we can compute it directly. To do so, we use:

$$\frac{\text{Net cost of}}{\text{deductible expense}} = \frac{\text{Deductible}}{\text{expense}} \times \left[100\% - \frac{\text{Marginal}}{\text{tax rate}} \right]$$

Using this equation, we find that Susan's $100 contribution is:

$$\$76 = \$100 \times [100\% - 24\%]$$

Do you need more practice? What is the net cost of $500 of deductible property taxes if the taxpayer's marginal rate is 44 percent? Net cost should be $280.

You should understand several facts about deductible expenses.

First, the higher the taxpayer's marginal tax rate, the lower the net cost of each dollar of deductible expenses.

Second, this reduction applies only to expenses that qualify as itemized deductions.

And third, the reduction in net cost applies only if your total itemized deductions exceed your zero bracket amount. Recall that you can subtract only excess itemized deductions, and you thereby benefit from lowered taxes when your total itemized deductions exceed the zero bracket amount.

Benefits From Long-Term Capital Gain   Recall from our earlier discussion that a taxpayer has to pay taxes on only 40 percent of a long-term capital gain. On a short-term gain, on the other hand, taxes are assessed on the entire amount. Therefore, a taxpayer, after paying taxes, will have much more left when the gain is long term rather than short term. The top half of Exhibit 6-16 dramatically illustrates that advantage. Despite both gains

---

EXHIBIT 6-16

Potential benefits when the capital gain is long term or when the capital loss is short term.

CAPITAL GAIN (OR LOSS)	SHORT- OR LONG- TERM	PERCENTAGE INCLUDED FOR TAX PURPOSES	MARGINAL TAX RATE	ADDED TAX ON GAIN	TAX SAVINGS WITH LOSS	NET AFTER- TAX GAIN (OR LOSS)
$1000	Long	40%	40%	$160	—	$840
$1000	Short	100%	40%	$400	—	$600
($1000)	Long	50%	40%	—	$200	($800)
($1000)	Short	100%	40%	—	$400	($600)

being equal to $1000, significantly more of the long-term gain, $840, remains in the hands of the taxpayer after paying taxes.

STRATEGY

Where possible, concentrate on long-term capital gains. When you have a capital asset with a gain, try to extend the holding period to more than a year in order to receive favorable tax treatment.

Benefits from Short-Term Capital Loss   Recall that on a short-term capital loss the entire amount can be deducted from other sources of income. When the asset has been held more than 1 year, the loss becomes long term. And only 50 percent of a long-term loss can be deducted from other income sources. The bottom half of Exhibit 6-16 shows the decided advantage of a $1000 short-term loss over a $1000 long-term loss. That advantage comes from the substantially higher tax saving, $400, which reduces the net loss to $600. The guidelines for capital losses are exactly the opposite of capital gains. A taxpayer with a loss on a capital asset that has been held for less than 1 year might want to consider selling the asset. In that way, the loss is kept short term, so the net cost of the loss is reduced.

STRATEGY

Carefully review all losses on capital assets you have owned less than 1 year. It may be better to take the loss before it becomes a long-term one.

Tax Planning: Concentrating Your Deductions

If your itemized deductions are regularly about the same year after year and if they seem to add up to just a bit less than your zero bracket amount every year, you might try what we call **concentrating deductions**. By that we mean it might be possible to pay expenses due this year and also pay in this same year some expenses that are due and are ordinarily paid next year. Does this sound crazy? Not really. What you are doing is paying what you have to pay anyway, but perhaps a bit earlier. What does that gain you? Your itemized deductions this year will exceed your zero bracket amount, and those excess itemized deductions very nicely reduce the taxes you have to pay this year. You won't have those deductions to take next year, but you can still elect the zero bracket amount; that won't change. Let's see how concentrating deductions, which is really like prepaying those expenses, works.

Assume that Max and Susan Kowalski have $3400 of itemized deductions in a normal year. The $1600 of property taxes on their house is billed in December, but they generally pay it in four installments: January, March, May, and July. Susan has her $200 professional teaching dues deducted from her paycheck, $20 per month, during the 10-month school year. Likewise, they also pay their $480 church donation spread over the entire year. They decide to try concentrating their itemized deductions during 1983. They will pay their 1983 property taxes in the usual four installments. But they will also pay their entire 1984 taxes when billed in December. At the start of the school year in September, Susan will pay her entire year's professional dues in a lump sum. By prepaying the dues that would normally have been withheld next year (January through June), their itemized deductions rise by $120 (6 months' dues at $20). Last, the Kowalskis will make their $480 church donation for 1984 in a lump sum during December. Their itemized deductions now total:

$5600	= $3400	+ $1600	+ $120	+ $480
△	△	△	△	△
Total itemized deductions	= Regular itemized deductions	+ 1984 property tax payment	+ Teaching dues: $20 × 6 months	+ 1984 charitable contribution

The best way to illustrate the potential benefits is to compute the Kowalskis' taxes with and without concentrating their deductions. Exhibit 6-17 shows these tax computations: deductions are concentrated in the top section, but not in the lower half. To keep the results consistent, we used 1983 tax rates for all computations. By concentrating deductions, the Kowalskis reduce their taxes by $506—clearly a worthwhile tax maneuver. Furthermore, unless the Kowalskis' tax circumstance changes drastically, they should use concentrating again in 1985, in 1987, and so forth.

STRATEGY

If your total itemized deductions nearly equal your zero bracket amount, try concentrating your itemized deductions.

AN AUDIT BY THE IRS

Each year the Internal Revenue Service informs a number of taxpayers that their tax returns have been selected for review and examination by the IRS:

EXHIBIT 6-17

Potential income tax savings from concentrating deductions.

YEAR	ADJUSTED GROSS INCOME	EXEMPTION DEDUCTION	TOTAL ITEMIZED DEDUCTION	ZERO BRACKET AMOUNT	EXCESS ITEMIZED DEDUCTIONS	TAXABLE INCOME	TAXES OWED (EX. 6-12)
Total Taxes with Concentrating							
1983	$26,000	$2,000	$5,600	$3,400	$2,200	$21,800	$3,058
1984	26,000	2,000	2,200	3,400	0	24,000	3,564
							$6,622
Total Taxes without Concentrating							
1983	$26,000	$2,000	$3,400	$3,400	0	$24,000	$3,564
1984	26,000	2,000	3,400	3,400	0	24,000	3,564
							$7,128

an audit. And the taxpayers panic! People will do anything to avoid the possibility of being called for an audit. Some people even cheat themselves by not using every opportunity to lower their taxes when preparing their tax forms, believing that doing so will ensure that they won't be audited. We strongly believe such measures are unwarranted; a tax audit should not present a major crisis.

Who Is Selected for Audit?

A small percentage of the tax returns are selected for an audit on a random basis. But the majority are singled out for audit by a computer; the computer selects a return either because it is not typical of returns in its income category or because it has certain unusual features. Unfortunately, the IRS never reveals what those identifying features are.

Generally, the higher your gross income, the more likely you are to be a candidate for an audit. Also, if your itemized deductions are unusually large for taxpayers in your income group, the possibility of your being audited increases.

What Is Examined?

Most audits are directed to just one or two specific items. They may be a particular deduction or a question about a gross income item. Rare is the audit that examines a return item by item.

Audit Procedures

When a taxpayer is notified that his or her return is being audited, the notice specifies which item is under scrutiny. The notice will request that supporting details be mailed to the IRS office, or will set a date when the auditor would like to meet with the taxpayer. At this conference, the auditor will explain whether additional tax is believed due and will explain

why. At this point, the taxpayer can either accept the auditor's findings or appeal the decision to a higher level.

Preparing for an Audit

When you receive the audit notice, carefully review your copy of your tax return form for errors or omissions. Next, review your supporting documentation for the items under review. If anything is incomplete or missing, now is the time to put that file in order. The best evidence to support your position at an audit are documents such as invoices, canceled checks, and professional appraisals.

Surviving an Audit

When dealing with the IRS, remember that the auditor is neither questioning your integrity nor conducting an inquisition. The auditor is merely trying to determine whether additional taxes are due. Most auditors are easy to talk with—in fact, so easy that many people say far too much. The first rule at an audit is to discuss only the item being questioned. Do not volunteer information about other items on your return; it might encourage the auditor to extend the audit. By preparing your supporting documents and your arguments justifying your position before the audit meeting, you should be able to win your case. An audit is really not the terrifying experience some people think it is.

SUMMARY

1   Taxpayers are entitled to use all legal means to reduce the taxes they must pay.

2   Tax rates ranked from the highest, or most expensive, to the lowest, or least expensive, are:

   a   Married couple filing separate returns

   b   Single taxpayer

   c   Head of household

   d   Married couple filing a joint return

3   Three common adjustments to gross income are contributions to retirement plans, moving expenses, and employee business expenses.

4   The two-earner married-couple deduction reduces the tax that a working couple pays compared with the taxes they would pay on two single returns.

5   All taxpayers are allowed the zero bracket amount.

6   Major categories of itemized deductions include interest and finance charges, taxes, contributions, medical and dental expenses, education expense, job-search expense, and casualty and theft losses.

7   Five tests must be met to qualify someone as a dependent: relationship, support, gross income, citizenship or residency, and the dependent's not filing a joint return.

8   When total itemized deductions are less than the zero bracket amount (the most frequent case), the basic income tax structure is: *Gross income* less *adjustments to gross income* equals *adjusted gross income. Adjusted gross income* less *exemption deduction* equals *taxable income.*

9   When total itemized deductions exceed the zero bracket amount, the basic income tax structure is: *Gross income* less *adjustments to gross income* equals *adjusted gross income. Adjusted gross income* less *excess itemized deductions* (total itemized deductions minus zero bracket amount) less *exemption deduction* equals *taxable income.*

10   The most common methods for computing the amount of taxes are the tax table, tax rate schedules, and income averaging.

11   Income averaging can substantially reduce the tax for an individual having wide fluctuations in income from year to year.

12   Taxpayers who qualify for tax credits—the child and dependent care credit, the residential energy credit, or both—can deduct the tax credit amount directly from their tax payment.

13   An estimated tax payment is generally required when an individual receives substantial income not covered by payroll withholding, or when the taxes withheld are significantly less than the tax amount that must be paid.

14   Advanced planning, coupled with complete tax records and a helpful tax reference book, can substantially reduce the burden of tax preparation.

15   The marginal tax rate is the proportion of your last dollar of taxable income you paid in taxes.

16   Income taxes reduce the effective cost of a deductible expense: interest and finance charges, most taxes, donations, medical and dental expenses, and education expenses.

17   When the IRS audits an individual's tax return, the auditor generally concentrates on one or two lines, not on everything in the tax return.

REVIEW YOUR UNDERSTANDING OF

Avoiding taxes

Evading taxes

Gross income

Net purchase price

Net sale price

Short-term capital gain or loss

Long-term capital gain or loss

Adjustments to gross income

Self-employed pension plan (Keogh)

Individual Retirement Account (IRA)

Moving expenses—deductible items

Employee business expenses

Two-earner married-couple deduction

Zero bracket amount

Itemized deductions

  Interest and finance charge

  Taxes

Contributions

Medical and dental expense

Education expense

Job search expense

Casualty and theft loss

Exemption

Filing status

  Single

  Married—joint return

  Married—separate returns

  Head of household

Excess itemized deductions

Taxable income

Tax tables

Tax rate schedules

Income averaging

Tax credit

Child and disabled dependent care credit
Residential energy credit
Tax withholding
Estimated tax payment

Underpayment of taxes
Marginal tax rate
Concentrating deductions

DISCUSSION QUESTIONS

1   Which of the following items would be included in gross income?

a Prize won in the state lottery

b Proceeds from life insurance policy

c Salary

d Interest on U.S. Treasury note

e Gift from an aunt

f Short-term capital gain

g Interest on a municipal bond

h Sales bonus

2   Although Jean Whitecloud is qualified to establish her own retirement plan, she has always felt she would be further ahead if she just saved and invested her money. Do you agree? Why? Do you think most people can establish an IRA plan? A Keogh plan?

3   What tests must be met in order to qualify moving expenses as a deductible item? What are the major types of expenses that can be included? Can most recently graduated college students qualify?

4   What are the major features that distinguish between adjustments to gross income and itemized deductions? Why would an individual who claims only the zero bracket amount want a particular item classified as an adjustment to gross income rather than as an itemized deduction?

5   What tests must be met in order for a taxpayer to be able to deduct education-related expenses?

6   Why do the majority of taxpayers take the zero bracket amount rather than itemize their deductions? What are some typical events that might boost a taxpayer's itemized deductions above the zero bracket amount?

7   Would the following individuals qualify as exemptions? Why?

a The individual is the taxpayer's uncle; his gross income was $1500; he is a United States citizen; the taxpayer paid $2000 toward the uncle's total support of $3500; the uncle is single.

b The individual is an aunt; her gross income was $600; she lived the entire year in Canada; the taxpayer paid $1000 toward her total support of $1900; she is unmarried.

c The individual is a brother; his gross income was $700. The taxpayer, together with four other brothers and sisters, paid $3000 of the brother's total support of $4000; the taxpayer paid $300; the brother is a United States citizen and is single; the other brothers and sisters agree that the taxpayer should claim the deduction.

8   What are the major requirements for filing as an unmarried head of household? What is the advantage to qualifying as a head of household rather than as a single person? Give several examples of when the head of household filing status would be appropriate.

9   Under what circumstances would a taxpayer use the tax table? The tax rate schedule? Which is easier to use? For a given income, will you get the same amount of tax from the tax table as from a tax rate schedule?

10   What is the advantage of using income averaging? Why does it give lower taxes for qualifying taxpayers?

11 Under what circumstances might you want more tax withheld than necessary? When might you want less tax withheld?

13 The taxpayers listed in the table below would like to know whether they will have to pay a penalty for the underpayment of taxes.

TAX-PAYER	TAXES FOR CURRENT YEAR	Amount of Taxes Paid by:		TAXES FOR PREVIOUS YEAR	IS THERE AN UNDERPAYMENT PENALTY?
		WITHHOLDING	ESTIMATES		
A	$1800	$1530	$ 0	$1850	?
B	2650	1700	400	1975	?
C	1650	700	600	1400	?

12 Pamela Manlee expects to earn $1000 from giving piano lessons in her home. Since no taxes have been withheld on that money, should she file an estimated tax return? Is there a specific penalty for not filing? What type of penalty might she be assessed for underpaying her taxes?

14 How would you react to the comment, "I cannot possibly earn that extra $500 because it would put me into the next tax bracket and my taxes would skyrocket"?

PROBLEMS

6-1 Fred and Becky Bear sold the following common stocks during the year:

CORPORATION	QT, INC.	PIGEON, INC.	IMPORTS LTD.	ZUG CO.
Net purchase price	$1200	$1300	$1900	$1500
Net sale price	$1500	$ 700	$1100	$2000
Holding period	13 months	5 months	3 years	11 months

a What is their net gain or loss on each sale?

b What is the impact on their gross income (ignore any implication from having gains and losses within the same year) of the following sales:

QT, Inc.?   Imports Ltd.?

Pigeon, Inc.?   Zug Co.?

6-2 Sharon Jones had the following medical expenses during the year: health-insurance premiums of $550, unreimbursed doctors' and dentists' bills of $700, and prescription drug charges of $125. Her adjusted gross income was $12,000, and she plans to itemize. What is her medical expense deduction?

6-3 Jan Swartz's tax details are summarized as follows:

Her total itemized deductions are $3,000.

Her adjusted gross income is $15,400.

She is single and has one exemption (herself).

a What is her taxable income?

b Will she use a tax table or a tax rate schedule to compute her taxes?

c When computing the tax, how will she handle her exemption allowance? Her zero bracket amount?

6-4   Listed below is the tax information for three taxpayers.

TAXPAYER– FILING STATUS	GROSS INCOME	ADJUSTMENTS TO GROSS INCOME	ITEMIZED DEDUC- TIONS	NUMBER OF EXEMPTIONS	TAXABLE INCOME	AMOUNT OF TAXES
A–Single	$16,600	$ 500	$3,400	1	?	?
B–Married	$28,500	$2,600*	$3,000	2	?	?
C–Head of household	$13,500	0	$2,000	2	?	?

*Includes the two-earner married-couple deduction

a What is the taxable income for each taxpayer?

b How much tax does each taxpayer owe? (*Hint:* Exhibit 6-12 can help.)

6-5   Al and Susan Bach are reviewing their eligibility for a child care tax credit. Details on their situation include:

They paid a baby-sitter $2800 to care for Al, Jr., in their home.

Al, who works full-time, had an adjusted gross income of $14,000.

Susan, who works full-time, had an adjusted gross income of $8000.

Their itemized deductions total $3000.

a Can they qualify for a child care credit?

b If so, what is the dollar amount of their credit?

c How will they handle the credit on their tax return?

6-6   Ralph Zuggo expects that his taxable income will be $17,000 this year. As he is single, what taxes will he pay? What is his marginal tax rate? Due to a great year-end push, he qualifies for a $1000 bonus. Should he accept it or tell the firm he cannot "afford" it?

6-7   Wilma Smith is single and her taxable income is $16,000. Her total itemized deductions were substantially larger than the zero bracket amount. What is the net cost of the $1000 of property taxes she paid during the year? What would be the effective cost of her donating $100 to her favorite charity?

6-8   On the basis of his income and deductions for the current year, Sang Fu estimated that his taxes for the year were $5000. That is substantially more than the $3000 that was withheld from his salary during the year. The major reason for the shortfall was that no taxes were withheld from the earnings of his part-time business. The previous year, when he did not have the business, his total taxes were only $2900, and $2800 of that $2900 was withheld during the year.

a Should Sang have filed an estimated tax form? Why?

b Will he be subject to a penalty for underpayment of taxes?

c Can Sang avoid the penalty? How?

6-9 Mike Stuart is considering three possible $1000 investments. Option A pays 10 percent interest and is fully taxable at Mike's 40 percent marginal rate. Option B pays 7 percent interest, but is fully tax-exempt. Option C pays 10 percent interest that is tax-deferred until retirement. Which option will provide the best return? Discuss the principal tax considerations for each investment option.

6-10 Assume we sold the following two similar-sized capital assets during the year:

	TRANSACTION I	TRANSACTION II
Net sale price	$6000	$6000
Net purchase price	$4000	$4000
Holding period	15 months	5 months

a Would the transactions be equally attractive if our marginal tax rate is 30 percent? Why or why not?

b Would one of the transactions become more attractive if our tax rate is 50 percent? Why or why not?

c Discuss the comment: The return on a short-term investment will have to be substantially above that for a long-term one before it will appeal to a high-income individual.

6-11 Ned and Noreen Notcertain would like to compute how much the recently enacted "two-earner married-couple deduction" would save them in taxes in 1983. They also want to know how much more taxes they will pay when they file a married joint return than they would pay if each of them filed as a single person. Ned's gross income is $14,000, while Noreen's is $12,000. Their itemized deductions total only $2000, so they plan to use the zero bracket amount. They qualify for only two exemptions: themselves.

a Compute the tax savings that the two-earner married-couple deduction would provide. (*Hint*: Compare their taxes from filing a joint return with the deduction to their taxes on a joint return with no deduction.)

b How much additional tax do they pay by filing a married joint return (ignore the two-earner married-couple deduction) rather than the combined tax from their each filing as a single person?

c Did the tax savings from the deduction—part **a**—completely eliminate the added tax you computed in part **b**? Is there still a "penalty" for their filing a married joint return rather than two single returns?

CASE PROBLEM

Herb and Grazelda Procrastinator are beginning their April 13 income tax marathon; it usually lasts well into April 14, if not April 15. They both work full-time and have

a young daughter. A glance through their checkbook and scant records revealed the
following for 1983.

OUTFLOWS

Purchase of new car	$4000	Health insurance	$ 250
Medical expenses (unreimbursed)	100	Contributions	300
		Property taxes	1650
Gasoline taxes	75	Automobile insurance	250
Dental expenses	100	Life insurance	450
Professional teaching dues for Grazelda	150	Interest on home mortgage	3400
Sales taxes	360	Veterinary expenses for McKenzie, their dog	100
Utility bills for the house	450	Gifts for their parents	300
		Safe-deposit box rental	10
Daughter's nursery school fee (monthly)	$ 200	Prescription drugs	50
		Tax reference book	5
Finance charges on various loans and credit cards	400	Grocery bills	2300

In past years, the Procrastinators have taken the zero bracket amount on their joint return. Their combined adjusted gross income for 1983, after subtracting the two-earner married-couple deduction, will be $24,000.

1   On the basis of the information given, do you feel they should itemize their deductions this year? Why or why not? Should they use a joint return? Why or why not?

2   If they itemized, what would their total deductions be? How much can they deduct as excess itemized deductions?

3   What would their taxable income be for the year? What would their total tax be?

4   Can they qualify for any tax credits? Based on the total tax you computed in part **3**, how much tax will they actually pay?

5   Would you have any recommendations for Herb and Grazelda for next year's tax return? What advantages can they expect from your suggestions?

INCOME TAX REFERENCE BOOKS

Your Federal Income Tax—for Individuals, Publication 17, Department of the Treasury, Internal Revenue Service, Washington, D.C., published annually.
    Very thorough coverage of most tax topics with sufficient examples to make the material reasonably easy to understand. Publication assumes that you already have some backgound in taxes and therefore know which questions you need answered. Can be obtained from your local IRS office or from the IRS by mail. At the price—free—it is hard to beat.

J. K. Lassser's Your Income Tax, Simon & Schuster, New York, published annually. Provides very thorough coverage of income taxes with numerous examples to illustrate major points. Contains a good section outlining strategies that can be used to save taxes during the next year. This volume works best if you already have some knowledge of taxes.

The H & R Block Income Tax Workbook, Macmillan, New York, published annually. Provides complete coverage of major tax topics. The book is easy to follow with sufficient examples to illustrate the major points. A useful glossary can aid those of you who do not have a strong tax background.

Sylvia Porter's 19XX Income Tax Book, Avon, New York, published annually. This guide explains income taxes by taking you through forms line-by-line. Because of this format, you may have more difficulty finding an answer to a specific question than with the other tax guides. It also becomes dated quickly since tax forms are revised so frequently.

CHAPTER 7

CREDIT: HOW TO GET IT AND HOW TO USE IT

**AFTER COMPLETING THIS CHAPTER
YOU WILL HAVE LEARNED**

How both the *finance charge* and the *maturity* of a loan affect the amount you have to repay

When you should use *credit* and when you shouldn't

What a *safe debt limit* is and how to determine your own by an *analysis of your budget*

How to *analyze the various sources of credit* and determine which one offers *credit at the lowest cost*

How to *calculate the refund from the finance charge* when you *repay a loan before its maturity*

How to evaluate whether you should *save* or *use credit* to buy an *expensive item*

How *finance charges* are computed on *charge accounts* and *credit cards*

What *truth-in-lending legislation* is all about

The *criteria* that lenders use in deciding who does and who doesn't get credit, and how much

What the special provisions for *women's credit rights* are

What the *consumer's rights* under the *Fair Credit Reporting Act* are

What to do when you find that you have taken on *more credit than you can handle*

SOMETHING TELLS ME WE WENT OVER OUR ALLOWABLE LIMIT.

CONSUMER credit has become so wide-

spread and so generally available that nearly everyone uses it at some point. The extent of usage, however, varies widely among different people. Some restrict credit usage to periods when they need extra money for emergencies or unexpected expenses. Others use it for emergencies, but also for buying cars, appliances, furniture, and other major durable goods. Still others use credit not only for these reasonable purposes, but also for many of their small day-to-day transactions. Regardless of usage, credit has become an integral part of nearly everyone's spending process.

Because of the importance of credit, this chapter and the next will discuss its various aspects in considerable detail. We think this discussion is essential for several reasons.

First, you should know what credit sources are currently available.

Second, you should have a basis for deciding whether to use credit in a given situation. If you decide to use it, you should be able to evaluate the merits and disadvantages of competing credit offers.

Finally, like any other service, credit can be overused. And while you are unlikely to do so, you should know what corrective actions are necessary should you overuse credit.

There are several kinds of credit; the two principal distinctions among them center on the purpose or reason for borrowing the money and the way in which the money will be repaid. The major types of credit include:

Mortgage loan: Money is borrowed to purchase a house. Repayment is made in equal monthly payments over the life of the mortgage.

Consumer cash loan: The lender gives the borrower a check equal to the amount of the loan. Repayment is typically in equal monthly payments over the life of the cash loan.

Consumer sales loan: Money is borrowed to purchase a major item or service such as a car, furniture, or an appliance. Repayment is by equal payments over the life of the sales loan.

Open-ended consumer credit: Examples of open-ended credit include the borrowing you do when you use a credit card or a charge account to purchase merchandise or some service. It is called "open-ended" because the customer decides the amount of credit he or she will use and the frequency of its use. Repayment can be either a single lump sum that repays the entire amount or a series of payments that spreads the repayment over a period of months.

Our discussion centers on three principal credit categories: (1) consumer cash loans, (2) consumer sales loans, and (3) open-ended consumer credit. (The discussion of mortgage loans is deferred until Chapter 11, where we cover housing, because a mortgage loan is directly associated with the purchase of a housing unit.) Our emphasis in this chapter is on the general attributes of credit and on correcting a credit overextension. The next chapter builds on this base to explore each of the three credit categories.

THE CONCEPT OF CREDIT

Whenever you use credit, you are temporarily borrowing money from some lender. By obtaining those monies now, you expand your current purchasing power. But that expansion is a temporary one because the borrowed money must be repaid in the future. Your total purchasing power is not raised; only the timing of your purchasing power is altered. If you increase your purchasing power now, your future purchasing power is reduced. Lenders not only expect to be repaid the money advanced; they also expect to collect a finance charge during the period the money was borrowed. A **finance charge** is a fee paid for money borrowed. That fee is essentially similar to the fee for renting an automobile, the major difference being that it covers the rental of money rather than the rental of an automobile. Because of the finance charge, the amount repaid exceeds the initial amount borrowed. Consequently, your total purchasing power is actually decreased.

An example will illustrate this point. Assume an individual expects to earn $14,000 this year and the subsequent year. The top portion of Exhibit 7-1 shows that person's total purchasing power for the 2 years to be $28,000. Another option is to borrow $10,000 in the current year with a promise to repay that amount 1 year later. This procedure is shown in the bottom half of Exhibit 7-1. The lender, however, also expects to be paid a 10 percent finance charge for that year. The total repayment will consist of:

$$\$11,000 \quad = \$10,000 \quad + (\$10,000 \times 10\%)$$

$$\begin{array}{llll} \text{Total} & = & \text{Amount} & + & \text{Amount} & \times & \text{Annual finance} \\ \text{repayment} & & \text{borrowed} & & \text{borrowed} & & \text{charge} \end{array}$$

Finance charge on borrowing

Thus the person will have only $3000 left from next year's earnings after making that repayment. During the first year, the borrowing option raises total purchasing power to $24,000; that is significantly more than the $14,000 that is available without any borrowing. But after repayment of the amount borrowed plus payment of the finance charge, the $3000 remaining from next year's earnings will bring total purchasing power for the 2 years to only $27,000. Clearly, borrowing has reduced the combined purchasing power for the two years.

Finance Charge The finance charge is an all-inclusive term that takes in all costs associated with a particular credit transaction. When lenders quote their finance charge, it must include the interest charge and any other fee that is part of the credit transaction. For example, it would have to include the application fee, any processing fee, premiums on credit life insurance, and any other fee that is a required part of the credit offer.

Repayment Terms   The **repayment terms** of any loan involve two things: the duration of the loan and how frequently and in what amounts the loan will be repaid within that duration.

First, there is the total time between the point when the money is initially borrowed and the point when it is completely repaid: the **maturity.** With consumer credit, that maturity typically ranges from a few days to 5 years.

Second, there is the timing and the size of the required repayments. They may be monthly, weekly, or annually; likewise, they may be equal in size or they may consist of unequal amounts. Generally, most consumer cash and sales loans require equal monthly payments over the loan's maturity. Throughout the next two chapters, we assume that a loan requires equal monthly payments, unless stated otherwise. The user typically has considerably more latitude on payment size and timing with open-ended consumer credit. Open-ended credit means that the user can borrow either very little or extensively. Given that flexibility, payments can range from a single lump-sum repayment to a small, lender-specified minimum payment. Consequently, maturity can be as short as 30 days, or it can extend over several years.

How the Finance Charge and the Maturity Affect the Payment

The total amount of the finance charge and the amount of the monthly payments are determined by the annual rate of the finance charge and the maturity. Using a $1000 consumer cash loan requiring equal monthly payments, we will illustrate the effect that a change in the finance rate or the maturity has on the total finance charge and monthly payments.

EXHIBIT 7-1

Reduction in future purchasing power due to finance charge on the amount borrowed.

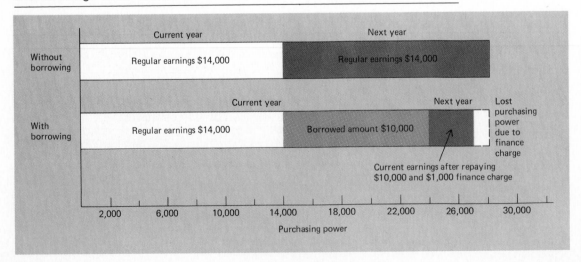

The Impact of the Finance Charge   Initially, we assume the $1000 loan has a 24-month maturity. Exhibit 7-2 illustrates the monthly payments and the total finance charge for six different annual finance rates between 9 and 30 percent. The left-hand portion of Exhibit 7-2 shows the required monthly payment for each finance rate. The right-hand side illustrates the total finance charge over the 24 months of the loan for each of the six rates. For example, at an 18 percent annual finance charge, the monthly payment is $49.92 and the total finance charge is $198.18.

Exhibit 7-2 demonstrates that increasing the annual finance rate raises the monthly payment by only a small amount. But repeated over the 24 months, that small increase in the monthly payment substantially boosts the total finance charge. For example, the difference between the monthly payment on an 18 percent loan and the payment on a 12 percent loan is only:

$2.85   = $49.92   − $47.07

⬆   ⬆   ⬆

Added payment _ Payment on _ Payment on
on 18% loan   =   18% loan   12% loan

EXHIBIT 7-2

Total monthly payments and finance charges on a 24-month $1000 loan at 9 to 30 percent finance charge.

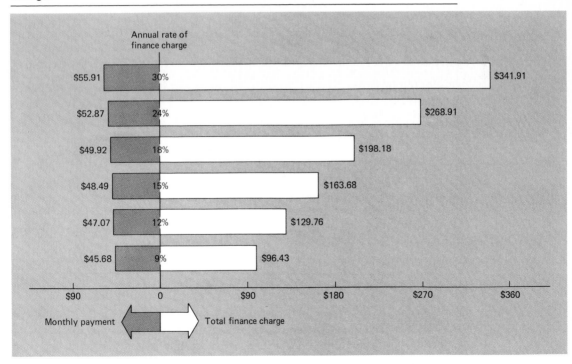

Yet, extended over 24 months, the total finance charge for the 18 percent loan is more than 50 percent greater than that for the 12 percent loan:

$$52.7\% = (\$198.18 - \$129.76) \div \$129.76$$

| Percentage increase in finance charge | = | Finance charge on: 18% loan − 12% loan | ÷ | Finance charge on 12% loan |

The message from Exhibit 7-2 seems clear: A small change in the annual finance charge rate has a sizable effect on the total finance charge. That's the main reason why you should carefully compare the annual rate on competing credit offers. The savings can be sizable.

The Factor of Maturity   Now we assume that the $1000 loan has a fixed 18 percent annual finance rate, but that the maturity can have a duration from 12 to 60 months. Exhibit 7-3 illustrates the effect of these different maturities on the monthly payment and the total amount of the finance charge. The left-hand portion shows the monthly payments for various maturity periods; the total finance charge is shown on the right-hand side for these maturities.

The left side of Exhibit 7-3 shows that for a given loan amount, the monthly payments are smaller for longer maturities. We can also see, however, that they don't get very much smaller as the maturity gets longer. Thus, extending maturity from 18 to 24 months lowers the payment from $63.81 to $49.92, or almost 22 percent:

$$21.8\% = (\$63.81 - \$49.92) \div \$63.81$$

| Percentage decline in monthly payment | = | Payment for 18-month loan | − | Payment for 24-month loan | ÷ | Payment for 18-month loan |

But extending the maturity from 54 to 60 months drops the monthly payment only 6.5 percent:

$$6.5\% = (\$27.15 - \$25.39) \div \$27.15$$

| Percentage drop in monthly payment | = | Payment for 54-month loan | − | Payment for 60-month loan | ÷ | Payment for 54-month loan |

Yet the total finance charge, shown on the right side of Exhibit 7-3, rises $50 or more for each 6-month extension of the maturity. While an extension may initially increase monthly purchasing power by lowering the required payment, it merely creates the illusion of easing the payment burden. The higher total finance charge actually raises the total repayment burden.

STRATEGY

If your only purpose in getting a longer maturity on your loan is to make the payments fit your budget, carefully consider whether you should use that credit at all.

USING CREDIT

There is no simple and definite answer to questions about when credit should be used or about how much credit is appropriate. You must answer those questions in light of your own individual situation. But some general guidelines should help you make those decisions for yourself.

Credit: The Cost-Benefit Trade-Off

There are two costs that should be considered when making a credit decision.

First, there is the direct cost of using credit—the finance charge. We illustrated this impact in Exhibit 7-1. Because the finance charge reduces future purchasing power, your gain in current purchasing power is less than your sacrifice in later purchasing power.

Second, there are the indirect costs of reduced flexibility and increased

---

EXHIBIT 7-3

Monthly payments and total finance charges for $1000 loan with 18 percent finance charge and 12- to 60-month maturities.

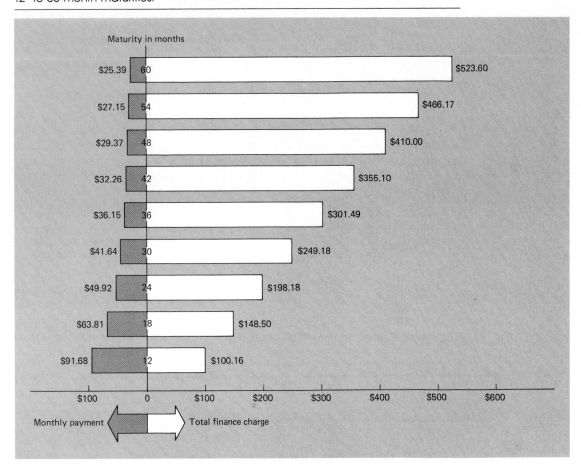

risk. Since most credit alternatives entail a fixed repayment schedule, the borrower might be unable to meet those payments. The consequences of that failure can be considerable: The lender will likely make a concerted effort to collect those payments. You may be bombarded with a whole series of letters demanding payment. It may also mean frequent telephone calls reminding you of the unpaid amount and requesting immediate payment.

On the other hand, using credit can provide several benefits.

First, by buying an item—car, appliance, furniture—on credit, you receive the service from those items immediately.

Second, by using credit, you can take advantage of a sale price on an item even when you do not have the money in hand, provided the saving on the sale price is greater than the total finance charge.

Third, when you expect a price to rise rapidly in a short while, it may be more economical to use credit to purchase an item immediately rather than to wait and buy later when the price has increased.

Last, there are the conveniences of using credit: It eliminates the need to carry large sums of money, you receive a single bill each month, and you have a record of your monthly purchases.

The decision to use credit essentially entails a **cost-benefit trade-off.** That decision hinges on whether the benefits from today's increased purchasing power coupled with the decreased flexibility and increased risk that are part of every credit transaction are great enough to offset your reduced future purchasing power.

Is Credit Justified?

The questions in Exhibit 7-4 provide a guide to help you decide whether credit can be properly used for a particular expenditure. Although the questions seem rather basic, it is amazing how few people stop and ask: Is credit really justified in this circumstance? Many people seem hypnotized by the lure of a "bargain"—"Price reduced 20 percent and just say charge it"—and "easy" credit terms—"Only $5 down, and this $500 Gumbat is yours, no payments for 2 months and then a low, low $16.01 for 60 months." They never ask themselves whether they really need the item. Nor do they consider the alternatives to credit: Delay the purchase, save money until you have the purchase price, or decide not to purchase the item at all.

We are not suggesting that credit be restricted only to major, long-lived, durable goods, such as appliances, cars, or furniture. But when credit is used as a convenience, we believe that the repayment period should be short. If you use credit for short-lived consumer goods and services that will last a year or less, such as clothing, children's toys, automobile operating expenses, restaurants, travel, and gifts, make plans to repay the entire amount when billed. Extended repayment terms are rarely justified in these circumstances.

STRATEGY

If the majority of your responses in Exhibit 7-4 are "Yes," using credit is probably justified. On the other hand, if many questions draw a "No," especially Questions 2 and 3, further consideration is in order.

EXHIBIT 7-4

Guide to deciding whether credit is justified.

	(YES)	(NO)
1 Do you really need the item?	( )	( )
2 Is the item a necessity that cannot be postponed?	( )	( )
3 Is purchasing on credit the only alternative?	( )	( )
a Would it be impossible to use money from your savings instead of using credit?	( )	( )
b Is it impossible to defer the purchase and save the money to buy later?	( )	( )
4 When the credit has extended payment terms:		
a Is the item's useful working life reasonably long (3 to 5 years)?	( )	( )
b Does its life equal or exceed the loan's maturity?	( )	( )
c Is the item's price such that it cannot be fitted into the monthly budget?	( )	( )
5 When the credit has flexible repayment terms:		
a If the item is short-lived (food, entertainment, clothing), can you repay the entire amount of the loan when billed?	( )	( )
b If credit is used to meet a temporary cash shortage, can you repay the borrowed amount when you are billed?	( )	( )

SETTING DEBT LIMITS

Unfortunately, many people rely on the lender to set their debt limits. By that we mean they do not decide the maximum amount of debt they can handle—their **upper debt limit**—based on their present income. If the lender is willing to extend additional credit, these people feel they may as well borrow up to their credit limit. True, most lenders are excellent judges of how much credit an individual can handle. But obtaining credit is so easy and so widespread that a lender may not be fully aware of how much credit from other lenders a borrower currently has outstanding. Consequently, a person can become grossly overextended before a lender signals a halt. Even then, many people put off the inevitable by trying various lenders until they find one who will grant them additional credit. Allowing the lender to set your debt limits is imprecise, and it can be an invitation to disaster. You know your personal finances best, so you should set the limits.

Estimating Your Limits

The questions in Exhibit 7-5 can guide you as to whether you are nearing your debt limit. If nearly all your responses are no, you are probably within your debt limit. We think Question 1 deserves special emphasis. If the new credit causes you constant worry or sleepless nights, you are paying a high price for that credit. In general, if you can identify where the money for the new payment will come from, and if you will not be forced into a major revamping of your present expenditure and savings plans, you are probably within your limits.

Use Your Budget to Set Your Debt Limits

We have already introduced the instrument that will help you decide whether you are approaching your upper debt limit: **a personal budget.** As you will recall, we stressed that the main purpose of a budget is to plan how you will spend your available income during the next year. Since the monthly payments on a proposed consumer loan will have to be part of your entry under "Planned expenditures," a budget is a good place to decide whether you have sufficient income to make those monthly payments.

The first step is to compare the total of your current planned expenditures as shown in your present budget, plus savings for long- and short-term goals, plus any current loan payments, with your currently available income. By deducting the total of planned spending from your income, you can compute how much money you currently have left for additional debt payments. If you now have enough money to cover the monthly payments

---

EXHIBIT 7-5

Checklist for upper debt limit.

	(YES)	(NO)
1 Will adding more debt make you feel uncomfortable?	( )	( )
2 Will you have difficulty fitting the new payment into your budget?	( )	( )
3 Will the new payment:		
a Take money away from essential expenditures (food, clothing, housing, savings)?	( )	( )
b Make it difficult for you to meet your current debt payments?	( )	( )
c Require major changes in the spending patterns you outlined in your budget?	( )	( )
d Reduce or eliminate your budgeted savings?	( )	( )
4 Will the added debt sharply reduce the net worth you show on your personal balance sheet?	( )	( )

on the proposed new loan, you are probably not at your upper debt limit; you can proceed with the new loan. On the other hand, if you do not have sufficient money to cover the payment, you are probably at your upper debt limit and should not undertake the new loan.

STRATEGY

Before deciding on a new loan, review your present budget to see whether you have money available to make the loan's monthly payments.

Let us give an example to show how a budget can be used to set an upper debt limit. Gus and Dimitra Alevas want to borrow $4400 to buy a boat. The $4400 loan would require $146 monthly payments over the next 36 months. A review of their present budget shows their expected monthly income is $1800, while their monthly planned spending totals $1650. So the Alevases have $150 a month that they can use for the new loan payment. If Gus and Dimitra want to borrow the money, they can do so because they are not at their upper debt limit.

Let's change the details and assume that Gus and Dimitra's current budget shows planned spending of $1749. Now the Alevases have only $51 available, far short of the $146 loan payment. Clearly, they are at their upper debt limit and should not proceed with the loan.

But suppose Gus and Dimitra still want to consider the loan. What should they do now? They will have to ask themselves whether they want to reduce their present planned expenditures by the $95 needed to complete the loan payment. If they decide they want to do that, they should identify exactly where the money will come from. All too often, people use some easy generalization like "The money will come from somewhere" or "We will just have to be more thrifty." What is needed is a detailed plan that shows what expenditures will be cut and by how much. And those proposed cuts should be reviewed to make certain they are feasible. If, in our example,

Gus and Dimitra decide they cannot, or do not want to, reduce their current planned spending by $95, they should forget the loan. But if they can identify the necessary cuts and are willing to make them, they can proceed with the loan.

STRATEGY

When you must reduce your current planned spending to obtain the money for a new loan payment, identify precisely which expenditures you will cut and by how much.

Longer Repayment Periods

In Exhibit 7-3 we demonstrated that for a longer maturity, the required monthly payments are smaller. But that should raise an immediate question: Does that payment reduction expand your debt capacity? Certainly, lower monthly payments would make the payment easier to fit into your budget. But has your debt capacity really expanded? In nearly all cases, we would say no. As we emphasized earlier, extending the maturity reduces the amount of each monthly payment, but it also prolongs them for several more years. About the only time an extension truly expands debt capacity is when the original repayment terms were abnormally short.

STRATEGY

Except for special circumstances, extending the maturity does not raise your effective debt capacity. If you must extend maturities to stay within your debt limit, you are probably overextended on credit.

COST OF CREDIT

Most lenders must specify their finance charges in dollars as well as in terms of an annual percentage rate. And that finance charge must include any and all costs associated with the credit transaction.

Annual Percentage Rate (APR)

The **annual percentage rate** (APR) that a lender quotes expresses the annual finance charge associated with a credit transaction as a percentage of the amount borrowed. Thus, the finance charge for 1 year on a $1000 loan with an APR of 12 percent is:

$$\underset{\substack{\text{Annual} \\ \text{finance charge}}}{\$120} = \underset{\substack{\text{Amount} \\ \text{of loan}}}{\$1000} \times \underset{\text{APR}}{12\%}$$

if the loan is repaid in a single lump-sum amount at the end of the year. (We are using a single year-end payment to simplify the example.)

The principal advantage to an APR is that it can be used to compare the borrowing cost of competing loan offers—it is a relative-cost measure. That is, APR gives the annual cost of credit as a percentage of the amount borrowed. Stated another way, a loan's APR is the cost of borrowing $1 for 1 year. Thus, the APRs on two competing credit offers can be compared directly, so you can decide which is cheaper. And this holds regardless of whether the offers are identical in all respects or different in some respects. For example, we can compare a 21-month loan of $500 with an APR of 14 percent to a 24-month loan of $600 with an APR of 12 percent. Despite the fact that the loans are for different amounts and have different maturities, we will conclude that the first loan, because its APR is 14 percent versus an APR of 12 percent for the second loan, costs more per dollar borrowed.

Comparative Shopping

Too often, people accept the first loan offer they receive. They never check to see if the same amount is available from other lenders at a lower APR. Few people buy a car from the first dealer who quotes a price, yet they seem reluctant to shop for the lowest APR. When you borrow money, the lender is performing a service, and you pay a finance charge for that service. So why not shop for the lowest cost? If your income, amount presently borrowed, and other essential personal financial details are such that you would be considered a good potential loan customer, you should be able to obtain offers of loans from a number of lenders. Probably, some will quote a lower cost than others.

STRATEGY

Before deciding on a lender, check the rates of other lenders in your area. Compare the APRs on competing credit offers to find the lowest cost.

Bargaining with the Lender

Few people consider the possibility of bargaining with the lender for a lower APR. Yet, the heavy competition in the personal consumer-lending market has made this a useful technique. Some lenders may be surprised when you ask them whether they are quoting you the best APR they can offer. Go ahead and surprise them with the question. It might mean a lower rate. If another lender has quoted a better rate, you might mention that in the negotiations. But be honest when quoting a competitor's rate. Lenders know what their competitors are doing.

Impact of Taxes on the Cost of Credit

Recall from the discussion of income taxes in Chapter 6 that the finance charge on all types of credit qualifies as an itemized deduction. In order for you actually to benefit from deducting the finance charge, your total itemized deductions must exceed your zero bracket amount. But if they do, including the finance charge as part of your itemized deductions can sharply reduce its effective cost. An example will illustrate why.

Assume Rose McLain borrowed $2000 on which she expected to pay an annual finance charge of $300: an APR of 15 percent. Rose's present

itemized deductions exceed her zero bracket amount, so she can deduct the entire $300. Since that reduces her taxable income by $300, and assuming that her marginal tax rate is 40 percent, the reduction in her taxes payable is:

$$\$120 \quad = \$300 \quad \times 40\%$$

| Reduction in taxes payable | = | Finance charge for the year | × | Marginal tax rate |

One way of looking at the saving of $120 in taxes that need not be paid is that it represents an effective reduction in the cost of the loan. That is, because you have to pay $300 to the lender in finance charges for the loan, you will pay $120 less in taxes; the effective cost of the loan is:

$$\$180 \quad = \$300 \quad - \$120$$

| Effective finance charge | = | Finance charge for the year | − | Reduction in taxes |

The saving in taxes can also be thought of as a reduction in the effective APR on the loan. But remember, it applies only when your itemized deductions exceed your zero bracket amount, so you can deduct the finance charges as an excess itemized deduction.

STRATEGY

If you can deduct the finance charge on your tax return, be certain to consider the sizable reduction it makes in the cost of credit.

Computing the Finance Charge: Cash and Sales Loans

Lenders compute the finance charge on a sales or cash loan using one of two techniques. The selection of the computational method partially depends on the lender's choice and partially on what a particular state allows a lender to do. To illustrate the two methods, we use a $1200 loan that carries a finance charge (APR) of 10.9 percent and is to be repaid in 12 equal monthly payments.

Precomputed Finance Charge With the **precomputed finance charge** technique, the lender computes the finance charge at the time the loan is made. And, on the basis of that finance charge, the lender sets the required monthly payment. In the case of the $1200 loan with an APR of 10.9 percent, the 12 monthly payments will be $106. The borrower is expected to make that payment by the due date each month. If the payment arrives late, the lender assesses a late payment penalty. But, should the payment arrive several days early, the borrower receives no credit for sending that payment in early. Consequently, on most loans the lender receives the finance charge that was computed at the time the loan was made.

Simple Interest With **simple interest**, the computation of the finance charge is based on the precise amount borrowed for the exact length of time it was borrowed. To illustrate the simple interest method, we will use the same $1200 loan. First, the 10.9 percent APR on that loan is converted to a daily finance charge:

0.0299%	= 10.9%	÷ 365 days
⬆	⬆	⬆
Finance charge on a daily basis	= Finance charge on an annual basis	÷ Number of days

We will round that to 0.03 percent for our calculations.

Let's take a look at Exhibit 7-6, which shows how to calculate the

EXHIBIT 7-6

Finance charge on a $1200 loan with an APR of 10.9 percent, using simple interest.

PAYMENT NUMBER (1)	DAYS SINCE LAST PAYMENT (2)	BEGINNING LOAN BALANCE (3)	FINANCE CHARGE: COL. 3 × COL. 2 × 0.03% DAILY FINANCE RATE (4)	LOAN PAYMENT (5)	REMAINING LOAN BALANCE: (COL. 3 + COL. 4) − COL. 5 (6)
1	30	$1200.00	$10.80	$106	$1104.80
2	35	1104.80	11.60	106	1010.40
3	25	1010.40	7.58	106	911.98

finance charge using the simple interest method, and what the remaining balance is after each payment.

Let's start by assuming that the beginning balance outstanding on the loan is $1200 and that the required monthly payment is $106. Further, we assume that the first payment is made exactly 30 days after the start of the loan. So, if the $1200 has been borrowed for 30 days and the finance rate is 0.03 percent per day, the finance charge for those 30 days is:

$$\$10.80 = \$1200 \times 0.0003 \times 30 \text{ days}$$

$$\underset{\substack{\text{Finance} \\ \text{charge}}}{} = \underset{\substack{\text{Amount of} \\ \text{loan}}}{} \times \underset{\substack{\text{Daily finance} \\ \text{rate (decimal)}}}{} \times \underset{\substack{\text{Number of} \\ \text{days}}}{}$$

This calculation is shown in column 4 of line 1 in Exhibit 7-6.

Using simple arithmetic still, we can now calculate what the remaining loan balance is after the first payment. Since the finance charge is added to the loan balance, part of the first payment repays the finance charge, while the remainder reduces the original loan balance. After the first payment, the remaining loan balance is:

$$\$1104.80 = (\$1200 + \$10.80) - \$106$$

$$\underset{\substack{\text{Remaining loan} \\ \text{balance}}}{} = \underset{\substack{\text{Beginning loan} \\ \text{balance}}}{} + \underset{\substack{\text{Finance} \\ \text{charge}}}{} - \underset{\substack{\text{Loan} \\ \text{payment}}}{}$$

The computation of the remaining loan balance is shown in column 6 of line 1 in Exhibit 7-6. The entire set of calculations is summarized on line 1 of the same exhibit.

Now assume that instead of making the second payment of $106 exactly 30 days after the first payment, it is made 35 days later. Can you calculate what the finance charge is at this second payment and what the remaining loan balance is after the second payment and finance charge? Check your calculations with the figures on line 2 of Exhibit 7-6.

The simple interest technique can provide several advantages. One is if a payment is made a few days early, the borrower is not assessed a finance charge for those days.

Of course, with the simple daily interest method, if the payment is several days late, the borrower pays interest for those days. But that is generally much less than the sizable late fee many loans with precomputed finance charges assess for a late payment. In short, a borrower generally benefits from a simple interest loan. *A word of caution:* Check the lender's procedures for early and late payments; a few have instituted penalties and restrictions that effectively cancel the benefits ordinarily offered by a simple interest loan.

STRATEGY

Provided that a simple interest loan's APR is competitive with other sources, it offers certain advantages over loans with precomputed finance charges.

Rebate of the Finance Charge

When a loan with precomputed finance charges is repaid before maturity (for example, when a 12-month loan is repaid in 6 months), a portion of the finance charge is refunded. Most lenders compute the refund using the so-called **"rule of 78"** or some variant of it. The refund, and the source of the 78, is computed as followed: (1) the months are numbered consecutively: the first month = 12, the second month = 11, the third = 10, etc.; (2) these numbers are added: for 1 year, the sum is 78 (12 + 11 + 10 +...+ 1 = 78). The second step is to compute the sum of the months for which the loan has been outstanding. A loan outstanding for 2 months would equal 23 (12 + 11). This sum, taken as a percentage of 78, represents the finance charge on the loan; the balance of the finance charge would be refunded.

To illustrate, assume that a 12-month loan of $1200 that had a $60 finance charge is repaid at the end of 6 months. Exhibit 7-7 shows what portion of the $60 finance charge would be refunded.

Some lenders charge a penalty fee when a borrower repays a loan prior to its original maturity. Thus, on the previous 12-month loan, they would charge a prepayment penalty because it was repaid after 6 months. While the refund rule is reasonably equitable, the addition of the prepayment fee can mean that the borrower pays a substantial penalty for early repayment of a loan.

If you have a reasonable belief that you might prepay your loan, you should take out a loan with a maturity that reflects how soon you expect to repay the loan. Or, you should consider a simple interest loan if it doesn't have a prepayment penalty. When a loan has a prepayment penalty, don't take a long maturity if you fully expect to repay the loan in less than the maturity period.

ESTIMATING MONTHLY PAYMENTS

Exhibit 7-8 shows the approximate monthly payments required on a $1000 loan at different maturities and different APRs. Since they have been rounded to the nearest penny, they are not exact, but they are accurate enough for our purposes.

EXHIBIT 7-7

Refund of the finance charge.

1	Sum of the months until the loan's final maturity:	
	12 + 11 + 10 + 9 + 8 + 7 + 6 + 5 + 4 + 3 + 2 + 1 =	78
2	Sum of the months for which the loan has been outstanding:	
	12 + 11 + 10 + 9 + 8 + 7 =	57
3	Percentage of the finance charge applicable to the time the loan has been outstanding: 57 ÷ 78 =	73%
4	Total finance charge	$60.00
5	Finance charge to date: $60 × 73%	$43.80
6	Finance charge refund: line 4 − line 5	$16.20

By using the appropriate maturity and APR, Exhibit 7-8 can be used to estimate the monthly payment on most loans. For example, assume we want to know the monthly payment for a 24-month, $2000 loan that has an APR of 12 percent. By using Exhibit 7-8, we know that the monthly payment is:

$$\$94.14 = \$47.07 \times (\$2000 \div \$1000)$$

| Required monthly payment | Payment on a $1000, 12%, 24-month loan | Loan as a multiple of $1000 (loan amount ÷ $1000) |

Do you need more practice? Compute the monthly payment on a $3600, 18-month loan with an APR of 15 percent. The answer should be $224.57.

Exhibit 7-8 can also be used to estimate the total finance charge for a given loan. Previously, we determined that a 24-month loan of $2000 with an APR of 12 percent would have monthly payments of $94.14. Over its 24 months, the loan's total payments are:

$$\$2259.36 = \$94.14 \times 24 \text{ months}$$

| Total payments | = | Monthly payment | × | Months to loan's maturity |

Since $2000 of those payments represents repayment of the initial loan, the remainder is the total finance charge:

$$\$259.36 = \$2259.36 - \$2000$$

| Finance charge | = | Total payments | − | Initial loan |

EXHIBIT 7-8

Monthly payments on a $1000 sales or cash
loan with different maturities and APRs.

MONTHS TO MATURITY	Annual Percentage Rate (APR)							
	9%	12%	15%	18%	21%	24%	27%	30%
12	$87.45	$88.85	$90.26	$91.68	$93.11	$94.56	$96.02	$97.49
18	59.60	60.98	62.38	63.81	65.24	66.70	68.18	69.67
24	45.68	47.07	48.49	49.92	51.39	52.87	54.38	55.91
30	37.35	38.75	40.18	41.64	43.13	44.65	46.20	47.78
36	31.80	33.21	34.67	36.15	37.68	39.23	40.83	42.45
48	24.88	26.33	27.83	29.37	30.97	32.60	34.28	36.00
60	20.76	22.24	23.79	25.39	27.05	28.77	30.54	32.35

Note: Payments are rounded to the nearest penny.

Do you need more practice? Work through the previous 18-month, 15 percent APR loan of $3600; its finance charge is $442.26.

SAVING: AN ALTERNATIVE TO CREDIT

As an alternative to borrowing, you can delay the purchase until you save the money to buy the item. In making this suggestion, we first assume that there is no emergency or pressing need which makes it essential that you purchase the item or service immediately. Second, we assume that the cost of the item or service is not rising sharply because of inflation or some other cause. Finally, we will ignore the effects of taxes on finance charges (an itemized deduction) and on the interest earned on savings (income). Later, we will indeed see how taxes affect the comparison between borrowing to buy and saving to buy.

Cost Differential: Saving versus Credit

The difference in cost between saving for an item and purchasing it on credit is best illustrated with an example. Suppose that Fred and Becky Vanderhoop are considering buying new furniture costing $1000.

One option is to use credit and repay the $1000 in 12 monthly payments. The lender has quoted an APR of 18 percent, so the total finance charge is:

$100.16　　 = ($91.68　 × 12 months) − $1000

| Total finance charge | = | Monthly payment | × | Number of months | − | Initial loan |

Alternatively, the Vanderhoops can wait 12 months until they have saved the required $1000. We assume that the savings account pays 6 percent interest.

Exhibit 7-9 illustrates how to calculate the cost difference between saving and buying on credit. The $1100.16 total cost of the credit alternative, shown in the top half of the exhibit, includes repayment of the loan and associated finance charge. For the savings alternative, we need the amount that must be deposited at the end of each of the 12 months in order to achieve the $1000 goal. The required monthly deposit for the desired goal, $1000 in this case, can be computed using Exhibit 1-7. From that exhibit, we can determine that $81.07 must be saved each month to have the required $1000 after 12 months.

Of course, once that first savings deposit is made, it will earn interest for the 11 months that remain until the purchase is to be made. Likewise, the second savings deposit earns interest for 10 months, and so forth for the other deposits. The net effect is that after 12 months, the balance in the savings account is:

$1000　　 = ($81.07　 × 12 months) + $27.16

| Balance in savings | = | Monthly deposit | × | Number of months | + | Interest earned on savings |

EXHIBIT 7-9

Cost differential: Saving the money to buy a
$1000 item versus borrowing $1000 to buy it.

DESCRIPTION	CREDIT	SAVING
Cost Differential—Ignoring Income Taxes		
Loan required for purchase	$1000.00	
Finance charge on loan	100.16	
Savings balance needed for purchase		$1000.00
Portion from savings deposits: 12 payments @ $81.07		972.84
Portion provided by interest earned on savings deposits		27.16
Total cost of credit alternative:		
Repayment of loan and finance charge	$1100.16	
Total cost of saving alternative:		
Required savings deposits		$972.84
Cost differential: $1100.16 − $ 972.84	$ 127.32	
Cost Differential—Considering Income Taxes		
Total cost of credit alternative:		
Loan repayment and finance charge	$1100.16	
Less: Reduction of income taxes due to finance charge:		
$100.16 × 30%	30.05	
Net after-tax cost of credit alternative	$1070.11	
Total cost of saving alternative:		
Required savings deposits		$ 972.84
Add: Additional deposit needed to offset income tax on		
interest earnings: $27.16 × 30%		8.15
Net after-tax cost of savings alternative		$ 980.99
Cost differential: $1070.11 − $980.99	$ 89.12	

Initially, the extra cost of buying on credit rather than saving for the
furniture is:

$127.32 = $1100.16 − $972.84

⬆ Added cost of credit = ⬆ Total cost of credit − ⬆ Total cost of saving

Impact of Income Taxes   Up to this point, we have ignored income taxes
in this example. Recall that if the Vanderhoops's itemized deductions
exceed their zero bracket amount, they can deduct the finance charge; we
will assume that they do. The bottom half of Exhibit 7-9 shows the tax effect

if their marginal tax rate is 30 percent. By deducting the $100.16 finance charge, they reduce their taxable income by a similar amount and therefore lower their income taxes by:

$$\underset{\substack{\text{Reduction in} \\ \text{income taxes}}}{\$30.05} = \underset{\text{Finance charge}}{\$100.16} \times \underset{\substack{\text{Marginal} \\ \text{tax rate}}}{30\%}$$

Consequently, the net cost of the credit alternative is:

$$\underset{\substack{\text{Net cost of} \\ \text{credit alternative}}}{\$1070.11} = \underset{\substack{\text{Total cost of} \\ \text{credit alternative}}}{\$1100.16} - \underset{\substack{\text{Reduction in} \\ \text{income taxes}}}{\$30.05}$$

Income taxes affect the savings alternative in the opposite way. Part of the interest earned on their savings is lost to taxes because it is income that is taxable. Since the Vanderhoops have to pay taxes on any interest they earn, the additional amount they will have to deposit to replace interest lost to taxes is:

$$\underset{\substack{\text{Additional} \\ \text{deposit}}}{\$8.15} = \underset{\substack{\text{Interest} \\ \text{earnings}}}{\$27.16} \times \underset{\substack{\text{Marginal} \\ \text{tax rate}}}{30\%}$$

That raises the net cost of the saving alternative to:

$$\underset{\substack{\text{Net cost of} \\ \text{saving alternative}}}{\$980.99} = \underset{\substack{\text{Saving} \\ \text{deposits}}}{\$972.84} + \underset{\substack{\text{Additional} \\ \text{deposit}}}{\$8.15}$$

While the comparison still favors saving over obtaining credit, the cost differential between the two is narrowed to:

$$\underset{\substack{\text{Cost} \\ \text{differential}}}{\$89.12} = \underset{\substack{\text{Net cost of} \\ \text{credit}}}{\$1070.11} - \underset{\substack{\text{Net cost of} \\ \text{saving}}}{\$980.99}$$

It is interesting to note that a higher marginal tax rate will narrow the cost differential even further. At 50 percent, the cost differential drops to $63.66 between the credit and the savings alternative. As practice, you can compute the net cost of the credit option—it should be $1050.08—and the net cost of the saving option—it should be $986.42. High marginal tax rates remove much of the incentive to defer the purchase. A high tax rate sharply lowers the net cost of borrowing while simultaneously taxing away much of the interest earnings.

Estimating Cost Differentials

Exhibit 7-9 can readily be modified to fit any specific situation you may want to evaluate. The required monthly savings deposit can be computed using Exhibit 1-7. And from that figure, the expected interest earnings can be computed. Likewise, the total payment and the finance charge for the credit option can be estimated using the payment details shown in Exhibit 7-8.

STRATEGY

If you have some flexibility, consider savings as an alternative to using credit. Granted, you forgo immediate use of the item you want, but the cost reduction can be considerable.

FINANCE CHARGE: CREDIT CARD ACCOUNTS

In this section we will examine how finance charges are calculated on the credit card accounts offered by nationwide retailers (such as Sears Roebuck, J. C. Penney, and Montgomery Ward), large department stores (such as Gimbels, Dayton Hudson, and Macy's), oil companies such as (Exxon, Mobil Oil, and Gulf), and bank-affiliated cards (such as MasterCard and Visa).

Calculating the finance charge on a credit card account isn't as simple as calculating the finance charges on a consumer sales loan or a cash loan. With either of these loans, a fixed amount of money is borrowed in a lump sum for a specified length of time; that amount is then repaid in equal amounts at regular intervals during the time period of the loan. It's not quite the same with a credit card account. To begin with, there is not a single transaction date; each time the credit card is used, there will be another transaction date. That means that you are, in effect, borrowing money a number of times. And, although you must repay a certain minimum amount each month, you can repay more than the minimum amount without paying a penalty.

Billing Cycle

To illustrate how to calculate the finance charge, we must first review the monthly **billing cycle** on which most credit card companies base their finance charge. There are two key dates in that cycle: (1) the billing date, also referred to as the closing date, and (2) the due date. Exhibit 7-10 is a sample monthly billing statement which shows these dates as well as other essential information needed to demonstrate the billing cycle.

Billing or Closing Date The **billing,** or **closing, date** is the last day of the month that any purchase you made with your credit card or any payment you made on the account has been recorded in the account. In Exhibit 7-10, the billing date is shown at point (A) as 9-2-8X. Since most credit cards use a

EXHIBIT 7-10

CHAPTER 7

197

CREDIT: HOW TO
GET IT AND HOW
TO USE IT

Sample monthly statement for a typical credit
card account.

MONTHLY STATEMENT

Ralph Smith
456 Dead End St.
Nowhere

Account Number
123-4567-890

Date	Reference Number	Description	Amount	
8-23-8X	305F-402319	Ajax Lumber Co.	100	00

Previous Balance	New Purchases	Finance Charge	Payments	New Balance	Past Due Balance	Minimum Payment
0	100.00	0	0	100.00	0	10.00

Annual Percentage Rate	Billing Date [A]	Payment Due date [B]	Card Limit	Balance of Limit Remaining
18 percent	9-2-8X	9-27-8X	500	400

calendar month, the billing or closing date on last month's statement would likely have been 8-2-8X. Consequently, the September statement shown in Exhibit 7-10 would include all credit card purchases as well as payments that were posted to the account between August 3 and September 2. Any purchase or payment that was posted to the account on September 3 would appear on the October statement.

Due Date The **due date** typically falls 25 days after the billing date. In Exhibit 7-10, this date is shown at point (B) as 9-27-8X. The payment is due on or before this date. In reality, you usually can pay several days after that date and still be on time. Some credit card companies allow 4 to 5 days after the due date to process the customers' payments. But if you pay much later than this, you may be assessed a finance charge.

Grace Period For regular purchases made during the current billing period, most credit card accounts consider the 25-day period between the billing and due dates as a **grace period.** If the card holder has no unpaid balance from the previous statement, has made credit purchases that were billed on the current statement, and, further, has paid the entire balance of the current statement by the due date, no finance charge is assessed. We think it is important to take a moment and stress the significance of this "no finance charge" feature. In effect, the card holder is essentially borrowing money during the grace period without paying any finance charge. This is a notable exception to the statement at the beginning of the chapter in which we said that borrowing involves a finance charge. Unlike the situation we illustrated in Exhibit 7-1 in which the borrower had to repay the loan and a finance charge, here the borrower has to repay only the borrowing, which is represented by the credit card purchases, within the grace period, and there is no finance charge.

We emphasize that the grace period applies only to regular purchases billed on the current statement. If the card holder had an unpaid balance from the previous month's statement, there would be a finance charge on this previous balance even if the entire balance was paid by the due date. The grace period for Exhibit 7-10 extends from September 2 through September 27. In this exhibit, Ralph's previous balance is zero. To avoid the finance charge on the credit purchase he made during the current period ($100 purchase on 8-23-8X), he would have to pay the entire current balance of $100 by September 27. If Ralph Smith had had a $200 previous balance, he would have been assessed a finance charge on that $200 even if he had paid the entire balance by September 27.

By concentrating purchases immediately after the billing date, the card holder can extend the effective grace period beyond 25 days. To demonstrate, assume that Ralph Smith, in Exhibit 7-10, made a $400 purchase on September 3. Since his billing date is September 2, this item would not be billed until the October statement. Because that statement's due date is October 27, his effective grace period is 54 days: September 3 to October 27. That provides $400 of credit for 54 days with no finance charge.

STRATEGY

CHAPTER 7

199

CREDIT: HOW TO
GET IT AND HOW
TO USE IT

Concentrate your purchases immediately after your billing date in order to maximize your effective grace period.

Computing the Finance Charge

Most credit card accounts compute their finance charge by using one of three methods: previous balance, average daily balance, and adjusted balance. Their similarities and differences can best be illustrated by continuing the example from Exhibit 7-10. We will assume Ralph Smith made a single $50 payment on September 17, leaving a $50 unpaid balance. We will also assume that Ralph made no other purchases during this statement period. The computation of the finance charge using each of the three different methods is summarized in Exhibit 7-11.

Previous Balance The **previous balance** method gives no credit for partial payments. Unless the entire balance is paid by the due date, a finance charge is assessed against the unpaid balance as of September 2 (the unpaid balance includes the previous balance, plus all new purchases, less all payments), even though part of the balance was paid during the current period. In effect, this method ignores the fact that the unpaid balance was only $50 after September 17. In most cases, previous balance has the highest finance charge of the three methods. Some credit card accounts still use this method.

EXHIBIT 7-11

Computation of the finance charge using the previous balance, average daily balance, and adjusted balance.

	PREVIOUS BALANCE	AVERAGE DAILY BALANCE	ADJUSTED BALANCE
Closing balance, September 2	$100.00	$100.00	$100.00
Payments, September 17	50.00	50.00	50.00
Ending balance	50.00	50.00	50.00
Balance on which finance charge is based	100.00*	75.00†	50.00‡
Finance charge for September (1½% per month)	1.50	1.13	0.75
Credit for partial payment	None	Partial	Complete

*Represents unpaid balance on September 2, 198X.
†Represents average daily balance during the period:
  15 days (9/3 to 9/17) @ $100 = $1500
  15 days (9/18 to 10/2) @ $50 =   750
            Total $2250
  Average daily balance = $2250 ÷ 30 days = $75
‡Represents unpaid balance on October 2, 198X.

Average Daily Balance   Using the **average daily balance** method, the finance charge is based on the average outstanding balance during the period. This average is computed by taking the balance each day during the regular billing cycle. Since payments during the period reduce the unpaid balance, the finance charge under this method is lower than the finance charge under the previous balance method. Of the three, this method is the most frequently used.

Adjusted Balance   With **adjusted balance,** the finance charge is based on the unpaid balance at the end of the billing cycle. In this example, that is the unpaid balance as of 10-2-8X, which was $50 after the $50 payment on September 17. Because it provides full credit for all payments during the period, it generally has the lowest finance charge. Unfortunately, it is also the least used method of the three.

Minimizing Finance Charges

You can do several things to minimize your finance charge.

First, you should try to obtain credit cards using the adjusted balance method.

Second, you should always pay within the grace period.

Third, make certain that your payment arrives in time. While most creditors allow several days past the due date, you are risking a finance charge. And paying an extra 1½ percent seems a high price for being 1 or 2 days late.

STRATEGY

When possible, pay the entire balance within the grace period and avoid the finance charge. If you are 1 or 2 days late, call the issuer of the credit card and explain your oversight. This approach does not always work, but the issuer might cancel the finance charges when you are that close.

TRUTH IN LENDING

Prior to the passage of truth-in-lending legislation as part of the Consumer Credit Protection Act of 1968, potential borrowers generally lacked information sufficient to enable them to directly compare and evaluate competing credit offers. The information they did receive was generally fragmented and lacked uniformity. But the passage of truth-in-lending legislation has greatly improved this situation.

Coverage   The act on **truth in lending** covers all credit transactions of $25,000 (or less) that are extended for personal, household, or agricultural purposes. Further, all mortgages on personal residences are covered, regardless of the amount borrowed. The legislation covers any individuals or organizations that regularly extend credit: banks, credit unions, savings and loan associations, retail and service charge accounts, credit card issuers, doctors, and dentists.

Disclosures   The Consumer Credit Protection Act requires lenders to disclose specific information about their loans. The principal disclosures are outlined in Exhibit 7-12. Typically, these disclosures are contained in the credit agreement you sign. So it is imperative that you read and understand the information contained in the agreement.

STRATEGY

When comparing competing credit alternatives, obtain complete information on every offer before you make that final choice. If you are unclear about the meaning or the intent of a lender's disclosure, ask for an explanation.

EXHIBIT 7-12

Disclosures a lender must make to a borrower
under truth-in-lending legislation.

REQUIRED DISCLOSURE	Type of Credit		
	HOME MORTGAGE*	CASH AND SALES LOANS	CHARGE ACCOUNTS AND CREDIT CARDS
Cost of credit			
Finance charge stated as:			
Annual percentage rate (APR)	Yes	Yes	Yes
A total dollar amount	Yes	Yes	No
Method of computing finance charge	No	No	Yes
Description of grace period	No	No	Yes
Finance charge refund if paid before maturity	Yes	Yes	No
Payments			
Number of payments	Yes	Yes	Yes
Amount of each payment	Yes	Yes	No
Due date of payments	Yes	Yes	Yes
Total amount of payments	Yes	Yes	No
Minimum payment	No	No	Yes
Penalties			
Fee for late payment	Yes	Yes	No
Fee if paid before maturity	Yes	Yes	No
Security			
Description of borrower's property pledged as security	Yes	Yes	Yes

*These are the required disclosures for the first mortagage a homeowner places on the residence. Chapter 11 will discuss mortgages in more detail.

QUALIFYING FOR CREDIT

Lenders use two broad criteria to decide whether credit should be extended: the borrower's ability to repay, and the borrower's willingness to repay.

Ability to Repay   When considering **ability to repay,** the lender compares the borrower's current debt obligations with his or her financial resources in order to decide whether the credit can be repaid. The top half of Exhibit 7-13 illustrates some typical questions used in this evaluation.

Willingness to Repay   Merely having the ability to repay does not necessarily mean that the credit will be repaid. Consequently, lenders review a borrower's payment record to see whether previous obligations were paid on time. The bottom half of Exhibit 7-13 illustrates some typical questions used in that review of the borrower's **willingness to repay.**

Applying for Credit

The best response you can give to a lender's questions, such as those in Exhibit 7-13, is a candid, complete answer. The lender will not be impressed by finding out later that you altered or omitted some important information. If you feel that a question is too personal or not relevant, tell the lender. When discussing your credit application, emphasize your strengths and be positive about your ability to handle the new credit. After all, if you

EXHIBIT 7-13

Evaluation of borrower's credit ability.

Ability to repay
1   Current income
    a   Regular income?
    b   Outside income?
    c   Length of present employment?
    d   Previous employment record?

2   Current obligations
    a   Present debts?
    b   Number of dependents?
    c   Unusually high expenses?
    d   Other fixed expenses?

3   Financial resources
    a   Savings account?
    b   Regular deposits in that account?
    c   Stocks or bonds?
    d   Homeownership?
    e   Property other than a home?

Willingness to repay
1   Current and previous credit transactions
    a   Were previous credit obligations repaid?
    b   If paid late, was lateness justified?
    c   Amount of prior credit experience?
    d   Prior lenders' opinion of borrower?

2   Payment record on recurring monthly expenses
    a   Payment record on rent, utilities, telephone, etc.?
    b   If there were delays, were they reasonable and justified?

do not believe you deserve the credit, the lender is not likely to believe you do, either. Before you apply for any form of credit, do your homework by answering the questions in Exhibit 7-13. In addition, decide in advance the amount, the maturity, and the reason why you need the credit.

Under the **Equal Credit Opportunity Act,** a lender must notify an applicant within 30 days as to whether or not the credit has been approved. So, once you complete the credit application, you can expect to receive an acceptance or a rejection in 30 days or less.

If Your Application is Rejected Should your credit application be rejected, the Equal Credit Opportunity Act requires a lender to furnish a written statement of the reason for rejection if you request that statement— and you should always request it! The reasons given to you can be very helpful in deciding your next course of action. Many lenders rely heavily on a report about the prospective borrower that is provided by a credit bureau. These bureaus specialize in gathering information on the payment records, credit history, and financial background of individuals. If a lender rejected your credit application on account of a credit bureau report, you must be told the name and address of that bureau.

The reasons that the lender supplies to justify the rejection are a good starting point to reevaluate your situation. Ask yourself: "Was the refusal unwarranted? If there is indeed a weakness or shortcoming in my ability to repay, how can I correct it? Are there specific steps I should take to improve my present 'ability to pay' image?" Depending on your answers, you may have several options. The first is to try a different lender. One lender's refusal should not discourage you from trying another. By going to another lender, you can learn for sure if your record has a serious weakness that needs to be corrected.

Credit Rights for Women

Before the Equal Credit Opportunity Act was passed, unmarried women who applied for credit had to meet higher standards than men applying for the same credit. Married women frequently found they could obtain credit only if it was "guaranteed" by their husbands. And some lenders refused even to consider a wife's income when judging a couple's credit worthiness. Married women who suddenly found themselves divorced, widowed, or abandoned had no credit record with which to face reluctant lenders. The Equal Credit Opportunity Act does not guarantee a woman that her credit application will be approved. But it attempts to ensure that she will receive the same credit rights as any male in the same situation.

Applying for Credit A lender cannot reject a woman's credit application simply because she is a woman or because she is married. Furthermore, lenders must use the same qualifying standards to judge male and female credit applicants. When a married woman applies for credit, she does not have to disclose her husband's income; she doesn't even have to disclose the fact that she is married unless her husband's income is the basis for granting the credit or unless both mates plan to sign the loan agreement. An exception is a woman living in a community property state such as California. In those states, a lender can require these disclosures.

As one of the contributors to a two-income household, a working woman should not hesitate to apply for credit in her own name. Too often, couples make all credit applications under only the man's name. If a particular credit application is primarily for the woman's use, she should make the application. In that way, she is assured of establishing her own credit record and keeping her credit history current.

A Woman's Income   When judging credit worthiness on a couple's application, lenders must consider both the woman's and the man's income. And that stipulation holds regardless of whether the woman works full-time or part-time. Further, lenders cannot ask a couple how many children they have or if they plan to have children.

When a woman is separated, widowed, or divorced, the lender must consider whatever income she receives from child support, alimony, or Social Security if she lists these as sources of income. Again, the lender is under no obligation to approve the credit application. But the lender cannot just summarily reject a woman's application because she lists one or more of these sources as contributing to her income.

Personal Credit History   A married woman should make certain she has a credit history in her own name. One way that she can do so is to ask a creditor to report credit information on all credit accounts in both her own and her husband's name. And make certain you use your legal name. For example, when Becky Smith married Fred Bear, she could elect to use Becky Bear, Becky Smith Bear, or a number of other combinations. But for business and legal purposes, she is not Mrs. Fred Bear.

Once a woman has established a good credit history, she should keep that history current. Should she marry, she will want to inform her creditors if she changes her name, but there is no special reason to close her present credit accounts.

STRATEGY

A married woman should establish her own credit history. She can accomplish this by applying for credit on her own record, or at least by making sure that the information on all credit applications that she and her husband complete is reported in her own credit record.

CONSUMER CREDIT FILES

Every individual who has used credit, or applied for it, probably has a personal data file at a local credit bureau. Typically, that file contains data on previous credit experience, payment record, employment, lawsuits, arrests, and personal bankruptcies.

Fair Credit Reporting Act

The **Fair Credit Reporting Act** was enacted to protect the consumer from possible personal damage resulting from misleading credit information. It was directed toward two areas. First, the Fair Credit Reporting Act was intended to protect the individual against the circulation of inaccurate or incomplete information. Second, it established a series of procedures you can use to correct or remove biased or bogus data from your file at the credit bureau.

Your Rights If you are denied credit, or if your cost of credit was increased because a lender was influenced unfavorably by information in a credit report, the lender must disclose the name of the credit bureau that compiled that report. You can then request an interview with a representative of the bureau in order to learn the substance of the information in your file. A bureau representative must discuss the contents of the file and must reveal the bureau's sources except for certain personal interviews. In addition, the bureau must provide a list of organizations and people who have received your credit report during the past 6 months.

Incorrect Information If the information is incorrect or incomplete, you can request that the bureau reinvestigate the item. If the alleged information cannot be verified, it must be removed from your file. In addition, you can ask the bureau to send a correction to everyone who has received a credit report during the last 6 months; there is no charge for this service.

Disputed Information When there is disputed information that cannot be resolved, you can request that your version be placed in the file. Future credit reports must contain your version of the dispute. For a nominal fee, you can request that the credit bureau send copies of your version to anyone who has recently received your credit report.

Obsolete Information In general, all adverse information is considered obsolete after 7 years and therefore must be deleted at that time. Bankruptcy information, however, can be retained for 14 years.

Fees If a credit bureau's report was the basis on which you were denied credit, the bureau must review your file with you, free of charge. But the review request must be made within 30 days of the denial. Even if you have not been refused credit, you can still review your file for a nominal fee: typically, from $15 to $25.

Joint Credit Accounts Used by Both the Man and the Woman

The Equal Credit Opportunity Act places special reporting requirements on credit accounts used jointly by a man and a woman. For joint credit accounts opened after June 1, 1977, all credit information must be reported in both the woman's and the man's credit file. Prior to the passage of the act, only the man had a credit file. Thus, the woman was placed at a disadvantage if the man died or they separated. Even when the woman may have provided a significant part of the family's income and therefore its credit rating, she often found herself without any credit record. Therefore, she might face restarting as a first-time credit applicant with the problems that such an application entails. But that is now unlikely because the joint credit accounts are reported in both names.

OVEREXTENDED WITH CREDIT

Recently, a sharp increase has occurred in the number of people who have become grossly **overextended with credit.** (They borrowed too much and are at or beyond their debt limits.) For many of these people, the wide availability of credit was just too enticing. They never stopped and asked themselves how they were going to make the payments on the new credit they were considering. They just shrugged off that question by telling themselves that the money would come from somewhere. Unfortunately, by the time they realized the full implications of the payment load, they were so overextended that only a drastic change could correct the problem.

Overextended? The questions shown in Exhibit 7-14 can provide an early warning signal of impending credit problems. *"Yes"* responses to five or six questions suggest that you may be approaching the point where you are using too much credit.

Correction and Retrenchment

Before any correction plan can succeed, you must want to correct the problem.

Self-Study and Evaluation Your first step is to stop using any more credit; you simply cannot borrow your way out of debt. Next, do a thorough study of your current debts, together with their repayment schedules. If you do not have a detailed budget, make one immediately. It should be an

EXHIBIT 7-14

CHAPTER 7

207

CREDIT: HOW TO
GET IT AND HOW
TO USE IT

Early warning signals: If the majority of answers
are "yes," you may be heading for credit
problems.

	(YES)	(NO)
Savings		
1 Have your cash reserves decreased sharply?	( )	( )
2 Are you forced to draw on your savings each month?	( )	( )
3 Do you rarely make deposits toward your savings?	( )	( )
Monthly payments		
1 Do you make only the minimum payment on credit cards?	( )	( )
2 Has your bill paying slowed?	( )	( )
3 Are any of your debts delinquent?	( )	( )
4 Do you need overtime or an extra job to make ends meet?	( )	( )
5 Are you unclear about where your money goes?	( )	( )
6 Are you always short of money before payday?	( )	( )
7 Do you need the overdraft provision on your checking account each month?	( )	( )
Use of credit		
1 Do you have many charge accounts and other debts?	( )	( )
2 Are you uncertain as to how much you owe?	( )	( )
3 Have you started receiving past due notices?	( )	( )
4 Do you have any debt consolidation loans?	( )	( )

emergency budget that reduces all nonessential expenditures to a minimum. You will then know how much money you have available for debt payments.

Deciding Who Should Be Paid   Exhibit 7-15 summarizes some positive and negative factors that we feel should be considered when deciding which payments to make. We have ranked the payments, suggesting which ones can be put off temporarily or paid in partial amounts. Items heading the list command first priority when you are making payments. These you *must* pay when due and usually in the full amount. Items further down the list can be deferred, but there may be a direct cost from a finance charge and also indirect cost of an unfavorable comment entered in your credit record. Should there be enough money to make more than the minimum payments, concentrate on repaying those debts with the highest APR finance charge. Once you have decided on a course of action, contact each creditor and explain your plan. A well-documented plan can convince your creditors that you recognize the seriousness of your situation and that you intend to correct it.

EXHIBIT 7-15

Selecting who should be repaid when your credit is overextended.

	Factors to Consider When Establishing Order for Paying Creditors	
CREDITOR	POSITIVE FACTORS	NEGATIVE FACTORS
Landlord	May not report slow payment to credit bureau	May move rapidly to evict slow-paying tenants Eviction may mean you have no place to live
Mortgage lenders	May delay collection effort 30 days or more May allow a payment deferral of several months May not immediately report slow payment to credit bureau	May damage your relationship with what is a long-term lender Can repossess house, but it may take several months May evict you, which can be traumatic
Utilities: electric, gas, and telephone	Typically allow 30 to 60 days past due date with little penalty Frequently make no finance charge on late payment	May disconnect utilities, a major inconvenience Usually make reasonably thorough collection effort, which can be annoying
Automobile, furniture, and appliance dealers	Frequently will negotiate a new payment schedule with extended maturity	May repossess car, furniture, or other assets pledged as security for loan May charge sizable late-payment fee Late payment immediately reported to credit bureau
Credit card lenders	Will be appeased by minimum payment May accept nonpayment for several months	Make very thorough collection effort, which is very annoying Have a very high finance charge: 18 % APR Report late payment immediately to credit bureau
Charge account lenders	May not start collection effort for 30 days or more May accept several months of nonpayment Make relatively mild initial collection effort, and therefore tolerable	Begin finance charge immediately: 12 to 18% APR Slow payment may be reported to credit bureau After several months, debt collection agency may begin aggressive collection effort
Doctors, dentists, hospitals	May not start collection effort for 30 days or more Typically make no finance charge on late payments Collection effort is usually mild	May impair relationship with a professional on whom you rely

Debt Consolidation Loan   The purpose of a **debt consolidation loan** is to provide money that the borrower can use to repay existing debts that are past due. Some lenders advertise a debt consolidation loan as if it were the final solution to all debt problems. They suggest, "Consolidate all your debt payments into a single loan payment, and the problem disappears." But does it? We think not. At best, you obtain breathing space to work out a long-term solution. But the cost is high: APRs of 20 to 30 percent are common. And you still have to repay that loan. If you use this source, you should absolutely not use additional credit until the consolidation loan is totally repaid.

STRATEGY

You should consider a debt consolidation loan only when it is part of a long-range plan to eliminate your overuse of credit. And the maturity on any consolidation loan should be as short as your emergency budget will allow.

Nonprofit Credit Counseling   Many medium- to large-sized cities have a **nonprofit credit counseling agency** that assists people with credit problems. The fee is nominal, generally less than $30. The agency works with the individual to design a repayment plan. If the counselors feel that they cannot help, they tell the person. Their role is strictly advisory; they do not negotiate with the individual's creditors. The individual must contact the creditors and explain the plan. Your local United Fund, Legal Aid Society, or Community Chest can tell you whether there is a credit counseling agency in your area.

Debt Consolidators   **Debt consolidators** are in business to make a profit, and their fees reflect this goal. They do not advance money to pay off their customers' debts. Rather, they negotiate a repayment schedule between the customer and the creditors. We strongly recommend that you avoid this group. They typically charge the customer a fee equal to 10 or 20 percent of the customer's debts. Thus, if a person's debts were $5000, the fee could easily run from $500 to $1000. That is astounding, considering the little they do for the customer. And their reputation is generally poor among creditors. If you could afford that fee, you would do better by using it to pay off your debts.

Debt Collection Agencies

The Fair Debt Collection Practices Act places considerable restrictions on the practices of **debt collection agencies.** These agencies specialize in collecting past due payments from individuals. Typically, a lender will turn a borrower's account over to one of these agencies when the lender's efforts at collecting the payments on the account have been unsuccessful. Generally, the agency's fee is a percentage of the amount it collects from the borrower. So it has a vested interest in "encouraging" prompt payment from the borrower. The past abuses and highly questionable tactics of these agencies were major reasons for the Fair Debt Collection Practices Act.

Collectors cannot call at unusual hours, use deceptive practices to force payment, make threats, or use abusive language. Further, the act limits what they can discuss about your debts with outside parties such as your neighbors, employer, or other creditors. Even within these limits, the collection efforts of an aggressive agency can be highly discomforting or even intolerable for some debtors. And there are still a number of unscrupulous operators who will readily step beyond the limitations of the law in pursuit of a collection. The restrictions imposed by the Fair Debt Collection Act do not apply to creditors who operate their own collection agencies.

STRATEGY

By keeping your credit usage within safe limits, you will avoid the highly irritating, and sometimes questionable, practices of debt collection agencies.

Bankruptcy Proceedings: A Last Resort

Individuals who are unable to work out a solution to their problems from overextended credit should consider seeking protection under the Federal Bankruptcy Act. We consider this step to be a last resort. The two courses of action under the act are the Wage Earner Plan (if the borrower qualifies) and straight bankruptcy.

Wage Earner Plan   The purpose of the **Wage Earner Plan** is to allow the individual to pay off part, or all, the credit obligations from future income. Once a Wage Earner Plan is accepted, the individual is protected from (1) lawsuits, (2) creditors who might attempt to collect the payment directly from the person's wages by contacting his or her employer, (3) physical repossession of property—car, furniture, appliance—that the borrower pledged as security for the loan, and (4) other legal actions that creditors might institute to collect what is due them. To qualify for the plan, you must show that you can set aside 20 to 30 percent of your disposable income to repay your credit obligations. Furthermore, the amount set aside from income to pay off the debts has to be sufficiently large so that those debts can be repaid in full within a reasonable period. Generally, a majority of your creditors must accept the plan; most will do so, since a viable plan offers at least some prospect of being repaid. Once the court accepts the plan, each pay period the individual will pay the amount agreed on to a court-appointed trustee; the trustee distributes that amount to the various creditors.

The cost of establishing a Wage Earner Plan can be sizable. Depending on the amount owed, the combination of court costs and attorney's and trustee's fees can easily exceed $1500.

STRATEGY

Individuals who have difficulty devising a debt repayment plan, or who lack the will power to stick to their own plan, should consider the Wage Earner

Plan. The combination of detailed structuring, court supervision, and high implementation cost may be enough to produce results with such a plan.

Straight Bankruptcy **Straight bankruptcy** is not so much a solution as an end to your debt obligations. Bankruptcy is generally advised when an individual's credit difficulties are so severe that no viable repayment plan can be devised. For example, the amount owed may be so large that even if the person could set aside 30 percent of each month's wages or salary to repay the debts, repaying all the debts would take 10 or more years. Or possibly the person's income has declined drastically, so any amount set aside for debt payments cannot begin to repay the large amounts that the person owes. With straight bankruptcy, the debtor's assets (except for certain items exempted under federal and state regulations) are sold by the court-appointed trustee. All money received from the sale is then distributed to creditors; typically, a creditor receives much less than the full amount owed. The unpaid portion of all debts is then canceled as part of the bankruptcy proceedings. Certain debts and other obligations are not canceled under bankruptcy; examples include such things as child support, alimony, most unpaid taxes, fines or penalties owed to governmental units, and education loans. Another limitation is that a person can file for bankruptcy only once every 6 years. Thus, if Borris Bumbler goes through bankruptcy in 1984, he cannot file for bankruptcy again until 1990. Therefore, if Borris immediately goes out and again overuses credit, he cannot use bankruptcy for at least 6 years, and his new indebtedness may mean a long stretch of telephone calls, letters, and other collection efforts from Borris's lenders.

If you decide that this drastic step is warranted, contact an attorney for advice and for complete details on what is required.

SUMMARY

1   Borrowing increases your immediate purchasing power but simultaneously reduces your future purchasing power.

2   The finance charge includes all costs of borrowing: interest, collection costs, record keeping, and required insurance.

3   Longer maturity periods mean lower monthly payments, but the total finance charge rises sharply.

4   To decide whether or not to use credit, compare the increase in today's purchasing power versus the reduction in future purchasing power.

5   Your budget should help you decide whether you are nearing your debt limit. A budget can also answer the question: Can I make the payment on the new consumer credit that I am considering?

6   A borrower should shop for credit the same as for any other service.

7   You should compare the APRs on competing credit offers to decide which has the lowest cost.

8   The finance charge on credit card accounts is computed by one of three techniques: previous balance, average daily balance, and adjusted balance.

9   Most credit card accounts provide a grace period with no finance charge.

10   Truth-in-lending legislation requires that lenders disclose information on the cost of credit, the required payments, and the penalties.

11   Lenders evaluate the credit worthiness of an individual by using two criteria: ability to repay, and willingness to repay.

12   The Equal Credit Opportunity Act attempts to ensure that women receive the same credit treatment as men.

13   If your credit file contains incorrect or unsupportable information, you can force the credit bureau to remove it. If it contains disputed information, you can require that the agency include your version of the disputed item.

14   A thorough study and evaluation of your personal finances is an important first step in correcting an overuse of credit.

REVIEW YOUR UNDERSTANDING OF

Finance charge
Repayment terms
Maturity
Credit: the cost-benefit trade-off
Upper debt limit: a personal budget
Annual percentage rate (APR)
Finance charge computation
   Precomputed finance charge
   Simple interest
Rule of 78
Billing cycle
   Billing or closing date
   Due date
Grace period
Finance charge computation
   Previous balance

Average daily balance
Adjusted balance
Truth in lending
Ability to repay
Willingness to repay
Equal Credit Opportunity Act
Fair Credit Reporting Act
Overextended with credit
Debt consolidation loan
Nonprofit credit counseling
Debt consolidators
Debt collection agencies
Bankruptcy
   Wage Earner Plan
   Straight bankruptcy

DISCUSSION QUESTIONS

1   How would you answer the criticism that borrowing encourages you to live beyond your means? Do you agree that borrowing is fraught with risks of eventual bankruptcy? Why or why not?

2   What types of items do you feel you should buy and pay for by borrowing and repaying over a long period? Which items do you feel least qualify for this kind of borrowing?

3   Briefly describe how a budget can be used to decide whether an individual is nearing his or her debt limit. What are the strengths of using a budget to set an upper debt limit?

4   Comment on the statement, "Extending the repayment period expands your debt capacity."

5   Under what situation can income taxes reduce the cost of borrowing? Why? Does the federal income tax system subsidize borrowing? Which taxpayers receive the largest subsidy—those with high marginal tax rates or low marginal tax rates? When do taxes have no effect on borrowing costs?

6   What is the difference between calculating the finance charge by using the simple interest method and the precomputed method? Under what circumstance might simple interest provide an advantage? Why?

7   What causes the cost differential between borrowing the money to purchase a $2000 item immediately and taking 1 year to save the necessary $2000 to buy the same item? Do income taxes change that cost differential? Why or why not? If the price of the item is expected to rise during the next 12 months, how will the anticipated increase affect the cost differential?

8   Some people argue that the federal income tax system encourages the use of credit, while at the same time it discourages saving. What evidence can you offer to support this point?

9   What is the principal difference between using the average daily balance and the adjusted balance techniques in the computation of the finance charge on a credit card account? As a borrower, which would you prefer? Why?

10   Give an example of how the grace period on a credit card works. How can you make use of the grace period? How can you get the maximum benefit from it?

11   What benefits do you see in the truth-in-lending legislation? How can the consumer make maximum use of the disclosures?

12   What special laws have been enacted to ensure the rights of women to obtain credit? What reasons and changes likely motivated the enactment of these laws?

13   Discuss what your rights are under the Fair Credit Reporting Act if you find that inaccurate or obsolete information is in your credit file.

14   What are some early warning signs that you may have taken on too much credit? Do you think some indicators are more valid than others? Why?

15   What is the principal difference between the Wage Earner Plan and straight bankruptcy? Can you give a circumstance where each would be appropriate? What advantages might a Wage Earner Plan have over a debtor's own personal repayment plan? Might there be any disadvantages?

PROBLEMS

7-1   Ralph Zuggo is considering two credit options to finance $2000 worth of new furniture for his apartment. The furniture dealer has offered a 24-month loan with a 24 percent APR. Ralph's credit union has offered a 24-month loan with a 12 percent APR. When Ralph asked about the difference, the dealer suggested it probably was not a good comparison. Besides, the monthly payments differed by only slightly more than $10.

a   Is the APR comparison valid?

b   What is the monthly payment for each loan?

c   How much more will Ralph have to pay each month with the dealer's loan than with the credit union's loan? How much more will Ralph pay over the total life of the dealer's loans?

d   Which type of loan would you recommend?

7-2   Listed on the following page are partial details on loan offers from three different lenders:

	LENDER X	LENDER Y	LENDER Z
Amount of cash from loan	$2000.00	$2000.00	$3000.00
Monthly loan payment	$94.14	$99.84	$137.04
Number of months	24	24	24

a What is the APR for each loan (*Hint:* Exhibit 7-8 may be helpful.)

b Would it be correct to compare the APR among the three loans?

c Which loan would you recommend?

7-3 Burton Swift plans to repay her 12-month, $2000 cash loan at the end of 4 months. The loan specifies that refunds are made using the rule of 78.

a What portion of the loan's original $156 finance charge will she receive?

b Since Burton has had the loan for one-third of its original maturity—4 months out of 12 months—why is her refund less than two-thirds of the original fee?

7-4 Susan Banks is considering two different $4000 loans for her new car: (*a*) a 36-month loan with an APR of 18 percent, and (*b*) a 60-month loan with an APR of 18 percent. The lender has stressed how much "easier" the payments would be on the loan with the longer repayment period.

a What are the monthly payments on the respective loans?

b Is the 60-month loan cheaper?

c If Susan can make the payments on either loan, which would you recommend she take? Why?

7-5 Clyde Padro would like to compare the following two purchase alternatives on a $2000 rug for his apartment.

1 Purchase immediately with a $2000, 12-month loan at 12 percent APR.

2 Save the money over the next 12 months in his 6 percent credit union account. That requires a $162.13 deposit at the end of each month so that the total deposits plus accumulated interest will equal $2000 at the end of the twelfth month

Clyde's current marginal tax rate is 40 percent, and his present itemized deductions exceed the zero bracket amount.

a If income taxes are ignored, what is the cost differential between options **1** and **2**? What is the cost differential between **1** and **2** when taxes are considered?

b Which would you recommend? Why?

c Without working through a detailed solution, how would that differential change if his tax rate declined to 30 percent?

7-6   Lee Chang has received offers from three car dealers for a new Piggo sport coupé.

CHAPTER 7

215

CREDIT: HOW TO
GET IT AND HOW
TO USE IT

	DEALER A	DEALER B	DEALER C
Cash price	$9,000.00	$10,000.00	$11,000.00
Credit option monthly payment	$293.40	$278.30	$289.64
Number of payments	48	48	48

All three dealer prices are for the same car model equipped in a similar manner. And Lee anticipates that each dealer will provide comparable service.

a   If Lee were buying the car outright with cash, which dealer should he choose?

b   If Lee selects the credit option, which dealer should be his choice? Why?

c   What is the APR quoted by each dealer? (*Hint*: Exhibit 7-8 may help.)

d   Can the APRs be compared for the three credit alternatives? Which option has the most attractive APR? Why?

CASE PROBLEM

Ralph and Grazela Smith are currently evaluating whether they should buy a $4000 camping trailer. Although they have decided that they would like the trailer, they still have reservations about whether their outstanding debts are becoming excessive. The Smiths have no children and are both working full time.

Their combined annual available income is $18,600 ($1,550 monthly). Their average monthly expenses are: rent, $265; utilities, $60; food, $250; clothing, $105; transportation (excluding their car loan payment), $200; entertainment, $100; donations, $40; insurance premiums, $30; and savings, $100.

Their present monthly debt payments include (the months remaining to the loan's maturity are shown in parentheses): car payment (30), $200; furniture (20), $100; and television and stereo (35), $70. Since their savings balance is limited, they plan to finance $3645 of the trailer's $4000 cost. The dealer has offered a 36-month sales loan of $3645 that carries an APR of 24 percent; it requires monthly payments of $143.

1   Do you think they should take on this new debt? Would you recommend any alternatives?

2   How can the Smiths use their present balance sheet to analyze the desirability of the new loan? When including the trailer as a possible asset, what dollar amount should the Smiths use to record the trailer? Why might it be less than $4000?

3   Prepare a brief budget for the Smiths to see whether they are nearing their upper debt limit. What is your conclusion?

4   Basing your judgment on what you learned from their budget, what would you recommend that the Smiths do? Do you think that the new debt will fit into their budget? Why?

5   One of Ralph's friends has suggested a debt consolidation loan to clean up their old debts. He maintains that the longer maturity on that loan will ease their present payment burden and permit them to take on the new debt. What are the strengths and weaknesses in that argument?

CHAPTER 8

SOURCES OF CONSUMER CREDIT

**AFTER COMPLETING THIS CHAPTER
YOU WILL HAVE LEARNED**

What a *consumer cash loan* is and where to get this kind of loan

What makes a *secured loan* different from an *unsecured loan*

How to *evaluate the advantages and disadvantages* of different types of *cash loans* and decide which loan best meets your needs

What a *consumer sales loan* is

How to evaluate the *life insurance* and *disability insurance* that lenders try to sell to borrowers

What *open-ended consumer credit* is

The similarities and differences between the major types of *credit card accounts*

How to design a *personal financial plan* that effectively uses the potential *benefits* from *credit cards* and *charge accounts*

How to avoid the potential *problems* and *pitfalls* of using *credit cards* and *charge accounts*

What to do if you *lose your credit card*

Consumer credit encompasses all the dif-

ferent types of credit that consumers use to finance their purchases of goods and services. The use of credit by consumers has increased dramatically during the past decade. That rapid growth can be attributed to several factors.

First, many consumers have changed their attitude toward the use of credit. In the past, many people felt that they should use credit sparingly and then only for emergencies or for purchasing life's necessities when it just was impossible to wait until they could save sufficient money to pay cash. Gradually that attitude has been changing. Most consumers no longer feel that using credit is a clear signal of inept management of their personal finances. At the same time, people broadened the range of those goods and services they felt to be qualified as potential credit purchases. Life's necessities remained the central focus, but the range widened to include those "extra" goods and services that we have begun to accept as fundamental parts of our generally high standard of living. The widespread use of credit cards and charge accounts has added another dimension to credit: the convenience aspect. Many consumers now consider these credit sources a substitute for paying cash for each purchase. The net effect of the changes is that consumers have increased their willingness to use consumer credit.

Still, to complete the growth picture, we needed the other side: lenders who were willing to extend the credit to consumers who wanted to use it. Some lenders, such as commercial banks and savings and loan associations that had previously limited their volume of consumer credit, greatly expanded their consumer credit offerings. Part of their expansion was through the promotion and expansion of consumer cash and sales loans, which they had traditionally offered but for which they had never aggressively recruited potential borrowers. The balance of the expansion was through the development of new forms of consumer credit, such as bank credit cards and automatic overdrafts on checking accounts.

This chapter examines three principal categories of consumer credit: consumer cash loans, consumer sales loans, and open-ended consumer credit.

CONSUMER CASH LOANS

With a **consumer cash loan,** the borrower receives cash from the loan. While the borrower may later spend the cash for a particular good or service, that purchase is not a prerequisite for granting the loan. Cash loans are available in amounts of as little as $10 or as much as $10,000 and more. Maturities can be as short as a few days or as long as 5 years. Generally, loans in very small amounts or with very short maturities have the highest APR. The APRs on some cash loans can be as low as 8 percent, yet can exceed 30 percent on others. Nearly all consumer cash loans must be repaid by equal monthly payments spread evenly over the time the loan is outstanding.

Cash loans can be either secured or unsecured, depending on the amount and the borrower's credit record. The difference between a secured and an unsecured loan centers on what guarantees the repayment promise.

Secured Loan A **secured loan** requires two things: (1) the borrower's written promise to repay, and (2) the pledge of some of the borrower's property or the added repayment promise of another person—a cosigner. A **cosigner** is a person who agreed to repay the lender should the borrower fail to repay the loan. The purpose of this second repayment provision is to give additional assurance to the lender that the loan will be repaid. The loan is secured by this second repayment option.

Property that can be pledged as security on a loan can be shares of common stock or a government bond, or it may be the borrower's personal property, such as a car, household furniture, a boat, or similar personal property. Normally, the value of the collateral must equal or exceed the loan amount. Often, the property securing the loan is the item the borrower plans to buy with the loan proceeds.

Regardless of the property or the cosigner, the borrower's ability and willingness to repay are still the principal criteria the lender uses in deciding whether to grant the loan.

If the borrower fails to repay the loan, the lender can take possession of the borrower's property as complete or partial payment of the loan. Where there is a cosigner, the lender will initiate action against the cosigner in

WE DON'T HAVE THE FACILITIES TO STORE YOUR FIRST BORN EVEN IF WE WOULD ACCEPT HIM AS COLLATERAL FOR YOUR HOME IMPROVEMENT LOAN.

order to force payment. A lender will insist the loan be secured by property or a cosigner when the amount is large or when the borrower's credit record is limited or questionable.

A secured loan exposes the borrower to the possibility that the property will be taken or that the cosigner will be forced to repay the loan.

Unsecured Loan   The lender's only repayment assurance behind an **unsecured loan** is the borrower's promise. Neither the pledging of property nor the promise of a cosigner is required. The borrower's ability and willingness to repay are the lender's sole assurance. Unsecured loans are typical when the amount is small or when the borrower's credit record is top grade and well established.

STRATEGY

A secured loan is probably the best choice in most cases because its APR should be lower than the APR on an unsecured loan. If the APRs are identical, take the unsecured loan.

Automatic Overdraft or Advance   An **automatic overdraft** or **advance** is merely a special variation of a consumer cash loan. Its major distinguishing feature is the way it operates. For customers who have checking, NOW, or share draft accounts, many lenders now offer an automatic overdraft or advance on one of those accounts. Customers who want an overdraft loan on their account normally complete a credit application which is then submitted for the lender's approval. Lenders typically use the same general criteria—ability to pay and willingness to pay—that they use for other types of consumer credit to decide whether they will approve the customer's overdraft application.

Depending on the customer's credit record, lenders usually agree to cover any overdraft from $100 to $5000. The overdraft "ceiling" that the lender places on a customer's account is determined by the customer's credit record. This kind of borrowing is called "automatic" because once the ceiling is approved, the customer can initiate a credit transaction—get a cash loan—by writing a check without notifying the lender that the overdraft is being used. An overdraft or advance is usually unsecured.

To get the overdraft feature, you do not pay an additional application fee or maintenance charge. But for any overdraft you use, there is a finance charge based on the amount of the overdraft—the loan—and the number of days for which it is outstanding. This finance charge is calculated in the same way as the simple interest finance charge illustrated in Exhibit 7-6 of Chapter 7.

As a review, assume that we have a $200 overdraft or advance that charges an APR of 12 percent on any amount borrowed, and that the overdraft has been outstanding for 21 days. Converting that 12 percent to a daily finance rate gives:

0.0329%	= 12 %		÷ 365 days
⬆	⬆		⬆
Daily finance rate	= Annual finance rate (APR)	÷	Number of days (Lender may use 360)

For the 21 days, our finance charge is:

$1.38	= $200	× 0.000329	× 21 days
⬆	⬆	⬆	⬆
Total finance charge	= Amount of the overdraft	× Daily finance rate (decimal)	× Days overdraft was outstanding

Most lenders charge an APR of 12 to 18 percent on overdrafts, although some charge as much as 24 percent.

The amount of the overdraft determines the amount that the lender requires to repay the overdraft. Most lenders set your required monthly payments so that you will repay the entire amount in 12 to 24 months. The customer can, of course, make much larger payments to repay the entire amount in as short a time as a few days.

The mechanics of the repayment take one of two forms: Either the repayment is automatically deducted from the customer's next deposit to the account, or the customer mails in a payment and specifically identifies it as a payment on the advance. Of the two forms, the first form is not only more convenient, it also eliminates the possibility of the borrower's forgetting the payment and thus saves on the finance charge.

With some overdraft checking accounts, the lender advances just enough cash to cover the overdraft in the customer's account. On other overdraft accounts, however, the lender provides an advance of even $100 multiples. Thus, a $205 overdraft will trigger a $300 advance to the account. Of course, the finance charge is based on $300. With the first type of overdraft account, the finance charge will be based on just the required $205 advance. Clearly, an overdraft account that advances the exact amount needed is more desirable than one using $100 multiples.

STRATEGY

When considering an automatic overdraft account, try to find one that advances only the overdraft and automatically uses the next deposit to your checking account to repay all, or part, of the advance.

Advantages and Disadvantages   The major advantages of an automatic overdraft are its convenience and flexibility. Its convenience arises because the customer (borrower) initiates the loan and also sets the repayment. And because that repayment can range from a few days to a few months, it is flexible. Further flexibility is provided by the feature allowing the customer to borrow any amount from a few dollars right up to his or her approved maximum limit. Combine these features and the overdraft loan makes an ideal short-term cash reserve. Should you find yourself short on dollars in some particular month, drawing on the overdraft can tide you over. Or should you need the money for a longer period, you can use the overdraft as a temporary borrowing source until you obtain a traditional consumer cash loan. Since most lenders do not charge a fee to obtain the overdraft, you pay for only the time and dollar amount that you borrow. Typically, the APR on overdrafts is competitive with other short-term cash loans.

The very flexibility and convenience that make an overdraft desirable can, for some people, be its major disadvantage, however. Some borrowers overuse the overdraft to the point that they become dependent upon it to carry them through to their next paycheck. For some, it becomes a permanent debt that never is repaid. Their unpaid balance gradually becomes larger and larger, as they never completely repay the previous advance before drawing another. They use the overdraft to cover that part of their spending that exceeds their available income. If you find your use of an overdraft beginning to follow this pattern, immediately stop drawing further advances. And once the balance is repaid, you should cancel your overdraft privilege.

STRATEGY

Properly used, an automatic overdraft provides a highly convenient, flexible short-term source of cash.

MAJOR SOURCES OF CONSUMER CASH LOANS

The major sources of consumer cash loans are summarized in Exhibit 8-1. For each source, it shows the range of APRs, the range of maturities, the range of available loan amounts, and whether loans must be secured or can be unsecured. The next section briefly discusses each type of lender; if one type has any special features or limitations, we will point them out.

Commercial Banks: Direct Consumer Lending

Some people have the notion that commercial banks lend only to upper-income wage earners. This is simply not true. Commercial banks have moved aggressively into the consumer-lending area, and most are ready to serve any credit-worthy consumer.

Mutual Savings Banks: Direct Consumer Lending

Many mutual savings banks used to offer only a narrow range of financial services to their customers. That range is broadening as mutual savings banks move aggressively to provide their customers with all the financial services that they expect from a one-stop personal finance center. But since such banks are concentrated in the New England and Mid-Atlantic states, you may not have one in your area.

Savings and Loan Associations: Direct Consumer Lending

Traditionally, savings and loan associations (usually referred to as S&Ls) have been required to restrict their consumer lending to cash loans that are secured by an equal amount in the borrower's savings account. Many S&Ls, however, wanted to expand their range of lending options to include more consumer credit alternatives, such as credit cards, overdrafts on a NOW account, and all types of consumer cash loans. They quite convincingly argued that they needed these broader lending powers in the consumer-credit area to enable them to become one-stop personal finance centers. Their efforts have recently been successful.

Currently, all federally chartered S&Ls have the authority to offer consumer cash loans as well as overdrafts on their NOW accounts if they have them. Generally, you can identify a federally chartered S&L by the use of the word "federal" in its name: e.g., First Federal Savings. Consumer lending by S&Ls that are chartered by the states is more mixed. Most states have authorized consumer lending, but exactly what type of loans each state allows its state-chartered S&Ls varies.

When shopping for a consumer cash loan or an overdraft account, do check with the S&Ls in your area. But don't be surprised if some S&Ls do

EXHIBIT 8-1

Summary of major sources for consumer cash loans.

SOURCE	FINANCE CHARGE APR	AVAILABLE MATURITIES	RANGE OF LOAN AMOUNTS	LOANS AVAILABLE: SECURED (S), UNSECURED (US), AND OVERDRAFT (OD)
Commercial bank	10– 22%	1 month– 5 years	$ 100– $10,000*	S US OD
Mutual savings bank	8– 20%	1 month– 5 years	$ 100– $10,000*	S US OD
Savings and loan	8– 20%	1 month– 5 years	$ 100– $10,000*	S US OD
Credit union	9– 20%	1 month– 5 years	$ 100– $10,000*	S US OD
Consumer finance company	18– 42%	1 month– 3 years†	$ 50– $ 2,000‡	S US
Second mortgage	12– 30%	6 months– 10 years	$ 1,000– $10,000	S
Life insurance	5– 10%	Flexible§	Set by§ policy	S
Loan sharks et al.	Devastating	Rarely long enough to repay	Negotiable	S (but their idea of security can be bruising)

*Larger amounts may be available if the borrower qualifies.
†Maximum maturity varies according to the regulations of the different states.
‡Maximum loan amounts are higher when state regulations permit.
§Loan has no set repayment schedule. The amount available usually equals the policy's cash value.

not offer these loans. Federally chartered S&Ls have had this authority only since 1980. To date, some S&Ls have elected not to participate in consumer lending.

Credit Union: Direct Consumer Lending

A credit union is a specialized financial institution that provides accounts (usually called "share accounts") in which its members can save their money. It also offers share draft accounts that members can use to make payments. And it lends money to its members. Only members can use the credit union, and to be a member you must share some "common bond" with the other members.

Consumer Finance Companies

Consumer finance companies are not one-stop personal finance centers; they limit their activities solely to lending money to individuals. And they are usually willing to lend money to people who ordinarily would not meet a bank's qualifications for borrowing money. The catch is that, while finance companies will lend money to people who are not able to borrow from a bank, they require borrowers to pay a higher finance charge.

Typically, finance companies will extend credit to people with poor credit records who cannot borrow from other lenders. Because they specialize in weaker borrowers, their collection efforts must be greater and their losses on uncollected loans are higher. Both problems boost their operating cost, which is then reflected in their higher finance charge.

Most states heavily regulate and control the lending activities of consumer finance companies. State laws set the maximum amount that these companies can lend, although some states are leaving this amount up to each company. State laws also regulate the maximum finance charge that a finance company can charge on a loan. Some states also specify a maximum maturity, but here, too, states are increasingly leaving maximum maturity to the lender's discretion.

Second Mortgage or Home Equity Loan: Cash Loan

Before we tell you about getting a cash loan using a **second mortgage**, we have to introduce you to a few things, such as what a second mortgage is. We'll discuss these points very briefly because they will be covered in more detail in Chapter 11 when we talk about homeownership.

A mortgage is a specialized form of borrowing that allows you to borrow money by using a home as security for the loan. The most frequent use of a mortgage is to purchase a house. For example, when you buy a house, you may pay 20 percent of its price with your own money, while the remaining 80 percent of the money you obtain from a mortgage. You own the house, but the lender who granted you the mortgage has a claim on the house to the extent that you still owe the money you borrowed. This is called a first mortgage because the lender has first claim against the house should you be unable to repay the mortgage.

But it is also possible to use a mortgage to obtain a secured cash loan.

The borrower can do so even when the first mortgage, used to purchase the house, has not been repaid. Because these loans involve a home, many lenders call it a **home equity loan.** When you obtain a cash loan using a second mortgage, it is the dollar amount of equity that the lender uses to decide how large a loan to grant. It is called a second mortgage because this lender's claim is second to the claim the original lender has with the first mortgage. Should the borrower have some problem repaying the two mortgages, the first mortgage lender would have first claim on the money obtained from selling the house. It would be used to cover any and all unpaid amounts on that first mortgage. Only then would the lender with the second mortgage be able to claim any of the money obtained by selling the house.

Generally, the loan is limited to 60 to 80 percent of the borrower's equity in the house. We will discuss the topic of your equity in a house further in Chapter 11, but an example will illustrate how a cash loan on a second mortgage works.

Assume your house is presently worth $60,000 and the unpaid balance on your first mortgage is $45,000. Your equity in the house is:

$15,000   = $60,000   − $45,000

⇧   ⇧   ⇧

Your equity = Current market − Unpaid balance on
in house   value of house   first mortgage

The maximum amount some lenders would provide on a second mortgage is:

$9,000   = $15,000   × 60 %

⇧   ⇧   ⇧

Maximum = Your equity × Maximum %
loan   in house   from lender

Some lenders require equal monthly payments that will repay the entire amount borrowed over the loan's maturity. Other lenders require only very small monthly payments that do little more than cover the loan's finance charge; as a result, the borrower must make a very large lump-sum payment (often called a balloon payment) when the loan matures. On a loan of a few thousand dollars, this amount can be a tremendous lump to pay at one time.

Some past lending practices in secondary mortgages came very close to being unscrupulous. Consequently, it is imperative that you be extremely knowledgeable and cautious when considering this type of borrowing.

Life Insurance: Cash Loan

A loan against your life insurance is the most restrictive of all the loan options discussed thus far. First, you must have the type of life insurance that accumulates a cash value as part of the policy. Some typical names for such policies include: straight life, cash-value life, and limited-pay life insurance. Second, the maximum you can borrow is limited to the cash value you have accumulated in the policy. One special feature of this loan is

EXHIBIT 8-2

Principal advantages and disadvantages for major consumer cash loans.

SOURCE OF LOAN	Principal Factors and Points to Consider		
	ADVANTAGES	DISADVANTAGES	STRATEGY
Cash loan: commercial banks, mutual savings banks, and S&Ls	APR is generally very competitive. Borrower can develop credit record for other financial services.	Lender often requires strong, well-established credit record. Marginal borrowers may not be eligible.	For a cash loan, always check commercial banks, mutual savings banks, and S&Ls.
Cash loan: credit union	APR is generally among the lowest. Credit life insurance is included on most loans. Loan can be small or can have a short maturity.	Borrower must be a member of credit union. Borrower develops a credit record with a lender whose range of financial services is somewhat limited.	By all means, consider a credit union if you qualify.
Cash loan: consumer finance company	Borrower can have a weak credit record or limited credit history. Loan can be small, but the APR can be very high.	The APR is usually among the highest. Highly restrictive state regulations can limit loan's usefulness. Lender does not offer additional financial services.	If you have a poor or unestablished credit record, this may be the only choice. But try other sources first.
Second mortgage or home equity loan: finance company, commercial bank, mutual savings bank, S&L	Loan is readily available. Loan can be sizable when borrower has a large equity in a house.	APR on finance company loans is very high. Risk exposure is considerable because borrower might lose house if loan is not repaid. Few borrowers plan final giant payment on lump-sum repayment loans.	Loan is best reserved for major borrowing needs. Thoroughly investigate other lending sources first.
Cash loan: life insurance	APR is among the lowest of all sources. Policyholders automatically qualify. Lack of set repayment schedule provides flexibility.	Only policyholders qualify. Policy must be sizable or purchased some time ago, to allow a large loan. Loan reduces insurance coverage. Lack of set repayment schedule may encourage postponing repayment.	An excellent short-term emergency cash source. If used for longer-term purposes, it requires discipline to repay.
Loan shark	None.	Too many to list.	Forget it!

that its repayment terms are the least restrictive, most loans do not require you to repay within a specified period. We will descuss life insurance loans further in Chapter 14.

Loan Sharks

A **loan shark** is a private individual who lends money at enormous rates and who is not regulated in any way, except perhaps by the "lords" of organized crime who usually give him whatever support he may need in his operations and collections.

Despite the large number of legitimate lenders, there still seem to be people who are willing to, or who must, borrow from loan sharks. Loan sharks have low qualifying standards, provide the loan quickly, and require a lump-sum payment at the end of a very short maturity—sometimes as brief as a week. Also, the cost of borrowing from a loan shark can be devastating: Annual rates range from 120 to 1000 percent per year! And sometimes the loan sharks will not let you repay the loan amount; instead, they "prefer" and insist that you keep on paying the high finance charge. This is a crime called "extortion." But, should you fail to cooperate with a loan shark, his collection efforts can be quick, brutal, unrelenting, and sometimes fatal.

STRATEGY

Our recommendation is an absolute and unequivocal DON'T. There are plenty of other lenders to try. And if they all refuse you, your finances are probably in such dire condition that a loan shark is not going to rectify your financial problems.

Selecting a Cash Loan

Exhibit 8-2 summarizes the principal advantages and disadvantages for each of the cash loans we just discussed. In addition, there is a strategy statement for each loan listed in that exhibit that summarizes the special features or points we believe you should consider.

Shopping for a Cash Loan

The checklist in Exhibit 8-3 can help you find a suitable source for a cash loan. You should answer the questions in the preliminary section before you visit any lenders. Many borrowers fail to decide clearly in their own minds what they are looking for before they begin their search. Also, be certain you have current data on yourself. An income statement and a recent balance sheet (similar to those in Exhibits 2-2 and 2-3 of Chapter 2) provide a good summary that lenders understand.

To obtain the information that you will need to compare competing loan offers, you will probably have to ask the lenders some direct questions. The questions in the lower half of Exhibit 8-3 should provide this key information. Many borrowers simply never ask them because they do not realize they should obtain and use this information. Lenders usually do not volunteer the information.

You should check at least three lenders, even if the first lender's offer seems attractive. There is no loan offer so good that it cannot stand a few hours of careful thought before being accepted. In making your decision, select the loan that has the lowest APR, yet whose terms match your needs.

CONSUMER SALES LOAN

Consumer sales loans are always associated with the purchase of big-ticket durable goods, such as an automobile, furniture, a major home appliance, or a recreation vehicle. With a sales loan, the borrower does not receive cash, but, instead, immediately receives the merchandise in exchange for a repayment promise. A sales loan is always secured by the merchandise that is being purchased with the loan. While most sales loans originate with the dealers who sell the merchandise, few stop there. They generally have a standing agreement with a finance company or a bank to purchase any sales loan the dealer originates. By selling the loan, the dealer obtains immediate cash without waiting 12 to 60 months while the buyer repays the loan. Unfortunately, the dealer is therefore out of the picture after you buy the merchandise and continue paying for it.

EXHIBIT 8-3

Checklist to use when shopping for a cash loan.

Preliminaries

1 How will the money be used?

2 How much money is needed?

3 For how long do you need the loan?

4 If required, what security can you pledge on the loan?

5 Do you have current data on yourself (income, rent, present debts, monthly payments, savings)?

6 Do you have a list of prospective lenders you have ranked by preference?

7 Have you prepared a current balance sheet and income statement? Does the balance sheet show all your assets?

Questions to Ask Prospective Lenders

1 What is the loan's finance charge (APR)?

2 What are the repayment terms?

3 Does the loan require security? If so, what?

4 Are there late-payment penalties?

5 Is there a penalty for repaying the loan before maturity?

6 If repaid early, how is the finance charge refund computed?

7 Is credit life insurance required?

The price of the item purchased determines the size of the loan. Typically, the buyer pays a small fraction of that purchase price as a down payment and finances the balance with a sales loan. The loan may be as little as $50 when it involves a small household appliance, or it may exceed $10,000 for an expensive automobile or a large boat. Maturities can range from 3 to 60 months but 24 to 36 months are more common. The increased availability of the longer 48-to-60 month maturities is a recent development. The APR of the finance charge ranges from 12 to 36 percent, although many average between 24 and 36 percent. All sales loans require equal monthly payments over the loan's maturity.

Sales Loan: Role of the Lending Institution that Purchases the Loan

While most sales loans have three parties—the buyer, the dealer, and the lending institution that provides the loan—they rarely participate simultaneously in the loan transaction. Typically, the buyer negotiates with the dealer and has no contact with the lending institution until after the loan has been sold; at that time, the buyer becomes a borrower. The fact that the lending institution is not part of the original transaction and has had only a limited role in these negotiations has raised the following questions.

Rebate When a bank or finance company purchases a sales loan from a dealer, it generally rebates a portion of the loan's finance charge to the dealer. In part, this rebate compensates the dealer for work on the required loan documents. In addition, the rebate encourages the dealer to sell other loan contracts to that particular institution. Because dealers get these rebates, it is easy to understand why they actively push sales loans. The arrangement also creates a situation where a dealer might be interested in selling loans to the lender offering the largest rebate rather than to the lender that offers the lowest APR to the borrower.

STRATEGY

To be sure that the dealer is not getting a large rebate at your expense, make certain that the APR on the dealer's sales loan that you are considering is competitive with other credit alternatives.

Corrective Action From the Dealer   Prior to the Federal Trade Commission ruling that became effective in 1976, a buyer had limited opportunities to force the dealer to take corrective action once the loan was sold. An example will illustrate why. Assume that Thelma Thrifty used a sales loan to buy a home freezer complete with 600 pounds of select, tasty beef; at least that is what the dealer claimed. Further, assume that the dealer who sold the freezer and beef immediately sold the loan to a finance company. Unfortunately, Thelma soon found that the freezer did not operate properly and that the beef was so tough and tasteless that her dog refused even the first serving, let alone any seconds. Prior to the 1976 ruling, Thelma could not withhold the loan payments from the finance company in order to force the dealer to repair the freezer and replace the beef with something edible. If Thelma did, the finance company would cite either the *holder in due course* or a *waiver of defense* (you need not know the meaning of these terms) to show that it was not responsible for unsatisfactory performance by the dealer. The finance company could then legally force Thelma to make the payments on the sales loan.

The new ruling has completely changed this possibility. Now Thelma can successfully withhold her loan payment from the finance company, and she can continue to do so until the dealer takes the necessary action to correct the problem. In our example, this responsibility would include repairing the freezer and delivering beef that matched the dealer's sales claims. This change has significantly improved the borrower's bargaining position when there is a dispute with the dealer. Now the lender is a full party to unsatisfactory performance by the selling dealer.

STRATEGY

Your best defense is still to buy from a dealer that you know will perform satisfactorily. But if a dispute does arise where a sales loan was part of the purchase, you can withhold payment until the dealer takes corrective action.

Caution: Problems With Sales Loans

Despite considerable state and federal legislation, some consumer sales loans still contain burdensome provisions that can be very costly to the borrower. The following section describes some of these problem areas.

Repossession The exact steps a lender must take to repossess the property you have pledged as security for a loan are heavily influenced by the regulations and controls established by the state in which you live. But the final result is nearly always the same: The lender physically takes possession of the property. One standard limitation is that lenders cannot resort to illegal means to repossess the item.

Once the lender has physical possession of the item, most states have rules which detail how the lender may proceed. Frequently, the lender can sell the item at a public or private sale. If the money from the sale exceeds the unpaid loan balance, the borrower receives the excess. Should the proceeds be insufficient, the borrower is generally required to repay the difference.

In most cases, **repossession** is a poor way to repay a loan. First, you lose the services of the repossessed item; you might then be forced to purchase those services elsewhere at a higher cost. Second, if the sale proceeds are insufficient, you end up repaying the loan, even though you no longer have the merchandise. Third, some lenders make only halfhearted efforts to obtain the highest price when they sell the repossessed item. Finally, the tactics some lenders use to repossess an item range from questionable to illegal.

If it looks as though you might be headed for this kind of situation, discuss your problem with the lender as a first step. Whenever possible, try to make at least a small monthly payment; most lenders will not repossess as long as the borrower shows some progress in making payments. If you are unable to do even that, consider obtaining a short-term cash loan to repay the debt; then you can sell the property yourself and use the proceeds to repay the short-term cash loan.

STRATEGY

Avoid repossession if at all possible. Arranging your own debt rescue is nearly always less expensive than having the lender repossess an item.

Balloon Note A **balloon note** has deceptively small monthly payments while the loan is outstanding. But at maturity, the borrower must make a final giant payment to repay the loan. For example, a 24-month, $4000 loan with an APR of 24 percent might have the following repayment terms: (1) 23 monthly payments of $80 and (2) a very large lump-sum payment of $4080 at the end of the twenty-fourth month. Most people simply would not be prepared to make the final $4080 payment. Unfortunately, at the time the loan is taken out, those low $80 monthly payments appear very attractive because they are much less than the $211.48 payment (computed using Exhibit 7-8 in Chapter 7) that would be required on a normal cash loan that had 24 equal-sized monthly payments.

Caution: If you start thinking that you need a balloon note to be able to make the small monthly loan payment, you probably cannot really afford to buy the item.

Acceleration Clause An **acceleration clause** makes the entire loan due immediately should the borrower fail to make a payment. If the borrower misses one payment, not so much by oversight as because of financial hardship, that buyer is not very likely to be able suddenly to repay the entire amount; therefore, the lender may repossess the merchandise. *Beware:* Many sales loans have this kind of acceleration clause.

CREDIT LIFE INSURANCE

Credit life insurance repays any unpaid balance on a cash loan or sales loan should the borrower die before completing the repayment. The money from the credit life policy is paid directly to the lender, so the borrower's survivors are not involved. The amount paid equals the unpaid loan balance. For example, assume that a borrower had originally taken out a $4000 loan but had repaid $2000 of that loan at the time of death. The credit life insurance policy would pay only the $2000 that would be required to repay the balance of the loan.

Most lenders offer credit life insurance on their cash and sales loans. A few lenders require that you buy their credit life as a condition for obtaining the loan; in this case, the cost of the credit life insurance must be included as part of the finance charge that the lender quotes. But most lenders offer it as an option that can be purchased at extra cost. It is this latter group to which our discussion is primarily directed.

Coverage Credit life insurance repays the unpaid balance due on the loan if you die before the loan is repaid. With this kind of insurance, the actual insurance coverage declines because the unpaid balance is reduced each month as you make the regular monthly payments on the loan. Thus, the coverage on a 3-year, $3000 loan may be $3000 at the moment you take it out, but as the loan approaches maturity, the coverage is only several hundred dollars because repayment is nearly complete. Effectively, the average coverage for the 3 years is closer to $1500.

Cost Individual states set the maximum cost that lenders can charge for credit life insurance, and they are very generous. Typically, the cost for each $100 of loan balance is 60 cents to $1 for each year that the loan is outstanding.[1]

At first glance, those premiums do not seem large, and because they don't, many borrowers just say yes when offered credit life insurance. Before agreeing, take a closer look at just how much this insurance really costs. Let's assume that a lender has offered a $5000 loan for 60 months with an 18 percent APR. As an option, credit life insurance is available with a premium, or cost, of 80 cents per $100 of coverage per year.

The first major surprise is that most lenders compute your premium using the amount borrowed plus the finance charge. Using Exhibit 7-8, we can compute the total amount for this $5000 loan thus:

---

[1] "Credit Insurance: The Quiet Overcharge," *Consumer Reports,* July 1979, p. 416.

$$\$7617 \quad = (\$5000 \div \$1000) \quad \times \$25.39 \quad \times 60$$

Loan plus   = Loan   ÷ Multiples × Payment on × Months
finance charge   of $1000 $1000 loan

The insurance premium is based on $7617, not on the $5000 that many people commonly believe. And the higher the APR or the longer the maturity, the larger that total amount—loan plus finance charge—is relative to the loan.

The second surprise is that the annual premium does *not* decline as the loan is repaid. Despite the fact that the insurance coverage is dropping as you repay the loan, you continue to pay an annual premium based on the initial loan. For our $5000 loan, these two surprises combine to give a total insurance premium of:

$$\$304.68 \quad = (\$7617 \quad \div \$100) \quad \times \$.80 \quad \times 5 \text{ years}$$

Total premium = Loan plus   ÷ Multiples × Premium per × Years to
            finance charge   of $100 $100 per year   maturity

A premium that started out looking deceptively small has become quite sizable. That causes the third surprise: For the amount of insurance coverage provided, the premium is extremely high. This is very expensive insurance!

There is even a fourth surprise for the borrower: Most lenders want to collect the whole credit life premium immediately. That is $304.68 in our example. Few borrowers are prepared to pay that amount. Not to fear—the lender just smiles and tacks it on to the $5000 loan. So the borrower ends up paying finance charges at the rate of 18 percent on the insurance as well. So, the total credit life premium, plus the finance charge, ends up costing the borrower $464.15 over the life of the loan. As practice, use Exhibit 7-8 and see whether you can compute this $464.15.

A Substitute: Term Life Insurance Let us jump ahead a few topics to term life insurance—Chapter 14 covers it in detail—to show why credit life insurance is usually a very poor buy. First, a word on what **term life insurance** is. It is pure, straight life insurance. If the person who is covered by the policy dies, the policy pays its coverage to the beneficiary named in the policy. If the insured person does not die during the covered year, the insurance company will renew the policy. Or course, there is a premium for the next year's coverage. There is no refund of last year's premium and no buildup in a saving's feature called "cash value." Since term insurance provides only insurance coverage, we can compare its premium with those on credit life insurance to answer the question: Is credit life insurance a good buy?

The best comparison is to figure the cost of term insurance that is exactly equal to the coverage under credit life insurance. But that could be a bit involved; remember the coverage under credit life drops as the loan is repaid. To simplify the comparison, we ignore the fact that credit insurance declines as the loan is repaid. And later, we will show that term insurance would be even cheaper if we allowed the coverage to decline as the loan is repaid.

We will use our previous $5000, 60-month loan to make the comparison. As a rough approximation, the annual premiums on term insurance would likely be 20 cents per $100 for borrowers in their twenties, 35 cents per $100 for borrowers in their thirties, and 50 cents per $100 for borrowers in their forties. If the borrower is 35 years old, the total premiums on a $5000 loan will be:

$$\$87.50 = (\$5000 \div \$100) \times \$.35 \times 5 \text{ years}$$

Total premium = Loan ÷ $100 × Premium per × Number of
$100 per year years

That is a far cry from the $304.68 premium that we computed in the last section. Thus, term insurance costs less than one-third as much as credit life. A saving of over two-thirds in premiums certainly more than repays taking a few minutes to compare the cost of credit life with term life insurance.

Actually, the premiums on term insurance would be even less than our computations indicate. During the first year of the loan, we would need $5000 of coverage. But during the second year the coverage could be lower because now part of the loan has been repaid: The unpaid balance on the original $5000 loan is $4322 at the start of the second year. And, during the third year, coverage can be lowered further because more of the loan had been repaid. Consequently, the premiums would be less than the $87.50 we showed because we would not need $5000 of coverage for each of those 5 years. Obviously, substituting term life insurance for credit life is an even better choice.

STRATEGY

Before accepting optional credit life insurance on a loan, try substituting a similar amount of term life insurance. The saving can be substantial.

Is Credit Life Necessary?   We don't think so! Not if you plan your life insurance needs along the lines we will show you in Chapter 14. If you plan all your insurance requirements properly, credit life will likely be an unnecessary and costly duplication of coverage you already will have.

Two cases come to mind that might be exceptions. First, the borrower's health may be so poor that no company will provide term life insurance. For such a borrower, credit life insurance may be a bargain. A second exception is the borrower who is in his or her late fifties or sixties. Term insurance can be very expensive at those ages. For this group of borrowers, credit life may be the best choice. But in either case, the borrower should always ask: "Do I really need the insurance coverage?"

DISABILITY INSURANCE

Some cash and sales loans offer disability insurance as an extra cost option. With **disability insurance**, the loan payments will be paid in full if the borrower becomes disabled and cannot work during the period of the loan. Depending on the policy, the coverage may begin immediately when the borrower becomes disabled or only after a waiting period following the date on which the insured person became disabled. Obviously, policies with a waiting period cost less.

Is Disability Insurance Necessary?   We have many of the same reservations about disability insurance that we voiced in the previous discussion on credit life insurance. Purchasing disability insurance from the lender is generally more expensive than purchasing it directly from an insurance firm. Also, the coverage may unnecessarily duplicate the disability insurance that borrowers may already have through their employers. If you decide that disability insurance is necessary during the period of your loan, check several insurance sources to see whether you can obtain the same coverage that the lender offers, but at a lower cost.

OPEN-ENDED CONSUMER CREDIT

Open-ended consumer credit includes a wide range of charge accounts and credit cards. With most open-ended credit, the lender assigns a limit to how much will be lent to the customer; the limit depends on the customer's current financial position and past credit record. The customer can borrow any amount within that limit. Most open-ended credit is intended for small, recurring transactions, rather than the single transaction that typifies cash and sales loans. However, some credit cards now allow customers to charge large purchases on their accounts and set up a repayment schedule that allows them several years to repay the entire amount. Therefore, the distinction that credit cards and charge accounts are used to borrow only small amounts is no longer completely true.

Most open-ended credit has very flexible repayment terms. The borrower generally has a choice of repaying over several years, of repaying the entire balance within 30 days, or of repaying on some schedule between these two extremes. When repayment extends beyond 30 days, the customer usually pays an annual finance charge of 12 to 24 percent. However, by paying the entire balance within the 25- to 30-day grace period, the customer generally avoids any finance charge; this is a major advantage of open-ended credit.

Charge Accounts

Charge accounts are offered by individual businesses, such as a department store, drugstore, doctor, dentist, or utility company. When you want to borrow through a charge account, you can do so only through the particular business that offers the account. Most charge accounts can be grouped into two general categories: regular charge accounts and revolving accounts.

Regular Charge Account   The **regular charge account**, also called the 30-day account, is the oldest and most common. When an item is charged to the account, the customer immediately receives title to the item in exchange for a promise to pay at a later date, usually not later than 30 days. Purchases are accumulated and billed monthly. The customer is expected to pay the entire balance within 30 days of being billed, and there is no finance charge. Failure to repay within the 30-day grace period may entail a monthly service fee of 1 to 1 1/2 percent on the past-due balance.

Revolving Account   The **revolving account** allows the customer to extend repayment. Typically, the account requires a minimum monthly payment which may be either a fixed amount, say $25 on a $300 account, or a percentage of the outstanding balance. Typically, the range is between 3 and 10 percent. A monthly finance charge of 1 to 1 1/2 percent is charged against the unpaid balance at the end of the month.

As the balance is repaid, the customer can make new purchases up to the credit limit on the account. The revolving account is primarily intended as medium-term credit—12 to 24 months.

STRATEGY

Match the charge account to the type of item you are purchasing. Use a regular charge for short-lived and low-priced items. For longer-lived, more expensive items, use a revolving charge.

Credit Card Account

Credit card accounts vary from the very specialized cards used only at a single business, such as a local department store, to cards that are accepted by businesses nationwide and worldwide. A credit card entitles you to a very versatile and convenient type of borrowing. We will discuss three major types of credit cards:

1   Bank cards: MasterCard and VISA (the two major ones).

2   Cards of nationwide retail stores: J. C. Penney; Sears, Roebuck; Exxon; Mobil Oil.

3   Travel and entertainment cards: American Express, Diners Club, and Carte Blanche.

Bank Credit Card   The two major **bank credit cards** are offered by a group of affiliated financial institutions that extends throughout the United States. Although bank credit cards are accepted nationwide, the individual accounts are administered and controlled by the institution that issued the card. For example, if I obtain a VISA card from the bank in Hell, Michigan,

MY TRAVELERS' CHECKS..
MY CREDIT CARDS..
THEY'VE BEEN STOLEN..
WHAT WILL I DO?
WHAT **WILL** I DO?

that bank will likely send me my monthly statements and handle any special details on the account. Yet I should be able to use my card at any business in the United States that accepts VISA.

All card holders are assigned an upper credit limit which is based on the holder's income and credit record: $300 to $1000 is a typical limit, although higher limits are available. Most banks allow a small overrun of that limit as long as the borrower continues to make payments on the account promptly.

Most financial institutions charge an annual membership fee of $10 to $25 for a credit card. But that fee is less than one-half the fee for a travel and entertainment card. Except in a few states, there is no transaction fee when the card is used. If the entire amount borrowed is paid within the 25- to 30-day grace period, there is no finance charge. Balances not paid within that grace period carry a monthly finance charge of 1 to 1 1/2 percent, depending on the size of the unpaid balance on the credit card.

All credit card accounts require that the holder make at least a minimum payment each month.

Extended Payment Supplement   Both nationwide bank credit cards offer an extended payment supplement. With this supplement, you can borrow for large, expensive items whose cost would exceed or largely exhaust your regular credit limit. There is no specified dollar limit for items charged on the extended payment supplement, but the merchant or dealer must obtain approval from an affiliated bank before charging the item to your account. Also, there is no grace period; the 1 to 1 1/2 percent monthly finance charge begins on the day of purchase. The card holder specifies the desired repayment period, usually 6 to 36 months. Borrowing and repayments in the extended payment supplement are shown separately and identifed as such on the holder's monthly statement.

Overall, the supplement operates much like a sales loan.

STRATEGY

Before using the extended payment supplement, compare its APR and terms with cash or sales loan to see which one best meets your needs.

Cash Advance   A bank credit card holder can also obtain a short-term cash advance, but the amount of cash borrowed cannot exceed the account's unused credit limit. There is no grace period; monthly finance charges of 1 to 1 1/2 percent begin when the advance is made. The nearest competitor to borrowing through a cash advance is borrowing through the automatic overdraft on a share draft, NOW, or checking account.

STRATEGY

Before using the cash advance on your credit card, compare its APR with the APR for the overdraft on your checking account, share draft, or NOW account.

National Retail Store and Major Oil Company Cards   Credit cards of national retail stores and major oil companies allow immediate borrowing over a wide geographic area, but the credit can be used for only a limited range of products and services. All accounts have a credit ceiling based on the card holder's income and credit record. The card holder can repay the entire balance within the 25- to 30-day grace period and thereby avoid any finance charge. Or the repayment period can be extended up to 36 months, but that entails a 1 to 1 1/2 percent monthly finance charge.

Travel and Entertainment Cards   The three major travel and entertainment (T&E) cards are American Express, Diners Club, and Carte Blanche; they are widely accepted by hotels, motels, restaurants, airlines, major department stores, and other businesses in the United States and many foreign countries. The main purpose of these cards is to cover your food and lodging expenses when you are traveling.

To qualify for a travel and entertainment card, the holder generally must have an annual income of $12,000 or more. In addition, the holder pays an annual membership fee of $30 to $50. The account has an upper limit depending on the holder's income and credit record. Except for certain major purchases, the entire balance must be repaid within 30 days. Although there is no finance charge, there is a late payment fee of 1 1/2 to 2 1/2 percent per month if the amount is not paid within 60 days. Failure to repay the balance promptly can be grounds for canceling the card. While the cards provide cash advances, the dollar amount the holder can obtain and the period allowed for repayment are less than they are for bank credit cards.

Potential Benefits from Using Credit Cards and Charge Accounts Effectively

We believe that if credit card and charge accounts are used properly, they can provide some worthwhile benefits for managing your personal finances.

Finance Charge-Free Grace Period   The grace period is one of the major benefits offered by most credit cards and charge accounts. By paying within the prescribed grace period, usually within 25 to 30 days of billing, you essentially receive an interest-free loan from the day of purchase to the day of payment. Furthermore, you can easily stretch the grace period to 50 or 60 days by concentrating purchases immediately after your account's billing or closing date.

It is an interesting fact that the merchant that accepts your credit card can also affect the number of days you have before you must pay for the item you charged. How? Merchants who are timely and prompt will immediately submit your charge slip to a financial institution that operates your credit card. That institution will waste no time in posting, or adding, the item to your monthly statement. But if you are lucky enough to have selected a merchant who delays, it may take a few days or several weeks to submit your charge slip to the financial institution. This delay gives you more time before you have to pay for the charged item. After all, the standard 25-30-day grace period does not begin until the charge is posted to your account. And the longer the time spent in entering the charged item on your account, the longer time you have before you must pay.

Minimizing the Finance Charge Given a Temporary Cash Shortage
In all cases, you should make every effort to pay by the due date. Even if you must use the automatic overdraft on your checking account or NOW account for a few days, do so; you will still be ahead.

For example, assume that Sandy Smith's average daily balance on her bank card was $300. But she is short of money on the due date and does not expect to have the $300 until 10 days later. Missing the due date will cost her:

$$\$4.50 \; = \; \$300 \; \times \; 1.5\,\%$$

Finance charge	= Unpaid credit card balance	× Finance charge per month

Yet, if she drew the $300 as a cash overdraft on her checking account or NOW account for 10 days (we assume that she has the option and its APR is 12 percent), her finance charge would be:

$$\$0.99 \; = \; \$300 \; \times \; (12\,\% \; \div \; 365 \text{ days}) \times 10 \text{ days}$$

Finance charge	= Amount of cash advance	× Finance charge	÷ 365 days	× Days for the advance

By using the overdraft, she would substantially reduce the finance charge.

Convenience   All credit cards and charge accounts provide several convenience features. First, you avoid the need to carry large sums of money. Second, most sellers agree to accept credit cards and will readily accept a card as payment, while personal checks are becoming increasingly unacceptable and difficult to use in some areas. Third, in situations where you are temporarily short of the necessary funds at the time you want to buy an item or service, you can use your credit card or charge account to pay for it. That, of course, assumes you will have the money a few days later.

Improved Record Keeping   The billings on credit cards and charge accounts provide a ready record of your expenditures. This record can be especially helpful when you are summarizing monthly expenditures into the different expense categories for your budget. (We discussed this process in Chapter 3.) Further, you will also have a ready record of when, where, and for what purpose you spent the money. Last, by consolidating a number of payments into one or two credit cards, you reduce the number of checks you write each month.

Potential Problems and Pitfalls with Credit Cards and Charge Accounts

Although credit cards and charge accounts provide many advantages and benefits, they also present problems and pitfalls you must beware of.

Billing Disputes   Many of you have heard or read some horror tales about a borrower battling a creditor for months over an error in a credit card or charge account billing. Supposedly, the Fair Credit Billing Act now makes it less difficult to deal with creditors when you have a **billing dispute.** This law requires creditors to establish a set of procedures for a customer to follow when there is an error in his or her billing statement. Possible errors may include such things as a charge you never authorized, a payment that was recorded in someone else's account, a charge for merchandise which you returned but which was never credited to your account, a charge for which you want to see the original signed charge slip, a simple arithmetic error, or a charge entered as the wrong amount.

Exhibit 8-4 summarizes the steps and the timetable that must be observed by both the customer and the creditor when there is a disputed item. The creditor's role is outlined on the left of the exhibit, while the customer's role is shown in the center and on the right.

Defective Articles or Services   The Fair Credit Billing Act has corrected a potential abuse of customers who bought defective articles or services. Should a merchant or dealer be unable or unwilling to correct the defective article or service, you can refuse to pay the cost listed against the credit card or charge account you used to purchase the article or service. And you can

Exhibit 8-4

Steps the creditor and the customer must follow to
resolve a billing dispute on a credit card or charge account.

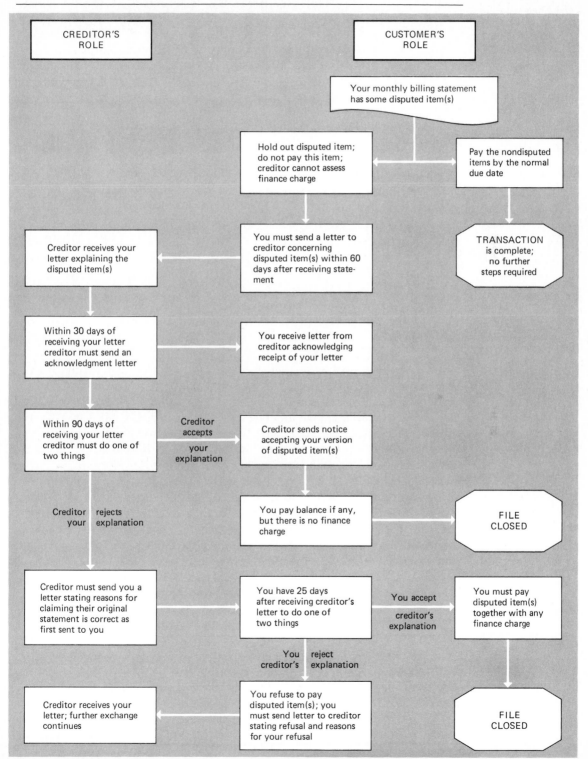

continue to withhold payment until the seller has corrected the defective article or service. However, two limitations apply on sales that involve a credit card: Under the law, the purchase must have been made within your home state or 100 miles of your home, and the purchase price must be over $50.

Excessive Use of Credit   Unfortunately, because credit cards and charge accounts are so easy and convenient to use, they frequently can also lead to major problems for some people. Those people find it too easy just to "charge it" and too difficult to pay cash. By charging it, they avoid facing the hard reality that they, and only they, must pay for that item at some point. They thus face the risk of using too much credit.

There are several things you can do to avoid finding yourself using credit cards and charge accounts excessively.

First, you should know exactly the amount you have charged at any point in time; doing so will likely require your keeping a running record of all outstanding charges.

Second, avoid charging an expensive item on impulse or when you feel you "deserve a reward."

Third, resist purchasing a highly touted sales item on credit unless you really need it. Even a sale that claims 50 percent off may cost too much if you buy an unnecessary item.

And fourth, if you cannot resist the continual temptation of a credit card, maybe you should just close the account and ceremonially cut your card in half.

"Minimum Payment Rut"   Most credit card and charge accounts require that the holder repay a minimum amount each month. The minimum may be based on a percentage of the balance (for example, 5 percent of a $300 balance) or a small fixed payment (say, $15 on a $300 balance). Typically, the minimum payment is established to repay the entire balance in 24 to 36 months, assuming there are no other charges during that time. For some people, however, this option can become the **minimum payment rut,** a distinct liability.

Assume that Fred Bear charged $280 on his credit card during the past month. His bill arrives, and since he is short of cash, he elects to make only the required $10 minimum payment. The finance charge is 1 1/2 percent per month on the balance. We assume that he continues to make the same $10 minimum payment each month.

During the early months, about $4 of each $10 payment goes to pay the finance charge; only the remaining $6 or so reduces the unpaid balance. Even after 12 months, $3 of the minimum $10 payment is still going for the finance charge and the remaining unpaid balance exceeds $200. If Fred continues the $10 payments, it will take him more than 36 months to repay the entire balance. In effect, his credit card account has become a long-term loan. With an APR of 18 percent (1 1/2 percent × 12 months), this is an expensive credit source.

STRATEGY

CHAPTER 8

243

SOURCES OF
CONSUMER
CREDIT

You should limit your use of the minimum payment option to periods of temporary financial emergency. If you need 24 to 36 months to repay the balance, consider repaying the balance through a cash loan. Often its APR will be less than the APR on the credit card.

Insurance Coverage: Credit Life, Disability, and Other Perils The types of insurance coverage offered on credit cards and charge accounts vary widely. Some credit card and charge account issuers offer straight credit life insurance that either covers any unpaid balance in the customer's account or provides some flat dollar amount—$500, $1000, $2000, etc.—to pay off the balance in the event of the death of the account holder. Other credit card or charge account issuers combine credit life and disability into a single policy covering the customer's unpaid account balance. Still others roll a whole series of coverages into a single policy: death, disability, robbery, unemployment, fire, and other perils. Reading the claims of some issuers, one gets the impression that about the only thing not covered is damage from a herd of recalcitrant elephants or the wake of the Titanic should it be raised and sunk a second time. If the purpose of grouping all those different insurance policies were to provide good coverage, we would be reassured. But we rather suspect that the more likely purpose is to divert the customer's attention from horrendously high premiums by offering seemingly robust insurance coverage.

The dollar amount of the coverage is small, and in the insurance industry, small dollar amounts of coverage nearly always mean stratospheric premiums per dollar of coverage. Depending on extent of coverage, you can easily pay $1.20 to $6 per $100 of insurance coverage with credit card or charge account insurance.

STRATEGY

Most people should avoid the credit life insurance and disability insurance offered on credit cards and charge accounts. This insurance coverage should be part of your overall insurance plan.

Lost or Stolen Credit Cards When you have a credit card, you are liable for up to $50 of charges that anyone charges on your card without your permission. Thus, should you lose your card or should someone steal it, you might have to pay up to $50 of bills that someone else charged on your account. We say you *might* have to pay, because there are four conditions or qualifications that must exist before you can be forced to pay:

1   You were given either a stamped, self-addressed envelope or a telephone number to notify the card issuer that you lost your card.

2   The charge someone made to your account occurred before you notified the card issuer of your missing card.

EXHIBIT 8-5

Steps you should follow to report a missing
credit card.

1 Call the card issuer to report the loss.

2 Obtain the name of the person with whom you discuss the loss.

3 Send a certified letter to the card issuer. Save the receipt as proof of notification.

4 Carefully examine subsequent monthly billings for any account charges that were made by someone else.

5 Should you suffer a loss, check your homeowners or renters policy. Many cover losses up to $500.

3　Your signature is on the credit card.

4　You were informed of your potential $50 liability when the credit card was issued.

The steps shown in Exhibit 8-5 should be followed if you lose a credit card.

There are several steps you can take to reduce the amount you may have to pay because of a missing credit card. First, keep a current file of the addresses and telephone numbers of the issuers of the credit cards you have. Thus, you are prepared for a lost or stolen card. Second, notify all the card issuers immediately of your missing credit cards. Last, keep only the credit cards that you really need and use frequently.

SUMMARY

1　Consumer credit transactions can be either secured or unsecured. With a secured loan, the borrower either pledges some personal asset or has someone cosign the note.

2　A consumer cash loan involves two people, the borrower and the lender, and the loan is given to the borrower in cash.

3　Borrowers should shop for credit just as they shop for any purchase. They should obtain price quotations, compare features, and get an explanation when they do not fully understand a feature.

4　The salient features of a sales loan are: *(a)* The loan is used to purchase large-ticket items; *(b)* the loan provides no cash; and *(c)* generally, there are three parties—the borrower, the dealer, and the lender.

5　All sales loans are secured by pledging the merchandise that is being purchased with the loan. In nearly all cases, the lender can repossess the pledged asset should the borrower fail to repay the loan.

6　Buyers can legally withhold payment on a sales loan to force corrective action from the dealer.

7   Credit life insurance can cost several times as much as term life insurance.

8   Credit life insurance or disability insurance offered by lenders is worthwhile only when coverage is needed and the insurance cannot be obtained elsewhere at less cost.

9   With open-ended credit, the lender sets a ceiling on the amount of credit available to a consumer, but the consumer decides when and how to use the credit.

10   Credit cards offer more flexibility than charge accounts because they are accepted by a wide range of retail and service businesses.

11   Major benefits offered by credit cards and charge accounts include a grace period with no finance charge, convenience, and improved record keeping.

12   When a customer disputes an item on the monthly credit card or charge account statement, the issuer must take specific steps to resolve the dispute.

13   If a buyer finds that some merchandise or service that was purchased with a credit card is defective, payment on that item can legally be withheld until the seller corrects the problem.

14   The ease and convenience of using open-ended credit can encourage some people to overuse credit.

15   By making only the minimum payment required on a credit card account, the card holder greatly extends the repayment period, and greatly increases the finance charge.

16   Credit card holders' maximum liability for the unauthorized use of their cards is $50 per card.

REVIEW YOUR UNDERSTANDING OF

Consumer cash loan
Secured loan
Cosigner
Unsecured loan
Automatic overdraft or advance
Consumer finance company
First mortgage
Second mortgage or home equity loan
Loan shark
Consumer sales loan
Repossession
Balloon note
Acceleration clause

Credit life insurance
Disability insurance
Open-ended consumer credit
Charge accounts
 Regular
 Revolving
Bank credit card
 Extended payment supplement
 Cash advance
Finance charge-free grace period
Billing dispute
Minimum payment rut

DISCUSSION QUESTIONS

1   What advantages and what disadvantages do you see for the lender in making a secured consumer cash loan rather than an unsecured loan? What about the borrower?

2   Why is the APR on cash loans from consumer finance companies generally higher than the APR on cash loans from banks and credit unions?

LOAN OPTION	A	B	C
Lender	Commercial bank	Credit union	Consumer finance company
Special notes	Will use automatic overdraft on his checking account	Straight personal loan	Straight personal loan

3 Halmut Maki is considering the three lenders listed above as potential sources for a 12-month, $1000 cash loan. What are the principal differences among the three loans? Are there any particular advantages or disadvantages to each loan that Halmut should know about?

4 What potential problems and pitfalls are associated with a cash loan using a second mortgage?

5 If a good friend asked you to rank sources of cash loans from the most desirable to the least desirable, what would your recommended list look like? Why?

6 What preliminary steps should a prospective borrower complete before shopping for a cash loan?

7 When shopping for a cash loan among competing sources, what features and provisions would you concentrate on?

8 What are the principal differences between a consumer cash loan and a sales loan? What key factors should you consider in deciding between the two loans?

9 How have the changes in federal legislation improved the buyer's bargaining position with the seller once the sales loan has been sold to a bank or finance company? Why were these changes necessary?

10 Do you agree that allowing the lender to repossess the item that is pledged as security on a loan is a poor way to repay that loan? Why?

11 What criteria should a borrower use to decide whether to purchase credit life insurance? Does credit life have any disadvantages? Some argue that the practice of rebating a portion of the insurance premiums to the lender can cause a conflict of interest. Why or why not?

12 What advantages does a card holder obtain from having a bank credit card? What benefits does the bank that issued the credit card hope to obtain? What factors account for the rapid expansion of bank credit cards? What future do you see for these cards?

13 Explain the major advantages gained from using credit cards and charge accounts properly and effectively.

14 While reviewing her bank credit card statement for the month of May, Betty Perfection noted that her previous month's payment had been credited as $135.35 rather than the $135.37 she wrote on the check. Because of this error by the lender, she failed to pay the entire $135.37 balance within the grace period; so she was assessed a $2.03 finance charge. How should Betty proceed? Will she likely prevail?

15 What advantages are offered by the small minimum-payment feature most credit cards provide? Are there disadvantages?

16 Fred Forgetful has just discovered that he "mislaid" one of his credit cards. How would you suggest Fred proceed? Despite speedy action, assume Fred later finds that someone has charged two one-way airline tickets to Casablanca, with a total cost of $2060. Discuss the consequences.

PROBLEMS

CHAPTER 8

247

SOURCES OF
CONSUMER
CREDIT

8-1 Orphial Parchenski has the following three options for obtaining the $1000 cash loan she wants:

	Option		
	1	2	3
Lender	Bank credit card	Mutual savings bank	Life insurance company
Description of loan	Cash advance	Personal cash loan	Loan on life insurance policy
APR	18%	12%	9%
Repayment period	1–24 months	12 months	As long as borrower desires

Orphial expects to pay the loan off in about 12 months. However, she may elect to repay it sooner if her finances permit.

a What is the monthly payment for each option, assuming repayment in 12 months? (*Hint:* Exhibit 7-8 may help.)

b What would the total finance charge be for each loan?

c Which loan would you recommend? Why?

d Do any of the loans have special features that Orphial should consider?

8-2 Morris Bumbler is having difficulty deciding whether he should elect to take credit life insurance on his $6000, 3-year, 18 percent APR cash loan; he plans to use the money from the loan to buy a new car. The lender has stressed the "financial security" and "peace of mind" the credit life insurance coverage will give because it completely repays any unpaid loan balance. Morris is amazed at the lender's concern for his well-being! When pushed, the lender volunteers that the premiums are 80 cents per $100 of initial loan. The lender also points out that the initial loan amount would include the entire finance charge plus the $6000. And the lender notes, "Since you will likely elect to pay the premium over the life of the loan—most of our borrowers do—there is a small finance charge on the premiums. But your monthly payment is only a low, low $6.77."

a What initial amount would the lender use to compute the insurance premiums? (*Hint:* Exhibit 7-8 may help.)

b Should Morris select the "low, low payment option," how much will he actually pay in total for the insurance?

c Assume that the repayments drop the unpaid balance to roughly $4345 at the end of the first year and to about $2366 at the end of the second year. Approximately how much true insurance coverage does Morris receive?

d Morris has found that term life insurance from an insurance company would cost him about $4 per $1000 of coverage each year. What is the annual cost of purchasing term insurance equal to the original loan ($6000)? For the entire period?

e What do you recommend that Morris do? Why?

8-3   Liz Krantz has price quotes from two dealers on the new camera and accessories she wants to take along on her vacation. The offers include:

	LOCAL CAMERA DEALER	MAIL-ORDER DEALER
Total cash price	$700	$650
Credit offered	Bank credit card or sales loan	None

Since Liz does not have the money, she will need to finance the purchase for about 12 months. Her credit alternatives include:

	Alternative			
	A	B	C	D
Source	Dealer	Credit card	Commercial bank	Credit union
Description of credit offer	Sales loan	Extended payments	Automatic overdraft	Personal cash loan
Maturity	12 months	12 months	12 months	12 months
APR	15%	18%	15%	12%
Special notes			Will accept more rapid repayment	Includes credit life insurance

   a   What is the appropriate monthly payment for each alternative? What is the total cost of each one?

   b   What are the strengths of each credit alternative? The weaknesses?

   c   Which option would you recommend? Why?

8-4   Ken Montgomery's bank credit card account currently has a $415 balance that is due July 20. Because he spent more money on his vacation than he intended, Ken cannot make the entire payment.

   One option is to make the $15 minimum payment. That will, of course, subject him to the finance charge, since there will be no grace period. Terms of the credit card agreement specify a 1 1/2 percent per month finance charge on the average daily balance. (Ken's daily balance is $415.)

   Another option would be to draw the required $415 by using the automatic overdraft on his checking account. It carries a 15 percent APR finance charge that is computed on the daily balance of the outstanding overdraft. Ken expects to repay the overdraft in about 20 days.

   a   What finance charge will Ken pay for missing the grace period? (*Hint:* Exhibit 7-11 may be of interest.)

   b   Is the checking overdraft a viable option? How does its cost compare with the penalty incurred by missing the grace period?

c Assume, for the moment, that Ken continues to make the $15 minimum payment. How many months will it take to repay the balance? (*Hint:* The 18 percent APR column in Exhibit 7-8 should help.) What total finance charge will Ken pay during that period?

CASE PROBLEM

Eric and Ingrid Svensen have decided to replace the kitchen stove and refrigerator that came with their house. The stove and refrigerator they want are handled by the local appliance dealer. The dealer's price for the two units is $1800, and he has assured them that he will handle all the financing problems. Eric and Ingrid think that the dealer's sales loan seems a bit costly: a 24-month loan with an APR of 30 percent, and credit life and disability insurance are included as extra cost items. After including the cost of the insurance coverage, the monthly payment on the dealer loan will be $103.88. But they feel they are fortunate that the dealer will make the small loan. Both doubt that their bank or credit union would make an $1800 loan.

1   Is a sales loan their only option? Could you recommend an alternative?

2   What is your opinion of the above loan? Do you see any problems with the dealer-arranged loan?

3   What would be the potential saving if the Svensens could find the same 24-month loan with an APR of 12 percent? Of 15 percent? (*Hint:* Exhibit 7-8 may be helpful.)

4   The Svensens have considered charging the two units on their bank credit card (their limit is $2000) and making the minimum monthly payment. What are the strengths and weaknesses of this option?

5   How should the Svensens decide about the credit life and disability insurance? If they decide that the coverage is needed, what would you recommend?

PART
3
CONSUMER
EXPENDITURES

CHAPTER

9

TRANS-PORTATION: YOUR AUTOMOBILE

**AFTER COMPLETING THIS CHAPTER
YOU WILL HAVE LEARNED**

The *five major categories of automobiles*

The *costs* of owning an automobile

How a *subcompact, compact,* or *midsize* car can *reduce your auto costs*

How to judge whether a particular automobile will *fit your budget*

How to *shop* for and *order* an automobile

Whether a *used car* will do a satisfactory job

What the *standard automobile warranty* covers

How to obtain satisfaction when you have a *warranty claim*

How to evaluate the cost of *automobile ownership* as compared with the cost of *leasing* the same kind of car

FOR many people, the automobile

is what the automobile advertisements want them to believe it is—a confirmation of their social status, a mark of their success in life, and something that can make them appealing to other people. Nevertheless, despite 50 years of this kind of advertising, the purpose of an automobile is still transportation—to carry you from one place to another. People have only recently begun to rediscover the purpose of an automobile. And it has been the skyrocketing costs of owning and operating an auto—the high costs of the auto itself, gas and oil, repairs, and insurance—that have encouraged people to reconsider what an automobile is really used for.

Because these costs are increasing sharply and will most likely continue to rise, people are beginning to pay keen attention to selecting an auto that adequately meets their transportation needs, yet does so without unduly high costs.

CLASSIFYING AUTOMOBILE MODELS

In the past, automobiles were generally classified according to size, but the size classification was based on exterior dimensions, without regard to the amount of usable interior space. Consequently, a car that was very large on the outside was called a "full-sized" car, regardless of how small its interior space might be. That same full-sized car might offer less interior space for passengers and luggage than a smaller car that was several feet shorter and hundreds of pounds lighter. The bigger car, even though it provided less usable space than the smaller car, was designated a "big car." The smaller car, despite its greater interior space, was considered a "small car."

That criterion has changed. Now an automobile is classified according to the amount of usable interior space it offers. After all, if the real purpose of an automobile is to carry you, your passengers, and any luggage, it is only fair that you be given the information to judge it on the interior space that it provides.

The United States government's five classifications for automobiles are based on usable interior space: **minicompact**, **subcompact**, **compact**, **midsize**, and **large**.[1] To qualify for a classification, a car must meet or exceed an established amount of passenger space and luggage capacity.

Exhibit 9-1 was constructed to show the similarities and differences among the automobiles in the five size classifications currently used by the United States government. The exhibit shows the typical overall length, total weight, and usable space of cars in each of the five classifications. Clearly, there are considerable differences among the various classifications.

---

[1] If you want to know how a particular automobile is classified, or would like some examples from each of the classes, you should look in the booklet called *1983 Gas Mileage Guide*. (A new booklet is usually published for each model year, e.g., 1983, 1984.)

EXHIBIT 9-1

Comparison of vehicle weight, length, and usable passenger and luggage space for the five major size classifications of automobiles. *Source:* Data on the size categories are based on a selected sample of representative autos in the various size categories in *1983 Gas Mileage Guide.* Data for usable passenger and luggage space were obtained directly from the *1983 Gas Mileage Guide.*

Car model		Typical overall length	Typical total weight	Usable passenger and luggage space
Mini compact		152 inches	1880 pounds	Less than 85 cubic feet
Subcompact		165 inches	2158 pounds	85 to 100 cubic feet
Compact		175 inches	2500 pounds	100 to 110 cubic feet
Mid-size		185 inches	2800 pounds	110 to 120 cubic feet
Large		216 inches	3780 pounds	More than 120 cubic feet

COST OF AUTOMOBILE OWNERSHIP

Any discussion of the **costs of automobile ownership** must include *all* the costs of ownership. Regular operating expenses, such as the costs of gasoline, oil, and normal maintenance, are considerable. But so are the less frequent expenses, such as the costs of insurance, new tires, repairs, and registration, when you add them all up. Many people seem to ignore these less frequent expenses. And just about everyone fails to recognize that a car begins to decline in value from the first day you own it. For example, even though you paid $9000 for a car 3 years ago, you can be sure it is worth much less today. A decline in value like this is called **depreciation**. And depreciation is indeed a cost. As the next few pages will show, depreciation is often the single largest cost of automobile ownership.

Unless you evaluate all the costs of owning and operating an auto, you will not know the true cost of your automobile transportation. You will believe that it costs less than it actually does to commute 20 miles to work or to drive 8 miles for one item at a special sale. If you only considered gasoline, you might conclude that it costs just 6 cents per mile to drive your car; therefore, you would incorrectly believe that the cost of commuting 20 miles by car would be only $1.20, or that driving to that special sale would cost only 48 cents. But the cost of gasoline isn't the only expense of transportation by car. If all the costs of automobile ownership are included, the true cost can easily exceed 24 cents per mile. That 20-mile commuting trip takes on an entirely different magnitude now that we know the real cost to be $4.80. Likewise, the item you wanted to buy on sale may no longer be a bargain when you consider that the trip to the sale costs $1.92.

Automobile Ownership Costs

A convenient way to analyze automobile ownership costs is to analyze those that are **fixed costs** (costs that don't change with the amount you use your auto) and **variable costs** (costs that do indeed depend on how much you drive your auto). This is the way in which ownership costs were analyzed in a 1982 U.S. Department of Transportation study.[2] The automobile ownership costs we will use in this section are drawn from the estimates published in that study.

Fixed Costs of Ownership The principal feature that distinguishes a fixed ownership cost is that the amount essentially remains fixed each year regardless of how many miles you drive during the year. By far the largest fixed cost is depreciation, or the decline in the market value, of the car during the year. We will demonstrate this in a moment. Other fixed costs include the premiums you pay for insurance, the fees for registering the auto, and any personal property tax you have to pay on your auto.

Variable Costs of Ownership Variable ownership costs tend to vary directly with the number of miles you drive your car. Thus, at the end of the year, a variable cost would be much higher if you drove a great many miles each year than if you drove only a few.

Cost Estimates From the Study Exhibit 9-2 graphically illustrates the fixed costs—depreciation cost and costs for insurance, registration fees, and taxes—of owning and operating automobiles of four different sizes. The variable costs—gas, oil, tolls, parking, and maintenance costs—are graphically illustrated in Exhibit 9-3. Costs are shown for four car models: subcompact, compact, midsize, and large. Before we analyze these cost estimates, we first need to discuss how this ownership study was put together, some of the study's basic assumptions, and some of its limitations.
Features and Limitations It was assumed in the cost estimates shown in Exhibits 9-2 and 9-3 that the respective cars would be owned for 12 years, during which time they would be driven 120,000 miles. The location chosen for the study was a medium-sized city in Maryland. Consequently, these auto ownership and operating costs could be considered typical for a

[2] *Cost of Owning and Operating Automobiles and Vans—1982*, Washington, D.C.: U.S. Department of Transportation, 1982.

EXHIBIT 9-2

Fixed cost per mile to own and operate a sub-compact, a compact, a midsize, and a large automobile. *Source: Cost of Owning and Operating Automobiles and Vans—1982*, Washington, D.C.: U.S. Department of Transportation.

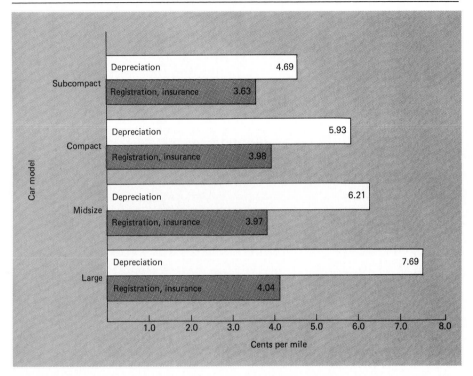

medium-sized suburban area. The study was based on the costs that prevailed during 1981; each cost component was converted to a per-mile figure. For example, assume that the estimated premium for insurance coverage during the first year of ownership is $313. Further, assume that we expect the car to be driven 14,500 miles during that first year. The insurance cost per mile is then:

2.16 cents = $313 ÷ 14,500 miles

Insurance cost = Total insurance ÷ Estimated miles
per mile   premiums   to be driven

A similar set of computations was made for each of the costs of owning and operating an automobile. The results of these computations are what we see summarized in Exhibits 9-2 and 9-3.

Assumed Ownership Period Another assumption that we need to point out is the assumed **ownership period**—12 years. As a later section will

EXHIBIT 9-3

Variable cost per mile to own and operate a subcompact, a compact, a midsize, and a large automobile. *Source: Cost of Owning and Operating Automobiles and Vans—1982,* Washington, D.C.: U.S. Department of Transportation.

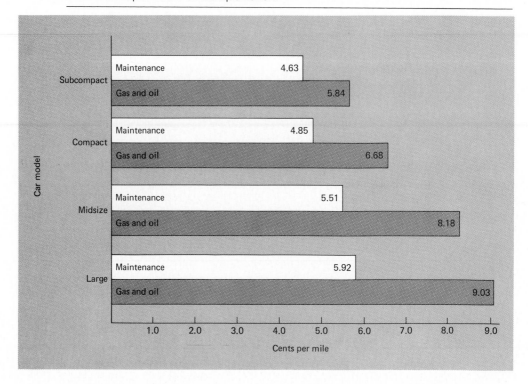

illustrate, the market value of a car declines much more rapidly in its early years than in its later years. Its depreciation cost is therefore higher during those years. And that means that someone who trades in a car for a new one every 1 to 3 years will likely have higher depreciation expense per mile than would someone who owns a car for 5 or more years. Since the depreciation costs in Exhibit 9-2 are based on owning the same car for 12 years, these costs are probably too low for someone who frequently trades in a used car.

Costs as They Were During 1981 Another thing you should know about the study is that it was based on the costs that prevailed during 1981. By the time you read this, these costs will have risen substantially. If recent experience is any indication, you can probably expect these costs to rise at least as rapidly as, if not more rapidly than, consumer prices in general; so annual increases of 5 to 10 percent per year will probably occur for the next several years.

Location for Study Finally, you should realize that this study was conducted in Maryland. Of course, costs such as those of licensing, gasoline, and registration taxes will differ considerably depending on where you live. Car owners in New York City or Boston pay much higher insurance costs than car owners pay for the same insurance in Poland Springs, Maine; Fish Creek, Wisconsin; or Missoula, Montana. Maintenance costs may also be higher in very large metropolitan areas and lower in small towns or rural areas.

The Study: How Much Confidence?   Although we have noted some limits on the data in the study, we do believe that the information contained in Exhibits 9-2 and 9-3 can be extremely useful if you know how to use it. First, your actual costs per mile will not be exactly the same as those shown in the exhibits, but they probably won't be far off. Second, the two exhibits vividly illustrate that the cost of owning an automobile is much greater than the regular expenses of gasoline and oil. Third, even if the cost estimates in these exhibits are dated when you read this, if you know the recent annual inflation rate you can adjust these estimates so that they more accurately reflect today's costs.

EXHIBIT 9-4

Total cost per mile to own and operate cars of four different sizes for three different ownership periods. *Source: Cost of Owning and Operating Automobiles and Vans—1982,* Washington, D.C.: U.S. Department of Transportation.

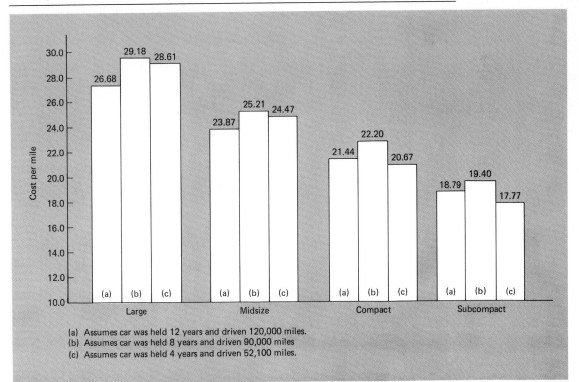

(a) Assumes car was held 12 years and driven 120,000 miles.
(b) Assumes car was held 8 years and driven 90,000 miles
(c) Assumes car was held 4 years and driven 52,100 miles

TOTAL COST OF OWNERSHIP

Exhibit 9-4 is designed to show you the total cost per mile to own and drive a subcompact, a compact, a midsize, and a large car. The total cost per mile shown includes the fixed costs from Exhibit 9-2 plus the variable costs from Exhibit 9-3. In addition to the 12-year, 120,000-mile ownership period, which we have used as a basis for our discussion up to this point, Exhibit 9-4 also shows the total costs per mile for two other ownership periods: you own the car for 8 years, during which time you drive it 90,000 miles, and you keep the car for 4 years and drive it 52,100 miles. For each size of car, column (*a*) shows the cost per mile for the 12-year ownership period, column (*b*) for the 8-year period, and column (*c*) for the 4-year period. You can make two immediate cost comparisons with the details shown in Exhibit 9-4. First, you can compare the cost per mile for each of the four different-sized cars. Second, for a particular car, you can compare the cost per mile for three different ownership periods.

The message from Exhibit 9-4 seems clear. The total ownership cost per mile for the subcompact is less than the ownership cost for the compact, considerably less than the cost for the midsize, and much less than the cost for the large car. This decline in cost holds for all three ownership periods. Similarly, the compact's total ownership cost per mile is less than the cost for the midsize and considerably less than the cost for the large car. Again, this relationship holds for all three ownership periods. Finally, the ownership cost for the midsize car is less than the cost for the large car.

Cost Savings: Midsize, Compact, or Subcompact?

The best way to understand what it really costs to own a particular size car is to look at how much you can save by owning a smaller car. Exhibit 9-5 graphically portrays the annual cost savings between a midsize and a large, a compact and a midsize, a subcompact and a compact, and a subcompact and a midsize car. For example, if you plan to keep your car for 4 years, the exhibit suggests you can save $539 each year by owning a midsize rather than a large car.

Source of the Savings   If you review the variable costs shown in Exhibit 9-3, you will notice that the maintenance cost per mile rises with the size of the auto driven. Also, the combined cost of gas, oil, and tolls rises as the car size increases. It is lowest for the subcompact and, as you might expect, it increases as the car becomes larger and weighs more. A major part of the saving that is shown in Exhibit 9-5 is due to the lower variable costs for the smaller car models.

Lower depreciation costs for the smaller car models also contribute to the savings shown in Exhibit 9-5 from switching to a smaller car. A review of the fixed costs in Exhibit 9-2 indicates that the cost of depreciation does indeed rise with the size of the car. Why does it rise? The major reason is that the purchase price of a car typically rises with the size of the car: Compacts cost more than subcompacts, midsizes more than compacts, etc. We say it typically rises, but there are some exceptions. Rolls-Royce has a subcompact model and it is hardly cheap to buy.

EXHIBIT 9-5

Annual cost savings from switching between the
four different sized automobiles for three different
holding periods.

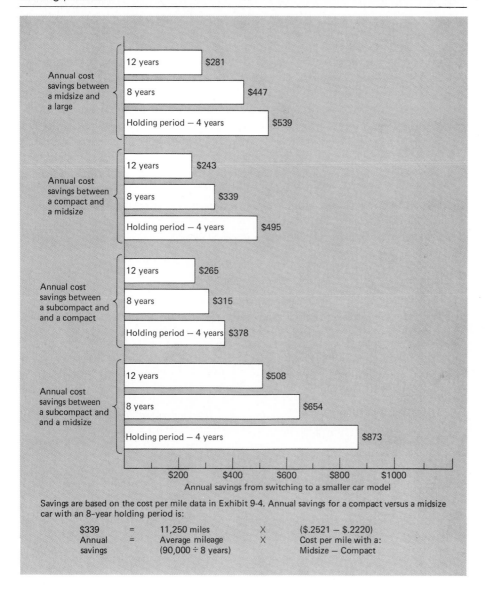

Savings are based on the cost per mile data in Exhibit 9-4. Annual savings for a compact versus a midsize
car with an 8-year holding period is:

$339	=	11,250 miles	X	($.2521 − $.2220)
Annual	=	Average mileage	X	Cost per mile with a:
savings		(90,000 ÷ 8 years)		Midsize − Compact

Which Ownership Period?

There is no "optimum" ownership period. That is, contrary to what some
people may believe, owning a car for a short period and selling it before any
repairs can be expected yields no lower ownership costs per mile than does
owning a car for 12 years and paying for those repairs. Exhibit 9-4 shows

this: Owning a car for 4 or 8 or 12 years produces no great differences in total ownership costs per mile.

Nevertheless, if your anticipated future repair bills will apparently be enormous, it may be time to trade your car. Your recent repair experience may provide a guide to such future costs. For example, if you have recently had several major repairs that cost $300 to $500, the time may be ripe to consider replacing your car. Or if your present car has begun to require a continuing series of $50 to $100 repairs, so that you only have the car for several weeks before it is back in the auto service shop for repairs, it may be a signal that it is time to replace your present car. A competent and trustworthy auto mechanic may be able to help you decide when replacing your present car will be cheaper than trying to keep it running.

Remember: Even when the most expensive cars get old or are driven for many miles, they become costly to keep in operating condition. There is one caveat, however. We stress the words "major repairs" and "recurring repairs." Some people will spend $5000 for a new car just to avoid replacing the $70, 5-year-old battery in their present car. That is not our idea of a major or recurring repair, nor does it signal the need to trade cars.

EXHIBIT 9-6

Estimated future cost per mile to own and operate a subcompact, a compact, a midsize, and a large auto.

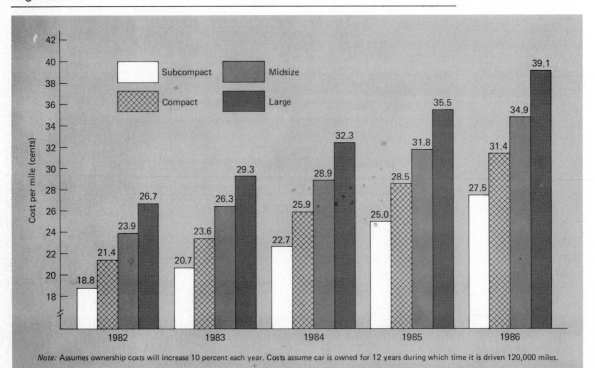

Note: Assumes ownership costs will increase 10 percent each year. Costs assume car is owned for 12 years during which time it is driven 120,000 miles.

can use to judge the relative importance of operating cost for a particular appliance you may be considering.

Comparative Operating Costs   The cost comparision, shown at (2) in Exhibit 10-5, illustrates the unit's operating cost efficiency relative to the efficiency of similar, competing models. All manufacturers must estimate the operating costs of their appliances using the same standard test and the same energy costs. The operating efficiency of all similar appliances can be compared using their **comparative operating costs**.

However, the label only compares appliances that are operated by the same energy source. Electric hot-water heaters are compared with other electric hot-water heaters but not with natural-gas hot-water heaters. Nevertheless, you can easily make your own comparison.

For example, suppose you want to compare an eletric hot-water heater with a natural-gas hot-water heater. By comparing the annual operating cost for the electric heater—it would be shown at point (1), Exhibit 10-5, on the energy-cost label—with the same annual operating cost from the label for the natural-gas heater, you can readily decide which heater will cost the least to operate.

Range of Operating Costs   Because the cost per unit of energy can vary considerably in different parts of the United States, the label provides a **range of operating costs** based on various energy costs. This is shown at (3) in Exhibit 10-5. Thus, people living where the cost per unit of energy is high or low relative to the national average will have some data for estimating what a particular appliance's operating cost will be.

EXHIBIT 10-6

Potential annual saving in operating cost from
using energy-efficient appliances.

APPLIANCE	RELATIVE EFFICIENCY RANK	COST PER YEAR*	Potential Savings in Operating Cost					
			MOST EFFICIENT VERSUS MIDRANGE		MOST EFFICIENT VERSUS LEAST		MIDRANGE VERSUS LEAST	
			ANNUAL SAVING	LIFE-TIME	ANNUAL SAVING	LIFE-TIME	ANNUAL SAVING	LIFE-TIME
Refrigerator: Top-freezer (capacity 16.5–18.4 cubic feet)	Most	$45	$21	$315				
	Midrange	$66			$43	$645	$22	$330
	Least	$88						
Freezer: Upright (capacity 15.5–17.4 cubic feet)	Most	$40	$18	$270				
	Midrange	$58			$36	$540	$18	$270
	Least	$76						

*Computed using 5.64 cents per kwh. Potential savings will be much larger where the cost is higher. Annual cost is rounded to nearest dollar.

Potential Savings

The more energy efficient the appliance, the greater your saving in operating costs. Exhibit 10-6 shows the range of estimated annual operating costs for top-freezer refrigerators and for upright freezers. The appliances tested were very similar in size, capacity, and features, so their operating costs can be meaningfully compared. The second column of the exhibit identifies the classifications: the least efficient, the midrange efficient, and the most efficient models. The third column shows the operating costs corresponding to each caliber of efficiency.

As Exhibit 10-6 illustrates, the cost differential among the three efficiency rankings can be sizable. Selecting the most efficient of the top-freezer refrigerator models rather than the least efficient model would save $43 annually. Saving this much each year during a refrigerator's typical 15-year life could produce total savings of $645. Even the refrigerator with midrange efficiency generates $22 in annual savings compared with the least efficient model; that means a lifetime saving of $330.

STRATEGY

When deciding which appliance to buy, be sure you consider energy efficiency. Over its lifetime, a high-efficiency model can produce sizable operating cost savings compared with a lower-efficiency model.

High Efficiency: How Much Is It Worth?

Some appliance manufacturers have introduced new models that have been specially designed to minimize the amount of energy they use and thereby to lower their annual operating costs. The purchase price on some of these new **high-efficiency appliances** may be higher than the price for a more traditionally designed model. An immediate question is: Will you save more in lifetime operating costs than the extra price you will have to pay for the most energy-efficient model? The easiest way to answer that question is simply to add up the annual savings in operating cost each year and compare that total with the difference in purchase price between the standard model and the most energy-efficient model. If the operating cost savings really exceeded the difference in purchase price, the energy-efficient model would be the best choice. But this comparison is not entirely accurate because it assumes that a dollar that you will save in operating costs 10 years from now is equal in value to a dollar now. You already know that a dollar 10 years from now may be worth much less than a dollar today.

One way to handle the difference in timing between the immediate extra purchase price and the future operating savings is to calculate how many years it will take to recover the added cost of the more efficient model from its annual operating cost savings. For example, assume that a particular high-efficiency model costs $90 more than a competing standard model, but its annual operating cost is $15 less than the other model. The number of years it will take to recover the added purchase price from operating savings is:

6 years   = $90   ÷ $15

⌂   ⌂   ⌂

Years needed to   Added   Annual
recover added   = purchase ÷ saving in
purchase price   price   operating cost

Our general decision rule is that the extra cost is justified if you can recover it from the operating cost savings in:

9 years or less on appliances with a 15-year life

8 years or less on units with a 12-year life

7 years or less on units with a 10-year life

Of course, the shorter the recovery period, the bigger the advantage from purchasing the more efficient model.

An example is the best way to illustrate how this decision rule works. Assume that we are considering two competing refrigerators, each having a 15-year life. Brand X's price is $700 and it costs $50 to operate each year. Brand Y is lower-priced, $640, but has a higher operating cost, $60 per year. Brand X's $60 higher price is recovered in:

6 years   = $60   ÷ ($60 − $50)

⌂   ⌂   ⌂

Years to _ Added _ Annual operating
recover   = cost ÷ cost savings

Since 6 years is considerably shorter than our 9-year cutoff for 15-year appliances, Brand X is clearly the refrigerator you should buy.

Too often, people never look beyond that higher initial price. They may claim that they can invest the extra purchase price and be further ahead. But is that true? Take our previous example, where you saved $10 in operating costs each year by paying an extra $60 for the more efficient refrigerator. But you would have to earn a return of approximately $10 each year for the next 15 years in order to justify buying the less efficient Brand Y. To do that, you would need to earn an annual rate of interest of 14.4 percent, and that kind of return is just not very common on most investments.

STRATEGY

Buy that energy-efficient appliance if your total savings in operating cost over the next 7 to 9 years will exceed the unit's added purchase price.

Operating Cost: The Future

As the cost of all forms of energy—electricity, natural gas, and fuel oil—rises, you will pay more and more to operate an inefficient appliance. And indications are that energy costs will rise 10 to 15 percent every year over the next few years.

Exhibit 10-7 projects what will likely happen to the difference in operating costs between the most efficient refrigerator and the least efficient one. We assume that the cost of a kilowatt hour of electricity will rise 10 percent annually. Given that increase, in 5 years the cost differential will have widened from $43 to $70. Exhibit 10-7 contains two messages. Operating efficiency will become increasingly important as energy costs continue their upward spiral. And the upward spiral of energy costs may make the purchase of a higher-priced, yet more efficient, appliance, even more attractive in the long run.

APPLIANCE PRICES

As you might expect, the appliance industry doesn't make it easy for you to decide what is a fair price to pay for a particular appliance. For example, manufacturers rarely indicate to the public the year in which an appliance was produced. The year of production is coded in the model number.

Another problem is determining exactly what the price of an appliance is. Some dealers heavily discount their prices while others charge full list price. Further, to complicate this problem, many manufacturers do not publish a "suggested retail price." The net effect of all these practices is that buyers have limited price information and must estimate what seems to be the "right" **appliance price**.

EXHIBIT 10-7

Projected future operating cost differential between the most energy-efficient refrigerator and the least energy-efficient refrigerator.

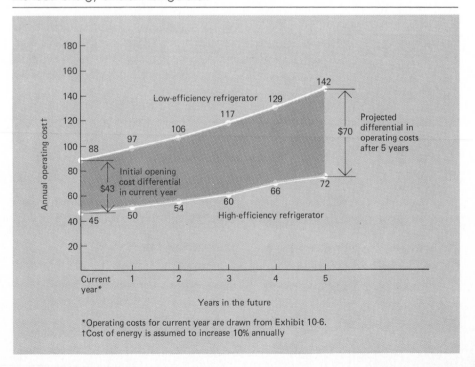

*Operating costs for current year are drawn from Exhibit 10-6.
†Cost of energy is assumed to increase 10% annually

Estimating a Reasonable Price

When trying to establish the price you should pay for a particular appliance, you generally encounter two extreme situations. On the one hand, large department stores and nationwide retail chains typically have a tag on the unit showing its price, and their salespeople have little, if any, latitude to bargain with you on that price. On the other hand, small retailers frequently do not post their prices, and their salespeople usually have some latitude in quoting prices to you. Usually, they are permitted to negotiate, at least beyond the first round of haggling, until they settle on a price with you.

Average Price   Estimating a reasonable price to pay would be much easier if you had some idea of the **average purchase price**. The comparative appliance tests reported in *Consumer Reports* are a good source for an average price. In addition to test data, *Consumer Reports* also gives the price range for each model tested. Frequently, the difference between highest and lowest price exceeds $100, so shopping for the lowest price is usually worth the time.

Haggling   The choice of whether to **haggle** over the price is a personal one. Some people love to haggle; others abhor doing so. Should you decide to haggle, be certain you know the local average price. Otherwise, you might suffer the fate of Borris Bumbler. The dealer initially quoted $850 on a television; Borris, sensing a quick $100 saving, countered with $750. After faking great distress, the dealer yielded to that price. Later, Borris found the same unit at a competing store for $700.

Trade In Your Used Appliance[2]   Some appliance dealers encourage trade-ins; others do not deal in them at all. Dealers who do take trade-ins will more readily accept appliances such as refrigerators and stoves. They're not too keen about accepting used dishwashers and clothes washers because selling them is difficult.

Trade-In Allowance: Dealer   The dollar amount that the dealer will give you as a **trade-in allowance** on your present appliance can significantly change the amount you pay for the new appliance. For example, assume that you are considering a new $700 refrigerator. The dealer has offered a $50 trade-in allowance on your present refrigerator. The net cash difference for the new appliance, then, is:

$$\underset{\substack{\text{Net cash} \\ \text{difference}}}{\$650} = \underset{\substack{\text{Purchase price} \\ \text{of new unit}}}{\$700} - \underset{\substack{\text{Trade-in allowed} \\ \text{on old unit}}}{\$50}$$

Some people are happy only when the dealer quotes a very high

---

[2] The trade-in practices discussed in this and subsequent sections are based on the conclusions in Larry R. Lang, "Trade-In Practices for Major Home Appliances," *Proceedings of American Council on Consumer Interest*, 25th Annual Conference, 1979.

trade-in allowance on their used appliance. Unfortunately, that might lead to the following: Suppose that you, the customer for the above $700 refrigerator, go to a second dealer complaining about the first dealer's low $50 trade-in allowance. This dealer senses that a "high trade-in allowance" may clinch the sale. She agrees with you about the "low trade-in allowance" and offers $125, and your eyes light up. But the dealer quotes a price of $800 on the new refrigerator (we assume that the price is not posted on the unit). Mesmerized by the larger trade-in allowance, you might purchase the refrigerator from the second dealer. Is it really a bargain? No. You would be paying a net cash difference of $675 to the second dealer. Yet, even with the lower trade-in allowance, the first dealer wanted only a $650 cash difference. The message is clear: You should have concentrated on minimizing the net cash difference, not on maximixing the trade-in allowance.

STRATEGY

When trading in a used appliance on a new one, purchase the new appliance from the dealer who offers the lowest cash difference.

METHOD OF PAYMENT

Most dealers make available two or three payment alternatives: straight cash, deferred payment same as cash, and consumer sales loan.

Cash By paying straight cash, you avoid any and all finance charges. Cash payment is generally less expensive than using credit since the cost of credit exceeds the interest that your money could earn in a savings account.

Deferred Payment Same as Cash With a **deferred payment** plan, you take possesion of the appliance even though you pay only part of the price at the time of the sale. You pay the balance of the price over the next 30, 60, or 90 days. Typically, there is no finance charge, so the terms of payment are indeed the same as cash. For those people who can fit the payment into their budget, it is the best form of payment.

Consumer Sales Loan   Most dealers aggressively push sales loans. No doubt, part of their enthusiasm is due to the rebate they receive from reselling the loan to a bank or finance company. If you are going to use a loan, shop for it among several lenders and compare its costs with the cost of the sales loan offered by the dealer.

STRATEGY

Deferred payment is generally the best way to pay for an appliance if you can fit the short-term payments into your monthly budget.

DESIGN AND OPERATING FEATURES

Among the four criteria for evaluating appliances, design and operating features constitute the hardest category for us to specify and for you to evaluate. The reason is that these features are as important as you want them to be. Because manufacturers know this, they design appliances with many different minor or convenience features supplementing the basic service of the appliance. For example, refrigerators are available with such extra features as ice-water dispensers and crushed-ice dispensers. How important these features are is entirely up to you, given your needs and preferences. Rather than review specific appliances, we will suggest ways for you to evaluate whether you will need or use extra features like these and whether they are worth the extra cost.

Information Sources   The results of comparative appliance tests reported in *Consumer Reports* and *Consumers' Research Magazine* provide a wealth of information on each model's various features. In addition, *Consumer Reports* highlights the major advantages and disadvantages for each model. Test data cover how well each model performs the basic task it was designed to do, as well as the model's various supplemental and convenience features. Both publications test each type of major appliance every 2 or 3 years. Therefore, their information is reasonably up to date. Since most libraries subscribe to one or both magazines, the information is readily accessible.

Evaluation   The reports in *Consumer Reports* and *Consumers' Research Magazine* generally group the models according to the extent of their supplemental features, and they recommend these models according to their usefulness. Their lists of recommendations, advantages, and disadvantages are an excellent place to begin your evaluation. Frequently, the reports note the features that most people otherwise may overlook. You can make the best use of these reports by following these suggestions: Do not include the negative comments and disadvantages of a model until you first ask yourself: Is that disadvantage important to me? Does that negative comment apply to my situation? Should you answer yes, you should include these negative comments in your evaluation of that particular model. Likewise, ask yourself whether the advantages reported in the publications will benefit you. We are not suggesting that you summarily reject the findings; instead, we recommend that you decide whether or not these comments apply to your own situation.

SHOPPING FOR APPLIANCES

There are three considerations to keep in mind when shopping for appliances:

1   Relative importance of service, operating cost, price, and design features

2   Type of appliance you need

3   Whether you are buying at a sale price

If you pay careful attention to each of these considerations, you should get maximum satisfaction at minimum cost.

Importance of Service, Operating Cost, Price, and Design Features

The relative importance of service, operating costs, price, and design features varies among different appliances. In Exhibit 10-8, we list the relative importance of the three considerations for the major home appliances. While the rankings in that exhibit are our value judgments, we believe

EXHIBIT 10-8

Shopping guidelines to help you decide the relative importance of service, operating cost, purchase price, and design features.

		Criteria		
APPLIANCE	SERVICE*	OPERATING COSTS*	MINIMIZING PURCHASE PRICE*	DESIGN FEATURES— ADVANTAGES AND DISADVANTAGES*
Air conditioner	V	E	M	M
Clothes washer	V	V	M	M
Clothes dryer	L	L	V	L
Dishwasher	V	V	M	M
Freezer	M	E	M	L
Kitchen range	L	L	V	M
Refrigerator	M	E	M	M
Television	E	M	M	V
Water heater	L	E	V	L

*Degree of importance:
E = Extremely   M = Moderately
V = Very   L = Little

they can provide general shopping guidelines for anyone. Our overall goal is to minimize life-cycle cost, yet still deliver adequate appliance performance. Not everyone will agree with our emphasis on minimizing cost; you may decide that other things are more important.

Selecting What You Need

The goal in selecting an appliance should be to find the one that exactly meets your needs—no more and no less. Too many people buy appliances that provide more features than they require. Try to "think simple" when shopping for an appliance. We are not suggesting that everyone buy the bare-bones model. Instead, we think you should decide what your needs are and select a model that meets those needs but no more. When in doubt, ask yourself: "Do I really need that added feature? Will I use it?"

"Trading You Up" In general, most people will be best served by the model midway between the manufacturer's most deluxe model and the simplest model. Unfortunately, the dealer and the salesperson both have an incentive to **trade you up**—to get customers to buy a higher-priced model. Why? Larger profits for the dealer, and a higher commission for the salesperson.

STRATEGY

Before deciding on that deluxe model the dealer is pushing, ask yourself if you need it.

Bait and Switch Unfortunately, the **bait-and-switch** routine is sometimes used as a sales tactic. Although in its most blatant form it is illegal, a restrained form is still around. The routine goes something like this: First there is the "bait"—a heavily advertised appliance that entices the customer because of its super low price; then comes the "switch"—the customer's interest, once attracted, is switched from the bait to a more expensive appliance. The switch techniques are numerous and ingenious.

The salesperson may claim the store is out of the bait. Alternatively, he or she may expound on the weaknesses and shortcomings of the bait. Or the dealer may present the bait in the worst possible light: poor display, ghastly color, missing parts.

Regardless of the exact switch technique used, you can protect yourself by just refusing to be switched. If you really are interested in the bait, fine—stick to your original plan. Should you decide that the bait is not what you want, or if you find that the appliance is unobtainable, look elsewhere. Chances are that you will not be missing any great bargains by passing up the substitutes. If you encounter this practice, report it to your local Better Business Bureau or the consumer protection agency in your state.

STRATEGY

Avoid being switched by demanding the bait if it really fits your needs. If it is not what you want, drop that store and shop a competitor.

Judging Claims About Price

"Closeout," "Manufacturer's Clearance"—everyone has read advertisements announcing an "appliance sale" using these or similar words. But when is a sale really a sale? We think that a real sale occurs much less often than the advertisements would have you believe. The best way to judge whether an appliance is really on sale is to know what the regular price is when it is not "on sale."

STRATEGY

Before you buy an appliance at a dealer's highly advertised sale, try to find out what the regular price is for that same appliance. Then you will know whether the sale will really save you any money.

SUMMARY

1   The four principal factors you should think about when deciding which appliance to buy are (a) service, (b) operating cost, (c) purchase price, and (d) design features.

2   Life-cycle ownership cost for an appliance includes three costs: purchase price, operating cost, and service costs.

3   In evaluating service for an appliance, you should consider frequency of service, the unit's serviceability, and service availability.

4   With a service contract, you don't have to think about what to do when you need repairs or how much they will cost. But the cost of a service contract is high.

5   The annual operating cost for certain types of appliance can be readily obtained from the energy-cost label which manufacturers are required to provide on them.

6   For appliances that use lots of energy, an energy-efficient model can save several hundred dollars in operating costs over its lifetime.

7   Although a high-efficiency appliance may cost more, it will be worth the higher price if the savings in annual operating cost will recover the difference in price in 7 to 9 years.

8   As energy costs continue to rise, operating cost will become increasingly important in deciding on the appliance model you should buy.

9   Comparative price shopping for appliances is essential. The results can turn up differences of $100 or more on identical models in competing stores.

10   The average price cited in *Consumer Reports* is a good starting point when estimating a reasonable price to pay for an appliance.

11   When comparing price quotes from different dealers, you should concentrate on obtaining the lowest net cash difference:

$$\frac{\text{Net cash}}{\text{difference}} = \frac{\text{Dealer's price on}}{\text{new appliance}} - \frac{\text{Trade-in allowance}}{\text{on your present appliance}}$$

12   Deferred payment same as cash is typically the best payment option if you can fit the payments into your budget.

13   *Consumer Reports* and *Consumers' Research Magazine* publish comparative appliance tests that discuss each model's design features as well as of its advantages and disadvantages.

14   Select the appliance model that just meets your needs.

15   Many dealers and salespeople will try to get customers to buy a more expensive model.

16   Beware the old bait-and-switch technique. If the dealer's bait meets your needs, insist that the dealer sell you that particular appliance.

REVIEW YOUR UNDERSTANDING OF

Life-cycle ownership cost
Appliance decision criteria
   Service cost
   Operating cost
   Purchase price
   Design features
Warranty
Service contract
Operating cost efficiency
Energy-cost label
   Estimated annual operating cost
   Comparative operating costs

Range of operating costs
High-efficiency appliances
Appliance prices
   Average purchase price
   Haggling
Trade-in allowance
Deferred payment same as cash
Trading you up
Bait and switch
Closeouts,
   manufacturer's clearance

DISCUSSION QUESTIONS

1 Which cost element—purchase price, operating cost, or service cost—do you think consumers most frequently consider when selecting an appliance? Why? What is meant by life-cycle ownership cost? Do you think the importance of life-cycle cost will increase or decrease in the future?

2 Do you agree with the comment that a service contract will end your service worries for only a few pennies per day? Why or why not?

3 What kinds of appliances must carry an energy-cost label? Why is it not required on all appliances? What information does a label show? How can this information be used when you shop among competing appliances?

4 Why is it difficult to compare prices of appliances? What steps can be used to estimate a reasonable price?

5 The dealer has quoted Ralph and Grazelda Swift two payment options on their new $700 appliance: (a) 90-day deferred payment same as cash, and (b) a 24-month sales loan with an APR of 24 percent. Which would you recommend? Why? Which option would the dealer likely stress? Why?

6 Should everyone rigidly follow the recommendations in *Consumer Reports* and *Consumers' Research Magazine*? Why or why not?

7 In buying what types of appliances is service an important consideration? What steps would you use to assign the importance of services to the various competing brands? What service factors should be considered? Give examples of appliances for which service should be an important consideration in the selection decision.

8 What degree of importance would you assign to purchase price, operating cost, service, and design features for the following: (a) refrigerator? Why? (b) clothes dryer? Why? (c) color television? Why? (d) hot-water heater? Why?

9 What does "trading up" an appliance customer mean? Why is this practice a problem? Is there any loss to the customer who is traded up to a deluxe model with more features than needed?

10 Fast Phil's Appliance Outlet has recently announced the start of its "super colossal clearance sale." How would you decide if it is a legitimate sale?

PROBLEMS

10-1 Stanley Snodgrass is off to replace his recently expired television set. He feels that the three most important considerations when shopping for any appliance are price, price, and price.

   a Approximately how many years can he expect to own the new color television?

   b What percentage of the television set's life-cycle cost does purchase price represent?

   c Are there other factors that you feel Stanley should consider?

10-2 Tim and Margaret Sudowski have been offered the following service contract on a new clothes washer: $65 for the first and second year, $43 for the third, $46 for the fourth year; the cost rises $3 for each year beyond the fourth year.

a Assuming that they keep the contract in force for the clothes washer's expected life, what total will they pay?

b The dealer has stressed that they can always lower the total fee by dropping coverage once the fee becomes large. Do you agree? Why or why not?

c If an average service call costs $40, how many service calls will they have to use during the lifetime of the washer before the contract can be considered a bargain? Do you think that the service contract would turn out to be a bargain for most people?

10-3   Susan McKenzie is going to replace the refrigerator in her condominium with one of three models:

MODEL	PURCHASE PRICE	ESTIMATED MONTHLY OPERATING COST
Standard (freezer on top)	$700	$5.50
Standard (freezer on side)	800	6.50
Superefficient (freezer on top)	800	4.00

a   What is the annual operating cost for each unit?

b   How long will it take to recover the added cost for the superefficient model? For the standard with freezer on side?

c   Which would you recommend? Why?

d   What is the highest purchase price you could justify for the superefficient refrigerator? (*Hint:* Consider the maximum recovery period for an appliance with a 15-year life.)

10-4   Maude Mesmerized has recently returned from a shopping trip to replace her vintage kitchen stove. When she had it repaired 2 months ago, the repair person jokingly suggested that she should donate it to the local museum for its "antique appliance display." Maude has three price quotes:

DEALER	KITCHEN STOVE	TRADE-IN ALLOWANCE	PRICE OF NEW KITCHEN STOVE
Fast Phil's	Le Gourmet	$27.50	$659.50
Honest Helen's	Le Gourmet	$72.00	$714.95
Low-priced Leo's	Le Gourmet	Zero; takes no trade-ins	$641.95

Maude is perplexed by all this information; she needs your help to decide which dealer she should select. (Assume all the dealers offer similar service after the sale.)

a   Which dealer do you recommend? Why?

b Assume Maude lives in a very large metropolitan area where disposing of an old appliance costs $40; she can avoid that expense by trading her stove on a new one. Knowing that, would your answer to question **a** change? If not, why not?

10-5 Herman Andrews has received sales offers from three dealers for a new Super Scrub dishwasher. Herman would like to trade in his old dishwasher and get a large trade-in allowance. Details on the offers include:

	DEALER A	DEALER B	DEALER C
Trade-in of current unit	$20 allowance	dealer refuses trade-ins	$80 allowance
Payment options	cash, credit cards (extended terms), sales loan (18 percent APR)	cash, deferred payment same as cash, sales loan (12 percent APR)	cash, deferred payment same as cash, sales loan (24 percent APR)
Price of new dishwasher	$570	$560	$650

a Which sales offer would you recommend? Why?

b What payment option would you recommend? Why?

c *Optional:* Assume that Herman finds a local charitable group that will take his old dishwasher as a tax-deductible donation. The charity estimates its fair market value to be $50. Herman's marginal income tax rate is 40 percent this year. Assuming that he itemizes his deductions (total itemized deductions exceeds zero-bracket), will he reduce his taxes by donating the unit? (*Hint*: Recall the discussion of deductible expenses in Chapter 6.) Would your answer to question **a** change? Why or why not?

CASE PROBLEM

Fred and Jan Smith need major appliances for their new home. A local dealer has quoted them a price of $3900 for a total package, which includes refrigerator, kitchen range, clothes washer, and clothes dryer. The dealer has assured them that the appliances are super deluxe models with numerous options and extras. The dealer maintains that all appliances are basically similar, so the only thing to consider is price. (Of course, she quickly emphasizes, that her price is the lowest available.)

Since the Smiths are short of cash, the dealer has offered an "easy" 3-year sales loan (APR 30 percent). The $165.56 monthly payment comes to a "low, low $5.44 per day." "Not much to pay for all that service," the dealer notes. Because they are "good" customers, the dealer has offered them a service contract covering any repair and service needs on all four units for only 50 cents per day. The Smiths' combined annual income is $33,000.

1 Do you agree with the dealer's point that price is the only consideration? Why?

2 How would you recommend that the Smiths shop for each of the appliances?

3   What guidelines would you recommend they use to decide which models best meet their needs?

4   How much will those "easy" terms cost the Smiths? How much is the finance charge?

5   What credit alternatives would you recommend? Why?

6   What is the annual cost of the service contract that the dealer offers? Is it likely to remain at that level throughout the lifetime of all the appliances? Assuming that the service contract fee remains constant, approximately how much will those fees total over the next 15 years (a reasonable estimate of the appliances' lifetime)?

CHAPTER
11
THE HOUSING DECISION

**AFTER COMPLETING THIS CHAPTER
YOU WILL HAVE LEARNED**

What the *three principal rental options* offer

The major *advantages and disadvantages* of *single-family houses, condominiums,* and *mobile homes*

How to decide whether to *rent or buy*

How to compute the *annual cost of rental*

How to compute the *annual cost of ownership*

How the *tax benefits of ownership* lower its annual cost

Why the *long-term cost of ownership* is less than the current *out-of-pocket cost*

What you should consider when *selecting a rental*

What you should consider when *selecting a single-family house, condominium, or mobile home*

How you use a *mortgage table* to estimate the monthly payment

The major distinguishing characteristics among the *principal types of mortgages*

How to select the *best mortgage* for you

WELL.. YOU DID ASK TO SEE SOMETHING FOR UNDER $35 THOUSAND...

SELECTING the housing unit you will live

in is one of the most important decisions in your life. Housing is crucial for several reasons. Most people spend between 25 and 35 percent of their gross income on housing; for many, it is their largest single expenditure. Your housing decision also involves a number of nonmonetary aspects. It determines how much time you will spend commuting to work. Your home's location determines the availability of shopping and cultural activities near to where you live. It also will have a significant impact on your social contacts. If you have children, it usually determines the school they will attend and who they may have as friends. Last, you will be spending considerable time in your home, so you should be comfortable with your choice.

THE HOUSING ALTERNATIVES: RENTAL OR OWNERSHIP

The two basic housing alternatives are **rental** and **ownership**. Each of these alternatives has its advantages and disadvantages. Some people always rent and never seriously consider ownership. For others, ownership is the *only* housing choice. But most people do not fall neatly into one or the other of these extremes. This group must weigh the benefits and drawbacks of the two housing alternatives to decide which is best. We assume that you are in the group that considers either option possible.

In this chapter, we will develop guidelines that can help you answer the question: "Which housing option—rental or ownership—is best for me at this time?" Before we do so, however, let's explore these two housing alternatives in more detail.

Rental

Most **rental options** can be grouped into one of three categories: apartments, duplexes and townhouses, and individual houses. The major differences among them center on the amount of living space, the availability of recreational facilities, the inclusion (or absence) of appliances, yard space (if any), the degree of privacy, and the tenant's or renter's responsibility for repairs and maintenance.

Apartment An **apartment** usually offers the least amount of living space. While there are exceptions, generally the largest apartment available is one with three bedrooms. Newer apartment developments provide extensive recreational facilities: swimming pools, tennis courts, community buildings, and putting greens are not uncommon. Older apartment buildings tend to have fewer rental units and typically provide few recreational facilities. In many apartments, you avoid the cost of buying major kitchen appliances because they are furnished. Also, most large developments offer pay-to-use laundry facilities. An apartment renter does not have a private yard. And because of its high-density design, an apartment generally gives you the least privacy. An advantage to an apartment is that you have little, if any, responsibility for repairs and maintenance. The yard, what there is of it, will be cared for; the building will be maintained; and all repairs will be taken care of by the landlord or building owner.

Duplex and Townhouse A **duplex** apartment or a **townhouse** generally offers considerably more living space. Often the living space in these units is located on two or three floors, thus increasing the interior privacy. With some, there is a private basement that substantially expands the renter's storage space. But most duplexes and townhouses provide no special recreational facilities. A few units will furnish major kitchen appliances, but you are more likely to find that they are not furnished. A private yard or inner court comes with many duplexes and townhouses. While the area may not be overly large, it can provide some outdoor privacy. Either a duplex or a townhouse offers considerably more privacy because it is not a high-density living unit; consequently, you are not forced to live in such close proximity to your neighbors. The renter, however, has more repair and maintenance responsibility with either a duplex or a townhouse. You may be expected to do yard work and some maintenance on the living unit.

Individual House An **individual house** contains the most living space, which typically comes in a considerable variety of floor plans. A house offers no special recreational facilities, nor does it usually include major kitchen appliances. The tenant must provide these items. A house may provide a private yard, together with a parking space that may include a garage. Privacy is greatest with a house. Because it is set on an individual lot, you generally have some space between yourself and the neighbors. And you do not have someone living above or below you. But the tenant usually must do the yard work plus some, or all, the repairs and maintenance on the house.

Ownership

We will examine three **ownership alternatives** in this chapter: the single-family house, the condominium, and the mobile home. We begin with a brief discussion of the major attributes for each of them. Next, we compare the three housing ownership alternatives by discussing their advantages and disadvantages. For simplicity, we'll use the term *"home"* to encompass all three ownership options.

Single-Family House The **single-family house** is still the most popular housing unit. It's what many people immediately envision when you mention ownership. While it is unlikely that the single-family house will be displaced as the preferred unit in the near future, both condominiums and mobile homes have become more popular.

With a single-family house, the buyer purchases both the living unit and the land on which it sits. Living space in a house covers the entire size spectrum. It ranges from compact, single-bedroom units with less than 1000 square feet of living space up to large units with five or more bedrooms that offer more than 4000 square feet of living area. Land on which the house stands can be so small that there are only a few feet between your house and your neighbor's, or it can have a country setting that includes several acres. As you would expect with such variety, prices may range from a low of $20,000 to $30,000 for a small "handy person's house" (that means it will be a lot of work) up to prices in excess of $150,000. The size of the house, its construction, the amenities it offers, and its location can all affect the price.

Advantages and Disadvantages of a Single-Family House   The top section of Exhibit 11-1 summarizes the major advantages of a single-family house. Its disadvantages are shown in the lower part of the exhibit.

Condominiums   **Condominium** ownership involves two different property areas: the individual living unit and the common property area. The individual living unit is what you purchase when you buy a condominium. The common property areas are what you are allowed to use as part of your condominium purchase. We will discuss both.

Individual Living Unit   The **individual living units** are generally part of the larger multiunit building. But they are considered separate entities within the development, so each purchaser receives a deed to his or her specific living unit. Since it is an identified area, a condominium can be financed with a standard home mortgage. Real estate taxes are assessed on the living unit the same as they would be on a house.

Individual owners are responsible for the taxes and mortgage payment on only their own living unit. In other words, each individual owner is responsible solely for his or her own debts and obligations and for no one else's.

Common Property Area   The **common property area** encompasses the land where the condominium development is located and all property items not

---

EXHIBIT 11-1

Advantages and disadvantages of a single-family house.

Advantages

1   Large selection of new and existing houses with different designs, sizes, and locations

2   Lengthy history of how the market price of single-family houses has changed during periods when inflation was moderate, as well as when it was high

3   Freedom to redecorate and remodel the house and to change landscaping to suit you

4   Widest range of alternatives to finance your purchase because of lending institutions' extensive experience with financing houses

Disadvantages

1   Large monthly mortgage payment, coupled with sizable property taxes, that can make a single-family house prohibitively expensive

2   Owner's responsibility for all repairs and maintenance on house and surrounding property

3   Downpayment and other costs at time of purchase that can easily exceed $5,000 to $10,000

4   Unavailability or undesirability of units near the business district of major cities included in the living units. Normally, this property includes structural parts of the buildings (exterior walls, stairways, roof, hallways), sidewalks, parking lots, and recreation facilities (swimming pool, tennis court, meeting hall). In some condominiums, however, parking lots and recreation facilities are owned by an outsider who leases them to the residents.

As part of the purchase, condominium buyers receive an undivided interest in the common property area. By an "undivided interest" we mean that no owner can claim specific segments of the common property. For example, an owner cannot claim one corner of the swimming pool or part of a tennis court. All owners share the maintenance and repair costs for the common property items. To provide for such expenses, each owner in the development is assessed a monthly fee. Part of the fee is also used to provide ongoing services, such as security, lobby personnel, and parking attendants.

Advantages and Disadvantages of a Condominium The advantages of a condominium are summarized in the top portion of Exhibit 11-2. The lower section of that exhibit briefly lists its disadvantages.

EXHIBIT 11-2

Advantages and disadvantages of a condominium.

Advantages

1 All maintenance and repairs of common property area are contracted to an outside firm.

2 Condominium developments frequently offer extensive recreational facilities.

3 The limited use of land, coupled with cost savings from the building's high-density design, generally means a square foot of living space in a condominium costs less than it would in a comparable single-family house.

4 Since a development requires only a limited amount of land, condominiums are available near major downtown business sections.

5 One can find specialized condominium developments that restrict purchasers to a select clientele; e.g., singles, married without children, retired.

Disadvantages

1 High-density living means less privacy, so you may have to make compromises in your living style.

2 Monthly cost of ownership—mortgage payment, maintenance fees, and property taxes—can be very high.

3 Personal choice in decorating and landscaping is reduced; condominium owners jointly decide how the common property is decorated and how the grounds are landscaped.

4 Some developments place restrictions on how and to whom you can sell your unit.

5 Down payment and costs associated with purchasing a condominium, while possibly less than those involved with buying a single-family house, can be sizable.

6 Owner is responsible for repairs, maintenance, and cleaning of his or her individual living unit.

7 Condominiums have not compiled a sufficiently long record to accurately predict how their market price will react to periods of moderate to high inflation.

Mobile Homes One of the fastest-growing segments of the housing industry is the **mobile home** (MH) market. The homes are "mobile" only in that each one is towed to its permanent location. Mobile homes are popular because of their relatively low cost. A fully equipped mobile home can range in price from a low of $12,000 to over $50,000. At the top of the price range, they provide over 1000 square feet of comfortable, sometimes opulent, living accomodations. A "small" single-family house (living room, kitchen, three bedrooms, and bathroom) contains about 1100 square feet. Many people who cannot afford, or do not wish to buy, a conventional house can obtain excellent living space and comfort in a mobile home.

Mobile home owners generally have several choices on where to locate their units. First, and most frequently, they may rent a site in a mobile home park. Typically, these parks are exclusively for mobile homes and are equipped with everything needed to attach and set up a home. But not all parks are open to every mobile home owner. Some rent only to people who purchased their home from the dealership that operates the park; that restriction narrows the choice significantly. All repair and maintenance costs for the park are covered by the monthly rentals of space. Repair and maintenance of your mobile home itself are, of course, your responsibility.

A second option is to purchase the site on which to set your mobile home. Again, the site will likely be in a park that is exclusively for mobile homes, but each mobile home owner purchases the individual site. That arrangement still leaves a considerable amount of common property: driveways, parking lots, recreational facilities, meeting rooms, and so forth. Typically, that common property is handled the same as it is with a condominium: all the mobile home owners in the park share in its ownership. Purchasing an individual site in this type of park will give you an undivided interest in the common property. Every owner is assessed a monthly fee to cover maintenance and repairs for that property.

Advantages and Disadvantages of a Mobile Home The top section of Exhibit 11-3 summarizes the advantages of a mobile home. The lower part of the exhibit lists its disadvantages.

THE BASIC DECISION: RENT OR BUY

The starting point in the rent-or-buy decision is to understand the major factors that influence whether renting or buying your housing is best for you. We divide those factors in two broad subcategories: the nonmonetary and the monetary factors. The first, of course, concerns those factors that do not involve a specific dollar cost. Nevertheless, they represent an essential consideration in your decision to rent or buy. The second subcategory concentrates on the dollar costs. The factors include the down payment, the other costs of purchasing a home, and the annual cost to continue owner-ship. We will develop a worksheet to summarize the costs of rental and ownership for your buy-or-rent decision. Our goal is to develop sufficient guidelines and standards so that you can combine both sets of factors and decide what is best for you in your present circumstances.

EXHIBIT 11-3

Advantages and disadvantages of a mobile
home.

Advantages

1 The cost per square foot of living space is the lowest of the three ownership alternatives.

2 Most mobile homes come equipped with major home appliances as well as furniture. These provisions minimize the initial cost of moving into the unit.

3 The monthly net cost of owning a mobile home is the lowest of the three ownership options.

Disadvantages

1 Unlike single-family houses and condominiums, the market value of a mobile home may decline while you own it.

2 The potential decline in market value may offset some, or all, of the potential savings due to the mobile unit's lower purchase price.

3 There are fewer options to finance the purchase of a mobile home; those that are available have a shorter maturity (time in which to repay the loan) and a higher finance charge (APR).

4 The materials used in some mobile homes and the quality of construction have been poor in the past. Questions have also been raised about the safety of some units and the possibly detrimental effect of the materials used on the occupant's health.

5 Availability of sites is reduced by the practice that some mobile home parks accept only people who purchase their units from the park's dealership.

6 The combination of poor maintenance and operation has made some mobile home parks resemble slums.

7 Mobile homes are anything but "mobile." Few are ever moved when the owner shifts to a new location.

Advantages and Disadvantages of Rental

This section discusses the major advantages and disadvantages of rental except one: its annual cost. A later section develops the worksheet needed to summarize that cost.

Advantage: Extensive Recreational Facilities Newer apartment developments often include such things as a swimming pool, tennis courts, a putting green, and a club house. The average homeowner could not begin to provide similar facilities. Depending on your personal preference, these added facilities may substantially enhance the attractiveness of renting.

Advantage: Restrictions on Types of Tenants Some rental developments limit the persons to whom they will rent their apartments or townhouses. Typical restrictive developments include those that cater to young singles, married couples without children, or mature couples whose grown children no longer live at home.

OH OH..
HERE
COMES
THE
NEIGHBORHOOD.

Advantage: Repairs and Maintenance   When you rent, you do not avoid the cost of repairs and maintenance: your monthly rental cost certainly includes them. But you do avoid the work and responsibility for them. Here is a possible scenario: You stand inside your warm apartment or townhouse while watching your neighbor swaying on a 25-foot extension ladder with a 40-pound storm window in hand; a chilling 38° wind is blowing from the north. Ah, to miss one of the joys of home ownership!

Advantage: Greater Flexibility   With most rentals, you are required to sign an agreement, the lease, that obligates you to rent the unit for a specified period—12 months is typical. Once that lease period is over, you are free to move somewhere else. Even if you have not completed the entire lease period, the landlord may cancel the balance of the lease if you pay a cancellation fee. Even if you must cancel, doing so is clearly much easier than having to sell a home.

Advantage: Low Initial Cost to Rent   Most rentals require that the tenant, or renter, pay from 1 to 3 months' rent in advance as a security deposit on the rental unit. Should the tenant move and leave the rental unit unusually dirty or seriously damaged, the landlord will deduct the costs of correcting those conditions from the security deposit. But that expense is much less than the down payment needed to purchase a home. Furthermore, since many rentals furnish major appliances and carpets, you also have to spend less to move in. On many rentals, $1,000 will cover the initial costs. Not so with ownership. When you buy a home you can easily spend 4 to 10 times that much.

Disadvantage: Restrictions on Personal Freedom and Life-Style

Nearly all rental situations involve high-density living. In many instances, you may learn all about your neighbor's loud, boisterous 3:00 A.M. party; you were not invited to it but you only have to try to sleep to hear it through your bedroom wall. Also, if the landlord likes shocking pink on the building's trim, or thinks that battleship-gray walls do not show spots or dirt, you will probably have to put up with that choice. If another tenant's visitor parks in your parking place, you just may have to settle for the street. Clearly, your personal freedom is likely to be less, and you may well find yourself sharing a building and facilities with some people you may not like.

Advantages and Disadvantages of Ownership

In this section we review all the major advantages and disadvantages of ownership save one: the annual cost of ownership. We postpone discussing it until we compare the costs of rental and ownership.

Advantage: Psychological Factors

The principal nonmonetary advantage of home ownership is the psychological reward. This includes the pride and personal satisfaction that owning a home can provide. By owning, you know that your housing arrangement is reasonably permanent. No landlord can refuse to renew your lease or raise your rent so high that you must move. Your home is yours until you decide to sell. Furthermore, all three ownership options allow you freedom to change the interior decor to your liking. The greater privacy of ownership also means that you are more free to pursue the life-style that you want.

Disadvantage: Responsibility for Repairs and Maintenance

Whether you rent or buy, you will pay the costs of repairs and maintenance in the housing unit. When you own, you write out the checks to pay those costs directly. When you rent, you write your rent check to the landlord who will use part of that monthly payment for the repairs and maintenance on your rental unit.

Ownership adds a second dimension: The owner is responsible for part or all of the repairs and maintenance on the housing unit. For a single-family house, the owner must do all the work, or at least hire someone to do it. With a condominium or mobile home, you have to handle repairs and maintenance only in your individual living unit. Repairs and maintenance on the exterior, the grounds, parking lots, sidewalks, and similar common property items are handled by someone else. But, one way or another, you still pay the bill.

For people who are very busy or who do not particularly enjoy doing this type of labor, the added work and responsibility of repairs and maintenance may be a decided disadvantage.

Disadvantage: Reduced Flexibility   When you own your living unit, you have less flexibility if you want to move to a new location. First, it generally takes time to sell your home. You may need several weeks, several months, or several years. Next, there are the costs for the sale. Plan to pay 6 percent of the home's market value as the selling commission if you have someone else sell it for you. On a $50,000 unit, those commissions are a not-insignificant $3000.

As a general rule, anyone planning to own a home for less than 3 years should probably rent. For most people, it takes that long to justify the hassle of selling the unit. Also, several years are needed for the market value of the home to rise enough to offset the considerable cost of the realtor's commission for selling it.

Disadvantage: High Initial Cost to Purchase   To purchase a housing unit, you have to make a down payment that can range from 5 percent to more than 20 percent of the purchase price. Even with a 5 percent down payment, you may still pay $3,000 when the purchase price is $60,000; that price is not unusually high for either a single-family house or a condominium. Had the purchase required 20 percent down, the amount would soar to $12,000! Many people simply do not have the money for a down payment of several thousand dollars. For them, buying just may not be a viable option until they have had time to accumulate the required down payment.

There are other costs that you will likely have to pay at the time of purchase. On a single-family house or condominium, there are the costs to close and complete the purchase. We will talk more about these later, but for now we note that these costs can run to several thousand dollars. For everything but a mobile home, you may also have to buy things like major home appliances, carpeting, draperies, and lawn equipment. Again, several thousand dollars in costs would not be uncommon.

The net effect is that these initial costs—down payment, closing fees, appliances, etc.—can mean that you will need more than a few thousand dollars on hand when you buy a home. For people who have not saved the money, buying a home may be out of the question. Furthermore, as we pointed out when discussing both financial goals (Chapter 1) and budgeting (Chapter 3), saving the necessary money to buy a home requires planning coupled with a lengthy accumulation period.

Comparing Estimated Annual Costs of Renting and Ownership

We still need one more input to make the rent-or-buy decision. That is a comparison of the estimated annual cost of renting with the estimated cost of owning. This is easiest to make if we develop a worksheet that summarizes the annual costs of renting and of ownership. Exhibit 11-4 will be our worksheet. All the costs shown there cover 1 year's activity. And, since the worksheet will be prepared before actually renting or buying, all the costs are estimates.

Cost Estimates: Renting

You would use the middle column of Exhibit 11-4 to estimate the cost of a prospective rental unit. To provide practice, we will run through an example. Our example is a three-bedroom townhouse that rents for $600 per month. According to the lease, the tenant pays all utilities—heat, light, and water—but the landlord covers all repair and maintenance expenses.

The annual rent is entered on line 1 of Exhibit 11-4. Since our rental

EXHIBIT 11-4

Worksheet for estimating the annual costs of renting and of ownership.

LINE	DESCRIPTION	RENTAL, TOWNHOUSE	OWNERSHIP, $75,000 HOUSE
	Costs		
1	Rent	$7,200	—
2	Mortgage payment	—	$9,600
3	Maintenance and repairs	—	750
4	Utilities	1,080	1,200
5	Insurance	100	340
6	Property taxes	—	1,200
7	Interest lost on security deposit or downpayment (after deducting taxes)	84	525
8	Gross cost: Total of lines 1 through 7	$8,464	$13,615
	Tax Savings		
9	Property taxes	—	$1,200
10	Mortgage interest paid	—	9,450
11	Total deductions: Line 9 + line 10	—	$10,650
12	Marginal tax rate	30%	30%
13	Tax savings: Line 11 × line 12	—	$3,195
	Net Cost		
14	Net cost: Gross cost (line 8) − tax savings (line 13)	$8,464	$10,420
	Long-Term Cost		
15	Appreciation in market value $75,000 × 4% = (current value) (annual appreciation)	—	$3,000
16	Less: Repayment of mortgage balance: Line 2 − line 10	—	150
17	Long-term cost: Net cost (line 14 − line 15 − line 16)	$8,464	$7,270

example has no maintenance or repairs, there is no entry on line 3. But if, in your rental agreement, you agreed to do some of the maintenance and repairs, an estimate of those annual costs would be entered on line 3. Line 4 contains the rental unit's estimated utility costs for the year. Sources for that information may be the landlord or a current tenant in a similar rental unit. Next, there is the required insurance. The landlord's insurance covers only the building and surrounding grounds, because these are the landlord's central concern. Every renter will need a renters insurance policy that covers his or her personal property. The estimated annual premium for that insurance goes on line 5. For our example, the annual premium was estimated to be $100. There is no entry on line 6 because the landlord pays the property taxes.

The interest on the security deposit for line 7 needs some explanation. As we noted earlier, most rental agreements require that the renter, or tenant, pay at least 1 and sometimes 2 or more months of rent in advance as a security deposit. This is a cost, because you have paid money to the landlord that will probably not earn any interest for you. So, had you not rented this unit, you would have earned interest on your security deposit money. Of course, you would have to pay income taxes on that interest. The true cost is the interest that remains after paying taxes. Let us return to our townhouse example and assume that a security deposit equal to 2 months' rent must be paid in advance. We expect the tenant could have earned 10 percent interest on the security deposit money. Further, we assume the renter's marginal tax rate is 30 percent. That means the tenant keeps 70 percent of the interest on the security deposit money. For our example, the after-tax interest is:

$$\$84 = \$1200 \times 10\% \times (100 - 30\%)$$

$$\text{After-tax interest} = \text{Security deposit} \times \text{Interest rate} \times \left[\begin{array}{c} \text{Proportion for renter:} \\ 100 - \text{marginal tax rate} \end{array} \right]$$

We enter that interest ($84) on line 7 of Exhibit 11-4.

The gross cost of renting is the total of lines 1 through 7. That comes to $8464 on our townhouse.

No Tax Savings with Rental Unfortunately, the tax regulations do not allow you to deduct any of the costs of renting on your tax return. Mark that as a major disadvantage to renting. From the discussion of itemized deductions in Chapter 6, you will recall that individuals can take the interest paid on mortgages and property taxes as an itemized tax deduction. But when you rent, you do not pay these items directly. Without question, they are part of the rent, but the landlord pays them and takes the deduction. Consequently, renting offers no tax savings, so lines 9 and 10 of Exhibit 11-4 are blank. So the net cost on line 14 equals the gross cost on line 8.

No Market Value Appreciation with Renting Yet another disadvantage of renting is that you receive no benefit if the market value of your rented apartment, townhouse, duplex, or house increases. The market value of most rental units increases over time, especially when inflation is high and most prices are rising rapidly. But the landlord captures all that price appreciation. Therefore, appreciation in market value on line 15 remains blank for a rental unit. Likewise, because the tenants are not repaying a mortgage, line 16 also has no entry. The net effect is that the long-term cost of renting (line 17) is the same as the gross cost shown on line 8.

Cost Estimates: Ownership

The costs of ownership will be accumulated in the far right column of Exhibit 11-4. A worksheet like Exhibit 11-4 can be used to summarize the cost for any home you might want to consider. Let's use a $75,000 single-family house that will be purchased with a $7500 downpayment as an example. The $67,500 balance will be financed through a 30-year, 14 percent mortgage. For now, we will tell you that the monthly payment on this mortgage is approximately $800. Later in this chapter, we will develop a mortgage table (it's shown in Exhibit 11-9, if you want to look ahead) so you can compute the monthly payments for most mortgages.

The only ownership situation for which you might enter rent on line 1 is that of a mobile home that you are considering placing on a rented lot in a mobile home park. In this case, the annual lot rental will be entered on line 1. For our example, that line remains blank. On line 2, you will enter the total of 12 monthly mortgage payments. In our example, those 12 payments total $9600.

The maintenance and repair costs will differ depending on the type of housing unit you are considering. For a single-family house, most housing specialists suggest that you plan on spending roughly 1 percent of its purchase price on maintenance and repairs each year. If the house is quite old, 2 to 3 percent is probably more realistic, and if it needs substantial repairs, you may want to boost that to 3 percent or more. For our $75,000 house, we set maintenance and repairs at 1 percent of its cost, so $750 is entered on line 3.

For a condominium, there are two costs that need to be entered on line 3. First, condominium owners pay a monthly maintenance and service fee. An estimate of this monthly fee for the care of common property is readily available from the condominium's owners' association. Second, they pay the costs of maintaining and repairing their individual living unit. We suggest ½ of 1 percent of the condominium's purchase price as an estimate for those maintenance and repairs.

For mobile homes, you have direct costs only for maintaining and repairing the home itself if you rent your site. We suggest 1 percent of the home's purchase price as the estimate of annual maintenance cost. The mobile home owner who also owns a site has a second cost. As with a condominium, there will be a monthly maintenance and service fee. It should be combined with the mobile home's maintenance cost and placed on line 3.

Estimated utility costs are entered on line 4. Possible sources for that information may be the present owner, if you are buying a previously owned house or condominium. If the present owner asks them to do so, many utility companies will send a prospective buyer a summary of the monthly utility costs on a home for the past year. On a new housing unit, the builder or the seller may be able to provide cost estimates. For our sample house, the estimated annual utilities costs are $1200. Note that the costs for the rental townhouse are lower. We assumed that owing to its common walls (shared with the unit next door), it costs less to heat and cool.

The annual premium for a homeowners insurance policy to cover both the dwelling and your personal property will be shown on line 5. For our sample house, the annual premium was set at $340. A local insurance agent can readily supply an estimate of the insurance premium for a particular home. Line 6 shows the annual property taxes on the housing unit. Owners of single-family houses and condominiums typically receive a property tax bill once or twice each year. Mobile home owners who rent their sites frequently have their property taxes shown as a separate item on the monthly rent billing. For an existing house or condominium, the present owner may be willing to show you the prior year's property tax bills. Barring that, you may be able to obtain an estimate from the municipal or county assessor's office where the property is located. On a new house or condominium, the builder or developer can generally provide an estimate of the likely property taxes. For our sample house, the annual property taxes (line 6) are expected to be $1200.

Purchasing a home nearly always requires that the buyer make a down payment. While you own the home, that money continues to be tied up so that it earns no interest. One cost of ownership is the interest that you could have earned on the money which has been used for the down payment. Of course, the tax authorities would want to collect income taxes on that interest. The net cost is the interest that remains after paying those taxes. We continue to assume that the buyer could have earned 10 percent on the down payment money, and that the buyer's marginal tax rate is 30 percent. The annual after-tax interest that would be lost on our sample house's down payment is:

$$\underset{\substack{\text{After-tax} \\ \text{interest}}}{\$525} = \underset{\substack{\text{Required} \\ \text{down payment}}}{\$7500} \times \underset{\substack{\times \text{ Interest} \\ \text{rate}}}{10\%} \times \underset{\substack{\left[\text{Proportion buyer retains:}\right. \\ \left.100 - \text{marginal tax rate}\right]}}{(100 - 30\%)}$$

This lost after-tax interest on the down payment is entered on line 7 as an ownership cost. The higher the required down payment, the more important this cost component will be to the purchase decision.

The gross cost of ownership is summarized on line 8 of Exhibit 11-4. It includes the individual cost components from line 1 through line 7. If we stopped at line 8, the question of whether it will be better to rent or buy would be quite easily answered: Rental would be clearly much less costly in most cases. But we need to examine the tax benefits of ownership before we draw any conclusions.

Tax Savings Reduce Cost of Ownership One of the major advantages of ownership is that homeowners can deduct both property taxes and the interest paid on a mortgage loan on their income tax return. As you recall from Chapter 6, deducting those items lowers the income taxes that the homeowner must pay. How much they are reduced depends on the dollar amount of the deductions and the homeowner's marginal tax rate.

To compute the tax savings, we first need an estimate of the two deductible items: property taxes and mortgage interest paid. Property taxes are easy to estimate because they are the same as our estimate on line 6; no additional work is necessary. To estimate the interest on the mortgage, we divide the annual payments on the mortgage into two components: interest on the mortgage and repayment of the mortgage balance. A precise estimate of the interest on the mortgage is quite involved. But we do not need that accuracy. For our purposes, we can obtain a reasonable interest estimate if we multiply the unpaid mortgage balance by the mortgage interest rate. For the $67,500, 14 percent mortgage on our sample house, the estimated interest for line 10 is:

$$\$9,450 \qquad = \$67,500 \qquad \times 14\%$$

$$\Updownarrow \qquad\qquad \Updownarrow \qquad\qquad \Updownarrow$$

Approximate = Unpaid balance × Interest rate
annual interst   on mortgage   on mortgage

The actual interest on this mortgage would be $9440. So you can see that our estimate is sufficiently accurate. Of course, as the mortgage is repaid, the interest paid annually declines. But the repayment is so slow in the early years of the mortgage that the homeowner's interest deduction does not drop rapidly.

The tax savings resulting from ownership are computed by multiplying the buyer's marginal tax rate from line 12 by the total deductions from line 11. Chapter 6 explained how a taxpayer can estimate his or her marginal tax rate. For our sample house, the tax savings are $3195. The higher the buyer's marginal tax rate, the greater the tax savings with ownership. When the tax savings on line 13 are deducted from the gross cost of ownership on line 8, the **net cost of ownership** on line 14 drops sharply. For our sample house, the tax savings reduce total ownership cost more that 23 percent. Now the net cost of ownership on our sample house, $10,420, is closer to the cost of rental at $8,464. Still, ownership continues to be nearly 25 percent more expensive than renting.

Can You Afford to Own? There are really two parts to this question. Frequently, people concentrate on the long-term cost of ownership. It includes all costs less any gains from the day of purchase through the day of sale. We will compute long-term ownership cost on line 17 of Exhibit 11-4. But if the homeowner is forced into bankruptcy in the short run, there will be no long run. We think a prospective owner should be asking: "Can I afford the annual costs of ownership in the short run?" Prospective owners first need to develop a worksheet like Exhibit 11-4 for the home they are considering. Next, they need a detailed budget that includes all their living costs except housing. Now they can compare the net cost on line 14 with the available income their budget shows to decide whether they can afford to own.

STRATEGY

Before deciding that ownership is for you, carefully estimate your total net cost along the lines of Exhibit 11-4. Then see if you can fit that cost into your budget.

Historical Guides To Decide Affordability Some lenders and financial writers continue to use two general rules that have evolved over the years to decide whether an individual can afford a specific home. We think both rules are fraught with potential problems. The first rule is: Never buy a home whose purchase price exceeds 2½ times your income. While the rule sounds precise, it totally ignores the annual costs of owning that home. Purchase price and annual ownership cost are two very different concepts. The size of those annual costs can mean the difference between paying and not being able to pay. Both your income and the estimated annual cost of ownership must be considered together. We think a worksheet like Exhibit 11-4, together with a realistic projected budget as discussed in Chapter 3, is a far better way to answer the question: "Can I afford this home?"

The second rule does consider the annual cost of ownership and your income. The original rule was that you should not spend more than 25 percent of your income on housing. In recent years, the accepted level has been boosted to 28 or 30 percent of income. While this rule can serve as a rough guide, we think it still misses the most important input: *You*. Your spending plans for housing may call for more or less than the suggested 30 percent limit. We believe the best technique is the one outlined at the start of this section. Lay out your *spending plans* in a detailed budget and see whether the cost of ownership, figured from a worksheet like Exhibit 11-4, will fit into that budget.

Price Appreciation Lowers Ownership Cost One major benefit to ownership is that the owner receives any appreciation in the home's market value. If the home ultimately sells for more than its original price, the gain on the sale reduces the cost of owning that home. How much the market value increases depends upon such things as where the home is located, how well it is maintained, how well similar homes in that area are selling, and how rapidly inflation is pushing up consumer prices in general.

During the past decade, the market value of a single-family house has risen anywhere from 4 to more than 13 percent each year. Unfortunately, statistics for condominiums and mobile homes are far more scarce, and those that are available show widely divergent patterns. In some areas, condominiums have risen sharply in value, but in other areas the price increase has been much smaller. On mobile homes, the price pattern is less encouraging. In many areas, the market value of a new mobile home drops during the early years of ownership. After that, the price seems to plateau; at other times, there will continue to be small declines. But the market value of some previously owned units has actually risen. When the market value of a mobile home drops, it raises, not decreases, the cost of ownership. It is important to recognize the possibility of a price decline. The mobile home that at first appears to offer a bargain ownership cost may turn out to be a costly ownership option.

The widely different annual increases in the market value for single-family houses, condominiums, and mobile homes make it impossible to set a single appreciation rate, or even a single rate for each ownership option. Probably the best estimate of the likely future increase in market value is one based on what has happened to similar homes in the same area. Potential sources for that information include realtors, mortgage lenders, builders, and possibly the municipal or county tax assessor's office. You will likely find it easiest to develop an estimate for single-family houses, much more difficult for condominiums, and very difficult for mobile homes. Barring the availability of adequate information from local sources, we suggest the following annual appreciation guidelines:

Single-family house: +3 to +5 percent per year

Condominium: +2 to +5 percent per year

Mobile home: −4 to +2 percent per year

Two points about these rates: First, they are low if we compare them with actual appreciation rates during the past 5 years, but we prefer to be conservative rather than overly optimistic. Second, we intended the mobile home rate to be part negative and part positive. A misprint it is not. That wide spread in rates reflects the considerable difference depending upon where the unit is located and whether it is new or previously owned.

Our sample $75,000 house can demonstrate how price appreciation affects the cost of ownership. Suppose that, on the basis of a study of similar single-family houses that are located in the same area as our sample house, we estimate the house will appreciate 4 percent per year. Based on its current $75,000 value, the annual appreciation on line 15 is $3000.

There is one more adjustment before we compute the long-term cost of ownership on line 17. Recall that we said the mortgage payments on line 9 contain the interest payment (by far the largest amount) and the repayment on the mortgage balance (a very small proportion). We already handled the special tax savings the interest provided on line 10. It remains for us to recognize that part of the mortgage is being repaid each month. That repayment means that when the home is sold the owner pays less of the sale price to the mortgage lender and so gets to keep more. Consequently, that part of the monthly payment which repays the mortgage balance is not a true long-term *cost* of owning. It is long term, however, because the owner gets it back only after the house is sold. The repayment is computed by taking the total annual mortgage payment on line 2 and deducting the estimated mortgage interest shown on line 10. For the sample house, the repayment is $150. We said the repayment of the mortgage is slow, but $150 out of $9600? Yes, that is what has been repaid.

The net **long-term cost of ownership** for line 17 equals the net ownership cost from line 14 minus the price appreciation on line 15 and minus the mortgage repayment on line 16. For our sample house, the long-term cost on line 17 is $7270. If all the estimates are accurate, the long-term cost of ownership, after all tax benefits and after any price appreciation on the home, equals the amount on line 17. It is long term because this is the owner's cost after the home is sold. That could be 5 years, 10 years, or more than 20 years after the home was purchased.

Taxes on Selling a Home One question the previous section may have suggested is: What about income taxes when there is a gain on the sale of a home (when the sale price exceeds the original cost)? Again, the tax regulations favor homeowners. If you sell your home for more than you paid for it and buy a similar or more expensive replacement home within 2 years of selling the old home (it can be as much as 2 years before or 2 years after the sale), all or part of the tax on the amount you gained from selling your previous home may be deferred. Notice we said "deferred" because the tax on that gain is not canceled; it is postponed to a later time. But there is a good possibility that the taxes you have to pay will be less, or zero, at a later time. But if you sell the home at a loss, that *loss cannot be deducted.*

If you are 55 or more years old when you sell your home, up to $125,000 of any gain that you realize is tax-exempt. This exclusion can be used only once. Assume that when you sell a house you are over 55, so you elect to exclude from taxes the $50,000 gain from that sale. But some years later, you sell another home for a $50,000 gain; having once used your tax exclusion, even though it was not for the full $125,000, it cannot be used again.

STRATEGY

For most home sellers who are 55 or older and who do not plan to buy another home, or who plan to buy a much less expensive home, the wisest course of action is to use their one-time exclusion when next figuring their taxes.

Rent or Buy: It's Your Decision

In the end, you are the one who has to weigh the advantages and disadvantages of your different housing options. At one time, it was almost taken for granted that most renters were just frustrated prospective homeowners who were merely renting until the right purchase opportunity appeared. Similarly, it was assumed that only married couples seriously considered ownership. Not so today. We think most people will want to investigate both renting and owning rather than to accept some general rule of thumb.

When comparing the cost of rental and ownership, it is essential that you develop a cost worksheet similar to Exhibit 11-4. In our opinion, the emphasis in this exhibit should be the estimated net cost shown on line 14. This is the out-of-pocket cost either to rent or to buy. It is the annual cost that you must fit into your budget. When the net cost favors renting, as our townhouse versus a single-family house did, you will have to decide whether the other advantages of ownership, coupled with the disadvantages of renting, are sufficient to swing your decision to ownership. Where the cost comparison favors ownership, you will need to ask whether the other advantages of renting coupled with the disadvantages of ownership may swing the balance back to renting, even with its higher cost.

We place less emphasis on the estimate of long-run housing costs on line 17 of Exhibit 11-4. They are essential because they show the annual housing costs after the home is sold. In many cases, ownership will have the lower long-run cost. But the favorable effects of price appreciation and mortgage repayment only reduce the cost of ownership after the home is sold. In the meantime, your annual payment is the net cost shown on line 14. That is why we favor net cost as the major factor in the housing decision.

SELECTING A RENTAL UNIT

If, after careful analysis, you have decided to rent, you will need to select a rental unit, whether it be an apartment, a duplex, a townhouse, or a house. The more you know about that unit before you rent it, the more likely you are to be pleased with it after you move in. Often, the tenant who makes a more thorough investigation of the rental unit and its accompanying lease eliminates many of the problems that later arise between the tenant and landlord.

Investigating the Rental Unit   Although the checklist in Exhibit 11-5 is labeled for apartments, it can also be used for duplexes, townhouses, and houses. Granted, there will be several questions that do not apply, but it is likely that more than 90 percent of the items relate to all four rental options. By thoughtfully analyzing each of the points raised in this checklist, you will be more satisfied with your final rental choice.

EXHIBIT 11-5

CHAPTER 11

329

THE HOUSING
DECISION

Checklist for apartments. *Source*: Money Management Institute booklet, *Your Housing Dollar*, the Money Management Institute of Household Finance Corporation, Chicago, IL.

Building and Grounds
- Attractive, well-constructed building
- Good maintenance and upkeep
- Clean, well-lighted and uncluttered halls, entrances, stairs
- Reliable building management and supervision
- Attractive landscaping with adequate outdoor space for tenants
- Locked entrances, protected from outsiders
- Clean, attractive lobby

Services and Facilities
- Laundry equipment
- Parking space (indoor or outdoor)
- Receiving room for packages
- Convenient trash collection and disposal
- Adequate fire escapes
- Storage lockers
- Locked mail boxes
- Elevators
- Engineer on call for emergency repairs
- Extras — window washing, decorating, maid service, shops, doorman

Living Space in the Apartment
- Adequate room sizes and storage space
- Convenient floor plan
- Suitable wall space for furniture
- Soundproof — listen for talking, footsteps, plumbing and equipment noise from other apartments or hallways
- Attractive decorating and fixtures
- Pleasant views
- Windows located to provide enough air, light, and ventilation
- Agreeable size, type, and placement of windows
- Windows with blinds, shades, screens, and storm windows
- Easy cleaning and maintenance
- Attractive, easy-to-clean floors
- Furnished appliances in good condition
- Clean, effective heating, thermostatically controlled
- Up-to-date wiring
- Conveniently placed electric outlets
- Well-fitted doors, casings, cabinets, and built-ins
- Extras — air conditioning, carpeting, dishwasher, disposer, fireplace, patio

Rental Agreement The rental agreement between the landlord and tenant can be either a formal written agreement—a lease—or a less formal verbal agreement. A **lease** specifies the beginning and termination dates of the rental agreement; a year is typical, but leases of 2 or 3 years are also used. Verbal rental agreements typically continue the rental on a month-to-month basis. A typical lease specifies who the landlord is, lists the tenant, shows the monthly rental, explains the security deposit, sets the length of the lease, and provides a description of the rental property. Since there is no "standard" lease document, you will have to read each lease carefully to see what it includes. Some key questions that you should try to answer as you read the lease are:

What utilities are included in the rent?

Who takes care of repairs and maintenance?

What are the provisions if you must terminate the lease early?

Are there special restrictions, rules, and regulations?

What are the terms for renewing the lease?

What is the refund policy for the security deposit?

If a section of the lease is not clear, ask the landlord for an explanation. Do not rely on the landlord's verbal promises. If the landlord makes special promises about redecorating, repairs, or sublet rights, ask that they be written into the lease.

STRATEGY

Before signing any lease, carefully read it to see what you will receive and what the landlord expects of you.

Security Deposit   Security deposits are probably the single most troublesome area in a lease. Most leases require that a minimum of 1 month's or, increasingly, 2 or 3 months' rent be paid in advance as a security deposit. Problems often arise when the tenant is ready to move: What can be charged against the deposit? When will it be returned? What is the tenant's recourse if the deposit is unfairly withheld? While some states have passed legislation that outlines landlord and tenant rights in this area, many states have not. Tenants in those states are on their own.

STRATEGY

Carefully review the terms and conditions that govern the security deposit in your prospective lease. Ask the landlord exactly what can be charged against your deposit.

BUYING THE RIGHT HOME

If you decide to buy, you must consider a number of factors in selecting the best possible home. Some of the factors are universal to all three ownership options: single-family house, condominium, and mobile home. We will review those universal factors in this section.

Location

One of the oldest axioms about real estate is: The three most important factors to consider in buying a home are *location*, *location*, and *location*. While this statement undoubtedly exaggerates the importance of location relative to other factors, it points out how crucial most real estate people and lending institutions consider it to be. Even a well-designed, structurally perfect home can turn out to be a bad purchase if it is in a deteriorating neighborhood or too close to industry or major highways.

Zoning   Communities closely regulate the types of buildings which may be constructed in a given location. This is what "zoning" is. Zoning may have a significant impact on a property's value. A home that appears to be in a good neighborhood can deteriorate in value substantially if industry is permitted to develop nearby. Nobody wants a meat-packing plant next door. When buying a home, make sure it is in an area that is zoned for single-family or multifamily homes and that excludes industrial development.

Value of Surrounding Property   The value of your home is heavily influenced by its surroundings—therefore the emphasis on location and zoning. However, a $60,000 home in a good neighborhood of $40,000 homes will not be nearly so salable as a $60,000 home in a neighborhood of $80,000 homes.

STRATEGY

When buying a house, try to make sure that no more than 50 percent of the dwellings in the same neighborhood are of lower value.

Convenience   Distance to shopping, schools, church, work, or any other place that is important to you should be considered when selecting a home. With rising transportation costs, you must think carefully about buying a home whose location will increase your commuting costs. Be sure to calculate the transportation time and costs you will incur with any home you are considering.

Selecting a Single-Family House

The three general selection factors from the last section probably have their fullest application when selecting a single-family house. The very fact that there is such a wide variety of available single-family houses in such very different locations—rural, suburban, and metropolitan—gives you considerable latitude in your selection. You are far more likely to find the one house that just matches your needs and personal preference.

The previous general selection criteria were concerned primarily with the location of the housing unit. The checklist in Exhibit 11-6 is designed to help you systematically evaluate not only the house itself, but the yard and the surrounding neighborhood also. A few hours spent evaluating a house before you purchase it can help you avoid grief after you move in. Many of the unpleasant surprises, such as leaking roofs, decrepit plumbing, damp basements, and inadequate insulation, that some homeowners find after they move in can be spotted with a thorough prepurchase inspection.

Considering an Older House?   The checklist we introduced in Exhibit 11-6 applies to both new and older single-family houses. But you may want to take several additional steps when considering an older house. Very careful selection is essential because such a home can have far more shortcomings and problem areas than does a new house. First, a number of excellent books on selecting an older house have been written. Borrow one of them from your local library and review it before beginning your search. Second, consider having a qualified home builder or contractor examine an older house before you make any offer to purchase. The modest fee is

EXHIBIT 11-6

Checklist for houses. *Source:* Money Management Institute booklet, *Your Housing Dollar,* the Money Management Institute of Household Finance Corporation, Chicago, IL.

Outside House and Yard
- Attractive, well-designed house
- Suited to natural surroundings
- Lot of the right size and shape for house and garage
- Suitable use of building materials
- Compatible with houses in the area
- Attractive landscaping and yard

- Good drainage of rain and moisture
- Dry, firm soil around the house
- Mature, healthy trees — placed to give shade in summer
- Convenient, well-kept driveway, walks, patio, porch
- Yard for children

- Parking convenience — garage, carport, or street
- Distance between houses for privacy
- Sheltered entry — well-lighted and large enough for several to enter the house together
- Convenient service entrance

Outside Construction
- Durable siding materials — in good condition
- Solid brick and masonry — free of cracks
- Solid foundation walls — six inches above ground level — eight inches thick

- Weather stripped windows and doors
- Noncorrosive gutters and downspouts, connected to storm sewer or splash block to carry water away from house

- Copper or aluminum flashing used over doors, windows, and joints on the roof
- Screens and storm windows or Thermopane glass
- Storm doors

Inside Construction
- Sound, smooth walls with invisible nails and taping on dry walls, without hollows or large cracks in plaster walls
- Well-done carpentry work with properly fitted joints and moldings
- Properly fitted, easy-to-operate windows

- Level wood floors with smooth finish and no high edges, wide gaps, or squeaks
- Well-fitted tile floors — no cracked or damaged tiles — no visible adhesive
- Good possibilities for improvements, remodeling, expanding
- Properly fitted and easy-to-work doors and drawers in built-in cabinets

- Dry basement floor with hard smooth surface
- Adequate basement drain
- Sturdy stairways with railings, adequate head room — not too steep
- Leakproof roof — in good condition
- Adequate insulation for warmth, coolness, and soundproofing

Living Space
- Convenient floor plan and paths from room to room
- Convenient entry with foyer and closet
- Convenient work areas (kitchen, laundry, workshop) with adequate drawers, cabinets, lighting, work space, electric power
- Private areas (bedrooms and bathrooms) located far enough from other parts of the house for privacy and quiet

- Social areas (living and dining rooms, play space, yard, porch, or patio) convenient, comfortable, large enough for family and guests
- Rooms conveniently related to each other — entry to living room, dining room to kitchen, bedrooms to baths
- Adequate storage — closets, cabinets, shelves, attic, basement, garage
- Suitable wall space and room size for your furnishings

- Outdoor space convenient to indoor space
- Windows located to provide enough air, light, and ventilation
- Agreeable type, size, and placement of windows
- Usable attic and/or basement space
- Possibilities for expansion
- Attractive decorating and fixtures
- Extras — fireplace, air conditioning, porches, new kitchen and baths, built-in equipment, decorating you like

generally well justified. Last, we think it is a good idea to have an independent appraiser give you an appraisal on any older house you consider.

Selecting a Condominium

When selecting a condominium, your range of choices is likely to be more limited. Consequently, while you will still want to use the three general selection criteria—zoning, value of surrounding property, and convenience—of the previous section to decide on the suitability of the condominium's location, you will have less latitude in your choices. Condominiums also raise some special issues that need to be considered.

The first problem is to decide how important the added features of a condominium are to you. The checklist in Exhibit 11-7 has been developed to help you do that. If most of your answers are in the "yes" column, a condominium should be high on your list. If not, you may want to reconsider the appropriateness of a condominium.

Like choosing a single-family house, selecting a condominium means you will need to investigate the individual living unit you may be purchasing. You will not be evaluating the advantages of a private yard, but you

EXHIBIT 11-7

Evaluating a condominium's added features.

	YES	NO
1 Is the reduced maintenance feature		
a An appealing one?	( )	( )
b Critical to you?	( )	( )
c Eliminating work you dislike?	( )	( )
2 Are the recreational facilities		
a What you enjoy?	( )	( )
b Sufficient for everyone to use without long waits?	( )	( )
c Such that you will use them extensively?	( )	( )
d Such that you can drop your recreation club membership?	( )	( )
3 Will the unit's location		
a Reduce your commuting effort and expense?	( )	( )
b Put you closer to social and cultural interests?	( )	( )
c Benefit your family's interests and activities?	( )	( )
4 Do your present housing needs not require the		
a Larger living area of a single-family house?	( )	( )
b Private yard of a single-family house?	( )	( )
5 Can you live where you		
a Have limited control over the common property?	( )	( )
b May have to alter your lifestyle (regarding noise, entertaining, hours, and pets, for example)?	( )	( )

should still investigate the common property items. We believe that most of the questions shown in Exhibit 11-6 can also be used to select a condominium. By dropping those questions that do not apply, you can systematically evaluate your prospective condominium.

Caution: Problem Areas Ahead   The past abuses and questionable tactics that have characterized some condominiums, such as the developer not providing the promised facilities or quoting unrealistically low monthly maintenance fees, make it essential that a buyer exercise extra care in each and every aspect of the purchase. The checklist in Exhibit 11-8 has sections for major problem areas. Too many "no" responses in a section may indicate problems ahead; consider and analyze that area further.

Selecting a Mobile Home

Prospective mobile home buyers have the choice of a wide range of models from a number of manufacturers. The same may not hold for the buyer's choice of locations for that home. In most areas, zoning regulations restrict mobile homes to designated parks; this limitation sharply narrows the available choices. Prospective buyers can still use the three location criteria from the opening section—zoning, value of surrounding property, and convenience—to guide them when selecting a location. But they will likely have to make some compromises on location.

Many of the questions developed in Exhibit 11-6 for selecting a single-family home can also be used to guide the selection of the mobile home itself. Granted, some items that deal with the yard and general neighborhood do not apply, but the rest of the questions can help a prospective buyer systematically evaluate a particular mobile home. A careful review is essential when selecting a mobile home. In the past, some serious questions have been raised about the quality of materials as well as the construction of some mobile homes. Without question, some manufacturers have consistently turned out quality units that have represented reasonable value for the money. But there have been enough shoddy units to warrant extra care.

EXHIBIT 11-8

Judging a condominium development.

	YES	NO
General development plans:		
1 Are the neighbors similar to you in status? (Are they chiefly singles, parents with young children, mature couples?)	( )	( )
2 Does the overall development		
a Appear attractive and well thought out?	( )	( )
b Provide adequate facilities and common area?	( )	( )
3 Is the design suitable for your climate?	( )	( )
4 When you want to sell		
a Are there restrictions?	( )	( )
b Must you work through a particular realtor?	( )	( )
5 Have the maximum number of units and the final completion date been set?	( )	( )
6 Are there many vacant units? If so, why?	( )	( )
Common facilities:		
1 Do the facilities meet your needs?	( )	( )
2 Are all recreation facilities part of common property?	( )	( )
3 If leased, are the fees reasonable?	( )	( )
4 If unfinished, is the completion date guaranteed?	( )	( )
Maintenance:		
1 Are the units well built?	( )	( )
2 Do the budgeted expenses include replacement of major capital items (roof, painting, sidewalks)?	( )	( )
3 Is the estimated cost per unit based on a realistic projected number of units?	( )	( )
4 Does the developer have a record of creating high quality, successful condominiums?	( )	( )
5 Can owners be forced to pay their maintenance fees?	( )	( )
6 If a new development, is the projected maintenance budget reasonable?	( )	( )
7 If an already-established complex, has the maintenance cost per unit remained relatively stable each year?	( )	( )

STRATEGY

Buy a mobile home from an established manufacturer whose products are recognized for their high quality. Try to talk to other owners who have purchased their mobile homes from the same manufacturer.

FINANCING YOUR HOME

Most people have to borrow a large portion of the purchase price of a home and pay it off over an extended period of time. Without mortgages, it would be virtually impossible for most people to consider home ownership. Because of the long-term nature of the commitment, careful analysis and selection of a mortgage are very important.

Common Features of Mortgages

Before discussing the various types of mortgages, it is important to understand the terminology used to describe mortgage contracts. Each of the following **mortgage features** is common to one or more of the mortgages discussed in this chapter.

Mortgage Tables   Exhibit 11-9 is a **mortgage table** for maturities of 20, 25, or 30 years (the most widely used maturities for home mortgage loans), and for interest rates ranging from 10 to 17 percent (the prevailing rates of the last few years). For a particular maturity and interest rate, the body of the table shows the monthly payment for a $1000 mortgage. Because the table gives the monthly payment for $1000, it can be used for a mortgage of any amount. To compute the monthly payment, simply divide the mortgage amount by $1000 and multiply the result by the monthly payment for $1000 from the table. For example, the monthly cost of a $45,500 mortgage at 14 percent for 25 years is:

$$\$547.82 \quad = \quad \$12.04 \quad \times (\$45,500 \div \$1000)$$

Monthly payment: =	Factor from	× Desired	÷ $1000
$45,500 mortgage	Exhibit 11-9	mortgage	

EXHIBIT 11-9

Monthly payment to amortize a $1000 loan for
different interest rates and loan maturities.

YEARS TO MATURITY	Rate (Percentage)							
	10	11	12	13	14	15	16	17
20	9.65	10.32	11.01	11.72	12.44	13.17	13.91	14.67
25	9.09	9.80	10.53	11.28	12.04	12.81	13.59	14.38
30	8.78	9.52	10.29	11.06	11.85	12.64	13.45	14.26

The actual mortgage payment for a $45,500 mortgage is $547.71; the small difference between that and our $547.82 estimate is due to rounding.

We can also use Exhibit 11-9 to compute the monthly payment when a mortgage's interest rate is between the values given in the exhibit. For example, suppose we want the monthly payment for a 13.25 percent, 25-year mortgage. To compute the payment on $1000, we take the payment at 13 percent and add to it one-quarter of the difference between 13 and 14 percent payments. The computation is:

$11.47   = $11.28   + [.25 ×   ($12.04   – 11.28)]

⌂   ⌂   ⌂   ⌂

$$\underset{\substack{\text{Monthly pay-}\\\text{ment for \$1000}}}{} = \underset{\substack{\text{Payment on}\\\text{13\% mortgage}}}{} + \left[.25 \times \left[\underset{\substack{\text{14\%}\\\text{mortgage}}}{} - \underset{\substack{\text{13\%}\\\text{mortgage}}}{}\right]\right]$$

Once we have the payment for $1000, we proceed as we did in the previous paragraph to find the payment for a mortgage of a particular size.

Amortization   Paying off a loan is called **amortization**. In the early years of a mortgage loan, most of your monthly mortgage payment goes toward paying the interest, with very little going toward paying off the loan. Exhibit 11-10 shows, for a 15 percent, $1000 mortgage, the amount remaining

EXHIBIT 11-10

Unpaid balance on a $1000 mortgage loan at 15 percent, with 20-, 25-, 30-year maturities.

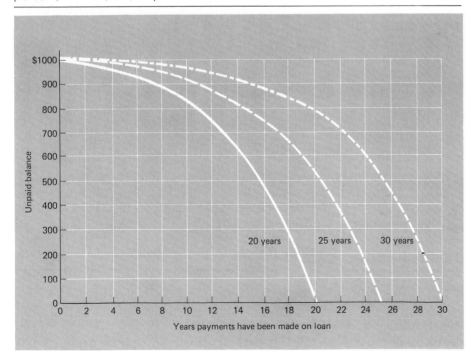

outstanding at the end of each year for maturities of 20, 25, and 30 years. Note how slowly the mortgage is reduced in the early years and how rapidly it reduces as the maturity date approaches. Note particularly that when the 20-year mortgage is paid in full, there is still $538 unpaid on the 25-year loan and $784 unpaid on the 30-year obligation. On the 30-year loan, only 21.6 percent of the mortgage has been repaid at the time the 20-year loan is completely repaid.

Acceleration Clause   Most mortgages stipulate that if the loan is in default (if payments are not made) for a period such as 60 or 90 days, the total amount of the loan becomes immediately due. This **acceleration clause** permits the lender to foreclose (repossess the property) in the event of default. It is not a negotiable provision.

Nonassumption Clause   Let's say you own a house, you want to sell it, you still have a large balance to repay on your mortgage loan, and you are paying a very low mortgage interest rate. Furthermore, let's assume that people who are buying houses today have to pay very high mortgage interest rates. The **nonassumption clause** means that when you sell your house, you will have to pay off the loan at the time of sale. The buyer cannot "take over" your mortgage; that is, the buyer cannot simply slip into the seller's mortgage and assume the balance of payments due.

Prepayment Penalty   During the period of a mortgage loan, a borrower might decide to repay part of the loan ahead of schedule—in other words, to prepay the mortgage. Most loans allow you to prepay a percentage of the unpaid balance without penalty; 10 percent is frequently allowed. Should you want to pay more than the allowed percentage, many mortgages assess a **prepayment penalty** that can be sizable if the prepaid amount is large. The purpose is to discourage borrowers from paying off the original loan because they have now found another loan that carries a lower interest rate. That is, interest rates may have dropped since the borrower took out the original mortgage loan. Without a penalty, the borrower may find it worthwhile to borrow at the new, lower rate and to use the money to repay the original loan. A sizable prepayment penalty can take away most, or all, of the savings you might gain from borrowing at a new rate.

STRATEGY

Try to find a mortgage that permits you to prepay a sizable part of the mortgage without a penalty.

Tax and Insurance Escrow Accounts   Some mortgage lenders will approve a mortgage only if the borrower also pays one-twelfth of the home's property tax to the lender each month. The lender then accumulates these property tax payments in a separate, non–interest-bearing (in most states) **tax escrow account**. Some lenders also require borrowers to pay one-twelfth of their homeowners insurance premium into the same non–interest-bearing tax escrow account each month. When the property taxes and

insurance premiums are actually billed, those bills go to the lender who pays them with the money in the escrow account. Lenders will tell you they are doing this to help you. But rest assured that the lender happily provides the service because the money in your escrow account can be loaned out to earn interest. It remains loaned out until it is used for a tax or insurance payment. Even lenders who do not require an escrow account on a mortgage will often "strongly recommend" it to the buyer.

Lenders claim that tax and insurance escrow accounts are necessary because a borrower might be unable to pay the property taxes and insurance premiums when they come due. Granted that escrow accounts do force the borrowers to accumulate the money for those two payments on a regular basis, but they earn no interest on that money—a major disadvantage. Left on their own, most home buyers should have enough discipline to accumulate the money in a savings account or a money market mutual fund (discussed in Chapter 20) where it earns interest right up to the time it is used for a payment.

STRATEGY

Always try to avoid a tax and insurance escrow account on a mortgage. If you cannot do so, try to find a lender who pays interest on escrow accounts.

MAJOR TYPES OF MORTGAGES

Before we discuss specific mortgage loans, there are several things we need to point out. First, the seven types of mortgages that we discuss are the major ones that are widely available as this is written. We emphasize this because the whole field of mortgages is in a state of flux. New types of mortgages continue to be introduced, and changes continue to be made in present mortgages. Consequently, we cannot guarantee that, by the time you read this, there will not be additional types of mortgages, or that existing mortgages will not have been modified.

Second, the mortgages we discuss are generally available throughout the United States. But that does not mean that within a given geographical area all of the mortgages will be available. Often, lenders within a particular area will offer several different mortgages but not the entire range. At least the home buyer will have several mortgage options from which to choose. We continue our previous definition that "home" encompasses all the ownership alternatives: single-family house, condominium, and mobile home. But we want to reiterate our earlier point that the range of mortgage options for mobile homes is likely to be more restricted than for either a single-family house or a condominium.

Our final point is that the major types of mortgages differ in these three significant ways:

The down payment the mortgage requires

Whether the interest rate on the mortgage changes over time

Whether the monthly payment on the mortgage remains fixed at the level when the mortgage started

To help you fully appreciate the differences among the various mortgages, we discuss these three points before we move to the specifics of the mortgages themselves.

Required Down Payment   The required down payment that a potential buyer must pay is set as a percentage of the home's selling price. At one extreme, there are government-guaranteed or insured mortgages that require a down payment that can be 3 percent or less of the selling price. At the other end of the spectrum, down payments on traditional mortgages may equal or exceed 20 percent of the selling price.

Potential home buyers and mortgage lenders tend to have opposite views on down payments. Lenders prefer to have a large down payment because it minimizes their potential loss should they be forced to repossess a home when the buyer is unable to make the mortgage payments. Buyers who want to minimize their costs at the time they buy the home prefer the opposite: a minimal down payment. A combination of government-sponsored insurance and guarantees, together with insurance from private companies, has reduced required down payments from the higher levels that lenders preferred to amounts closer to those that buyers wanted. Lenders accept those lower down payments because the insurance or guarantee program assures repayment should the buyer encounter difficulty repaying the mortgage.

Interest Rate over the Life of the Mortgage   Traditionally, mortgages had a fixed interest rate that was set when the mortgage was obtained and remained unchanged thereafter. If it started at 10 percent, it remained at 10 percent until the mortgage was repaid. Both the borrower and the lender were locked into the mortgage loan's fixed rate.

Increasingly, home mortgages have adjustable interest rates that allow the rate to be adjusted upward or downward over the life of the mortgage. A major reason for this change is that mortgage lenders have become more and more reluctant to commit themselves to a fixed interest rate over the lengthy life of the mortgage. Should interest rates in the marketplace rise after a mortgage loan is made, lenders will want to raise the interest rate on their previous mortgage loans. Of course, should interest rates decline after a mortgage loan is made, the borrower would want the interest rate lowered. An adjustable interest rate on the mortgage allows either possibility.

Actual adjustments in a mortgage's interest rate can be made in two ways. One way employs a formal automatic approach. With it, the interest rate on the mortgage is tied (or *indexed*, to use financial jargon) to some interest rate in the borrowing and lending marketplace. Should demand for borrowed funds increase, or should the supply of available funds for lending decline, interest rates in the marketplace will likely rise. If the mortgage's interest rate is indexed to some marketplace interest rate, that mortgage's rate will also rise. Conversely, should market interest rates decline because of either reduced borrowing or an increased supply of funds to be loaned, the mortgage's interest rate will also decline. The only question that remains is how often the mortgage's interest rate is adjusted. At present, the interest rate on most adjustable rate mortgages is adjusted every 6 or 12 months.

The second technique for rate adjustment is not automatic. It relies on a series of renegotiation sessions between the lender and the borrower to adjust the rate. Often, this type of adjustable rate mortgage (frequently called a renegotiated rate mortgage) covers 20, 25, or 30 years. But within that mortgage period, the interest is set by a series of 1- to 5-year notes. The borrower must negotiate a new note with the lender each time the existing 1- to 5-year note expires. During that renegotiation session, the lender may well raise the rate if market interest rates have risen since the last note was signed. Or, if market rates have fallen, the lender will lower the rate of the new note. The borrower usually has a choice on the maturity of the note: 1 to 5 years may be available. But lenders may not offer all these maturities.

When mortgages with adjustable rates were first introduced, state and federal regulators set a number of restrictions. Frequently, they limited the amount a mortgage's interest rate could rise in a 6- to 12-month period. Likewise, they placed a maximum on how much the interest rate could be raised during the life of the mortgage. Many of those limits have now been phased out, as a part of the move to deregulate financial institutions. The net effect is that borrowers are now basically on their own. Today, a potential borrower must judge whether the interest rate adjustment on a particular mortgage seems fair and reasonable, making it essential that borrowers know how a mortgage's adjustable rate operates.

STRATEGY

Carefully review how a mortgage's adjustable interest rate operates. Try to determine whether it treats the borrower fairly.

Monthly Payment over the Life of the Mortgage With a traditional fixed interest rate mortgage, the monthly payment was set at the start of the loan and did not change. But that no longer holds. An adjustable rate mortgage is likely to have differing monthly payments during the life of the mortgage. Payments will rise when the mortgage's interest rate increases to cover those higher interest charges. Conversely, the monthly payment can be decreased if the mortgage's interest rate drops, because there will now be less interest to pay.

Some mortgages also have a changing monthly payment built right into them. These mortgages begin with a very low monthly payment, so that more potential home buyers can afford the payments. The payments do not remain there, however; they rise by a prescribed amount each year. The assumption is that the home buyer's ability to pay will rise over time, so the monthly payment can be raised to reflect that increased ability. On some mortgages, the yearly payment increase continues for the first 5 to 10 years of ownership. Other mortgages continue their annual increases right up to the point the mortgage is repaid.

Features of Currently Available Mortgage Loans

Exhibit 11-11 uses the three attributes from the last section to summarize the differences and similarities for seven currently available types of mortgage loans. The specifics for each mortgage are discussed in the next section.

EXHIBIT 11-11

Features of currently available mortgage loans.

TYPE OF MORTGAGE	TYPICAL DOWNPAYMENT	INTEREST RATE ON MORTGAGE	MONTHLY PAYMENTS OVER LIFE OF MORTGAGE
Conventional	20% or more	Fixed when loan is obtained	Fixed at the time loan is obtained
FHA and VA	0% to 5%	Fixed when loan is obtained	Fixed at the time loan is obtained
Conventional insured	5% to 10%	Fixed when loan is obtained	Fixed at the time loan is obtained
Graduated payment (GPM)	5% to 15%	Fixed when loan is obtained	Increases each year during first 5 to 10 years
Growing equity (GEM) (rapid payoff)	5% to 10%	Fixed when loan is obtained	Increases 2½% to 7½% each year of mortgage loan
Adjustable-rate mortgage (ARM)	10%	Varies with interest rates in the marketplace	Varies as the interest rate on the mortgage changes
Second mortgage from seller	5% to 10% (set by first mortgage)	Fixed rate but often less than market rate	Some are fixed, others are fixed for 3 to 5 years with a final balloon payment of the entire loan balance

Conventional Mortgage   **Conventional mortgages** are made by a savings institution to a borrower, the homeowner; the mortgage contract is between the lender and the homeowner, and there are no other parties to the loan. The lender's only protections on the loan are the value of the property and the equity or down payment the purchaser has been required to make in order to get the loan. Consequently, the required down payment is substantial.

FHA-Insured and VA-Guaranteed Mortgages   The Federal Housing Authority (FHA) makes loans to all buyers on **FHA loans**, and the Veterans Administration (VA) makes **VA loans** to veterans. FHA and VA loans both involve a third party in the loan transaction. A savings institution makes the loan to the borrower, but the FHA insures or the VA guarantees to repay the loan should the borrower be unable to repay it. Because the federal guarantee promises to cover losses on the loan, the lender will accept a much smaller down payment. The FHA and VA specify what minimum down payment they will accept from a buyer; it can range from zero for a veteran purchasing an inexpensive house to 5 percent of the selling price on a more expensive home. The buyer pays an annual fee of ½ percent of the unpaid mortgage balance for FHA insurance or the VA guarantee. The annual fee on a mortgage with a $50,000 unpaid balance is:

$$\underset{\text{Annual fee}}{\$250} \quad = \quad \underset{\text{Mortgage balance}}{\$50,000} \quad \times \quad \underset{\text{Annual rate}}{½\%}$$

Of course, as the mortgage is repaid, the fee decreases.

There are two additional restrictions on FHA and VA loans. First, FHA and VA will loan money on houses only when the selling price is less than the maximum set by the two agencies (currently $70,000). Since this maximum has typically been about equal to the average cost of a new house, this limit would be a problem only on an expensive house. The second restriction is that government regulations place a ceiling on the interest rate that a lender can charge on an FHA or a VA loan. To give the appearance of a "bargain," the maximum rate is nearly always less than the rate lenders are offering on conventional and adjustable rate loans. Faced with the choice of making a lower-paying FHA or VA loan or a higher-paying conventional or an adjustable-rate loan, lenders would prudently avoid FHA or VA loans. However, the regulators, in a burst of wisdom, created an obtuse device to minimize the lender's reluctance: **points**.

Points   Our explanation will be somewhat involved, but bear with us a bit. First, one point equals 1 percent of the mortgage loan. Thus, one point on a $50,000 mortgage equals $500; eight points on that mortgage equals $4,000. So far, so good.

Next, recognize that FHA and VA rules specify that only the *seller* of the home can be required to pay points on an FHA or a VA mortgage; the buyer or borrower does not pay them. Consequently, if our previous $50,000 mortgage was FHA or VA, the seller would have to pay the points: $500 if it were one point and $4000 if it were eight points.

Now let us see how the lender can use points to raise the interest rate on an FHA or a VA loan to an amount equalling the rate on competing loans. The lender is forced to use points for two reasons. First, the FHA and VA maximum interest rate is often less than the current interest rate on competing mortgages. Second, because of the rate ceiling, the lender cannot raise the interest directly. For each point the lender charges on an FHA or a VA loan, it raises the lender's effective rate of return on that mortgage approximately ⅛ percent. We say "effective rate of return" because the stated interest rate, the one quoted to the borrower, remains unchanged. But the lender's rate of return rises roughly ⅛ percent for each point.

An example is the best way to demonstrate how points work. Suppose Bob Buyer has agreed to buy Sue Seller's house, using a $50,000 FHA mortgage. Recognize that the home's actual selling price is higher than that, because Bob also has a down payment. But we can ignore that. Assume the current FHA and VA maximum interest rate is 14½ percent, while the interest rate on a conventional or adjustable-rate mortgage is 15 percent. Lenders would be reluctant to accept 14½ on a FHA loan when they could earn 15 percent interest on a conventional or adjustable-rate mortgage. So the lender charges enough points to raise the effective rate of return from 14½ to 15 percent on the FHA loan. Since charging one point raises the rate ⅛ percent, the lender will charge four points to raise the return the desired ½ percent. That means Sue will be charged:

$$\$2,000 = \$50,000 \times 4 \times 1\%$$

$$\text{Dollar} = \text{Mortgage} \times \text{Points} \times \text{Rate per}$$
$$\text{charge} \quad \text{amount} \quad \text{charged} \quad \text{point}$$

Why is Sue the victim? Because she is the seller.

Let us follow how the transaction would be completed. With either a $50,000 conventional or adjustable-rate mortgage, Sue would receive a check for that amount from the lender. But in our FHA loan example, Sue owes the lender $2,000 for the points. She receives only $48,000. The lender's return is improved because only $48,000 was paid out on the loan. Yet Bob, the borrower, will be making payments on a $50,000 mortgage at 14½ percent because those were the terms of the loan. The combination of those payments raises the loan's effective return to approximately 15 percent. And how about Sue? She will likely be so "impressed" (probably *de*pressed is closer) with FHA loans that, on the next house sale, she will raise the selling price. How much? About enough to cover the points. And most sellers do exactly that. So who pays the points in the end? The buyer, through the inflated selling price.

STRATEGY

The next time some lender quotes what sounds like a "bargain interest rate," check to see if the seller will have to pay points. If so, how many? In all likelihood, the selling price will actually be higher to cover those points.

Conventional Mortgages: Insured One weakness of the FHA and VA programs has been the extensive paperwork for the loan application and the length of time—often as long as several months—that is needed for approval. As a result, private insurance companies developed a new variation by combining their primary business—insurance—with standard mortgages: a **conventional insured mortgage**. Paperwork was reduced and approval time shortened to a few days. Because the loan is insured, a much lower down payment is required.

Privately insured mortgage loans call for either a 5 or a 10 percent down payment. The insurance company insures the first 20 percent of the loan. If the lending agency has to foreclose, it is in exactly the same position as if it had a conventional mortgage. On a $70,000 home, the bank could sell the house for as little as $56,000 and still recover the amount of the loan.

The *buyer* pays the insurance premium: for 95 percent loans, a typical premium is 1 percent of the loan for the first year and .325 percent each year thereafter; for 90 percent loans, the premium is ½ of 1 percent for the first year and .325 pecent thereafter. For example, if the loan is a 95 percent mortgage for $50,000, the first year's premium is:

$$\$500 \quad = 1\% \quad \times \$50,000$$

$500	= 1%	× $50,000
⬆	⬆	⬆
First year's premium	= Initial fee	× Amount of mortgage

Graduated Payment Mortgage A **graduated payment mortgage** (GPM) is designed to enable home buyers to purchase a more expensive house than they could normally afford with their current income. To do that, the initial monthly payment on a GPM is set below the amount needed to repay the mortgage over its 20- to 30-year life. Consequently, during each of the first 5 to 10 years, the monthly payment increases gradually; typically, it rises 2½ to 7½ percent per year. On most loans, the initial monthly payment is set so low that it does not even pay the interest on the mortgage. So the unpaid balance on the mortgage actually rises rather than declines during the early years. Each year's unpaid interest is merely added to the mortgage balance. As the payment is increased, it comes ever closer to meeting the mortgage's interest. Once all the 5 to 10 years of planned increases are in place, the payment is sufficiently large so that it will repay the entire balance over the remaining life of the mortgage.

An example is the best way to illustrate a GPM. All the mortgages in Exhibit 11-12 are for $60,000, carry a fixed 14 percent interest rate, and mature in 30 years. The monthly payment on the conventional mortgage begins at $710.92 and remains constant throughout the loan's life. The initial payment on the GPM is only $553.52, a sizable saving over the conventional's $710.92. But the monthly payments increase 7½ percent each year during the first 5 years. By year 6, the GPM payment has risen to $794.65, where it stays for the remaining years of the loan. Now the payment is considerably more than it is on the conventional mortgage. In

EXHIBIT 11-12

Monthly payments during first 10 years for a conventional mortgage, a graduated payment mortgage, and a growing equity mortgage.

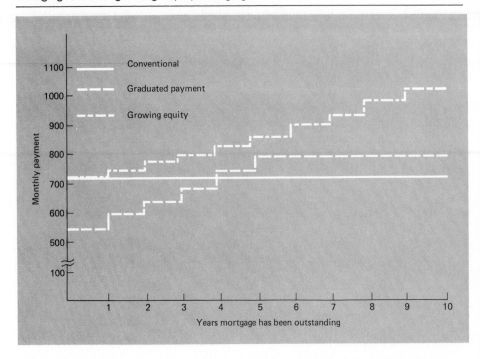

effect, the borrower must now pay for those bargain monthly payments of the first 5 years.

Growing Equity Mortgage A **growing equity mortgage** (GEM) has monthly payments that increase by a specified percentage each year that the mortgage is outstanding. The initial payment on a GEM is the same as the payment on a similar-sized conventional mortgage with a maturity of 25 or 30 years. But each year after that, the monthly payment will rise by 2½ to 7½ percent annually. Those larger payments will repay the balance on the loan much more quickly. For example, if the monthly payment rises 2½ percent annually, the loan will be completely repaid in approximately 14 years. Raising the payment 7½ percent annually repays the loan in approximately 10 years. A GEM will appeal to buyers who not only expect their incomes to rise sharply during the next few years but who also want to use part of their additional income to repay their home mortgages more quickly. The GEM enables them to do so by incorporating a systematic accelerated repayment plan.

The operations of a GEM can best be illustrated through an example. Let us return to Exhibit 11-12, where we have already illustrated the conventional mortgage and GPM. To those we will add a $60,000 GEM. Its interest rate is also 14 percent and the initial payment is based on a 30-year maturity. The monthly payment on this GEM is scheduled to rise 4 percent each year. The initial payment on the GEM in Exhibit 11-12 is $710.92. This is the same as for the conventional mortgage. Every year, however, that payment rises by 4 percent. By the fifth year, it is $831.68, and by the tenth, it reaches $1011.86. By that time, the payments are nearly 45 percent higher than those on the conventional mortgage. It is easy to see why the mortgage is being repaid rather quickly. In fact, the GEM in Exhibit 11-12 will be repaid before the end of the thirteenth year. At that point, the conventional mortgage still has 17 more years of payments.

Adjustable-Rate Mortgage   The interest rate on **adjustable-rate mortgages** (ARMs) changes during the mortgage's lifetime. An ARM protects the lender if interest rates in the marketplace rise because the mortgage's interest rate can be adjusted upward. Similarly, during a period of declining interest rates it protects the borrower because the interest rate on an ARM would be adjusted downward. Of course, if market interest rates remain relatively stable, the interest rate on an ARM remains basically unchanged.

Some ARMs index, or tie, the interest rate on the mortgage to some market interest rate. The mortgage's interest rate is then adjusted in accordance with changes in that market interest rate. One frequently used market interest rate is the rate on certain U.S. Treasury securities. Another often-used rate is the rate on recent mortgages within a particular area. Other ARMs rely on negotiations between the lender and the borrower to adjust the rate on the mortgage. Those renegotiations typically occur every 1 to 5 years. Regardless of which adjustment technique is used, a change in the interest rate often means a different monthly payment. If the new rate is higher, the monthly payment will rise. Conversely, a decline in the rate on the ARM will decrease that payment. To lessen the possibility of wide swings in the monthly payment, some lenders include a promise in the mortgage that the monthly payment cannot increase by more than 25 percent at any one time.

Second Mortgage from Seller   Some new buyers are able to get a **second mortgage from the home seller** as partial payment on the house. Sellers may be willing to accept this mortgage in order to help the new buyer purchase the house. Often, the second mortgage carries an interest rate that is below the rate currently offered by other mortgage lenders. By accepting a lower rate, the seller reduces the cost of the home by subsidizing the buyer's financing package. The saving to the buyer comes from the below-market interest rate on the second mortgage. Also, the required down payment may be less because the lender who is granting the principal first mortgage may be willing to count the second mortgage as part of the down payment. Sellers will frequently offer a second mortgage to help clinch the sale of the home.

The monthly payments on a seller-offered second mortgage may have two parts. The initial monthly payment is set so that the loan will be repaid in 25 to 30 years. Thus, on a $10,000 second mortgage with an interest rate of 10 percent, the required payment will be $87.80 (based on Exhibit 11-9 with a 30-year maturity). But the surprise comes with the second part of the

payment. After 3 to 5 years of these monthly payments, many second mortgages have a single final balloon payment equal to the entire unpaid mortgage balance. That balloon payment means that the borrower must repay the entire unpaid loan balance all at one time. To show the sheer size of such a payment, assume our previous $10,000, 10 percent second mortgage has a balloon payment after the end of 5 years. For 5 years our borrower placidly pays a manageable $87.80 monthly. But then the surprise! After 5 years, the unpaid balance on the second mortgage is still $9654. So the balloon payment is $9654. And it must be paid immediately! Obviously, the borrower probably cannot pay that amount. In all likelihood, when the borrower accepted this mortgage, he or she hoped to be able to borrow the money for that balloon payment, and to borrow it at a lower interest rate than the mortgage interest rate of 5 years ago.

Second mortgages with balloon notes must be considered a short-term temporary financing source. The consequences can be disastrous—the borrower may lose the house—if he or she is unable to make the final balloon payment.

STRATEGY

Because the risks are sizable, home buyers who accept a seller-provided second mortgage with a final balloon payment should proceed with extreme caution.

Selecting the Right Mortgage

Selecting the right mortgage requires joint consideration of what is best for the borrower and what is best given the present economic environment. To decide what mortgage is best for you, the potential borrower, you will need to ask:

What is the required down payment?

How large is the initial monthly payment?

Will the monthly payment change during the life of the mortgage?

If so, by how much is it likely to change?

Part of these questions can be answered by a review of your present financial position:

How much cash do you have available for the down payment?

What income is currently available for your monthly payments?

What is your future income likely to be?

Will it rise?

If so, how rapidly?

The worksheet (Exhibit 11-4) for estimating the cost of ownership can help you decide whether you can afford to own. You can use the worksheet to examine what happens if certain things change. For example, you might examine how a different down payment changes the cost, what the impact of a rise in mortgage interest rates may be, or the effect on the cost if your marginal tax rate increases.

To select the best mortgage in light of the present economic environment, you will need to compare the interest rates on competing mortgages. For adjustable-rate mortgages, you will have to consider what the future direction of interest rates will likely be: Will mortgage interest rates rise? Decline? Or remain unchanged?

Exhibit 11-13 summarizes the major strengths and weaknesses of the seven mortgages shown in Exhibit 11-11 and discussed in the prior section. The far right column of Exhibit 11-13 provides guidelines on determining when a particular mortgage will likely be most appropriate. A review of the strengths and weaknesses of the various types, together with the guidelines, should help a borrower select the best mortgage.

Land Contract: An Alternative to a Mortgage

With a **land contract**, the seller finances the buyer; that is, the seller agrees to receive the home's selling price in a series of monthly payments that typically extend over 20 to 30 years. Often, the down payment is very small. The interest rate is nearly always fixed. So, since it does not change, the monthly payment will remain the same during the life of the land contract. On these points a land contract resembles a mortgage, but there is a major difference. Unlike a mortgage, when the buyer uses a land contract, title to

EXHIBIT 11-13

Guidelines to evaluate currently available
mortgage loans and to decide when to select
each mortgage.

STRENGTHS	WEAKNESSES	WHEN TO SELECT
Conventional Mortgage		
Widely available	Very large down payment	Future interest rates
Payment remains fixed	Interest rate may be	will likely rise
Easily predicted	higher than ARMs	Buyer wants fixed terms
future cost		
Higher down payment may		
lower interest rate		
FHA and VA Mortgages		
Extremely low down	Long approval time	Future interest rates
payment	Seller may refuse if	will likely rise
Payment remains fixed	points are high	Buyer needs low down
Future cost is	Annual premium on FHA	payment
predictable	or VA coverage	
Conventional Mortgage, Insured		
Very low down payment	Interest rate higher	Future interest rates
Widely available	than with larger down	will likely rise
Payments remain fixed	payment	Buyer needs lower
Future cost easily	Annual premium on	down payment
predicted	private insurance	
Graduated Payment Mortgage		
Initial payment is	Interest rate may be	Buyer needs lower
lower	higher than with	initial payments
Payments are fixed	conventional mortgage	Buyer expects future
Payment rises with	Not offered by some lenders	income to rise
buyer's ability to pay		
Future cost is predictable		
Growing Equity Mortgage		
Rapid payoff	Very large payment	Buyer expects future
minimizes interest	in later years	income to rise
paid	Repayment is very diffi-	sharply
Lender may offer	cult if borrower's future	Buyer wants to repay
"bargain interest	income rises only	quickly
rate" to promote GEM	moderately	Buyer expects to sell
		in 7 years or less
Adjustable-Rate Mortgage		
Interest rate falls	Interest rate rises with	Future interest rates
with market rates	market rates	will likely fall or
Interest rate may be	Sizable payment increase	be unchanged
lower than conventional	if market rates rise	Buyer expects to sell
mortgage rate	sharply	in 7 years or less
Widely available	Future cost is hard to	
	estimate	

EXHIBIT 11-13 *Continued*

CHAPTER 11

351

THE HOUSING
DECISION

STRENGTHS	WEAKNESSES	WHEN TO SELECT
Second Mortgage from Seller		
Interest rate is often less than prevailing market rates	Borrower may be unable to make balloon payment	Borrower can make balloon payment
Payment is lowered by below-market interest rate	Refinancing balloon payment with another mortgage may be difficult	Buyer needs the lower payment provided by second mortgage
Below-market interest rate lowers cost of home		

the home does not pass to the buyer until the final payment on the land contract is made. The buyer who defaults (fails to pay the land contract) has little recourse to recover all the money that has been paid to date. The buyer does not own the home, so that cannot be sold. The seller retains the money the buyer has paid up to this point and continues to own the property; the buyer is typically out of all the money he or she has paid. There are numerous cases where buyers paid on a land contract for 10 or 15 years only to lose everything they paid on the property because they could not continue the payments.

STRATEGY

Consider a land contract only in the rare circumstances when (1) you are certain you can make all the required monthly payments, and (2) you have thoroughly exhausted all sources of mortgage financing.

FINDING MORTGAGE MONEY

After deciding which home you want to buy (and, assuming you are like most of us, you are without the cash to pay for it), you will have to obtain a mortgage to finance the purchase. The primary sources of mortgage loans are (1) savings and loan associations, (2) commercial banks, (3) mutual savings banks (primarily in the Northeast), (4) **mortgage bankers** (organizations that originate mortgages and then sell them to others), and (5) credit unions.

During periods of high interest rates, when mortgages are hard to obtain, some preliminary steps can be important in applying for a loan. Things that you can do to help you get mortgage money are:

1   Make sure the property is worth what you have offered for it. You can help to ensure that you will not overpay by having the home appraised.

2   Have funds for the down payment. For a conventional loan, this should be at least 20 percent of the purchase price.

3   Use the net cost of ownership of the home you want to develop a new budget that can cover that cost.

4   Be a customer of the lender where you are applying for the mortgage; you can become one through a checking or a savings account, or through previous consumer loans.

Legal Aspects: The Actual Purchase

Prior to and at the time of the purchase, you should consider a number of legal factors. These involve (1) earnest money, (2) deeds, titles, and abstracts, (3) legal assistance, (4) title insurance, and (5) other closing costs.

Earnest Money   Sam Splitlevel, after months of looking, found his dream house. He offered the owner $58,000 and accompanied his offer with a check for $1000 as evidence of good faith. This advance is called **earnest money**. Later that same day, Sam found another house he liked even better and offered the seller $63,000 with $1000 earnest money. If both offers are accepted by the sellers, Sam has just lost $1000. Earnest money becomes the seller's if the buyer fails to complete the transaction. Unless Sam is ready to buy two houses, he will have to sacrifice the earnest money on one of them. There is one out, and it should be written into every offer to purchase. Make the earnest money contingent on obtaining satisfactory financing. If Sam had done this and then could not find a mortgage, both sellers would have had to return his earnest money.

Deeds, Titles, and Abstracts   A written document called a **deed** is the instrument which conveys the **title** (right to ownership) to a piece of property from the seller to the buyer. In all states, the deed is recorded by the registry of deeds, usually a unit of local government, to notify any interested parties of the status of the property. If there is some question as to the quality of the deed, you may be required to purchase title insurance. We'll discuss this more fully in a later section.

An **abstract** of title consists of a historical record of all transactions involving a piece of property. A *title search* involves examining the abstract or other documents to ensure that the title is clear. This is usually done by an attorney. In fact, most lenders will be unwilling to give you a mortgage unless an attorney gives an unqualified opinion of title based on an examination of the abstract.

Legal Assistance   Without exception, a lawyer should be retained to assist a home buyer. The lawyer represents the buyer when the actual title is transferred; this process is called the "closing." The lawyer protects your interests in all aspects of the purchase and makes sure that you receive clear title to the property. It is your attorney who is responsible for ensuring that you receive a clear title to your property.

STRATEGY

Before signing any agreements for the purchase or sale of a house, be sure to retain legal counsel. Also be sure that you and the attorney agree on the lawyer's fee before using any attorney.

Title Insurance When Carol Colonial buys her dream house, she is concerned that somebody may later prove to have a legal right to the property or a portion of the value of the property. For example, assume a carpenter did extensive remodeling work for the previous owner and had not been paid. The carpenter would file a claim against the property for the unpaid bill. This is called a "workman's lien," and it is generally recorded at the registry of deeds to inform anyone who is interested that there is a claim against the value of the property. Unfortunately, the lien may not have been properly recorded or may have been overlooked when the lawyer searched the title. By buying **title insurance** from a title insurance company at the time Carol buys the house, she ensures that if anyone does come forward claiming a right to the property, she will not lose her equity in the property.

The premium for title insurance is paid only once, at the time the title is conveyed to the buyer. The insurance protects the buyer for as long as he or she owns the property. Thus, if someone proves an interest in your property, the title insurance will reimburse you for the loss. A separate title insurance policy protects the bank that gave you the mortgage loan. If title insurance is required by the bank, make sure you buy two title insurance policies—one to protect the bank, and one to protect your equity. One final caution: Your title insurance policy protects only your initial equity—your down payment. As you amortize the mortgage, and as the home appreciates in value, the insurance policy protects a decreasing percentage of your equity in the property.

Closing Costs Upon Purchase

In analyzing how much to pay for a home, you must also include the costs which are incurred at the time the property is transferred from the seller to the buyer. These are called **closing costs**. Depending on geographic location, the closing costs may range from a low of approximately $500 to more than $3000. Exhibit 11-14 lists the major closing costs and estimates each cost for a typical $70,000 house.

Lenders are required to give you an itemized estimate of the closing costs when you apply for a mortgage loan. Since some of the costs may be negotiable, this advance notice should enable you to check the cost among

EXHIBIT 11-14

Estimated price ranges for closing costs on a
$70,000 home.

CLOSING COSTS	PRICE RANGE	CLOSING COSTS	PRICE RANGE
1 Title search fee	$ 50–150	**6** Recording fee	$15–30
2 Title insurance	$300–600	**7** Credit report (on buyer)	$25–75
3 Attorney's fees	$ 50–500	**8** Termite inspection	$50–150
4 Survey of property (if required)	$200–400	**9** Lender's origination fee	1% to 3% of mortgage
5 Appraisal fee	$100–300		

competing sources before the purchase is completed. Also feel free to discuss these costs with your attorney before you complete the purchase.

STRATEGY

Carefully investigate alternative sources and professionals to handle the various closing costs. It can save you hundreds of dollars.

OWNERSHIP: AN INVESTMENT OR A SHELTER?

The rapid rise in the market value of single-family houses, and to a much lesser degree condominiums and mobile homes, during the past few years has encouraged some people to view ownership as primarily an investment. Certainly, as Exhibit 11-15 illustrates, the market price of single-family houses rose very sharply during the mid- and late-1970s. The exhibit shows the annual rise in the median price of existing houses as well as the annual rise in consumer prices during the period 1975 through 1983. During that

EXHIBIT 11-15

Annual percentage increase in consumer prices
and the median price of an existing home.

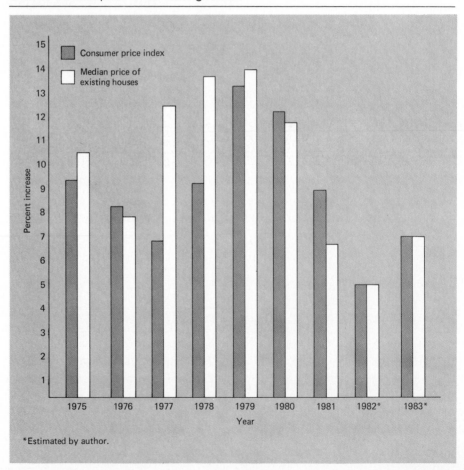

*Estimated by author.

time, home prices rose considerably faster than consumer prices in general. Many people watched happily as the value on their homes rose steadily each year, outpacing consumer prices in most years. Many more conventional investments failed to do even that well. And the favorable tax treatment for the gain on homes made the attraction even greater. Many who were not homeowners waited for the opportunity to plunge into the housing market.

But before you become totally sold on the merits of home ownership as an investment, look at the second half of Exhibit 11-15: the early 1980s. For the past several years, the rise in home prices has barely matched the rise in general consumer prices. In our opinion, the next several years are likely to be ones where that trend continues. Our expectation is that consumer prices and the median value of single-family houses will rise at about the same rate. Because of that, we believe ownership should be considered first and foremost as purchasing a *living unit*. In the end, the home may well prove to be a good investment. But we are not convinced that that possibility warrants making the considerable annual outlay that ownership entails if that is your only motive for buying a home. We think home ownership should be considered for its shelter potential first, with its investment potential a distant second.

SUMMARY

1   The four major rental options are apartments, duplexes, townhouses, and individual houses.

2   The three major ownership alternatives are single-family houses, condominiums, and mobile homes.

3   The major advantages of renting include:

Extensive recreational facilities
Development's restriction of its clientele to certain people
Landlord's responsibility for repairs and maintenance
Low initial cost to rent

4   The principal disadvantages of rental units include:

Restrictions on personal freedom and life-style
Rent payments not deductible on income tax return
No participation in price appreciation of rental unit

5   The major advantages of ownership include:

Psychological rewards of owning
Some of major costs of ownership can be deducted on income tax return
Appreciation in a home's market value

6   Principal disadvantages of ownership include:

Owner's responsibility for repairs and maintenance
Reduced flexibility for owner
High initial cost to purchase

7   The gross cost of ownership is substantially reduced by the tax savings from including mortgage interest and property tax as itemized deductions on the owner's income tax return.

8   To decide whether you can afford to own, estimate the annual cost of ownership and see whether you can fit it into your budget.

9   Appreciation in the market value of a home reduces the long-term cost of ownership.

10   When selecting a rental unit, you should carefully evaluate both the living unit itself and the rental agreement.

11   Picking the right home requires that you carefully evaluate the location of the home, the features it offers, and the yard, if there is one.

12   The three main attributes that distinguish the different mortgages are:
Down payment that is required
Interest rate over the life of the mortgage
Monthly payment over the life of the mortgage

13   Currently, widely available mortgage loans include: (a) conventional, (b) FHA and VA, (c) conventional, insured, (d) graduated payment (GPM), (e) growing equity (GEM), (f) adjustable-rate (ARM), and (g) second mortgage from seller.

14   Selecting the best mortgage requires the prospective borrower to consider both his or her current financial situation and the present economic environment.

15   Major sources for mortgage money are: (a) saving and loan associations, (b) commercial banks, (c) mutual savings banks, (d) mortgage bankers, and (e) credit unions.

16   Closing costs can easily equal 3 to 4 percent of the home's purchase price. Those costs can include: (a) title search fee, (b) title insurance, (c) attorney's fee, (d) survey fee (if required), (e) appraisal fee, (f) recording fee, (g) credit report, (h) termite inspection, and (i) lender's origination fee.

17   Purchasing a home should be based primarily on the buyer's need for shelter rather than a desire for an investment.

REVIEW YOUR UNDERSTANDING OF

Rental options
 Apartment
 Duplex
 Townhouse
 Individual house
Ownership alternatives
 Single-family house
 Condominium
 Mobile home
Individual living unit
Common property area
Net cost of ownership
Long-term cost of ownership
Lease
Mortgage features
 Mortgage table
 Amortization
 Acceleration clause
 Nonassumption clause

Prepayment penalty
Tax escrow account
Mortgages
 Conventional
 FHA/VA
 Conventional, insured
 Graduated payment (GPM)
 Growing equity (GEM)
 Adjustable-rate (ARM)
 Second mortgage from seller
Points
Land contract
Mortgage banker
Earnest money
Deed
Title
Abstract
Title insurance
Closing costs

DISCUSSION QUESTIONS

1 What are the differences in the features and facilities in a rented apartment versus renting a townhouse?

2 What are the major advantages of a condominium over a single-family house? Are there any disadvantages?

3 What principal advantages does ownership provide? What are its disadvantages?

4 Some people maintain that the income tax regulations encourage ownership rather than renting.

   a What does the tax system offer for owners?

   b Is the cost of ownership reduced by the income tax regulations? How?

   c Do renters receive similar benefits from the tax system?

5 What additional costs will there be in the annual net cost of ownership that are not in the net cost of rental? Are there some savings in the net ownership cost that are not in the net rental cost?

6 What causes the long-term cost of ownership to differ from the annual net cost of ownership (after taxes)? What factors can make a considerable difference between the two annual costs?

7 A local mortgage lender is encouraging Gus Gullible to adopt the lender's optional tax escrow account.

   a What advantages does the escrow account offer?

   b Are there likely to be disadvantages?

   c Should Gus consider an alternative?

8 What features do FHA and VA mortgages and insured conventional mortgages have in common? What is their principal difference (or differences)? What type of borrower will likely be best served by one of these mortgages?

9 A graduated payment mortgage has some features that are similar to a growing equity mortgage. What are they? How are they different? What type of borrower will likely want to use a graduated payment mortgage? A growing equity mortgage?

10 Mortgage lenders have increasingly shifted from offering conventional to adjustable-rate mortgages (ARM).

   a How do the two mortgages differ?

   b Why have lenders shifted toward ARMs?

   c In what situation does the borrower benefit from having an ARM rather than a conventional mortgage? When may the lender benefit?

11 What are the differences between a mortgage and a land contract?

12 Some people maintain that a home should be considered more as an investment than as a place to live.

   a What developments over the past 10 years have encouraged this view?

   b Do recent trends suggest that a home is becoming a better, or a poorer, investment?

PROBLEMS

11-1 Orelia Option is deciding between two $60,000 conventional mortgages: a 20-year, 14 percent loan and a 30-year, 14 percent loan.

   a What is the monthly payment on each of the two loans?

   b Over the life of the mortgage, what are the total payments on the 20-year loan? On the 30-year loan?

c Why are total payments on the 30-year loan so much higher? What happened to those additional payments?

d How should Orelia decide between the two loans?

11-2 Assume that Harve Hightax (whose marginal tax rate is 45 percent) and Ron Recentgrad (whose marginal tax rate is 25 percent) are both considering a particular condominium. Annual costs for the condominium include:

Mortgage payments	$7,235	Interest on mortgage	$7,005
Property tax	1,035	Homeowners insurance	240
Utilities	960	Maintenance cost	600
Interest lost on down payment (after-tax)	400		

a What is Harve's net cost of owning? Ron's net cost of owning?

b Why are the two net costs different?

11-3 Betty Bungalow plans to use a 30-year, $45,500 FHA mortgage to purchase a house. Currently, the maximum interest rate allowed on FHA mortgages is 11 percent, while the prevailing interest rate on conventional mortgages is 11¾ percent.

a Will the lender charge points on the FHA mortgage? If so, how many?

b If there are points, how many dollars are involved and who will pay them?

c Why would the lender accept an 11 percent interest FHA mortgage when conventional mortgages offer 11¾ percent interest?

11-4 Hal Halfdone has developed the following cost worksheet on his two housing options:

	RENTAL	OWNERSHIP
Housing unit	Duplex	$60,000 house
Net annual cost*	$5,880	7,155

*Amount from line 14 on a worksheet similar to Exhibit 11-4.

On the basis of the appreciation on a comparable house in the area, Hal expects that the house should appreciate approximately 3 percent per year. During the early years of ownership, Hal will be repaying approximately $120 of the mortgage each year.

a What is Hal's long-term annual cost of ownership?

b Which housing option offers the lowest long-term cost?

c When does Hal receive the benefits of long-term ownership?

11-5 Wilma Dixon is considering an apartment with the following features:

Monthly rental	$350	All maintenance and
Annual premium on		repairs provided by landlord
renter's insurance	110	Security deposit of 2 months'
Monthly utilities	95	rent in advance

Wilma plans to draw the money for the security deposit from her money-market fund, which currently pays 10 percent interest. Her marginal tax rate is 30 percent.

a What is the net annual cost of the apartment?

b Does the apartment give Wilma any tax benefits?

c Will the apartment's long-term cost differ from the net cost in part (a)? Why?

11-6 Fran Fasttrack, who recently graduated from a prestigious university with a master's degree in business administration, is considering the purchase of a condominium with one of the following two mortgages:

MORTGAGE	INTEREST RATE	MATURITY OF MORTGAGE	ANNUAL RISE IN PAYMENT	PAYMENTS WILL INCREASE:	INITIAL PAYMENT
Graduated payment	12%	30 years	7½% per year	During first 5 years	$338
Growing equity	12%	30 years	7½% per year	Each year of mortgage	$458

a Compute the annual payments on each mortgage for the following years (round to nearest dollar):

YEAR	1	2	3	4	5	6
Graduated payment	$338	____	____	____	____	$485
Growing equity	$458	____	____	____	____	$658

b Which loan will be repaid most quickly?

c How should Fran decide between the two loans?

CASE PROBLEM

Alice Crosely is a professional buyer for a major department store. She currently earns $28,500 a year. Her income should at least keep pace with inflation, and if she receives promotions as expected, her income could rise sharply in the future.

Alice lives in a one-bedroom apartment situated near stores, theaters, and her work. The rent on the apartment is $500 a month. This includes water and sewerage, but not heat and electricity, which run about $80 a month. Renters insurance for the apartment costs $100 a year.

She is concerned that, when renting, she has very little to show for her living costs except a pile of canceled checks. Nevertheless, she has not bought a single-family house because she does not want to get involved in caring for a yard and she prefers the city to a suburban location.

A new condominium building is being constructed near her present apartment building. One-bedroom units, similar to her apartment, are being sold for $58,400. A down payment of $5,900 is required, and the balance can be financed with a conventional mortgage at 14 percent for 25 years. In addition to the monthly mortgage payment, taxes are $820 a year, the monthly maintenance and service fee is $75, and utilities will likely average $85 per month. In addition, Alice expects maintenance and repairs on her living unit will average ½ percent of the unit's $58,400 purchase price. Annual premiums on a homeowners policy for the unit will be $140.

Alice estimates that her marginal tax rate will be 30 percent. The money for the down payment will come from her money-market fund, which is currently paying 9 percent interest.

Based on a study of similar condominiums in the area, Alice expects the market value of the condominium will increase about 4 percent per year.

1　How does the annual net cost of the condominium compare with the same cost for the apartment?

2　Roughly what percent of her income would Alice be spending on the condominium? How should she decide whether she can afford to own it?

3　What is the long-term annual cost for the condominium? (*Hint*: You will need to estimate the interest on the mortgage.)

4　What is the condominium's long-term cost if it appreciates only 3 percent per year? If it rises 5 percent? Does the assumption about appreciation have a major impact on the unit's long-term cost?

5　When will Alice receive the benefits of any appreciation in the condominium's market value? Of repayment of the mortgage?

6　If you were Alice, what would be your choice between the two options? Why?

PART
4
SAFEGUARDING YOUR RESOURCES

CHAPTER

12

THE INSURANCE DECISION

**AFTER COMPLETING THIS CHAPTER
YOU WILL HAVE LEARNED**

What *insurance* is and how it operates

How to avoid *underinsurance* and *overinsurance*

How to use *personal risk management* to select
your insurance coverage

How to *select a good insurance company*

What *deductibles* are and how they can be used
to *reduce insurance costs*

When to *purchase insurance* and when to *retain a
particular risk*

How to *buy the insurance* you need at the *least cost*

When to *review your insurance coverage*

MANY people think they know what

insurance is all about. But they very often don't. At least they don't understand the most basic purpose of insurance and how it works in its simplest, purest form.

To understand what insurance is, let's consider a small fictional town in which there are 200 homes, each home valued at about $80,000 including the structure, furniture, and usual appliances. Let's further assume that the 200 homeowners get together and decide to put $400 each into a "pot," the total in the pot amounting to $80,000. They also agree that whichever one among them suffers a total loss of house and contents, due to a fire or similar catastrophe, gets the money to help rebuild the house and buy new furnishings.

Insurance is a means whereby a number of people agree to pool their losses; to do that, every person in this group pays a premium that will be used to cover the individual losses of each group member. The premiums of everyone cover the losses of a few. However, everyone in the group is reasonably assured that any member who personally suffers a loss during the period will be able to collect from the dollars in the pool of premiums. Some would argue that only those lucky devils who have a loss receive anything from the insurance. We don't agree. As members of the group, individuals receive the assurance that, should they be unlucky enough to suffer a loss, they will be compensated. In our opinion, all people who participate in the insurance plan receive one of two worthwhile benefits:

> Those who do not undergo a loss have the peace of mind that comes from knowing that they will be compensated should they have a loss.

> Those who suffer a loss are compensated for part or all of the loss.

In addition to understanding what insurance does, a knowledge of some basic concepts about insurance is important for making the best use of your insurance dollars. To know how to buy insurance effectively and economically, you must know the purpose of insurance and understand the fundamental principles of risk management. Unfortunately, most Americans have very little understanding of what is involved in a sound insurance program. Rather, they simply accept insurance as necessary and they allow others to tell them what they need and how much to spend on maintaining it. Few people understand the policies they buy, and most are not even sure why they are buying them. This is unwise because insurance is important in maintaining your economic welfare. Without insurance, you may suffer devastating financial losses: Your death could impose severe financial hardship on your dependents, or a fire could destroy your possessions. Insurance, tailored to the specific needs of the family or individual, can make it easier to deal with the financial consequences of such unhappy events.

To make an informed insurance decision, you must ask yourself, and develop answers to, such questions as:

1   What should be insured?

2   How much should it be insured for?

3   Where should the insurance be purchased?

4   What are the specific details that should be included in the insurance policy for my particular case?

The technical term for answering these questions is **risk management**. It is an organized and systematic approach to analyzing and evaluating the pure risks which confront people. First, it concentrates on identifying and analyzing the loss exposures that the individual faces. Second, it attempts to identify the best method for dealing with each of these loss exposures.

Pure Risks and Speculative Risks   A **pure risk** has only the possibility of a loss or of no change; there can be no possibility of a gain. It is the one type of risk against which you can be insured. Let's use an example to clarify. Donna Development's condominium is exposed to the risk of loss from fire. It is a pure risk because Donna cannot gain if the condominium is destroyed by fire. Consequently, she will be able to buy insurance against the risk of fire. Since you can only buy insurance to protect against pure risks, they are the principal concern of this chapter.

By contrast, a **speculative risk** has the possibility of a loss, no change, or a gain. Assume that Donna, in our example, goes to the race track and places a $20 bet on Fleet Foot to win the fifth race. Donna creates a speculative risk when she places the bet. Depending on Fleet Foot's performance, she can profit handsomely, break even, or lose. An insurance company would be unwilling to cover this speculative risk. First, Donna might profit from taking that speculative risk. Second, it might be difficult to judge the extent of her loss or the exact point when the loss occurred. We will not talk further about speculative risks in this chapter since you cannot insure against them.

INSURANCE: REIMBURSEMENT FOR LOSSES

Insurance is not designed to make money for you. All that it will do is indemnify you. The word "**indemnify**" means to compensate for insured damages or loss.

Thus, all that indemnification will do is return you to the same financial position you were in prior to the loss. The maximum a policy will pay is the loss that you suffer or the policy's dollar limit, whichever is less. If you own a home worth $50,000 and you insure it for $80,000, the maximum the insurance will pay is $50,000. There is no point to overinsuring a property because you will never collect more than its value. This is the most basic lesson in learning how to buy insurance. If you want to insure the house for $80,000, the insurance company won't argue with you. It will gladly take your money. However, should you suffer a total loss, the company will pay only for the value of what you have lost.

Buying two or three policies will not help, either. Almost all insurance contracts contain a clause stipulating that in the event you have more than one policy (multiple coverage), the insurers together will split the total value of the loss among themselves.

Life insurance represents the one major exception to indemnification. Unlike the appraisal of a car or home, there is no satisfactory way to place a value on a person's life. Therefore, you can buy just about as much life insurance coverage as you want or as much as the insurance company will accept. And you can buy from different companies.

The insurance industry guards against the possibility of a person insuring his or her own life solely to provide immediate money for someone else. A suicide clause disallows claims if the insured commits suicide within the first 1 or 2 years of the policy. And there are laws that prohibit individuals named to collect the insurance (the beneficiaries) from collecting life insurance proceeds when they are responsible for the insured's death. Protected as they are by these provisions, insurance companies place no limits beyond normal health standards on the amount of insurance they will sell to an individual. In fact, there are a number of people in this country who carry $1 million or more in life insurance.

What Can You Insure?

Just about anything can be insured as long as the potential loss meets certain conditions and is a *pure* risk, not a *speculative* one.

The loss has to be financially measurable and it must be definite.

It must be fortuitous or accidental; that is, it must result from something that may happen, not something that is certain to happen or is intentionally caused.

Finally, the loss must be personal, not one affecting everybody at the same time. In other words, it cannot be a catastrophe. (This is why flood insurance was impossible to buy until recently, when it was made available as a result of a government-sponsored program. Only those people in low-lying areas would buy it—and everybody would be affected when a flood occurred.)

Protect against Large Losses

The primary purpose of insurance should be to protect against catastrophic losses which have a low probability of happening. These are the large losses that can financially ruin an individual. For example, the probability of being sued for $250,000 for an automobile accident is very low. Yet, if you should be sued and you lose the case, it would probably be impossible for you to pay such a judgment without insurance.

The idea of protecting against large losses is central to the development of a sound personal insurance program. It means that **policy limits** (the maximum amount the policy will pay) should be set higher than most people would expect. Fortunately, the cost of increasing policy limits from $10,000 or $20,000 to $200,000 or $300,000 is very low.

Do Not Underinsure

A frequent mistake people make is to buy insufficient insurance. That is, they **underinsure** by setting the limits on their insurance policies too low to protect against large losses. In our opinion, buying only $10,000 of liability insurance on an auto is underinsurance; it does not provide sufficient protection for the very large dollar settlements that are being awarded in many automobile accident cases. We think a limit of $100,000 to $300,000 of auto liability insurance is fully justified; it protects against a possible large loss. Losses where the likelihood of their occurrence is limited, but where the potential cost is very large, are prime candidates for insurance—and insurance with a high dollar coverage.

STRATEGY

When there is the possibility of very large dollar losses, thoroughly consider the advisability of raising the policy limits on your insurance coverage.

But Also Avoid Overinsuring

We define **overinsuring** as buying insurance to cover very small losses which you could cover out of income or your emergency cash reserve. Again, the problem centers on buying the right amount of insurance. We are not saying that paying those small losses is pleasant or easy, but it generally can be done without undue financial hardship. As an example, many people buy insurance to cover the loss of a contact lens. Yet, over several years the cost of the insurance frequently exceeds the cost of replacing the lens yourself. Lenna Looselens might find the insurance a "good buy" (she loses one lens a week). But even she will likely be disappointed because the insurance company will probably cancel her coverage after several losses.

How do you decide whether the coverage is likely to be overinsurance? Ask yourself: Does the insurance cover a loss where the likelihood of its happening is quite high, yet the potential dollar loss is quite low? Can you afford (even though you may find it unpleasant) to pay for the loss out of your current income or emergency cash reserve? If the answer to both questions is *yes*, then the coverage is probably overinsurance.

STRATEGY

Rather than use scarce insurance premium dollars on overinsurance, use those dollars to eliminate underinsurance in other areas.

PERSONAL RISK MANAGEMENT

Perhaps the best way to determine what the right amount of insurance is for you is through personal risk management. The objective of a personal risk management program is to minimize the cost of insurance coverage while maximizing the amount of protection. A systematic approach to personal risk management involves four steps. Each of them is important in obtaining the right type of protection for the risks involved.

Step 1   Identify the Risks

No insurance program should be implemented without **risk identification**— that is, without actually listing what must be insured. Most people find they need insurance in the following categories:

HELEN.. DO YOU REMEMBER MAILING
THAT INSURANCE PREMIUM I GAVE YOU LAST MONTH?

1   Loss of health through either sickness or accident

2   Loss of money resulting from personal liability

3   Loss of property through theft, fire, or accident

4   Loss of income owing to premature death

5   Loss of income through sickness or accident

You may insure against each of these risks since they meet the criteria of insurable risks. The types of insurance available to protect against these risks are discussed below.

1   *Health insurance* protects a person against the expenses caused by an illness or accident. Reimbursement for medical expenses is one of the most important insurance protections a family or an individual can buy.

2   *Liability insurance* protects individuals from financial loss arising from personal liability caused by improper or negligent behavior on their part. Running over a pedestrian is an example of negligent behavior producing a personal liability. Both automobile insurance and homeowners insurance include liability protection.

3   *Property insurance* provides financial protection for the value of automobiles, homes, and personal property. It reimburses the insured for damages or theft of the property involved even if the loss is the insured's fault. Collision and comprehensive insurance on a car and homeowners property insurance are examples of this type of coverage.

4   *Life insurance* pays a beneficiary a sum of money when the insured dies. In its purest form, life insurance is designed to replace a family's income when one of the main wage earners dies.

5   *Disability income insurance* provides a monthly income should the insured become physically disabled. The amount and duration of the payments are determined by the particular disability insurance purchased.

Exhibit 12-1 shows the breakdown of the major forms of personal insurance into their respective property, liability, and personal categories.

Step 2 Evaluate the Risks

After assessing the possible risks confronting you, you need to evaluate the financial impact a particular risk would have on you if it should occur. When undertaking **risk evaluation**, the question you must answer is: How severe is the financial burden for each risk? To determine the **financial burden**, consider two facets: (1) What is the potential size of the dollar loss? and (2) how frequently is the loss likely to occur over a set period of time? Let's look at several examples to illustrate those two concepts. The dollar loss from having your home and your personal belongings destroyed is indeed very large; it could be a severe financial burden. The dollar loss from

EXHIBIT 12-1

Major types of personal insurance.

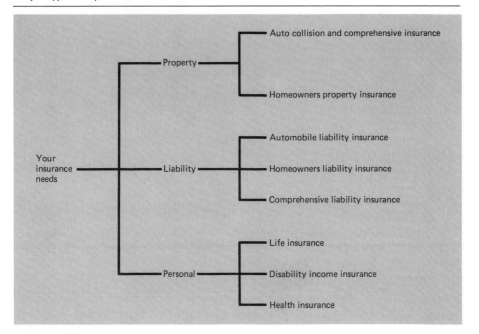

having to pay the first $50 if one of your credit cards is stolen is small; we rate that as a limited financial burden. As would be expected, the larger the dollar loss, the greater the financial importance of a particular risk. The likelihood that a loss will occur also affects the financial burden of that loss. In general, the more frequently a loss may happen, the greater its financial importance. The fact that Paul Poordiet often has sizable health-care expenses means that he has a high likelihood of losses from sickness. And that strong likelihood could make the financial burden of Paul's health risk very significant. On the other hand, the possibility that Brenda Badluck will be hit by a satellite plunging out of the sky is very remote—so remote that Brenda would not consider the financial burden of that risk unduly high.

Determining the financial burden for a particular risk situation requires considering both the severity of the loss and the likelihood of its occurring. The financial burden will be high in a situation where the potential dollar loss is large and the loss is likely to occur. Similarly, the financial burden remains high when the dollar loss is large even though the possibility of loss is low. When the financial burden is high, the dollar consequences of a loss may be so severe that insurance may be required. The next section discusses this situation in detail. In those situations where the dollar loss is limited and the likelihood of its occurrence is high, the financial burden is moderate. Here, the dollar consequences of a loss are likely to be much less. If you can endure this loss yourself, insurance, if necessary at all, would be far less critical. Finally, the financial burden is low in those risk situations where both the dollar loss is limited and the possibility of its occurring is remote. Here, the dollar consequences of a loss would be so limited that you probably could handle this loss on your own; insurance would rarely be needed.

Exhibit 12-2 evelutes the financial burden for the basic types of insurance. For each one, it summarizes the possible dollar loss together with the likelihood that a loss will occur. It also indicates those individuals who should consider buying each of the insurance policies.

Step 3 Determine Whether You Should Buy Insurance

After evaluating potential losses, you are in a position to determine what you should do with a particular risk. You have four possibilities:

1 *Eliminate the risk* entirely, thereby making insurance protection unnecessary. Selling an automobile or a boat to eliminate the need for insurance is an example of this strategy. If you have nothing to insure, you don't need the insurance.

2 *Reduce the risk*, thus reducing the cost of the insurance. For example, insurance companies charge a higher premium when you use your car to commute to work. Using public transportation rather than driving is an example of risk reduction. Risk reduction does not eliminate the need for insurance.

3 *Retain a risk* that cannot be eliminated or cannot be reduced further. **Risk retention** means that you accept the financial consequences of the loss.

Deciding *not* to buy an insurance policy which protects you against the potential $50 liability when you lose a credit card is one example.

4 *Transfer the risk* without reducing or eliminating it. **Risk transfer** means transferring the risk from yourself to someone else, which is the insurance company. Hence, risk transfer simply means buying insurance. The purchase of an automobile liability insurance policy is an example of this alternative.

Step 4 Selecting the Right Coverage

If you decide that you should insure the risk, you must then select a policy and an insurance company. Policies differ and rates of many companies for the same coverage vary considerably. The differences in coverages and rates may have a significant impact on the adequacy and total cost of your insurance program. Deciding what insurance is needed and how to buy it will be the topic of Chapters 14 through 16.

Personal Risk Management: A Summary Exhibit 12-3 shows a flow-chart that summarizes the four steps of personal risk management. Evaluating your insurance needs by using this approach can help you save a

EXHIBIT 12-2

Risk evaluation for basic insurance contracts.

TYPE OF INSURANCE	MAXIMUM POSSIBLE LOSS	LIKELIHOOD OF LOSS	INDIVIDUALS WHO SHOULD CONSIDER
Life insurance	Depends on income (might be $250,000 or more)	Low, increasing with age	Major wage-earners with dependents
Health insurance	$50,000 or more	Small losses almost certain, large losses less likely	Everybody
Disability income	Same as life insurance	1 chance in 10 before age 65	Everybody who earns a living
Auto, liability	$300,000 or more	Low	All auto owners
Auto, collision and comprehensive	Value of car	High	Owners of valuable cars
Homeowners, liability	$100,000 or more	Low	All homeowners and renters
Homeowners and renters, property	Value of property plus contents	Small losses likely; total losses less likely	All homeowners and renters
Scheduled property	Value of property	Low	Owners of jewelry, antiques, fine art, etc.

EXHIBIT 12-3

Steps in personal risk management.

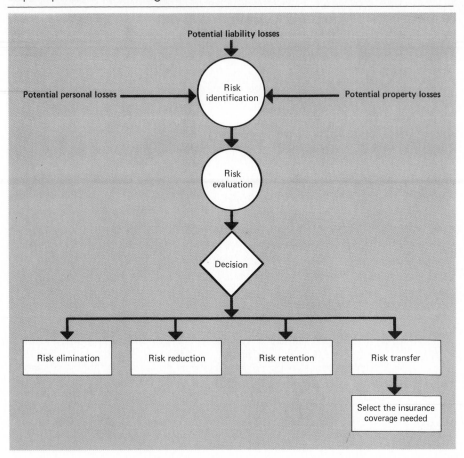

substantial amount of money when you buy insurance. And remember that insurance is something you buy every year, so the savings recur every year.

MANAGING YOUR INSURANCE PROGRAM

The steps outlined in the section Personal Risk Management are the preliminaries for a sound personal insurance program. After you set your priorities, you must select a good sales agent who represents a sound, low-cost insurance company from which to buy your insurance. Your job does not stop there, however. You should review your insurance coverage periodically to see that it still meets your needs. Last, should you have a loss, you will need to know when and how to submit a claim.

Buying Insurance

You should have a good idea of what you need before contacting an insurance sales representative. A good agent can certainly assist you in meeting your insurance needs, but you need to know enough about these needs to give the representative adequate information to work with. Most people find they need two insurance agents, one who specializes in personal (life and health) insurance, and another who specializes in property and liability insurance. We believe that the following suggestions will be helpful in finding and dealing with both types of agents:

1   *Do not buy* from insurance agents who are part-timers. Insurance is complex and should be handled only by people who know what they are doing. The unemployed rock musician who is trying to make a few bucks selling insurance is not the individual to entrust with your insurance needs.

2   *Do* make the agent work for *you*. Agents should be willing to answer your questions, tell you the rates on different policies, and offer advice in setting up a sound insurance program. If the agent makes these services sound like a favor, find somebody else. You are doing the insurance salesperson a favor by buying insurance from him or her—not vice versa.

3   *Do* make sure the agent works for a reputable, low-cost company. By and large, the better agents work for the better companies. Always make certain the company is sound before selecting the agent: do not select an agent without considering the company.

4   *Do* try to deal with agents who have demonstrated technical competence by passing professional examinations. The designation CLU, **Chartered Life Underwriter,** is a strong indicator that the life agent is a real professional. The same is true for the property agent qualifying as a **Chartered Property and Casualty Underwriter** (CPCU).

5   *Do* ask the opinions of friends and relatives. They may have some good ideas on possible agents. But be wary of overreliance on their recommendations—they may be making all the mistakes we are warning you to avoid.

Selecting the Right Company

Thousands of companies sell insurance in this country. Some companies specialize in life insurance, while others handle only property and liability insurance. Selecting the right company for each type of protection can save you a substantial amount on your insurance each year.

Financial Strengths   When selecting an insurance company, you want to choose a company that will be able to make good on its promise to compensate you for losses. In brief, you must select a firm with the financial resources to back up its promise. There are two excellent sources for this information: *Best's Insurance Reports* and *Best's Life Reports* (both published by A. M. Best and Co.). Both volumes are available in most public libraries.

The two publications use a **General Policyholder Rating** to judge the different insurance companies. Most larger insurance companies are rated. A sizable number of factors are incorporated in this rating, and you would do well to refer to one of the two volumes for a more detailed explanation. The actual rating scale is similar to a truncated grading scale: A+ and A are excellent, B+ is very good, B is good, C+ is fairly good, and C is fair. Most professionals suggest that you concentrate on those insurance companies that are rated A or A+.

STRATEGY

Always select an insurance company with a strong financial rating. As a general rule, policies from strongly financed companies cost no more than those from weak companies.

Settlement of Claims   What you want is a company that will quickly and fairly settle your claim for a loss. A loss is traumatic enough without adding the complication of a battle with the insurance company to obtain a settlement. One source of information on how various insurance companies settle their claims exists in the surveys and reports contained in *Consumer Reports*. Typically, a report discusses different aspects of how the magazine's subscribers felt their insurance company handled their claim. A second source is the insurance commissioner's office in your state. Frequently, a call to that office can alert you to those companies about which there have been an unusually large number of complaints. And do not be afraid to ask your insurance agent about his or her experience in settling claims with the insurance company he or she represents; a good agent should be straightfoward with you.

Net Cost   When selecting an insurance company, it is essential that you compare the net cost of comparable insurance coverage among competing companies. Detailed cost studies have confirmed, and continue to confirm, that for similar coverage, costs differ tremendously among companies. And differences in financial strength and policyholder satisfaction do not begin to explain, or justify, those sizable cost variations. In fact, companies with the strongest financial rating frequently are the ones with the lowest net

ROGER...THE
MAN FROM THE
INSURANCE COMPANY
IS INSISTING ON
3 WRITTEN ESTIMATES....

costs. Comparison is definitely the order of the day: the net cost of insurance coverage is not the same in all the companies you might consider.

STRATEGY

Compare the costs of competing insurance coverage to ensure that you select a company that handles policies with a low net cost to you.

Reducing Insurance Costs

The cost of a personal insurance program can be overwhelming unless you take definite steps to keep expenses down. You can do a number of things with all types of insurance, in addition to carefully selecting the lowest net cost company, to ensure that you get the insurance you need for the least cost.

Use Deductibles The simplest definition of a **deductible** is that it is that part of a loss that you are willing to pay yourself. The higher the deductible, that is, the greater the amount of the loss you are willing to pay, the lower the cost of the insurance. For example, let's suppose that you pay a $100 premium for insurance where, in case of a loss, the insurance company will pay the excess over $50. Now let's assume that the same insurance company offers coverage with $100 deductible, which means you pay that amount if you have a loss. But the premium is reduced to $65. Of course, if you suffer $500 of damages or losses, you now have to pay the first $100 rather than $50. The insurance company pays the remainder. In effect, you retain part of the risk of a loss. And the higher your deductible, the greater your risk retention.

There are several reasons why the premium drops as the deductible rises. First, the insurance company has less to pay because the insured pays more of the loss. Second, the company avoids the considerable administrative and settlement costs associated with very small claims. Third, it encourages the insured to be extremely cautious because, if a loss occurs, the insured will have to cover part of the loss.

Deductibles are available on auto collision and comprehensive insurance, health insurance, and homeowners property insurance. They may be set at $50, $100, $250, $500, and larger amounts. Selecting a deductible requires a review of your present situation; that is the topic of the next section.

Selecting a Deductible The decision to select a particular deductible requires that you consider three things: your present financial resources, the saving in premiums from increasing the deductible, and the dollar amount of your added risk exposure.

The first point requires that you ask yourself, "Can I afford to pay the deductible amount?" For your answer, look at your emergency cash reserve to see whether it will cover the deductible amount. We will never claim that paying a larger deductible will be pleasant or easy. But remember: If you ask the insurance company to pay that deductible amount, it charges for it. And the cost can be substantial.

Assuming that you have decided you can afford the larger deductible, the next step is to consider the saving in premiums from the higher deductible versus the potential dollar loss if a loss happens. We will label that potential dollar loss as your **added risk exposure**. An example is the best way to illustrate how to make the comparison. Assume you are deciding between an auto collision policy with a $100 deductible and annual premiums of $149 and a $200 deductible policy with premiums of $120 per year. Note that your auto collision insurance covers damage to your auto when the accident was your fault. We want to know the point at which the savings from the higher deductible will offset your added risk exposure from the higher deductible. Exhibit 12-4 answers that question by comparing the total cost for each auto policy under differing accident scenarios. The first cost column assumes that you expect one accident each year; a disastrous record. The second column assumes premiums are paid for 2 years, during which time you expect one accident. The third and fourth columns are, respectively, premiums paid for 3 years with one accident and premiums for 4 years with one accident. The results in Exhibit 12-4 show that if you expect to have an accident (your fault) every 3 years or less, the lower deductible is the policy of choice. If, however, you believe you will likely go more than 3 years without an accident, you should switch to the $200 deductible. The reason is that in slightly more than 3 years, the $29 ($149 − $120) in premium savings will offset the added $100 loss from the higher deductible. For the person who can go 10 years without an accident, the total

EXHIBIT 12-4

Comparison of premium savings with added
loss from higher deductible.

	One Auto Accident Within			
	1 YEAR	2 YEARS	3 YEARS	4 YEARS
Cost: $200 deductible				
Total premiums paid	$120	$240	$360	$480
Deductible payment	200	200	200	200
Total cost [A]	$320	$440	$560	$680
Cost: $100 deductible				
Total premiums paid	$149	$298	$447	$596
Deductible payment	100	100	100	100
Total cost [B]	$249	$398	$547	$696
Added cost (savings) of $200 deductible: Total cost [A] minus total cost [B]	$ 71	$ 42	$ 13	($16)

savings of $290 will far more than offset the added $100 loss during those 10 years.

One parting comment before we leave Exhibit 12-4. Do the highly favorable cost results in column 1 suggest that Fran Fenderbender (who averages one accident every year) should always select the lowest deductible? Probably not. If Fran's driving record is that poor, she may well find it difficult to find any insurance, let alone quibble about the deductible. But that is not all bad. If the insurance should continue to cover Fran and similar drivers, the other policyholders would have to pay those horrendous losses!

A worksheet similar to Exhibit 12-4 can be used to analyze the deductibles on all insurance whether it be homeowners, health, or auto comprehensive coverage. To do a comparison, you need the annual premiums for the competing policies, together with an estimate of your likely dollar loss for that particular risk. Often, your recent loss experience can provide an estimate of how often you have had a loss. And a comparison of the two deductibles will give you the potential dollar loss. Deductibles of $250 or $500 may be appropriate in some cases.

STRATEGY

Carefully compare the cost (higher deductible) with the benefits (lower premiums) to decide whether you should accept a higher deductible on an insurance policy. A worksheet like Exhibit 12-4 can help you make this comparison.

Do not be surprised if some insurance agents try to discourage you from accepting a higher deductible. Some are conditioned to the idea that $100 is a "large" deductible. Some are concerned that insured persons may be bitter when they have to pay for a loss. And some may be concerned that a lower deductible means lower premiums and thus may reduce their commission on the policy.

STRATEGY

If you believe the potential savings from a higher deductible justify that policy, stick to your decision even when an agent is only lukewarm to the higher limit.

Retain the Risk on Small Losses Do not buy (that is, do not transfer the risk on) insurance against small losses; those are the losses that you should handle yourself either from current income or your emergency cash reserve. The primary purpose of insurance is to cover major losses where the financial burden is so enormous that you could not begin to pay for the loss yourself. There are several rules to remember when considering insurance:

The poorest insurance buys frequently are those that cover risks where the dollar losses are small yet the likelihood of the risk's occurring is moderate to high.

Conversely, the better insurance buys are typically those where the risk covered involves a severe dollar loss, yet the likelihood that the loss will occur is moderate to limited.

Let's use an example to show why retaining part, or all of a loss, is often the best course. Assume you are considering a dental insurance policy that covers an annual dental examination and cleaning. Why would that be a poor insurance buy? First, the potential loss—the cost of the annual exam and cleaning—is rather limited. Second, nearly everyone who purchases the policy will have a claim. That means a lot of claims for the insurance company. The company must charge sufficient premiums to pay those claims, plus possibly an equal amount to administer and process them. The net effect is that the premiums on the policy might equal, or even exceed, the cost of paying that dental expense yourself. So you should retain the risk.

We are not advocating that you retain the risks that have a very large dollar loss but a remote possibility of happening. Instead, we suggest retention of those risks where you can cover the potential loss from income or your emergency cash reserve. As your cash reserve increases, you may be able to retain a larger amount of the risk yourself. In fact, the balance in your emergency cash reserve is a good way to judge whether you should retain a risk. We suggest a rough rule: If the potential dollar loss equals 25 percent or less of your cash reserve, that risk probably should be retained.

STRATEGY

Do not cover small potential losses with insurance; retain these risks and, if necessary, cover them with your emergency cash reserve.

Pay Premiums Annually Most insurance premiums are set on the assumption they will be paid in one lump sum each year. Often an insurance company will also offer the option of semiannual, quarterly, or even monthly billings. It may seem like a good idea to spread out your payments, but there is a cost. Companies add a service charge to the premiums if you elect semiannual, quarterly, or monthly payments. In effect, the service charge is much like the finance charge on a loan. The interest that you might earn by investing the money from not paying the full premium in one payment rarely offsets the service charge for the more frequent billings.

STRATEGY

In nearly all cases, you are further ahead when you pay insurance premiums in one lump sum rather than in a series of payments spread throughout the year.

Use Group Insurance Many companies provide **group insurance** programs for their employees as part of a fringe-benefit program. The employer purchases or helps the employees purchase the insurance. Because of the cost reductions available when a company sells to a large group rather than to individuals, group insurance is generally less expensive than comparable individual policies. Moreover, the group policy often provides better coverage than is available from an individually purchased policy. This is particularly true with health insurance.

If the entire cost of the program is paid by the employer, all employees should accept the insurance. If the employee contributes to the cost, he or she generally has the option of accepting or rejecting the coverage. Probably the only reason to reject available group coverage is lack of need. A woman may not need health insurance if she is covered by her husband's health insurance. Or a single person may find little need for much life insurance. If you need insurance, the group plan will undoubtedly be less expensive and you should buy it.

Nevertheless, there are a few words of caution about group insurance. The principal drawback is that you are no longer insured when you leave the group, that is, when you leave your job. Your new employer may not have a group insurance program, or if the company has one, you may not be eligible to participate in it until you have been employed for a specified period. In either case, you may suddenly find you have serious gaps in your insurance program which could be difficult to fill. You can minimize that possibility by taking a few precautionary steps before you change jobs. First, see whether you can convert the group policy to an individual policy when you leave your present job. If so, that individual policy can provide the necessary insurance coverage until you are covered at your new job. If conversion is not permitted, you should purchase insurance coverage to fill the gap caused by the termination of the group insurance.

When you decide to purchase insurance, look into some possible ways of getting the best value for your dollar.

Buy Big Policies Quantity discounts are available on some types of insurance. Life insurance is a prime example where savings can be realized by buying large policies. A $50,000 life insurance policy will cost less than five $10,000 policies. Look into the possibility, when buying insurance, of getting preferred rates by buying high-policy-limit coverages.

Try Buying Direct There are a number of ways that you can save money by purchasing insurance direct from a company, rather than from a sales agent. Companies that deal directly do not have agents, so you must seek them out. Unfortunately, there is no central source of information listing companies which sell direct. Discussed below are some of the possibilities for buying life insurance, health insurance, and automobile insurance direct from the companies. The list is far from inclusive, but it does give an idea of the sources for direct purchase of insurance.

Life Insurance In Wisconsin, the state runs a life insurance fund and amounts up to $10,000 may be purchased at very low rates. In Massachusetts, Connecticut, and New York, low-cost life insurance is offered through savings banks. For educators, the Teachers Insurance and Annuity Association (TIAA) offers low-cost life insurance on a direct basis. Also, many professional associations and college alumni groups are making insurance available to their members at extremely competitive rates.

Health Insurance   Blue Cross and Blue Shield is a nonprofit direct seller of health insurance. The rates may be higher than some competing, profit-oriented insurance companies. However, the policies are well designed and represent good health-insurance coverage for most people.

Auto Insurance   A few companies sell insurance through their own salaried sales personnel. The rates for these direct policies may be below the rates for companies selling through commission agents.

An innovation in auto insurance is group coverage. Several insurance companies have started selling group auto insurance, and a number of employers are making it available as an employee fringe benefit. The cost of group auto insurance can be substantially below the cost of individual policies. If it is available to you, strongly consider it.

STRATEGY

Always check to see whether the insurance coverage you need is available directly from the insurance company; your savings can be sizable.

When to Review Your Insurance

Your insurance program should not be static. It should change as your needs change. As a good rule of thumb, you should contact your life insurance agent or property insurance agent (depending on the insurance affected) when you do any of the following: (1) get married, (2) get divorced, (3) have children, (4) buy a house, (5) move, (6) buy a boat, a car, or other major item, or (7) change jobs. In addition, it is wise to reassess insurance needs every 2 to 3 years, even if no major changes have taken place.

Collecting Insurance Claims

The ultimate purpose of insurance is to reimburse you for losses or damages. But you must make a claim to collect the reimbursement. Paradoxically, one of the best pieces of advice that can be given is, do not submit all claims. Technically, you may be entitled to reimbursement for small losses, but in the long run you will be better off ignoring them. For example, if you have $100 deductible collision insurance and you find your car in the parking lot at the supermarket with fender damage that costs $135 to repair, the insurance company will pay $35 of the loss. If you collect the $35, you will have a claim on your record which may boost your premium by more than the amount you received. Also, people often make claims they should ignore for small losses covered by their homeowners policy. If $120 of lawn furniture is stolen, they submit a claim for $20 ($100 deductible for theft). The companies consider these to be nuisance claims and will cancel or not renew the policy of someone who submits such claims too often. Think twice before you make a claim. Is it worth the possibility of higher rates or a canceled policy? If the answer is no, absorb the loss yourself.

Documenting Claims   All claims should be accompanied by complete documentation. Auto claims require the greatest care since the accident may involve some measure of negligent behavior on your part. In the event

WHAT LUCK, HONEY.. IT'S OUR INSURANCE AGENT.

of an auto accident, care should be taken to get the names and addresses of all witnesses; they can be crucial to whether or not you will collect.

Health claims should be supported with receipted bills for services. It is also important to know when the claim should be submitted directly to the insurance company by the doctor or hospital.

Disability income claims depend heavily on statements by attending physicians. The start of the disability should be clearly documented since benefits will not begin until after a waiting period. Without an accurate record that precisely determines the beginning of the disability, the start of the waiting period will be difficult to determine.

Life insurance claims must include a copy of the death certificate for the insured and, surprisingly, some proof of birth, preferably a copy of a registered birth certificate. This is necessary since premiums for life insurance are based on a person's age at the time the policy was issued. An understatement of age means that policy benefits are overstated and ultimately must be reduced. The companies are willing to accept questionable proof of birth when selling the policy, but they require accurate proof when paying the proceeds.

SUMMARY

1 Insurance may be purchased to protect against the possibility of loss from a pure risk. A pure risk has the possibility of a loss or no change, but no possibility of gain. Speculative risks, on the other hand, have the possibility of loss, no change, or gain.

2 Insurance indemnifies you against loss. That is, it will pay benefits only up to the amount of the loss or the policy limit. It is not possible to make money by insuring a property for more than its current value.

3 If you own two or more policies for the same purpose, the insurance companies share any reimbursement according to the amount each insured.

4   The primary purpose of insurance is to protect against large losses.

5   A frequent error is that some people underinsure by setting an insurance policy's limit too low to protect against large potential losses.

6   Some people err by overinsuring; they purchase insurance to cover small losses that should be paid out of income or their emergency cash reserve.

7   Personal risk management has four steps. They are (a) identifying the risks, (b) evaluating each risk, (c) determining whether to buy insurance, and (d) selecting the right insurance coverage.

8   There are four courses of action relating to each risk. You may (a) eliminate the risk, (b) reduce the risk, (c) retain the risk, or (d) transfer the risk.

9   When buying insurance, care should be taken in selecting qualified agents and buying from financially sound insurance companies.

10   Selecting a higher deductible (the amount of the loss that you pay) can substantially reduce insurance costs.

11   Avoid purchasing insurance to cover small losses; individuals should retain these risks and pay the losses from income or their emergency cash reserve.

12   Other ways to reduce insurance costs are (a) to pay premiums annually, (b) to buy insurance directly from the companies, (c) to select one large policy rather than several small ones, and (d), when possible, to use group insurance.

13   Your insurance program should be reviewed every 2 to 3 years and when you experience a major event, such as a change in jobs, a large purchase, marriage, or the birth of a child.

14   The ultimate purpose of insurance is to be reimbursed for loss. Paradoxically, there are many instances where claims for small losses should not be submitted.

REVIEW YOUR UNDERSTANDING OF

Risk management	Risk retention
Pure risk	Risk transfer
Speculative risk	Added risk exposure
Indemnify	Chartered Life Underwriter (CLU)
Policy limits	Chartered Property and Casualty
Underinsure	Underwriter (CPCU)
Overinsure	General Policyholder Rating
Risk identification	Deductibles
Risk evaluation	Added risk exposure
Financial burden	Group insurance

DISCUSSION QUESTIONS

1   Who provides the dollars that an insurance company pays to indemnify people with losses? Would it be possible for an insurance company to refund the premiums of all insured persons except those with a loss? Why?

2   What benefit do you obtain from

purchasing insurance? If you do not have any claims on that insurance during the year, does it mean you received no benefit?

3 What does it mean to underinsure? Give several examples of underinsurance. How does overinsurance differ from underinsurance? Give several examples of overinsurance.

4 Sue Smalltime's insurance strategy is to (a) insure against the small losses that happen frequently because she then will always get back part of her premiums through claims, and (b) never insure against the large losses that happen less often because she will probably never collect. What do you think of Sue's strategy? Do you have any suggestions?

5 What are the major steps in personal risk management and what is the principal objective of each step?

6 Once you have identified and evaluated a particular risk, what are your four options for dealing with that risk? Give an example of a risk that might be handled in each of four different ways.

7 What factor is the most important in determining whether a risk should be retained or transferred? Give an example of a risk that may be retained, then one of a risk that should be transferred.

8 What specific factors do you feel are significant when selecting an insurance agent?

9 What major factors should be considered when selecting an insurance company? Where can you obtain information on each factor?

10 What are deductibles? How do they lower the cost of insurance?

11 What response would you have to the statement, "A very small or no deductible is best because then the insurance company will pay the entire loss"?

12 What steps would you suggest to help someone decide whether or not to raise the deductible on his or her insurance policy?

13 Under what conditions should your insurance program be reviewed? Name specific events that would make you reassess your life insurance program, your homeowners insurance, and your health insurance.

14 What factors should you consider when deciding whether to submit a claim for a particular loss? Give several examples of instances when you might decide not to submit a claim even though you are entitled to do so.

PROBLEMS

12-1 Brenda Ross is concerned that the loss of one of her recently fitted contact lenses would be financially devastating. Her friend has just purchased an insurance policy that will replace her lenses after she pays a $25 deductible. The annual premium for the insurance is $25. Currently, a replacement lens costs $50.

a What is Brenda's financial loss if she loses a lens when she doesn't have insurance? When she has insurance?

b Should she purchase the lens insurance? Why or why not?

12-2 Ron Avery is doing a complete review of his present insurance coverage. The list on the next page outlines some of the risks that he is currently evaluating. For the first items, Ron has summarized his potential dollar loss and the likelihood that a risk will occur.

RISK	POTENTIAL DOLLAR LOSS	LIKELIHOOD OF RISK OCCURRING
Theft of personal property from apartment	$12,000	Moderate
Prolonged illness	$10,000 or more if lengthy	Limited
Annual dental examination	$45	High
Disability that causes income to cease	$10,000 or more (depending on duration)	Moderate
Loss if $200 deductible on auto collision is substituted for $100 deductible	$100	Limited
Loss of contact lens	?	?
Liability for stolen credit card	?	?
Rusty 1971 Ford Pinto destroyed in a collision	?	?

a For the first five risks on the list, outline for Ron whether each should be retained or transferred.

b For each of the final three risks on Ron's list, estimate the potential dollar loss as well as the likelihood the loss will occur. For each risk, would you recommend retention or transfer?

12-3 Debra Diligent has two options for the collision coverage on her automobile. If she selects a $100 deductible, the premium for 6 months is $65.95. Should she raise the deductible to $250, the 6-month premium would drop to $47.20. During the past 5 years, she has had only one accident that was her fault.

a Which deductible should Debra choose? Why?

b Are there any other things that Debra should consider before selecting a deductible?

12-4 Arnold Sweatypalms has noted that most of his friends have a routine dental examination and cleaning once or twice each year. With the cost averaging $30 per visit, Arnold figures it would be a great idea to form Sweatypalms Dental Insurance Limited to cover those losses. To date, 1000 of Arnold's friends (he is very gregarious) are interested in the insurance. Each of those friends averages 1.5 routine exams (some go twice, some once, some not at all) during a regular year. Before launching the firm, he has asked for your counsel.

a Is the risk of the routine dental examination and cleaning a pure risk? Why?

b Does this risk seem to be one that should be transferred to an insurance company? Why?

c With 1000 subscribers, how many dollars of benefits will Sweatypalms pay out each year?

d What annual premium should the firm charge each subscriber?

e What lucky subscribers will benefit from having the insurance? Which ones will lose by having it?

f Arnold expects the cost of running the firm will about equal its yearly benefit payments. How much will this added cost increase each subscriber's premium?

g Considering the premium in **f**, will Arnold's friends join?

CASE PROBLEM

Susan Shortfall has decided her insurance program needs a major review. One problem is that she never seems to have enough money to pay her insurance premiums. Consequently, she does not have some insurance coverage that she thinks may be essential. Her chief reason for not purchasing the coverage is the lack of premium dollars. She hopes that a review of her present insurance coverage will reveal areas of savings that she can use to buy some other insurance policies. She has outlined her present insurance coverage:

INSURANCE COVERAGE	CURRENT POLICY DETAILS
Homeowners insurance on $50,000 condominium	Two policies with $50,000 of coverage. There is no deductible on either policy. Premiums are paid monthly.
Auto collision coverage	Policy has a $50 deductible. Premium is paid monthly.
Life insurance	Five policies with very low dollar limits. Premiums are paid monthly.
Insurance on liability for lost credit card	Premiums are paid as part of monthly credit card billing. Policy provides similar coverage to homeowners insurance.
Dental insurance (maximum annual payment is $100)	Premiums are paid monthly. Policy has no deductible.

Susan listed the insurance areas shown on the next page as ones where her present coverage may be inadequate or lacking.

1 Does Susan have gaps in her present insurance coverage? If so, what are they?

2 Would you recommend any changes in Susan's present insurance coverage? What are they?

3   Will your suggested changes in **2** reduce Susan's current insurance premiums?

4   Do you think Susan and her insurance agents have developed a good insurance program? How might she select new insurance agents if that appears necessary?

INSURANCE COVERAGE	COMMENTS
Health insurance	Premium seems too high.
Disability insurance	Is it really needed?
Auto liability	To minimize premiums, her present upper dollar limit is $20,000.
Auto, comprehensive (covers theft, fire, wind, and other risks)	Would comprehensive insurance be better than collision insurance?

CHAPTER
13

SOCIAL SECURITY: AN INTEGRAL PART OF YOUR PERSONAL FINANCIAL PLAN

AFTER COMPLETING THIS CHAPTER YOU WILL HAVE LEARNED

Who is covered by Social Security

The general guidelines that determine the amount of *Social Security payments*

When Social Security payments aren't taxable as income

How Social Security payments are adjusted for inflation

How the Social Security system is financed

What a *quarter of work credit* is

Who qualifies for *survivors benefits* and what they are all about

How the earnings of a surviving spouse affect the survivor benefits he or she receives

Who qualifies for Social Security *disability benefits*

How to figure out which *dependents* are *eligible* for disability payments, *how much* they are eligible for, and *for how long* they are eligible

What Social Security *payments* you can receive following your *retirement*

IF WE COMBINE YOUR PENSION WITH OUR SOCIAL SECURITY BENEFITS, SHUT OFF THE ELECTRICITY AND CASH IN OUR GREEN STAMPS WE CAN KEEP OUR SCENE TOGETHER FOR A WHILE..

IN order to understand the Social Security system as it is now, as well as perhaps the direction in which it is heading, you may want to look briefly at what it was when it started and how it developed.

The original purpose of the Social Security legislation was to ease the economic hardships, caused by insufficient income, that affected many people during the 1930s. The people suffering the most then were the elderly, the retired, and the unemployed. Therefore, the objectives of the original Social Security system were aimed at helping them. But during the past 50 years, the Social Security coverage has broadened considerably, affecting more and more of us—even those of us who have steady jobs and regular income and are nowhere near retirement age.

Initially, Social Security benefits were available only to retired workers at 65 or more years of age. Within a short time, coverage was extended to dependent survivors of workers who died before retirement. In 1957, the act was expanded to include permanent disability—for workers who became ill or injured and as a result were unable to earn income. Hospital and medical coverage for people 65 and over was the next expansion of the Social Security system; we commonly refer to this as Medicare.

If you are working and earning income, chances are 9 out of 10 that you are paying part of your income into the Social Security fund whether you like it or not. But you can get a lot of benefits out of the Social Security system if you know your rights.

BASIC STRUCTURE OF THE SOCIAL SECURITY SYSTEM

From the beginning, the Social Security system was designed as a "pay as you go" program: Any payments the system makes as benefits will come out of the taxes currently being collected from almost everyone who is working. Consequently, the Social Security taxes you pay into the system during the present year are not accumulated in an account like a savings account. Instead, these taxes are used immediately to make Social Security payments to people who are currently receiving benefits. When you qualify to receive a Social Security payment, whether for retirement or disability, the Social Security taxes paid by people who are working at that time will be used to pay *your* benefits. The net effect is that today's workers pay the benefits of yesterday's workers, and today's workers expect that tomorrow's workers will pay their benefits.

BENEFIT LEVELS: HOW TO DETERMINE WHAT AND HOW MUCH YOU ARE ELIGIBLE FOR

When we say **benefit levels**, we mean the dollar amount of the payments an individual receives when he or she is eligible for Social Security. The amount of the benefits that you are entitled to varies directly with your past earnings record. Thus, for example, when Jan Smith applies for benefits, the actual dollar amount she receives will depend on two **principal determinants**.

First, the higher Jan's annual earnings during the years she worked, the larger her benefits will be. Therefore the general rule is that the more you earn during each year of your working career, the larger the benefit payment will be when you become eligible for Social Security. Later in the chapter, we will modify this rule slightly, but for now it is sufficient.

Second, the more years that Jan has worked and therefore the more she has paid in Social Security taxes, the larger her benefit payments will be. This is a general rule that applies to everyone who has earned income and paid Social Security taxes. We will modify this rule slightly too, but for our present purposes it is adequate.

Indexing Earnings: Adjusting Past and Present Earnings So They Are Comparable

In the past, the Social Security system merely added up a worker's annual earnings and divided by the number of working years to determine his or her average earnings. That served reasonably well as long as those earnings did not change drastically from one year to the next. But the recent bout of high inflation altered that approach. During these high inflationary periods, nearly everyone's wages rose rapidly. Such increases, however, placed older workers with a lengthy work history at a decided disadvantage because their earnings record included those early years when wages were low. Younger workers had a decided advantage because their earnings record consisted primarily of recent years when incomes were high owing to rapid inflation.

The solution lies in **indexing prior years' earnings** so they are comparable with today's earnings. By using a series of *index factors*, a worker's earlier lower earnings are adjusted so that they capture the annual increase in the average person's "typical annual income" during the years prior to the current date. The net effect is that the earnings from prior years are restated into today's dollars. Indexing the prior years' earnings means that an individual with a long work history will be treated fairly by the Social Security system. It does so by ensuring that the income an individual earned in a prior year receives the full credit it deserves without being distorted by the inflation of recent years.

Before the Social Security system computes your average earnings, it indexes all your prior years' earnings. Once it has done so, it computes your average indexed earnings. Benefits are then calculated on the basis of those average indexed earnings (more on this later). The appendix of this chapter presents the steps and worksheets needed to index earnings from prior years.

Indexing Benefit Payments So They Keep Pace with Inflation

In the past, when someone became eligible for Social Security benefits, the amount of the payments was determined; that amount remained the same although, every year, inflation increased prices. Because the value of the dollar decreased every year, the value of the payment also tended to decline. Infrequently, the Social Security system increased the amount of the payments, but often not enough to keep pace with the rate of inflation. However, in 1972, legislation was passed that automatically increased benefits in relation to the consumer price index (CPI). Each year, benefits are automatically adjusted upward by an amount equal to the percentage increase in the CPI to compensate for higher living costs. **Indexing Social Security benefits** means that if the CPI rose 10 percent during the year, the dollar amount of the benefit payments would also increase 10 percent. That cost-of-living adjustment is made once each year, with the higher benefits beginning in January.

It is important to distinguish clearly between the two indexes.

The *CPI index* is used to increase your Social Security benefits once you have started to receive them.

The *index factor* is used to determine your average annual indexed income before your benefits begin.

The cost-of-living index that we just discussed is designed to ensure that once benefit payments begin, they keep pace with the higher cost of everyday living expenses caused by increasing prices.

The index factor that was developed to adjust prior years' earnings is used before any benefits begin. This index is designed to update your earnings record for increases in the typical wage which occurred during the years you were working. Thus the index adjusts your past earnings so that when your benefits do begin, you will receive proper credit for them.

Obtaining Benefits

Social Security benefits do not begin automatically. Whether you become disabled, or you retire, or you are a dependent survivor, if you wish to receive benefits, you must notify your nearest Social Security office and apply for them. If possible, you should apply several months before you expect to become eligible for benefits. First, there can be considerable delay in processing your application. Second, there are generally limits on the number of months of back payments the system will make. Last, even if a claim for past benefits is honored, the Social Security system does not pay interest on those payments.

STRATEGY

You should apply for benefits 2 or 3 months before you retire, or immediately if you become disabled or a dependent survivor. If you're uncertain whether you qualify for benefits, discuss your status with your local Social Security office.

Taxability of Benefits

Prior to 1984 all Social Security payments received the same income tax treatment: They were not subject to either federal or state income taxes. But 1983 legislation changed that in order to "rescue" the Social Security system. Now up to one-half of your Social Security retirement benefit may be subject to federal income taxes if you have a substantial income. Both disability and survivor benefits still have their previous nontaxable status.

Disability and Survivor Benefits   All Social Security disability and survivor benefits continue to be exempt from federal and state income taxes. And of course they are not subject to Social Security taxes, either. That nontaxable feature can substantially enhance the actual spendable income that a dollar of benefits actually provides. Let's assume that Andre Dumas presently earns $13,000, on which he pays $3,000 in various state, local, and federal taxes. He estimates that should he become disabled, he would qualify for annual disability benefits of $5,400. First, it would be grossly incorrect to compare his $13,000 of before-tax earnings with the $5,400 of Social Security benefits. From his current earnings, Andre's spendable income is only:

CHAPTER 13

391

SOCIAL SECURITY:
AN INTEGRAL
PART OF YOUR
PERSONAL
FINANCIAL PLAN

$$\$10,000 \quad = \$13,000 \quad - \$3,000$$

$$\begin{array}{ccc} \text{Spendable} & = \text{Before-tax} & - \text{Taxes: state} + \\ \text{income} & \text{earnings} & \text{local} + \text{federal} \end{array}$$

Andre's spendable income would not drop from $13,000 to $5,400 as it initially appears. Instead his spendable income would drop from its previous $10,000 to $5,400 if he begins collecting disability benefits. Another way to look at this issue is to ask: What percentage of Andre's current spendable income has Social Security benefits replaced? In his case, it is approximately:

$$54\% \quad\quad = \$5,400 \quad\quad \div \$10,000$$

$$\begin{array}{lll} \text{Replacement of} & = \text{Estimated Social} \div \text{Current spendable} \\ \text{spendable income} & \text{Security benefit} & \text{income} \end{array}$$

Retirement Benefits   Not all retirees will have to pay income taxes on their Social Security benefits. Up to a prescribed amount of income, those benefits continue to be nontaxable. Above that limit, a retiree may have to pay income taxes on up to one-half of the Social Security benefits. Let us see how this works. For 1984, if a retiree's income from all sources is less than $25,000, then the person pays no income taxes. If a couple files a joint return, their combined joint income from all sources can be up to $32,000, and they will pay no income taxes. Once over the limit, your taxes are the lesser of two amounts:

1   One-half of the dollars that you are over the limit:

$$\begin{array}{l} \text{Taxable} \\ \text{portion} \end{array} = \begin{bmatrix} \text{Total income} & - \text{Upper income} \\ \text{from all sources} & \text{limit} \end{bmatrix} \times \text{½}$$

or

2   One-half of your Social Security benefit:

$$\begin{array}{l} \text{Taxable} \\ \text{portion} \end{array} = \begin{array}{l} \text{Social Security} \\ \text{(retirement benefit)} \end{array} \times \text{½}$$

Before we illustrate how those amounts are computed, an explanation is in order. "Total income from all sources" includes all the items that usually must be included in gross income: wages, pensions, interest, dividends, and capital gains. In addition, it includes one-half of the Social Security benefit. And it also includes interest on municipal securities. That is completely opposite of how that item should be treated for income taxes purposes before retirement, as we explained in Chapter 6. The actual interest itself still would not be included on your tax return. But to determine if you must pay income taxes on your Social Security retirement benefits, it must be counted. Of course, when a couple files a joint tax return, total income includes *all* the income that both of them have. Now let's look at several examples of how to figure out taxes on your Social Security.

Exhibit 13-1 computes the taxable portion of Social Security retirement benefits using three examples for single individuals—the top section of the exhibit—and three examples for couples—the lower section of the exhibit. Column 2 of the exhibit shows one-half of the Social Security benefits. Column 3 takes this amount, together with other income, to give "total income from all sources." Column 4 shows the upper income limit. The excess of total income over that income limit is shown in column 5. The final column shows the portion, if any, of the Social Security benefit that is subject to income taxes.

We can conclude from Exhibit 13-1 that many people will not be subject to any federal income tax on their retirement benefits. But those individuals who have substantial retirement income from non-Social Security sources will now have to begin paying some taxes on their Social Security benefits. We have intentionally not commented on how state income taxes will treat these benefits because, as this is being written, no such information is available to us. The states could continue their prior practice of not taxing them at all. Or they could adopt a system like the above, and tax part of those retirement benefits if the recipient's income exceeds some prescribed amount.

Financing the Social Security System

The Social Security system is financed by a payroll tax that is assessed against every person who works in an occupation that is covered by the

EXHIBIT 13-1

Taxability of Social Security Retirement Benefits for 1984.

SINGLE OR MARRIED	ONE-HALF SOCIAL SECURITY BENEFIT	TOTAL INCOME: ALL SOURCES	UPPER INCOME LIMIT	EXCESS OVER LIMIT	BENEFITS SUBJECT TO TAXES: ½ BENEFIT OR EXCESS
Single	$3,000	$21,000	$25,000	0	0	0
Single	$3,600	$26,000	$25,000	$ 1,000		$ 500
Single	$4,200	$35,000	$25,000	$10,000	$4,200	
Married	$5,400	$30,000	$32,000	0	0	0
Married	$7,200	$35,000	$32,000	$ 3,000		$1,500
Married	$8,400	$50,000	$32,000	$18,000	$8,400	

Social Security law. Since more than 90 percent of the jobs in the United States are covered, nearly everyone pays Social Security taxes. Whereas we have been using the term "Social Security taxes," you should be aware that the more correct title is Federal Insurance Contributions Act taxes: FICA for short. And since the word "contribution" was used in the legislation, your payments into the Social Security system are often called **contributions** rather than taxes. Throughout the rest of the chapter we will use the terms "Social Security taxes" and "contributions to Social Security" interchangeably.

When you work for someone—a corporation, an individual, or a partnership—**employer-employee matching contributions** are paid into the Social Security system. You make a contribution to the system in your name, and your employer also makes an equal, or matching, contribution in your name. The **Social Security tax for the self-employed** consists of a single contribution equal to the combined contribution of an employer and an employee. But self-employed persons receive some relief from those sizable Social Security taxes through a credit on their income taxes. Self-employed persons qualify for the same benefits as those received by an employee who works for someone else.

Income Subject to Social Security Contributions   You are required to make Social Security contributions only up to a certain earnings level. Once your earnings reach the **maximum wage subject to tax**, you make no contributions on wages above that cutoff. The second column of Exhibit 13-2 shows the maximum income that is subject to Social Security taxes for

CHAPTER 13

393

SOCIAL SECURITY:
AN INTEGRAL
PART OF YOUR
PERSONAL
FINANCIAL PLAN

EXHIBIT 13-2

Current and projected Social Security levels: tax rates, maximum wage limits, and maximum tax.

YEAR (1)	MAXIMUM WAGE SUBJECT TO TAXES* (2)	Tax Rate (percent)		Maximum Tax	
		EMPLOYEE (3)	SELF-EMPLOYED (4)	EMPLOYEE† SHARE (5)	SELF-EMPLOYED† (6)
1979	$22,900	6.13%	8.10%	$1,404	$1,855
1980	25,900	6.13	8.10	1,588	2,098
1981	29,700	6.65	9.30	1,975	2,762
1982	32,400	6.70	9.35	2,171	3,029
1983	35,700	6.70	9.35	2,392	3,338
1984	38,200	7.00	14.00	2,674	5,348
1985	40,500	7.05	14.10	2,855	5,710
1986	42,900	7.15	14.30	3,067	6,135
1987	45,500	7.15	14.30	3,253	6,506

*Amounts through 1983 are actual; maximums after 1983 are the authors' estimate.
†Beginning in 1984, self-employed individuals qualify for an income tax credit that offsets part of their Social Security taxes.

the 9 years from 1979 to 1987. A review of that column shows that the maximum has risen sharply during the past several years; those maximums will continue to increase at the same rate as the national "average wage" increases.

An example will show how the earnings maximum works. Assume that Jan Smith earned $34,000 in 1982. Since the 1982 maximum was $32,400, she pays Social Security contributions only on her first $32,400 of salary. Of course, since Jan paid tax on only $32,400, her Social Security earnings record will show only $32,400. It is that $32,400 of earnings that the Social Security system will use to calculate Jan's benefits.

With the rise in the maximum for earned income, more and more workers find that they must pay Social Security taxes all year long. That is, most people find their earned income just never exceeds the increased maximum, so they must continue paying Social Security taxes. Only those individuals with very high salaries exceed the maximum during the year, and therefore can stop paying Social Security taxes on those excesses.

Rates for Social Security Contributions   Column 3 of Exhibit 13-2 shows the **tax rate** for employees. And since employers match each employee's contribution, it is also the employer's rate. Column 4 of the same exhibit shows the **tax rate** for self-employed persons. A review of either column shows that rates have risen steadily—more than 16 percent—over the 9 years shown in Exhibit 13-2.

Maximum Contributions to the Social Security System   By combining the maximum earnings income subject to Social Security taxes (column 2 in Exhibit 13-2) with the tax rate for employees (column 3), we can compute the maximum amount an employee would pay in each of the 9 years shown in the exhibit. Column 6 calculates the maximum tax for self-employed individuals by combining the maximum income from column 2 with the tax rate for the self-employed from column 4.

The maximum taxes shown in columns 5 and 6 of Exhibit 13-2 dramatically illustrate the sharply higher burden of Social Security taxes. During the 8 years from 1979 to 1987, the income subject to these taxes is scheduled to nearly double, a rise of 98 percent. Over the same period, tax rates will rise more than 16 percent. The net effect is that the maximum Social Security tax will rise a whopping 131 percent in just 8 years! The increase more than doubles the burden of Social Security taxes within that short period.

YOUR WORK CREDITS IN THE SYSTEM

There are many different Social Security benefits, and each one has a certain minimum work credit that must be accumulated in order to qualify for it. The Social Security system uses 3-month calendar quarters as the basic measure of work credit. The work credit measure works this way:

You receive 1 **quarter of work credit** in 1983 for each $370 earned, up to a maximum of 4 quarters for the year. Therefore, by earning $1480 at any time during 1983, you receive the maximum 4 quarters of work credit. It does not matter if you earn the $1480 in 1 day or spread over 365 days.

As wage levels continue to increase, the Social Security system will likely raise the amount from the present $370.

Fully Insured Status   Individuals are considered fully insured when they have accumulated 40 quarters of credit. The term "**fully insured**" signifies that the person has gained certain rights under the Social Security system.

The 40 credits required to qualify you as fully insured do not have to be consecutive. For example, you can earn 20 quarters and then temporarily withdraw from the work force. You retain those 20 quarters and can add to them whenever you return to work. And there is no limit on the number of employers you may have had while accumulating the 40 quarters. Once you become fully insured, you never lose that qualification, even if you never work another day.

Currently Insured Status   To be **currently insured**, an individual must have received credit for 6 quarters (1 1/2 years) out of the most recent 12 quarters (3 years). Unlike the previously described fully insured status, you will have to continue to meet these credit standards—6 quarters out of the last 12 quarters—to remain eligible for the benefits that come with a currently insured status. As would be expected, a currently insured status entitles you to a smaller range of benefits than does a fully insured status.

A Record of Your Credits

You can verify the number of credits you have accumulated with the Social Security system by mailing a request to the Social Security Administration in Baltimore, Maryland. Your local Social Security office will provide a standard postcard on which you can fill in the required information—your complete name, address, Social Security number, and date of birth—to request your insured status.

STRATEGY

Request a copy of your quarterly credit record every 3 years as part of your normal financial record keeping.

BENEFITS FOR SURVIVORS

Should you die before age 62, your dependents may qualify for monthly Social Security payments for a number of years.

Standards for Eligibility

Generally, you must be fully insured in order for your dependents to have **eligibility** for what are called "income continuation payments." The income continuation designation is used because those payments are intended to replace part of the income you and your dependents would have received had you survived. There are, however, special provisions for younger workers who will not have worked long enough to accumulate 40 quarters of credit. Exhibit 13-3 summarizes the credit requirements specifically intended for workers who are relatively young at the time of their death. One general exception is available to everyone: You only need to be

FIRST THINGS FIRST, MADAM.. **FARFIE** IS **NOT** AN ELIGIBLE SURVIVOR..

currently insured when your survivors include minor children or when your surviving spouse is caring for minor children.

Benefits for Your Survivors

Next, we will examine the two principal categories of **survivors benefits** for **qualifying dependents**: the benefits for your spouse; and the benefits for your children, if any. You should be aware that your parents may also qualify as survivors; your local Social Security office will explain the necessary qualifications.

Surviving Spouse A recent major court decision regarding survivors benefits has recognized the equality of men and women as well as the emerging pattern of two-income families; the decision requires equal treatment of the surviving marriage partner, whether it's the wife or the husband. Now a husband may qualify for survivors benefits under his wife's

EXHIBIT 13-3

Years of work credit you need to qualify your survivors for income continuation payments.

	Born After 1929					
	Age at death					
	28 OR LESS	30	34	38	42	46
Required years of work credit	1½	2	3	4	5	6

work record in the same way that a wife may qualify for benefits on her husband's work record.

CHAPTER 13

397

SOCIAL SECURITY:
AN INTEGRAL
PART OF YOUR
PERSONAL
FINANCIAL PLAN

The surviving spouse qualifies for monthly income continuation payments for as long as the dependent children are younger than 16 years old. When the youngest of the children reaches 16 years of age, the spouse's payments generally cease. The surviving spouse does not qualify for any further payments until age 60. This period between the time when benefits cease because the youngest child is 16 and the time when the surviving spouse reaches 60 years old and therefore again receives benefits is called the "blackout period." The blackout period has special significance when estimating life insurance needs; we will discuss it further in Chapter 14.

There are also special qualifying rules that permit the surviving spouse to receive benefits as early as age 50, should the surviving spouse become disabled. Check with your Social Security office if you feel you might qualify.

Children   Your unmarried children qualify for dependent children's benefits. up to age 18. And they can qualify under the work record for either parent, regardless of whether it's the father or the mother who is deceased.

Benefit Reduction: Surviving Spouse Works   If the surviving spouse has a paying job, the amount earned will determine how much in Social Security benefits the spouse will receive. A portion, or all, of those benefits may be lost if his or her earnings exceed a prescribed amount. As shown in the top half of Exhibit 13-4, the reduction takes place in several steps. Up to the base amount, $4920, in 1983, no reduction is made in the amount of benefits. Beyond that, benefits are reduced by $1 for each $2 of earnings that exceed the base amount. Thus, a spouse earning $7920 would exceed the base by:

$3000   = $7920   − $4920

⬆   ⬆   ⬆

Earnings above   = Spouse's − Base amount of
the allowed base   earnings   allowed earnings

By exceeding the earnings base by $3000, the spouse's annual benefits would be reduced by:

$1500   = $3000   ÷ $2

⬆   ⬆   ⬆

Reduction in   = Amount earnings ÷ Reduction:
spouse's   exceed the allowed $1 in benefits
annual benefit   base   for each $2
                                                    of excess earnings

Generally, when the spouse's earnings reach the $14,000 to $18,000 range, the benefits are reduced to little or none at all.

Earnings include all wages and salary, but exclude interest income, dividend payments, payments from private pension plans, and rental income. It is important to note that only the surviving spouse's benefit is

EXHIBIT 13-4

Reduction in Social Security benefit payments
when surviving spouse or a retired person works.

BENEFIT RECIPIENT	MAXIMUM EARNINGS ALLOWED IN 1983	BENEFIT REDUCTION IF EARNINGS EXCEED MAXIMUM
Surviving spouse with child under 16	$4920*	$1 reduction for each $2 of earnings above the maximum
Retired individual, age 65 to 70. No earnings limit above age 70	$6600*	$1 reduction for each $2 of earnings above the maximum†

*Amount will automatically rise each year as wage levels increase.
†Reduction is scheduled to fall to $1 for every $3 of earnings over the maximum.

reduced. Benefit payments specified for minor children are not affected by the surviving parent's income.

Lump-Sum Payment   When workers who are covered by Social Security die, their estate receives a **lump-sum payment** of up to $255. This payment was originally intended to provide a minimum amount for burial expenses.

Computation of Benefits

Our central purpose in this section is to help you make a reasonable estimate of the income continuation payments your survivors would receive in the event of your death. Before we begin, you should be aware of the following in order to appreciate what the estimates are all about:

The following calculations rely heavily on estimates and our judgments.

The dollar benefits that we will calculate can be applied only to situations concerning persons who died in 1983. Nevertheless, the dollar amounts computed using 1983 results can be used to estimate the dollar benefits for persons who die in later years.

The entire area of Social Security benefits is changing. We have summarized the latest changes we are aware of. And we've tried to suggest how to use anticipated future changes. Therefore, you should be in a good position to use this information as part of your overall personal financial plan.

Social Security Survivors Benefits: Primary Insurance Amount   The Social Security legislation uses the term "**primary insurance amount**"—PIA for short—to describe the basic monthly Social Security survivors' benefit. From it the system derives the amount to be paid to the survivors of a deceased worker. Before we examine how a PIA benefit is computed and used, let us briefly review what determines an individual's PIA. First, the Social Security system indexes the person's earnings from prior years. As you recall, this process adjusts these earnings so that they are comparable with today's wage levels. Next, the system divides those prior earnings by the number of months the person had worked to compute the person's average earnings. That average is called the **average indexed monthly earnings** (AIME). The appendix of this chapter provides a detailed explanation together with worksheets that show precisely how that AIME is computed; we will defer discussion of that topic to the appendix. Once the AIME has been computed, the PIA is based on that AIME amount. The larger the AIME, the larger the PIA. Since the actual computation is a bit involved, we'll not perform it here. What we have done, however, is to show a range of AIMEs in Exhibit 13-5 and to compute the PIA for each one. These PIAs are shown in column 2 of that exhibit.

Several comments about the PIA computation: First, your PIA is a percentage of your AIME, but as your AIME rises, the percentage declines. For example, the PIA for an AIME of $1000 is less than double what the PIA is when the AIME is $500.

Let us use several examples to show how Exhibit 13-5 can be used. Suppose Rob Waller's AIME is $900. It will be no problem to go directly to the exhibit and see that his PIA is $435. But suppose Rob's AIME is $925. We can interpolate between the $900 and $950 shown in Exhibit 13-5 to estimate Rob's PIA:

$$\$443 = \$435 + [\tfrac{1}{2} \times (\$451 - \$435)]$$

| Estimated PIA | = | PIA if AIME is $900 | + | [Fraction of difference | × | PIA when AIME is: $950 - $900] |

Our estimate may not be the precise PIA, but it is sufficiently accurate for our purposes.

Social Security Survivors Maximum Family Benefit

The Social Security system has established a maximum monthly benefit for which a worker's family can qualify; it is appropriately called the **maximum family benefit**. This maximum benefit typically averages 150 to 200 percent of the PIA that we calculated in the last section. A family qualifies for the family maximum when there is a surviving spouse with at least two children under 18 years of age and one child must be under 16 years of age.

Benefit Payments for Your Survivors

The monthly benefit payments your survivors can receive depend on two things: (1) your primary insurance amount (PIA) or your maximum family benefit and (2) the age and relationship of the survivors. Columns 3 through 8 of Exhibit 13-5 list the benefit to which each survivor of a deceased worker is entitled. Columns 3, 4, and 5 are used when there is a surviving spouse but no children under 16. Columns 6 and 7 are used when there is a surviving spouse with one child. Column 6 shows the surviving spouse's benefit; it continues until the child

CHAPTER 13

399

SOCIAL SECURITY:
AN INTEGRAL
PART OF YOUR
PERSONAL
FINANCIAL PLAN

is 16 years old. Column 7 shows the child's benefit; it continues until he or she is 18 years old. Column 8 is used when the surviving spouse has more than one child under 18 and at least one child is under 16.

An example will show how Exhibit 13-5 works. Assume that Wilma Green is married and has one child, age 4. Wilma knows that her average indexed monthly earnings (AIME) are $1000. Should something happen to her during 1983, her widower would qualify for a monthly benefit of $350, and it would continue until the child is 16. In addition, the child also qualifies for a monthly benefit of $350, which continues until the child is 18. Suppose Wilma had had two children: one aged 4 and the other 7. The family's benefit—widower plus the two children—would equal the family maximum of $876 monthly.

EXHIBIT 13-5

Monthly Social Security benefits for survivors, disabled workers, and retired workers, 1983.

		Benefits for Survivors of Deceased Person					
		SPOUSE'S BENEFIT					
AVERAGE INDEXED MONTHLY EARNINGS (AIME) (1)	PRIMARY INSURANCE AMOUNT (PIA) (2)	WITH NO CHILD UNDER 16			WITH CHILD		WITH 2 OR MORE CHILDREN
		AGE 65 (3)	AGE 60 (4)	DISABLED (5)	SPOUSE (6)	CHILD (7)	(8)
Percentage of PIA paid		100%	71.5%	100%	75%	75%	Family maximum
$ 500	$307	$307	$220	$307	$230	$230	$ 461
600	339	339	243	339	254	254	528
700	371	371	265	371	278	278	615
800	403	403	288	403	302	302	702
850	419	419	300	419	314	314	745
900	435	435	311	435	326	326	789
950	451	451	323	451	338	338	832
1000	467	467	334	467	350	350	876
1050	483	483	346	483	362	362	898
1100	499	499	357	499	374	374	920
1200	531	531	380	531	398	398	963
1300	563	563	403	563	422	422	1005
1400	595	595	426	595	446	446	1048
1500	627	627	449	627	470	470	1098
1600	647	647	463	647	485	485	1136
1700	662	662	473	662	497	497	1163
1800	677	677	485	677	508	508	1189

Estimating Survivors Benefits for Future Periods The benefit amounts shown in Exhibit 13-5 are based on wage levels and benefit cutoffs existing in 1983. That is, if a worker died during 1983, the benefits for survivors would be based on the amounts shown in Exhibit 13-5. After 1983, those wage levels and cutoffs will be revised. Consequently, the dollar benefits for survivors will be altered. You could use the amounts shown in Exhibit 13-5 for a very rough estimate, but you might want to be more accurate.

We expect that survivors benefits will rise about as rapidly as overall consumer prices. One such estimate of the increase in consumer prices is the consumer price index (CPI) compiled by the federal government. Each month, the *Federal Reserve Bulletin* publishes details on the change in the CPI. Most libraries have copies of the *Bulletin*. If you can't find it there, the

CHAPTER 13

401

SOCIAL SECURITY:
AN INTEGRAL
PART OF YOUR
PERSONAL
FINANCIAL PLAN

EXHIBIT 13-5 *Continued*

Benefits for Disabled Worker and Dependents				Benefits for Retired Worker			
BENEFIT FOR WORKER	1 OR MORE MINOR CHILDREN	BENEFIT FOR SPOUSE OF WORKER		BENEFIT FOR WORKER		BENEFIT FOR NONWORKING SPOUSE	
		AGE 65	AGE 62	AGE 65	AGE 62	AGE 65	AGE 62
(9)	(10)	(11)	(12)	(13)	(14)	(15)	(16)
100%	50%	50%	37.5%	100%*	80%*	50%*	37.5%*
$307	$154	$154	$115	$307	$246	$154	$115
339	170	170	127	339	271	170	127
371	186	186	139	371	297	186	139
403	202	202	151	403	323	202	151
419	210	210	157	419	335	210	157
435	218	218	163	435	348	218	163
451	226	226	169	451	361	226	169
467	234	234	175	467	374	234	175
483	242	242	181	483	387	242	181
499	250	250	187	499	399	250	187
531	266	266	199	531	425	266	199
563	282	282	211	563	451	282	211
595	298	298	223	595	476	298	223
627	314	314	235	627	502	314	235
647	324	324	243	647	518	324	243
662	331	331	248	662	530	331	248
677	339	339	254	677	542	339	254

*Percentage of basic benefit.

reference specialists at your library can probably help you determine how much the CPI has risen each year. Those who do not want to spend the time and effort needed to determine exactly what has happened to the CPI may use an adjustment of 6 to 8 percent. In our opinion, that is a reasonable estimate of how much consumer prices are likely to rise each year over the next 3 to 4 years.

An example is the best way to illustrate how the benefits in Exhibit 13-5 can be adjusted. Assume that Earl Estimate wants to know what his survivors—a child and spouse—might receive should he die during 1985. Earl's AIME is $1200. A review of Exhibit 13-5 shows that both the surviving spouse and the child (age 4) will receive monthly benefits of $398 if Earl died in 1983. Based on the expected rise in consumer prices between 1983 and 1984, Earl decides that benefits probably have risen 6 percent each year; that is the lower end of our 6 to 8 percent range. So his survivors' monthly benefits in 1985 would be approximately:

$$\$445.76 = \$398 + (\$398 \times 6\% \times 2 \text{ years})$$

| Survivor benefit: 1985 | = Survivor benefit, 1983 | + Survivor benefit, 1983 | × Growth rate | × Years since 1983 |

Of course, if Earl wants a more accurate estimate of the rise in consumer prices, he can use the actual CPI increases for 1984 and 1985. The combined increase for those 2 years can then be used to adjust the 1983 benefit shown in Exhibit 13-5.

SOCIAL SECURITY BENEFIT: AN INTEGRAL PART OF PLANNING SURVIVORS BENEFITS

We can best illustrate the key role of Social Security benefits in personal financial planning through an example.

Assume that Bob and Jean Webster are both 30 years old and have one daughter, Kristy, age 3. Since both of the Websters work full time, they want to know what benefits their survivors will receive if one of them should die. Specifically, they want answers to the following questions:

What are the surviving spouse's benefits? How long will they last?

Would Kristy receive any benefits?

Is there any impact on the spouse's retirement benefits?

CHAPTER 13

403

SOCIAL SECURITY:
AN INTEGRAL
PART OF YOUR
PERSONAL
FINANCIAL PLAN

Our example will concentrate on the benefits that Jean's survivors might receive beginning in 1983. The starting point here is to estimate Jean Webster's average indexed monthly earnings (AIME). We will assume that Jean knows her AIME is $1400. In the appendix of this chapter, we will show how that computation can be made.

Available Survivors Benefits: The Websters

Exhibit 13-6 summarizes the entire range of survivors benefits that Bob and Kristy Webster would be entitled to should Jean die prematurely in 1983.

It is assumed in section 1 of the exhibit that Bob earns less than $4920, the maximum earnings a surviving spouse can have in 1983 and still receive the full Social Security benefit: $446 in this case. Had Bob worked full time so that he earned $14,520, his annual benefit would be reduced by:

$4800	=	($14,520 − $4920)	÷	$2
⇧		⇧	⇧	⇧
Annual reduction in benefits	=	Earnings during 1983	− Maximum earnings allowed	÷ Reduction: $1 in benefits for each $2 over maximum

Converting that annual reduction to a monthly amount gives:

$400	=	$4800	÷	12 months
⇧		⇧		⇧
Monthly reduction	=	Annual reduction	÷	Conversion to monthly reduction

That $400 monthly reduction would nearly eliminate his $446 Social Security benefit.

Regardless of how much Bob earns, Kristy would be eligible for $446—her portion of the Social Security benefits. Section 2 of the exhibit covers the period until Kristy reaches age 18.

STRATEGY

Consider Social Security survivors benefits when planning your family's potential income sources should you or your spouse die prematurely.

EXHIBIT 13-6

Schedule of survivors benefits Bob and Kristy
Webster could receive.

SECTION	DESCRIPTION OF PERIOD	Recipient's Age During Period		PERCENTAGE OF PIA BENEFIT	MONTHLY* BENEFIT PAYMENT
		START	FINISH		
1	Family income				
	Bob	30	43	75%	$446
	Kristy	3	16	75	$446
2	Child continues				
	Bob	43	45		0
	Kristy	16	18	75	$446
3	Blackout period				
	Bob	45			0
4	Retirement				
	Bob	60		71.5	$426

*From Exhibit 13-5.

BENEFITS IF YOU BECOME DISABLED

If you become disabled before age 62, you and your dependents may qualify
for income continuation payments from Social Security during the period of
disability.

Qualifications for Eligibility

To qualify as disabled, you must meet two general requirements: You must
be unable to perform any substantial work, and your disability must be
expected to last for 12 months or to be a probable cause of your death. These
are the two basic requirements for **disability benefits**; you must meet them
both no matter how old you are. (They are shown in the upper part of Exhibit
13-7.) The younger you are when you become disabled, the fewer quarters of
work credit you will need to become eligible for disability payments. This is
a way of recognizing that young workers will have had less opportunity to
accumulate quarters of credit; these special provisions are shown in the
lower half of Exhibit 13-7. Disabled individuals who are younger than 22
may qualify for benefits under one of their parents' records.

It is important to note that the work credit requirement specifies that
all workers age 31 or older must have earned at least five years of work credit
during the 10 years preceding their disability. A person might have 10 years
of credit, be fully insured, yet not qualify for disability because of not having
earned five years of credit during the most recent 10 years.

There is a minimum 5-month waiting period on all disability payments. If you were disabled in December, your minimum waiting period
would be January through May, so June would be the earliest you could
expect a benefit payment.

EXHIBIT 13-7

CHAPTER 13

405

SOCIAL SECURITY:
AN INTEGRAL
PART OF YOUR
PERSONAL
FINANCIAL PLAN

General requirements and work credit needed
to qualify for disability payments.

| | **Age of Covered Individual** | | |
REQUIREMENT	LESS THAN 24	24 THROUGH 30	31 AND OVER
General: Disability prevents substantial work	Required	Required	Required
Disability expected to last 12 months or cause death	Required	Required	Required
Special: Years of required work credit	1½ years dur- ing preceding 3 years	Half the time between age 21 and year of disability	At least 5 years credit during the 10 preceding years. If over 42, additional years may be needed.

Benefits for Yourself and Your Dependents

There are three categories of **qualifying individuals** for disability benefits: (1) yourself, (2) your spouse if married, and (3) your children, if any.

Disabled Person   If you are disabled, you yourself will be eligible to receive Social Security income continuation payments during the disability period. Generally, the benefits will terminate when you are able to return to work and when your earnings are sufficient so that you are considered to be doing "substantial gainful work."

If you are married, your spouse's earnings, no matter how large they are, will not affect your disability benefit payments.

Spouse's Benefits   Just as survivors benefits were broadened, so also were disability benefits. For example, a husband may be eligible for benefits as a result of his wife's disability. Of course, in order to qualify for any type of disability payment, his wife would have to meet the general requirements and the work experience we outlined in Exhibit 13-7. A wife may be eligible for disability payments because of her husband's disability. In either case, these benefits do not begin until the spouse is 62, assuming that the partner is still disabled at that time.

Children   Unmarried children who are less than 18 years old qualify for benefits arising from the disability of either working parent. To collect benefits, the child's disabled parent must have met the qualifications in Exhibit 13-7.

Where there are no children, or none under 18, the total benefit equals the payment to the disabled person.

Computation of Benefits

We will now make some estimates and do some calculations to determine disability benefit payments for certain situations. However, just as with survivors benefits, changes may have occurred in the Social Security regulations since this book went into production.

Remember, the dollar amounts are computed using rules and dollar cutoffs that really apply only when estimating disability benefits for 1983. As such, they assume that the covered individual is disabled in 1983. We will show later how these amounts can be modified to estimate disability benefit payments in subsequent years.

Primary Insurance Amount   As with survivors benefits, the Social Security legislation also describes the basic disability benefit as the "primary insurance amount" (PIA). From that PIA, the system determines the payments to the disabled person and his or her dependents, if any. At this point, you might ask: Is the PIA used for someone's survivors benefits different from the PIA used for disability benefits? Yes, in most cases it is. To explain why, we will briefly review the steps in computing a PIA. Both PIAs start at the same point: the Social Security system indexes your earnings from prior years. When those indexed earnings are summed and divided by the years in the earnings records to compute an AIME, the difference arises. When averaging earnings for survivors benefits, the system eliminates years with low or zero earnings; that keeps low years from pulling down average earnings. The rules for both survivors benefits and disability benefits allow the dropping of low or zero years. But the disability rules are much more restrictive. Consequently, with fewer years excluded, your AIME for disability purposes may be smaller than your AIME for survivors purposes. And the smaller your AIME, the lower your PIA benefit. The appendix of this chapter explains how the rules for the dropping of low years differ.

Once your AIME has been determined, the computation of your PIA for disability benefits involves the same steps as your PIA for survivors benefits. Instead of showing you how to compute the PIA, Exhibit 13-5 gives the PIA for a series of AIMEs. Column 1 of Exhibit 13-5 shows AIMEs, while the corresponding PIA disability benefit is shown in column 9 of that exhibit. You will see that column 9 is titled "Worker"; since the disabled worker's benefit is 100 percent of the PIA, column 9 serves the dual purpose of being both the PIA and the disabled worker's benefit.

Some additional comments about the PIA benefit in column 9 need to be made: First, the PIA is not a straight percentage of the AIME; as the AIME increases, the percentage declines. Thus, the PIA for an AIME of $1400 is not double that for an AIME of $700. Nevertheless, if you need to compute the PIA for an AIME that is between two AIME values given in Exhibit 13-5, you can interpolate between those AIMEs. Usually, the resulting PIA will be sufficiently accurate for your needs. An example will illustrate. Suppose Jan Van Mueller's AIME is $1150. We know from Exhibit 13-5 that the disability PIA (column 9) is $499 when the AIME is $1100 and $531 when it is $1200. By interpolating between the two, Jan estimates her PIA is $515. For purposes of financial planning, that estimate is accurate enough.

Family Maximum   The **maximum family benefit** a disabled person and his or her family can receive is 150 percent of the PIA benefit.[1] Since the worker is always entitled to 100 percent of the PIA, that leaves 50 percent for the worker's family. To emphasize that, we labeled column 10 in Exhibit 13-5 as "Minor Children: One or More." It shows that they qualify for the remaining 50 percent of the PIA from the family maximum. The column shows that one child would receive 50 percent of the PIA. But since the family maximum only allows 50 percent of the PIA for dependents, the benefit payment to children, even if there are more than one, is limited to 50 percent of the PIA. In the event of disability, Bob Beaucoop's six minor children together would receive the same 50 percent of PIA as Octavia Larson's one child would receive.

CHAPTER 13

407

SOCIAL SECURITY:
AN INTEGRAL
PART OF YOUR
PERSONAL
FINANCIAL PLAN

Disability Payments for You and Your Dependents   Columns 9 through 12 in Exhibit 13-5 summarize the benefits that you and your dependents would receive should you become disabled. Several points need to be emphasized. The disabled worker automatically receives a benefit equal to the PIA amount, as in column 9. Each child who is under 18 is theoretically entitled to a benefit equaling 50 percent of the PIA. But, since the family maximum limits payments to 150 percent of the PIA, only one child can actually receive a benefit. Consequently, column 10 shows the total benefit for all minor children in the disabled worker's family. Last, it is important to note that the spouse's earliest time to receive benefits begins at age 62. Columns 11 and 12 show the spouse's monthly benefit at age 65 and 62, respectively.

An example will illustrate the use of Exhibit 13-5. Sue Becker is married and has two children, aged 6 and 10. Sue knows her AIME is $1300. Should she become disabled in 1983, she would receive a monthly benefit of $563. Since the children are under 18, their total monthly benefit would be $282. That benefit would continue until the youngest child is 18 years old. Sue's husband would not qualify for any benefits until he is at least 62 years old.

Estimating Disability Benefit for Future Periods   Exhibit 13-5 has the same limitation on disability benefits that we discussed in the section called "Benefits for Survivors"; the benefits in that exhibit apply only to someone disabled in 1983. Those amounts need to be modified to estimate benefits for years after 1983. As we suggested in the section on survivors benefits, raising the benefit by the percentage increase in overall consumer prices seems a reasonable way to proceed. Since the adjustment is identical to that discussed in the earlier section on adjusting survivors benefits, we will not repeat it here. If you need a refresher or want details on how to make the required adjustment, refer back to the subsection "Estimating Survivors Benefits for Future Periods."

---

[1] In special circumstances, the family maximum may be limited to 85 percent of the AIME if that is less than 150 percent of the PIA.

INCORPORATING PROJECTED DISABILITY PAYMENTS INTO YOUR FINANCIAL PLANS

Because Social Security payments often replace a sizable percentage of a person's income, they are an essential factor that you should consider when planning where your income will come from and how much it will be should you become unable to work. We can best illustrate this point by working through an example.

You are already familiar with Bob and Jean Webster and their daughter Kristy, whom we introduced in our calculations for survivors benefits. Now, let's estimate what benefits they would qualify for starting in 1983 if Jean were to become disabled during that year.

The first thing we need to decide is whether Jean Webster can qualify for Social Security disability benefits; to do so, she must meet the qualifications we listed in Exhibit 13-7. If she were actually applying for benefits, she would have to meet both general qualifications: she must be (1) unable to do substantial work, and (2) expect to be disabled for at least 12 months. For our present estimate, we can ignore these requirements. But Jean, who is 30 years old, would have to meet the special requirement for persons between 24 and 30 years of age: work credit for half the years between age 21 and the year of disability. Since we are completing the calculations for 1983, we assume that would be the year of disability. From a review of Jean's earnings record, we see that she has worked for five full years. That means she has accumulated work credit for more than one-half the years since she turned 21, and so could qualify for disability benefits.

To start our example, we need to compute Jean Webster's average indexed monthly earnings (AIME) for disability purposes. Recall our saying that the rules are more restrictive when dropping years with low or zero earnings when computing the AIME for disability benefits. Earlier, we had said that Jean's AIME for survivors purposes was $1400. In recognition of

WELL, I'LL SAY
THIS MUCH... IT'S
ONE OF THE MOST
UNUSUAL DISABILITIES
WE'VE EVER PAID..

the disability program's tighter rules, we assume her AIME is only $1300 for disability purposes.

CHAPTER 13

409

SOCIAL SECURITY:
AN INTEGRAL
PART OF YOUR
PERSONAL
FINANCIAL PLAN

Available Disability Benefits   The complete schedule of disability benefits the Websters will receive, assuming that Jean remains disabled, is summarized in Exhibit 13-8.

Family Income Period   The benefits shown for the family income period in Exhibit 13-8 assume that Jean remains disabled the entire period. The amount that Bob earns during this period has no impact on Jean's or Kristy's benefits; they remain the same whether Bob earns nothing or a lot.

Middle Period   For the middle period, we assume that Kristy has reached 18 years old, so she no longer qualifies for any benefits. Bob, of course, still is not eligible for a benefit. Only Jean, whom we assume remains disabled, will continue to receive benefits during this period.

Retirement Period   The retirement benefit payments were calculated as though Bob qualified under Jean's work record. In all likelihood, his continuing to work would mean he would qualify under his own earnings record because of the larger retirement benefits it would provide. Regardless of his working or not working, he would be eligible to receive whichever benefit was larger.

An Interesting Note   Using the amounts shown in Exhibit 13-8, we can estimate that the Websters could collect as much as $266,952 in total Social Security benefits by the time they were both 62 years old, assuming that Jean remained disabled from age 30 to 62.

STRATEGY

Social Security payments are very important when planning how much income you will receive and where it will come from should you become disabled.

EXHIBIT 13-8

Schedule of the Websters' disability benefits at three stages in the family's development.

TIME PERIOD	AGE AT START OF PERIOD	AGE AT FINISH OF PERIOD	PERCENTAGE OF PIA BENEFIT	MONTHLY PAYMENT
Family income period				
Jean, disabled	30	45	100%	$563
Kristy	3	18	50	282
Middle period				
Bob	45	62	—	—
Jean	45	62	100	563
Retirement period				
Bob	62	Death	37.5	211
Jean	62	Death	100	563

RETIREMENT BENEFITS

We now will cover retirement income, which many people think is the only benefit provided by the Social Security system. It was not the original purpose of the Social Security Act, nor is it currently intended that **retirement benefit** payments should cover your complete retirement income needs. You will have to supplement Social Security retirement benefits through retirement income from private pension plans, income from investments you accumulated during your working career, or other sources.

Qualifications for Benefits

The most basic requirement to establish **eligibility** for Social Security retirement income payments is that you be fully insured, meaning that you have 40 quarters of work credit. Under no condition do you need more than 40 quarters of work credit.

The 40 quarters of work credit qualify you only for retirement benefits. They do not guarantee that you are entitled to receive the maximum benefit. That is still determined by averaging your annual indexed earnings for a prescribed number of years.

Benefits for You and Your Dependents

Although 65 years has been the traditional retirement age, you can begin to receive Social Security payments at any time after you are 62 years old. Should you decide you want to start receiving the benefits at age 62, you will receive only 80 percent of the benefits you would otherwise receive at age 65. Should you decide on some date between age 62 and age 65, your monthly retirement benefit will be reduced a small fractional percentage for each month you begin to receive benefits before you reach 65. For example, if you elect to start receiving Social Security retirement income at exactly 63½ years of age—18 months before you reach age 65—your monthly benefit check will be exactly 90 percent of what it would be if you wait until age 65 to start receiving benefits.

Delaying the start of retirement benefits until after age 65 increases the benefits by 3 percent for each year beyond that age. For example, your benefit payment at age 70 would be:

115%	= (3%	× 5 years)	+ 100%
⇧	⇧	⇧	⇧
Benefit as a percentage of the benefit at 65	= Percentage increase for each year beyond age 65	× Years beyond age 65: 70 years − 65 years	+ Normal benefit at age 65

Retired Worker's Benefit Columns 13 and 14 of Exhibit 13-5 summarize the benefit a retired worker will receive at age 65 and age 62, respectively. In both cases, the benefit is given as a percentage of the retirement PIA benefit. Let's use an example to demonstrate Exhibit 13-5. Assume that Saul Goldberg has determined that his AIME is $900. By going down column 1 of Exhibit 13-5 until we encounter $900 and reading across to column 13, we find that Saul would qualify for a monthly benefit of $435 at age 65. That is also his PIA, since the retirement benefit at age 65 equals 100 percent of the PIA. Should Saul decide to retire at age 62, his monthly benefit would be $348, or 80% of the PIA.

CHAPTER 13

411

SOCIAL SECURITY:
AN INTEGRAL
PART OF YOUR
PERSONAL
FINANCIAL PLAN

Spouse's Benefit   Columns 15 and 16 summarize **spouse's retirement benefits** for a wife or a husband based on the working spouse's Social Security record. At age 65, the wife or husband qualifies for 50 percent of the working spouse's PIA. At age 62, the spouse's benefit is only 37.5 percent of that PIA. Spouses who work outside their homes can select the highest retirement benefit; either the one based on their earnings record or the benefit based on the earnings record of the husband or wife.

Estimating Retirement Benefits

Estimating benefit levels is considerably harder for retirement benefits than for either survivors benefits or disability benefits. Much of the difficulty arises because the earnings record that must be included when computing average annual earnings for retirement is much longer than the earnings record for survivors benefits or disability benefits. Currently, people born after 1930 must include 35 years of earnings. Since most people have not yet worked that many years, there are two unattractive options for calculating retirement benefits.

1   We could estimate the benefit using the person's actual earnings to date and assume that the future years' earnings needed to complete 35 work years will be at the same rate as the average of the past actual earnings.

2   We could attempt to estimate the future annual earnings for all the years needed to bring the person's earnings record up to 35 years. For many people, that calculation may entail projecting earnings that are 20 years or more in the future.

We suggest that you not do either. Instead, we recommend that you use Exhibit 13-9 to get an idea of what your retirement income from Social Security will be in future years. The previous two estimates required that you make some guesses about what you expect your future annual earnings might be. Exhibit 13-9 gives estimates that, while they are not precise, are probably more accurate than either option mentioned above. And it requires far fewer computations to estimate your projected monthly retirement benefit.

Please note that Exhibit 13-9 specifically applies to someone who was 65 in 1980 and therefore beginning retirement that year. That's probably not your present circumstance. For those of you who are less than 65, the replacement percentages could change by the time you retire. Nevertheless, we doubt there will be sweeping changes in these percentages over the next several years. Consequently, we believe they are sufficiently accurate to allow you to estimate approximately what Social Security retirement benefits you can expect.

EXHIBIT 13-9

Percentage of household's gross income that
Social Security retirement benefits will replace.

HOUSEHOLD'S TOTAL GROSS EARNINGS*	SINGLE WORKER	MARRIED: ONE WAGE-EARNER	COUPLE: TWO WAGE-EARNERS†
$10,000	49%	73%	63%
$15,000	42%	64%	54%
$20,000	34%	51%	49%
$30,000	23%	34%	42%
$50,000	14%	21%	27%

*Based on a continuously employed worker retiring at age 65 in 1980
and, if married, a spouse of age 65. Prior earnings were assumed
to increase at 6% per year.
†Assumes each wage-earner contributed one-half the household's
income.
Source: President's Commission on Pension Policy, November 1980.

Let us use an example to demonstrate how Exhibit 13-9 can do that.
Assume Lisa Wolf is single and, furthermore, her gross earnings are $15,000.
Based on Exhibit 13-9, Lisa's retirement benefit would be approximately:

$6,300   = $15,000   × 42 percent

Social   = Present   × Replacement
Security   earnings   percentage
benefit

While not a precise estimate, it is accurate enough to help Lisa plan her
retirement. We cover that in Chapter 21.

Need another example? Ron and Ann Dunn currently earn about
$10,000 each, or approximately $20,000 between them. The Dunns' combined Social Security retirement benefit would be roughly:

$9800   = $20,000   × 49%

Social   = Household's × Replacement
Security   income   percent
benefit

Again this estimate is primarily to help Ron and Ann plan their retirement.
Of course when Lisa, Ron, Ann or anyone else using Exhibit 13-9
actually retires, their actual earnings will likely be much higher than those
shown here. Nevertheless, single individuals would probably find that
Social Security retirement benefits replace between 14 and 49 percent of

their pre-retirement earnings. Married couples would likely find Social Security retirement benefits replace 21 and 73 percent of their household's pre-retirement earnings.

CHAPTER 13

413

SOCIAL SECURITY:
AN INTEGRAL
PART OF YOUR
PERSONAL
FINANCIAL PLAN

SHOULD SOCIAL SECURITY BENEFITS BE PART OF YOUR FINANCIAL PLAN?

After reading this chapter, we think you will answer that question with a resounding **YES**. Our intent was not to make you a Social Security specialist; that would be impossible in a single chapter. What we wanted to do was to increase your awareness of the range of benefits, how these benefits are determined, and the general qualifying standards for them. Anyone paying Social Security taxes should definitely consider the available benefits when planning his or her financial future. In our opinion, the guidelines presented in this chapter are sufficiently detailed so that you should be able to incorporate Social Security benefits as part of your financial plan. If you are unclear what a benefit's standards for qualifying are, or how a benefit is determined, by all means call your local Social Security office. It is staffed by experts on the system who can provide a wealth of useful information. Certainly, if you feel you might currently be eligible for a particular benefit, you should immediately call that office.

We will consider our goal of increasing your Social Security awareness as accomplished if, during the discussion of life insurance, disability insurance, or the planning of retirement income, you reflect a moment and then say, "Ah, but have we considered the Social Security benefit in each of these areas?"

SUMMARY

1 Social Security benefits are an important part of your overall personal financial plan.

2 The amount of the benefit payments you will receive is determined by the earnings on which you have paid Social Security taxes.

3 Your annual earnings are indexed to adjust income from early years to amounts comparable with the higher average incomes of more recent years.

4 Benefit payments for Social Security recipients are increased in January of each year by an amount equal to the percentage increase in consumer prices during the past year.

5 If your occupation is covered by the Social Security Act, you are required to pay Social Security (FICA) taxes on your wages up to a prescribed maximum amount. Your employer, if you are not self-employed, must match your tax payments.

6 The Social Security taxes which self-employed people pay equal the combined total amount of taxes paid by an employee plus those paid on his or her behalf by the employer.

7 You need 40 quarters of work credit in order to be fully insured.

8 Currently insured status requires work credit for 6 quarters during the most recent 12 quarters.

9   Should you die while covered under Social Security, your unmarried children will receive income continuation payments until they reach age 18.

10   A surviving spouse receives benefits only while caring for a child who is less than 16 years old. Otherwise, the surviving spouse's benefits do not begin until age 60.

11   When a surviving spouse's earnings exceed a prescribed maximum, his or her benefit is reduced; benefits to minor children of the surviving spouse are entirely unaffected by that income.

12   Your basic monthly Social Security benefit, the primary insurance amount (PIA), is determined by averaging your indexed earnings from prior years.

13   The maximum family benefit to survivors is generally 150 to 200 percent of the PIA.

14   Social Security survivors benefits should be an integral part of your life insurance planning process.

15   To be eligible for disability benefits, your disability must (a) prevent your doing any substantial work and (b) be expected to extend for 12 months or more.

16   Unmarried minor children of a disabled person may qualify for disability benefits until age 18.

17   Social Security disability benefits should be incorporated into the planning process when you establish your disability income insurance plan.

18   Retirement benefits can begin as early as at 62 years of age, or the start of Social Security retirement income can be delayed past 65 years of age if desired.

19   A spouse's retirement benefits are the higher of (a) 50 percent of the husband's or wife's benefit, or (b) the benefits computed using the spouse's earnings record.

20   Social Security retirement benefits typically will amount to 40 to 45 percent of the income you earned during the years just before you retired if your preretirement earnings were near the national average.

REVIEW YOUR UNDERSTANDING OF

Benefit levels: Principal determinants
Indexing prior years' earnings
Indexing Social Security benefits
Contributions to Social Security
Employee-employer matching
  contributions
Social Security tax for the
  self-employed
Maximum wage subject to tax
Tax rates
Quarter of work credit
Fully insured
Currently insured
Survivor benefit
  Eligibility
  Qualifying dependents

Schedule of benefit payment
Maximum family benefit
Benefit reduction: Surviving spouse works
Lump-sum payment
Primary insurance amount (PIA)
Average indexed monthly
  earnings (AIME)
Disability benefit
  Eligibility
  Qualifying individuals
  Schedule of benefit payments
  Maximum family benefit
Retirement benefit
  Eligibility
  Spouse's benefit
  Estimating benefit level

DISCUSSION QUESTIONS

CHAPTER 13

415

SOCIAL SECURITY:
AN INTEGRAL
PART OF YOUR
PERSONAL
FINANCIAL PLAN

1 Some people criticize Social Security retirement benefits on the ground that they are so low you can barely subsist on them. Do you agree? Is the criticism valid?

2 Assume that Ralph Chad paid $1200 in Social Security taxes during 1984. What will likely happen to that $1200? When Ralph collects retirement benefits in 30 years, who will contribute the monies for those benefits?

3 Are Social Security benefits subject to income taxes? Why is this factor important? Give a numerical example to illustrate the difference between receiving $20,000 of fully taxable income (assume a 20 percent average tax rate) and receiving $10,000 of Social Security benefits. Does the $20,000 income really provide twice as much spendable income as the $10,000 of Social Security benefits?

4 If Daisy Tsi receives a promotion in late 1984 that raises her annual salary from $13,000 to $26,000, what happens to her Social Security tax contributions? To her employer's contributions? Will the Social Security benefits she will eventually be eligible to receive double? Why or why not?

5 Why is it necessary to index the earnings from prior years? Before indexing, the dollar amount of the Social Security benefit for a young disabled individual who had only worked several years was often substantially larger than the dollar amount a retired worker with a long work record received. Explain why and how this could occur. How does indexing correct the problem? (*Hint:*

Consider what has happened to average earnings, especially during the recent periods of high inflation.)

6 Some people claim that once a person begins receiving Social Security benefits, those benefits from now into the future are "inflation-proof." Is that true? If so, how is it achieved?

7 Are Social Security tax rates progressive? Does the tax rate rise with income levels? Does everyone pay the same amount of Social Security taxes? How is the Social Security tax structure changing? (*Hint:* Exhibit 13-2 may be of help.)

8 When are you credited with a quarter of work credit? Why are quarters of work credit important? Can you check your own record of work credits?

9 Why is it difficult to estimate what your Social Security retirement benefits will be when you retire in the future? How can you make a rough approximation of your retirement benefits?

10 Which of the individuals listed in the table below would qualify for survivors benefits?

a List those individuals who cannot qualify and explain why they can't.

b Approximately what percentage of the PIA benefit would each of the qualified individuals receive?

c How long will the benefits last for each qualified person?

COVERED INDIVIDUAL	AGE	SPOUSE	AGE	CHILDREN	AGE	ACCUMULATED WORK CREDIT
Fred	30	Janet	28	None		8 years
Gretal	28	Hans	32	Hans, Jr.	8	6
Allan	42	Robin	40	Sue	19	14

COVERED INDIVIDUAL	SPOUSE (AGE)	ELIGIBLE	PERCENTAGE OF PIA	CHILDREN AGE	ELIGIBLE	PERCENTAGE OF PIA
Ralph	Sue (30)	___	___	None	___	___
Brenda	Fred (26)	___	___	Dan (3)	___	___
Tom	Ronda (46)	___	___	Sue (17)	___	___
Sandra	Bob (49)	___	___	Ted (9)	___	___
Vince	Debra (38)	___	___	{ Jim (4)	___	___
				{ Cindy (4)	___	___

11 The people listed in the table above have already determined that they have sufficient quarters of work credit to meet the requirements for the survivors benefits portion of Social Security. But they are uncertain whether their dependents would qualify and, if so, for how much.

a Which of the dependents is eligible for survivors benefits?

b For those who are eligible, what percentage of the covered individual's PIA would each receive?

12 Listed in the table below are four sets of circumstances for four individuals covered by Social Security. All of them are trying to determine what benefits they might receive should they become severely disabled.

For each situation, determine:

a Is the covered individual eligible for disability benefits?

b What percentage of the PIA benefit will the disabled individual and dependents, if any, receive?

c In each case, how long will the benefits last?

COVERED INDIVIDUAL	AGE	Dependent SPOUSE	AGE	CHILDREN	AGE	WORK CREDIT
Lawrence	30	None		None		2 years
Linda	32	Jim	32	None		6
Susan	28	None		None		5
Terry	35	Lee	34	Lisa	1	8

PROBLEMS

13-1 Lewis and Rachel Finestein both work; Lewis is self-employed, while Rachel is employed at Ajax Corporation. During 1984, Lewis expects to earn $40,000, while Rachel anticipates earnings of $20,000. How much Social Security taxes will the Finesteins pay? What total amount—from both employee and employer shares—will be paid into the Social Security system?

13-2 Juan Lopez estimates that his current monthly disability benefits of $430 amount to only 43 percent of the $1000 in monthly earnings he has been averaging when he was able to work. Last year Juan paid $2400 in Social Security, federal, and state income taxes. Are Juan's calculations correct? If not, what percentage of his spendable income before disability has been replaced by the Social Security benefit he currently receives? Are there other factors that Juan should consider?

13-3 Ron and Becky Issuzi are estimating the impact of Ron's continuing to work should Becky die in 1983. They have one child, Pattie, aged 10. On the basis of Becky's earnings record, they estimate Becky's average indexed monthly earnings (AIME) are $1100.

a If Ron does not work at all, what is his benefit? Pattie's benefit?

b If he earned $9720, what would his benefits be? Pattie's benefits?

c How much can Ron earn before losing the entire benefit? (*Hint*: Maximum = (benefit × $2) + surviving spouse's income allowance.) How much can he earn without disturbing Pattie's benefit?

13-4 Ed and Erma Easytime have recently retired. Ed's AIME is $1050 based on his work history. He is currently 62. Since Erma worked outside the home for a limited number of years, her AIME is $800. She is currently 65.

a What retirement benefit does Ed qualify for at age 62?

b What retirement benefit does Erma qualify for at age 65?

c Whose earnings record—Ed or Erma's—is Erma's benefit based on? Why?

13-5 Burno and Wanda Trent want to estimate the disability benefits they might receive should Burno become disabled in 1983. The Trents have two children: Sue, aged 14, and Tammie, aged 10. On the basis of Burno's earnings record, they estimate his AIME is $1500.

a What disability benefits would Burno receive?

b Would Sue receive a disability benefit? What about Tammie? What is their combined disability benefit?

c How long would the benefits to Burno's children continue?

d Would Wanda receive any benefit? If so, when would it begin?

13-6 At a recent cookout in the Golden Years recreation center Ron Allan, Bob Sweet, and Tom Young were talking about what portion, if any, of their Social Security retirement benefits would be subject to federal income taxes. Ron is single. Bob and Tom are both married and file joint tax returns with their spouses. Details on their respective incomes include:

INDIVIDUAL	TOTAL INCOME OTHER THAN SOCIAL SECURITY	SOCIAL SECURITY BENEFIT	AGE	FILING STATUS FOR TAXES
Ron	$20,000	$8,400	66	Single
Bob and Alice	$11,000 $14,000	$7,200 $8,400	67 68	Joint return
Tom and Joan	$23,000 $20,000	$8,000 $7,400	66 65	Joint return

a What portion, if any, of Ron's Social Security benefit is taxable? How about Bob and Alice's retirement benefit? And finally Tom and Joan's retirement benefit?

b Had Bob and Alice been single, what amount of each of their respective Social Security retirement benefit would have been subject to income taxes? Does it seem as though two people filing as single people or the same two people filing as a married couple on a joint return would most likely be subject to income taxes? Why?

c Prior to 1984 none of the retirement benefit would have been taxed at the federal level. Based on your results in part **a**, which income group is likely to be most affected by the recent change in taxability of benefits? Which income group will be least affected?

CASE PROBLEM

Joe and Sandra Smith want to estimate the survivors benefits they would qualify for should something happen to one of them during 1983. They have two daughters aged 2 and 6. Joe and Sandra have both worked full time since they were 25 years old until their present age of 32. Their earnings are:

YEAR	JOE'S EARNINGS: EMPLOYEE OF SLUG PRODUCTS	SANDRA'S EARNINGS: SELF-EMPLOYED
1976	$12,000	$ 6,000
1977	14,000	7,000
1978	16,000	8,000
1979	18,000	9,000
1980	20,000	10,000
1981	21,200	10,600
1982	23,200	11,600

On the basis of their earnings records, Joe's AIME is $1800 while Sandra's AIME is $900.

Since Joe's earnings are double Sandra's, they expect that the survivors payments based on his earnings record should be double the payments that would be due using Sandra's record. Even at that, the Smiths have expressed concern as to what portion of the benefits would be left after paying taxes. During 1983, their combined federal and state income taxes plus Social Security taxes were $10,500. The Smiths are also troubled as to how the surviving partner would pay the costs of raising their two daughters.

1 What survivors benefits, if any, would the Smiths qualify for on the basis of Joe's record? On Sandra's?

2 What is the primary insurance amount using Joe's earnings? Using Sandra's earnings?

3   On the basis of your answer in question **2**, can you support their expectation that the benefits based on Joe's earnings record would be double the benefits using Sandra's earnings record? Why or why not?

4   Design a table of benefits, similar to Exhibit 13-6, to show the payments that the Smiths can expect under Joe's record. Do the same for payments under Sandra's earnings.

5   (Optional) Will your tables in question **4** change if the surviving spouse works full time? What payments will Sandra and her children receive if she works and earns approximately the amount she earned in 1983? What payments can Joe and the children anticipate if Joe works and earns the amount he did in 1983?

6   Are their concerns about income taxes well founded? Why or why not?

7   Would the Smiths' Social Security payments make a significant contribution to the costs of raising their two girls?

APPENDIX:
INDEXING PRIOR YEARS' EARNINGS FOR SOCIAL SECURITY BENEFITS

In this Appendix, we will outline the steps that the Social Security Administration uses to index a worker's earnings from prior years. Chapter 13 first introduced the concept of indexing the prior years' earnings and examined the rationale for its use. But it did not present the actual computations. Your immediate response might be, "Why not let the Social Security system do the indexing computations for me?" A meritorious suggestion. Unfortunately, the system is so overburdened with handling current and ongoing claims that it does not have the time to estimate your benefits in the event of your death or disability. It only indexes your earnings if you are actually filing a claim for benefits.

In our opinion, that will be too late. For example, to plan your life insurance requirements (our topic in Chapter 14), you need an estimate of what Social Security benefits your survivors might receive. Thus the survivors of old Terry Toosoon (may he rest in peace) cannot do anything about Terry's inadequate life insurance once he is gone. If Terry had estimated his Social Security benefits by indexing his prior earnings, he might have known he needed more life insurance, and he could have bought it in time. Likewise, you need an estimate of your Social Security benefits to systematically and logically plan your disability insurance coverage. Again, the Social Security Administration will tell you those disability benefits *after* you are disabled. But that is too late. You cannot then buy disability insurance to supplement your Social Security disability payments should they prove to be inadequate. If the Social Security office cannot, or will not, estimate your benefits *before* you need them, *you* must make the estimate. That is the purpose of this appendix. It provides sufficient information and worksheets to estimate your approximate benefits. We underscore *approximate*! We make no claim that our procedure will provide a *precise*, to-the-penny benefit. In our opinion, it will give you a sufficiently accurate benefit estimate so that you can plan both your life insurance and your disability insurance.

The Why and How of Wage Indexing

Let us go back and see why we need to index in the first place. To do that, we will use two workers. Sam Average started work in 1970, while his younger brother Tom started work in 1980. When Sam began working in 1970, the $6200 he earned was about the average wage for a United States worker. Sam continued to work each year through 1980, so that he has a reasonably lengthy work record. During those years, his wages rose at about the same rate as those for an average American worker. By 1980 he was earning $12,500. When Tom started in 1980, his $12,500 earnings also approximated the average wage of a United States worker. During the next 4 years, both of their wages rose at about the same rate as the average wage in the U.S.

Now suppose that both Sam and Tom filed for Social Security benefits. As Chapter 13 has pointed out, the benefit is based on the worker's average monthly earnings over his or her work career. If we did not adjust, or index, the prior years' earnings, Sam's average monthly earnings would be much lower. The reason is that he had all those years during the 1970s when the average wage was much lower. Tom, on the other hand, would only count his earnings during the 1980s. His average earnings will be much higher. Is that fair? No. Both Sam's and Tom's wages equaled those of an average worker during their work careers. It would be unfair to penalize Sam for his lower earnings just because he has been in the work force for a longer period. What we need, then, is an index factor that corrects for the doubling of the average wage during the 10 years that Sam had worked before Tom started.

Computing an Index Factor   One possible index factor is to compare the average wage of a typical worker in an earlier year with a typical worker's current average wage. The actual index value is:

$$\frac{\text{Index}}{\text{factor}} = \frac{\text{Average wage, current year}}{\text{Average wage, prior years}}$$

We can return to Sam's and Tom's averages to show how an index factor is actually computed. Recall that while the average wage in 1970 was $6200, it had risen to $12,500 by 1980. The index factor would be:

$$2.0161 = \frac{\$12,500}{\$6,200}$$

$$\frac{\text{Index}}{\text{factor}} = \frac{\text{Current year's average wage}}{\text{Prior years' average wage}}$$

How do we use the index factor? We multiply it by the individual's actual earnings for the prior year; that adjusts those earlier earnings so they are comparable with today's earnings. In Sam's case, we would index his 1970 earnings as follows:

$$\$12,499.82 = \$6200 \times 2.0161$$

| Index earnings | = | Prior year's earnings | × | Index factor |

Now Sam's 1970 earnings have been indexed so that they are comparable with average earnings in 1980. To complete the computation, we can index all Sam's prior years' earnings. Once that is done, we can compute Sam's average monthly earnings. After indexing, Sam's average earnings will likely be much closer to Tom's average.

We will now examine Social Security index factors and how they are used.

Social Security Index Factors

Because the average wage of a typical worker changes each year, the Social Security system develops a separate set of index factors for each year. Consequently, the index factors used to adjust the prior years' earnings to 1983 wage levels will be different from the factors used to adjust those earnings to 1982 wage levels. So the Social Security Administration issues a new set of index factors each year. The factors published for 1982 would be used for all workers or survivors who applied for Social Security benefits in 1982. At the start of 1983, the system published a new set of factors to be used for all workers or survivors who were expected to apply for benefits in 1983.

Columns 3 and 4 of Exhibit A13-1 show the actual index factors used by the Social Security Administration during 1982 and 1983, respectively. Index factors for 1984 through 1986 (columns 5, 6, and 7) were estimated by the authors. If you wanted to compute your disability benefit for 1983, you would use the factors in column 4 to index your prior years' earnings for those benefits.

Before we demonstrate the use of the index factors, we need to explain the purpose of column 2 in Exhibit A13-1. Recall from our discussion of Social Security taxes that only those wages up to a specified level are subject to tax. A worker pays taxes only on wages up to the maximum and therefore receives credit only for those wages on which taxes were actually paid. Let us use several examples to illustrate the point. Suppose that during 1983, Sue Smalltime earned $7500. When indexing Sue's earnings, we use $7500 because that is what she paid taxes on. But suppose Becky Bigbuck earned $38,000 during 1983. On the basis of the maximum in column 2 of the exhibit, she would have paid taxes only on $35,700. So, when indexing Becky's earnings, we would use $35,700 because that is the amount on which she paid taxes. From these we can develop a general strategy.

STRATEGY

When indexing a prior year's earnings, always use the lower of that year's actual earnings or the maximum earnings that were subject to Social Security taxes that year (column 2 of Exhibit A13-1).

EXHIBIT A13-1

Index factors to adjust prior years' earnings to reflect the general rise in average earnings.

YEAR (1)	MAXIMUM EARNINGS SUBJECT TO SOCIAL SECURITY TAX (2)	1982 (3)	Index Factor* for Death or Disability			
			1983 (4)	1984 (5)	1985 (6)	1986 (7)
1970	$ 7,800	2.02	2.23	2.39	2.53	2.68
1971	7,800	1.93	2.12	2.27	2.40	2.55
1972	9,000	1.75	1.93	2.07	2.19	2.32
1973	10,800	1.65	1.82	1.95	2.06	2.19
1974	13,200	1.56	1.72	1.84	1.95	2.07
1975	14,100	1.45	1.60	1.71	1.81	1.92
1976	15,300	1.36	1.49	1.59	1.69	1.79
1977	16,500	1.28	1.41	1.51	1.60	1.70
1978	17,700	1.19	1.30	1.39	1.47	1.56
1979	22,900	1.09	1.20	1.28	1.36	1.44
1980	25,900	1.00	1.10	1.18	1.25	1.32
1981	29,700	1.00	1.00	1.07	1.13	1.20
1982	32,400	†	1.00	1.00	1.06	1.12
1983	35,700	†	†	1.00	1.00	1.06
1984	38,200‡	†	†	†	1.00	1.00
1985	40,500‡	†	†	†	†	1.00
1986	42,900‡	†	†	†	†	†

*Index factors for 1982 and 1983 are actual; all other years are estimates. All factors have been rounded to two decimal places.
†There are no index factors for these years; only those earnings prior to death or disability are counted.
‡Maximum earnings for 1984 through 1986 are estimates.

Average Indexed Monthly Earnings (AIME)

The purpose of indexing prior years' earnings is to compute an individual's average indexed monthly earnings (AIME). Once you know your own AIME, you can compute your Social Security benefits using a benefits table similar to Exhibit 13-5. Before we can compute an AIME, we need more explanation.

To lessen the possible negative impact of years with low or zero earnings, the Social Security system allows several adjustments. First, when computing your average earnings, you need to include only the full years beginning with the one you turned 22 years of age. We say "full years," because you do not include the year in which you are making the computation.

Let us illustrate with an example. Suppose Allan Green wants to estimate his likely disability benefits should he have become disabled in 1983. Allan turned 22 in 1978, so he is now 27 years old. While he was in college, Allan worked part-time, so his work history began before age 22. The Social Security system allows Allan to ignore the earnings for all years prior to 1978 (when he became 22). And he would include earnings only through 1982 because he was making the computation in 1983. Allan's list of earnings would show the 5 years from 1978 through 1982. But Allan might be able to drop even more years with low or zero earnings.

Dropping Years with Low or Zero Earnings As a basic minimum, the Social Security system generally requires that you include at least 2 years of earnings when computing your AIME. Thus Allan, from our previous example, must have at least 2 years of earnings when he computes his AIME. The Social Security system allows you to drop up to 5 years of low or zero earnings when computing your AIME. The exact number of years you can drop depends on two things: how many years your earnings record contains and whether you are computing survivors or disability benefits. Exhibit A13-2 shows the number of years of credit you must have in order to drop from 1 to 5 years. The first line of this exhibit gives the rules for survivors benefits. The rules for disability benefits are on the second line. A quick review of the two lines shows that the rules for disability benefits are considerably more restrictive than those for survivors benefits. We will again use Allan Green to illustrate this point: Since Allan turned 22 in 1978, his work record includes the 5 years from 1978 to 1982. He can therefore drop 3 years of low or zero earnings when computing his AIME for survivors benefits. But Allan can drop only 1 year when he computes his AIME for disability benefits. And generally, the fewer years he can drop, the lower his AIME will be. Thus we expect Allan's AIME for survivors benefits will exceed his AIME for disability.

From this example, we can make the following generalization. In most cases, you must compute two AIMEs: one to use for survivors benefits and

EXHIBIT A13-2

Years of low or zero earnings that can be dropped when computing AIME.

SOCIAL SECURITY BENEFIT	To Be Able To Drop				
	1 YEAR	2 YEARS	3 YEARS	4 YEARS	5 YEARS
Survivors— must have in records:	3 years	4 years	5 years	6 years	7 plus years
Disability— must have in records:	5–9 years	10–14 years	15–19 years	20–24 years	25 plus years

the second AIME to use for disability benefits. Furthermore, your AIME for disability benefits will nearly always be less than your AIME for survivors benefits.

Estimating Your AIME

Up to this point we have discussed (1) the index factors for prior years' earnings, (2) what earnings are included for indexing, and (3) how many years of low or zero earnings can be dropped. Now we need to pull all these parts together to show how an actual AIME is computed. Exhibit A13-3 will be our worksheet for that computation. While our sample worksheet covers

EXHIBIT A13-3

Worksheet to calculate average indexed monthly earnings: survivors and disability benefits.

Part A: Indexing Earnings

YEAR (1)	ACTUAL WAGES (2)	WAGES TO BE INDEXED* (3)	INDEX FACTOR: EXHIBIT A 13-1† (4)	INDEXED EARNINGS: COL. 3 × COL. 4 (5)	YEARS THAT CAN BE DROPPED FOR AIME‡	
					SURVIVORS (6)	DISABILITY (7)
1976	$15,900	$15,300	1.36	$20,808	√	
1977	16,400	16,400	1.28	20,992		
1978	7,800	7,800	1.19	9,282	√	√
1979	12,844	12,844	1.09	14,000	√	
1980	20,300	20,300	1.00	20,300	√	
1981	22,900	22,900	1.00	22,900		

Part B: Computing AIME

		SURVIVORS AIME	DISABILITY AIME
1	Years that can be dropped	4	1
2	Years that remain in computation	2	5
3	Sum of remaining indexed earnings, survivors, 1977 and 1981	$43,892	
4	Survivors AIME: $43,892 ÷ 24 months	$ 1,828.83	
5	Sum of remaining indexed earnings, disability, 1976, 1977, 1979, 1980, and 1981		$99,000
6	Disability AIME: $99,000 ÷ 60 months		$ 1,650

*Lower of actual earnings or maximum wages subject to Social Security taxes: Exhibit A13-1, column 2.
†Indexing factors for 1982: Exhibit A13-1, column 3.
‡Years to be dropped were determined by using Exhibit A13-2.

only the number of years in our example, by the end of our discussion you will have no problem modifying that worksheet to fit most work histories.

Don Scanlon wants to estimate his Social Security benefits for two circumstances: (1) if he becomes disabled during 1982, and (2) if he dies during 1982. Column 2 of the worksheet in Exhibit A13-3 summarizes Don's wages since he turned 22 in 1976. His earnings were low during 1978 and 1979 because he attended graduate school during those years.

A quick note to review the reason for column 3 in Exhibit A13-3: Recall that when indexing earnings, we always use the lesser of actual wages or the maximum earnings that were subject to Social Security taxes that year. By doing this, the wages that are indexed are in fact the wages on which Social Security taxes were paid. For 1976, Don enters the maximum wages subject to those taxes from column 2 of Exhibit A13-2 because his wages exceeded the maximum. But for all the other years, Don's earnings were less than the maximum ceiling; so his actual wages are entered for those years.

The index factors used in Exhibit A13-3, column 4, are those for 1982 since that is the year Don assumes the disability or death might occur. Had he been estimating benefits for a possible disability or death in 1984, he would use the index factors for 1984. Column 4, "Index Factor," multiplied by column 3, "Wages to Be Indexed," gives Don's indexed wages in column 5. Don now must decide whether he can drop some of his years with low or zero earnings.

Since Don reached 22 in 1976, his work history includes all full years up through 1981 (the last complete year before the computation); his record contains 6 years. Based on the rules for survivors benefits from Exhibit A13-2, Don can drop 4 years from his 6-year work history. Column 6 of Exhibit A13-3 shows the 4 years—they are marked with a √—that he should drop. Because of the more restrictive rules for disability, he can drop only 1 year. The selected year is shown with a √ in column 7 of Exhibit A13-3.

The lower half of Exhibit A13-3—Part B—outlines the steps to compute the AIME for survivors benefits as well as for disability benefits. For survivors benefits, Don would add the indexed earnings for the 2 years that were not dropped; this is done on line 3 of Part B. Those total indexed earnings are then divided by the number of months in the years that were not dropped. Dividing his total indexed earnings by 24 months gives Don his AIME of $1828.83 Considerably more years are included in the AIME for disability benefits because fewer years were dropped. Line 5 of Part B summarizes the total indexed earnings for the 5 years that remain: 1976, 1977, 1979, 1980, and 1981. Those total indexed earnings are then divided by 60 months to give the AIME of $1650 shown on line 6. Don's smaller disability AIME of $1650 versus his $1828.83 survivors AIME is due solely to disability's stricter rules for the dropping of years with low or zero earnings.

Benefit Payment Based on Your AIME   As we discussed in Chapter 13, Social Security benefits are based on your AIME. Once you have used a worksheet similar to Exhibit A13-3 to compute your AIME, you can readily go to a table of benefits like Exhibit 13-5 in the chapter text to determine the benefits for which you are eligible. In all likelihood, you will have two AIME amounts to work with: one for survivors benefits and another for disability benefits. Typically, the AIME for survivors benefits is the largest of the two. This would be especially true if you only worked some of the years since you turned 22 and your earnings have fluctuated sharply during your work career.

PROBLEMS

A13-1   Terry Weber would like to know, should he become disabled or die in 1983, how many years of low earnings would be dropped when computing his AIME. The table below summarizes his earnings from the year he turned 22 (1975) up through 1982.

		Years to Drop for AIME:	
YEAR	EARNINGS	SURVIVORS	DISABILITY
1975	$0	_____	_____
1976	$0	_____	_____
1977	$0	_____	_____
1978	$15,400	_____	_____
1979	$16,500	_____	_____
1980	$18,150	_____	_____
1981	$18,700	_____	_____
1982	$19,580	_____	_____

a What year(s) can he drop when computing his AIME for survivors benefits?

b What year(s) can he drop when computing his AIME for disability benefits?

A13-2   Sue Shorterm, who is 26 years old, has been working full-time since she turned 22 in 1980. She would like to compute her AIME for both survivors and disability benefits should she become disabled or die in 1984. She has started a worksheet similar to Exhibit A13-3 but is unclear about how to proceed.

		WAGES TO BE INDEXED	INDEX FACTOR	INDEXED EARNINGS	Years to Drop for AIME:	
YEAR	ACTUAL EARNINGS				SURVIVORS	DISABILITY
1980	$12,500	_____	_____	_____	_____	_____
1981	$30,500	_____	_____	_____	_____	_____
1982	$32,300	_____	_____	_____	_____	_____
1983	$34,000	_____	_____	_____	_____	_____

a How should Sue proceed with her worksheet?

b What will her AIME be for survivors benefits?

c What will her AIME be for disability benefits?

CHAPTER 13

427

SOCIAL SECURITY:
AN INTEGRAL
PART OF YOUR
PERSONAL
FINANCIAL PLAN

A13-3   By using his tax returns from prior years, Homer Healthy has determined that his earnings were $18,000 for 1978; $19,000 for 1979; $20,000 for 1980; $18,000 for 1981; $20,000 for 1982; and $9,500 so far in 1983. As part of his benefit estimate, Homer would like to index those earnings, assuming that he might be disabled in 1983; he is currently 27 years old.

a   What are Homer's indexed earnings for the years 1978 through 1983?

b   For disability benefit purposes, how many years would Homer include in his earnings record?

c   How many of those prior years of low or zero earnings can he drop?

d   Which years should Homer drop when computing his AIME?

e   What is Homer's AIME?

A13-4   Suppose that Homer Healthy in problem A13-3 also wants to index his earnings, assuming that he might die in 1983. All other data are the same as given in problem A13-3.

a   For survivors benefit purposes, how many years will Homer include in his earnings record?

b   How many years of low or zero earnings can he drop?

c   Which years should he drop when computing his AIME?

d   What is his AIME?

e   Why are the two AIME amounts—Part **e** in problem A13-3 and Part **d** in problem A13-4—different? (You must have worked Problem A13-3.)

CHAPTER

14

LIFE INSURANCE

**AFTER COMPLETING THIS CHAPTER
YOU WILL HAVE LEARNED**

What the principal *reasons* are for *purchasing life insurance*

The *differences* among the *six major types* of *life insurance contracts*

What *nonforfeiture options* are available when you surrender an insurance policy

How to *evaluate* the *supplementary provisions* a policy offers

The different ways that *insurance proceeds* can be paid to beneficiaries

The impact of *taxes on life insurance policies*

How to *estimate* your *life insurance needs*

How to *develop an insurance program* which reflects the insurance protection you need

How *inflation is incorporated* into a life insurance program

The steps to *evaluate* which *type of life insurance* is most appropriate for you

How to *select* a competent *insurance agent*

AS A MATTER OF FACT,
I WAS JUST THINKING
ABOUT NEEDING TO GET
MY LIFE INSURANCE
PROGRAM ORGANIZED...

misunderstood, poorly managed, and often wasteful uses of a family's income. Unfortunately, many people who should have substantial amounts of protection have far too little; they are woefully underinsured. At the same time, others have much more life insurance than they need: they are overinsured. The reason why people find it so difficult to evaluate life insurance properly is that there are so many different forms of life insurance offered by more than 1800 companies in the United States. Some life insurance policies are excellent, but others provide very poor insurance protection. Moreover, the costs of competing life insurance contracts vary substantially among companies.

The purposes of this chapter are to explain the basics of life insurance, to develop a framework for calculating the amount of insurance you need (if any), and to provide guidelines for buying the protection at the lowest possible cost.

WHAT LIFE INSURANCE IS ALL ABOUT

Some people think that life insurance is like gambling. From the insured's perspective, perhaps that's so. But from the perspective of the insurance company (the insurer), that is certainly not the case. Insurance companies don't gamble; their work is strictly business, and it is business based on history and math—statistics and probability.

Let us use an example to illustrate how a hypothetical life insurance company might operate. Suppose that the 1000 members of the Loyal Order of the Lost Moose Lodge decide they want to establish a life insurance company for the members. For the sake of simplicity, let's assume that all lodge members are 27 years of age and each wants a policy that pays $1000 if a member dies during the year. The payment will be made to the beneficiary the deceased member has specified.

Recall from Chapter 12 that insurance companies operate under the principle that a large number of people pay in premiums to cover the losses of the unlucky few. It is the pool of paid-in premiums that covers the losses. The question we need answered is: What annual premium must each lodge member pay our proposed Lost Moose Insurance Company to cover the benefits for those who die during the year? To start, we need to find out how many members are likely to die during the next year. The answer has already been made available to us in a mortality table. This table shows, for each age group in the population, how many people may be expected to die during the year in a group of 1000 people that age. Assume we look in the mortality table and find that in a group of 1000 people, all 27 years old, 2 are likely to die during the year. Therefore, the potential dollar losses our Lost Moose Insurance Company might expect next year are:

$2000 = 2 members $\times$ \$1000

⬆   ⬆   ⬆

Potential = Number $\times$ Loss from each death
loss   likely to die

To cover that loss, the company needs to collect \$2000 in premiums. Therefore, each member's annual premium would be:

$2 = \$2000 \div 1000$

⬆   ⬆   ⬆

Annual premium = Total $\div$ Total
losses   members

In real life, the insurance company would charge each customer more than \$2 because it needs to cover the costs of operating the company, selling the insurance, and paying the claims. Also, the firm would want far more than 1000 people in the insured group. By having a very large group of people, the insurance company can better predict likely future losses. Nevertheless, our example shows how the premiums from many individuals are used to pay for the losses of the few unlucky ones. Also, it shows that insurance is not some magic process but a series of mathematical calculations that determine what annual premiums must be charged.

Before we leave our example, try to think what will happen to the annual insurance premium as the members of the Lost Moose Lodge grow older. For example, what will the annual premium be when all the Lost Moose members are 48 years old? Clearly, as our group of 1000 people ages, the number who are likely to die during the next year increases. In fact, our mortality table suggests that at age 48, seven members will probably die during the next year. For the Lost Moose Insurance Company, that probability raises potential losses to \$7000. Consequently, each of the 1000 will have to pay a \$7 annual premium for \$1000 of insurance coverage at age 48.

Some Key Insurance Provisions   Before we continue our discussion of life insurance, let us first define a few key insurance ideas. Each of these provisions is cited throughout the chapter, and it's necessary to understand them in order to understand life insurance.

Face Amount (of Policy)   The **face amount** is the amount that will be paid if the insured dies. When an individual purchases a \$5000 life insurance policy, that \$5000 is the face value and that is what the policy will pay should the person die.

The Insured   The individual whose life is insured by the policy is **the insured.** Usually, the insured selects and pays for the insurance.

Beneficiary   The **beneficiary** or **beneficiaries** are the individual or individuals who will receive payments at the time of the insured's death. The beneficiary can be anyone named by the owner of the policy. If children are named as beneficiaries, some sort of guardianship or trustee arrangement is also necessary. This provision is made outside the provisions of the insurance contract. Also, if the insured is a parent whose children are named as beneficiaries, a beneficiary clause should include any unborn children of the marriage. Without this provision, if a policy is issued naming only Johnny and Susy as beneficiaries, and Billy is subsequently born, he will be excluded from benefits.

For most people, deciding on the beneficiaries is uncomplicated. However, it is a decision that should be reevaluated every few years so that as circumstances change, the beneficiary is still appropriate.

Owner   Generally, the insured is the **owner** of a policy. But the beneficiary or someone else may be the owner. Ownership often involves tax considerations because the proceeds of the insurance will be in the insured's estate if he or she is the owner. Ways to minimize the tax consequences are discussed in a later section. The owner, not the insured (if they are different people), is the person who can make changes in the policy.

Premium   The amount paid to purchase the insurance is called the **premium.** Premiums are generally quoted on an annual basis. The premium is determined at the time the policy is purchased, and the amount of the premium depends on the insured's age and the type of insurance being purchased. There are wide differences in premiums among insurance companies for virtually the same insurance coverage. So shopping for insurance is very important and very worthwhile.

Insurability   To purchase insurance at standard rates (premiums), you must have **insurability;** that is, you must be in good health and not be involved in a dangerous occupation. If you meet these requirements, you are insurable. If you are in poor health or work in a dangerous occupation, you may be uninsurable or have to pay a surcharge to obtain insurance.

Cash Surrender Value   Certain types of policies provide insurance and a savings feature. The buildup in the savings part of the policy is the **cash surrender value.** For now, note that those policies that have a cash value can be surrendered, or cashed in, for the value of the savings accrued.

Rider   Often, a policy will have another policy attached to it—usually for a specified time period. The insurance added to the basic policy is called a **rider.**

Proceeds   The **proceeds** are simply the amount paid out by the life insurance company. If the insured should die, it would be the face amount of the policy plus premium refunds, terminal dividends, and any interest, less any policy loans. If the insured terminated a policy with a cash surrender value, it would be that cash value.

Double Indemnity   **Double indemnity** is a provision in a life insurance policy that stipulates that the death benefit will be doubled if the insured should die accidentally.

Why Buy Life Insurance?

Purchasing a life insurance policy can provide at least two, and with some insurance policies three, benefits. First and foremost, if the insured dies prematurely, proceeds from that life insurance policy can replace part or all of the insured's income that has now ceased because of death. Explained another way, it replaces the stream of income that the insured would have earned had he or she survived. Life insurance provides *protection against the loss of income due to premature death.* Second, the proceeds from life insurance can be used to pay the costs of settling a deceased person's financial affairs or estate. Typical expenses are burial costs, debt repayment, estate or inheritance taxes, and legal and probate expenses. Life insurance provides *money to settle the deceased individual's estate.* Of much less importance, some insurance policies provide a third benefit: the policy accumulates cash value during the years it is owned (more on this later). If the insured survives, that investment component can be withdrawn. For example, when the insured retires, it can provide retirement income. Life insurance can provide *a savings plan.*

TYPES OF INSURANCE CONTRACTS

One thing that makes life insurance an involved, and at times a confusing, topic is the tremendous range of different policies that are available. While details of individual policies vary, they all have one common component: each provides death protection in the event of the insured's death. Some policies add a second common component, an investment segment called the cash value.

Pure Death Protection All life insurance policies provide pure **death protection**—a promise to pay some amount should the insured die while covered by the policy. With some policies, the death protection remains *fixed* during the life of the policy. It starts at some dollar amount and remains unchanged throughout the policy's life. Should the insured want to increase the dollar amount of that protection, some life insurance companies must issue a new policy. Often, it also may be necessary to issue a new policy to decrease that protection. Other insurance policies provide *flexible* death protection under which the dollar amount varies during the life of the policy. On some, the changes in death protection are stated in a schedule that comes with the policy when you buy it. On others, the insured has the option of raising or lowering the death protection. Frequently, the policy will prescribe limits on how large a change the insured can make.

Investment Feature or Cash Value Some insurance policies provide an investment component whereby part of the annual premium is invested in an account, the **cash value**, from which the insured can withdraw money at some point. The insurance company pays interest on the account balance. Here, also, the dollars that are contributed from the premiums each year can be either *fixed* or *variable.* When they are fixed the insured cannot designate that more or less money than initially specified can be invested in the account. Also, the insurance policy will contain a detailed schedule that specifies what the policy's accumulated cash value will be after the owner has maintained it for a set number of years. For example, the schedule on a $10,000 life insurance policy might show that 3 years after the policy is purchased, its cash value is $156. After the insured has owned it 10 years, the policy's cash value will be $1400.

Life insurance policies that have a *variable* cash value allow the insured to determine how rapidly the cash value will accumulate. That is, the insured decides how large an annual premium he or she wants to pay each year. In years when the payment is relatively small, most or all of it will be needed just to cover the cost of the policy's death protection. If the insured invests only a limited amount, little if any is invested in the policy's cash value; it will grow rather slowly. Quite the opposite happens when the premium payment is large; then, a sizable dollar amount can be invested in the cash value, and that means it will increase much more quickly.

Having discussed the two common features in general terms, we will now see how they are combined in the six major types of life insurance policies. This background is essential for you to make an informed choice as to which insurance contract is best for your specific circumstances.

Level Term Insurance

Level term insurance provides only death protection; it has no cash value component. It gives a fixed dollar amount of protection for the *term*, or set period, of the policy. During this term, the annual premium for that fixed amount of coverage remains unchanged. Typical terms for such insurance are 1 year, 5 years, 10 years, and 20 years. That means if an individual purchases a $10,000, 5-year term policy, its death protection remains at $10,000 and its annual premium will be unchanged for the next 5 years. But after 5 years, the insurance policy will have to be renewed, and at that time the premium will rise. Why? Because the insured person is now 5 years older and therefore more likely to die during the next 5-year term. To cover that increased probability, the premiums rise to cover those larger expected losses. Had it been a 1-year term policy, the annual premium would have been fixed for only 1 year. So, each year the premium will rise as the insured becomes older.

Many insurance companies refuse to offer term insurance once you are over 65. They have several reasons for limiting its availability. First, as you can imagine, the cost of term insurance will be quite high when everyone in the insured group is over 65 years of age; the annual losses, or death benefit payments, will likely be sizable. Many policyholders will probably decide to drop their policies because of the high premiums. The number of people who still want the product will be limited. Second, as the next section will discuss, many people find that their need for life insurance coverage decreases once they reach 65 years of age. That further thins the ranks of potential buyers who are interested in continuing their insurance after they reach 65. Given a limited demand, many insurance companies have decided not to offer term insurance for people who are past 65.

Decreasing Term Insurance

Decreasing term insurance, like level term coverage, only provides death protection without any investment component. This kind of coverage differs in that its annual premium remains fixed even as the insured grows older. In order to allow that, the dollar amount of death coverage is variable:

it declines as the insured grows older although its annual premium remains the same as when the policy was purchased.

How rapidly does the death coverage under a decreasing term insurance policy decline? Insurance companies offer policies in which the coverage drops from the initial amount to zero over a period of 5 to 30 years. An example is the best way to illustrate the decreasing coverage feature. Suppose Wanda Wane purchased a $10,000 decreasing term insurance policy that will drop to zero over a 20-year period. Her initial annual premium started at $450 and it remains that for each of those 20 years. While her death protection started at $10,000 for the first year, it falls each year so that, by the tenth year, it is only $7200. Further annual decreases will bring her coverage down to $1000 by the twentieth year. No coverage remains after that because the 20 years are up.

Decreasing term insurance policies are like level term policies in that most are typically not available once the insured individual reaches 50 to 60 years of age.

Ordinary Life Insurance

Ordinary life insurance, which is also called **straight life,** is the type of insurance policy familiar to most people. This policy provides both death protection and an investment component, or cash value. Under the basic ordinary life policy, you pay the same premiums every year during your lifetime and your insurance protection equals the face amount of the policy, that is, the amount your beneficiaries would receive in the event of your death. Each year, a portion of the premium payment is used to provide the death protection, while the balance is accumulated as part of the policy's cash value. Since this split of premiums is part of the policy, the insured cannot choose whether or not to contribute. Consequently, we say that it is a "forced savings" plan. Once you purchase an ordinary life policy, your annual premium and the insurance protection remain unchanged as long as you continue the policy.

The buildup, or accumulation, of cash value in an ordinary life insurance policy is possible because the annual premium exceeds the amount needed to provide death protection during the early years of the policy. For example, for someone aged 25, the premium for $1000 of ordinary life may be $14 per year and the premium for 1-year term insurance may be $2. The difference, $12, represents what you might consider a "reserve" on the straight life policy. Most of the reserve goes into the cash value or the savings part of the policy. It is the accumulation of this reserve in the policy's early years that permits the fixed annual premium during the entire life of the insured. In effect, the policyholder pays more than the cost of insurance coverage at the beginning of the policy and less than the cost of coverage during the later years. Exhibit 14-1 uses the example of $1000 of insurance coverage for a 25-year-old male to contrast the fixed premium of an ordinary life insurance policy with the increasing annual premiums for an equivalent level term insurance policy.

One question that Exhibit 14-1 raises is: How can the premium on the ordinary life policy remain at $14 when, in later years, the premium for term

EXHIBIT 14-1

Comparison of ordinary life and level term premiums for $1000 insurance.

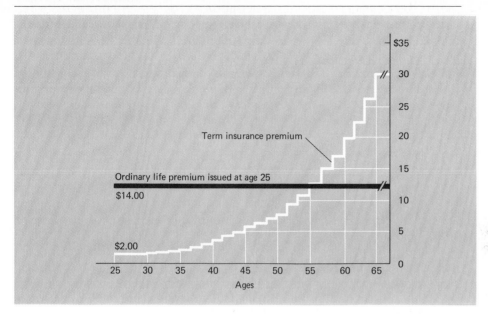

insurance is substantially higher? The answer is: the accumulated cash value. To demonstrate this point, we will use Exhibit 14-2 to illustrate graphically the accumulation of cash value in an ordinary life policy. We use the example from Exhibit 14-1 and assume that Calvin Covered bought a $1000 ordinary life policy at age 25. He plans to continue to pay the annual premium until age 60, at which time the policy will have a cash value of $430. This is shown in Exhibit 14-2. In the euphoria of learning about that increased cash value, Calvin inadvertently steps in front of a crosstown bus. Unfortunately, he becomes a traffic statistic, so the insurance policy pays $1000 (the policy's face value) to Calvin's beneficiary. But where does the $1000 come from? The $430 is from Calvin's investment element or cash value; the balance, $570, is from the policy's death protection element. That means that when Calvin reaches age 60, his $14 annual premium has to purchase only $570 of death protection and to make that year's contribution to the policy's cash value. Now can you see why the $14 premium was sufficient? From the diagram in Exhibit 14-2, it is clear that as the cash value accumulates (lower half of exhibit), the required death protection (top half of the exhibit) declines. That is why the premium can remain constant. As the insured becomes older, the ever-rising cash value will pay an increasingly larger part of the policy's total benefit should the insured die.

An immediate question is: What happens to the cash value if the insured does not collect the insurance? In a later section, we will discuss those options in detail, but for now, suffice it to say that Calvin could surrender his policy—losing his insurance protection when he does so—in order to collect its accumulated cash value. And, as Exhibit 14-2 illustrates, the longer Calvin waits, the higher the accumulated cash value will be.

All ordinary life policies contain a detailed schedule showing the dollar amount of the policy's accumulated cash value. For each year that the policy has been in force, it shows the policy's cash value. Thus, a $1000 whole life policy, purchased by a 25-year-old male, might have a $70 cash value after 10 years of ownership; after 20 years, it might be worth $200. With most policies, the accumulated cash value and the face value are equal when the insured is 95 to 100 years old. Thus, if Calvin Covered continues his payments on that $1000 policy, its cash value will equal $1000 when he is 95 or 100 years old.

Limited-Pay Life Insurance

Limited-pay life insurance provides both death protection and a cash value investment component. Like ordinary life, the policy can be continued until the insured reaches 100 years old or dies. And, like ordinary life, each year the policy remains in force and the premiums are paid, the cash value continues to grow.

But the two policies differ in the number of years the premium must be paid. Ordinary life requires payments right up to the day the insured dies, surrenders the policy, or reaches 100—whichever event occurs first. But, as the name suggests, a limited-pay life policy requires only that the premium be paid for a prescribed period. For example, it might be "20 pay life," which requires that premiums be paid for the next 20 years. Because all the policy's

EXHIBIT 14-2

Accumulated cash value on $1000 ordinary life
policy purchased at age 25.

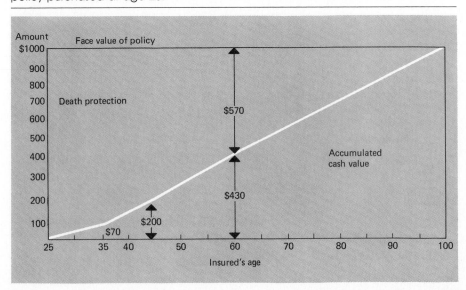

ONE HUNDRED PERCENT
COVERAGE OF YOUR FINANCIAL
WORTH IS CERTAINLY RECOMMENDED..
..BUT I'M NOT SURE WE CAN
WRITE A $50 INSURANCE POLICY....

premiums will be paid in that period, the policy's insurance protection continues until the insured is 100 years of age or dies. Another variation might be a "paid up at 65" policy. Here, the insured pays premiums until age 65 but the protection continues until death or age 100.

Necessarily, with a limited-pay policy, the insurance company has a shorter period in which to collect the necessary premiums to provide both the policy's death protection and to accumulate its cash value. The annual premium on a limited-pay policy will then be higher than the premium for an ordinary life policy of similar size. Because of those higher premiums, a limited-pay life insurance policy provides less insurance protection for each premium dollar than does an ordinary life policy.

Endowment Policy

An **endowment policy** emphasizes the investment component first and death protection second. While the policy combines the two features, it emphasizes the accumulation of a sizable cash value within a relatively short time; death protection is a secondary concern with this type of policy. An endowment policy specifies a set period: 10 years, 20 years, and to age 65 are typical time-spans during which a fixed annual premium must be paid. If the designated payments are made, at the end of the period the accumulated cash value equals the policy's face value. That is a much more rapid buildup of the cash value than that of either ordinary life or limited-pay life. The "insurance protection" arises if the insured dies during the specified accumulation period; then the policy's face amount is paid to the beneficiary.

An example will illustrate. Assume that Carol Careless purchases a 20-year $1000 endowment policy that calls for annual premiums of $43. If she pays the premium each year, she can surrender, or cash in, the policy for

$1000 after 20 years. But suppose that in a moment of euphoria upon finding that the policy's cash value is $400 after 10 years, Carol drives through a red traffic light. At that point, the policy will pay $1000 to her beneficiary. Of that total, $400 is from the policy's cash value and $600 is from the policy's death protection. Had Carol ignored that stop-light one day after purchasing the policy, it would still have paid $1000 to her beneficiary. Of course, nearly all of that $1000 would have been death protection.

Because an endowment policy is designed to accumulate a rather large cash value within a reasonably short time, the annual premium for a given-sized policy is very high. The cost of providing life insurance protection through an endowment policy is much more expensive than it is through a limited-pay policy, which itself is more expensive than a straight life policy.

Universal Life Insurance

Universal life insurance combines death protection with an investment component. But, unlike the three previous cash value insurance policies—straight life, limited-pay life, and endowment—that combine the two, this policy has considerably more flexibility. First, the death protection component is flexible; each year, the insured can raise or lower the death protection the policy provides. Some policies require that the insured take a medical examination to prove insurability if the added amount of protection is large. But the feature does allow you to raise or lower the protection element as your insurance needs change.

The second flexible feature is the annual premium. All the policies discussed thus far have a set premium prescribed in the policy. With universal life, the insured can, within limits, decide how large a premium he or she wants to pay each year. You might decide to pay a large premium this year; yet one year later, if your finances were strained, you could elect to pay a smaller premium. What happens to the additional premium when your payment is sizable? First, the insurance company always removes an amount sufficient to cover the cost of your requested death protection. Whatever premium remains is invested in the policy's cash value. In years when premium payments are large, the cash value will accumulate rapidly. When the premium payment is small, the growth in cash value is limited. In fact, if you have a really difficult year, you can skip the premium. Provided your policy's cash value is sufficient, the insurance company will deduct enough from the cash value to cover that year's death protection. Moreover, you can continue skipping annual premiums until you have exhausted the policy's cash value.

Lest we leave you with the idea that the annual premium decision is entirely up to you, we must point out that this is not true because most insurance companies require a minimum initial premium to begin the policy. Furthermore, most provide a "suggested annual premium" when the insurance policy is purchased. But most companies do not require that you pay the suggested premium each year. Many insurance companies also limit the amount of the premium you can pay for a given amount of death protection. Thus, they prevent someone from purchasing a policy with limited death protection while making very large premium payments. If a company should premit this, the insurance program would be first and foremost an investment plan with only a minor insurance element.

Most universal life policies do not pay a fixed rate of return on the investment component. Instead, they may tie that rate of return to the current return for U.S. Treasury securities. As the return on those securities changes, the return on the investment component also changes. Over a period of time, the rate of return may be quite variable, depending upon what happens to the return on U.S. Treasury securities. Predicting the likely future return on the investment component will be difficult, if not impossible.

The combination of flexible premiums, coupled with a variable rate of return on the investment component, makes it difficult to predict a particular policy's future cash value. Unlike the three previously discussed policies, which have schedules that spell out a policy's cash value, a universal life policy has no set schedule. If you make large premium payments with sizable additions to the policy's cash value and if the policy's rate of return remains reasonably high, then, after 5 to 10 years, the accumulated cash value will be large. On the other hand, the combination of limited annual premium payments, coupled with a low rate of return, can mean that the accumulated cash value remains small.

Universal life insurance can be continued until the insured reaches 95 or 100 years of age. As long as the annual premium is paid each year, or as long as the policy has sufficient cash value to cover the annual premium, the insurance coverage continues. Unlike straight life or limited-pay life, the accumulated cash value on a universal life policy will not necessarily equal the policy's face value at age 100. For one thing, since the policy's face value is flexible, it may have been altered several times during the time the policy has been in force. Second, given the flexible premium feature, there may have been substantial additions to the policy's cash value, moderate additions to that cash value, or almost no additions to that cash value. Last, depending on the rate of return, the cash value may have increased rapidly, moderately, or slowly during the years it has been accumulating.

PARTICIPATING AND NONPARTICIPATING INSURANCE CONTRACTS

The life insurance industry consists of two major types of organizations: stock insurance companies, which are owned by stockholders, and mutual companies, which are owned by the policyholders. Any profit earned by a stock company goes to the company's shareholders, whereas, with a mutual company, the profit belongs to the policyholders. Generally, stock companies issue nonparticipating policies; mutual companies issue participating contracts.

Participating Insurance **Participating policies** are insurance contracts that return any premium overcharges to the policyholders in the form of *nontaxable* **dividends**. Since the premiums for insurance are based on estimates, it is impossible to set the premium in advance at the exact figure that the insurance will finally cost. Investment earnings, actual mortality experience, and expense of operations (the three factors that determine insurance costs) are unknown and only approximately estimated at the time the insurance is sold. Mutual companies approximate these costs with an overestimate, and when the actual costs are determined at the end of the year, the overcharges are returned to the policyholders in the form of dividends.

Dividend Options   The dividend paid on participating policies can be used in a number of ways. The available alternatives are (1) payment in cash, (2) reduction of premium for the next period, (3) deposit with the company to earn interest, (4) purchase of paid-up additional insurance, and (5) purchase of a 1-year term insurance. Option 5 has the effect of increasing the face amount of the policy by an amount equal to the added term coverage.

While each of the options has something to recommend it, the only ones that should be seriously considered are options 2 (reduction of premium and 5 (purchase of term insurance). By using the dividend to reduce the premium, insurance costs can be reduced. This is desirable as long as adequate insurance has been purchased. By using the dividends to purchase "paid-up adds" (the technical nickname) or term insurance, you can obtain increased insurance protection at a small additional cost.

Nonparticipating Insurance   **Nonparticipating policies** do not rebate any overcharges to the policyholder. Any charges in excess of the true cost of the insurance accrue for the benefit of the insurance company's stockholders, not its policyholders.

Usually, the initial premium will be lower for a nonparticipating policy. However, in the long run, participating policies usually have a lower net cost, resulting from the dividend payments. When comparing insurance policies, do not be misled by the seemingly lower initial cost of the nonparticipating policies.

STRATEGY

Since participating insurance policies have historically cost less than comparable nonparticipating policies, you should carefully compare the net cost (premium minus dividends) of participating policies with the cost of a nonparticipating policy before deciding on either one.

MAJOR POLICY PROVISIONS

The insurance policy is a very technical instrument that has a number of important provisions that affect the insured and the beneficiaries protected by the contract. There are two basic types of provisions that you must consider: provisions that affect the policy while it is in force, and those that may take effect when the insurance is terminated either because the insured dies or the policy is surrendered for its accumulated cash value.

Nonforfeiture Options

Four of the insurance policies that include a cash value component—ordinary life, limited-pay life, endowment, and universal life—offer several

nonforfeiture options to ensure that the insured would receive the policy's accumulated cash value should he or she stop paying the premiums. These options guarantee that if you stop paying the premium on an insurance policy, you won't lose the cash value it has accumulated up through the last premium payment. The three basic nonforfeiture options are (1) to surrender the policy for cash, (2) to convert it to paid-up insurance, or (3) to use the cash value to purchase extended term insurance. Some contracts also have automatic premium loans which can be considered a fourth nonforfeiture option.

Cash Surrender Value With this option, the owner receives a check for the cash value of the policy. To receive the payment, you must return the policy to the company; that is, you "surrender" the policy. The advantage of this option is your receipt of the cash. The disadvantage is that the insurance protection ceases with your surrender of the policy.

Paid-Up Insurance The owner has the option of converting the life insurance policy to paid-up status. The company uses the accumulated cash value from the current policy as a single premium to purchase a new policy requiring no additional payments. By electing this nonforfeiture provision, the insured continues to receive protection, although it is reduced, but no longer pays any premiums.

Extended Term Insurance Under this option, the cash value is used to purchase term insurance equal to the policy's face amount for as long as the cash value lasts. For example, a person aged 45 with a $10,000 policy having a cash surrender value of $3000 may use it to purchase extended term insurance in the amount of $10,000 for 20 years without additional premium payments. This option is desirable when you want to continue the original insurance protection. Its disadvantages are the loss of the cash value and the limited duration of the protection. Once the extended term period is over, the policy expires with no value.

In most instances, extended term is selected by individuals who believe they are going to die in a short time; they withhold payments on their whole life policies and exercise the extended term option. The insurance companies are faced with the problem of adverse selection. That is, poorer risks select this form of insurance. Consequently, the insurance companies set the rate per $1000 somewhat higher for extended term insurance purchased under this option than for term insurance purchased under ordinary circumstances.

Exhibit 14-3 gives approximate values for the three nonforfeiture options at various ages for an ordinary life policy issued to a person 25 years of age.

Automatic Premium Loan The automatic premium loan is sometimes considered a fourth special nonforfeiture option. With this feature, when you miss a premium payment, the insurance company automatically borrows that payment from the cash value of the policy in order to keep the

EXHIBIT 14-3

Approximate nonforfeiture values per $100,000
of insurance for an ordinary life insurance policy
issued at age 25.

PREMIUMS PAID TO AGE	CASH VALUE	PAID-UP INSURANCE	EXTENDED TERM INSURANCE
30	$ 2,340	$ 9,050	7 years–183 days
35	7,850	26,200	20 years–300 days
40	15,200	39,400	25 years–110 days
45	23,400	54,600	24 years–211 days
55	40,500	64,300	20 years–175 days
65	61,000	86,700	16 years– 83 days

contract in force. For example, on a $10,000 policy with a $200 annual premium and $3,000 of cash value, that premium would be borrowed from the cash value. After one such automatic premium loan, the company would pay $10,000 less the $200 loan, or $9,800, if the insured should die. If the insured should surrender the policy, the cash value would be $2,800.

Policy Loan Provisions

Life insurance policies that have a cash value include **policy loan** provisions: they permit the policyholder to borrow the cash value at 5 to 10 percent simple interest; the interest rate charged depends on when the policy was issued. This is frequently cited as a benefit of owning life insurance with a cash value. But that claim is somewhat misleading, since the insured is, in fact, borrowing his or her own money. For example, an individual who has a $10,000 policy with $3,000 of accumulated cash value may borrow $3,000 without a credit investigation and with no stipulated repayment schedule. If the insured should die while a loan is outstanding, the face amount will be reduced by the amount of the indebtedness. In this example, the beneficiary would receive $7000 in the event of the insured's death.

Extra-Cost Policy Provisions

Buying a life insurance policy is similar to buying a new car. You can buy a stripped-down model or one having special options which will cost substantially more. Unlike the special options on a car, which are paid for only once, the special features on a life insurance policy must be paid for every year for as long as you have the policy. As a result, it is very important to analyze the options carefully when buying a policy. The most common extra provisions are (1) waiver of premium, (2) guaranteed insurability, and (3) accidental death benefit.

Waiver of Premium If you select the **waiver of premium** option, the insurance company will pay the premiums on your life insurance policy if you become disabled and can no longer work.

Given the limited cost of this option, it is probably worthwhile for most people. But carefully review how the contract defines "disability." Some are so restrictive that you might have difficulty qualifying for the waiver.

Guaranteed Insurability This option of **guaranteed insurability** guarantees gives you the right to purchase additional life insurance, at specified intervals, at some multiple of the face amount of the original policy, without providing evidence of insurability. A policy for $10,000 issued at age 25 may permit you to buy an additional $10,000 every 3 years until the total amount of insurance reaches $60,000. The benefit of this provision is that if you develop a serious health problem after buying the initial policy, you will still be able to purchase additional insurance at standard rates in the future. The feature is most valuable for younger people who are beginning an insurance program and who expect their need for life insurance will increase in the future.

STRATEGY

If you expect your future insurance needs will rise, you should consider this option. It is highly recommended if you have symptoms or a family history of serious health problems.

Accidental Death Benefit The accidental death benefit feature, also referred to as **double indemnity** or **triple indemnity,** stipulates that if, prior to a certain age (usually 65), the insured is killed in an accident, the company will pay double or triple the face amount of the policy. For example, the beneficiary of a person with a $10,000 policy who dies in a plane crash on a regularly scheduled flight would receive not $10,000, but $20,000 or $30,000.

At first glance, this option seems appealing; for a small added premium, a policy's death benefit is doubled or tripled. But if you have a soundly structured life insurance program, the extra protection is unnecessary. A good insurance program should meet all your insurance needs regardless of how you depart this world.

STRATEGY

Avoid the temptation of the double indemnity option; doubling or tripling the coverage for select circumstances of death merely duplicates coverage in a well-developed insurance program.

Settlement Options

At the time a life insurance contract matures, either by the insured's death or surrender of the policy, the payment of the face amount can be made in a number of ways other than a lump-sum payment. Each of the **settlement options** has something to recommend it, but care should be exercised in selecting the best method.

Interest Option

With the **interest option,** the proceeds are left on deposit with the insurance company, and the company periodically pays the interest to the beneficiary. This is usually a temporary settlement until the beneficiary has had time to select the best option. *Note:* In the event that the policy was surrendered, rather than maturing as a result of the insured's death, the recipient of the income would be the owner.

Installments For a Fixed Period

Under the provision for **installments for a fixed period,** the company agrees to make payments for a specified number of years or months until the proceeds are exhausted. With a participating policy, this settlement option provides an additional advantage: during the payment period, dividends are added to the remaining balance to be paid.

This option would be appropriate for a beneficiary who can determine that the proceeds will provide a sufficient regular income to support the family during the payment period. It would be suitable, for example, for a middle-aged surviving spouse who must support several teenage children. In

5 or 6 years, when the children's education is complete and they are working, the surviving spouse with a skill or trade can return to work. This option would not be appropriate, however, for a beneficiary who needs an income for life because she or he cannot earn an income; the proceeds could be depleted while the beneficiary is still alive.

STRATEGY

The option of installments for a fixed period is best suited for a beneficiary who requires an annual income for a set period and who can specify the length of that period with some degree of certainty.

Installments of a Fixed Amount   Installments of a fixed amount are just a minor variation of the installments for a fixed period. Instead of specifying the number of periods, the beneficiary specifies the amount of each periodic payment, and the payments will be made until the proceeds are depleted.

We cannot see any circumstances in which this option would be superior to the installments for a fixed period.

The Life Options   None of the previous three options is designed to guarantee an income for the life of the beneficiary. Insurance companies using the same principles of risk sharing that are applicable in all other kinds of insurance can guarantee a life income for a beneficiary even if the beneficiary lives longer than the funds would provide for. This is the case simply because some people will die before they have exhausted their funds. Some form of life income option is desirable for people who need the security of a guaranteed lifetime income.

A straight **life income option** guarantees the income for as long as the beneficiary lives. If an individual were to start receiving payments of $100 per month under this option and should die after receiving one payment, most of the money would be lost. If the initial principal were $10,000, then $9,900 would revert to the insurance company upon the beneficiary's death. While this option provides the largest monthly benefit of the guaranteed settlement options for life, there is a distinct possibility that the beneficiary may die before payment of the original principal is completed. This loss can be avoided; the life option can also be written with guaranteed payments for a stated period, such as 10 years, or with a lump-sum cash refund feature. Had a 10-year guaranteed period been selected in this example, the monthly payment would continue to be made to another designated beneficiary for the duration of the 10 years. Had the lump-sum option been selected, $9900 would be paid to the beneficiary's heirs.

The payments under either the guaranteed payment option or the refund option are slightly smaller than would be received from a straight life option. The refund guarantee options are advantageous, however, if the beneficiary dies shortly after payments start; in that case, the principal amount will not be sacrificed but will be distributed to the beneficiary's heirs.

STRATEGY

Beneficiaries who are near retirement age should select one of the life options with a refund or guarantee feature.

Taxes on Life Insurance

We will discuss the effects of two types of **taxes on life insurance:** federal and state income taxes and federal estate taxes. For each tax, we will examine the potential tax liability in three different life insurance situations:

First, the taxability of the proceeds paid to beneficiaries upon the death of the insured

Second, the taxability of the cash value the policy owner receives when the insurance policy is surrendered

Last, the taxability of the interest earned on the cash value while it is accumulating in the insurance policy

Life Insurance Death Benefit The proceeds a life insurance policy pays when the insured dies—the **death benefit**—are exempt from both federal and state income taxes. This is true regardless of who is named as the policy's beneficiary. Thus, if Marvin Mishap dies while covered by a $10,000 life insurance policy, the $10,000 death benefit will not be subject to either federal or state income taxes.

Two factors determine whether the death benefit from a life insurance policy is subject to federal estate taxes. First, who owned the policy? If anyone other than the insured owned it, there will be no federal estate taxes. Thus, in our previous example, if someone other than Marvin had owned the policy (such as his spouse or his children) the $10,000 will not be part of Marvin's estate and therefore will not be subject to estate taxes. Had Marvin owned the policy, that $10,000 would be included in his gross estate. Depending on the size of that estate, there may be federal estate taxes. The top section of Exhibit 14-4 summarizes the tax treatment for a life insurance policy's death benefit.

Cash Value from a Life Insurance Policy If you surrender a life insurance policy for its cash value, you pay income taxes only on that portion of the cash value that exceeds the combined premiums you paid while you owned the policy. Let's illustrate with an example. Assume that Lizz Lucky surrendered her life insurance policy for its $980 cash value. During the 10 years she owned the policy, she paid annual premiums of $133: $1330 in total. She owes no income taxes because the cash value was less than the total premiums she paid. But suppose, that instead of $980, her policy's cash value had been $1530. Now Liz would include $200 in her income and pay taxes on that amount. There is no federal estate tax on a life insurance policy's cash value. The middle section of Exhibit 14-4 summarizes the taxability of a life insurance policy's cash value.

EXHIBIT 14-4

CHAPTER 14

447

LIFE INSURANCE

Taxability of proceeds from a life insurance policy.

SITUATION	POLICY OWNER	INCOME TAX	ESTATE TAX
Death of insured	Insured	None	Included in insured's estate
Death of insured	Other than insured	None	None
Surrender for cash value	Anyone	Only on the excess of cash value over the total premiums paid	None
Interest on policy's cash value	Anyone	None	None

Interest Earned While Accumulating a Policy's Cash Value   During the period a life insurance policy is in force, all **interest on its cash value** is sheltered from taxes. That means that you do not have to pay income taxes on that interest, so the entire amount can be added to the policy's cash value. As long as the interest continues to accumulate in the policy's cash value, it remains sheltered from income taxes. There would be no estate tax on that interest while it is accumulating. The bottom half of Exhibit 14-4 summarizes the taxability of the interest earned on the policy's cash value.

DETERMINING YOUR LIFE INSURANCE NEEDS

Rather than just pick some arbitrary amount of life insurance and hope for the best, or worst, leaving your survivors also "hoping for the best," we suggest a more systematic approach. Some insurance counselors use a rule that tells you to purchase an amount of life insurance equal to several times your salary. Thus, they might advise: Buy life insurance equal to 4 times your annual income. While a rule like this one is appealing for its simplicity, it totally ignores what your special needs may be and it does not consider your present financial position or your financial resources. For some people, such as a single person with no dependents, that much insurance may be woefully excessive. Yet, for someone who has several young dependents, that coverage might represent gross underinsurance. And the solution is not to raise the multiple to 5 or 6 times your salary. Instead, the answer is to consider your insurance requirements on the basis of your unique insurance needs as well as your financial resources. We will call this process the **life insurance needs approach** to estimating your required life insurance coverage.

The Needs Approach

The needs approach concentrates on the two principal benefits of life insurance: settling a deceased individual's financial affairs and replacing that individual's income stream that premature death has terminated. For most people, these two benefits can be divided into seven broad categories:

1 Cleanup fund   **5** Income: Middle years

2 Emergency fund   **6** Income: Retirement

3 Mortgage redemption   **7** College education fund

4 Income: Family years

If you have an additional special need, make another category and add it to your list.

We will develop an insurance program for Carl and Connie Green to demonstrate this system. They both are 32 years old and work outside the home. They have one child, aged 2 years. Our example will develop Carl's life insurance needs to provide for his survivors. And when we complete that, we will show how Connie's life insurance needs would be calculated.

Our example has intentionally been made a bit complex so that it demonstrates all seven needs categories. We believe that if you can master a complex example, you can readily estimate the insurance needs given a simpler situation. One final point: We will plan Carl's insurance needs as though something might happen to him tomorrow. It would clearly be inappropriate to base Carl's insurance needs on his likely situation 5 to 10 years from now.

The decision on how much life insurance the Greens need requires that they jointly consider their current standard of living as well as what standard of living they feel the family should have if Carl dies. Clearly, one limiting factor on insurance protection is the amount the Greens can afford to spend on insurance premiums. The next sections will estimate the life insurance coverage needed for each of the seven categories. Exhibit 14-5 summarizes the insurance required for each category.

Coordinating Life Insurance and Social Security As you recall from Chapter 13, survivors of a deceased worker may be able to qualify for Social Security benefits. Typically, those benefits are available to children of a deceased worker until they are 18 years old. A survivor's spouse qualifies only when there are minor children under 16 years old or when the spouse is at least 60 years of age. It is essential that your insurance program be coordinated with Social Security survivors benefits. To the extent that your lost earnings will be replaced by these benefits, life insurance will not have to replace those earnings. To integrate Social Security coverage into your insurance plan, the first step is to estimate the benefits your survivors might receive from Social Security; Chapter 13 outlined how you can estimate those benefits.

Cleanup Expenses Money should be readily available in a **cleanup fund** to pay (1) funeral expenses, (2) the unpaid balance on loans, (3) other debts, and (4) medical expenses where there was a final long illness. Initially, we assume that the entire need must come from life insurance. Later, we will show how the Greens' present financial resources may cover some or all of this amount.

Carl has excellent health insurance, so large medical expenses will not be a concern. The Greens estimate that $8000 would be needed to repay the car loan, other debts, and the funeral expenses. Their cleanup fund of $8000 is shown as the first entry in Exhibit 14-5.

Emergency Fund   An **emergency fund** provides money for the survivors to meet unexpected expenses. Examples include costly, unexpected automobile repairs, major repairs to the home, or a major medical expenditure not covered by insurance. By establishing such a fund, the survivors will have the peace of knowing that they are prepared to handle a financial emergency.

Let us assume that Carl and Connie already have a $2000 emergency fund. But they decide that fund should be raised to $4000 for purposes of insurance planning. We continue our earlier treatment by asssuming that the entire $4000 must come from life insurance. This amount is shown in the second section of Exhibit 14-5. At the end of our discussion, we will show how the Greens' current $2000 fund is incorporated in their insurance plan.

Mortgage Redemption: Repaying the Mortgage   When planning life insurance, we assume that the entire unpaid balance of the home mortgage,

EXHIBIT 14-5

Estimated life insurance needed to settle Carl Green's financial affairs and to replace his income.

REASON FOR INSURANCE	TOTAL AMOUNT NEEDED	SPOUSE'S EARNING	SOCIAL SECURITY	AMOUNT STILL NEEDED	PERIOD NEEDED	POTENTIAL LIFE INSURANCE REQUIRED
		Amount Provided by:				
1 Cleanup fund	$ 8,000	0	$255	$ 7,745	One time	$ 7,745
2 Emergency fund	4,000	0	0	4,000	One time	4,000
3 Mortgage redemption	50,000	0	0	50,000	One time	50,000
4 Family period: Child is under 16	2,000	$1,300	466	234	168 months	39,312
Child is 16 to 18	2,000	1,300	466	234	24 months	5,616
5 Middle years	1,400	1,300	0	100	144 months	14,400
6 Retirement years	1,000	481	444	75	300 months	22,500
7 College fund	4,500	0	0	0	4 years	18,000
Total required life insurance coverage						$161,573

if there is one, will be repaid; part of the life insurance will be earmarked for this **mortgage redemption.** With the mortgage repaid, the survivors have several options: they may stay in the home; they may retain it for a period, then sell it; or they may sell it immediately. For those who have not purchased a home, this section will be blank.

Carl and Connie own a $70,000 house with $50,000 remaining to be paid on their mortgage over the next 20 years. Their mortgage redemption fund is set at $50,000 and is the third entry in Exhibit 14-5.

Income: Family Period   The **family income period** extends from today until the family's youngest child reaches 18 years of age. It has two parts. The first extends from now until the youngest child is 16. During this time, the surviving parent may qualify for Social Security survivor's benefits. The second period runs from the point the youngest child turns 16 until he or she reaches 18 years of age. The division is necessary because, while Social Security survivors benefit payments to the surviving parent cease at the child's sixteenth birthday, the child's benefit continues until he or she is 18. For a family with young children, this family period is frequently the time when the need for life insurance is most crucial. This need will likely be especially large when the surviving spouse does not earn money in any way. Should the primary wage-earner for that family die, the only source of income other than Social Security benefits will be the proceeds from life insurance.

The continued sharp rise in the number of households with two wage-earners has lessened the amount of insurance required because the surviving spouse's earnings add a third income source during the family period. To allow for the earnings of the surviving spouse, we added column 3 to Exhibit 14-5. Those earnings are deducted from the total required income to compute the net amount life insurance must provide. Unfortunately, those earnings may reduce or eliminate the spouse's Social Security benefits. Recall that when a surviving spouse earns more than the maximum allowed income ($4920 in 1983), $1 of benefits is lost for each $2 of income over the limit. There is, of course, no family period for individuals without children, or where children are 18 or older; these persons can skip to the next section.

To compute the life insurance coverage required during the family period, we need an estimate of the after-tax income (amount after income and Social Security taxes have been paid) the family requires. When estimating your income, you need to recognize that with the insured's death, there will be one less member in the family. And the mortgage, if there was one, will be repaid; that further lowers the family's living expenses. These two things will likely reduce the required income to less than what the insured individual currently earns. We assume that Carl and Connie have decided that the survivors need a monthly after-tax income of $2000 if Carl dies.

Next, we need to estimate the length of the family income period. The first part lasts until the youngest child is 16. The second part begins at that sixteenth birthday and runs until the child turns 18. For Carl and Connie, the first part lasts 14 years, or 168 months. The second part extends an additional 24 months; their child will be 18 at that point.

Next we identify where the money will come from. Throughout our needs estimate, we assume that the proceeds from life insurance will be the balancing figure. That is, we will first use Social Security benefits and any surviving-spouse earnings to meet the family's income needs. If they are not sufficient, life insurance will make up the shortfall.

Let us use again Carl and Connie Green to illustrate. Exhibit 14-6 is designed to show the income needs of the survivors, using a time line from the present to the cessation of those needs in the future. The first section shows the $2000 of income that the Greens estimate for the family period. The Greens estimate that Carl's primary Social Security benefit (his primary insurance amount, or PIA) would be $621. Connie could potentially draw a $466 monthly survivors benefit until the child is 16. We say "could" because Connie's $19,000 salary exceeds the maximum allowed income ($4920 in 1983) by such an amount that it completely eliminates her Social Security benefit. Regardless of what Connie earns, the child's survivors benefit of $466 runs until she reaches 18. That benefit is shown in Exhibit 14-6. Connie expects that she would go on working full-time, so her present monthly earnings of $1583 will continue. Before that amount is entered in Exhibit 14-6, it was adjusted for federal and state income taxes plus Social Security taxes; the resulting $1300 of after-tax monthly income was entered

EXHIBIT 14-6

Projected future income needs for Connie Green and child during family years, middle years, and retirement years.

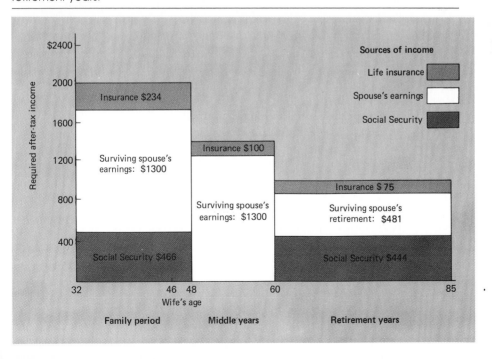

in Exhibits 14-5 and 14-6. Based on total income needs of $2000, life insurance must cover:

$234   = $2000   − $466   − $1300

⬆   ⬆   ⬆   ⬆

Shortfall for = Total required − Social Security − Surviving spouse's
life insurance   income   benefits   earnings

This insurance amount is highlighted in Exhibit 14-6.

In the final column of Exhibit 14-5, we compute how much life insurance is needed to cover that income shortfall. To meet the needs of his survivors, Carl should purchase life insurance equal to:

$39,312   = $234   × 168

⬆   ⬆   ⬆

Required   = Monthly × Number of
life insurance   income   months needed

For Carl Green's survivors, their needs during the second part of the family period are the same as the first; required income and sources of income are unchanged. To meet his survivors' needs, Carl should purchase life insurance equal to:

$5616   = $234   × 24

⬆   ⬆   ⬆

Required   = Monthly × Number of
life insurance   income   months needed

Income: Middle Years   The **middle years income** must cover the period between the point at which Social Security survivors benefits for raising children cease (when the youngest child turns 18) and the point when the surviving spouse can again qualify for Social Security benefits—typically, age 60. During this period, the survivor's entire income must come from two sources: earnings together with proceeds from life insurance. Consequently, the need for life insurance depends heavily on the surviving spouse's earnings. Given limited or no earnings, a large amount of life insurance will be required. Given sufficient earnings, the need for insurance can be slight. Even with substantial expected earnings, you might want to be conservative and provide some life insurance. That can cover situations where the surviving spouse cannot work full-time, or when earnings fall short of what was originally estimated.

The first step is deciding what after-tax income the survivor might require during the middle years. The Greens decided that $1400 a month would be adequate if Carl should die. That estimate recognizes that the house will be fully paid for and that their child will be self-sufficient at this point.

Next we compute how long those middle years will last. It will be relatively short for surviving spouses who are in their mid-fifties. At the opposite extreme, for surviving spouses who are in their twenties or thirties with no children, the middle years period will be lengthy. For Connie Green, that period will run from the time she is 48 (when the child is 18) until she is 60 years old: a total of 12 years, or 144 months.

The middle section of Exhibit 14-6 shows the monthly $1400 that the Greens estimate Connie would need during the middle years. Of that total, $1300 is Connie's after-tax earnings from continuing to work full-time. That leaves $100 to come from life insurance. That same information is shown in columns 2 through 5 of Exhibit 14-5. The amount of life insurance that Carl needs to provide for his survivors is:

$$\$14{,}400 \quad = \$100 \quad \times \ 144 \text{ months}$$

| Required life insurance | = Income required | × Period income will be required |

This amount is shown in the far right column of Exhibit 14-5.

Income: Retirement Period The **retirement period** begins when Social Security benefits again become available for the surviving spouse and runs until the spouse dies. During this period, the survivor's income will come from some combination of three sources: Social Security benefits, pension payments (if the spouse has worked), and proceeds from life insurance. If the spouse has worked extensively so that pension benefits are substantial, less income has to come from life insurance. Surviving spouses who have worked will have compiled their own Social Security work record. Survivors can take whichever benefit is larger: the one based on their own record or the one based on their deceased spouse's record. While we used the earliest point when Social Security survivors benefits can be restarted, spouses may elect to work until age 62 or 65 and draw Social Security retirement benefits based on their own record. Let us assume that the spouse, rather than begin Social Security survivors benefits at age 60, decides to work until age 65. In that case, the survivor will begin receiving Social Security retirement benefits at age 65 on the basis of his or her own record. When you are planning your life insurance needs, figure your survivor's middle years as extending until he or she is 65 years old. At the same time, that individual's retirement period will be shortened because it will not start until age 65.

The first step is to estimate what income the survivor will need during the retirement years. That estimate should recognize that Social Security benefits are generally exempt from income taxes. Also, since the survivor will probably not be working, all work-related expenses cease. The Greens have decided that Connie will need a retirement after-tax income of $1000 monthly.

Next we estimate how many months the retirement period will last. That requires an estimate of how long the survivor will live—not an easy, or necessarily pleasant, task but essential to complete the insurance plan. One way to make this estimate is to consult a mortality table (we discussed this table earlier in the chapter) to see how long the survivor is expected to live.

We assume the Greens, after consulting such a table, decide to use 25 years (300 months) as Connie's life expectancy. That is entered in column 6 of Exhibit 14-5.

The remaining step is to identify where the income will come from for the retirement years. Again we consider life insurance as the balancing amount to cover the shortfall from other income sources. The far right section of Exhibit 14-6 shows the sources for the Greens' required $1000 of after-tax income. On the basis of Carl's present Social Security PIA of $621, Connie will qualify for a $444 monthly survivor benefit. That amount is shown in both Exhibits 14-5 and 14-6. The Greens estimate that Connie's retirement plan from her current employer will provide a monthly after-tax retirement income of $481. After deducting the $444 Social Security and the $481 retirement payments, they find that $75 will have to come from life insurance. Based on those payments extending over 25 years, or 300 months, the required life insurance is:

$$\underset{\substack{\text{Required} \\ \text{life} \\ \text{insurance}}}{\$22,500} = \underset{\substack{\text{Income} \\ \text{required}}}{\$75} \times \underset{\substack{\text{Period income will be} \\ \text{required}}}{300 \text{ months}}$$

This amount is shown in the far right column of Exhibit 14-5.

College Education Fund The **college education fund** is designed to provide money for a child, or children, to complete a university education. Necessarily, the decision as to whether life insurance should provide an education fund raises some difficult questions. Is the child capable of completing college? Will he or she be interested in doing so? Do you want to provide this opportunity? Will the child be ineligible for other sources of financial assistance? Assuming that all the answers are *yes*, the next step is to estimate the size of the education fund. Given today's tuition and fees, one year at a state-supported university can easily cost $4500, while the same year at a private college can exceed $9000. We assume that the Greens feel they want to provide a college fund; they estimate the annual tuition and fees at $4500. To provide for 4 years of attendance, the college fund should be:

$$\underset{\substack{\text{College} \\ \text{fund}}}{\$18,000} = \underset{\substack{\text{Cost per} \\ \text{year}}}{\$4500} \times \underset{\substack{\text{Years in} \\ \text{attendance}}}{4 \text{ years}}$$

This amount is shown at the bottom of Exhibit 14-5.

Estimating What Additional Life Insurance You Need to Purchase
The worksheets developed in Exhibits 14-5 and 14-6 estimate your total required life insurance for all seven major categories. Before you shop for

that much life insurance, you should ask, "Have I already covered part of those insurance needs?" First, you may currently have some life insurance; if so, reduce your total insurance needs by that amount. Second, some of your present assets (such as savings accounts, money-market mutal funds, common stocks or mutual funds) can be used to meet part of your projected insurance needs. The larger those assets, the larger the reduction in the life insurance required. What remains is the net new life insurance you require to meet your projected insurance needs. The process can be summarized as:

Total life insurance required

Less: Current life insurance coverage

Less: Qualifying assets

Equals: Net new life insurance required

The Greens can use a similar worksheet to decide on the additional insurance Carl should purchase. His present job provides $36,000 of life insurance (twice his salary) as a fringe benefit. Further, Carl and Connie Green have $10,573 of assets that could be liquidated to meet part of the projected insurance needs. Therefore, the additional life insurance that Carl will need is:

Total life insurance required: (Exhibit 14-5)	$161,573
Less: Existing life insurance	−36,000
Less: Qualifying assets	−10,573
Additional life insurance required	$115,000

Life Insurance Planning for Women: Is It Different from Planning for Men?

The answer, in one word, is *no*. A woman who must provide for survivors would use the same needs approach that we developed in the previous section. The steps and process for men and women are identical. While our example used Carl Green, it could have just as easily used Connie Green. For each of the seven major needs categories, we would estimate what the survivors need and how many of their needed dollars must come from life insurance. The only difference is that now Carl and the child would be the survivors and the family's needs would be based on them. And it would be Carl's earnings, as the surviving spouse, that would meet part of those income needs.

What can we generalize from this example? That planning a woman's life insurance needs, whether she does or does not work for wages or a salary, requires the same steps as those for planning a man's insurance needs. Granted, the dollar inputs will be different, but the process and steps are the same as those outlined in the prior section.

STRATEGY

Both men and women, whether married or single, should develop an insurance plan based on their respective needs.

Inflation and Life Insurance Needs

A frequently asked question is: How does inflation impact on my life insurance plan? There are two parts to that question. The first concerns how inflation alters your need for life insurance while you are living. Clearly, as inflation pushes up the cost of goods and services, the dollar amounts required for such things as your emergency fund, cleanup fund, and income for the survivors will rise. The life insurance that adequately meets today's needs may be insufficient for tomorrow's needs. To avoid that possibility, you should review your insurance needs along the lines outlined in Exhibits 14-5 and 14-6 every 2 to 3 years. When you do that review, you may find that your required life insurance rises in some of the seven categories and possibly falls in others. For example, the life insurance required to meet the needs for the family period may drop because that period will shorten as the children grow older.

STRATEGY

Review your life insurance needs every 2 to 3 years to check the adequacy of your present coverage; then make any required additions or reductions in insurance coverage.

The second part of the same question is: Given continued inflation, will the monthly income from a deceased individual's life insurance proceeds still adequately meet the survivors' needs a few years after that person's death? Now we are concerned with the impact of inflation in the years following the insured's death. Let us briefly return to the life insurance computations summarized in Exhibits 14-5 and 14-6. First, you should

recognize that all sources of income, other than life insurance, should partially or completely adjust for future inflation. For example, Social Security survivors benefits will rise with the consumer price index. Also, the surviving spouse's earnings should rise with inflation. As a result, life insurance should not have to provide a higher proportion of income in the future.

But will life insurance be able to provide higher benefits to offset inflation? We believe it can. We totally ignored any interest that might be earned on the proceeds from life insurance when estimating required insurance coverage. Those earnings can offset inflation. Let us go back to Exhibit 14-5 and use the $14,400 we estimated Carl needed to meet his survivors' needs during the middle years. In the event something happens to Carl, the example is set up as though Connie would deposit that $14,400 in a non–interest-bearing investment; from that she would draw $100 monthly over the next 144 months. In real life, Connie would deposit it in an interest-bearing account. And those dollars would continue to earn interest right up to the point they were withdrawn. By drawing on the two sources—the original investment and the interest it earned—she could withdraw more than the $100 shown in Exhibit 14-5. In fact, if the interest rate she earned equaled the inflation rate (and it should), she should be able to raise the monthly payment enough to offset inflation. Yes, you say, but what about the 16 years (our plan assumes that Carl might die tomorrow) until she starts drawing the funds? During those years, Connie would also invest that $14,400, and her interst rate should at least match the inflation rate. By ignoring interest earnings when developing the required insurance in Exhibit 14-5, we have, in effect, included an inflation adjustment in the life insurance plan.

SELECTING YOUR LIFE INSURANCE COVERAGE

The needs approach will answer the question: "How much life insurance coverage do I need?" But you still must decide: "Which life insurance policy should I purchase?" Wouldn't it be easy if we could give you a single rule, such as "Always buy level term insurance" or "Always buy limited-pay life," or even, if we could narrow the field, "Never buy an endowment policy"? Sorry: we do not think any such neat rule or rules exist. Given the right circumstance, a case can be made for each major type of insurance. This section develops guidelines that should help you select the insurance that is best for you.

"Buy Your Life Insurance"—Don't "Be Sold" It

It seems straightforward: You decide the amount and type of life insurance you need, then shop for that coverage. But all too often, it goes like this: (1) Ed Easytouch receives a call from Fran Fastbuck, local agent for Last Bet Life Insurance Company; (2) midway through their conversation, Frans says, "Ed, have you considered your financial security lately? We have this great new insurance product, and it is just what *you* need"; (3) Ed protests that he is "kind of short of dough"; (4) "Not to worry, Ed. We will sell you this tiny (call it woefully inadequate) policy to start with. Then, in 5 or 10 years, you can buy more." In the end, Ed probably buys the policy without shopping, without determining whether it meets his needs, or without even estimating what coverage he needs.

Our intent is to make you an informed insurance buyer who decides how much coverage you need, what type of insurance is best for you, and last, but most important, to compare the cost on competing policies. Exhibit 14-7 summarizes the major provisions for each of the six principal types of insurance.

Pure Death Protection Versus Death Protection Combined With a Cash Value

Pages have been written extolling the clear superiority of purchasing an insurance policy that provides only death protection; level and decreasing term policies are examples. Probably an equal number of pages has acclaimed the absolute superiority of insurance policies that combine both death protection and an investment component; examples include ordinary life, limited-pay life, endowment, and universal life. We don't think either position is always correct. You need to analyze your own circumstances to decide which insurance policy is best for your individual needs.

EXHIBIT 14-7

Features of the basic life insurance policies.

TYPE	COVERAGE PERIOD	ANNUAL PREMIUM	AMOUNT PAID AT DEATH	CASH VALUE COMPONENT
Level term	Terms of 1 to 20 years; typically not offered past age 65	Fixed for the term, but rising at each renewal	Fixed for life of policy	None provided
Decreasing term	Periods of 5 to 30 years; typically not offered past age 65	Fixed for period of policy	Declines to zero over period of policy	None provided
Ordinary life	Until age 100 or death	Fixed and continuing to age 100	Fixed at policy's face value	Increases at fixed rate set by policy
Limited-pay life	Until age 100 or death	Fixed; continuing for set period, e.g., 20 years	Fixed at policy's face value	Increases at fixed rate set by policy
Endowment	Set period, such as 10 years, 20 years, or to age 65	Fixed for period of policy	Fixed at policy's face value	Increases at fixed rate set by policy
Universal life	Until age 100 or death	Flexible: within limits, insured can specify	Variable: insured can decide	Flexible; buildup depends on premium and rate of return

The first step in your selection process is to ask: "What kind of insurance can I afford to buy?" The answer to that question may well eliminate some policies as simply too expensive. For the insurance alternatives that are still viable, the next stage is to evaluate each policy's strengths and weaknesses relative to your specific needs.

Can You Afford Life Insurance that Accumulates a Cash Value? The annual premium on an insurance policy that both provides death protection and accumulates a cash value will be higher than that of a policy that gives you just death protection. Exhibit 14-8 dramatically illustrates this point by comparing policies with just death protection (the top two in the exhibit) with those that provide protection plus a cash value (bottom part of Exhibit 14-8). For someone who needs a large amount of insurance coverage, the annual premium on one of the combination policies may be simply too high. The logical solution is to switch part or all of the insurance coverage to one of the first two policies listed in Exhibit 14-8. Regrettably, rather than switch policies, some people reduce their insurance coverage until they can afford the premium. In our opinion, that solution is completely backward; for example, if you need $50,000 of insurance, switch to a policy with just death protection to lower the premium. Only after you have exhausted that option and the premiums are still unaffordable should you reduce coverage further to lower your premiums.

Suppose Carl Green, from the previous example, originally planned to buy $115,000 of ordinary life at an annual cost of $1978. After reviewing their budget, the Greens decide that premium is much too expensive. They

EXHIBIT 14-8

Approximate annual premium* for $25,000 of insurance protection.

TYPE OF INSURANCE	Age When Policy Was Issued			
	20	25	35	45
Level term: 5-year	$ 85	$ 87	$ 107	$ 189
Decreasing term: 20-year	52	56	89	198
Ordinary life	305	348	477	702
Limited-pay life: 20 years	562	618	767	1000
Endowment: 20 years	1018	1022	1062	1143
Universal life	120	152	277	548

*The listed premiums are typical. Your actual premium may be higher or lower; some companies may not offer a policy as small as $25,000.

should consider switching all or part of the coverage to term insurance. Unfortunately, some insurance salespeople might suggest that the Greens use their $400 or $500 of available premium dollars to purchase a $25,000 ordinary life policy. No matter how attractive that policy's cash value, its insurance coverage is pitifully inadequate.

STRATEGY

First, buy insurance coverage to meet your estimated needs. You may find that you must use a more affordable term policy to provide most or all of your desired coverage.

Selecting Term Life Insurance Coverage

Since both level term and decreasing term insurance have a number of characteristics in common, we will first discuss them; later, we will cover the unique features of each type of insurance. Exhibit 14-9 outlines the major strengths and weaknesses that you should consider when deciding whether one or both of these term life insurance policies can meet your insurance needs. While most of the points are straightforward, several of the weaknesses need further explanation.

One weakness—coverage cannot be continued past age 65—will not be a major concern for everyone. Many people, after laying out their survivors' income needs on a time line similar to the one we used in Exhibit 14-6, may find that those income needs after age 65 are limited. The reason is that, often, many of the sources that provide income after age 65 will continue even if the individual dies. Social Security benefits, survivors pension

---

EXHIBIT 14-9

Strengths and weaknesses of level term and
decreasing term life insurance.

Strengths

1 These policies provide the largest amount of insurance protection per premium dollar.

2 Comparative shopping among competing policies is reasonably straightforward.

3 Many professional associations offer these policies.

Weaknesses

1 Many policies do not offer coverage after age 65.

2 Policies do not accumulate any cash value.

3 They do not force you to save.

4 The annual premium becomes sizable once the insured individual reaches his or her mid-fifties.

5 Coverage declines to zero over a set period (decreasing term).

payments, and income from investments are good examples. Since those income sources will continue, at least partially, the income stream that life insurance would have to replace can be rather small. Hence, the need for life insurance for many people after 65 is limited.

How do you decide whether term insurance's restricted availability past 65 is important to you? First, put your income needs on a time line like those in Exhibit 14-6. Then review the retirement period to see how large those needs are when based on today's circumstances. If they are limited, the restricted availability may not be serious.

As to the point that term insurance lacks any investment component, ask yourself if you truly want and need this feature. For example, do you really need a forced saving plan? Or can you accumulate the necessary money for your financial goals through your own initiative? Even if you think a forced savings plan is desirable, you might be able to accomplish the same thing through a substitute stategy, such as direct payroll withholding.

Level Term Insurance   Level term insurance is at its best when you need large dollar coverage for a period that does not extend much beyond the time you reach 60. As Exhibit 14-8 dramatically illustrated, level term insurance is among the least expensive sources of insurance protection. Even the premiums on a $100,000 policy for a 45-year-old male, while not inexpensive, remain within the realm of the affordable. Frequently, there are some real economies of scale such that the cost per $1000 of coverage is significantly less on high dollar-coverage policies. With its fixed death protection, level term insurance is best able to meet needs that require constant dollar coverage for an extended period.

Level term insurance is not suitable when you expect the insurance need will extend well past your sixtieth birthday. The annual cost rises sharply and you probably cannot continue beyond age 65.

STRATEGY

Carefully consider level term insurance to meet your major insurance needs; it provides the high dollar coverage at the reasonable premium cost that many people find essential.

Decreasing Term Insurance   Decreasing term insurance is ideally suited to meet a need you expect to decline systematically over some set period; repayment of a home mortgage and insurance protection while accumulating a child's education fund are good examples. In both cases, the need for life insurance decreases with time—in the first example, because the mortgage balance is being repaid, and in the second, because the required money should be accumulating in the education fund, lessening the reliance on insurance. By selecting a decreasing term policy whose period parallels the declining need, you will provide the necessary coverage with a minimum premium.

Decreasing term insurance does not work well for a need where the required dollar coverage remains constant over time. Nor will it meet an insurance need that you expect will extend beyond your sixty-sixth birth-day.

STRATEGY

Buy decreasing term insurance to meet those insurance needs that decline systematically over time.

Renewable and Convertible: Essential Options When shopping for level term insurance, concentrate on policies that give *you*—not the company—the right to **renew** or not renew the policy at the end of its set term (typically 1, 5, or 10 years). Allowing the insurance company to approve or deny your renewal is highly undesirable because it might deny your renewal when, owing to deteriorating health, you most need insurance and probably can least qualify for it elsewhere.

The **convertible** feature permits you to convert your term policy to either ordinary life or limited-pay life. By converting, you extend coverage past age 65 and you avoid having to prove insurability at that point. Of course, the annual premium on either one of those new policies can be very substantial.

STRATEGY

Make certain that any term insurance you are considering is renewable at *your* option. Also, a policy that permits you to convert to an ordinary life policy is highly desirable.

Selecting Ordinary Life, Limited-Pay Life, and Endowment Coverage

Since ordinary life, limited-pay life, and endowment policies have a number of common features, we will discuss them first. Later, we will examine the features that are unique to each type of insurance. Exhibit 14-10 summarizes the major strengths and weaknesses that you should consider in deciding whether one (or more) of these three policies is suitable for your insurance needs. Most of the points in Exhibit 14-10 are straightforward, but several warrant an explanation.

A major selling point for each of these three types of insurance is the cash value you accumulate while holding the policy. As part of this feature, the avoidance of income taxes on the interest the cash value earns is a plus. The automatic savings (we prefer to call it "forced") factor is also noted. To judge the merit of the cash value feature, ask yourself: "Do I want an investment vehicle?" If the answer is *yes*, the next question is: "Do I need one that forces me to save?" If you answered the first question *no*, cash value life insurance, whether it be ordinary life, limited-pay life, or endowment, is probably not for you. You may have answered no because (1) you presently have other investments, (2) your present financial situation does not permit an investment plan for now, or (3) none of your present financial goals requires an ongoing investment plan. Regardless of the reason, cash value life insurance may not match your present needs.

EXHIBIT 14-10

CHAPTER 14

463

LIFE INSURANCE

Strengths and weaknesses of ordinary life,
limited-pay life, and endowment life insurance.

Strengths

1 Coverage can be continued until age 100.

2 The premium remains constant throughout the life of the policy.

3 The policy provides a forced savings vehicle.

4 The policy accumulates a cash value, which provides an investment component.

5 Income taxes are deferred on any interest earned while the policy's cash value is accumulating.

6 The insured can borrow against the policy's cash value.

7 The annual premium on limited-pay life is paid for only a set period.

8 Endowment policies accumulate a sizable cash value in a reasonably short period.

Weaknesses

1 The annual premium can be prohibitively costly when the required insurance coverage is large.

2 Accumulation of cash value during the first 5 years is very limited; dropping a policy during that time is very expensive.

3 Rate of return on the investment component can be dismally low.

4 Estimating the rate of return on the investment component (cash value) is difficult.

5 Heavy emphasis on the investment component makes an endowment policy extremely expensive insurance coverage.

6 Limiting the payment period raises premiums on limited-pay policies substantially above those for ordinary life.

Even if you are interested in an investment vehicle, purchasing ordinary life, or limited-pay life, or an endowment policy is not a foregone conclusion. You need to consider how good an investment vehicle one of these cash value insurance policies is. After all, if that investment provides a very poor return, you would likely be further ahead if you split the insurance decision:

> Obtain insurance coverage through a policy that just provides death protection, such as term insurance.

> Develop your own investment program to meet your investment needs.

We hasten to add that estimating the rate of return on a cash value insurance policy is involved and requires a number of assumptions. But an extensive, well-documented comparative study of cash value insurance policies in *Consumer Reports*[1] provides some revealing, if not downright discouraging, data. First, the rate of return varies tremendously among companies. Second, the returns range from being reasonable for the best companies to being absolutely dismal for the poorer companies. As an example, the researchers found that if a $25,000 participating policy were purchased by a 25-year-old male and held 29 years, the return could be as high as 6 to 8 percent annually. But, at the opposite extreme, it could be less than 4 percent: that is poor! And had the same policy been held only 9 years, the return could be a resounding minus 3 to 5 percent. That is hardly an investment to be pursued with zeal. In essence, you would do better by throwing the money you would normally pay into the cash value in a shoe box and burying it for 9 years. In fact, to match the above performance, you would need to throw some of that saved money away when you opened the shoe box.

How should you incorporate these findings into your life insurance plan? First, make certain that you really want an investment component. Second, since the rates of return on many policies are very poor unless they are held for close to 20 years, make certain you plan to keep the insurance policy in force for at least that long. Third, if your plans include cash value life insurance, review a comparative study, such as the previously cited one in *Consumer Reports*, to single out policies that provide a reasonable return. Last, carefully compare your likely rate of return on life insurance policies with those available on competing investments.

Insurance advertisements and salespeople frequently extoll the fact that any interest earned on a policy's cash value is sheltered from income taxes. However, the value of that tax shelter depends heavily on your marginal tax rate. For someone in the 40 to 50 percent bracket, that feature has considerable value. But someone in the 20 to 30 percent bracket will find that tax shelter much less valuable. For example, a fully taxable investment offering a 10 percent return may be more valuable to someone with a 35 percent marginal tax rate. Even after paying taxes, the return is still 6.5 percent; that may be as high as, if not higher than, the return on many life insurance policies.

Even if you decide that the tax shelter is attractive, you should fully investigate alternative investments that also provide a shelter against income taxes. One of these alternative investments might provide a rate of return that is considerably better than that provided by a cash value life insurance policy. Present tax-advantaged investment alternatives might include Individual Retirement Accounts (IRA), salary reduction agreements (we discuss both of these in Chapter 21), United States savings bonds (Chapter 18), and mutual funds that concentrate on capital gains (Chapter 20).

---

[1] *Consumer Reports*, "Life Insurance, a Special Two-Part Report," March 1980, pp. 163–186.

Don't be oversold on the tax-shelter feature that ordinary life, limited-pay life, and endowment policies offer. Even with tax sheltering, a dismal return is still a dismal, albeit tax-sheltered, return.

Ordinary Life Insurance   Ordinary life is ideal for someone who wants to combine death protection with an investment component. For those who have difficulty saving money, its required premium payments can encourage savings. Because interest earned on the policy's cash value is sheltered from income taxes, it can appeal to people with marginal tax rates in the 40 to 50 percent range. Finally, with the continued payment of premiums, the coverage can be long term.

A straight life policy is at its worst when it will be held only a few years; with the brief holding period, the rate of return is little short of a disaster. Even with a long holding period, the rate of return on many ordinary life policies is disappointingly low. Also, for someone who needs high dollar insurance coverage, the premiums can be prohibitively high.

STRATEGY

Before selecting ordinary life, make certain that you want an investment component, that you plan to continue the policy for more than 15 years, and that the policy's rate of return is competitive with alternative investments.

Limited-Pay Life Insurance   Limited-pay life insurance is well suited to someone who wants both death protection and an investment component that will be paid for in a limited length of time. The very large premium this entails makes limited-pay life insurance prohibitively expensive for many people. Someone who would be interested in limited-pay life typically wants an investment component, plans to hold it for an extended period, may want a forced savings plan, and is in a high marginal tax bracket.

STRATEGY

Unless you really want the limited-payment feature and can afford its considerably higher annual cost, you will likely be better served by one of the other insurance alternatives.

Endowment Policy   An endowment policy is appropriate for someone who wants an investment that also provides some death protection. When judging an endowment policy, your major question should be: How good an investment is it? Unfortunately, all too many endowment policies just have not delivered a rate of return that is competitive with other investments. We question whether many people wouldn't be as well off by purchasing a decreasing term insurance policy to provide the death protection while accumulating the investment component on their own. By selecting an investment that also provides some tax shelter (we gave some examples in an earlier section), you might get a rate of return considerably higher than you would get from an endowment policy.

As your principal life insurance vehicle, an endowment policy is a very poor choice. Its high annual premium makes it exorbitantly expensive if you need high dollar insurance coverage.

STRATEGY

Unless you really need the forced savings feature of an endowment policy, we think you can do better by selecting your own investment vehicle.

Selecting Universal Life Insurance

Exhibit 14-11 summarizes the major strengths and weaknesses that you should consider in deciding whether universal life insurance would be

---

EXHIBIT 14-11

Strengths and weaknesses of universal life
insurance.

Strengths

1 Within limits, the insured can vary the life insurance coverage a policy provides.

2 The insured can change the annual premium payment to vary the amount contributed to the policy's cash value.

3 The policy's accumulated cash value can be used to pay the annual premium.

4 Income taxes are deferred on interest that accumulates as part of the policy's cash value.

5 The insured can borrow against the accumulated cash value.

6 Coverage can be continued after age 65.

7 The rate of return on cash value is tied, or indexed, to some interest rate set by the financial markets.

Weaknesses

1 Some policies have a very sizable first-year fee to establish the policy; that lowers your return on the cash value.

2 A percentage of each premium payment is used to pay fees and expenses; that further lowers the return on the cash value.

3 Some policies set a minimum cash value balance. Amounts below the minimum receive a low guaranteed rate, while amounts above the mimimum receive the advertised market-determined rate; that further lowers the return on the cash value.

4 The minimum insurance coverage on some policies is $100,000.

5 It is nearly impossible to accurately predict a policy's future cash value given the policy's variable rate of return.

suitable for your insurance needs. Universal life insurance is a relatively recent product that is far more flexible than previous insurance products. While the number of companies offering it is somewhat limited, indications are that it will be sufficiently popular to encourage other companies to develop a similar policy. Certainly universal life has some attractive features. By making a policy's death protection flexible, you can better tailor the coverage to your present needs. Similarly, you can adjust your annual premium from just enough to cover the cost of the death protection up to a large payment that adds a substantial amount to the policy's cash value. Furthermore, the practice of tying the rate of return on the policy's cash value to some market interest rate is a major improvement over more traditional insurance products. But, lest we leave you with the idea that universal life is the answer to everyone's insurance needs, we hasten to note some major drawbacks. First, current policies deduct a substantial fee—typically, 5 to 10 percent—from each premium payment. So less money remains to be invested in the policy's cash value. That reduces your rate of return on the policy's cash value. Next, some policies charge a sizable one-time fee when you purchase the policy. Some also restrict the return you receive on your first $1000 of accumulated cash value. Both requirements further reduce your rate of return. Using a realistic hypothetical example, a study in *Consumer Reports*[2] found that after deducting the fees and restrictions from a universal life policy that advertised a 12 percent return, the actual return with a 4-year holding period would be only 1.8 percent. That is a far cry from 12 percent! When considering universal life insurance, you should critically review a policy's fees and restrictions to see what impact they can have on your realized rate of return.

In our opinion, universal life insurance has some decided advantages over more traditional cash value life insurance products. But, even with its greater flexibility and its improved cost and cash value disclosure, we feel it still appeals to a select audience. To help you decide whether it is for you, you should ask yourself some questions. First, "Do I want an insurance product with an investment component? And, since it does not have a fixed premium, will I make a sufficiently large premium payment to utilize that investment feature?" Second, "Will I need the life insurance for an extended period?" If not, the rate of return on the investment component will be disappointingly low. Third, "Due to minimums on policy size, are my insurance needs sufficiently large to warrant a large policy? Even if they are large, can I afford the suggested annual premium for a universal life policy?" Then, "Will the investment component provide a competitive rate of return?" To answer that, you will need to carefully estimate your likely return after paying any fees, one-time charges, and any investment restrictions. Last, "How does that return compare with what is available on other investments?" It may well be that the policy's net after-expense return is attractive only to people who have a high marginal tax rate.

---

[2]*Consumer Reports*, "Universal-Life Insurance," January 1982, pp. 42–44.

STRATEGY

Despite the current push to sell universal life, you should still evaluate whether you need:

Pure death protection for an extended period
An investment component
The added flexibility that universal life provides

SHOPPING FOR LIFE INSURANCE

There are several things that can help make you a more effective insurance shopper. First, before you begin your search, know how much insurance coverage you need; the estimating procedure outlined in Exhibits 14-5 and 14-6 can help you decide that figure.

Second, review the strengths and weaknesses of the various types of insurance to decide which insurance policy, or policies, will meet your needs. In doing your review, ask yourself whether a particular weakness or strength really applies to you. Where possible, concentrate your coverage in a few policies. Typically, you can make major savings by purchasing one large, rather than several small, policies.

Third, *compare, compare, compare* the premium and features on competing policies. There are tremendous differences in the costs of insurance protection. A study of competing cash value insurance policies, also published in *Consumer Reports*,[3] found, for example, that a 35-year-old male purchasing a $100,000 participating cash value policy could pay a theoretical cost over 20 years of $10,520 for the lowest-cost policy while the highest-cost policy's theoretical cost was a whopping $33,469. More than 3 times as much! Does it pay to shop? A resounding *yes!* An earlier issue of *Consumer Reports*[4] carried a study that compared the annual costs of term insurance policies. While the cost differences were less dramatic, the annual cost on a $100,000 participating term policy for a 35-year-old male with the highest-cost policy was still *more than twice* as expensive as the similar-sized lowest-cost policy. Here, also, the message is, *shop for life insurance.* Exhibit 14-12 summarizes the potential savings that careful shopping for life insurance can provide; it shows representative premiums for high- and low-cost policies issued at the same age. For each one, we calculated what those premium savings would be worth had they been reinvested to age 65.

A good starting point to single out the desirable low-cost policies is a comparative study such as the two previously cited ones in *Consumer Reports*. Also check the commissioner of insurance for your state to see whether the commission has done a comparative cost study of life insurance policies. Another excellent source for comparative cost information is *Best's Flitcraft Compend 1983* (it is revised each year), published by A. M. Best Company. Your local library will likely have a copy.

---

[3]*Consumer Reports*, "Life Insurance, A Special Two-Part Report," March 1980, p. 165.
[4]Op. Cit., February 1980, pp. 79–106.

Last, before you make a final commitment, make certain the annual premiums will fit your budget. It will be one very expensive learning experience if you pay the premiums for several years on some high-cost, cash value life insurance and then decide it is too expensive. Dropping the policy will probably mean a negative, and often a large negative, rate of return on the policy's cash value. You are worlds ahead when you start with and continue a policy you can afford even if it is term life insurance.

STRATEGY

When purchasing life insurance:

Determine your insurance needs
Select the type of insurance that meets your needs
Shop and compare costs on competing policies
Make certain the premium fits your budget

SELECTING AN INSURANCE AGENT

The complexity of life insurance makes professional assistance very important. To obtain a second opinion on the amount of insurance you need a competent life insurance agent to complete a questionnaire with the essential characteristics of the needs approach. The agent who fails to delve deeply into the client's personal financial affairs is more interested in selling a policy than in developing a complete and sound insurance program. Remember, selling insurance will obviously be the agent's primary objec-

EXHIBIT 14-12

Differences in annual premiums for $100,000 nonparticipating policies issued at ages 25, 35, and 45.

AGE OF INSURED	TYPE OF POLICY	Premium* HIGHEST	Premium* LOWEST	DIFFERENCE BETWEEN HIGHEST AND LOWEST	Difference Invested Annually to Age 65 7%	Difference Invested Annually to Age 65 9%
25	Term	$ 420	$ 220	$200	$39,927	$ 67,576
25	Ordinary life	1,350	850	500	99,818	168,941
35	Term	560	260	300	28,338	40,892
35	Ordinary life	1,830	1,300	530	50,064	72,243
45	Term	900	560	340	13,938	17,394
45	Ordinary life	2,750	2,100	650	26,647	33,254

*These premiums are representative of the least and most expensive offered by insurance companies. Actual premiums for individual companies will generally fall in this range.

tive. Nevertheless, a good agent will admit when additional insurance is unnecessary or present coverage is excessive. Finding a good agent requires more than recommendations from friends and relatives. They may be making the same mistakes you are trying to avoid. Some of the most important things to consider when selecting an agent are discussed in this section.

Affiliation With a Large, Reputable Insurance Company   Good agents seem to gravitate toward the better and larger companies simply because it is easier to sell for a well-known firm than for a small unknown organization, and, as a result, they earn more.

CLU Designation   Life insurance sales agents who pass a series of examinations that test their competence in all aspects of life insurance are awarded the designation **chartered life underwriter (CLU)**. While designation as a CLU is not a guarantee that the agent will be helpful, it is a measure of achievement in the field.

The Agent's Sales Presentation   The agent who will not spend an hour assessing your present financial condition and discussing what your insurance needs are is doing a poor job. (Remember that just because you ask an agent to make a sales presentation, you are not obligated to buy insurance.)

The Agent's Willingness to Sell Term Insurance   Because the commissions for term are lower than for ordinary life policies, some agents are extremely reluctant to sell term insurance. This is unfortunate because term represents the best insurance for most people. An agent who is really interested in your welfare should be willing to sell you term insurance.

STRATEGY

After listening to the sales agent's presentation, never sign a policy application for at least 2 days, or until you have completely thought over your decision and what it means. The agent can wait, and so can you.

RUSES AND ABUSES

This section examines some of the common misunderstandings, questionable sales pitches, and outright misrepresentations that are used to sell life insurance.

"Buy Life Insurance When You Are Young"   Sales representatives point out that if you buy ordinary life when you are young, you will obtain a lower premium than if you buy it at a later age. This is very true, but it also means that you are paying for life insurance when you may not need it; also, you will pay that premium for many more years. If you do not need the insurance, do not buy it just to realize a lower premium.

"Do Not Drop In-Force Policies"   The insurance industry has aggressively promoted the idea that there is something sinful about dropping a life insurance policy. If you do not need the insurance, there is no reason to keep the policy in force. If you have insurance but find a policy which is less expensive, take it and drop your current insurance.

"Insurance for College Seniors"   Several major companies aggressively try to sell policies to graduating seniors. The sales pitch makes the policy look like an excellent bargain. In fact, it is often one of the poorest insurance buys on the market. The attraction of these policies is what appears to be a very low first-year premium: $10 is typical. But that is misleading because you are asked to sign a promissory note for the balance of the premium. Later, you have to pay the note plus interest. To make matters worse, most of these policies are very high-cost. Furthermore, most college seniors have little, if any need for life insurance at graduation. That makes it expensive *and* unnecessary!

"Insurance for Children"   Children do not need life insurance. Insurance agents may stress the need for insurance to cover the cost of a funeral if the child should die. To purchase insurance for such a remote possibility represents a very poor way to spend money. Remember, the basic purpose of insurance is to replace income; children do not earn money.

"Sharking"   Sharking is a term that is frequently used to describe a problem that can arise when a salesperson wants you to replace your present life insurance policy or policies. In one situation, an insurance salesperson suggests replacing your present cash value insurance policy or policies with a comparable insurance policy that provides no added benefit for you. The salesperson, however, benefits handsomely: there is a sizable commission on that new policy. But, because it is a new policy, its cash value will build up slowly during the first few years you own it. You may suffer because the cash value on the new policy may not accumulate as rapidly as it would have had you continued your previous policy or policies.

We intentionally said "may" because not all policy replacements are a poor idea. For example, if your prior policy was providing a very low return, the new policy may be an improvement. Nevertheless, any time a salesperson suggests that you swap your present policy or policies, you should carefully review the financial consequences. Ask the salesperson to demonstrate exactly what benefit the policy swap will provide.

A variation on "sharking" is where the salesperson suggests that you surrender your present cash value insurance policy or policies for the accumulated cash value. The salesperson then proposes that you replace them in two ways:

> Purchase term life insurance to provide the death protection the previous policy provided.

> Invest the accumulated cash value in a load mutual fund (the "load" is the commission that the investor pays to buy the mutual fund).

We foresee several possible problems with this swap. First, as we discussed earlier in the chapter, that term insurance can become expensive if you need coverage in your later years. Second, investing in a mutual fund is very different from accumulating a cash value in a life insurance policy. Comparing the returns on the two investments is like comparing apples and oranges. Also, as Chapter 20 will amply demonstrate, there are any number of no-load mutual funds that will probably do as well as the suggested load mutual fund. And no-load funds do not carry the 5 to 8½ percent commission that you must pay to purchase a load mutual fund.

STRATEGY

Carefully evaluate exactly what you will receive if some salesperson suggests you swap your present life insurance policy or policies for a term policy coupled with a load mutual fund.

SUMMARY

1   Life insurance is primarily designed to:

    a replace an insured's income stream that has been terminated because of premature death.

    b Provide money to settle the insured's financial affairs.

2   The major types of life insurance include (a) level term; (b) decreasing term; (c) ordinary life; (d) limited-pay life; (e) endowment; and (f) universal life.

3   Life insurance policies can be either participating or nonparticipating. Participating policies refund a portion of the annual premium as a nontaxable dividend.

4   Dividends on participating policies can be (a) collected as cash; (b) used to reduce the premium; (c) left with the company to earn interest; (d) used to purchase additional paid-up insurance; or (e) used to purchase 1-year term insurance.

5   Nonforfeiture options that protect a policy's cash value include the opportunity to (a) surrender the policy for cash value; (b) purchase reduced paid-up insurance; (c) buy extended term insurance; or (d) obtain an automatic premium loan.

6   Extra-cost options available on many life insurance policies include (a) waiver of premium, (b) guaranteed insurability, and (c) accidental death benefit.

7   The proceeds from a life insurance policy can be (a) left on deposit with only interest paid; (b) paid as installments for a fixed period; (c) paid as installments of a fixed amount; or (d) paid out over the life of the beneficiary.

8   Death proceeds from a life insurance policy are exempt from federal and state income taxes. The cash value from a policy can be either partially or fully exempt from income taxes.

9   Determining life insurance needs requires a dollar estimate for (a) cleanup expenses; (b) an emergency fund, (c) redemption of a mortgage, (d) income for the family period, (e) income for the middle years, (f) income for the retirement period, and (g) a college education fund.

10   The additional life insurance an individual requires is computed as:

Total life insurance required
Less: Current life insurance coverage
Less: Qualifying assets
Equals: Net new life insurance required

11   Planning a woman's life insurance involves the same steps and needs approach as planning for a man.

12   Life insurance planning should be repeated every 2 or 3 years as needs and circumstances change.

13   Selecting the type of life insurance that is best for you requires a detailed anaylsis of each policy's strengths and weaknesses.

14   The cost of life insurance varies so widely from policy to policy that comparative shopping is essential.

15   A good insurance agent should help you estimate your needs and tailor a program to meet them all.

REVIEW YOUR UNDERSTANDING OF

Face amount
The insured
The beneficiary
The owner
Premium
Insurability
Cash surrender value
Rider
Proceeds
Double indemnity
Death protection
Cash value
Level term insurance
Decreasing term insurance
Ordinary, or straight life, insurance
Limited-pay life insurance
Endowment policy
Universal life insurance
Participating policies
Dividends
Nonparticipating policies
Nonforfeiture options
Policy loan

Waiver of premium
Guaranteed insurability
Double or triple indemnity
Settlement options
      Interest option
      Installments for a fixed period
      Installments of a fixed amount
      Life income option
Taxes and life insurance
      Death benefits
      Cash value
Life insurance needs approach
      Cleanup fund
      Emergency fund
      Mortgage redemption
      Income: Family period
      Income: Middle years
      Income: Retirement
      College education fund
Renewable
Convertible
Chartered life underwriter (CLU)
Sharking

DISCUSSION QUESTIONS

1   Can someone other than the insured be the owner of an insurance policy? Under what circumstance(s) might you want to name another person as owner? Why should caution be exercised when naming that owner?

2   What are the two principal reasons for purchasing life insurance? What is the third reason for purchasing selected types of policies?

3 What common component do all types of insurance policies offer? How can that component vary among different types of policies? What second component do some policies offer? How can it vary among different types of policies?

4 What do level term and decreasing term insurance have in common? How do the two differ? Describe an insurance situation where decreasing term would be better than level term insurance.

5 What features do an ordinary life and limited-pay policy have in common? How do the two policies differ?

6 What features of a universal life policy are similar to the features of traditional ordinary life policies? How is the policy different?

7 Gail Gullible is impressed that the annual premium, $275, on a $100,000 nonparticipating "Guaranteed Life" policy is less than the $375 initial premium for a $100,000 participating "Refund Life" policy. Are you equally impressed by the lower premium? Why? Would you suggest anything else to Gail?

8 Why are there nonforfeiture options on some life insurance policies? Under what situation might you use one of those options? Why are these options not included on a term insurance policy?

9 One frequently cited advantage of cash value life insurance policies—ordinary life, limited-pay life, endowment, and universal life—is that you can borrow against the cash value. What are the advantages of that opportunity? Does it have any negative aspects?

10 Sidney Startup estimates that his present life insurance needs are limited but expects they may rise in the future. He is concerned that if his health deteriorates, purchasing additional coverage might be difficult. What would you recommend? Are there any special guidelines Sidney should observe to implement your recommendations?

11 Ted Troubled notes that $24,000 of his present life insurance is intended to provide $100 each month during his survivor's middle years. Ted is worried about what inflation would do to that $100. If he should die today, what would happen to that $24,000 during the 10 years until those middle years begin? What will happen during the 20 years when those middle years' benefits are paid? Are the $100 benefit payments protected against inflation?

12 What are the seven major needs categories that make up the needs approach to estimate the life insurance you require? Can you outline a circumstance where an individual may find that one or more of these categories is zero or not applicable?

13 Stan and Sue Equal, both working outside the home, recently completed a life insurance plan for Stan based on the needs approach. How would you suggest they plan Sue's insurance needs? Why?

14 What is meant by the criticism, "Far too much life insurance is sold and not enough life insurance is purchased?" What are the potential deficiencies of being "sold" a policy rather than "buying" a policy?

15 After a sterling sales pitch by Hal High Commission, Linda Lamb (age 35) is sold on using a $125,000 straight life policy to meet her needs. Hal claims, "You always get back the cash value, whereas term insurance just gives you paid premium receipts." Will Linda always get back her cash value? Are there other things she should consider before buying the straight life policy?

16 Some financial advisors have described universal life insurance as the "ideal" policy for nearly everyone. What aspects of universal life have probably encouraged that positive acclaim? Are there any drawbacks to this policy? Can you decribe the buyers who would likely be well served by this policy?

14-1   Using the needs approach, Rodney Rogers has estimated that his life insurance needs include:

Cleanup fund $3000

Emergency fund $2000

Middle period: $300 per month during 20 years

Retirement period: $200 per month during estimated 30 years

a   How much life insurance should Rodney purchase to cover these needs?

b   In planning that amount, did you assume interest would be earned on the proceeds from that life insurance? Why?

14-2   Marvin Matched (age 25) is considering the following two nonparticipating insurance policies:

TYPE OF INSURANCE	INSURANCE PROTECTION	ANNUAL PREMIUM	CASH VALUE AT AGE 65
Straight life	$25,000	$300	$14,725
Term to 65	25,000	145*	0

*Premium remains constant to age 65.

a   If Marvin plans to keep a policy in force until age 65, what is the total premium for each policy?

b   If he should die at age 45, what would each policy pay his beneficiaries?

c   What are the strengths and weaknesses of each policy?

d   Approximately what rate of return would Marvin have to earn on the premium savings (straight life minus term to 65) from the term policy to match the straight life policy? (*Hint:* You will need Exhibit 1-6 to solve this problem.)

14-3   Wade and Wanda Welch want to estimate how much life insurance Wanda should have on herself to meet her survivor's income needs during the family period. The Welchs have a 6-year-old child. Other details include:

Monthly after-tax income required during period, $1400

Wanda's Social Security PIA benefit, $500

Wade's monthly before-tax earnings, $1235

Social Security benefit to surviving spouse reduced $1 for every $2 that annual earnings exceed $5400

Wade's monthly after-tax earnings, $950

Wanda's monthly before-tax earnings, $1300

The Welches expect Wade would continue to work should something happen to Wanda.

a How much of the monthly income must life insurance provide?

b How many years will the family period last?

c How much insurance should Wanda consider buying?

14-4 Clem and Ann Tomkin estimate that to provide $1200 for each year of Ann's 25-year retirement period, he currently needs $30,000 of life insurance. The Tomkins are concerned about what benefit Ann can actually draw when that period begins in 30 years.

a Assuming that something happens to Clem tomorrow, what amount will that $30,000 have grown to if it is invested at 8 percent? (*Hint*: Exhibit 1-4 may help.)

b Based on your answer in **a**, how much can Ann draw during the retirement period? (Ignore any interest she might earn *during* the retirement period.)

c Does your answer in **b** suggest that Clem can lower his insurance coverage? Why?

14-5 Ed Exact wants to avoid purchasing unnecessary life insurance, so has asked your help. A complete detailed needs analysis indicates that Ed requires $75,000 of life insurance to meet those needs. Other details on his finances include:

Ed's present life insurance coverage	$20,000
Savings account balance	400
Wholesale value of car	750
Balance in common stock mutual fund	6,000
NOW account balance	600

a What amount of life insurance should Ed purchase?

b How can it be less than $75,000 and still meet his needs?

14-6 Delbert Doubtful (age 25) wants you to compute what income taxes might be due on his $25,000 ordinary life policy (annual premiums $300) if:

a He surrenders it after 10 years for its $1780 cash value?

b Delbert should die at age 45 and the $25,000 is paid to his beneficiary?

c He surrenders it at age 65 for its $12,900 cash value?

CASE PROBLEM

Jason and Jan Burns are both 35 years old and they have one child, Sandra, who is 5 years old. Jason is just completing a graduate degree and has recently accepted an engineering position that will pay $18,000 a year. Jan continues to work as a computer programmer, earning $24,000 annually. The Burnses have not done a complete review of their life insurance for a number of years. The only life insurance that they now have are the level term policies provided by their respective employers. The face value of Jan's policy equals twice her salary, while Jason's policy will equal his salary once he is working in his new position. Given Jan's sizable contribution to the family's combined income, the Burnses are concerned about whether her present life insurance coverage is adequate.

The Burnses have been encouraged to review their insurance coverage by the many calls Jason has recently been receiving from various life insurance agents. After talking with several of them, Jason and Jan feel more befuddled than enlightened. One agent stressed the need for an endowment policy to provide for Sandra's education. Another agent suggested that straight life insurance with its cash value feature is clearly the best choice for them. Yet another agent said their insurance program should be based on a foundation of term insurance, with additional policies added on top of that foundation. The net effect has been to confuse the Burnses as to what they should do in the life insurance area.

One of their friends has suggested that they begin by listing their needs. On the basis of these needs, the friend suggests they can estimate how much life insurance coverage they require. Since the Burns' initial concern is with Jan's coverage, they want to plan what life insurance she should carry on her life. Details on their needs include:

Required cleanup fund, $6000

Mortgage repayment, $0 (they rent)

Emergency fund desired, $2000

Required monthly after-tax income for Jason and Sandra as survivors during family years, $2050

Jan's estimated PIA, or basic Social Security monthly benefit, $600

Spouse's annual earnings without losing Social Security survivors benefit, $5400

As the survivor, Jason's expected monthly after-tax earnings during middle years, $1200

If Jason works until age 65 as planned, expected monthly Social Security retirement benefit, $600

Sandra's 4 years' college education costs will total $20,000, with $4000 provided from other financial sources; the Burnses will provide the balance

Family's present monthly after-tax income (Jason and Jan both working), $2600

Jason's monthly after-tax earnings (he and Sandra in household), $1200

Required monthly after-tax income for Jason during middle years, $1400

Jason's projected monthly after-tax pension payment, $550

Required monthly after-tax income for Jason during retirement years, $1200

Jason's projected retirement period, 15 years

Lump-sum Social Security payment on Jan's death, $255

To further assist in planning the additional life insurance Jan should buy, the Burnses have made a detailed balance sheet. Their friend has suggested that some of their present assets might be counted as covering part of their projected total life insurance needs. The Burns' list of assets include:

NOW account, $500

Money market fund, $1500

Common stock mutual fund (current market value), $1800

1   Estimate what life insurance Jan should carry to meet the needs of Jason and Sandra in the following areas:

Cleanup fund, mortgage redemption, and emergency fund

Family years income

Middle years income

Retirement years income

College fund

2   What is the total amount of life insurance that Jan should currently carry to meet the family's needs?

3   How much additional life insurance should Jan consider buying?

4   What basic guidelines should Jason and Jan follow to help them decide whether they should concentrate on term life insurance or one of the cash value types of life insurance for Jan's additional insurance requirements?

5   Assume that Jan survives and that she and Jason are reviewing her life insurance needs 5 years from today. In actual practice, the Burnses would update all the previous dollar estimates. But, rather than do that, set up a needs worksheet similar to Exhibit 14-5, using the dollar estimates you worked with in **1** but with an altered time period, because it is now 5 years later. Has their total required insurance increased or decreased?

CHAPTER
15
HEALTH INSURANCE AND DISABILITY INCOME INSURANCE

THIS IS THE MOST IMPORTANT PART OF YOUR PATIENT'S MEDICAL RECORD – HIS FINANCIAL STATEMENT!

MEDICAL costs have risen so fast in the

last decade that a hospital confinement of 1 or 2 weeks could prove financially catastrophic for most families without health insurance. Two weeks in the hospital following surgery can easily cost $4000 to $8000 or more. That expense would wipe out most families' emergency cash reserve. For an extended illness, medical costs in excess of $50,000 are not unusual.

The best insurance against high medical costs is good health. You have heard all the advice: Do not smoke, do not drink to excess, eat a balanced diet, get regular exercise. Unfortunately, even these precautions do not eliminate the possibility of sickness or accident. The objective of this chapter is to convince you that health insurance is an absolute necessity, and to discuss the provisions, advantages, disadvantages, and costs of standard health-insurance programs.

The second section of this chapter examines the need for disability income insurance to replace your income should you be unable to work because of an accident or a prolonged illness. The possibility of becoming disabled during your working lifetime is extremely high: as many as 1 out of 3 workers experiences some period of disability before reaching age 65. Disability income insurance is as important as life insurance, because as much income can be lost through disability as through premature death.

HEALTH-INSURANCE POLICY PROVISIONS

Since there are no standard health-insurance contracts, it is essential to understand the major features of a contract before you buy it. This section discusses the most important **policy provisions** of a health-insurance contract: deductibles, coinsurance, policy exclusions, waiting periods, renewability, policy limits, and benefit payments.

Deductibles   Many health-insurance contracts specify an amount that the insurance company will deduct from the amount of the claim. Typically, the **deductible** amount will range from $100 upward. The policyholder must pay that amount; the company pays the balance. The objective of the deductible is to eliminate small claims. If insurance paid all medical expenses, there would be little incentive for people not to see a doctor at the first sign of a sore throat or cold—and to claim reimbursement for the cost of each visit.

The deductible amount forces policyholders to accept responsibility for at least the first $100 of their medical expenses. If there were no deductible, the companies would have to increase the cost of the insurance by more than $100, since they must collect an amount sufficient to pay these small claims as well as to cover their administrative costs. Deductibles vary widely among companies. Watch for the following:

First, for how long does the policy allow you to accumulate bills in order to reach the deductible amount? Some policies put a 3- or 6-month limitation on the deductible. For example, if in the 3-month period your bills did not exceed the deductible amount, you would have to start accumulating expenses from zero at the start of the next 3-month period. Hazel Hypochondriac's health-insurance policy had a $100 deductible and a 3-month deductible period. During the first 3 months she had the policy, her medical expenses were $98. In the next 3 months, she had another $85 in medical expenses. Despite the "$100 deductible," she could not collect her $183 in expenses from the policy because of the deductible period.

Second, check to determine whether the deductible amount can be accumulated from the charges only for a single illness or for any number of separate illnesses that fall within the period when deductions are allowed. If you are restricted to accumulating expenses for only one illness, the policy will be less beneficial than if it covers all illnesses of a family member. Hazel's policy permitted her to accumulate expenses for each family member for only one illness. When her son was sick with four different illnesses in one 3-month period and she had over $375 of expenses, she still couldn't meet the deductible because no one illness had cost more than $100.

An even better deductible permits you to accumulate expenses for all family members. If one member has high medical expenses, the deductible can be reached for the entire family through the expenses of that one person. Moreover, modest expenses for each member will also fulfill the deductible provision.

Coinsurance Clauses   After excluding the deductible amount from the amount of your claim, the insurance company may only pay you a part of the balance, not the entire amount. This is called **coinsurance.** In a health-insurance contract, the coinsurance agreement will specify that the company will pay from 70 to 90 percent of all claims, after the deductible; the insured pays the remaining 10 to 30 percent. Here is a brief example: If you have a $50 deductible, 80–20 percent coinsurance, and a claim for $550, how much will the insurance company pay you? First it will deduct $50 from the claim, leaving $500, and then pay 80 percent of the $500, or $400.

$$\$400 \quad = (\$550 \quad - \$50) \quad \times 80\%$$

Amount = Total claim − Deductible × Coinsurance
paid   percentage

In this case, you must pay $150 out of your own pocket: $50 for the deductible and $100 for your portion of the coinsurance. Exhibit 15-1 shows the relationship of the deductible and the coinsurance provision for a typical policy.

Whereas the deductible provision discourages trivial claims without inflicting financial hardship on the insured, the same cannot be said for coinsurance. The economic impact of coinsurance can be quite severe. Exhibit 15-2 assumes that Sue Serious incurred $10,200 of medical expenses while covered by an insurance policy with a $200 deductible and an 80–20 percent coinsurance clause. Even with a small deductible and a high coinsurance agreement, she still must pay $2,200 of the costs. Sue's policy highlights a distinct weakness of coinsurance: On large claims, the insurance does not protect the person against large dollar losses, which is its primary purpose.

STRATEGY

If possible, try to purchase a policy which does not have a coinsurance clause. The policy may cost a little more, but it will protect you against large losses.

Coinsurance with a Maximum   Some insurance policies correct the coinsurance shortcoming by specifying a maximum dollar amount that the insured must pay. For example, the policy might say that the most the insured will pay through a combination of the deductible plus the coinsurance amount is $1000. Had Sue's policy, like the example in Exhibit 15-2, had this maximum, or cap, she would have had to pay only $1000 of her medical claim. Clearly, the maximum eliminates the possibility of very large losses and thus makes a coinsurance clause much more acceptable; it may not make your share of the costs pleasant to bear, but a maximum can hold those costs to a manageable level.

Policy Exclusions   Before buying any health-insurance policy, make sure you know its **exclusions**—that is, whether certain illnesses and medical procedures are excluded from coverage. Some policies do not cover normal pregnancy, but do cover any complications which arise from childbirth. For

EXHIBIT 15-1

Summary of health-insurance deductibles and coinsurance.

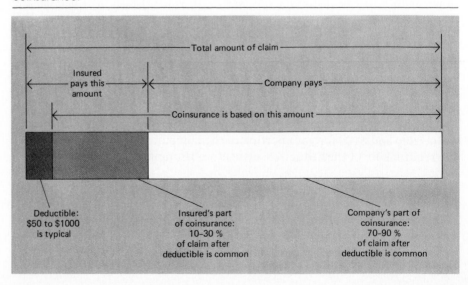

CHAPTER 15

483

HEALTH
INSURANCE AND
DISABILITY
INCOME
INSURANCE

EXHIBIT 15-2

Sample claim calculation for a comprehensive
medical policy with a $200 deductible and an
80–20 percent coinsurance clause.

	TOTAL	YOUR SHARE	INSURANCE
Total expenses	$10,200	—	—
Deductible	—	$ 200	—
Amount subject to coinsurance (Expenses – deductible)	10,000	—	—
20% coinsurance	—	2,000	—
80% reimbursed	—	—	$8,000
Total payments		$2,200	$8,000

an additional fee, most companies will also cover usual and regular maternity costs. The cost of this coverage is reasonably high, because people who want it are undoubtedly contemplating having children. Consequently, the insurance companies must charge everybody a premium which about equals the actual medical and hospital costs of childbirth. As a result, you may be better off paying the costs yourself by assuming the risk for maternity expenses. After all, you should have at least 9 months to save for them.

Some exclusions are more acceptable than others. For example, a policy which does not cover elective cosmetic surgery, such as the removal of noticeable but otherwise harmless birthmarks, may be perfectly adequate in all other respects. But policies that exclude treatment of mental illness and coverage for convalescent expenses, such as home nursing care required after major surgery, may not suit many people's needs.

STRATEGY

Carefully review what an insurance policy excludes before you purchase it; there can be major differences among policies.

Waiting Periods   Most health-insurance policies require a **waiting period** —the insurance company will not pay a claim for certain illnesses or for maternity until a period of time has passed after the date on which the policy was purchased. Policies that cover maternity benefits are invariably written with a 9- or 10-month waiting period. Illnesses such as tonsillitis may have shorter waiting periods. For example, Hazel Hypochondriac needed to have her tonsils removed. She bought a health-insurance policy with a 60-day waiting period for tonsillectomies. If she has the operation before the sixtieth day, the policy will not pay any expenses for the surgery or hospital.

Imposing a waiting period on illnesses where treatment can be postponed for a short period forces people to have insurance prior to those illnesses. The waiting period prevents people from postponing medical treatment until they buy insurance. The procedure is fair.

Renewability   A policy which the insurance company can cancel at any time is far less desirable than one which guarantees continued protection. Policies that guarantee **renewability** are usually more expensive than those that may be canceled by the company. (Some policies may be canceled only if all policyholders in the same state are dropped at the same time.) The danger in buying a policy renewable at the company's option is that the company may cancel at just the time you most need the insurance. At that point, it may be difficult to qualify for health insurance, and you may be left unprotected and unable to get health insurance from another company.

STRATEGY

When selecting health insurance, make certain that the policy is renewable at your option and not the insurance company's; the higher premium is justified.

Policy Limits   What is the maximum amount the policy will cover? Does the maximum apply to each illness, or is it for the life of the policy? Policies that apply the limit for each illness are more desirable than ones which apply the limit to all claims. Obviously, the higher the **policy limits**, the better the policy.

Policy limits of $50,000 or more are not extravagant, considering today's high medical costs. Many insurance advisors are now recommending that individuals should have coverage of at least $100,000 and that $250,000 is not unreasonable. Fortunately, the cost of increasing the policy limits is very small. The increase from $25,000 to $100,000 in major medical coverage may cost only a few dollars more per year. The additional cost is a small price to pay for protecting against the possibility of catastrophic medical costs.

Some policies pay a maximum amount during any one calendar year; other policies will pay a maximum for any one illness. The latter are the most liberal. Here's why. If the limitation is applied to each illness and medical costs for each illness are at the maximum that is payable, the insurance company will pay the maximum costs every time they occur during the calendar year. If the limitation were on a calendar year basis, the insurance company would pay the maximum only once during the year, no matter how many times the illness recurred or how much it may have cost.

Some basic health-insurance plans specify low limits, such as $2000 to $5000. For example, if Hazel Hypochondriac has a basic policy with a limit of $2000 and she incurred $18,000 of medical expenses (not at all difficult to do), she would have to pay $16,000 of the expenses herself. Even worse, if her policy pays the maximum only once a calendar year and she suffers a second major illness during that same year, she would be totally uninsured.

Benefit Payments   Benefit payments under health-insurance policies can allow a specified amount, a cash benefit, or a service benefit.

Specified Amount   Some health insurance policies pay a **specified amount**, or a flat dollar benefit. For example, the policy might pay you $40 for each day you are hospitalized. What you do with that money is your choice.

Cash Benefit   Some health policies pay a **cash benefit** for each covered health care service up to some set maximum. For example, the policy might set the maximum at $400 on a tonsillectomy or $150 per day for a hospital room. If your actual health costs were less, your reimbursement would be the smaller amount. But if the cost exceeds that maximum, your reimbursement would be the maximum amount and you would pay the difference. Typically, the policy contains a detailed list of the maximums it pays for different health care services.

Service Benefit   If a health-insurance policy promises to pay *all* necessary and reasonable charges, it provides a **service benefit**. Thus, no matter what the doctor or hospital charges for a specific procedure, the insurance will pay all the costs—subject to any deductible and coinsurance clauses in the policy. Usually the payments under service contracts are made directly to the hospital or physician, rather than to the insured.

HEALTH-INSURANCE POLICIES

Health-insurance contracts fall into five distinct categories. Three are referred to as basic plans; they have modest policy limits on the amount of coverage and are designed to cover specific items such as hospitalization. Two of the contracts offer extended policy limits that provide coverage for a broad range of health services. In addition, there are special supplemental insurance policies and dental insurance policies that are becoming popular.

Hospital Expense Insurance

Hospital expense insurance covers the hospital's charges for room and board and may also cover additional expenses such as operating room fees, lab work, x-rays, and medicines. Limits are usually stated in terms of dollars per day and a maximum number of allowable days. For example, the policy may pay for your hospital costs up to $100 per day for 45 days. Any charges that exceed this amount will have to be paid by the policyholder. Hospital expense insurance is the most basic form of health insurance available. The important things to consider when purchasing this type of coverage are the maximum amount of daily payment and the number of days for which the payments will continue.

Surgical Expense Insurance

Surgical expense insurance covers the cost of a surgeon's fee. They are separate policies that are frequently combined with a hospital expense policy to provide basic health coverage. Some policies provide a cash benefit, while others provide a service benefit.

Regular Medical Insurance

Regular medical insurance pays part or all of the physician's fees for nonsurgical care. Since many medical procedures do not require surgery but can nevertheless be very expensive, the need for regular medical insurance

CHAPTER 15

485

HEALTH
INSURANCE AND
DISABILITY
INCOME
INSURANCE

to supplement the hospital insurance expense and surgical expense insurance is obvious.

Shopping for Basic Health Coverage

Basic health insurance policies frequently combine the coverages of hospital, surgical, and medical services into a single policy. Typically, the maximum policy limit is quite low and the deductible is usually small. Many policies do not have a coinsurance clause. The combination of these features typically holds the annual premium to a moderate amount. Exhibit 15-3 is a checklist to help you systematically evaluate a basic health insurance policy. If, instead of a single combined policy, you are evaluating separate insurance policies, you can use applicable sections of the exhibit for each type of policy.

When you are analyzing any health insurance policy to decide whether it is appropriate for your situation, we believe you should concentrate on three broad criteria:

Breadth of the health care services covered by policy

Adequacy of policy's payments for moderate claims

Adequacy of policy's payments for very large claims

The first criterion is concerned primarily with the policy's provisions for the services covered, exclusions, and waiting periods. A good policy should provide a broad range of coverages without being unduly restrictive. A basic health policy does a fair job of meeting this criterion; its biggest deficiency is likely to be gaps in coverage which leave some health care services uncovered. This can be especially true where there are separate policies for each of the service areas.

The second criterion is concerned chiefly with the policy's deductible and coinsurance clauses. A good policy should cover a sufficient part of the claim so that the insured will not be financially strapped by paying the remainder. Most basic health policies rate high on this criterion. The combination of small deductibles and the lack of a coinsurance stipulation means that most of a moderate claim will be paid.

The third criterion is mainly concerned with the policy's coinsurance clause and its upper dollar limit. A good policy should cover most of a large medical claim, leaving the insured to pay a manageable amount. Most basic health-insurance policies do a poor job on this score. Their major deficiency is that, with the typically low policy maximum, you may be woefully underinsured on a large medical claim; you could exhaust the policy's entire coverage and still have a sizable part of the bill to pay. For that reason, you may have to supplement this policy with a major medical policy.

Major Medical Insurance

Major medical insurance covers a broad range of medical services within a single policy. Its coverage includes nearly all the charges from the hospital, the doctor, and other costs such as drugs, blood transfusions, and similar medical needs.

EXHIBIT 15-3

CHAPTER 15

487

HEALTH
INSURANCE AND
DISABILITY
INCOME
INSURANCE

Checklist for analyzing basic health policy
provisions.

AREAS OF CONCERN	RECOMMENDATIONS
Hospital Expense Coverage	
1 How many days are covered?	Desirable policies cover 365 days.
2 What is the daily benefit?	Benefits should equal daily hospital cost in your area.
3 Are additional services, such as x-ray, lab work, and medication covered?	Desirable policies include these extras.
4 Is there a deductible?	If so, it should fit your ability to pay.
5 Is the policy automatically renewable?	It should be renewable at your request.
6 Is there a waiting period for certain illnesses?	Desirable policies have few illnesses subject to waiting periods, and these periods are short.
7 Are there policy exclusions?	Desirable policies have few exclusions.
Surgical Expense Coverage	
1 Does the policy pay a cash or service benefit?	Desirable policies have a service benefit.
2 Does the policy cover surgery only if you are hospitalized?	Desirable policies also cover procedures in a doctor's office.
3 What are the exclusions?	Desirable policies have few exclusions.
Regular Medical Coverage	
1 What is covered?	Policy should pay all nonsurgical medical expenses except routine office visits.
2 Are prescription drugs covered?	Coverage for medicine is important if prolonged medication is required.

Maximum policy limits under a major medical policy are always substantial; limits of $25,000 to $50,000 are typical, with coverages up to $250,000 not unusual. The maximum can be counted either during a calendar year, over the insured's lifetime, or for each illness or accident; the limit for each illness or accident is the preferred maximum.

Major medical policies frequently carry a sizable deductible that can range from $300 to $1000 or more. By specifying a large deductible, the company can hold down the policy's annual premium. If this policy is combined with a basic health policy, you can frequently meet the major medical policy's large deductible through the payment from the basic policy.

Major medical insurance usually has a coinsurance clause that requires the insured to pay anywhere from 10 to 30 percent of a claim. Again, the purpose is to hold down the premium while providing a policy with broad coverage and high dollar limits. The better policies set a maximum that the insured must pay on any one claim; $1000 to $2500 is typical. That upper limit substantially reduces the burden of the coinsurance feature.

Shopping for Major Medical Coverage Exhibit 15-4 provides a checklist to help you evaluate the provisions of major medical insurance policies. Major medical coverage can be purchased either as your sole health insurance or as a supplement to a basic health policy. Purchased as the sole health policy, major medical policies rate well on our first criterion: breadth of health care services provided. They rate less well on the second: adequacy

EXHIBIT 15-4

Checklist for analyzing major medical policy provisions.

AREAS OF CONCERN	RECOMMENDATIONS
1 What is the policy limit?	Maximum should be at least $25,000; maximum of $100,000 is suggested.
2 Size of deductible?	Match the deductible to your ability to pay.
3 Provisions of coinsurance clause?	Coinsurances of 80–20 or 90–10 are recommended; coinsurances with a maximum are highly desirable.
4 Renewability of policy?	It should be renewable at your option.
5 How is maximum policy limit computed?	Computation per illness is best; per calendar year, second; over your lifetime, is least desirable.
6 Are there policy exclusions?	It should provide broad coverage with few exclusions.

of the policy's payment for moderate claims. The combination of a sizable deductible coupled with a coinsurance clause may mean that you will have to pay a considerable percentage of small to moderate-sized claims. On the third criterion, adequacy of policy's payments for very large claims, these policies do reasonably well. The major problem centers on the coinsurance clause; it can mean that you still have to make a large payment even with insurance. That will be less of a problem if the policy sets a maximum that the insured must pay on a claim. But even without the maximum, major medical's high policy limits will protect you against catastrophic expenses. As long as you are prepared to pay the initial portion of a claim plus a percentage of that claim, major medical provides excellent protection against large medical expenses.

As a supplement to a basic health policy, a well-chosen major medical policy can remedy the deficiencies of most basic policies. Its broad coverage will likely fill the gaps in coverage that the basic policy might have. Also, its high policy limits will provide protection on very large claims after the basic policy's benefits have been exhausted. When selecting health insurance, take care that you are not unnecessarily duplicating coverage with the two policies; a good insurance agent can help you avoid this.

Comprehensive Medical Insurance

Comprehensive medical insurance covers a very broad range of health care services and does so with high policy limits. Generally, the deductible amount is moderate or zero. Likewise, most policies have a limited or no coinsurance provision. The combination of those two features makes the policy ideal for both small and large medical claims. Comprehensive policies are becoming the common form of health insurance offered through group insurance plans. As you might expect, a comprehensive insurance policy is more expensive than either major medical coverage or basic health coverage alone. But it may be less costly to buy a comprehensive policy than it would be to duplicate it through a separate basic health policy coupled with a major medical policy.

Shopping for Comprehensive Health Coverage   Since some comprehensive medical policies are sold only on a group basis, you may have more difficulty finding such coverage. Exhibit 15-5 outlines the checkpoints you should consider when selecting a policy. Comprehensive policies rate very well on our first criterion. Their combination of broad coverage, coupled with limited exclusions, gives them excellent breadth of coverage. They also score very well on our second and third criteria. Their moderate-to-low deductible, together with a lack of coinsurance, means that most small and moderate claims will be paid by the insurance company. At the same time, the policy's high dollar limit, along with low or no coinsurance, means that the insurance policy pays most of a very large claim.

Overall, comprehensive medical policies provide excellent insurance protection for most medical claims. So why are they not the recommended policy for everyone? Cost! The premiums are so high that many people just

EXHIBIT 15-5

Checklist for analyzing comprehensive policy provisions.

AREAS OF CONCERN	RECOMMENDATIONS
1 What is the policy limit?	Maximum should be at least $25,000, with $100,000 desirable.
2 Size of deductible?	It should range from $25 to $200.
3 Provision for coinsurance?	It should have either no coinsurance or coinsurance with a maximum amount the insured pays.
4 Renewability of policy?	It should be renewable if you remain in the group; if you depart, a conversion privilege is desirable.
5 Are there exclusions?	Coverage should be broad, with few exclusions.

cannot, or decide they do not want to, pay so much of their income for health insurance. Of course, if your employer pays most of the premium, the cost is not a problem. But for those to whom cost is a substantial concern, a major medical policy may better fit their financial means.

Accident Insurance

Originally, health insurance and accident insurance were sold as separate policies. The health policy covered medical costs owing to illnesses; reimbursement for medical costs resulting from accidents was made under **accident insurance.** Commonly, the provisions of the accident policy named the amounts that would be paid for specific injuries to the insured person. An insured person might receive $500 for the loss of a leg, $1500 for the loss of an eye, and so on, with a maximum payment of $10,000 if the insured died.

Accident insurance policies represent a poor insurance buy. The medical costs of accidents should be paid by health insurance, and if the injury is disabling, a disability income policy will provide the replacement income. Last, a life insurance policy would be a more efficient way of protecting against the economic consequences of the insured's death.

Dread Disease Insurance

Dread disease insurance policies are now being marketed that cover medical costs due to specific diseases or illnesses. The most common example is insurance covering the medical costs of treating cancer. You can also buy health insurance specifically covering kidney disease and other "dread" diseases. The limits on these policies are quite large. Moreover, the cost of the insurance is usually modest, often under $200. Nevertheless, these types of policies, like accident insurance, represent a poor insurance buy.

CHAPTER 15

491

HEALTH
INSURANCE AND
DISABILITY
INCOME
INSURANCE

YOU MUST BE THE
GENTLEMAN INTERESTED
IN THE ACCIDENT INSURANCE..

The probability of contracting the dread disease covered by the policy is small. This is why the policies cost very little to buy and also why they have high dollar coverage.

STRATEGY

Buy a good major medical or comprehensive health policy rather than use your premium dollars for a "dread disease" policy.

Supplemental Hospitalization Insurance

Many Sunday newspapers carry appealing ads for **supplemental hospitalization insurance** which you can buy by mail. The ads promise to pay you $600 or $1000 per month without explaining under what conditions the insurance company will make these payments. The large print also promises that the insurance company will pay up to a maximum of $50,000 or more.

These policies are not a good way to supplement your health-insurance policies. Many of these mail-order contracts will pay you only when you are hospitalized. Assuming a maximum benefit of $600 per month, you would have to be in the hospital for almost 7 years in order to receive the maximum $50,000 amount the policy promises.

Another deceptive feature of these policies is this: Many do not start paying you benefits until after you have been in the hospital for 6 days. You will receive benefits starting only from the sixth day. But the average hospital stay in the United States is 5 days.

Finally, many of the policies will not pay for certain illnesses until you have had the policy for 1 or 2 years. This waiting period effectively eliminates many claims that a policyholder might make during the first year or two that the contract is in force. Examples of the types of illnesses that may not be covered during the first 2 years are cancer and heart disease.

Further evidence of the poor protection offered by mail-order insurance is the claims-to-premium ratio. This figure is simply the total claims that are paid as a percentage of the total premiums paid to the insurance company. Blue Cross has a 90 to 95 percent ratio; for every $100 received in premiums, it pays back $90 to $95 to fulfill claims submitted to it. Mail-order insurers usually have claims-to-premium ratios as low as 20 percent; they pay only $20 in claims for each $100 in premiums. Good business for the mail-order company—bad insurance for people!

Dental Insurance

The fastest-growing segment of the health-insurance industry is **dental insurance**. Traditionally, health-insurance policies have excluded customary dental work, such as fillings or dentures. Treatment for diseases of the mouth and gums, however, is usually covered in health plans.

The growth of dental insurance probably started with labor unions. Recognizing the high cost of dental work, especially dentures and orthodontia (teeth straightening), labor unions began to insist on dental insurance as part of their contracts. As union members become covered under dental plans, many companies extend the dental benefits to their nonunion employees. Although employees are covered under group dental insurance plans, many insurance companies also sell dental plans to individuals.

The cost of dental insurance, like the cost of health insurance, is subject to many variables. Policy limits, deductibles, coinsurance clauses, and exclusions vary widely among policies.

Should You Buy Dental Insurance? Health insurance is certainly a must. Is dental insurance? The answer to that question is a qualified *no.* If

dental insurance is part of a group plan paid for by your employer, by all means take the coverage. However, if you are thinking about buying an individual policy, consider the decision carefully. Remember that the likelihood of catastrophic dental expense is limited. Major oral disease or structural repairs following an accident should be covered by your health insurance.

That leaves dental insurance to cover only normal fillings, dentures, and orthodontia. Fillings are relatively inexpensive. While dentures may be costly, they can be anticipated and budgeted for. And orthodontia, although expensive, is administered over a fairly long period. Thus you should be able to pay its cost out of current income.

CHAPTER 15

493

HEALTH
INSURANCE AND
DISABILITY
INCOME
INSURANCE

STRATEGY

You should only consider an *individual* dental plan if you cannot budget the costs required for dental care.

WHERE TO BUY HEALTH INSURANCE

In this section, we will present the major sources of health insurance and the insurance plans that each provides. And, of course, we'll offer some suggestions about what health insurance you may need and where to buy it. To begin with, there are private insurance companies that make a profit and nonprofit health-insurance organizations that do not. As an alternative to traditional health insurance, there are health maintenance organizations (HMOs).

Blue Cross and Blue Shield

The largest health insurer in terms of the amount of health insurance it provides is a group of nonprofit organizations known as Blue Cross and Blue Shield. Among the unique characteristics of the Blues, as they are often called, is the fact that everyone in the same geographic location may join, either on a group basis or an individual basis. The coverage provided under Blue Cross and Blue Shield is among the best available. As nonprofit organizations, their sole objective is sound insurance protection at the lowest cost. Premiums are set to cover only claims and administrative expenses.

Blue Cross   **Blue Cross** is the hospital expense insurance portion of Blue Cross and Blue Shield. In addition to paying for room-and-board charges, the insurance also covers lab fees, x-rays, operating room charges, and prescription medication.

The rates for Blue Cross vary, depending on the geographic location and the policy limits. Costs for hospital care show wide regional differences. The larger cities are usually more expensive than small towns, and the Northeast and California have higher medical costs than the South and the Midwest. The insurance rates must be set to recognize these differences.

Other variations include limits on the number of hospital days allowable (anywhere from 30 days to 1 year) and on the daily hospital cost payable. These factors are also incorporated in the company's insurance rate structure.

Blue Shield   **Blue Shield** is the surgical expense coverage of the Blue Cross and Blue Shield plans. It is really broader than just surgical expense coverage because it also reimburses for some physicians' fees which do not involve surgery.

Blue Shield contracts generally state that payment will be made for all "reasonable and necessary charges." This stipulation permits the physicians some latitude in setting their fees without forcing the policyholder to pay the difference between the actual charge and some maximum reimbursement by the company. For example, if Hazel Hypochondriac had surgery to remove her appendix, the Blue Shield reimbursement to the doctor would be for the total amount, no matter whether the bill was for $500 or $1500. If Blue Shield considers the bill excessive, it will negotiate directly with the doctor.

In those cases where benefits are stated as flat payments, most physicians agree to accept the stated benefit as full payment for services. They do so because the Blue Shield organization was begun and supported by doctors and, in many states, 90 percent of the physicians are sponsoring members of the plan. Nonparticipating M.D.'s may charge more than the set fee; however, they must collect the difference from the patient, not from Blue Shield. Many Blue Shield plans urge their policyholders to refrain from signing supplemental fee agreements (promises to pay more than the insurance coverage) and to refer any doctor's charges in excess of the stated levels back to Blue Shield for negotiation, even if the doctor is not a Blue Shield sponsor.

Private Insurance Companies

There are many reputable **private insurance companies** writing very acceptable health-insurance policies, although sometimes the legalistic garble written in their contracts can confuse even lawyers. Unfortunately, there are also companies that seem to be writing policies designed specifically to shortchange the policyholder and enrich the firm's stockholders.

One area in which deceitful insurers find it easy to fool people comprises the exclusions. These may be so broad that they leave dangerous gaps in the insurance protection. For example, many policies cover dependent children from 14 days to 19 years old. By excluding the first 14 days, the company shifts the costs of possible congenital birth defects to the parents. The costs of such illnesses can be unbelievably high.

Other private plans may either have a 2-year waiting period for certain illnesses or totally exclude existing illnesses from being covered at any time.

All the policy provisions we discussed earlier should be very carefully scrutinized when you are considering a policy sold by a profit-making insurance company. With the wide differences among policies and companies, uninformed insurance buyers can be sadly underprotected if they select a poor contract or buy from an unscrupulous company.

Cash Benefits   The major thing to keep in mind when buying private health insurance is that you will generally get cash benefits, not service benefits. Unless you select a policy which has a high benefit schedule, you may be woefully underinsured. The benefit schedule is the maximum amount the policy will pay. However, the amount that it will pay for a specific surgical procedure will vary proportionally with the maximum benefit payable under the policy. For example, a policy with a $700 maximum may pay $50 for a tonsillectomy, while a policy with a $2100 maximum will pay $150 for the same operation. If you buy the lower benefit policy and the doctor charges you $150 for the operation, you must pay the difference.

CHAPTER 15

495

HEALTH
INSURANCE AND
DISABILITY
INCOME
INSURANCE

Health Maintenance Organizations

Health maintenance organizations (HMOs) provide an alternative to long-established health insurance. Under traditional health insurance, three parties are involved in the health care process: the insured, the hospital or doctor who provides the service, and the insurance company. The insurance company does not have a direct role in deciding the extent of, or the delivery of, those care services. Some people criticize this third-party payment system on the ground that neither the doctor nor the hospital has any direct incentive to avoid possibly excessive medical procedures or unnecessarily long hospital stays. And the insurance company is not in a position where it can pressure doctors and hospitals to hold down health costs.

Under the terms of a typical HMO, a family pays the organization a flat amount for its total annual health care needs. Here the similarity between HMOs and conventional health insurance ends. The HMO provides medical care through the doctors it employs and the hospital it owns or through an agreement with other hospitals. The member, the insured, simply goes to the plan's clinic or hospital whenever in need of medical attention. The annual prepayment covers any services provided during the year. Since the HMO receives only a set amount each year, it has a strong incentive to eliminate unnecessary health care costs. Because the HMO is directly involved in providing health care services, it can work to reduce health care costs and therefore can benefit from any reduction.

HMOs have been both praised and damned. Praise has come from groups that see the plans as a low-cost and efficient way of delivering health care services. Opponents of the plans claim that they remove the individual's freedom of choice in selecting a personal physician. They further argue that a doctor should work on a fee-for-service basis and that working for a salary reduces his or her incentive to provide good medical care. Despite these arguments, HMOs appear to be providing sound medical care for their members. By and large, the members are satisfied, and there is no indication that the care HMOs provide is inferior to traditional medical services.

STRATEGY

If there is a HMO in your area, consider it as an alternative to traditional health insurance; judge its services using the same three broad categories that we outlined earlier for health policies.

EXHIBIT 15-6

Summary of health-insurance policies and
insurance carriers.

TYPE	GROUP OR INDIVIDUAL	AVAILABLE FROM
Basic: Hospital expense Surgical expense Regular medical Major medical Comprehensive	Both	Service organizations such as Blue Cross and Blue Shield or private insurance companies
Prepaid (HMO)	Both	Health maintenance organizations
Cancer insurance	Individual	Private companies
Accident insurance	Individual	Private companies
Dental insurance	Both	Service organizations or private insurance companies
Supplemental insurance	Individual	Private companies

Summarizing Health Coverages

The principal types of health-insurance coverage discussed in this chapter
are summarized in Exhibit 15-6. This exhibit shows three things: the types
of health insurance; whether each type is available on a group basis, an
individual basis, or both; and sources for each type of health insurance.

Costs of Health-Insurance Policies Generalizations about the cost of
health-insurance policies are impossible to make. Premiums vary depending
on the company, the coverages, the insured's geographic location, and
whether the policy is for an individual or a family. About the only thing that
can be said is that adequate health-insurance protection is very expensive: a
good family policy with maternity benefits can cost more than $2000 a year.

To complicate matters further, it is almost impossible to compare
health policies. Coverage under health-insurance policies has not been
standardized, so direct cost comparisons are nearly impossible.

Which Program Is Best? Perhaps the simplest and best way to obtain
good health coverage is to work for a company that provides its employees
with a comprehensive group insurance program. If you have to obtain your
health insurance on an individual basis, here are some rules of thumb for
selecting a good health-insurance policy:

1   Buy from a reliable nonprofit organization.

2   Buy a policy without a coinsurance clause or one with a maximum
that the insured pays.

3   Do not buy supplemental health-insurance policies.

4   Reduce the cost of the insurance by increasing the deductible up to the maximum you can afford.

5   Get the longest period allowed for accumulating the deductible.

6   Buy a major or a comprehensive medical policy with at least a $25,000 limit, preferably, $100,000.

7   Make sure the policy is renewable at your option.

8   Make sure the policy exclusions and waiting periods are minimal.

9   Make sure you understand the exclusions and that they are reasonable.

CHAPTER 15

497

HEALTH
INSURANCE AND
DISABILITY
INCOME
INSURANCE

Updating Your Health Insurance

When your personal or financial position changes, your insurance needs may also change. Health insurance, like all other insurance plans, should be reviewed periodically to make sure that coverages are adequate. This is true even if you are covered under a group health contract. In addition to reviewing coverage at least every 2 years, you should take a careful look at your policy when any of the following things happen to you.

Change of Jobs   If you are covered under a group plan, your protection will stop when you leave your current employer. If you may be out of work for a while, or if you will not be covered under a new plan during a waiting period, see whether you can convert your former group insurance to an individual policy. If this is impossible, consider buying a major medical policy to fill the gap. You will need some protection until you are covered by a new group policy.

Change in Family Status   Make sure your employer knows when you have children so that they can be covered under the group policy. If you have an individual policy, make sure to notify your agent of any family change.

Children Nineteen or More Years Old   Most health policies protect dependent children only until age 19. After that, an individual policy will have to be purchased for dependent children. College students can often buy adequate low-cost protection through their school. If they are under 19, do not consider additional insurance so long as they are covered under a family policy. It would duplicate the coverage, and you would waste your money.

Retirement   Protection under an employer's group plan may stop with retirement, or some form of reduced protection may continue as a part of the retirement benefits. It is important to check your coverage because the increased medical needs that often accompany the aging process can be devastating without adequate health insurance.

DISABILITY INCOME INSURANCE

Disability income insurance is intended to provide you and your family with an income in the event you become disabled by an accident or illness. Despite the rather high likelihood that a wage-earner will be disabled for some time before age 65, many people overlook the need for disability income insurance. While there are other sources that may replace part of your income during a disability—Social Security benefits or your spouse's earnings if you are married—it is essential that all these sources be coordinated into a systematic disability insurance plan that is based on your likely income needs during the disability. That plan is developed in the next section.

Calculating Disability Income Needs

The first step in calculating your **disability income needs** is to decide what income you and your dependents, if you have any, would require should you become disabled. Your figure should represent the total amount that you want to receive after paying all income and Social Security taxes. If you use a worksheet like the one in Exhibit 15-7, that required income is entered on line 1. When establishing your requirement, you should recognize that, with disability, all work-related expenses, such as commutation costs, work clothing, and purchased lunches would cease; these exclusions should place your income requirements below your present earnings.

We will use Seth and Susan Vinton to illustrate how disability income needs are computed. Both Seth and Susan work outside the home, and, together, their combined after-tax monthly earnings are $2050. They have one child, who is eight years old. After discussing their monthly income requirements, the Vintons determined that they would need $1850 after paying all taxes should Susan become disabled; that amount is entered on line 1 of Exhibit 15-7.

There are three principal sources of income to meet your disability income needs:

Social Security disability benefits

EXHIBIT 15-7

Worksheet to compute disability income needs.

1 Required monthly after-tax income		$1850
2 Less:		
a Social security benefits for:		
(1) Disabled person	$500	
(2) Dependent's benefit	$250	
b Spouse's after-tax income	$995	$1745
3 Income to be met with disability income insurance (line 1 − line 2)		$105

Your spouse's earnings, if you are married and your spouse works outside the home

Your payments from disability income insurance

CHAPTER 15

499

HEALTH
INSURANCE AND
DISABILITY
INCOME
INSURANCE

As with life insurance, we consider the payment from a disability income policy to be the residual, or balancing, amount that completes your income needs. That is, we use the first two income sources to meet disability income needs; only if they are insufficient will you use disability income insurance to make up the shortfall.

Chapter 13 outlined how you would estimate the Social Security disability benefit you would receive if you were disabled; it also provided guidelines to decide whether your dependent(s), if any, would be eligible for a benefit. Based on Susan's earnings record, the Vintons estimate her monthly disability benefit would be $500. Since their child is under 18 years of age, the child's monthly benefit would be $250 (50 percent of Susan's). These amounts are entered in line 2a (1) and 2a (2) respectively. Because Social Security benefits are not subject to taxes, they are entered without any adjustment.

When both people work outside the home, couples would count the nondisabled spouse's earnings as helping to meet the family's total income needs. But those earnings should be reduced by the federal and state income taxes and Social Security taxes that must be paid. The Vintons expect that Seth would continue to work. Thus, after deduction of all applicable taxes, his monthly earnings as the sole worker in the family are $995; this is entered on line 2b of Exhibit 15-7.

Disability income insurance will have to supply that part of the required income that Social Security and the spouse's earnings (if any) do not cover. Line 3 of Exhibit 15-7 summarizes this amount; income from other sources (line 2), is subtracted from the total income required (line 1). Susan Vinton should purchase enough insurance to provide $105 each month. Estimating how much insurance that entails is easy because the benefit under a disability income policy is stated as a monthly payment. Susan needs a policy that provides $105 of monthly disability income.

Limits on Replacement of Income The insurance industry does not want to give people an incentive to claim they are disabled after purchasing disability income insurance. To prevent that possibility, your total disability income—Social Security plus disability income insurance payments—typically cannot exceed 60 to 70 percent of your predisability earnings from working. Or, stated another way:

$$\begin{matrix} \text{Social} \\ \text{Security} \\ \text{benefit} \end{matrix} + \begin{matrix} \text{Disability} \\ \text{income insurance} \\ \text{payment} \end{matrix} = \begin{matrix} \text{Predisability} \\ \text{earnings from} \\ \text{work} \end{matrix} \times 60 \text{ to } 70\%$$

Let's go back to Susan Vinton to demonstrate this restriction. Susan's present before-tax income is $1300, so her maximum income replacement (assuming a 60 percent restriction) is:

$780   = $1300   × 60%

⬆   ⬆   ⬆

Maximum income = Predisability × Maximum
replacement   income   insurance allows

Based on the computation in Exhibit 15-7, Susan's planned income replacement is:

$605   = $500   + $105

⬆   ⬆   ⬆

Total income = Social   + Disability income
replaced   Security   insurance payment

Consequently, Susan is far below the $780 maximum that she could replace. As a point of explanation, only the disabled person's Social Security benefit is counted for the limitation; interest, dividends, and income from rental property are excluded.

Incidentally, a person cannot circumvent the replacement limitation by purchasing policies from several companies. In the event of disability, the insurance companies would likely find out that the person had several policies. As soon as they did, they would then pool their benefit payments so that the person's total disability income would be no more than 60 to 70 percent of his or her predisability earnings. In all probability, the person will merely have wasted premium dollars by purchasing insurance that will not be paid.

STRATEGY

Avoid purchasing excess disability income insurance by making certain that your Social Security benefits, coupled with the insurance payments, do not exceed the maximum the policy allows.

Inflation and Disability Income Payments Unfortunately, disability income insurance policies set the benefit in fixed dollars; even if inflation pushes up prices, that dollar amount remains the same. That raises a major problem in the case of an extended disability because benefits do not increase to offset the rising cost of living. Boosting the benefit payment to several times your present needs is not the answer, because you will likely exceed the policy's maximum replacement percentage and will be unable to collect those enhanced benefits. The only way to partially adjust for inflation is to review your insurance needs every 2 to 3 years and buy more insurance if they have increased.

Buying Disability Income Insurance

Disability income protection can be purchased either as a separate policy or as a rider (option) to an ordinary life or limited-pay life insurance policy. The second source is a bit cumbersome because benefits frequently are based on the policy's face value; that may or may not meet your needs. The next section will discuss the three major features you would be wise to consider when purchasing a policy.

CHAPTER 15

501

HEALTH
INSURANCE AND
DISABILITY
INCOME
INSURANCE

Definition of Disability   A policy's **definition of disability** heavily influences the probability of your qualifying as disabled; the more restrictive the definition, the less likely you will collect benefits. For example, one policy might say, "You are disabled if you are unable to do the work of your present occupation." That is a liberal definition because, if you cannot do your present job, you could collect disability benefits. If Dawn Doloop, a computer programmer, say, is unable to continue her programming duties, she is considered disabled. Contrast that with another policy that says, "You are disabled if you cannot perform any gainful employment." That is far more restrictive because, if you can do *any* work, you will *not* be considered disabled. Under this policy, Dawn Doloop would be defined as disabled only when she was not able to do even the most menial, low-paying work: sweeping floors, stocking shelves, operating an elevator. Clearly, a liberal definition of disability is highly desirable. Typically, the more liberal the definition, the higher the annual premium per dollar of income coverage.

STRATEGY

When possible, concentrate on policies that provide a reasonably liberal definition of disability; settle for the more restrictive definitions only if you are strapped for money to pay premiums.

Duration of Benefits   The longer a disability income policy will continue the benefits, the longer its **duration of benefits** and the better the protection. There are policies with benefit periods as short as 3 months and some with as long as "to age 65." Because most disabilities do not last that long, you can generally extend the benefits to the much more desirable long duration with only a moderate increase in premiums; that provision can improve a policy immensely.

STRATEGY

Concentrate on disability income policies with benefit payments that extend for at least 20 years or, better yet, to age 65.

Waiting Period for Benefits   Before benefits from your disability income policy will start, a **benefit waiting period** must elapse; typical periods are 31, 61, 91 and 182 days. This waiting period acts like a deductible because it shifts the burden for short-term disability losses to you. By extending the waiting period, you lower the annual premium for a given amount of income coverage.

How do you decide which waiting period is best for you? First, extend that period for as long as you can go without a monthly income. By comparing your budgeted monthly outlays with your cash reserve and any other sources of income, you should get an idea of how long a waiting period you can handle.

STRATEGY

Select a policy with as long a waiting period as you can handle given your present cash reserves and any other sources of income.

Integrating Benefit Duration, Disability Definition, and Waiting Period

Your first priority should be to select a policy that provides benefits for an extended period of time. That will protect you against the large financial losses of an extended disability. Even if that means extending the waiting period in order to reduce the premium, we think that is a good trade-off. Next, concentrate on obtaining a policy that has a reasonably liberal **definition of disability**. Again, if you must then extend the waiting period in order to lower the annual premium on the more desirable policy, we favor that trade-off. Our final priority is to shorten the benefit waiting period. If you still have extra premium dollars after implementing the first two guidelines, then consider shortening the waiting period. Waiting several months for benefits to begin may not be pleasant, but it is far more manageable financially than having benefits run out midway through a disability or, worse, having your disability claim denied because the policy's disability definition is so restrictive.

SUMMARY

1   Health insurance is the first and most important insurance coverage that everyone should have.

2   The most important things you should evaluate when buying a health-insurance policy are *(a)* deductible, *(b)* coinsurance, *(c)* policy exclusions, *(d)* waiting periods, *(e)* renewal terms, *(f)* policy limits, and *(g)* benefit payments.

3   There are five standard health insurance policies: *(a)* hospital expense insurance, *(b)* surgical expense insurance, *(c)* regular medical insurance, *(d)* major medical insurance, and *(e)* comprehensive medical insurance.

4   Health policies that cover only a narrow range of illnesses, or only accidents, or pay a low daily benefit only while you are hospitalized are poor insurance buys; examples include accident, dread disease, and supplemental insurance policies.

5   Dental insurance is one of the fastest growing health insurance areas. Dental insurance is not essential, because it is more of a prepayment plan than protection against catastrophic losses.

6   Health insurance can be purchased from a nonprofit organization, such as Blue Cross and Blue Shield, or from private insurance companies. As an alternative, health care services can also be obtained from an HMO.

7   As a general rule, the best health insurance buys are provided by the nonprofit health-insuring organizations. Those organizations return to their policy-holders a high percentage of premiums in the form of benefits; that factor is a sign of an effective insurance program.

8   The annual premium for a good comprehensive medical insurance policy is expensive; a family policy can easily cost $1500 to $2000 annually.

9   When purchasing health insurance, you should concentrate on:

First, obtaining broad coverage with few restrictions

Second, having a policy limit of at least $25,000 to $100,000

Third, raising the deductible to the maximum you can afford

CHAPTER 15

503

HEALTH
INSURANCE AND
DISABILITY
INCOME
INSURANCE

10   Your health insurance program should be reviewed when *(a)* you change jobs, *(b)* you have a change in family status, *(c)* your children reach 19 years of age, or *(d)* you retire.

11   Income needed for disability can be met through *(a)* Social Security benefits, *(b)* a spouse's earnings, if any, and *(c)* payment from disability income insurance.

12   Selecting a disability income insurance policy requires consideration of its definition of disability, its duration of benefits, and its waiting period.

REVIEW YOUR UNDERSTANDING OF

Policy provisions
Deductible
Coinsurance
Exclusions
Waiting periods
Renewability
Policy limits
Specified amount of benefit
Cash benefit
Service benefit
Hospital expense insurance
Surgical expense insurance
Regular medical insurance
Major medical insurance
Comprehensive medical insurance

Accident insurance
Dread disease insurance
Supplemental hospitalization
  insurance
Dental insurance
Blue Cross
Blue Shield
Private insurance company
Health maintenance organization
  (HMO)
Disability income insurance
Disability income needs
Definition of disability
Duration of benefits
Benefit waiting period

DISCUSSION QUESTIONS

1   Why do many health-insurance policies include a deductible? Would a $100 deductible seriously reduce the attractiveness of a policy? Why?

2   How does a coinsurance clause work? Why would an insurance company include such a clause in a policy?

3   Why do many individual health-insurance policies include a waiting period? How does it benefit the insurance company? If you already had a policy from a particular company (assume you have met the waiting period), would you benefit from the company's requiring the waiting period for new policyholders?

4   How do the three benefit payment methods—specified amount, cash benefit, and service benefit—differ? Which would you prefer? Why?

5   What are the principal strengths and weaknesses of the three basic health-insurance policies? What health care situation would they be the best for? The worst for?

6   Compare and contrast major medical insurance with comprehensive medical insurance. How would an individual decide which of the two policies to buy?

7 What are the major weaknesses of a dread disease insurance policy? What would you recommend as a substitute?

8 Why is it less important for an individual to purchase dental insurance than to purchase health insurance? What type of person should consider a dental policy?

9 What restrictions make a supplemental hospitalization insurance policy deliver less than its advertisements promise: "Generous daily cash benefits with a high upper policy limit, all for a modest premium"? What would you recommend as an alternative?

10 How does the health care an individual receives from a health maintenance organization (HMO) differ from that provided by a traditional health-insurance policy? What features make the HMO attractive?

11 Why should you review your health-insurance coverage (old and new) when you are changing jobs? How can you prevent lapses or gaps in the coverage?

12 Why is disability income insurance even more important than life insurance for most people?

13 Do insurance companies place any limits on the amount of disability income insurance you can buy? Why do they do that?

14 What are the three major features to consider when judging the merits of a disability income policy? How would you rank them according to their importance?

15 Why is the definition of disability so essential in determining the likelihood of collecting benefits under a disability income policy? What would you look for in a definition?

PROBLEMS

15-1 Ronald Rollo spent 14 days in the hospital with an illness that the doctors had difficulty diagnosing. The hospital room cost $150 per day. In addition, he incurred physicians' charges of $1200 and laboratory fees and x-ray charges of $750. Ronald has a comprehensive health-insurance policy with a $250 deductible and an 80–20 percent coinsurance clause. How much will he pay on the bill? How much will the insurance company pay?

15-2 For each of the two policies described below, calculate the reimbursement for medical expenses incurred as follows: January $150, February $400, March $0, and April $900.

POLICY #1	POLICY #2
1 $100 deductible	**1** $100 deductible
2 80–20 coinsurance	**2** 80–20 coinsurance
3 90-day deductible period	**3** Calendar year deductible period

15-3 Alberta Woo has narrowed her choice of major medical policies to the following three:

CHAPTER 15

505

HEALTH
INSURANCE AND
DISABILITY
INCOME
INSURANCE

	POLICY #1	POLICY #2	POLICY #3
Deductible	$100	$300	$500
Coinsurance	75–25	80–20	80–20
Maximum insured must pay	Unlimited	Unlimited	$2,500
Policy limit	$10,000	$25,000	$100,000

All the policies have similar annual premiums. And they all allow Alberta to accumulate her medical expenses over the calendar year to meet the deductible provision.

a What would Alberta pay under each policy if her medical expenses totaled $800 for the year?

b What would she have to pay under each policy if her expenses totaled $20,000 for the year?

c Which policy do you recommend? Why?

15-4 Philbert Piecemeal has the following three basic health insurance policies.

	POLICY #1	POLICY #2	POLICY #3
Expense covered	Hospital	Surgical	Medical
Policy limit	$100 per day for 20 days	$700 per surgery	$25 for each day in hospital
Deductible	$100	$50	$50

Philbert recently incurred the following expenses for surgery: *(a)* hospital room, $150 per day for 10 days; *(b)* surgeon's bill, $1500; *(c)* doctor's fee, $45 per daily visit in hospital.

a What amount will Philbert have to pay on these bills?

b After this experience, Philbert is considering switching policies. What guidelines would you give him for his search?

15-5 Sonya Single is planning the disability income she would need to replace her present earnings of $1500 before taxes and $1160 after taxes. She estimates that, if she should be disabled, her monthly after-tax income would have to be $960. On the basis of her prior earnings, she estimates her Social Security disability benefits would be $570.

a What disability income insurance should Sonya purchase?

b The policy Sonya is considering limits her combined Social Security benefits plus disability income payment to 60 percent of her preretirement income. Will that be a problem?

c Assume that she expects to receive $75 (after taxes) each month from the rental property she owns. What are her revised disability income insurance needs? Will the policy's 60 percent maximum replacement be a problem now? Why?

15-6   Earl and Fran Grey are outlining what disability income insurance Fran should carry. Selena, their daughter, is now six years old. They have compiled the following estimates:

Total family after-tax income required if disabled	$1950
Fran's Social Security disability benefit	$ 540
Earl's after-tax earnings (if Fran is disabled)	$1040
Fran's present after-tax income	$1020

a How much disability income insurance should Fran have?

b A local insurance agent suggests that since most disabilities do not extend for a long period, the Greys should concentrate on a policy that has a very short waiting period coupled with a short benefits period. Do you agree?

c The Greys are concerned that inflation may erode the purchasing power of those projected sources of disability income. Will it erode all the sources? Can the Greys compensate for this possibility in their insurance plan?

15-7   Clyde Closecall has narrowed his choice of disability income policies to the following:

	POLICY #1	POLICY #2
Maximum benefit period	1 year	20 years
Waiting period	30 days	90 days
Monthly benefit	$200	$200
Maximum income replacement allowed	60%	70%

Both policies define "disability" similarly and their annual premiums are comparable. Clyde presently earns $1350 monthly before any taxes; he estimates that his monthly Social Security disability benefit would be $600.

a Will Clyde have a problem with either policy's income replacement percentage?

b What is the maximum benefit with each policy?

c Clyde is confused as to why the two policies have similar premiums. Can you explain, given your answer in (**b**), why they do?

CASE PROBLEM

Neal and Nancy Shaw are considering several health insurance alternatives. The first option is not to buy any insurance. But, while they are both healthy at the present time, they are not certain that being uninsured is such a good idea.

Therefore, they have gathered the following details on four possible insurance policies:

CHAPTER 15

507

HEALTH
INSURANCE AND
DISABILITY
INCOME
INSURANCE

FEATURES	**Policies**			
	BASIC HEALTH	MAJOR MEDICAL	COMPRE-HENSIVE	SUPPLEMENTAL HOSPITAL
Deductible	$50	$500	None	None
Coinsurance	None	80–20 with $2,000 maximum	None	None
Benefit payment	Cash benefit	Service benefit	Service benefit	$40 per day after 6th day in hospital
Policy limit	$5,000	$50,000	$50,000	$50,000
Premium	$400	$700	$1,500	$200
Waiting period	10 days	20 days	10 days	2 years

1   Should the Shaws buy insurance? Why?

2   What are the strengths and weaknesses of each of the four health insurance policies?

3   If one of the Shaws should incur $800 of medical expenses without requiring hospitalization, what amount would they have to pay under each policy?

4   If one of the Shaws had a serious illness that included a lengthy, 30-day hospital stay with expenses totaling $19,500, what amount would they have to pay under each policy?

5   For each policy, list the guidelines you believe the Shaws should use to decide which policy they should choose.

6   If you were faced with the above choices, what policy would you choose? Why?

CHAPTER

16

PROPERTY INSURANCE AND LIABILITY INSURANCE

AFTER COMPLETING THIS CHAPTER YOU WILL HAVE LEARNED

What *homeowners insurance* is all about

What the *differences* are among the *six principal types of homeowners policies*

How to decide which *homeowners policy* best fits *your needs*

How your *reimbursement for losses* under a homeowners policy is computed

Why it is important to *shop* for *homeowners insurance*

What *auto insurance* is all about

How to get the *most protection* from your auto insurance at the *least cost*

How *deductibles* can help to reduce your *auto insurance costs*

The *factors* that determine your *auto insurance costs*

Why *shopping for auto insurance* is essential

CHAPTER 16

509

PROPERTY
INSURANCE AND
LIABILITY
INSURANCE

PROPERTY insurance and liability insur-

ance protect you, but in different ways.

Property insurance protects you against the loss of personal possessions, such as your car, your house, and your furniture. By "loss" we mean damage to or theft of your property. By "protect" we mean that the insurance company will reimburse (protect) you up to a specified amount for your property loss.

Liability insurance protects you from financial loss resulting from lawsuits brought against you by others who have suffered a loss caused by your negligence. In other words, should someone be hurt or suffer a loss in any way on account of you or your property, and should that person sue you in a court of law and it turns out you were "negligent," liability insurance would pay the claims granted to that person. The key word here is "negligent," which basically means that you weren't especially careful and so caused the other person to suffer a loss.

Technically, property and liability insurance are two distinct types of insurance. However, they are commonly sold together as a combination policy. Therefore, rather than treat property insurance and liability insurance coverages separately, we will discuss the two basic kinds of insurance policies that combine these coverages—the standard homeowners policy and the family auto policy.

HOMEOWNERS INSURANCE

Homeowners insurance is sold as a combination policy to protect you both against losses to your personal property and against personal liability losses. Examples of personal property losses that would be covered include damage to your home from a fire or the theft of a TV set from your living room. Liability protection would pay the medical expenses for someone who tripped over your child's bike which had been left on the sidewalk.

In most states, the homeowners policies are designated as HO-1, HO-2, HO-3, and HO-5 for people who own single-family houses; HO-6 for condominium owners; and HO-4 for renters. The policies differ primarily in the kinds and extent of the **perils** (causes of loss) which they insure against.

Homeowners Property Insurance

Exhibit 16-1 summarizes the perils that each of the different homeowners insurance policies covers. For those who own and live in a single-family house, the most limited coverage is provided by the basic policy, **HO-1**: it covers loss or damage caused by the 10 listed perils. Moving up to an **HO-2** policy provides coverage for those 10 perils, plus an additional 7 perils. The next step is an **HO-3** policy, which provides **"all risk"** coverage on the building and covers personal property against the 17 listed perils. Even with all peril coverage, the insurance policy will list some causes of loss that are excluded; typically, they include flood, earthquake, war, and nuclear accidents. Upgrading one more step, we have the comprehensive **HO-5** policy: it provides "all risk" coverage for both buildings and personal property. An HO-5 policy gives the most comprehensive, and therefore the most expensive, coverage of the policies discussed thus far.

The renters policy, **HO-4**, is designed to meet the special needs of those who rent their living units. It covers personal property against perils 1 through 9 and 11 through 17, as listed in Exhibit 16-1, but it provides no coverage on the building because the renter has no insurable interest in it. Condominium owners have special needs because they not only have their personal property; they also own their individual living units. The condominium policy, **HO-6**, covers personal property against perils 1 through 9 and 11 through 17, as shown in Exhibit 16-1.

EXHIBIT 16-1

Peril coverage provided by each type of homeowners insurance.

PERIL COVERAGE	Policy Type					
	HO-1: BASIC FORM	HO-2: BROAD FORM	HO-3: SPECIAL FORM	HO-4: RENTERS FORM	HO-5: COMPRE-HENSIVE FORM	HO-6: CONDO-MINIUM FORM
Buildings	1–10	1–17	All risks*	None	All risks*	None
Personal property	1–9	1–9, 11–17	1–9, 11–17	1–9, 11–17	All risks*	1–9, 11–17

Guide to Perils

1	Fire and lightning	**9**	Theft	**15**	Explosion of steam or hot-water system
2	Windstorm or hail	**10**	Glass breakage		
3	Explosion	**11**	Falling objects		
4	Riot or civil commotion	**12**	Weight of ice, snow, or sleet	**16**	Freezing
5	Aircraft	**13**	Collapse	**17**	Damage from artificially generated current
6	Vehicles	**14**	Accidental discharge or overflow of water of steam		
7	Smoke				
8	Vandalism or malicious mischief				

*All risk insurance is further explained in the text.

Property Coverages   The first section of a homeowners policy insures the property, and it is divided into four separate provisions which describe the type and extent of coverage.

Provision A   The insurance coverage under this provision pertains to the house and structures attached to it. Renters insurance, HO-4, and condominium owners insurance, HO-6, do not provide any protection on the building. The insured determines the amount of insurance protection on the building. There is no point in buying more insurance than the building is worth, because the insurance company will not reimburse you for more than the replacement value of the property in the case of total loss. The amount specified under this provision is referred to as the *"face amount"* of the policy.

Provision B   Detached garages, tool sheds, and similar outside buildings are referred to as **appurtenant structures** in insurance policies. Appurtenant structures are covered for an amount equal to 10 percent of the face amount of the policy. If the building structure of your house were insured for $50,000 (the face amount of the policy), your garage would automatically be covered for $5000. In the event both structures were totally destroyed by fire, you could collect $55,000.

Provision C   This portion of the policy specifies the coverage on the contents of the building, such as furniture, clothing, and other **personal property.** Altogether, these items are usually specified at 50 percent of the policy's face amount. For a home insured for $50,000, the contents would be covered for $25,000. Since the renters and condominium owners policies do not insure the building structure, the owner specifies the coverage on the contents. The minimum coverage for both HO-4 and HO-6 is $6,000. Beyond that, the policyholders can raise the limits to suit their needs.

Under all of the policies, the insured's personal property is also covered while away from home. Coverage equals 10 percent of the basic contents' coverage. Thus, if you had an HO-3 policy with limits of $50,000 on the dwelling, the contents would be covered for $25,000 and property away from home would be protected for up to $2500. Examples of property away from the premises would be your son's or daughter's possessions in a college dormitory and the luggage in your car. For example, if a stereo set worth $350 were stolen from your daughter's dormitory room, your homeowners policy would pay for the set just as though it were stolen from your home.

Provision D   This section defines **additional living expenses,** such as motel or hotel rentals and meals for you and your family, to be paid in the event that your home cannot be occupied because of fire or other perils. Limits are 10 percent of the face amount for HO-1; 20 percent for HO-2, HO-3, HO-4, and HO-6; and 40 percent for HO-5.

However, because there is no coverage on the dwelling for HO-4 and HO-6, living expenses are based on the coverage on the contents. Since this is usually significantly less than the coverage of the building, the reimbursement for living expenses can be quite limited.

CHAPTER 16

511

PROPERTY
INSURANCE AND
LIABILITY
INSURANCE

Summary of Policy Coverages

For the six types of homeowners policies, Exhibit 16-2 summarizes what is covered by each type of policy and the extent of that coverage. This list includes both the property and the liability features of the policies. In using this table, it is important to note that many of the property coverage limits depend on the amount that is specified for the basic dwelling. (The liability features will be discussed later.)

STRATEGY

The best insurance buy for most homeowners is either HO-2 or HO-3. The coverage under HO-1 is too limited, and the more extensive coverage under HO-5 is more appropriate for individuals who are willing and able to pay substantially higher premiums.

EXHIBIT 16-2

Types of homeowners policies and what each type covers.

	Policy Type					
COVERAGE ON	HO-1 BASIC FORM	HO-2 BROAD FORM	HO-3 SPECIAL FORM	HO-4 RENTERS FORM	HO-5 COMPRE-HENSIVE FORM	HO-6 CONDO-MINIUM FORM
Dwelling	You set amount	You set amount	You set amount	None	You set amount	None
Appurtenant structures	10% of dwelling	10% of dwelling	10% of dwelling	None	10% of dwelling	None
Trees and shrubs	5% of dwelling	5% of dwelling	5% of dwelling	10% of personal property	5% of dwelling	10% of personal property
Personal property*	50% of dwelling	50% of dwelling	50% of dwelling	You set amount	50% of dwelling	You set amount
Personal property off premises	10% of property on premises	10% of property on premises	10% of property on premises	10% of property on premises	10% of property on premises	10% of property on premises
Living expenses	10% of dwelling	20% of dwelling	20% of dwelling	20% of personal property	40% of dwelling	20% of personal property
Personal liability*	$25,000 or more	$25,000 or more	$25,000 or more	$25,000 or more	$25,000 or more	$25,000 or more
Damages to others' property	$250	$250	$250	$250	$250	$250
Medical payments*	$500 per person	$500 per person	$500 per person	$500 per person	$500 per person	$500 per person

*Higher coverage is available.

How Much Insurance?

CHAPTER 16

513

PROPERTY
INSURANCE AND
LIABILITY
INSURANCE

One thing most people don't understand about homeowners insurance is the fact that policy limits must be at least 80 percent of the replacement value of the property; otherwise, the insured becomes subject to **coinsurance.** That means that the company will pay for only a portion of the loss and the policy owner must pay the remainder—or, in effect, be self-insuring. In the event of a fire, the policyholder will only collect:

$$\text{Payment} = \text{Amount of loss} \times \frac{\text{Actual insurance}}{\text{Required insurance}}$$

For example, let's assume that Sally Wright bought her house 12 years ago, paid $35,000 for it, and insured it for $30,000. The 12 years pass, and the replacement value of the house increases to $75,000, which is what it is worth today. Sally never reviewed her insurance, so the house is still insured for the original $30,000. On a bitterly cold night this past winter, her furnace overheated, causing a fire which resulted in $20,000 of damages. Despite the fact that Sally had $30,000 of insurance, she collected only $10,000. Her payment for her loss was figured by the insurance company as follows:

$$\$10,000 = \$20,000 \quad \times [\$30,000 \quad \div \quad (\$75,000 \quad \times 80\%)]$$

$$\begin{array}{ccccc} \Uparrow & \Uparrow & \Uparrow & \Uparrow & \Uparrow \end{array}$$

$$\text{Payment} = \begin{array}{c}\text{Amount of}\\\text{loss}\end{array} \times \begin{array}{c}\text{Actual}\\\text{insurance}\end{array} \div \left\{\begin{array}{l}\text{Required insurance:}\\\text{Replacement} \times 80\%\end{array}\right\}$$

If Sally had maintained $60,000 of coverage on her home, she would have received the full $20,000 for the fire damage. With a policy face amount of $60,000, Sally would have received full payment for any damages up to that amount.

Despite the fact that complete compensation will not be received for a

SO SORRY I COULDN'T MAKE THAT APPOINTMENT YESTERDAY..

total loss unless the policy provides full replacement coverage, (for Sally's house, that would be $75,000 of coverage), it is generally recommended that homes be insured for 80 percent of their replacement value. This coverage provides full protection for any partial losses up to the face amount of the policy. Since most losses are partial, this coverage should provide adequate protection. Moreover, even with a "total loss," the foundation of the dwelling and other below-ground portions of the house should still be usable.

STRATEGY

Reevaluate your homeowners insurance each year to make certain that your coverage equals at least 80 percent of the current cost of replacing the house.

Compensation for Loss of Personal Property

A policy that insures a home for $60,000 will cover the family's personal property in the home for up to $30,000. That should be adequate coverage for most people. Unfortunately, the actual protection you get from the insurance company often falls far short of the amount stated in the policy. The explanation is that standard items of personal property are covered at replacement cost *minus* accumulated depreciation. The replacement cost is what the item would cost today. That seems fair, particularly given high inflation rates. However, the accumulated depreciation is the amount that the insurance company says the item has lost in value because it is no longer new. If the insurance company uses a life of 20 years for a particular item and the one you own is 19 years old, you would collect only 5 percent of the item's replacement cost. Since 19 years have elapsed, the company estimates that the item has only one-twentieth of its replacement value. Assume that a walnut dining room set was assigned a 20-year life; its annual depreciation, or decline in value, is 5 percent of the set's replacement cost. A 19-year-old dining room set having a replacement cost of $2000 would be covered for only $100 in the event of fire or theft. The calculation is:

$$\$100 \quad = \$2000 \quad - \quad [\$2000 \times (19 \text{ yrs} \div 20 \text{ yrs})]$$

$\Uparrow$	$\Uparrow$	$\Uparrow$	$\Uparrow$	$\Uparrow$

$$\begin{matrix} \text{Insurance} \\ \text{payment} \end{matrix} = \begin{matrix} \text{Replacement} \\ \text{cost: Dining} \\ \text{room set} \end{matrix} - \left\{ \begin{matrix} \text{Accumulated depreciation:} \\ \text{Replacement} \times (\text{Present} \div \text{Assumed}) \\ \text{cost} \qquad \text{age} \qquad \text{life} \end{matrix} \right\}$$

The problem is, a 20-year-old dining room set—in good condition—might very well have a *higher* actual value now than it did when it was new. Certainly it would cost far more to replace than it originally cost to buy. The insurer, even though living up to the policy's provisions, could leave the insured with a substantial loss.

Full Replacement for Personal Property   A number of insurance companies now sell homeowners insurance that provides **full replacement coverage** for personal property losses. No depreciation would be deducted; instead, you would be reimbursed for the full replacement cost of your personal property loss. Had the dining room set cited in the previous section been covered by a full replacement policy, it would be covered for its full $2000 replacement cost. The additional premium for one of these policies is 10 to 20 percent more than a standard homeowners policy.

If you are considering buying such a policy, carefully review the coverage to make certain there are not additional restrictions on the payment for losses. For example, a policy might limit your maximum reimbursement to 4 times the item's original price. If our previous dining room set had an original price of $300, the reimbursement would be only $1200.

STRATEGY

You should consider adding the full replacement option, if available, to your homeowners policy. This step is especially important if much of your personal property is 5 to 20 years old, because depreciation charges would sharply reduce your reimbursement.

Property Records   The fact that the settlement for loss of personal property can be such a small percentage of the property's value is an unpleasant surprise to many people. But an equal, if not more frustrating, shock is when you cannot be certain of what personal property you have lost. Suppose Debbie Disaster returns to her apartment to find that not only has it been ransacked by someone but, even worse, all her remaining worldly goods are in a 5-foot mound in the center of her living room. Unless Debbie has a good inventory of her personal property, it will be difficult to reconstruct precisely what she owned originally and, therefore, to know what is missing. Situations like this make it essential that you maintain a thorough, up-to-date set of personal property records along the lines we discussed back in Exhibit 2-4 of Chapter 2. Probably the easiest and most effective technique is to group your inventory cards (assuming that you are using index cards) according to each room in your house or apartment. And make certain that you store your inventory off the premises; a safe deposit box is ideal.

The point at which you are updating your inventory is also a good time to check the adequacy of your personal property coverage. First, total up the estimated replacement value for each item in your inventory; that covers the major property items. Next, make a rough estimate of the replacement value for all your personal property items that are not part of your inventory; that covers the smaller items. The total of these two groups is the personal property coverage you should have under your homeowners policy.

STRATEGY

When you update your personal inventory every 2 years, use the time to simultaneously review the adequacy of the insurance coverage on your personal property.

CHAPTER 16

515

PROPERTY
INSURANCE AND
LIABILITY
INSURANCE

Additional Limitations   Special types of personal property that actually appreciate in value (become worth more than their original cost as time passes), rather than depreciate in value, are always underinsured by the standard homeowners policy. Articles such as antiques and art, unless identified and specified in the insurance policy, will be evaluated as ordinary furniture and pictures. For example, let's say you own the painting of the Mona Lisa, which is probably worth about $10 million. Let's also assume that you forgot to mention this to your insurance company, and later a fire occurs. When the insurance company looks at the charred, empty frame, it will figure it owes you the cost of a mere copy of the original painting plus the frame, worth about $150.

Thus, in the event of loss, compensation would be limited to the depreciated value of the physical components of the item. Since real works of art appreciate in value, standard policies would grossly underestimate their true value. Loss of other articles, such as jewelry and silver, will be reimbursed only up to a maximum of $500 to $1000 on the homeowners policy. Types of property which are underinsured by the homeowners policy and which should be separately insured include:

Jewelry	Cameras	Guns
Furs	Arts and antiques	Stamps and coins
Silverware	Musical instruments	

Scheduled Personal Property Endorsement   The most common way to provide the additional coverage you need for special personal property items is by scheduling those special items on your existing homeowners policy. **Scheduling personal property** means that you provide a detailed list of the special items you want insured, together with the value of each item. For valuable items, most insurance companies require that you substantiate an item's worth. One way to do that is to have the item appraised, or valued, by a qualified expert. If it has been purchased recently, the company may accept your purchase receipt as evidence of the item's value. Regardless of which technique you use to establish the value, that amount is the amount of coverage you will have, and it will be your reimbursement if the item is lost or destroyed. Typically, all peril coverage is provided on scheduled property.

Personal Articles Floater Policy   Another way to cover your special personal property items is to purchase a separate **personal articles floater** policy. The operation of that policy is similar to the previously discussed scheduled personal property: The item is insured for its current value and you receive all peril coverage.

STRATEGY

If you have special personal property items, make certain that you obtain the necessary additional coverage either by scheduling them on your homeowners policy or by buying a separate floater policy; review that coverage every 2 to 4 years to ensure that each item is protected at its *current value.*

Recreational Vehicles Reimbursement for the loss of boats, motors, and trailers is limited to $500 under the terms of the standard homeowners policy. Consequently, separate policies should be purchased to cover these items.

Mobile Homes and Farms Mobile homes and farms cannot be insured under a standard homeowner's policy. However, there are policies that are designed specifically for such residences. The provisions will differ somewhat from those of the homeowners policies. If you are considering such a policy, it is important to recognize that the coverage may be different and to read its provisions.

Homeowners Liability Insurance

The **liability insurance** portion of the homeowners policy provides coverage for the following:

1 Personal liability—protection against the financial consequences when you may be at fault for someone else's injury or loss

2 Medical payments—the cost of medical attention for someone who may have been injured as a result of your actions

3 Property damage—when you may have been at fault for damage caused to someone else's property

Whether you rent or own, you are subject to the threat of financial loss if someone is injured in your home or on your property. Similarly, if you do something that results in damage to somebody else's property, you can also be held financially liable. In fact, in certain instances, even if you can prove that someone was injured on your property through his or her own negligence, you can still be financially liable. Such would be the case if a child was injured while trespassing on your property.

Personal Liability Standard homeowners policies have **personal liability** limits of $25,000, although this amount can be increased substantially for a small additional cost. The liability coverage includes protection for legal judgments against you and the legal costs incurred in your defense.

The cost of a liability judgment against you could be financially devastating. For example, if a neighbor, while having a drink in your home, should trip on a rug and sustain severe injuries, an award of $25,000 or $100,000 might result. Awards of these and often greater amounts are common. Could you afford to pay a settlement of that magnitude? Most likely, the answer is *no*. Even a $4000 or $5000 damage suit would be financially disastrous for most people. This is why the liability portion of the homeowners policy is so important.

STRATEGY

For a small additional cost, as low as $4 annually, you can increase the liability limit on your homeowners policy to $50,000 or $100,000 of protection.

Medical Payments   In addition to providing protection against liability judgments, the liability portion of the homeowners policy also provides **medical payments** to persons other than the insured and his or her family. These payments are made whether or not the insured is found to be negligent. For example, if a woman slipped on your sidewalk, she could receive medical compensation from your insurance company without proving you to be at fault.

Property Damage Liability   If you, or another member of your family, should accidentally cause minor damage (under $250) to somebody else's property, the claim for such damage is covered under the **property damage** liability portion of your policy. In the event that a child under thirteen years of age causes the damage, the claim will be paid even when the damage was intentionally caused. If the child is thirteen or over, claims will be paid only in the event that the damage was accidental.

Cost of Homeowners Insurance

There are a number of factors that affect the premiums on homeowners insurance policies. The factors we consider in this section include:

Construction of the home and its location

The type of policy that is selected

The company from which that coverage is purchased

The deductible amount on the policy

To obtain the best insurance coverage for your premium dollars, you need to be familiar with these factors and how they operate.

Construction of the Home and Its Location   The type of material used in a home's construction affects the insurance premium; generally: the more fire-resistant the material, the lower your premiums. Consequently, a home with a brick exterior typically has a lower rate than a frame home. At the same time, the location of the home can have a sizable bearing on the premium. If it is located in an area that is currently experiencing high losses, the premiums will be higher. Likewise, if the home is located in an area with only limited fire protection, the premium will also be higher. While you obviously cannot relocate the housing unit itself, you can be aware, when selecting a housing unit, that certain locations and types of construction can each raise your insurance premiums.

Type of Policy   Exhibit 16-3 summarizes the annual premiums for three different homeowners policies. It was compiled by the Insurance Information Institute, which is an organization that publishes information to increase consumers' understanding of insurance. The premiums are based on a house that is insured for $75,000 with $25,000 of liability coverage. The average premium is revealing because it shows that for a very small increase

I'VE GOT AN HO-5 POLICY — THAT PROTECTS ME AGAINST EVERYTHING BUT TIDAL WAVES!

in premiums, individuals can substantially enhance their homeowners insurance coverage by upgrading from an HO-2 to an HO-3 policy.

STRATEGY

Clearly, for many people the small increase in premiums justifies the much broader coverage of an HO-3 policy over an HO-2 policy.

Purchasing the Right Policy Selecting a low-cost homeowners policy can produce a dramatic savings in the annual premium. The range of premiums shown in Exhibit 16-3 illustrates the sizable premium differentials that can

EXHIBIT 16-3

Typical premiums for homeowners insurance coverage.

TYPE OF POLICY	**Annual Premium***			PREMIUM REDUCTION BY SWITCHING FROM $100 TO $250 DEDUCTIBLE
	LOW COST	AVERAGE COST[†]	HIGH COST	
Broad form HO-2	$182	$218	$283	10%
Special form HO-3	190	229	298	10%
Comprehensive HO-5	N/A	269	N/A	10%

N/A = Not available
*Based on home located in a suburban area with class 3 fire protection.
[†]Average cost based on sample of seven companies, except for HO-5, which is an in-house estimate.
Source: Insurance Information Institute, Chicago.

exist between low- and high-cost policies. Selecting the wrong policy could easily raise your premiums by 50 percent or more. And since homeowners policies are reasonably easy to compare for coverages, paying those sharply higher premiums is unnecessary.

STRATEGY

Always obtain price quotes from at least three insurance agents before you select a policy; the savings can be very worthwhile.

Deductibles   One way you can lower your homeowners insurance premium is to raise the deductible. To provide an idea of how large the savings can be, the far right column of Exhibit 16-3 computes the premium reduction you can get by switching from a $100 to a $250 deductible policy. It suggests that a reduction of 10 percent is typical. On a $250 annual premium, you would save $25. Since you can only deduct casualty losses that exceed 10 percent of your income, switching to a higher deductible is far less attractive now than it used to be. The reason is that you no longer gain the tax advantage from deducting those casualty losses. For that reason, we recommend switching to a higher deductible only if your premiums are very high and therefore a 10 percent reduction is worthwhile. Switching may also make sense if you are strapped for funds to pay premiums. Unless that is your case, we advise staying with the standard $100 deductible.

AUTOMOBILE INSURANCE

A major expense confronting automobile owners is the annual premium on the auto insurance policy. The cost of the policy is determined by two groups of factors: those over which you have no control (such as your age and place of residence) and those which you can influence (such as your driving record and the type of automobile you own). Each of these factors will be discussed later in this chapter. Careful selection of the coverages in your auto policy can also reduce your cost substantially. In this section, we will look at the provisions of the standard family auto policy and highlight the areas that can be of most importance to you in tailoring the policy to your needs.

The Family Auto Policy

The principal auto insurance policy issued in this country is the **family auto policy** (FAP). Its provisions, summarized in Exhibit 16-4, are standard from company to company and, for the most part, from state to state. The FAP is designed only for the protection of privately owned vehicles and is available only to individuals who satisfy very tough standards designed to eliminate high-risk drivers. Coverages under such policies fall into the following four sections:

1   Liability, which covers both bodily injury and property damage

2   Medical payments

3   Uninsured motorist protection

4   Property damage, both collision and comprehensive

CHAPTER 16

521

PROPERTY
INSURANCE AND
LIABILITY
INSURANCE

The top section of Exhibit 16-4 summarizes the bodily injury coverage that is provided by the various sections of the FAP. The bottom half of the same exhibit summarizes the property damages that are covered by the FAP's various sections.

Liability Coverages   The primary need for auto insurance is to protect yourself against legal liability arising from negligence on your part. Section 1 of the policy gives **liability limits** for the maximum payment the insurance company will make on **personal injury** and **property damage** that are a result of your negligence. For example, a policy with limits of $100,000/$300,000/$25,000, often stated as 100/300/25, will pay $100,000 to any one accident victim, a maximum of $300,000 to all victims in one accident, and $25,000 in property damages. If you hit another car with four occupants, the maximum personal liability coverage would be $300,000, even though the policy will pay up to $100,000 to any one victim. Exhibit 16-5 shows these liability coverages.

In addition to the basic liability coverage, the insurance company agrees to defend the insured in any accident case. This promise to defend is separate from any liability settlement. That is, the legal costs are separate from the amount of the legal judgment. Thus, if the judgment were for $300,000, the maximum under the policy, the insurance company would pay all court and defense costs as well as the $300,000 judgment.

The property damage liability portion of section 1 covers damages to

EXHIBIT 16-4

Insurance protection provided by various sections of the family auto policy.

	Protection given to	
BODILY INJURY COVERAGES	POLICYHOLDER	OTHER PERSONS
Personal injury liability	No	Yes
Medical payments	Yes	Yes
Protection against uninsured motorists	Yes	Yes
PROPERTY DAMAGE COVERAGES	POLICYHOLDER'S CAR	PROPERTY OF OTHERS
Property damage liability	No	Yes
Comprehensive physical damage	Yes	No
Collision	Yes	No

EXHIBIT 16-5

Automobile liability insurance limits for FAP.

LIMITS OF LIABILITY FOR PERSONAL INJURY		LIMITS OF LIABILITY FOR PROPERTY DAMAGE
$100,000	/ $300,000	$25,000
Maximum amount payable to any one person injured in accident	Maximum amount payable to all persons in one accident	Maximum amount payable for damage to others' property

other people's property in an accident caused by the insured. Running into another car, going through a storefront, or knocking down a telephone pole would all be covered up to the policy limits.

Medical Payments   Section 2 of the family automobile policy provides **medical payments** to the insured and to passengers in the insured's car. You can buy medical payments protection in amounts starting at $500; for a small additional premium cost, the amount of this protection can be increased to $5000. If you have regular health insurance and you are injured in your car, you will receive payments for your medical expenses from your auto insurance, and these payments will not reduce any payments that would be made from any health-insurance policies you own. This is one of the rare cases in insurance where you can collect more than the total amount of your loss—in this instance, your medical expenses. The important thing about section 2 of the auto insurance policy is that the medical payments provide immediate coverage for the insured (there is no waiting period as in health insurance) and that it provides coverage for the passengers who may not have health insurance.

Protection Against Uninsured Motorists   One of the dangers confronting drivers is that of being involved in an accident where the other driver is at fault but does not have automobile insurance. The **uninsured motorists** section of your own FAP is designed to reimburse you for personal injuries if you are involved in an accident with an uninsured driver. It is important to realize that this protection covers *only* personal injury, *not* property damage. Limited as the protection may be, it is a worthwhile addition to your insurance policy. Most companies will automatically include this feature on the policy. In some states, in fact, it is a mandatory coverage on the FAP.

Collision Insurance   This portion of the FAP reimburses you for damages to your car resulting from an accident in which you are at fault. **Collision coverage** always specifies a deductible amount. That is, you must pay a specified amount for damage repairs and the insurance company pays the rest. Standard deductible amounts are $50, $100, $250, and $500. With a $50 deductible, if you suffered $1000 of collision damages, you would collect $950, provided that your car was worth at least $1000. The maximum that the insurance company will pay is the wholesale price of the car. Thus, if a car valued at $500 is damaged and repairs will cost $1000, the maximum compensation with $50 deductible will be $450.

CHAPTER 16

523

PROPERTY
INSURANCE AND
LIABILITY
INSURANCE

Comprehensive Property Coverage   Comprehensive property protection reimburses you for damage to your car resulting from fire, theft, vandalism, hail, windstorm, flood, smoke, and similar perils. It even provides coverage for contact with birds and animals. Unfortunately, many people believe that the theft provisions of their comprehensive coverage also include personal articles in the automobile. This is not true. Only the automobile itself is covered by this portion of the policy. If luggage or other personal items are is stolen from your car, any reimbursement must come from your homeowners or renters insurance. And to collect on either of these policies, there usually must be visible evidence of forced entry into the car.

Who Is Covered?

The most important technical aspect of the FAP is the definition of who is covered by the insurance. The FAP is designed to provide protection for the insured when driving both owned and nonowned automobiles.

An **owned automobile** is one that is owned by the insured. The coverage for an owned automobile is extensive.

A **nonowned automobile** is one that is not owned by the insured, nor is it an automobile provided for the regular use of the insured. For example, if Mary Stone lends her car to Thelma Rock, Thelma is covered by Mary's policy since she is driving with Mary's permission. Thelma is also be covered under her own FAP if she has one. The car, as defined by the insurance companies, qualifies as an *owned automobile* for Mary and a *nonowned automobile* for Thelma. There will not be double coverage in this situation. However, if Thelma's policy had higher limits than Mary's policy, she would be protected up to the maximum protection of her policy. But if claims exceeded its limits, the excess would be covered by Thelma's insurance. The coverage by Mary's policy would be the *primary,* or first, coverage, while Thelma's policy would provide *secondary* coverage.

In summary, it is safe to assume that your FAP policy will cover you if:

1   You are driving your car.

2   Somebody else is driving your car with your permission.

3   You are driving a borrowed car with permission, provided that the car meets the definition of a nonowned automobile.

If you have a unique situation and have a question about whether you or another person will be protected by your insurance, check with your agent.

Policy Cancellation

You may, of course, cancel your family auto policy at any time. The company may also do so under certain conditions, and you should be aware of them. During the first 60 days a policy is in force, the insurance company can cancel by just giving you notice. Beyond those 60 days, the company can cancel under only two conditions:

The premium has not been paid.

The insured's driver's license has been suspended or revoked.

The latter provision means that if the insured's driver's license is suspended or revoked for too many moving traffic violations, driving under the influence of alcohol, a hit-and-run accident, or similar serious offenses, the company can cancel the policy.

We should also note that when the policy is up for renewal (typically every 3 to 6 months), the insurance company can generally refuse to renew it for almost any reason. Even if your policy is not canceled while it is in force, there is no guarantee that the company will renew it. However, some states have passed legislation that restricts the insurance company's right not to renew the policy.

STRATEGY

When you purchase an automobile insurance policy, you should carefully examine the cancellation and nonrenewal provisions.

Choosing the Amount of Auto Insurance Protection

Estimating the coverage that you need to protect your property (primarily your automobile) against damage is reasonably straightforward. But estimating the correct liability coverage for other people's property and personal injury to other persons is much more difficult. This section provides some guidelines on these two coverages.

CHAPTER 16

525

PROPERTY
INSURANCE AND
LIABILITY
INSURANCE

Personal Injury Liability   Our advice here is simple: Purchase very high dollar limits on the personal injury liability coverage. Granted that coverages can be obtained for as low as $10,000/$20,000, but the added cost to increase that coverage to $50,000/$100,000 or even $100,000/$300,000 is not that large. We recommend that you purchase the maximum personal injury liability coverage that the company will sell you. Those extra dollars are well spent because they protect you against the catastrophic losses that a large damage award might entail. Personal injury coverage is not the area to try to save premium dollars when purchasing insurance.

Property Damage Liability   Our advice on property damage liability is similar: Select a high dollar coverage. First, the added premium to raise the limit from the minimum $5000 to a more reasonable $25,000 is not very much. Second, with the cost of new cars easily exceeding $10,000, and with a number of them exceeding $20,000, that higher coverage becomes essential. We recommend that you buy the maximum property damage coverage that the insurance company will sell you. Property damage is another area where we think it unwise to try to save premium dollars.

Getting the Most for Your Insurance Dollar

We believe the central goal when purchasing auto insurance, as with all insurance, is to maximize protection while holding premiums at a reasonable level. Recognizing this fact, the first concern should be to protect against potentially large losses. If you still have premium dollars available, shift to reducing your loss exposure on smaller losses. The annual premiums shown in Exhibit 16-6 are for a representative family auto policy. Because premiums vary widely owing to differences in the age and location of the insured, we are not suggesting your premiums will necesssarily match the ones in the exhibit. Our principal goal in presenting Exhibit 16-6 is to illustrate how premiums change with changes in the coverage. Each of the four types of coverage will be discussed in the next section.

Personal Injury and Property Damage Liability   As the previous section emphasized, the potential losses from both personal injury and property damage can be large. For that reason, high dollar coverage limits are essential. As Exhibit 16-6 illustrates, you can get these with only a moderate increase in premiums. A premium increase of 20 to 25 percent will frequently double your liability protection; mark that a "good insurance buy." We think those added premium dollars are well spent.

Medical Coverage   Recall that the medical payments section covers many of the same things as a good health care policy. Consequently, if you have a good health policy and rarely carry anyone in your car, the coverage you need for this section will likely be limited or zero. If, on the other hand, you have a mediocre health policy, or if you frequently carry passengers who also may have poor health insurance coverage, do purchase medical coverage. With the high costs of today's health care, coverage limits of $5000 are not unreasonable. As Exhibit 16-6 illustrates, additional coverage can be purchased for a modest increase in premiums.

Collision Coverage Unfortunately, all too many people attempt to purchase excellent collision coverage at the expense of adequate coverage in the more critical liability area. Their major concern is to keep the deductible to a pleasant $50, even when that means shorting coverage in other areas to hold down their premiums. In our opinion, that emphasis is precisely backward. You need coverage to handle the potential $5,000, $20,000 or $50,000 losses, not the small $100 to $200 losses. For that reason, we suggest you consider raising the deductible to $250. First, as Exhibit 16-6 aptly illustrates, the saving in premiums can be sizable. While you do reduce your coverage by increasing the deductible, you decrease that coverage only $150 when going from a $100 to $250 deductible.

As a second point, many people continue to carry collision insurance long after the car warrants such coverage. When an older car is damaged in an accident, the most that the insurance company will pay under collision coverage is the current wholesale value of the car. Once your car's wholesale value falls below $800, you should seriously consider dropping your collision coverage. An example will show why: Assume you paid a $150 annual premium for $100 deductible collision coverage on your $800 (wholesale)

EXHIBIT 16-6

Representative premiums for family auto policy coverages.

COVERAGE	LIMITS (IN 1000s)	PERCENTAGE IMPROVEMENT IN COVERAGE	ANNUAL PREMIUM	PERCENTAGE INCREASE (DECREASE) IN PREMIUMS
Liability:				
Personal	$15/$30/$10		$108	
injury and	$50/$100/$25	233%	135	25%
property	$100/$300/$25	200	162	20
damage				
Medical	$1000		14	
	2000	100	16	14
	5000	150	22	38
Collision	50 deductible		148	
	100 deductible	*	126	(15)
	250 deductible	†	94	(25)
Comprehensive	Full		41	
	50 deductible	*	31	(24)

*Reduces coverage by $50.
†Reduces coverage by $150.

car. In the event of a total loss, the most you can collect is $700. The question becomes: Is it worth paying $150 to obtain $700 of protection? Unless you have an accident more than once every 5 years, you will be further ahead to drop the coverage and accept the risk yourself.

STRATEGY

Consider raising your deductible to $250; the saving in premiums can be much better used to purchase additional liability insurance.

Comprehensive Coverage   Increasing the deductible on your comprehensive insurance reduces your coverage somewhat, with the trade-off that you lower your premium. Because the cost per dollar of comprehensive coverage is significantly less than the cost of collision coverage, the actual dollars saved by raising the deductible is much less than you might save by raising your collision deductible. Nevertheless, you should still consider raising the deductible, especially if you need those premium savings to pay the higher costs of improved liability coverage.

Rates for Automobile Insurance

Insurance rates are adjusted for factors such as automobile usage and driving record. The major factors are discussed below. It is important to realize that you can lower your premium costs by taking advantage of these special rating factors.

Type of Car   If you own a high-performance car, you will have to pay a substantial surcharge to obtain insurance coverage. That means you will have to pay a lot more for your insurance than will your friend with an unimpressive, plain car used strictly for transportation. The surcharge may run 30 or 40 percent annually. Thus, if the insurance costs $300 for an ordinary car, and you decide to buy a high-performance car, you will add $90 to $120 per year to your insurance costs. You should ask youself, "Can I afford the extra insurance cost to drive a high-powered car?"

Driving Record   Many automobile insurance companies offer a discount to safe drivers and impose a surcharge on drivers with poor records. Their definition of a "poor record" includes not only drivers who have accidents, but also individuals with moving violations such as speeding tickets or arrests for drunken driving. Your next speeding ticket may add $50 or more to your insurance costs in addition to the $50 fine.

STRATEGY

Keep your driving record clean and save by avoiding a fine and an insurance premium surcharge.

Automobile Use   The less you use your car, the lower your insurance cost. Using your auto for commuting and/or business purposes can add substan-

CHAPTER 16

527

PROPERTY
INSURANCE AND
LIABILITY
INSURANCE

tially to your premium. The longer the distance you commute to work, the more costly the insurance. Given this fact, you may want to include auto insurance as one of the cost factors that you should consider when selecting a place to live.

City of Residence Auto insurance companies include your place of residence in calculating the insurance premium. In communities where drivers have few accidents, the insurance costs less than in communities where drivers have more accidents. This will be the case even when the communities are adjacent. For example, it may cost only one-half or even one-third as much to insure a car in Needham (a suburb of Boston) as it does in Boston. Again, selecting where you live can have a big influence on your insurance costs.

Two-Car Discounts If you own two cars, you should insure them with the same company. Most companies offer a second-car discount of as much as 10 percent. It could save you $20 or even $30 per year.

Driver Education Credits The premium surcharge imposed on young drivers can be reduced if they have completed a driver-training program. A reduction of 10 percent in premiums is typical.

Age, Sex, and Marital Status The hard facts are that in most states young drivers pay higher rates than do their older counterparts. Likewise, young men pay significantly higher rates than do young women. At the same time, the rates are higher for young unmarried drivers than for married drivers of similar age; the rate differential is especially pronounced for men. The net effect is that a young, unmarried male typically pays the highest premium. As he grows older, or if he marries, the annual premium will decline sharply. The additional premium for a young, unmarried female is substantially less than that for her male counterpart. So, while her premium will decline over time, or if she marries, the decline will be much less pronounced. Unfortunately, the data on frequency and severity of accidents

---

EXHIBIT 16-7

Rules for buying insurance.

Do get price quotes from four or five different agents. Eliminate agents whose price is not competitive.

Do ask friends and relatives to recommend a good agent. Someone's long-term experience can be invaluable in helping you find a good insurance agent.

Do contact four or five agents and ask them to help you plan an insurance program. A good agent should be willing and able to do so.

Do *not* buy insurance from the car dealer. Much of the insurance sold by dealers is not competitive with insurance you can purchase elsewhere.

Do *not* finance your automobile insurance through a dealer.

Do consider buying group auto insurance if it is available through your employer.

fully support the higher premiums: young drivers do have a poor accident record.

Buying Automobile Insurance

Shopping for auto insurance is just as important as shopping for homeowners or life insurance; the savings can be substantial. Even for the same driver with identical coverage, differences in annual premiums of 100 to 200 percent are not uncommon. The guidelines outlined in Exhibit 16-7 should help you in your search for good automobile coverage at a fair price.

No-Fault Insurance

Two long-standing complaints about auto insurance have been the delays and the costs of settling claims. Under the law, in order to collect in an auto accident, one party must prove the other to be at fault. Often this procedure requires lawyers on both sides and involves bitter legal action. In some cases, such as multicar collisions, it is virtually impossible to prove negligence by any one driver. As a result of the weaknesses and inequities in the current application of legal principles to auto insurance, there has been a gradually accelerating move to a system known as **no-fault insurance**.

Under no-fault insurance an insured collects from his or her own insurance company for injuries and damages sustained in an automobile accident. No-fault does not mean that you can't also sue and try to collect from the other person's insurance carrier. Rather, it requires that a specified amount of damages must be sustained before lawsuits are permitted. The intent of no-fault legislation is to reduce the costs of insurance by eliminating the costs, primarily the legal costs, of settling claims. And the way in which no-fault does this is simply for the insurance company to pay the claim without determining who is at fault. If the claim exceeds the no-fault limit (usually between $500 and $5000), a lawsuit will be permitted.

A number of states have enacted no-fault legislation. Results to date indicate that the plans have great potential for reducing insurance costs. At present, there is no uniform system of no-fault insurance in this country. If you live in a state which has adopted no-fault, it would be wise to familiarize yourself with the major provisions of the program.

SUMMARY

1   Both homeowners and automobile insurance policies are combinations of personal liability insurance and property insurance designed to provide protection against most perils facing homeowners and auto owners.

2   There are six forms of homeowners insurance: (a) four forms (HO-1, HO-2, HO-3, and HO-5) are designed exclusively for people who own a single-family house; (b) one form (HO-4) is for people who rent; and (c) one form (HO-6) is for owners of condominiums.

3   One major difference among homeowners policies is the range of perils against which the insured is protected. For owners of houses, moving to the higher policy numbers (HO-1 to HO-2 to HO-3) broadens the range of perils covered.

4   To be fully protected for a partial loss of a dwelling, the dwelling must be insured for at least 80 percent of its current replacement value. When an owner carries less than the required coverage, the reimbursement for a loss is:

$$\text{Payment} = \text{Amount of loss} \times \frac{\text{Actual insurance}}{\text{Required insurance}}$$

5   Reimbursement for loss of personal property is calculated as:

$$\text{Payment} = \begin{array}{c}\text{Current replacement}\\ \text{cost of item}\end{array} - \begin{array}{c}\text{Accumulated depreciation}\\ \text{on item}\end{array}$$

6   Many items of personal property, such as jewelry, antiques, art, silverware, and furs, will be underinsured by the standard homeowners policy. Additional coverage can be obtained by scheduling the items on your homeowners policy or by purchasing a separate policy.

7   The liability portion of the homeowners policy protects against financial judgments arising from injuries to people on the insured's property, whether or not the injuries were caused by the insured's negligence.

8   The cost of homeowners insurance is quite modest. It is influenced by the type of policy, the policy limits, the construction of the building, the location of the property, and the deductible.

9   The family auto policy (FAP) is one of the automobile insurance policies commonly sold throughout the country. It combines protection for personal liability and coverage for damage to your property.

10   The primary reason for automobile insurance is to protect you against lawsuits arising from *your* negligent behavior.

11   The insurance company can cancel an FAP if the insured does not pay the premium or if the insured's driver's license is suspended or revoked.

12   Auto insurance should be selected with the goal of providing maximum insurance at a reasonable annual premium.

13   For a small increase in premiums, most drivers can raise the dollar limits of coverage under the liability section to a much more acceptable level of protection.

14   Raising the deductible for the collision coverage can sharply reduce the annual premium; raising the deductible on comprehensive coverage provides a smaller reduction.

15   Owners of cars whose current wholesale value is less than $800 should seriously consider dropping collision coverage.

16   Your driving record, the type of car you drive, and whether you use the car for business or pleasure can have a major impact on your auto insurance costs.

17   Shopping for auto insurance is essential; premiums on the same policy can vary from 100 percent to more than 200 percent among different insurance companies.

REVIEW YOUR UNDERSTANDING OF

Property insurance
Liability insurance
Homeowners insurance
  HO-1, HO-2, HO-3, HO-4,

HO-5, and HO-6
Perils
All risk coverage
Appurtenant structures

Personal property
Additional living expenses
Coinsurance
Full replacement coverage
Scheduling personal property
Personal articles floater
Homeowners liability insurance
   Personal liability
   Medical payments
   Property damage
Family auto policy
   Personal injury liability

Property damage liability
Medical payments
Uninsured motorists
Collision coverage
Comprehensive property protection
Liability limits
Deductibles
Owned automobiles
Nonowned automobiles
Policy cancellation
No-fault insurance

CHAPTER 16

531

PROPERTY
INSURANCE AND
LIABILITY
INSURANCE

DISCUSSION QUESTIONS

1 Sue Smalltime and Bill Bigdollar are discussing their respective needs for homeowners insurance. Sue owns a small, rather inexpensive house while Bill owns a large, very costly house. Bill made the comment, "Expensive houses are always covered by an HO-5 policy, while small homes only need the coverage of an HO-1 policy." Do you agree? Why or why not? Can you give Sue and Bill some guidance on selecting homeowners policies that suit their respective needs?

2 Stephanie Studio told a friend that since she does not own a house but rents an apartment, there is no reason to purchase insurance. Do you agree or disagree with this statement? Why?

3 A recent fire in Borris Badluck's condominium destroyed $10,000 (current replacement cost) of his personal property. Borris is not concerned, however, because his HO-6 policy has $20,000 of coverage. Will he receive a check for $10,000? Why or why not?

4 What is the purpose of maintaining an inventory of your personal property? What should that inventory record show? How often should you update it?

5 Ronda Frank recently paid $4000 for an antique table that was made about 1820 in a Shaker community. Ronda is concerned about whether her HO-3 policy will adequately cover that table. Will the policy cover it? If not, what do you recommend?

6 While delivering mail to Albert Swift's house, Agnes Badback slipped on a roller skate left out by Albert's daughter and twisted her back. Agnes's parting words were, "My lawyer will be in touch." Will Albert's HO-3 homeowners policy cover this injury? Assuming Albert has standard coverage, what is the maximum the policy will pay? If Albert needs a lawyer to defend him, who will pay the fee?

7 Fred Firstime is about to begin his search for a single-family house. He is concerned that the cost of homeowners insurance may be high. What are some ways that Fred may be able to hold down the annual premium?

8 On her way to go hunting in northern Michigan, Brenda Biggame got her deer: she bagged it on the front end of her Volkswagon. For $800 the local bump shop will repair her car (she gets the deer, of course). Can she collect on her auto insurance? If so, under what coverage?

9 While testing the "impressive winter handling capabilities" of her new front-wheel drive car, Betty Bungled missed a curve, thereby wiping out (a) her car, (b) a fire hydrant, (c) Fast Phil's Popcorn Wagon, and (d) Phil's new 450SL Mercedes Benz. She also slightly injured (e) Phil and (f) herself. Which of these damages will be covered by Betty's auto insurance? For each damage that is covered, what section of the policy will cover it?

10 Why is it considered important to have high dollar coverage on the liability section of an auto insurance policy? Since $700 fender-bender accidents are far more frequent than $70,000 personal injury and property damage accidents, wouldn't it make more sense to insure against the first through a low deductible on collision, rather than insure against the latter through high liability coverage? Comment.

11 Irene Illused borrowed her mother's car for the evening. She lent the car to a friend who proceeded to smash into a new storefront, injuring three pedestrians in the process. Is Irene covered by her FAP? Why or why not? What about her mother's FAP?

12 Tom Morgan continues to carry collision insurance ($100 deductible) on his very tired 1972 Plymouth (current retail value is $900 and wholesale value is $600). If his car were totaled, what would Tom collect? Do you have any suggestions for him?

13 Marvin Bumpkin is concerned about his breathtakingly large annual premium for his auto insurance. Details include:

> In keeping with his sauve, debonair image, he drives a high-performance auto.

> Marvin has accumulated 11 points for moving traffic violations; when he reaches 12 points, he loses his license.

> Marvin is twenty-two years old and single.

> To minimize his losses, Marvin keeps his deductibles to $50 or less.

> Marvin uses the car in his business.

> Marvin lives in a large metropolitan area.

Can you explain Marvin's high premiums? Would you suggest any changes?

PROBLEMS

16-1 Betty Woe owns a home with a current replacement cost of $62,500. She has a HO-3 homeowners policy with a face amount of $40,000. Recently, her home was damaged by fire, and the repairs cost $8,000.

    a How much will she collect from the insurance company?

    b To collect the entire $8,000 for the fire damage, how much insurance coverage should Betty have had?

16-2 Because of extensive damage from the tornado that struck their house, the Timms family had to live in a motel for 2 months while repairs were being made; the total cost of that stay was $2,400. The Smiths' house was covered by a $40,000 (face value) HO-3 homeowners policy.

    a Are living expenses while the house cannot be occupied covered?

    b How much does their policy promise to pay for living expenses?

16-3 A recent fire in Linda Loser's apartment building destroyed her leather wingback chair (original purchase price $600, current replacement cost $1200). The chair was 8 years old and in excellent condition. According to the schedule used by her insurance company, overstuffed furniture (such as her chair) has a life of 10 years.

a What amount will Linda collect under her HO-4 policy?

CHAPTER 16

533

PROPERTY
INSURANCE AND
LIABILITY
INSURANCE

b For an added 15 percent over and above the standard HO-4's $150 annual premium, Linda could have purchased an HO-4 policy with full replacement on personal property. Had she opted for that policy, what would she have collected?

c Would you recommend the full-replacement HO-4 policy? Why?

16-4 While waiting for a traffic light to turn green, Marie Misfortune's car was struck by Borris Bankrupt's car. Unluckily, Borris has no insurance and there is little, if any, hope of recovering damages. Marie's auto coverage includes:

Liability: Personal, $50,000/$100,000
Property, $25,000

Comprehensive: $50 deductible

Uninsured motorist: $15,000/$30,000

Collision: $100 deductible

Marie lost 3 weeks' wages ($288 a week at her present salary) and her medical bills totaled $1800. Repair of her car cost $1300.

a What amount will Marie collect, if anything, for her medical expenses and lost income? What section of the policy will pay?

b What will she collect toward her automobile's damages? Under what section of the policy will she be paid?

16-5 Brian Dale has developed the following three coverage options for his automobile policy:

TYPE OF COVERAGE	A DOLLAR AMOUNT	A ANNUAL PREMIUM	B DOLLAR AMOUNT	B ANNUAL PREMIUM	C DOLLAR AMOUNT	C ANNUAL PREMIUM
Liability Personal injury	$25/$50*	$ 96	$50/$100*	$115	$100/$300*	$138
Property	10*	65	15*	67	25*	69
Collision	50†	194	100†	164	250†	132
Comprehensive	0†	70	50†	52	100†	46

*Amounts in thousands of dollars.
†Deductible amount on policy.

a What combination of coverages would you suggest to provide good coverage for a reasonable premium? What would your suggested policy cost?

b If Brian wants to hold down the annual premium, what would you suggest? What will be the cost of a policy that provides good coverage with a minimum premium?

CASE PROBLEM

Randy Jacoby's house recently suffered extensive fire damage. The dwelling had a replacement value of $55,000, and Randy carried insurance of $45,000 (HO-3 policy). The total damage to the house was $22,000. In addition, his detached garage was destroyed, and replacing it cost $3,200. His car was also ruined in the fire. It had a retail value of $2,800 and a wholesale value of $2,200, and Randy carried $50 deductible comprehensive coverage. As a result of the fire, Randy had to live in a motel for 2 months at a total cost of $2,450. While the firefighters were trying to save the burning house, their trucks and hoses damaged the trees and shrubs on the property. It cost Randy $2,500 to have the property relandscaped. His boat was also in the garage, so it was a total loss. Randy did not carry a separate policy on the boat, despite its wholesale value of $2,500.

Finally, as a result of the fire, Randy lost extensive personal property. The current replacement cost of those possessions was $8,000, but the insurance company paid only $3,100.

1   For each of the losses, indicate:

a Whether the loss is covered by insurance

b What Randy will receive if his loss is covered

c The reasons it is not covered if it is not

2   Why did Randy receive only $3,100 for the personal property when its current replacement cost was $8,000?

3   How could Randy have improved his personal property coverage?

4   What other recommendations would you make for Randy's insurance coverage?

PART
5

BUILDING FOR YOUR FUTURE

CHAPTER
17
INVESTMENTS: FUNDAMENTALS AND GOALS

**AFTER COMPLETING THIS CHAPTER
YOU WILL HAVE LEARNED**

That the two basic types of investments are *lending* and *ownership*

What the differences between the two types of investments are

What the *risk exposure* is on an investment and how to mearsure it

That there is a *trade-off* between the risk on an investment and its return

The *six criteria* that you should consider in order to evaluate an investment and compare it with others

How to develop a *set of investment goals* that cover your future plans

INVESTMENTS should be an important part of

everyone's personal financial program. We first introduced investments back in Chapter 1, when we discussed the importance of establishing financial goals. In connection with that discussion, we pointed out that during the time you are accumulating the money for a long-term goal, you should invest it. Furthermore, we stressed that by earning a high rate of return on those investments, you can reduce the amount of money that you have to save each month.

Clearly, selecting the correct investment is important. Throughout the chapters since then, investments have been mentioned in connection with a number of other personal finance topics. Investments are an integral part of many personal finance decisions. The more you know about the various kinds that are available, the better equipped you will be to select appropriate investments to meet your financial goals.

People who can afford to invest large amounts of money have more to gain or lose from their investments than do small investors. But, because small investors have less to invest, it is even more critical that their investments earn an adequate return. Furthermore, the return on an investment should be appropriate for the risk it entails. When we use the term "small investors," we mean someone whose total investments are worth less than $50,000. The term can also refer to anyone who has $10,000 or less to invest when considering making a new investment.

There are many investment opportunities available to small investors, and indications are that there will be even more opportunities in the future. As a small investor, you generally must be your own investment advisor. To advise yourself wisely and effectively, you need some basic background on investments. Chapter 17 through 20 can help you achieve this objective.

The study of investments is not an easy task. But we think that every small investor can acquire the basic knowledge and skills necessary to effectively manage his or her personal investments. Furthermore, we hope that, after completing these chapters, you will find managing your personal investments an interesting, challenging, and satisfying pursuit.

The next several chapters will not provide you with a formula guaranteed to make you rich. No book and no author can guarantee to bring you great wealth through investments, even though many make such a claim (and they make lots of money for themselves and their publishers by selling such books). We stress guidelines and strategies that will provide a respectable return on the money you invest with relatively limited risk.

SOME FIRST STEPS

Before you can decide on a particular investment goal, the first thing you must do is describe the goal in detail. It is not enough to say, "I want to earn all the money I possibly can." If you really invested toward that goal, it could take you into such risky investments as the common stock of companies like Lost Horizons Gold Mines, Boom & Bust Oil Wells Incorporated, and Last Flight Airlines. Granted, the potential returns may be sizable, but you also face the possibility of a complete loss. The risk that you might lose all your money may far outweigh the potential return, making the investments totally unacceptable to most people. What is needed is a set of specific goals which can assist you in answering the important questions:

How much do I have to invest?

Where should I invest?

When should I invest?

What investment alternatives are available to me?

What are the risks?

We will help you answer these and other questions in this and the next three chapters.

Do It Now   Even a relatively small annual investment can accumulate to a sizable sum over a period of years. For example, suppose that early in her life, Becky Bimstein decided she wanted to accumulate half a million dollars by her seventieth birthday. A little bit of math indicates that she could achieve that $500,000 goal by saving $72.62 each month, beginning at twenty years of age, and placing that money in an investment that earned 8 percent annually. Although few people aspire to having a half a million dollars at the end of 50 years, this example does demonstrate that even limited savings invested at a modest return will accumulate to a substantial amount over an extended period.

Let us work through a second example.

Suppose Winthrop Adams wants to accumulate $14,000 in 5 years to finance his daughter's college education. Assuming an annual 8 percent return, he will have to save $2,386.39 per year if he starts the investment program only 5 years before he needs the $14,000. Had he begun the program when his daughter was born, giving him 20 years to accumulate the money, he would have had to save only $305.93 each year.

This example illustrates a key point: Once you identify an investment goal, it is essential that you begin working toward that goal immediately, especially when the dollar amount of the investment goal is large.

A Tool for Every Purpose   For small investors, there are many investment alternatives; some are appropriate for certain investment goals, others are not. For example, the common stock of large corporations might be ideal for a long-term investment goal. However, it is likely to be inappropriate if the money is going to be invested for only 6 months.

Our objective in this chapter is to provide the basic guidelines for you to match your investments to your goals.

INVESTMENT ALTERNATIVES

You can invest your money in two basic ways: You can lend your money to some borrower, or you can use your money to purchase partial or full

ownership in some income-producing asset. For example, you might decide to use your money to purchase a duplex housing unit. The rents from that unit would provide you with a source of income. Or you might team up with someone else in a partnership and use your money to open a do-it-yourself car wash. The revenues from that business would provide a source of income to you and your partner. Although there are many, many different types of investments—savings accounts, government bonds, common stocks, real estate, corporate bonds (to name a few you may be familiar with)—each one can be classified as either a lending investment or an ownership investment.

Lending

When you lend money, your return comes from the interest the borrower pays you for using your funds. Most **lending investments** have a *fixed income* and a *fixed maturity*.

Fixed income means the borrower promises to pay you a specified rate of interest for the use of your funds. And that rate is usually established at the time the lending investment is originally made.

Fixed maturity means the borrower promises to repay the loan at some specified date in the future. That date is usually established at the time the loan is made.

The principal advantage to lending is that the investor knows with certainty what the rate of return will be, how long that return will continue, and when the borrowed funds will be repaid by the borrower. Of course, if the borrower suffers a major financial crisis, it can alter the amount of return the lender receives or the timing of the repayment.

The main disadvantage of a lending investment is that your return will never be more than the rate specified in the original lending agreement. Thus, no matter how successful the borrower may have been with the money you loaned, you will never receive a return larger than what you originally agreed upon.

Variable Return Lending Investments While the great majority of lending investments still have a fixed return, we have seen increasingly more variable return lending options. The term **variable return** means that over the life of the lending investment your return varies. The principal purpose is to have that return move up and down with interest rates in the financial markets.

Let us highlight the differences by comparing a traditional fixed return lending investment with a variable return one. Assume both investments are certificates of deposit (CDs) (more details on this investment later) from a federally insured bank; both have a maturity of 3½ years and require an initial investment of $500. The only difference is that the traditional CD promises a 10 percent fixed rate of return over those 3½ years. But a variable rate CD, while its return may begin at 10 percent, promises to adjust that rate once each month so that it equals the current return on U.S. Treasury notes with a 2½-year maturity; we call this **indexing** the return to the interest rate on 2½-year Treasury notes. Over the 42-month life of the variable rate CD, the return will be changed 41 times (the first month's return is 10 percent). What you do not know, of course, is what those 41 rate changes will be. Instead, each month the CD's return will be changed so that it equals the prevailing interest return on 2½-year Treasury notes. Let us suppose that, for whatever reason, the interest rates on 2½-year Treasury notes rise during the next 3½ years. Your rate of return will be adjusted upward each month so that your return always equals the return on those 2½ year Treasury notes. What is your actual return? It is the average of those different 42 monthly rates.

Why the growth in variable return lending investments? Because the recent bouts of rapid inflation, coupled with highly volatile interest rates, have made some investors reluctant to "lock into" some fixed interest rate. Investors become all too aware that today's 10 percent may be woefully inadequate next week, next month, or next year when interest rates rise to 14 percent. With a variable return investment, that is no longer a problem. With it your interest rate will vary with market interest rates. However, if inflation cools and interest rates fall, your variable rate CD would have a lower yield. Therefore, the desirability of a variable rate CD depends on what happens to the economy between the time you invest your money and the date of the certificate's maturity. In other words, you, as an investor, are faced with having to make an intelligent and informed *choice*. We will have more specifics on actual variable return lending investments in Chapter 18.

Ownership

There are several ways in which a person can invest through **ownership.** Examples include partial ownership of a corporation by buying its common stock; buying mutual fund shares (the money invested in the mutual fund is used to purchase the common stocks of many different corporations); ownership of a small business; a business partnership; ownership of real estate; and ownership of investment goods, such as gold, art objects, antiques, and stamps. Regardless of the particular ownership investment you select, your rate of return will depend upon how successful that particular investment is. Thus, in our earlier example of the duplex rental unit, your return will depend upon the success of that housing unit: Can you keep it occupied? Can you charge and collect reasonable monthly rents? How large are your maintenance and repair expenses relative to the rents you collect? Likewise, the success of the previously mentioned car wash is going to depend upon the ability of that ownership venture to produce revenues or income greater than the cost of operating it. In the end, the return on an ownership investment depends on its income-producing potential. If it does well, you, as partial or complete owner, will share in its earnings. However, should the ownership investment fare poorly, your return will be poor.

Although there is no guaranteed return with ownership, neither is there an upper limit on the return. If the investment is unusually successful, your return could be very high. This potentially unlimited return is the major advantage to ownership investments.

But the principal disadvantage stems from the same unlimited feature. If the ownership investment is unsuccessful, your return may be very small, zero, or even negative. It may be such a large negative return that you lose your entire investment; chalk this one up as an experience. Furthermore, in some business and real estate ventures, you, as an owner, may be liable for part of the business's debts.

EFFECTIVE RETURN ON AN INVESTMENT

Whenever you make an investment, you forgo the current purchasing power of the money you invest. In exchange for that, you expect to receive a return on your investment. That return can be annual income on the investment, or an increase in the investment's market value, or some combination of income plus increased market value. Regardless of where the return comes from, the total return must be included when computing an investment's effective annual rate of return. We use the combined **effective return**— annual income plus possible changes in market price—to compare one investment with another.

Rate of Return   Throughout this and the next three chapters, we are going to be using the terms *rate of return*, *return*, and *yield* on an investment; we will use them interchangeably in all our discussions. They all describe the profitability of a particular investment. Generally, that profitability is described in terms of a percentage return on the investment over a specified time period: We will always use 1 year as the measurement period, unless otherwise noted. When we say an investment's rate of return, or return, was 20 percent, we mean that over a 1-year period, the return provided by the investment was 20 percent of the actual investment. Thus, on a $1000 investment we would have:

$$20\% \quad = \$200 \quad \div \$1000$$

$$\overset{\displaystyle\Uparrow}{\underset{\text{return}}{\text{Rate of}}} = \overset{\displaystyle\Uparrow}{\underset{\text{dollars}}{\text{Return in}}} \div \overset{\displaystyle\Uparrow}{\underset{\text{investment}}{\text{Original}}}$$

The actual source of that return may have been an interest payment, a dividend payment, or a change in the market value of the investment. All these sources are discussed in the next two sections.

Income on Investments   In Chapters 18, 19, and 20, we will frequently use the following terms to describe the different types of investment income.

Interest   When you lend someone money, the borrower pays **interest** for the use of your money. The borrower may be a bank, savings and loan association, credit union, corporation, municipality, the United States government, an individual, or a host of other borrowers. Generally, interest income is stated in terms of an annual percentage return. Thus, if a $1000 lending investment pays interest of $150 per year, its annual return is:

$$15\% \quad = \$150 \quad \div \$1000$$

$$\overset{\displaystyle\Uparrow}{\underset{\text{return}}{\text{Annual}}} = \overset{\displaystyle\Uparrow}{\underset{\text{interest}}{\text{Annual}}} \div \overset{\displaystyle\Uparrow}{\underset{\text{invested}}{\text{Amount}}}$$

Dividends: Common Stock   When you purchase a share of common stock in a corporation, you become a part owner (it is likely that you own a very small part) of that corporation. As an owner, you share in the income that the corporation earns on its business activities during the year. But that does not mean you will necessarily receive part of the corporation's annual income. Payments by the corporation to its shareholders (people who own the common stock) are called *dividends*. And the corporation may decide to pay all its annual income, part of its income, or none of its income as **cash dividends.** Corporations are not required to pay a certain percentage of the company's annual income as dividends. They may decide to pay no dividends, which means they retain 100 percent of the income within the company. Furthermore, the company may continue to pay no dividends for years, even though its annual income was very large each year. If the corporation does decide to pay a dividend, those dividends are usually stated as a dollar amount per share of stock. Thus, Slug Products may decide to pay a dividend of $1 per common share. If you own 100 shares of Slug's common stock, your dividend check from Slug Products is:

$$\$100 \quad = \$1 \quad \times 100 \text{ shares}$$

$$\overset{\displaystyle\Uparrow}{\underset{\text{check}}{\text{Dividend}}} = \overset{\displaystyle\Uparrow}{\underset{\text{per share}}{\text{Dividend}}} \times \overset{\displaystyle\Uparrow}{\underset{\text{shares owned}}{\text{Number of}}}$$

Rent   When someone uses property you own, he or she is expected to pay **rent.** The rental agreement is commonly a written document called a *lease,* which specifies the monthly payment and the exact length of the rental period. Or the rental agreement may be informal, whereby the renter continues to rent the property on a monthly basis with no specified maximum or minimum rental period.

Changes in an Investment's Market Price   The investments discussed in Chapters 18, 19, and 20 are subject to varying **changes in market price.** By market price we mean the price that the investor would receive for a particular investment from some other investor or institution that would buy the investment. For some investments, such as common stocks, a wide range of investors and institutions might be interested in buying the stock. The market price of such an investment will be determined by that rather large group of potential buyers competing to purchase the stock. At the opposite extreme is the traditional savings account. You cannot sell it to someone else. The only institution interested in buying or redeeming it is the bank, savings and loan, or mutual savings bank where you have the account. In this case, market price is set by that one institution.

The amount of change that will likely take place in the market price of a particular investment varies widely. At one extreme is the balance in a bank savings account. Barring the bank's collapse (financial, not physical), that balance will not change except for the addition of interest earnings on the account. The market price of a savings account balance is highly stable. At the opposite extreme is the common stock of Last Ditch Gold Mines. Should the company strike it big, each share's market price would likely skyrocket. Of course, Last Ditch may find nothing; in that case, the shares price would probably plummet. The point here is that the market price of a share of Last Ditch Gold Mines could fluctuate widely.

Capital Gain   A capital gain is the difference between (1) an investment's sale price and (2) its initial purchase price including any selling expense. For example, assume that 40 shares of XQ Corporation were initially bought for $800, or $20 per share. Later, these shares are sold for $24 a share less a $30 selling expense. The capital gain was:

$$\$130 = (\$24 \times 40 \text{ shares}) - \$800 - \$30$$

$$\underset{\text{gain}}{\text{Capital}} = \underset{\text{Price per share} \times \text{Number of shares}}{\text{Proceeds from sale}} - \underset{\text{purchase}}{\text{Original}} - \underset{\text{expense}}{\text{Selling}}$$

Capital gains on investments held more than 12 months are long-term gains; for periods of 12 months or less, they are short-term gains. For tax purposes, the entire short-term gain must be included in income, and it is therefore fully taxable. On long-term gains, 60 percent of the gain can be excluded from income. You pay taxes only on the 40 percent of the long-term gain you must include.

Capital Loss   Although it would be nice if an investment's market price always increased, it does not always do so. Selling an investment for less than the combined total of its initial purchase price and the associated selling expense results in a capital loss. Thus, if the shares of XQ (from our previous example) had been sold for $15, the capital loss would have been:

$$\underset{\substack{\text{Capital} \\ \text{loss}}}{\$230} = \underset{\substack{\text{Proceeds from sale} \\ \text{Price per share} \times \text{Number of shares}}}{(\$15 \times 40 \text{ shares})} - \underset{\substack{\text{Original} \\ \text{purchase}}}{\$800} - \underset{\substack{\text{Selling} \\ \text{expense}}}{\$30}$$

As with the previous gains, if you hold the stock for more than 12 months, it is a long-term loss; for a period of 12 months or less, it is a short-term loss. But the tax treatment is unlike that for gains. Generally, you can deduct the full amount of a short-term loss (there is a maximum amount, however) from your taxable income. Only 50 percent of the long-term loss can be deducted from your taxable income.

Risk   Defining what we mean by risk in the context of investments is a bit involved. Let us begin with the definition of **risk** from *The American Heritage Dictionary:* "The possibility of suffering harm or loss." We can relate that idea to investments. If I invest in a 6 percent savings account at the local insured savings and loan association, I am virtually guaranteed I will receive my 6 percent return. The possibility that I might receive less than 6 percent is so remote that it is almost nonexistent. Therefore, the possibility that I might suffer a loss by receiving less than my expected 6 percent return is essentially zero. But suppose, instead, I had purchased 100 shares of Last Ditch Airlines; I originally expected that my return would be 15 percent. Now, any number of things could go wrong. Last Ditch might cut its dividends or the market price might plummet. Either or both events will sharply reduce my actual rate of return. Here, there is the strong possibility that my actual rate of return will be less than what I expected. Given the distinct likelihood of a loss, where the actual return is less than the expected return, we would conclude that this investment had considerable risk. We will define *risk* as the possibility that the expected rate of return on an investment will not develop; in particular, we are concerned that the actual return will be less than our original expected return.

Now that we have a basic idea of what risk is, the next step is to discuss how we measure risk. Without a quantitative measure of risk, it would be difficult to compare one investment with another. The simplest, most frequently used, and most widely accepted measure of risk is the variability in future returns. That is, we use the dispersion in an investment's expected future returns to describe that investment's risk. Thus, if an investment's future returns are closely clustered about a single value, as our previous savings account was, it is said to have little or no risk. The range of an investment's possible future return is one way to visualize the variability in that investment's return. If we plotted all the likely rates of return a savings account might provide in the future, we would find it to cover a very narrow range; in fact, it would be a single point. There is virtually no variability or dispersion, so it carries nearly zero risk On the other hand, an investment which has a very volatile rate of return—it can range from sharply positive one year to sharply negative another year— carries high risk. If we plotted the likely future returns on the common stock in our previous example, we would find it covered a wide range. Given the wide variability in those future returns, it is an investment that carries considerable risk.

You may have noted that we have been consistently using the term *future rates of return*. What we need to do is to estimate the variability of an investment's future return. Many investment professionals develop such estimates by examining an investment's historical rates of return. Throughout the following sections, we will use this generalization: The more variable the investment's return in the past, the higher the expected risk.

What Causes Returns to Vary?

Returns can vary for many different reasons. In the next two sections, we will give some examples of two very likely reasons: changes in the business environment and changes in interest rates.

Risks, Returns, and the Business Environment   Changes in the **business environment** cause variations in the returns on different investments, including the returns on lending and ownership in a profit-making business.

Major changes in the business environment include fluctuations in customer demand for a product or service, increased competition from other suppliers, the obsolescence of a product or service, and shortages of key materials or labor. Any of these events might have a favorable or an unfavorable impact on the revenue potential of the firm or organization you loaned your money to or bought ownership in. And, as the firm's revenue increases or decreases, you can expect the return from your investment to behave in the same way. Also, you can assume that the wider the swings in the investment's return, the greater the risk.

Risk, Return, and Interest Rate Changes While the rate of return on many lending investments is typically fixed over the life of that investment, the return that borrowers must offer varies over time. That is, at one particular point in time borrowers might be offering a 10 percent return on a certain investment; several months or years later that return may be quite different. Over time, the rate of return that is currently being offered changes as the demand by borrowers changes and as the willingness of lenders to loan money changes. These fluctuations in the prevailing market return can cause considerable variability in the rate of return on certain fixed-income lending investments. An example will illustrate why.

Suppose Sue Fine paid $1000 for a $1000 bond; this $1000 is usually called the *face value* of the bond. The bond promises to pay 10 percent interest each year, or $100 annually. The bond will do so for 20 years, at which time the person, company, or municipality that issued the bond promises to redeem it for $1000 (its face value); this 20-year period is called the *maturity* of the bond because it is the point when the lender is repaid. Because the bond is a fixed-income investment, it will continue to pay $100 interest each year for the next 20 years, regardless of whether the rate of return that prevails in the lending market rises, declines, or stays unchanged in the future. Likewise, despite any fluctuations in the market return, the bond will mature in 20 years. But the market price on the bond (recall that it was $1000 when Sue bought it) can change dramatically.

Assume that for some reason, prevailing rates of return on new bonds that are similar to Sue's bond rise to 15 percent. These new bonds will now pay 15 percent, or $150 interest, on a $1000 face-value bond. Since investors will receive $150 from a new $1000 bond, they are not willing to pay $1000 for Sue's bond with its $100 payment. In fact, the price of Sue's 10 percent bond would have to decline to $667 for its "effective" return to be 15 percent:

$$15\% = \$100 \div \$667$$

| Effective rate of return | = | Interest payment on the bond | ÷ | Market price of the bond |

At a price of $667, the older bond will be competitive with the new 15 percent bonds. In actuality, the price will not decline all the way to $667. Why not? Because at maturity (in 20 years), the investor who owns the bond receives its full face value—$1000 in our example. Now, if you paid only $667 for this bond, you would not only receive $100 interest each year for 20 years; you would also receive that $1000 at maturity. Since you paid only $667 for the bond, you have an additional $333 gain when the bond matures. That means the bond's price does not decline all the way to $667. In fact, if the price dropped to only $687, that bond would still provide a 15 percent return. The exact details of how that $687 price was computed are beyond the scope of this section, so we will not go into it here.

The above example clearly illustrates a general investment principle, however. It concerns **interest rate changes.** When the rate of return or interest rates that are prevailing in the market rise, the market price of existing fixed-income lending investments declines. That stands to reason because an investor can now obtain a higher rate of return on new fixed-income investments, so will be willing to pay less for an existing fixed-income investment. Conversely, when interest rates or market returns decline, the price of existing fixed-income investments should rise because potential investors would be willing to pay more.

Furthermore, the longer the maturity on the lending investment, the wider its price swing. Thus, if the prevailing interest rates rise 2 percent, the change in the price for a 20-year bond will be much larger than the change in price for a 1-year bond. For example, assume that we have two bonds: a $1000 bond that pays 10 percent interest ($100 per year) and matures in 1 year, and a $1000 bond that also pays 10 percent interest but does not mature for 20 years. We will assume that the prevailing market interest rate on similar bonds rises to 15 percent. Given that rise in interest rates, the price of the 10 percent bond with a 1-year maturity will decline to $957. But the 20-year bond will drop all the way to $687. While we are not going to show exactly how that price decline was computed, we can give you an intuitive feel for why the price of the 20-year bond dropped by so much more. First, if prevailing rates are 15 percent, we know that a new $1000 bond pays $150 in interest each year. Now, with our previous 1-year bond, you are asking an investor to accept an interest payment of only $100. Before an investor would be tempted, we would have to drop the price on the old 1-year bond to $957 to make it competitive with the new bonds. That discount—$957 versus the $1000 price on a new bond—compensates the investor for accepting $100 of interest when the new bond would have paid $150. But that 20-year bond is much less attractive; we are asking the investor to accept $100 in annual interest for the next 20 years! That means the investor sacrifices $50 in interest ($100 on the old bond versus $150 on a new bond) for each of the 20 years. To do that, the investor requires a much larger reduction in the price on that existing 20-year bond, and the price drop to $687 reflects that reduction.

Our second generalization from this example is that the longer the maturity on a particular fixed-income investment, the larger its change in market price for a given change in prevailing market rates of return.

RISK-RETURN TRADE-OFF

Given a choice, nearly all investors would prefer less risk to more risk, if all other things were the same. That is, most investors have an aversion to risk; they wish to avoid it as much as possible, but if they have to face risk, they want to be paid for it. Investors expect and demand a higher return as compensation for accepting higher risk on an investment. And since variability of return is the most frequently used measure of risk, the more variable the return on an investment, the higher the return on that investment must be to attract investors. Exhibit 17-1 illustrates this **risk-return trade-off** for different investments. When we use the term

EXHIBIT 17-1

General pattern of risk-return trade-off on investments.

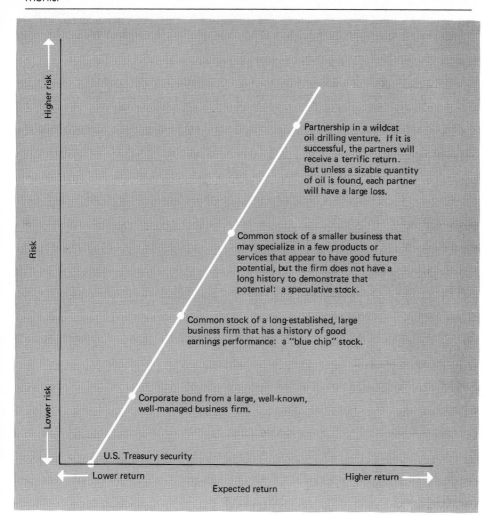

Partnership in a wildcat oil drilling venture. If it is successful, the partners will receive a terrific return. But unless a sizable quantity of oil is found, each partner will have a large loss.

Common stock of a smaller business that may specialize in a few products or services that appear to have good future potential, but the firm does not have a long history to demonstrate that potential: a speculative stock.

Common stock of a long-established, large business firm that has a history of good earnings performance: a "blue chip" stock.

Corporate bond from a large, well-known, well-managed business firm.

U.S. Treasury security

Higher risk

Risk

Lower risk

Lower return

Expected return

Higher return

"risk-return trade-off," we are describing the process by which you must accept more risk if you want a higher return: Your trade is higher risk for a higher return. If you want an investment with lower risk, you will have to accept a lower return: Here, your trade is a lower return to obtain lower risk. Investments on the upper segment of the line provide a higher return, as you can see on the horizontal axis, but look at the vertical axis, where you can see that these same investments also involve more risk.

The five points along the risk-return line in Exhibit 17-1 are used to demonstrate where five representative investments would likely fall. United States Treasury securities are generally considered to have very low risk or none at all, so that is the beginning point for our risk-return line. Of course, that low risk means they provide only a small return. As we move out toward the corporate bond in Exhibit 17-1, the return rises but so does the risk. And this process would be repeated if we continued on out that risk-return trade-off line.

For most investments, we can make this generalization: The higher the investment's potential return, the higher its risk exposure.

COMPOUND RETURNS

The principle of **compound returns** centers on the fact that not only does the initial balance continue to grow, but the interest you receive each period also goes on to earn interest the next period. Consequently, your balance in an investment comprises three parts: (1) the initial amount you paid for the investment, (2) the interest or return you earn on your initial balance, and (3) the interest you will earn on the interest that you earned last period and left in the investment. For example, assume that Ye Olde National Bank promises to pay interest at 10 percent[1] compounded annually. The top line in Exhibit 17-2 illustrates how an initial $1000 deposit would grow over a 20-year period if the interest were left to compound in the account. As you can see from Exhibit 17-2, the deposit not only continues to grow each year; it grows at an ever-increasing rate. Although you cannot read the exact figures from the graph, the balance increased $147 during the year between years 4 and 5; yet, between years 19 and 20, the balance rose by $612 during that one year—clearly a substantial increase in growth. Why the increased growth every year? The increases all center on the fact that the account pays interest every year on the initial balance and it also pays interest on all the accumulated interest.

Simple Versus Compound Return   The lower line in Exhibit 17-2 illustrates how a $1000 investment would grow with **simple interest** at 10 percent. With simple interest, interest earnings do not earn interest even if you leave the interest in the account.

Impact of Different Returns and Years of Compounding

The details in Exhibit 17-3 show the results of investing $1000 for 5, 10, 15, and 20 years at annual compound interest rates of 7.5, 10, and 12.5 percent. What first stands out in Exhibit 17-3 is the substantial impact that a small increase in interest rate can have on an investment's value over time. The added first year's interest for a 10 percent investment over that for a 7.5 percent investment is only $25. Yet, over the first 5 years, that added return raises the total interest on the investment from $436 to $611. That represents a 40 percent improvement! Even more impressive is the added interest from having the money invested for the full 20 years at the higher 10 percent return. That total interest, $5728, is more than 75 percent higher than the return for the 7.5 percent investment!

---

[1]Although we realize that 10 percent is not comparable with current bank rates—they are closer to 8 percent—using 10 percent simplifies the computations.

EXHIBIT 17-2

CHAPTER 17

551

INVESTMENTS:
FUNDAMENTALS
AND GOALS

Increase in $1000 invested at 10 percent compound interest and 10 percent simple interest for 20 years.

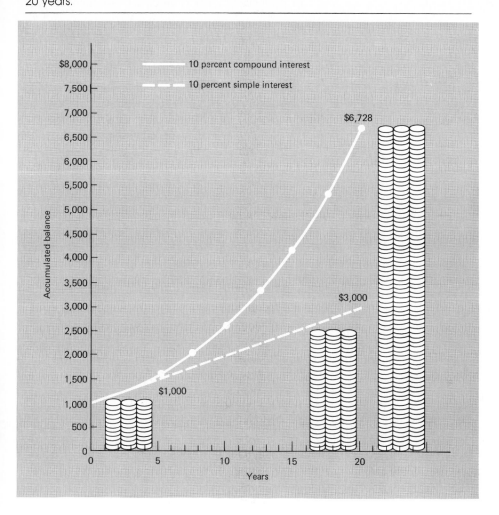

The results in Exhibit 17-3 illustrate two points.

1 A small increase in an investment's rate of return can have a sizable impact on its value over time.

2 The longer the investment period, the greater the impact a higher rate of return has on the value of the investment over time.

STRATEGY

Because the benefits from compounding are large when the investment period is long, you should begin saving for larger investment goals as soon as

possible. And when considering comparable investments, take the one with the higher rate of return.

Compounding More than Once Each Year

The return on many investments is compounded more than once each year. To see how the **frequency of compounding** alters the effective annual return, let's return to our example of $1000 in a savings account. Let's again assume that the account pays 10 percent annual interest, but now we will assume that the interest is paid at that annual rate every 6 months, or every

---

EXHIBIT 17-3

Interest earned on a $1000 investment with rates of return of 7.5 percent, 10 percent, and 12.5 percent.

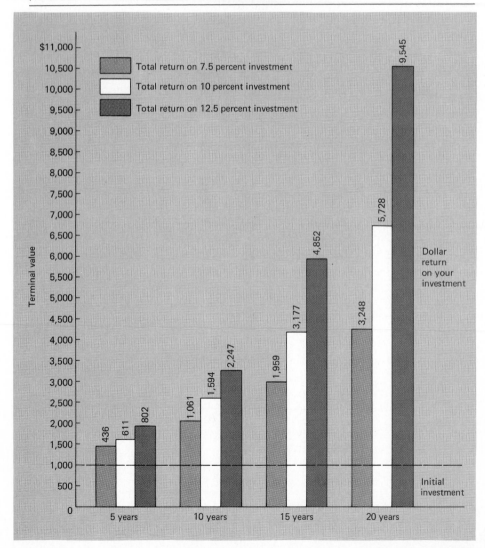

- Total return on 7.5 percent investment
- Total return on 10 percent investment
- Total return on 12.5 percent investment

half-year. So, after 6 months, you will receive $50, or one-half of that year's 10 percent interest. That $50 will then be reinvested so that it earns additional interest. During the second half of the year, you will receive an additional $50 interest for 6 months' interest on your original $1000 plus $2.50 added interest for the $50 you reinvested at mid-year. In total, your rate of return is:

$$10.25\% = (\$50 \quad + \$50 \quad + \$2.50) \quad \div \$1000$$

$$\frac{\text{Rate of}}{\text{return}} = \frac{\text{Interest received:}}{\text{6 months} + \text{6 months} + \text{additional}} \div \frac{\text{Original}}{\text{investment}}$$
$$\text{interest}$$

Would you expect the effective return for a 10 percent return, compounded quarterly (every 3 months), to be (1) greater than 10.25 percent, (2) less than 10.25 percent, or (3) equal to 10.25 percent? Not certain? Well, work it through.

Exhibit 17-4 shows effective annual returns for different compounding periods. Those results can be summarized in a short rule: For any rate of return, the more frequent the compounding, the higher the effective return.

STRATEGY

Given two comparable investments with identical rates of return, choose the one offering the most frequent compounding.

IMPACT OF INFLATION

We are reminded of inflation's impact every time we purchase an item. The question is rarely, "Has the price gone up?" Instead, the question is "How *much* has the price increased?" Although the effect of inflation on invest-

EXHIBIT 17-4

Effective annual rate of return on an investment
with earnings compounded more than once
each year.

STATED RATE OF RETURN	**Effective Annual Percentage Rate of Return When Compounding Period is:**				
	ANNUAL	SEMIANNUAL	QUARTERLY	MONTHLY	DAILY
5%	5%	5.06%	5.09%	5.12%	5.13%
6	6	6.09	6.14	6.17	6.18
7	7	7.12	7.19	7.23	7.25
8	8	8.16	8.24	8.30	8.33
10	10	10.25	10.38	10.47	10.52
12	12	12.36	12.55	12.68	12.75
14	14	14.49	14.75	14.93	15.02
16	16	16.64	16.99	17.23	17.35

ments is less direct than price increases, it can hurt your purchasing power just as much.

For example, assume that we deposit $100 in a savings account paying 5 percent annual interest. At the end of 1 year, the account balance will be:

$$\underset{\substack{\text{Account} \\ \text{balance}}}{\$105} = \underset{\substack{\text{Initial} \\ \text{deposit}}}{\$100} + \underset{\substack{\text{Interest earned:} \\ \text{Deposit} \quad \times \text{ Rate}}}{(\$100 \times 5\%)}$$

Yet, if prices have risen 3 percent during the same year, our real purchasing power from the investment has increased only 2 percent. Because prices have risen, we now need $103 to buy what $100 bought 1 year ago. Despite its promised 5 percent return, the savings account's "real" return (annual rate minus the inflation rate) is only:

$$\underset{\substack{\text{Real return} \\ \text{on investment}}}{2\%} = \underset{\substack{\text{Annual rate} \\ \text{of return}}}{5\%} - \underset{\substack{\text{Annual rate} \\ \text{of inflation}}}{3\%}$$

And it is not hard to imagine a situation in which inflation could reduce an investment's real return to zero or even to a negative return. For example, the 9 percent inflation rate during 1978 reduced the typical 5 percent savings account's real return to:

$$\underset{\text{Real return}}{-4\%} = \underset{\text{Annual return}}{5\%} - \underset{\text{Inflation rate}}{9\%}$$

Thus, if you had $100 in a 5 percent savings account during 1978, your purchasing power would have actually declined by $4.

Clearly, the impact of inflation must be considered in any investment decision. An immediate question is: Were the high inflation rates of the past several years unusual, or were they the first wave of the future? The top half of Exhibit 17-5 shows the inflation rate during recent years. The bottom half of the exhibit traces out the effect of those inflation rates on the purchasing power of $1.

Future Prospect During the past 30 years, inflation has averaged 3½ percent annually. However, for the past 10 years shown in Exhibit 17-5 the average inflation rate is approximately 8.5 percent. Unfortunately, we believe preliminary evidence suggests that the annual rate during the 1980s is likely to continue at the more recent 6 to 8 percent rather than at the historical 3½ percent. Given this distinct possibility, the impact of inflation on an investment's return should be one of your primary concerns.

Historical Experience: Real Rates of Return Exhibit 17-6 summaries the **real rates of return** that investors have received on five types of investments: standard savings account, U.S. Treasury bills, long-term U.S.

Treasury bonds, long-term corporate bonds, and common stocks. Three different investment holding periods, or investment ownership periods, were used to compute those returns: it is assumed for the first period that an investor held the specific investment for 5 years from 1974 through 1978; for the second, that the particular investment was held for 10 years from 1969 through 1978; for the third, that the investment was held for the 15 years from 1964 through 1978.

It is readily apparent from Exhibit 17-6 how poorly many investments have performed relative to the recent rates of inflation. For most investments, the question is not whether the real rate of return was negative; instead, the question was: *How* negative? Despite some noteworthy increases in the rates of return on most investments during recent years, these increases just have not been sufficient to offset even larger increases in the inflation rate. Consequently, most real returns were negative.

EXHIBIT 17-5

Annual percentage increase in consumer prices and purchasing power of a 1967 dollar. *Source: Federal Reserve Bulletin,* various issues.

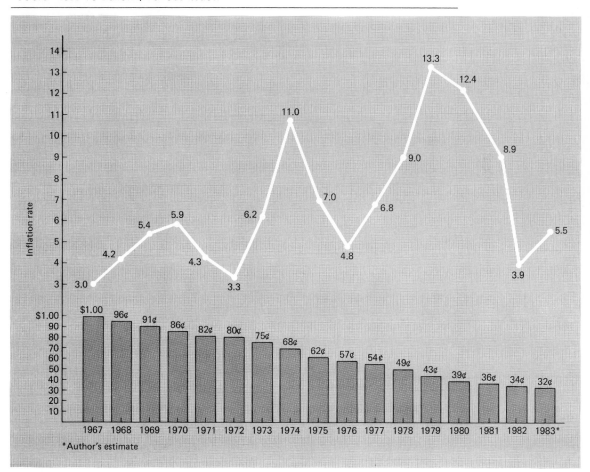

*Author's estimate

Hedge Against Inflation

While most of the real rates of return shown in Exhibit 17-6 were negative, we are not suggesting that you should not invest. As we saw in the section on inflation in Chapter 4, we believe that investments are essential to managing your personal finances. But we think it is essential that you

---

EXHIBIT 17-6

Real rates of return on selected investments.
Source: Roger G. Ibbotson and Rex A. Sinquefeld, "Stocks, Bonds, Bills, and Inflation: Updates," *Financial Analysis Journal,* July-August 1979, p. 41.

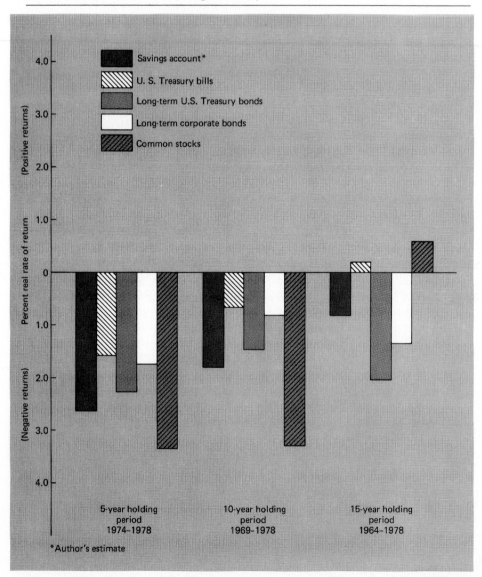

concentrate on investments that offer some hedge against inflation. To provide a **hedge against inflation,** we need an investment whose rate of return is not constrained by some arbitrary set of rules or regulations. Without constraints, when the rate of inflation rises, the return on the investment can likewise rise. In so doing, we not only want the real rate of return on the investment to remain positive, but it should also be sufficiently positive to compensate the investors for the risk they are accepting.

Lending Investments When the return on a lending investment is fixed, its real return declines as inflation increases. Thus, the return on a 6 percent 10-year bond remains at 6 percent regardless of inflation. If inflation ranges from 4 to 14 percent annually during those 10 years, the bond's real return may range from plus 2 percent to minus 8 percent. For this reason, some people maintain that fixed-income investments offer no protection against inflation and therefore are generally poor investment choices.

We don't quite believe that fixed-income investments are that bad. What the interest rate on a fixed-income investment must contain is a component to offset inflation. We will call this component the **inflation premium.** If that premium is set high enough to offset the impact of inflation, the investor's real rate of return should remain positive.

If investors expect that future inflation rates will be high, they should demand sharply higher interest rates which include a sufficiently large inflation premium to offset those future price increases. But that only affects the interest rates on investments that will be purchased in the future; investments purchased prior to the upward interest adjustments only pay the rates of return that were available when the investments were purchased. Therefore, we suggest that you avoid fixed-income investments with maturities longer than 10 years. Once purchased, you will be locked into that return for the entire period.

Even with an inflation premium, your rate of return on a fixed-income investment is likely to be poor when inflation rates fluctuate widely. When inflation rates reached levels of 10 percent and higher in past periods, interest rates on investments simply failed to rise sufficiently to compensate. Of course, that may change if high inflation rates persist.

The best defense against inflation is to avoid fixed-income investments with very long maturities. Certainly, the returns on the very short-term Treasury bills in Exhibit 17-6, while they were negative, were less negative than the returns on the longer-maturity Treasury bonds.

STRATEGY

The best way to deal with periods of high inflation, or with periods when inflation rates vary widely, is to concentrate on fixed-income investments with maturities of less than 6 years.

Lending: Variable Return One of the major advantages to a variable-return lending investment is that the investor does not become locked into some fixed interest rate. Instead, the interest rate on most variable-return investments is tied, or "indexed," to some market interest rate. Consequently, if the rate of inflation increases after you make the investment, you should not have a problem because market interest rates will likely rise to offset that higher inflation. The return on a variable-return investment will increase accordingly. That means a variable-return lending investment performs well during periods of rising inflation rates.

How do variable-return lending investments perform during periods of declining inflation rates? Unfortunately, not as well. As inflation subsides, interest rates typically decline. So the return on your variable-return investment declines accordingly. Had you selected a fixed-return investment, the return would have remained unchanged. Nevertheless, we favor variable-return lending investments. We think that the protection against the ravages of increasing inflation, at least in the present environment, more than offsets the disadvantages during periods of decreasing inflation.

STRATEGY

Consider a variable rate-of-return lending investment as an alternative to one with a fixed return—especially if you expect interest rates to rise during the life of that investment.

Ownership Investments   Theoretically, an ownership investment should provide a better hedge against inflation. Why? Because most ownership investments involve an income-producing asset or some real property, and their market value should increase as inflation increases.

For example, assume that Fred Fontana purchased a $60,000 duplex, which he plans to rent. If all prices double over the next 10 years, the property's market value should rise to at least $120,000. Assume it has done

so; Fred would not have a true $60,000 gain because, with prices doubled, that $120,000 would buy the same thing that only $60,000 bought 10 years earlier. Nevertheless, he would be in a much better position than he would have been had he held $60,000 in cash during that 10-year period. The cash would have lost half its purchasing power. Just owning the property itself has provided a hedge against inflation. But there is also the rental income that Fred can earn from the property. Since all prices have doubled, it is only fair that Fred should raise the rents of his tenants. (We assume his community does not have rent controls that prevent his doing so.) The net effect is not only does Fred's original investment—the duplex—rise in value; his returns—rentals—should also increase as all prices rise.

Have ownership investments worked in reality the way in which theory predicts they should? Regrettably, there is no single definitive answer. Some ownership investments, such as real estate, have fared reasonably well during recent inflationary periods. Others, such as common stock and mutual funds, have not done well. As the real rates of return in Exhibit 17-6 aptly illustrate, the real returns on common stocks during recent years have been decidedly negative; their returns provided a woefully inadequate hedge against inflation. In fact, common stocks tended to earn the best returns when inflation was low and the poorest returns when inflation was high.

What can we conclude from this mixed picture? Certainly, ownership investments offer no guarantee of protection against inflation. However, over a longer time period than the 15 years shown in Exhibit 17-6, they have provided at least some hedge against inflation. Therefore, we believe that ownership investments should be considered as potential investments for your future goals.

CRITERIA FOR EVALUATING INVESTMENTS

Throughout the next three chapters, we will use six **criteria to evaluate investments:** (1) risk, (2) rate of return or yield, (3) minimum maturity, (4) smallest dollar amount, (5) tax features, and (6) flexibility. These six criteria should help you decide whether a particular investment is suitable for a specific investment goal. The appendix, at the end of the chapter, has a table that summarizes the six criteria for different investments.

Risk   The variability of an investment's expected future rate of return will be used as our **risk** measure. You should be aware, however, that investment professionals do not unanimously agree that return variability is a valid measure of risk. Instead of a quantitative risk measure, we will use simple qualitative descriptions of risk exposure because they are sufficient for our purposes.

Rate of Return   The annual **rate of return** on an investment, or its yield, includes the investment's annual income, such as interest, dividends, or rent. In addition, it includes any loss or gain resulting from a decrease or increase in the investment's market price. For investments such as common stock, the change in market price may be the major source of its annual return. For others, such as savings accounts, market price does not change, so the entire return comes from annual interest payments.

Market-Determined Rates of Return   On some investments, the annual return is determined by the current supply and demand for investors' money. That is, the return is determined by how badly borrowers need money (demand) and how willing the lenders are to invest (supply). When the supply of funds is plentiful or the demand is light, the price (the annual rate of return) is likely to be low. On the other hand, if the supply is small or the demand is heavy, the price (the rate of return) will probably be high. Examples of this type of investment include the previously mentioned U.S. Treasury bills and bonds, corporate bonds, and common stocks of corporations.

Rate of Return Established by Regulatory Agency   On other investments, the rate of return is not established by the market forces of supply and demand, but is set by some federal or state regulatory agency that has been empowered to do so. Any change in these rates is entirely at the discretion of the regulatory agency. Examples of this type of investment include the traditional savings account offered by commercial banks, savings and loan associations, and mutual savings banks.

Minimum Maturity   Traditionally, an investment's maturity is the time period between the date of purchase and the date the borrower agrees to redeem it at face value (to pay back the amount borrowed). A few borrowers —mainly financial institutions—will redeem an investment before its maturity date, but that generally entails a penalty that lowers the amount of interest you will receive. That penalty drops the investment's return below the return the borrower promised to pay the lender for borrowing the money over the full maturity. Consequently, we will consistently use an investment's effective **minimum maturity:** the time for which the investment must be held in order to achieve its full rate of return as promised originally by the borrower.

Throughout our discussion, we will give greater emphasis to the minimum length of time you must hold a particular investment. Our reasons for concentrating on this minimum holding period rather than on the maximum are several:

1   Many of your goals will likely be in the 1- to 5-year range, so you will need investments with a short maturity.

2   An investment that requires only a short holding period is highly flexible. You can invest in it once, or several times if you have a longer investment period.

3   Investments with short holding periods are never far from their maturity date. Should an emergency arise, you could sell or redeem the short-term investment within a reasonably short time.

4   The considerable interest rate risk on an investment with a long maturity encourages the use of shorter maturities.

5   The inflation experience of the past several years is a strong argument for shorter maturities.

We group maturities into three broad categories: short-term—less than 1 year; intermediate—1 year to 10 years; and long-term—more than 10 years.

Smallest Dollar Amount   Many investments are only offered in certain specified or minimum dollar denominations. The **smallest dollar** amount on investments can require a minimum purchase of $1000 to $10,000 or more. In addition, some investments only come in increments of $1000 or $5000. For example, assume that an investment required a minimum purchase of $10,000 and, further, that it only came in increments of $5000. That means the smallest amount you could invest is $10,000, and your next alternative would be to invest $15,000. Beyond that you could choose $20,000, $25,000, and so forth. Clearly this investment would not fit the needs of someone who wanted to invest $4000 or even $14,500.

Even where there is no specified minimum, investing a small amount may be unattractive if you must pay a dealer's or broker's fee to purchase an investment. For example, suppose that you plan to invest $1000 in an instrument that can only be purchased through a dealer. Further, assume that the minimum fee to purchase it is $35. Even if that investment earns 10 percent during the next year, the effective return after deducting the fee is only:

$$6.5\% \ = \ [(\$1000 \ \times \ 10\%) \ - \ \$35] \ \div \ \$1000$$

$$\frac{\text{Effective}}{\text{return}} \ = \ \frac{\text{Return from investment:}}{\text{Investment} \times \text{Rate}} \ - \ \frac{\text{Dealer's}}{\text{fee}} \ \div \ \frac{\text{Original}}{\text{investment}}$$

The above example shows that having to pay a fee to purchase an investment may reduce the return to the point that you would only make that investment when you either have a sizable amount to invest or plan to hold it for several years.

Tax Features   The discussion of **tax features** centers on federal income tax regulations. The most important question about taxes and investments is whether an investment's return is exempt from federal income tax—or possibly whether the taxes on that return can be deferred for a number of years. Depending on the investment, some returns are taxable; some are not. And even where returns are taxable, some portions of the returns may be taxed at a lower rate. Of course, the higher an investor's marginal tax rate, the more important it is to determine whether the return on an investment is fully taxable, only partially taxable, not subject to any taxes, or tax deferrable for a period of time.

Flexibility   An investment's **flexibility** depends on how easily it can be converted into cash should the need arise. One aspect of flexibility is the speed with which the investment can be turned into cash. If a borrower agrees to redeem an investment at any time the lender requests, it has fast convertibility and the investment is highly flexible. For example, a savings account has good flexibility because banks, savings and loans, and mutual savings banks generally permit withdrawals without advance notice.

An investment with a well-developed secondary market also can be converted into cash in a short time. A **secondary market** is one where you can sell an investment to another investor or a dealer before it matures. For example, assume that Don Stein currently has a corporate bond from Zug Products that matures in 5 years. If Don waits the 5 years, Zug will pay off the face amount of the bond. But the company will be unwilling to do that before 5 years are up. Don, however, wants to sell the bond immediately because he needs the money for other purposes. What he needs to find is another investor who will be willing to buy the bond from him. The secondary market is specifically intended to handle transactions between individuals who want to sell an investment before it matures and individuals who are interested in buying these investments. In effect, we might say that a secondary market deals in "used investments." That is, investments sold in secondary markets have had at least one, and possibly more, owners and now they are being offered for sale to still one more investor. When we say an investment has a good secondary market, we mean that market has a number of buyers who are ready to purchase a particular investment should an existing owner, or investor, decide to sell.

Other factors that affect the flexibility of an investment are price concession, transaction cost, and penalties.

Price Concession   Price concession is the amount by which the investor must reduce the selling price of the investment in order to attract a prospective buyer. Price concession is another measure of an investment's flexibility. At one extreme is a specialized investment such as rental property. If an investor wants to sell the property in a hurry, the selling price may have to be substantially below the price that it could be sold for if there were time to wait for buyers. At the opposite extreme are U.S. Treasury notes. The resale market on these notes is so broad and extensive that they can be sold with little or no concession below the current market price.

Transaction Cost   Some types of investments can be converted to cash only through a dealer or broker. The fee or commission to sell the investment is the transaction cost, and it is a cost that must be considered when determining an investment's flexibility. In general, the higher the transaction cost, the less flexible the investment.

Penalty   A few types of investments assess a penalty fee when they are redeemed before their final maturity date. Of course, a high penalty fee reduces an investment's flexibility because you will be very reluctant to redeem the investment before maturity if you face a large penalty.

YOUR INVESTMENT GOALS

Many people think that a suitable investment goal is merely to accumulate the largest amount of money in the least time. All of us would love to be able to do that. But that's not a goal because it does not provide the

AN INVESTMENT SCOUT
IS CAUTIOUS,
HARD WORKING,
SELF CONFIDENT
AND LUCKY!..

necessary guidelines to help the investor decide what is to be done, how it is to be done, and when it is to be done.

Your investment plans should have a series of well-defined goals. Each goal should use three basic guidelines.

1 You should state the specific reason or purpose of each goal.

2 You should set a specific dollar estimate.

3 You need to specify a time horizon within which you plan to achieve the goal.

Purpose or Reason for Establishing the Goal Investment goals can encompass a broad range of purposes and reasons. By specifying the purpose of each goal, it is easy to rank them in importance. And generally, you should not group a number of different purposes under one investment goal. Instead, you can implement your goals much more clearly and easily if you limit each goal to a single purpose or reason.

Dollar Amount of Goal Once the purpose of a goal is specified, it should be relatively easy to estimate the **dollar amount** of that goal. When a goal extends a number of years into the future, the estimate should include the effects of price increases owing to inflation. For example, assume that your goal is to have a 20 percent down payment 3 years from now for a house that currently costs $60,000. If you expect the price of the house to rise 7 percent annually during those 3 years, that house will cost:

$73,800 = $60,000 × 1.23

⇧ ⇧ ⇧

$$\frac{\text{Expected cost of}}{\text{house in 3 years}} = \frac{\text{Current cost of}}{\text{house}} \times \frac{\text{7\% annual inflation:}}{\text{Exhibit 1-4}}$$

(Recall that Chapter 1 illustrated how the compound value table in Exhibit 1-4 could be used to estimate the future price of an item.) Because of the expected rise in prices, a 20 percent down payment in 3 years means you will need:

$$\$14,760 \qquad = \$73,800 \qquad \times\ 20\%$$

$$\Updelta \qquad\qquad \Updelta \qquad\qquad \Updelta$$

Down payment = Expected cost × Down payment

STRATEGY

The longer the time span of a goal, the more critical it is to estimate the impact of inflation on the future dollar amount.

Time Horizon The **time horizon** for an investment goal is the period you set to achieve that particular goal. For some goals, the time horizon will be relatively short (as when you plan to purchase a new car); for other goals, it may be fairly long (such as investing for a newborn child's college education).

SUMMARY

1 There are two basic ways to invest: lending money to a borrower, and purchasing ownership in an income-producing investment.

2 Some recently introduced lending investments have a variable rate of return that is tied, or indexed, to the current rate of interest in the financial markets; the return therefore changes as the market rate changes.

3 Income from investments includes interest, cash dividends from common stock, rent, and an increase in the market value of the investment.

4 The total effective return on an investment includes the annual income on the investment plus the difference, if any, between the investment's purchase price and sale price.

5 One measure of an investment's risk is the variability of its rate of return.

6 An investment's return can vary owing to changes in the business environment and changes in the interest rates that prevail in the marketplace.

7 All investments involve a trade-off between risk and return. Generally, the higher the potential return, the higher the risk on that particular investment.

8 With a compound return, the initial investment earns a return, which is reinvested and which also earns a return. In effect, the investor receives earnings on previous earnings.

9 The annual rate of growth in value from compounding is greater for each year the earnings are reinvested.

10 The greater the frequency of compounding during the year, the higher the annual rate of return.

11 Inflation reduces an investment's real rate of return.

12 The recent high rates of inflation have reduced the real return on many investments to zero or less than zero (negative returns or losses).

13 Ownership investments should, in theory, provide a better hedge against inflation than do borrowing investments. But recent experience has shown mixed results. Certainly there is no guarantee that ownership investments will be completely effective in coping with high inflation rates.

14 To evaluate an investment properly, you need information on six criteria: risk, rate of return, minimum maturity, smallest dollar amount, tax features, and flexibility.

15 A well-specified investment goal includes the purpose of the goal, an estimate of the dollar amount of the goal, and the time horizon in which you plan to complete the goal.

REVIEW YOUR UNDERSTANDING OF

Two basic types of investments
  Lending
  Ownership
Variable return
  Indexing or tying
Effective return
  Interest
  Cash dividend
  Rent
  Change in market price
Risk
Causes of varying returns
  Business environment changes
  Interest rate changes
Risk-return trade-off
Compound return
Simple interest

Frequency of compounding
Real rate of return
Inflation premium
Hedge against inflation
  Lending investments
  Ownership investments
Investment evaluation criteria
  Risk
  Rate of return
  Minimum maturity
  Smallest dollar amount
  Tax features
  Flexibility
Secondary market
Investment goals
  Dollar amount
  Time horizon

DISCUSSION QUESTIONS

1 Do you think investment planning for small investors is more important or less important today than it was 10 years ago? What reasons can you give to support your position? What trend do you see over the next 10 years?

2 Can you give examples of investments that derive most of their return from annual income? What investments derive most of their return from the change in market price?

3 Which of the two investment categories—lending and ownership—is likely to provide the steadiest return? Why?

4 What measure is most frequently used to describe the risk on different investments? Can you give a numerical example of what the pattern of annual rates of return might be for a high-risk investment? What would the return pattern be like for a low-risk investment?

5 If you invested in a bond several years ago that pays 10 percent interest and suddenly the prevailing interest rate in the credit markets on comparable new bonds rises to 15 percent, what happens to the market price of your 10 percent bond? Why? If you continue to hold the bond, will you eventually receive the full face value? Why or why not?

6 Based on the 11-year period from 1968 through 1978, rank the following investments from the highest to the lowest in terms of their real rates of return: long-term corporate bonds, U.S. Treasury bills, common stocks, and long-term U.S. Treasury bonds. What might be the explanation of the difference between Treasury bills and Treasury bonds?

7 Why have many banks and other financial institutions switched to more frequent compounding? Why is the effective rate higher with more frequent compounding?

8 Why have investors become more concerned with an investment's real rate of return? Do you think investors will become more or less concerned during the next 5 years? Why?

9 Many people maintain that ownership investments can better offset the impact of inflation. Do you agree? Why?

PROBLEMS

17-1 Fred Bear wants to accumulate a $4000 down payment in order to purchase a vacation retreat in about 5 years. The investment he is considering for this goal provides an 8 percent return.

a If Fred decides to start accumulating the necessary funds immediately, how much will he have to save each month during the next 5 years? (*Hint:* Exhibit 1-7 may help.)

b If he delays the start of his investment plan until 2 years before the planned purchase, how much will he have to save each month?

c Which would you recommend? Why?

17-2 Chris Woo is considering three alternatives for her $4000 cash reserve fund.

ALTERNATIVE	INTEREST RATE	FREQUENCY OF COMPOUNDING
1	6	Annual
2	6	Daily
3	8	Daily

a Assume that Chris deposits the initial $4000 and reinvests the interest in the same investment. What will Chris earn in interest for the year?

b Which account would you recommend? Why?

c While the information given is very limited, which alternative would likely have the highest risk?

17-3 Antone and Susan VanderMullen would like to accumulate enough money to make a down payment on a house. They would need $6000 for the house they want, based on current prices. They plan to put the money into an investment that provides an 8 percent rate of return during the 5 years it will take them to accumulate the money.

a How much will they have to save each month?

b If they expect the house prices, and therefore the required down payment, to rise by 6 percent each year, what size of down payment will they need in 5 years? (*Hint:* Exhibit 1-4 may help.)

c Assuming that prices do rise as suggested in question **b**, will the monthly savings in question **a** be sufficient? If not, how much would they have to save each month?

d Why does the expected price increase described in question **b** have such a large impact on the required monthly savings?

17-4   Assume Shawn York is considering two Ajax Corporation bonds. Details on the bonds include:

BOND	MATURITY	PRICE	ANNUAL INTEREST PAYMENT	INTEREST RATE	VALUE AT MATURITY
A	1 year	$1000	$80	8%	$1000
B	10 years	$1000	$80	8%	$1000

a If Shawn purchases bond A, what annual dollar income will he receive? What wil he receive with bond B?

b Assume that the prevailing interest rates on new bonds comparable with the above Ajax bonds increase to 10 percent. On a new bond, what annual dollar income does the investor receive on a 1-year bond? A 10-year bond?

c Why will the price of bond B decline more than that of bond A? [*Hint*: Compare the annual incomes over the lives of the various bonds in questions **a** and **b**.]

17-5   Carmine Cautious is considering the following three competing lending investments:

INVESTMENT	CURRENT RATE OF RETURN	FUTURE RETURN	MATURITY
A	10%	Fixed	10 years
B	9%	Fixed	2 years
C	9%	Variable*	3 years

*Interest is recomputed every 6 months; rate is based on the rate for 2-year U.S. Treasury securities.

All the investments have similar risk, and they can be purchased in similar denominations with comparable flexibility. One of Carmine's concerns is the likely future rate of inflation.

a If Carmine believes the inflation rate to be reasonably stable and to average 4 percent over the next 10 years, what real rate of return would she expect from each investment? Which investment would you advise? Why?

b If Carmine thinks the annual inflation rate will be highly volatile—very high for several years followed by several years of moderate rates—which investment would you advise? Why?

CASE PROBLEM

Carlos and Carla Zapata have been married for 4 years; they both work full-time and they have no children. Despite the fact that their combined annual salaries total

$33,000, they have accumulated only $500 in a savings account. They own their furniture and have completely paid off one of their cars but still owe a balance on the other. They would like to buy a house, but the prospect of accumulating the required 10 percent down payment on a $70,000 home has them worried. In addition, they think it would be nice to have a new boat, and possibly also a travel trailer to keep by the lake when they go boating. Of course, they could also use the trailer in the winter if they were to buy a pair of snowmobiles. They agree they could put all these things to good use when they start their family next year. After looking at their long list of needs, they realize they will have to save more. They decide that if they try to spend less, there should be more left at the end of every month for savings. Furthermore, they feel that they must earn the highest return possible if they are ever going to get ahead. Consequently, they have a single investment goal: to accumulate the largest possible amount of money in the shortest time.

1   Would you have any recommendations for Carlos and Carla on their investment goal? What changes, if any, would you recommend in their investment goal(s) for their projected purchases? What information would they need to set up the goals you have recommended?

2   Do you think their strategy for implementing a new savings plan is a good one? Why or why not?

3   Which of their future goals will be the easiest to achieve? The hardest?

4   How do you feel about their objective of earning the highest return on their investments? How would you go about setting the anticipated return for each goal?

5   Do you feel that a single investment will meet all the Zapatas' goals? Why? What features are likely to differ among their various goals?

6   How much will the Zapatas need each month to accumulate the desired house down payment of $7000 in 5 years, assuming a 9 percent return? (*Hint:* Exhibit 1-7 may be helpful.)

APPENDIX:
SUMMARY OF MAJOR INVESTMENT ALTERNATIVES

Exhibit A 17-1 summarizes the six criteria that we will discuss in detail throughout the next three chapter when we describe the major investment alternatives. The list covers those investments that would be of particular interest to most individuals.

EXHIBIT A17-1

Summary of major investment alternatives using six criteria.

INVESTMENT	RISK* (1)	1982–1983 RETURN (%) (2)	MINIMUM MATURITY (3)
Financial Institutions:			

Savings account
  NOW account
	None on insured
	  account
		5¼–7	Immediately
			redeemable

Money market
  deposit account;
  Super-NOW
	None on insured
	  account
		No experience;
		G-1
			Immediately
			redeemable

Certificate of deposit	None on insured account	8–10	7 to 30 days

Certificates of
  deposit
	None on insured
	  account
		8–15	31 days and longer

Direct Investments:			
U.S. Treasury	No risk; G-2		
Bills		8–13	90 days to 1 year
Notes		10–15	1 year to 10 years
Bonds		10–14	10 years and longer

Corporate notes and bonds
  Notes
	Low to moderate;
	  G-2
		11–15(Aaa)
		14–17 (Baa)
			Notes 5 to 10 years
			Bonds 20 to 30 years

Municipal bonds	Low to moderate; G-2	8–12 (Aaa) 10–13 (Baa)	2 to 30 years
Common stock	Moderate to high; G-3	8–9 (G-4)	No set maturity; investor decides holding period
Mutual Funds:			
Money market:			No set maturity; redeemable by check
General	Low	9–15	
U.S. Government	Very low	8–13	
Corporate bonds:	G-2 and G-5;		No set maturity
Investment grade	Low	11–15	
Aggressive	Moderate	12–17	

Common stock	Moderate to high,
	  depends on fund's
	  objective; G-3
		9–10 (G-6)	No set maturity

Municipal bonds,
  Investment grade
  Aggressive
	G-2 and G-5;
	Low
	Moderate
		9–13
		11–14
			No set maturity

*General Comments
G-1 Account created in late 1982. Likely return would have been in the 8–13 percent range.
G-2 Price will change as market interest rates change.
G-3 Market price subject to wide swings due to changes in the overall stock market.
G-4 12-year average for broad sample of common stocks. "1982 Mutual Fund Ratings,"
      Forbes, Aug. 30, 1982.
G-5 Low if fund buys high-quality bonds (rated A or better); higher if fund buys lower-
      quality bonds (rated Baa or lower)
G-6 12-year average for broad sample of mutual funds. "1982 Mutual Fund Ratings,"
      Forbes, Aug. 30, 1982.

INVESTMENT	TYPICAL MINIMUM INVESTMENT (4)	TAX FEATURE[†] (5)	FLEXIBILITY (6)
Financial Institutions:			
Savings account NOW account	No minimum	T-1	Highly flexible; no fees or penalties on withdrawals
Money market deposit account; Super-NOW	$2,500	T-1	Highly flexible; rate on balance below $2,500 is 5¼ or 5½
Certificate of deposit	$2,500	T-1	Limited flexibility; 31 days' interest lost but institution will redeem
Certificates of deposit	No minimum but institution may specify one	T-1	Limited flexibility; 31 days' interest lost (maturities of 1 yr. or less) or 90 days' interest lost (maturities of more than 1 yr.) but institution will redeem
Direct Investments:			
U.S. Treasury Bills Notes Bonds	$10,000 $1,000–$5,000 $1,000	T-2 and T-4	Can be sold in strong secondary market; dealer's fee on sale
Corporate notes and bonds Notes	$5,000	T-1 and T-4	Can be sold prior to maturity; secondary markets range from strong to weak; dealer's fee on sale
Municipal bonds	$5,000	T-3 and T-4	Can be sold prior to maturity; secondary markets range from moderate to weak; dealer's fee on sale
Common stock	$1,000; brokers fee can be prohibitive on small amounts	T-1, T-4, T-5	Readily salable in good secondary market; broker commission on all sales
Mutual Funds:			
Money market: General U.S. Government	$1,000 $1,000	T-1 T-1	Highly flexible; can be redeemed by check at any time; investor decides
Corporate bonds: Investment grade Aggressive	$1,000 $1,000	T-1 and T-4	Highly flexible; redeemable at any time; investor decides holding period; no-load fund has no fee; load fund has fee
Common stock	$1,000	T-1, T-4, T-5,	Highly flexible; redeemable at any time; investor decides holding period; no-load fund has no fee; load fund has fee
Municipal bonds, Investment grade Aggressive	$2,500 $2,500	T-3 and T-4	Highly flexible; redeemable at any time; investor decides holding period; no-load fund has not fee; load fund has fee

[†]*Tax Features*
T-1   Income is fully taxable for federal and state income tax purposes.
T-2   Income fully taxable for federal income taxes but exempt from state taxes.
T-3   Income is exempt from federal income taxes and from some state income taxes.
T-4   Only 40 percent of long-term capital gains (sale price > purchase) subject to federal income taxes.
T-5   First $100 ($200 of joint return) on dividend income is exempt from federal income taxes.

CHAPTER
18
FIXED-INCOME INVESTMENTS

AFTER COMPLETING THIS CHAPTER YOU WILL HAVE LEARNED

What *savings accounts, money market accounts,* and *share accounts* are all about, as well as their advantages and disadvantages

How a savings account, money market account, or share account can be used to meet some of your *financial goals*

What a *certificate of deposit* (CD) is, and a *CD's advantages* and *disadvantages*

What the principal differences are between *traditional certificates of deposit (CDs)* and *deregulated CDs*

Which *financial goals* can be achieved through a CD

What the various *U.S. Treasury securities* are and how they can be purchased

What a *U.S. Series EE savings bond* is and how it compares with *U.S. Treasury securities*

How a *secondary market* operates and how it differs from a *primary market*

What *corporate bonds* and *municipal bonds* are

ALL the fixed-income investments

we will describe in this chapter are lending arrangements whereby the investor lends a specific amount of money in exchange for:

1   The borrower's promise to repay the borrowed funds at some future date

2   The borrower's promise to pay in one of two ways:

    a   A fixed rate of return over the life of the loan

    b   A variable rate of return that is tied (indexed) to some current interest rate in the financial market.

3   The borrower's promise to pay the interest on the investment at regular intervals during the period of the loan

All three of the promises are established when the investor makes the investment.

There are several reasons why it is important to know the details of the various fixed-income investments. For one thing, many people underestimate the variety of fixed-income investments available to them. Too often, investors accept an investment that has a low return or is unusually inflexible because they fail to investigate it fully and to compare it with other investments. Another reason is that the range of fixed-income investments continues to expand. Part of this expansion is due to the development of new fixed-income investments. But the remainder is due to revisions and modifications of previously existing investments.

Before you can select which fixed-income investments best match your specific investment goals, you need information on what is available. One further reason why you should study the alternatives before investing your money has to do with the impact of inflation and taxes. Recent periods of double-digit inflation have clearly illustrated the necessity of selecting investments that provide the highest return for the particular amount of risk you are willing to assume.

The fixed-income investments covered in this chapter are suitable for most small investors—people with $500 to $3000 to invest each year. We will concentrate on those investments that have moderate to low risk. Typically, they provide a reasonable return without exposing the investor to the possibility of losing the entire investment should something go wrong. We will not cover fixed-income investments that (1) can be purchased only for a large minimum investment (i.e., $25,000 and up), (2) are not readily available to everyone, or (3) are high-risk investments.

The fixed-income investments that we will examine in detail are savings accounts and share accounts, certificates of deposit (CDs), and U.S. savings bonds. We will cover to a more limited extent U.S. Treasury securities, corporate bonds, and municipal bonds. We will evaluate each of these fixed-income investments, using the six basic criteria we developed in Chapter 17—risk, rate of return, minimum maturity, smallest dollar amount, tax features, and flexibility. Where special features or criteria apply to a particular investment, we will discuss them. We will also examine the major advantages and disadvantages of each investment, and we will suggest the kinds of goals for which each of the fixed-income investments seems most appropriate.

FIXED-INCOME INVESTMENTS THROUGH FINANCIAL INSTITUTIONS

The first two groups of fixed-income investments we will discuss—savings or share accounts and CDs—involve a financial institution. Exhibit 18-1 shows the role of these two investments in the on-going operations of a financial institution. We have already briefly discussed the major financial institutions that offer these two types of investments—commercial banks, mutual savings banks, savings and loan associations, and credit unions—in Chapter 5. Our emphasis in this chapter will be on the right side of Exhibit 18-1.

The left side of Exhibit 18-1 shows why financial institutions are willing to pay a return on the fixed-income investments they sell to investors. They relend that money through a number of different loans. By consolidating the dollars from a large number of smaller investors, financial institutions can loan rather large amounts to various borrowers. The borrower might be an individual who plans to use the money to buy a home (a mortgage) or a new automobile (a consumer cash loan), or to deal with a temporary cash shortage (an automatic overdraft on a checking account). Or it could be a much larger borrower, such as a business, a local municipality, or even the United States government.

It is important to recognize that when you invest in a savings account, a share account, or a CD, the promise to repay comes from the financial

EXHIBIT 18-1

Role of financial institutions in the lending and borrowing process.

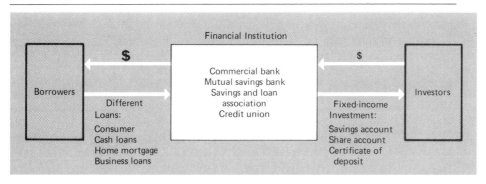

institution. And it is the financial institution that decides what rate of return it will pay on that particular investment. But the institution is not entirely free to set that return. There are a series of regulations and controls that set interest ceilings, or the maximum rate of return that the financial institution can pay on some investments.

Interest Rate Ceilings: The Future   Prior to April 1980, all the fixed-return investments that financial institutions offered to small savers had interest rate ceilings specifying the maximum return they could pay. In this highly regulated environment, the interest rates among competing institutions were much the same: typically, they were at the maximum allowed rate. But all that is changing and will likely continue to change over the next several years. Under the Depository Institutions Deregulation and Monetary Control Act of 1980, all interest rate ceilings must be removed by 1986. After that date, financial institutions can pay any interest rates they feel are appropriate. Once those interest rates are deregulated, they will be set by the forces of supply and demand in the financial markets. Since each financial institution may have a different view of exactly what the current state of the financial markets is, there are likely to be sizable differences in the interest rates that individual financial institutions offer. In this environment, investors will have to be much more actively involved in managing their money. Before making an investment, it will be essential that they compare the returns on competing investments. And once the investment is made, the investor will need to continue to monitor it to make certain its rate of return remains competitive.

STRATEGY

As we shift to deregulated interest rates, it is essential that you carefully compare returns on competing investments.

The next two sections, which deal with savings accounts and certificates of deposit (CDs), will outline those investments on which the interest rates have already been deregulated and discuss the likely timetable for the complete removal of all interest rate ceilings.

Savings Accounts, Money Market Accounts, and Share Accounts

Savings accounts, money market accounts, and share accounts are offered by a wide array of financial institutions: commercial banks, mutual savings banks, savings and loan associations, and credit unions.

Traditional Savings Accounts   **Traditional savings accounts** have been a standard form of investment for many small investors. They were widely available, could be opened for a small amount, and allowed immediate, and typically unlimited, withdrawals. But the maximum interest rate has always been tightly regulated. Unfortunately, even as other interest rates moved into double digits, the ceiling remained unchanged at 5¼ to 5½ percent. Because of those very low rates, many investors withdrew their money and moved to competing investments that provided a return that compared more favorably with market interest rates. Rather than raise, or even totally remove, the interest ceilings, the regulatory agency elected to create a new, deregulated account: the money market deposit account, the topic of the next section. We should point out, however, that by 1986, the ceiling must be removed from all savings accounts. But current indications are that traditional savings accounts will likely be the last investment vehicle that is deregulated.

Money Market Deposit Accounts **Money market deposit accounts** were introduced in 1982 as the first step toward deregulated savings accounts. We should note that while the deregulation advisory board used the term "money market deposit account," financial institutions are free to use whatever label or title they want. We have no doubt that marketing departments and promotional staffs, being what they are, will create a whole range of imaginative account names. So don't be surprised if you encounter a lot of different titles. For our purposes, we will shorten it to *money market account*.

As **deregulation** implies, the money market account has no interest ceiling. It allows the financial institution to decide what rate of interest it wants to pay on the account. Call that a definite plus. But to prevent a wholesale shift from the traditional savings account to this new account, the Depository Institutions Deregulation Committee (which developed the account) placed some restrictions on it. First, opening an account requires an initial deposit of at least $2500; the financial institution can set a higher minimum if it desires. Should your account balance drop below $2500, the return reverts to 5¼ percent. Once the account is established, you are free to make whatever deposits or withdrawals you want, unless your financial institution restricts them in some way. But each month you are permitted only six transfers from the account to a third party and only three of those can be checks. What does that mean? It says you can write up to three checks against this account each month to whomever you please for whatever amount your account will cover, but that is your limit. The remaining three transfers may be a combination of electronic transfers of money to some other business or financial institution, or a telephone transfer of money to another account—NOW, checking, savings—that you have at the same institution where your money market account is located. To summarize, you can make unlimited withdrawals from the account yourself and do what you please with that money. But if you want to instruct the institution to transfer that money (either through a check, a telephone call, or electronically) directly to someone else (a third party), you cannot do so more than six times each month. There are penalties if you exceed that number.

Clearly, the introduction of the money market account is a move toward deregulating savings accounts. But the restrictions limit the account to investors who have the sizable minimum initial deposit. We hasten to add that the restrictions and guidelines listed here are those that prevailed when this was written early in 1983. We expect that after a trial period, the regulators may relax those restrictions so that money market accounts are accessible to a wider range of investors.

Share Accounts Share accounts are comparable with savings accounts but are offered only by credit unions. The term **share account** is used to signify that you, as a depositor in the credit union, share the ownership of that institution. Rather than use the term *"interest"* to describe the earnings on a share account, the term *"dividend"* is used. Beginning in early 1982, all interest ceilings were removed on federally chartered credit unions (those that have received their operating charter from the federal government). These credit unions can set whatever interest rate they choose on their deregulated share accounts. But unlike the previous money market deposit account, this type of account does not have a required initial deposit unless the credit union itself sets one. Nor does it restrict the number of transfers to third parties. So not only is the account deregulated, it also is far less limited than its money market counterpart.

Major Investment Attributes: Savings and Share Accounts

We will use the six investment criteria that we established in Chapter 17 to review the major attributes of traditional savings accounts, money market accounts, and share accounts. Exhibit 18-2 summarizes the first five of those six criteria; we will discuss the sixth one a bit later. Since most of the criteria are self-explanatory, we will limit our comments to two areas.

Rate of Return While traditional savings accounts have a maximum return, or interest rate ceiling, the financial institution is *not* required to pay

EXHIBIT 18-2

Major investment attributes: Savings and share accounts.

INVESTMENT	MAXIMUM RATE OF RETURN	RISK EXPOSURE	MINIMUM MATURITY	TYPICAL MINIMUM INVEST-MENT	TAX FEATURE
Traditional savings account	5¼% or 5½%*	Zero if insured	No set minimum	$ 25	Interest fully taxable
Money market account	No set maximum†	Zero if insured	No set minimum	2500	Interest fully taxable
Share account	No set maximum	Zero if insured	No set minimum	25	Dividends fully taxable

*Commercial banks pay 5¼ percent; while savings and loan associations and mutual savings banks can pay 5½ percent.
†If account balance is less than $2500, the interest rate is only 5¼ percent.

that amount. So, if you open one of these accounts, make certain it does pay the maximum. The deregulated nature of money market accounts and share accounts requires some changes on the investor's part. First, before opening an account, investors will have to compare competing accounts to see whether interest rates differ widely among the various financial institutions. This step was typically not required on the old regulated savings account because investors generally found that all such accounts offered the same rate. But investor involvement does not stop with opening the account. After all, the institution is free to lower the return on a money market account or share account at any time. No longer can the investor just sit back and assume a particular account's return will continue to be competitive with other accounts. Investors must continue to monitor their money market accounts or share accounts to make certain that their returns remain competitive.

Risk When the saving account or share account is covered by federally sponsored insurance, the balance is insured up to $100,000. Should the financial institution be unable to repay investors their money, the **Federal Deposit Insurance Corporation** (FDIC) or the **Federal Savings and Loan Insurance Corporation** (FSLIC) will step in and redeem those accounts. Given the wide availability of either FDIC or FSLIC insured accounts, there really is no reason to accept anything less than an insured account.

Flexibility All three accounts—traditional savings, money market, and share—have excellent flexibility (our sixth investment criterion) because they can be readily converted to cash. None has a stated maturity, so the investor decides whether to hold the investment for 2 weeks, 2 months, 2 years, or even longer; since the institution promises to redeem the entire balance in the account, the market value of the account does not fluctuate. Generally, all three accounts permit unlimited withdrawals. Some, however, do assess a fee if your withdrawals exceed a set number during a month. In our opinion, the limitation that you can make only six transfers from your money market account to third parties is not overly serious. Should you exhaust all six transfers, you can always personally withdraw money and place it in some other account or use it directly to make a payment.

Special Features

Many financial institutions offer special features and services which can make it more advantageous to have a savings account or share account with them.

Deposit and Withdrawal Options Many institutions offer mail service for deposits and withdrawals. Obviously, this is a great convenience, saving you time and travel to transact your bank business. Some financial institutions even pay the postage.

Carrying this convenience one step further, some institutions will transfer funds between a depositor's savings account and checking or NOW account (all you have to do is make a phone call). In addition, upon your instruction, many institutions will automatically transfer a set amount of money from your checking account to your savings account each month.

Remote Electronic Terminals Increasingly, financial institutions are providing remote electronic terminals (RETs) as a service to their customers. The single largest advantage of having access to an RET is convenience: You can complete all the required transactions for your savings or share account—deposits, withdrawals, and transfers to or from your other accounts at that one financial institution. Also, you can carry out most of these transactions at hours when the financial institution is closed or at places where the terminal is closer to where you live than the institution itself is.

Savings, Money Market, and Share Accounts: Advantages and Disadvantages

The major advantages and disadvantages of savings accounts, money market accounts, and share accounts are listed in Exhibit 18-3. The benefits and drawbacks are generally self-explanatory. However, we need to make two comments on the rate of return. First, a comment on the disadvantage that traditional saving accounts "provide a very limited rate of return." We do not expect this rate to change until these accounts are deregulated. Given the present 5¼ or 5½ percent ceiling, they just are not providing a competitive return. Second, we intentionally qualified one of the advantages of a money market account or a share account: "Its interest rate *may* be competitive with open-market interest rates." While an institution can set the rates of return at whatever level it chooses, these accounts are so new that we lack enough experience to predict what return will actually be

EXHIBIT 18-3

Major advantages and disadvantages of savings accounts, money market accounts, and share accounts.

INVESTMENT	ADVANTAGES	DISADVANTAGES
Traditional savings	1 2 3 4 6	1
Money market	1 2 4 5 6	2 3 4
Share accounts	1 2 4 5 6	5

Advantages

1 Highly flexible and convenient
2 Unrestricted withdrawals; no set maturity
3 Low required initial deposits
4 Widely available
5 Interest rate sometimes competitive with open-market interest rates
6 Zero risk if insured

Disadvantages

1 Very limited rate of return
2 Very large required initial deposit
3 Rate of return is only 5¼ percent on account balance below $2500
4 Only six transfers to third parties permitted monthly
5 May not be insured

offered. The potential is there to provide a competitive rate of return, but it remains to be confirmed that the *actual* rate paid will be competitive.

Suitable Investment Goals for Savings, Money Market, and Share Accounts

Because the traditional savings account differs significantly from either the unregulated share account or the money market account, we will discuss it separately.

Traditional Savings Account For an investor who has only several hundred dollars to invest and who lacks access to a share account paying a competitive rate, a savings account may be the choice by default. If it is all that is available, the account can be used to accumulate money for short-term financial goals. It can also be the place you invest your emergency fund; recall that we discussed that fund back in Chapter 3. Similarly, it can serve as a temporary investment for money that you eventually plan to invest elsewhere. While the account can be used for all these applications, it does none of them well. It just does not provide a competitive rate of return. And during periods of high inflation, its real rate of return has been decidedly negative. Those who have more dollars to invest have alternatives that provide a higher return with little or no added risk.

Money Market Accounts and Share Accounts For those investors who can either meet the minimum deposit requirements of the money market account or qualify for a share account providing a competitive return (in a moment, we will explain what we mean by "competitive"), either of these accounts is much better than a traditional savings account. Both accounts would be a good investment for the emergency fund that we discussed in budgeting (Chapter 3). As long as their rate of return is competitive, they will also be a good investment for money that you ultimately plan to place in a more permanent investment. Or, they can be used to accumulate the necessary money for your various short-term financial goals, especially those that you expect to complete within the next 6 to 18 months.

At this point, however, a word of caution is in order. These comments are predicated on the assumption that the money market account or share account in which you plan to invest is providing a competitive rate of return. To be a recommended investment, the account's rate of return must be comparable with prevailing interest rates in the financial markets.

STRATEGY

In our opinion, the rate of return is probably competitive when it meets one of these two criteria:

It equals or exceeds the current interest rate on 90-day U.S. Treasury bills (which we will discuss later in the chapter).

It is slightly less than the return offered by money market mutual funds (discussed in Chapter 20).

CERTIFICATES OF DEPOSIT

Certificates of deposit (CDs) are offered by many of the same financial institutions that offer savings and share accounts. A CD is distinguished in that the depositor agrees not to withdraw the funds for a specified period; that period may range from 7 days to more than 7 years. In exchange for the investor's accepting this restriction on withdrawals, CDs typically pay a higher rate of return than either savings or share accounts. Generally, the longer the maturity of the CD, the higher the promised rate of return.

Two distinctly different types of certificates of deposit are currently available: traditional CDs and deregulated CDs. (We should point out that we created these labels so that we could distinguish between them in our discussion. Financial institutions may or may not use similar labels.) The second CD group was developed in response to two forces:

> An attempt to make the interest rate on CDs more closely parallel interest rates in the financial markets

> The ongoing deregulation of financial institutions, which continues to remove the previous interest rate ceilings

Traditional CDs Traditional CDs were the standard accounts that financial institutions offered for years. Interest rates on these CDs were closely regulated, with a maximum, or ceiling, interest rate being set for each different CD maturity (e.g., 90 days, 1 year, 2 years, etc.). Of course, the institution was always free to pay less if it chose. But, during the late 1970s and early 1980s, double-digit inflation with its accompanying double-digit interest rates raised havoc with traditional CDs. The prevailing interest ceilings meant that CD rates were not competitive and, furthermore, those maximums were not raised appreciably. As their CDs matured, more investors moved their money to other investments that were providing a more attractive return. Rather than sharply revise the interest ceilings, the regulators created a new account: the interest-indexed CD. We will not go into detail about those interest-indexed CDs because they were replaced in 1983 by deregulated CDs. While traditional CDs are still permitted, few financial institutions now offer them. Deregulated CDs have effectively replaced the traditional CD.

Deregulated CDs As the name suggests, **deregulated CDs** have no interest ceiling, and they are not indexed to some market interest rate. Instead, the financial institution can establish any interest rate that it wants on these CDs. Because each institution will use its own unique set of data and computations to establish its CD rates, competing institutions may well offer significantly different rates. So it is essential that you compare the rate of return offered by several financial institutions when selecting a deregulated CD. By late 1983, all CDs were deregulated.

Major Investment Attributes: Certificates of Deposit

We will continue to use the six investment criteria that we developed in Chapter 17 to discuss deregulated CDs. We intentionally omit traditional

CDs, in part because new CD forms have almost completely displaced them. Furthermore, in the present environment, the interest rates on traditional CDs are so low that they are not attractive investments. Exhibit 18-4 sumarizes the first five of the six criteria; the sixth is a bit more involved, so we will discuss it later in a separate section.

Rate of Return   The interest rate on deregulated CDs is left entirely to the discretion of the financial institution issuing it. Interestingly enough, some financial institutions decided *not* to offer any deregulated CDs when they first became available. Rather than venture into a totally new area, they opted for the easy way out: Do nothing except continue the available interest-indexed CDs. Now with all CDs effectively deregulated, those financial institutions will have no choice but to venture into the uncharted waters of "totally deregulated interest rates." Among institutions offering deregulated CDs, the interest rates have differed significantly at times. Their disparity points up the need to compare CD rates carefully before investing your money. We think that, as a general guide, a deregulated CD should offer a return roughly equal to the interest rate on a Treasury security of comparable maturity. For example, the rate on a 4-year CD ought to be about the same as the rate on a 4-year Treasury note.

Variable-Rate CDs   One potential concern about investing in a CD with a long maturity and a fixed interest rate is what happens when market interest rates rise after you purchase the CD. Owing to the CD's fixed return, you could end up accepting a below-market return over part, or all, of the CD's life. In fact, during the recent bout of sharply higher interest rates, many investors experienced exactly that. "Once burned," as the old saying goes, some investors have become very reluctant to purchase any fixed-rate CD that has a lengthy maturity. The solution was to create a **variable-rate CD** whose interest rate would vary over its life.

Rather than offer a single fixed-interest rate throughout its maturity, a variable-rate CD promises to change its return over its life, or maturity. Typically, the mechanism to accomplish this is to tie the CD's rate to some market interest rate such as a Treasury security. Or a financial institution may decide to establish the interest rate through its own deliberations.

EXHIBIT 18-4

Major investment attributes of deregulated certificates of deposit.

INVESTMENT	MAXIMUM INTEREST RATE	RISK EXPOSURE	MINIMUM MATURITY	TYPICAL MINIMUM INVESTMENT	TAX FEATURE
7 to 30 days	No set maximum	No risk if insured	7 to 30 days	$2500	Fully taxable
31 days and longer	No set maximum	No risk if insured	31 days	$ 100	Fully taxable

Further, the CD specifies the time intervals or points at which the interest rate will be adjusted.

Let us use an imaginery CD to show how this provision might operate. Waldo Wary is considering the following 3½-year, variable-rate CD: The CD's rate equals the interest rate on a 2½-year U.S. Treasury note and it is adjusted every 2 weeks. To begin, we assume the current return on 2½-year Treasury notes is 13 percent. For the first 2 weeks, Waldo receives a 13 percent return. For whatever reason, let's assume the rate on 2½-year Treasury notes rises to 15 percent; Waldo's CD return rises to 15 percent for the next 2 weeks. Now suppose that after those 2 weeks, the Treasury note rate plunges to 11 percent. Waldo's rate likewise falls to 11 percent for the next 2 weeks. During the 6 weeks he has owned the CD, Waldo's return has ranged from 11 to 15 percent. But the important thing is that it has moved with market interest rates: Waldo is *not* locked into a single rate.

In fact, this whole adjustment process will be repeated every 2 weeks during the entire 3½ years that the CD is outstanding. In the real world, interest rates probably would never swing through a range of 11 to 15 percent in such a short time. Nevertheless, our example illustrates how a variable-rate CD protects the investor during periods of rising interest. Of course, it also lowers the CD's rate during periods of declining interest rates. But, on balance, we believe the positive features of a variable rate more than offset its negative features. This would be especially true if you were buying a CD at a point when you expect interest rates were more likely to rise than decline over the life of that CD.

STRATEGY

If you are considering a CD with a lengthy maturity, especially during a period when interest rates are volatile or when there is the distinct

charted at the top simply follows the average price of the stock each year—it tells us nothing about the price of the stock with respect to inflation. (2) The index charted in the middle of the exhibit is the consumer price index—one measure of what is happening to inflation. (3) The index at the bottom is the average stock price index charted in "constant dollars." The constant dollar used in this index is the value of $1 in 1913.

To clarify our understanding of this exhibit, let's look at the real meaning of each of its parts. By using the consumer price index we eliminate that portion of the increase or decrease in the average price of common stocks—the Dow Jones Industrial Average shown in the top of the chart—that was due solely to the general increase in overall consumer prices. After eliminating the price increase due to the general rise in overall prices, we obtain a series of common stock prices that reflect constant dollars which have not been raised by the general upward trend in overall

CHAPTER 19

615

COMMON
STOCKS: A
VARIABLE INCOME
INVESTMENT

EXHIBIT 19-2

Inflation and the average price of common stocks: Dow Jones Industrial Average in current and constant dollars.

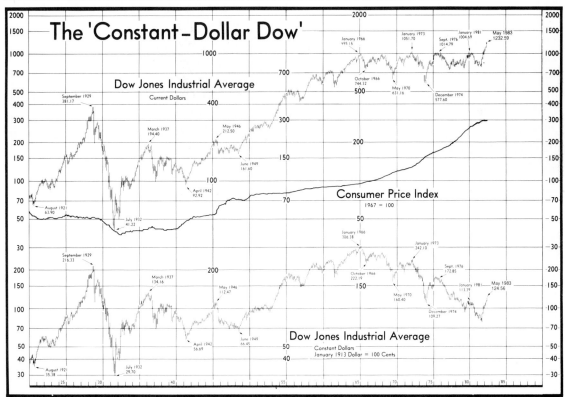

Source: The Media General Financial Weekly   Richmond, Virginia 23219

consumer prices. This is plotted in the bottom portion of Exhibit 19-2 as the Dow Jones Industrial Average—"Constant Dollars."

Several observations can be made from the stock price index shown in Exhibit 19-2.

One: During recent years, the constant dollar index tended to decline most sharply during periods when the consumer price index rose most rapidly. On the other hand, the price index generally performed best during periods when consumer prices were rising only moderately. Clearly, common stock prices have not provided a sufficient hedge against the sharp price increases of the late 1960s and 1970s.

Two: Despite several sharp advances in common stock prices during the past 25 years, most of those increases have been offset by inflation.

And three: The overall pattern of stock price changes during the 1970s was not encouraging. Investors who bought common stock during the late 1960s or early 1970s and held them have seen the price of those shares eroded by inflation. The exception consists of those investors who were wise enough—or lucky enough—to buy when stock prices were lowest during 1970 and 1974. But even professional investors and advisors are not wonderfully successful at detecting when prices are lowest and will again begin to rise.

Real Investor Return Because total investor return includes both a stock's cash dividend yield and the change in market price, we need to include dividend yield with what we have learned about inflation and stock prices from Exhibit 19-2.

Over the 20 years from the late 1950s to the late 1970s, an investor's annual real return (that is, total return cash dividends plus market price change less inflation) was approximately 2.2 percent.[2] That is less than the 4 to 4.5 percent real return that we feel a high-quality common stock should provide. During the 9-year span between 1969 and 1978, the real return was a negative 3.51 percent[3] (a loss!). If we consider the effects of inflation, investors lost money by holding common stocks during that decade.

Overall, our answer to the question of whether common stocks are a good hedge against inflation is: Historically, it seems that common stocks can provide a hedge against low inflation rates (not more than 5 percent inflation per year), but they are no protection against inflation rates in the 10 percent plus range.

Stock Valuation

At this point, we will explain several measures that are frequently used to describe a particular common stock.

Earnings per Share A stock's **earnings per share** (EPS) is computed by first dividing the corporation's total annual earnings after it has paid any

---

[2]Roger G. Ibbotson and Rex A. Sinquefield, "Stocks, Bonds, Bills and Inflation: Update." *Financial Analysts Journal*, July-August 1979, p. 41.
[3]Ibid.

federal and state income taxes by the total number of shares of common stock which that corporation has. Thus, if Zug Products had annual earnings (after payment of taxes) of $1,500,000 and if there are currently 300,000 shares of Zug common stock, its EPS would be:

CHAPTER 19

617

COMMON
STOCKS: A
VARIABLE INCOME
INVESTMENT

$5   = $1,500,000   ÷ 300,000

⇧   ⇧   ⇧

Earnings per = Annual earnings ÷ Shares of common stock
share (EPS)   after tax

This EPS computation used the firm's historical earnings—what Zug did last year. In addition, projected annual earnings for a future year may be used to compute the projected EPS for some future period.

Price-Earnings Ratio The **price-earnings ratio** (P/E) is computed by dividing the market price per share by the earnings per share. The price-earnings ratio indicates the relationship between the market price of a share and annual earnings of that share. Thus, the price-earnings ratio of a stock that currently sells for $10 and has EPS of $1 is:

10 times   = $10   ÷ $1

⇧   ⇧   ⇧

Price-earnings = Market price of ÷ Annual earnings
ratio (P/E)   common stock   per share

Another way of stating the same thing is to say the stock is selling at 10 times earnings. The P/E gives investors a way of evaluating a particular stock. At any point, some stocks sell at 30 to 50 times earnings while others sell at 3 to 5 times earnings. Why the big difference? It can be due to a number of things, such as future earnings' prospects, highly respected company management, a glamorous product line, more publicity, or many other factors.

Common Stock Categories

To group all common stocks into a few summary categories would be difficult, and in the end some placements would be arbitrary. Nevertheless, we will provide our definitions of three frequently used labels: blue chip stock, growth stock, and speculative stock.

Blue Chip Stock A **blue chip stock** represents a share in a large, well-regarded corporation. Most of these corporations have a long history of reasonably consistent earnings and steady dividends. Their earnings continue to grow, although the growth rate is generally not spectacular. The financial community regards these firms as well managed and prudently financed. Blue chip stocks typically present the lowest risk of all common stocks.

Growth Stock A **growth stock** represents a share in a corporation whose earnings have grown at above-average rates during recent years. A true growth stock must also offer the prospect of a continued above-average growth in the future. Merely increasing sales is not enough; the firm must also increase its earnings. With an earnings growth rate of 10 to 15 percent or more per year, you can expect that a firm cannot continue to grow at that rapid rate forever. For example, a firm growing at 15 percent annually would double in size every 5 years. Even if it started small, the firm would be 4 times its original size in 10 years.

Most growth firms pay low dividends because they need most of their earnings to pay for the costs of their continuing expansion. The P/E ratio on growth stocks, especially those of the large, highly respected firms, tends to be well above the market average. The prices of growth stock are very volatile: They drop sharply when the general market declines and rise sharply when the market advances.

Many investors are continually searching for "undiscovered" growth stocks. They hope to purchase the shares before their price reflects the firm's rosy future. Once a stock is "recognized" as a growth stock, its price rises sharply and early investors pick up a tidy profit. But identifying an "undiscovered" growth stock is no small task. All too often, many promising candidates turn out to be the work of the accountant's creative pen, management's financial maneuvers, or just plain unsupported rhetoric.

Speculative Stock   A **speculative stock** represents a share in a company that may, or may not, have good future potential earnings. In general, investors buy the stock on the prospect of its future earnings rather than on its past accomplishments. The company may have a new or revised product that may revolutionize the industry. Or, the firm may have been highly successful in the past, but is currently experiencing difficulty; if these problems can be resolved, the firm may be highly successful once more. But investors have no guarantee that a speculative stock will succeed in increasing its earnings and that eventually its price per share will rise sharply. For every stock that succeeds, dozens that looked equally promising never work out.

THE MARKETS WHERE STOCKS ARE TRADED

Common stocks can be purchased in either the primary market or in the secondary market.

Primary Market   New issues of common stock are sold in the **primary market**. The actual sale is handled by a specialized selling group called the underwriters; the corporation receives the sale proceeds minus a small commission charged by the selling group. A new company sells a new issue of common stock simply to obtain funds for beginning operation. A company already in operation may sell a new issue to finance a major expansion. Since most firms obtain the money they need by retaining a portion of their earnings, the number of new issues each year is small.

Secondary Market   The **secondary market** is the one where most investors buy and sell stock; it is what most people mean when they say "the stock market." Stocks traded in this market were issued previously and have been outstanding for various lengths of time. Secondary market transactions involve a shareholder who decides to sell a particular stock and a prospective investor who decides to buy that stock. The corporation has no role in the transaction, nor does it receive any of the proceeds. A stock's price on any day reflects the supply and demand for the stock at that precise moment. If many shareholders want to sell but only a few investors are interested in buying, the price will decline and will continue to do so until prospective investors are attracted. Conversely, a heavy demand by new investors and limited supply will cause the price to rise.

Reading a Secondary Market List Exhibit 19-3 provides a hypothetical example of a secondary market listing of common stocks. While the actual lists that appear in the *Wall Street Journal* and other metropolitan newspapers may differ in format, their informational content is similar to that in Exhibit 19-3. A company's common stock may be listed on one or more stock exchanges, including (1) the New York Stock Exchange; (2) the American Stock Exchange; (3) regional exchanges—Midwest, Pacific, Boston, and so on; and (4) the over-the-counter market.

To explain the information given in the listing, we will use as an example Atwood Chemical, which is near the middle of this exhibit. The first two columns show the stock's highest and lowest prices for the

CHAPTER 19

619

COMMON
STOCKS: A
VARIABLE INCOME
INVESTMENT

EXHIBIT 19-3

Hypothetical example of a secondary market listing of common stocks traded on October 14, 1983.

1983						
HIGH	LOW	STOCK	DIVIDEND	SALES 100'S	DIVIDEND YIELD	P/E RATIO
24⅛	21⅞	Algoma Products	1.00	13	4.3	10
19⅜	18¼	American Power	2.50	3	13.5	6
26⅜	18⅞	Atwood Chemical	0.95	78	4.1	11
9⅜	9	Azoor Finance	0.04	17	0.4	12
75¾	70⅛	Baker Foods	2.75	6	3.9	5
78⅛	45¼	Beeker Oil	0.10	33	0.2	45

STOCK	**Price**			
	HIGH	LOW	CLOSE	CHANGE
Algoma Products	23¼	23⅛	23⅛	−⅛
American Power	18·	18½	18½	—
Atwood Chemical	23⅜	22½	23	¼
Azoor Finance	9⅛	9	9	−⅛
Baker Foods	71¼	71⅛	71¼	½
Beeker Oil	47½	47⅜	47⅜	−⅜

previous 12 months. Atwood's stock ranged from 26 ⅜ ($26.375) to 18 ⅞ ($18.875). The dollar amount following the name of the stock—0.95—is the annual dividend in dollars. Following this, under "Sales 100's," is the number of shares traded that day in 100's. Thus, 7800 shares of Atwood stock were traded on October 14. Next comes the stock's current dividend yield:

$$4.1\% \quad = \$0.95 \quad \div \$23$$

$$\triangle \qquad \quad \triangle \qquad \quad \triangle$$

Dividend = Cash $\div$ Market price on
yield   dividend   day of listing

In the next column is the stock's P/E ratio, based on its current closing price and its most recent annual EPS. The day's price range follows: high, low, and closing prices. (The closing price is the price of stock at the last transaction on that day.) Last comes the net price change between the previous and the current day's closing prices.

Stock Market Indexes   The widely publicized **stock market indexes** show the current state and recent performance of the total market. All stock indexes are based on the market price of a sample of selected stocks, but the sample varies widely for different indexes. Some indexes concentrate on industrial stocks: Dow Jones Industrial Average (30 industrial firms), Standard & Poor's 425 Industrials (425 industrial firms). Other indexes, such as the Standard & Poor's 500 Index, New York Stock Exchange Index, and American Stock Exchange Index, cover a much broader cross section of stocks.

Danger! Here Come the Bulls and the Bears   When stock prices are rising, the trend is typically called a "bull market." On the other hand, declining prices indicate a "bear market." When these terms are translated to an individual investor, a **bear** is generally a pessimist who expects stock prices to decline; a **bull** is an optimist who expects stock prices to rise. So the next time someone begins discussing whether the current market is bullish or bearish, you can either pass the bull back or bear it.

SELECTING A COMMON STOCK

Techniques for evaluating and selecting common stocks can be grouped into two general categories:

> Those that rely on technical analysis

> Those that rely on fundamental analysis

We shall first discuss the principal points for each type of analysis. We will then raise questions about the efficacy of selecting common stocks through either type of analysis. In essence, can an investor operating in an efficient market (supporters of this theory argue that the market for common stock is indeed efficient) select common stocks, whether evaluating them through technical or fundamental analysis, with sufficient consistency to provide above-average returns?

CHAPTER 19

621

COMMON
STOCKS: A
VARIABLE INCOME
INVESTMENT

Technical Analysis

Supporters of **technical analysis** believe that the price of a common stock moves according to a series of definite patterns and flows. They argue that by identifying those patterns and flows, people can predict the likely future direction of stock prices. That prediction then becomes the basis for buying and selling common stocks. Advocates of technical analysis (who frequently refer to themselves as "technicians") believe that certain patterns of stock prices will repeat themselves in the market. So, by recording, or "charting," the price trend and volume of trading of a particular stock, they believe they can identify the emergence of those repetitive patterns and act accordingly. They maintain that the careful study of historical price and volume patterns provides definite clues as to the future direction of prices.

Fundamental Analysis

Fundamental analysis attempts to identify promising common stocks by analyzing the underlying factors that give a particular common stock its value. By analyzing these underlying factors, supporters of fundamental analysis maintain that an investor can estimate the intrinsic "value" of a particular stock. The only concern of the fundamentalist (a title frequently associated with advocates of fundamental analysis) regarding the current market price is its relationship to the intrinsic value that has been established through fundamental analysis. If the price is less than the value of the stock, it is a purchase candidate. Likewise, if the market price exceeds the fundamentalists' estimate of its value, it is a sell candidate. They believe that over time the two amounts—market price and intrinsic value—will converge as other market participants recognize the true worth of that

THE TROUBLE REALLY STARTED WHEN WE TRIED TO INVEST IN THE STOCK MARKET TOGETHER..

MARRIAGE COUNSELOR

particular stock. Those who can identify a price difference before other market participants will profit by buying (when they expect the price to rise) or selling (when they think the price will fall).

Fundamentalists are primarily concerned with estimating the future prospects of the company. To do that, they begin by estimating the prospects for the industry within which the firm is located. From there they move to a review of the company's future prospects, which includes an estimate of the likely sales for the firm's present products as well as its future products. Next, they want to estimate how profitable those future sales may be. This step requires reviewing the firm's operating costs, competition within the industry, import competition, and future changes in tax regulations, to mention a few areas. Needless to say, a detailed fundamental analysis will involve analyzing a very large amount of data and making a number of estimates. It is a lot of work; and even after that, there is no guarantee that the stock being analyzed will in the end be over- or undervalued relative to its current market price.

Efficient Market or Random Walk Theory   Supporters of the **efficient market theory,** also called the **random walk theory,** argue that the market price of a common stock already reflects the published information about that stock. Small investors as well as professional ones will have read and acted upon the information that is currently published on a particular stock. No one, relying on the same information, will be able to consistently glean some tidbit of data that will lead to a "superior projection" of what is going to happen to the market price of a particular common stock. The efficient market and random walk theorists maintain that even a diligent search, coupled with good analysis (whether technical or fundamental) of the data is just not going to permit an investor to select common stocks which will earn consistently higher rates of return. Granted, some of the time a selected common stock will rise, but random walk theorists would argue that there will be other, and frequent, times when the price of the selected stock declines. The net effect, these supporters suggest, is that the investor will likely earn an average return overall when all the selected stocks are averaged together.

Even the addition of new information on a particular common stock will not alter or improve the investor's chance for success. Supporters of the random walk theory say that as soon as that new information becomes known (and they argue that this happens rapidly), the market price of the affected common stock will adjust nearly instantly.

Assume for the moment that the stock market is highly efficient because it has already digested and reflected currently available public information. What implications does the efficient stock market have for an investor trying to select a winning common stock?

It suggests that we could select stocks successfully by merely putting any stock listing on a board and then throwing a dart at the list to select our common stock. With an efficient stock market, a stock selected using a dart board will do as well as a stock selected after an elaborate investigation and analysis. What are the implications for the investor who selects a stock in this way? For one thing, it means the investor must have skill and accuracy; after all, you have to hit the board with the dart! For another thing, it takes the suspense and excitement out of investing. Seriously, it raises a real question on whether the time spent searching for undervalued or undiscovered stocks is really worthwhile. Maybe an investor would do equally well, albeit with less suspense, using a random selection technique.

Certainly the often dismal performance of some investment organizations (pension funds, bank trust departments, mutual funds) that invest heavily in common stocks provides considerable support for the random walk theory. Despite their claim to professional expertise in the stock market, many of their investments have not consistently outperformed the average return for the stock market.

Information Sources

There are a number of major publications and many small newsletters that cover the stock market. Exhibit 19-4 lists some of the major sources for data on the principal groups of industries. Typically, they review recent performance, current status, and future prospects for each industry. In addition, many industries have a trade journal that discusses current developments and special topics within the industry. In Exhibit 19-5, we have summarized the major publications that provide information and data on individual corporations within the different industries. Nearly all these sources can be found in a public library of moderate size.

EXHIBIT 19-4

Information sources for data on specific industries.

TITLE	PUBLISHER	TYPE OF PUBLICATION
Industry Surveys	Standard & Poor's Corporation	Analyzes, in detail, major industries' operating statistics. Updated with quarterly supplements. Completely revised every 1 to 3 years
Value Line Investment Survey	Arnold Bernhard & Co., Inc.	Analyzes the current state and future prospects of four to six industries. Published weekly.
The Outlook	Standard & Poor's Corporation	Highlights several industries in each week's issue.
United Business & Investment Report	United Business Service	Analyzes current business trends and specific industry factors. Published every 2 weeks.
Business Week	McGraw-Hill, Inc.	Summarizes recent performance data on major industries on a recurring basis.
Forbes	Forbes, Inc.	Analyzes the past and prospective performance of major industries in one issue each year.

BUYING COMMON STOCKS

All purchases and sales of common stocks, whether in the primary market or the secondary market, require a stockbroker to execute the transactions. The broker's role is to bring together the buyer and the seller. Currently, there are two types of brokerage firms to execute your stock transactions: full-service brokers and discount brokers.

Full-Service Brokers   The **full-service broker** can be either a major national company with offices throughout the United States or a regional firm having offices throughout one region. In addition to the basic service of buying and selling common stocks, most full-service brokers also provide other customer services. Many publish a regular newsletter that discusses

EXHIBIT 19-5

Information sources for individual corporations
within the different industries.

TITLE	PUBLISHER	COMMENT
Stock Reports	Standard & Poor's Corporation	Detailed data on corporations listed on the New York and American stock exchanges, plus major issues from the over-the-counter market. Updated regularly.
Moody's Manuals	Moody's Investor Services, Inc.	In-depth historical sketch together with current data on all major corporations. Updated regularly.
Corporation Records	Standard & Poor's Corporation	In-depth historical sketch and recent operating data on major firms. Updated frequently.
Value Line Investment Survey	Arnold Bernhard & Co., Inc.	Comparative analysis of large firms within major industries. Each industry's review is updated every 13 weeks.
The Outlook	Standard & Poor's Corporation	Reviews major current events that affect an industry or specific stock. Also comparative analysis of a major industry and its firms.
United Business & Investment Record	United Business Service	Typically reviews individual companies within a selected industry or specialized area. Published every 2 weeks.
Forbes	Forbes, Inc.	The industry analysis issue, appearing early each year, covers the major firms within each industry. In addition, each issue discusses a number of companies.
Business Week	McGraw-Hill, Inc.	Summarizes the current performance and future prospects of several major firms each week.

the general state of the stock market as well as reviewing common stocks that may represent good investments. Frequently, they prepare research reports, or purchase reports, which analyze a company to help you determine whether you want to buy its stock.

Discount Brokers   **Discount brokers** have only begun to appear during the past few years. Many have only one office or, at most, a few offices. They concentrate on one single function—to execute your purchase or sale of a common stock. They do not provide investment advice on specific common stocks, nor do they recommend what stocks to purchase or sell. But as compensation for their reduced customer services, their commissions are considerably lower.

Brokerage Commissions   While brokerage firms are not required to charge the same commissions, the top half of Exhibit 19-6 (see page 626) shows that most large brokers charge nearly identical commissions. From a comparison of the two parts of this exhibit, it is clear that the discount firms provide sizable savings in commissions over the full-service firms.

One of the interesting things that can be done with the information in Exhibit 19-6 is to compute what the commission percentage is for each of the four sample transactions.

As an example, we will use the average commission for the big brokers. For the two different stock purchases we have:

NUMBER OF SHARES (1)	MARKET PRICE PER SHARE (2)	TOTAL PURCHASE PRICE: COL. (1) × COL. (2) (3)	COMMISSION CHARGED ON PURCHASE (4)	COMMISSION AS A PERCENTAGE OF THE PURCHASE PRICE COL. (4) ÷ COL (3) (5)
50	$30	$1500	$42	2.8%
50	50	2500	58	2.3
100	30	3000	67	2.2
100	50	5000	85	1.7

Since an investment in a common stock involves both the original purchase and eventually the sale of the shares, we have to pay one commission for buying and one for selling; the round-trip commission cost is double those commissions we just calculated. Thus, if you purchase a $30 stock from a full-service broker, its price will have to rise 4 to 6 percent or it will have to pay a 4 to 6 percent dividend just to cover a transaction cost. Likewise, a $50 stock will require either a dividend or a price increase of 3 to 5 percent merely to cover transaction cost. It is easy to see how commissions can devastate the return on a common stock unless it provides a large return.

Which Broker?   Since both full-service brokers and discount brokers can execute your purchase and sell transactions, the point on which you will

EXHIBIT 19-6

Brokerage commission to trade 50 or 100 shares
of common stock through a full-service broker
versus a discount broker.

BROKERAGE FIRM	50 Shares		100 Shares	
	$30 STOCK	$50 STOCK	$30 STOCK	$50 STOCK
Full-service brokers*				
Highest commission	$43	$60	$68	$90
Average commision	42	58	67	85
Lowest commission	42	56	66	81
Discount brokers[+]				
Highest commission	$32	$40	$44	$60
Average commission	27	31	34	41
Lowest commission	25	25	25	25

*Based on commission data from three large brokers.
[+]Based on commission data from five discount brokers.
Source: Unpublished study by authors.

make your decision is whether you prefer the extra service of the full-service
broker or the cost saving of the discount broker.

If you know what you want to buy or sell, a discount broker will serve
quite well. And if you trade actively (make frequent purchases and sales),
the lower commission charged by a discount firm can mean the difference
between a profit and just breaking even.

If, however, you require investment advice, or if you need and use
research reports, a full-service broker will be the choice.

But be sure that you get some benefits in return for the higher
commissions you pay the full-service broker. For example, if the firm's
research reports give you nothing but a simple data summary, rather than a
true analysis of a company's strengths and weaknesses, you're not getting
what you're paying for. You should also analyze the full-service broker's
latest recommendations to see whether they provide solid information and
justification for each selection rather than broad, sweeping generalizations
that reflect little sound research.

Timing of Stock Investments

Because common stock has no set maturity, investors face two questions:
When to buy? When to sell? The old Wall Street axiom to "buy low and sell
high" offers no guidance: Who decides what is "low," and at what point is
"high" reached?

Buy and Hold   Under the **buy-and-hold strategy**, common stock is held as
long as it continues to provide a return commensurate with its risk. Of
course, when an investor identifies a stock that appears to have more
potential, that stock should definitely replace the current stock holding. For

the great majority of small investors, the buy-and-hold strategy is probably the best.

CHAPTER 19

627

COMMON
STOCKS: A
VARIABLE INCOME
INVESTMENT

Short-Term Trading With **short-term trading**, the investor's objective is quite different. For one thing, the time horizon is days and weeks rather than years. For another, the potential profit is likely to center on a small but definite change in the stock's price. Short-term trading requires heavy investor involvement because identifying potential profit opportunities is time-consuming and the time to react is short.

Dollar-Cost Averaging **Dollar-cost averaging** avoids the question of whether the price is right. Rather than invest a single large amount, the investor invests a set amount of money to buy shares of a given stock at regular intervals. If the plan is followed consistently, the investor buys more shares when the price is down and fewer shares when the price is high.

An example is the best way to illustrate dollar-cost averaging. Assume that Wilma Swift decides to invest $600 in XQ Corporation every 3 months. Exhibit 19-7 shows the details of how that investment might proceed for 1 year. Had Wilma decided to purchase 24 shares each quarter at the price for that quarter, her average price for 96 shares purchased during the year would have been $22.50. But, by investing a set dollar amount each quarter, she purchases 114 shares at an average cost per share of $21.05. One advantage to dollar-cost averaging is that it forces the investor to buy when prices are low, even if overall market prospects may seem bleak at that point. For most people, buying stock when the total market is in a decline is far more difficult than buying when it is rising. Remember, if the stock was a good buy at $30 per share, it should be a great buy at $20, and one whale of a buy at $15. Of course, if a particular stock's future prospects have reversed, the investment should be discontinued.

EXHIBIT 19-7

An example of dollar-cost averaging, assuming that $600 is invested each quarter.

QUARTER (1)	SHARE PRICE (2)	AMOUNT INVESTED (3)	SHARES PURCHASED (4)	TOTAL SHARES (5)	CUMULATIVE INVESTMENT (6)	AVERAGE PURCHASE COST* COL. 6 ÷ COL. 5 (7)
First	$25.00	$600	24	24	$ 600	$25.00
Second	30.00	600	20	44	1200	27.27
Third	15.00	600	40	84	1800	21.43
Fourth	20.00	600	30	114	2400	21.05
Average[†]	$22.50					

*Cumulative investment divided by total shares.
[†]Simple average of the price for four quarters:

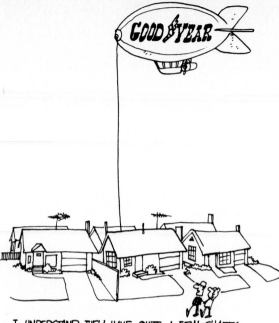

I UNDERSTAND THEY HAVE QUITE A FEW SHARES.

STRATEGY

To make dollar-cost averaging work, stick to your investment schedule during rising markets—when it's easiest—and during declining markets—when it takes courage and conviction.

Reaction to a Declining Market Certainly no one enjoys watching the price of his or her common stocks decline as the total market enters a downtrend. But it can be foolhardy and costly to panic and sell during an overall market downturn. Before you decide to sell your stock and switch to a different investment, consider the total cost of selling and possibly repurchasing a short time later. If you are merely "hoping" that a different stock will somehow not decline so much, it is likely that all the switch will do is cost you commissions.

COMMON STOCKS: ARE THEY FOR YOU?

Beause they are a specialized investment, common stocks are not for every investor. Their price volatility is just too high for some investors.

How Do You Measure Up? Some people are much better suited than others for investing in stocks. The checklist in Exhibit 19-8 should help you determine your own fitness for this type of investment. These questions place stress on the qualitative and psychological aspects of investing in stocks rather than on the financial points.

Most of your answers should be "yes" if you are thinking of investing in common stock. If your answers are mostly "no," you should seriously

EXHIBIT 19-8

CHAPTER 19

629

COMMON
STOCKS: A
VARIABLE INCOME
INVESTMENT

A questionnaire to help you judge your
common stock buying fitness score.

	YES	NO

Time commitment
Will you spend:

1   10 to 15 hours each week to review current
business developments?   ( )   ( )

2   The 10 to 40 hours needed to evaluate an
investment idea?   ( )   ( )

3   1 to 2 hours each month to reevaluate each of your
previous investments?   ( )   ( )

Investor interest
Will you:

1   Find financial reports and brokerage research
reports interesting?   ( )   ( )

2   Have sufficient confidence to raise questions if a
research report concludes with glowing, but
unsupported, conclusions?   ( )   ( )

3   Find the prospect of picking a winner exciting?   ( )   ( )

4   Have sufficient interest to analyze a stock
thoroughly?   ( )   ( )

Stock selection
Do you think:

1   That an average investor can pick successful
stocks?   ( )   ( )

2   That good investment opportunities exist in
industries that may not have a lot of glamour?   ( )   ( )

3   You could purchase a stock which appears to have
good potential even though it is not a current
market favorite?   ( )   ( )

4   That a thorough analysis is a better way to pick
investment candidates than someone's hot tip?   ( )   ( )

Anticipated rate of return
Can you:

1   Be satisfied with an average annual return of 10 to
14 percent?   ( )   ( )

2   Accept that a 20 to 30 percent annual return is
unrealistic?   ( )   ( )

3   Accept a price decline of 20 to 50 percent?   ( )   ( )

4   Sleep nights knowing that this year's return may
be a 20 percent increase or a 20 percent loss?   ( )   ( )

consider alternatives. If the prospect of sharp variations in your rate of return will cause you sleepless nights and possibly ulcers, you should restrict yourself to fixed-income investments. If you want to invest in common stocks, yet do not want to be involved in managing them, you should consider a mutual fund (discussed in Chapter 20).

Risk The risk on a common stock can range from moderate to very high, depending on the company whose shares you buy. Among all the types of investments we have discussed thus far, the risk on common stock will generally rank near the top. The rate of return on a common stock is subject to some wide swings—considerably greater than for other investments.

The variability in a common stock's return is caused by many factors. Since this return depends heavily on the operations of the company that issued it, anything that affects the company's fortunes will likely be reflected in the return on its common stock. One general factor would be declines and expansions in the overall economy; the price of most common stocks is affected by these changes. Other factors would include anything affecting the industry where the particular company operates, as well as anything that might affect that particular company itself.

Diversifying Your Stock Holdings Diversification means splitting your investments among several stocks; by diversifying, you can reduce your risk. In particular, we are trying to reduce the high variability in investor returns that characterizes common stocks. By doing that, we hope to avoid a situation in which the return is sharply positive one period and then is decidedly negative in the next period.

Selecting stocks for satisfactory diversification is a complicated process which involves considerable work. While the actual process is beyond this book's scope, we can give a highly simplified description to help you understand the central goal of diversification.

First, by spreading your investment among several companies, you reduce the possibility of losing your entire investment should a major financial crisis occur; it is unlikely that all the companies would simultaneously encounter financial difficulty.

Second, by selecting companies from different industries, the success of your total investment is not solely dependent upon the fortunes of a single industry. Even more important, by selecting companies from industries that have different expansion and contraction cycles, the return on your total investment will be more stable. When the sales in one industry are contracting, which is likely to sharply reduce the company's earnings, another industry may be expanding and its sales should provide much higher earnings.

Diversifying among a number of stocks has several implications for investors. In order to benefit from diversification, an investor would have to buy at least 5 to 10 different stocks. An investor who lacks a sizable amount to invest will not be able to purchase the required number of different stocks. Another consideration investors must understand is that spreading the investment among many issues may provide stable returns, but they will probably not exceed the average return for the total market. For some investors, this possibility may offset the benefits of diversification.

Tax Features   If a stock is held for more than 12 months and eventually sold at a profit, the difference in price (sale price minus purchase price) is taxable at the long-term capital gains tax rate; that rate is only 40 percent of what the tax is on short-term gains. This can be an attractive tax benefit on stocks that pay low dividends but have a good potential to increase in price.

The cash dividends on common stocks are taxed at the regular rate except that an investor can exclude the first $100 of dividends as tax-free ($200 on a joint return).

CHAPTER 19

631

COMMON
STOCKS: A
VARIABLE INCOME
INVESTMENT

SUMMARY

1   Common stock represents ownership in a corporation. As owners, the common stock shareholders are entitled to the corporation's earnings.

2   A stock's cash dividend and any change in the stock's market price provide the returns to the shareholder. Both should be included when determining the shareholder's total return.

3   The real return—current return less rate of inflation—on common stock has been highest during periods of moderate inflation and lowest during periods of high inflation.

4   During the last 10 years, common stocks have not provided an effective hedge against inflation.

5   Earnings per share and the price-earnings ratio are frequently used to describe the valuation of a stock.

6   Most common stock purchases and sales involve previously issued shares that are currently traded in the secondary market.

7   The widely publicized market indexes—the Dow Jones Industrial Average, Standard & Poor's 500, New York Stock Exchange Index—show the current state and the recent performance of a large sample of common stocks which should be representative of the overall stock market.

8   Techniques for analyzing and selecting common stocks can be grouped into two categories: those that rely on technical analysis and those that rely on fundamental analysis.

9   There is considerable evidence that stock prices move in a random fashion. Thus, even a professional investor cannot predict future changes in price with sufficient accuracy to earn a better-than-average return.

10   Because discount brokerage firms limit their services to executing a customer's purchase and sell transactions, their commissions are lower than the commissions charged by full-service brokerage firms.

11   Under dollar-cost averaging, a specific amount of money is invested at regular intervals in a particular common stock.

12   By diversifying among different common stocks, investors can reduce their total risk.

REVIEW YOUR UNDERSTANDING OF

Common stock shareholders' rights
  Corporate earnings
    Liquidating the corporation
Cash dividend
Dividend yield
Market price change
Stock dividend
Stock split
Earnings per share (EPS)
Price-earnings ratio (P/E)
Blue chip stock
Growth stock
Speculative stock
Markets for common stock
  Primary market

Secondary market
Stock market indexes
"Bulls" and "bears"
Technical analysis
Fundamental analysis
Efficient market theory or
  random walk theory
Full-service broker
Discount broker
Buy-and-hold strategy
Short-term trading
Dollar-cost averaging
Diversification

DISCUSSION QUESTIONS

1   If the general public were asked what annual rate of return a common stock investment should yield, do you think the most frequent answer would be (a) less than 10 percent, (b) between 10 and 20 percent, or (c) more than 20 percent? Do you think those expectations are realistic? Why?

2   Are there advantages to the corporate form of business organization? Does the corporate form offer any specific advantages for the common stock shareholders?

3   How does a shareholder benefit when the company retains part of its earnings? In future periods, how will the shareholder actually benefit? What form will those benefits take?

4   Who is entitled to a corporation's earnings? Who decides what part of the earnings is paid as dividends? What factors affect the decision to pay out dividends?

5   During the past 5 years, XQ Plastics has grown rapidly and has paid no cash dividends. But it has paid a 10 percent stock dividend each year. In addition, there was a 2-for-1 stock split 3 years ago. How do these actions affect the shareholder? Has the shareholder's dividend return been 10 percent? Why or

why not? Why would a company declare a stock dividend or split?

6   Why should a common stock be a better hedge during an inflationary period than a fixed-income investment? Has recent experience supported this contention? Why or why not?

7   What is the difference between a blue chip stock and a growth stock? Which kind of investors would probably be most satisfied with a blue chip stock? With a growth stock?

8   Assume that the evening newscast reported that the Dow Jones Industrial Average has risen 5 points that day. What does that information mean? How could you use it? What is the reason for having a Dow Jones Industrial Average?

9   The market price of a common stock already reflects the currently available information. What is meant by the statement? What should happen to the market price of a certain common stock if a piece of highly favorable information about that company appears in today's newspaper? Will an investor likely be able to earn above-average returns by reviewing and analyzing existing, widely distributed data about a particular common stock? What implications does this statement have for stock selection techniques?

10   What are the principal differences between full-service brokerage firms and discount brokers? What type of investor would probably be best served by the discount firm?

11   What are the advantages of dollar-cost averaging? Are there disadvantages? What investors should use dollar-cost averaging?

12   What are the advantages in diversifying your stock investments? Are there disadvantages and constraints?

PROBLEMS

19-1   Sandra Carmine purchased 50 shares of Glug Petroleum Products 2 years ago at $30 per share. Since then, Glug has been highly profitable, and its shares currently sell for $36. It also paid a quarterly dividend of 15 cents per share during those 2 years. Because of several recent developments, however, Sandra has decided that she should sell her shares.

    a What annual dividend yield did Sandra receive during her holding period?

    b What was her approximate annual return (in percent) from the increase in the market price of Glug's common stock? (Ignore any compounding.)

    c What was Sandra's combined overall rate of return for each of those years? (Ignore selling commissions and compounding.)

    d What would be the difference in the income tax treatment of the dividend return and the return from the market price increase if Sandra should sell her shares?

19-2   Arvin Absent temporarily mislaid his shares in Speciality Plastics Corporation when he moved to a new apartment. Arvin knows he purchased 100 shares 3 years ago. Furthermore, he remembers that Specialty declared the following stock dividends and splits:

PERIOD	DIVIDEND OR SPLIT
End of 1st year	20 percent stock dividend
End of 2d year	10 percent stock dividend
End of 3d year	2 for 1 split

When Arvin originally purchased his shares, Speciality Plastics Corporation had a total of 10,000 shares of its common stock outstanding.

    a How many shares should Arvin currently own?

    b What fraction of the company does he now own?

    c Is the fraction of ownership now greater than the fraction he owned 3 years ago? Why or why not?

    d How many shares of stock does Speciality Plastic currently have outstanding after all the splits and dividends?

19-3   Leonard Longshot has recently received a hot tip that the common stock of Big Roller, Inc., is where the action is. The company hopes to franchise a series of gambling casinos (in much the same fashion as the fast food restaurants) that would be located throughout the United States. The financial section of his newspaper had the following stock market listing on Big Roller:

Price Range During the Year

HIGH	LOW	COMPANY	DIV	SALES 100'S	DIV YIELD	P/E RATIO	HIGH	LOW	CLOSE	CHANGE
85½	1¼	Big Roller, Inc.	$0.01	400	.02%	106	55¼	50⅛	53	−5

Since Leonard is a newcomer to the stock market, he is unsure what all those numbers mean.

a On the basis of the above prices for the year, what appears to have happened to the market price of the firm's stock?

b Does this stock provide a good dividend? If an investor is going to receive a reasonable overall return on this stock, where will it have to come from? Why?

19-4 Chantile De Brode currently holds 50 shares of Zug Corporation with a current price of $60 per share. She plans to sell her shares in the near future. She has narrowed her choice of brokers down to the following two firms:

FIRM	COMMISSION	CUSTOMER SERVICES
Fast Phil's Full-Line Brokerage House	2.3 percent of the sales proceeds	Gives investment advice, buy and sell recommendations Executes customers' buy and sell orders
Boris's Bargain Brokerage House	$15 flat fee and 18 cents per share	Just executes customers' buy or sell orders

a What will be the commission for each firm?

b Which one would you recommend? Why?

c Assume Chantile's combined rate of return on the stock is 10 percent before any commissions. What will her net return be after deducting the transaction cost if she uses Fast Phil? If she sells through Boris? (*Hint* You will need to compute what Boris's commission is on a percentage basis.)

CASE PROBLEM

Bill and Jan Stien are considering investing their $2000 savings account in common stocks. Although they earn $30,000 annually, their savings have averaged only $750 each year because they have needed much of their income to pay the high rent on their luxury apartment, to pay for their extensive travel, and to trade for a new car each year. (They currently own two cars.) Bill and Jan have heard that common stocks are where the action is. And they feel that the breathtaking rates of return on common stocks will encourage them to save more. They have identified three investment goals, and plan to use their expected earnings on common stocks to provide for:

CHAPTER 19

635

COMMON
STOCKS: A
VARIABLE INCOME
INVESTMENT

1 A short-term emergency cash fund of $500

2 A $2000 fund for Jan to complete a graduate degree beginning 2 years from now

3 A down payment of $6000 to purchase a house in 4 years

Given their limited savings, they feel that they need to earn 25 to 30 percent a year on their stock investments. On the basis of that return, they have estimated the following 4-year savings plan:

	1ST YEAR	2D YEAR	3D YEAR	4TH YEAR
Beginning investment balance	$2000	$3250	$2813	$4266
Earnings on balance (25%)	500	813	703	1067
Total	$2500	$4063	$3516	$5333
Add: New savings for year	750	750	750	750
Less: Withdrawals	0	2000	0	6000
Ending investment balance	$3250	$2813	$4266	$ 83

The Stiens are undecided about which stocks they should select. Bill favors conservative blue chip stocks, but Jan believes they should aim for the highest return by concentrating on speculative stocks, which might have a higher return. Their current list of stocks to evaluate includes the following (all hot tips):

STOCK	PRICE RANGE OVER PAST 3 YEARS	Current Information per Share			BUSINESS ACTIVITY
		PRICE	EARNINGS	DIVIDEND	
A	$15–$25	$20	$3.33	$2.00	Gas and electric utility
B	5–42	40	1.00	0	Manufactures slot machines for gambling casinos; has been in business 2 years
C	50–85	75	3.75	2.25	Soft-drink manufacturer
D	30–90	50	3.33	2.50	Auto manufacturer
E	0.25–1.35	1	None	0	Gold mining

The Stiens have seen a number of advertisements concerning the brilliant advice they can get from some of the large brokers. On the basis of advertisements, they expect to rely heavily on the broker for recommendations on which stocks they should buy. They are greatly interested in those undiscovered, undervalued growth stocks that double in a few months. They have not, as of yet, selected a brokerage firm.

1   What are the strengths and weaknesses of the Stiens's initial foray into the stock market?

2   Is their projected savings plan a good one? Would you recommend any changes? If so, how would your recommendations affect the Stiens's present goals?

3   Would you have any general comments about the list of stocks they are evaluating? Where could they find information about the five companies in their list?

4   Do you think that what the Stiens expect from the brokerage firm can be realized? What type of firm do the Stiens appear to need?

5   Overall, do you feel that the Stiens are ready for the stock market? Would you have any suggestions or recommendations for additional preparation?

CHAPTER
20
MUTUAL
FUNDS

**AFTER COMPLETING THIS CHAPTER
YOU WILL HAVE LEARNED**

What a *mutual fund* is and how it operates

How a *load fund* differs from a *no-load fund*

The *three potential returns* an investor can receive
from a *mutual fund*

What the *major types of mutual funds* are

How a small investor can benefit from the *advantages* provided by a *mutual fund*

The major *sources of information on mutual funds*
and what each provides

How you would select a *money market mutual fund*

How you would pick a *bond mutual fund*

How you would select a *common stock mutual
fund*

During a subcommittee investigation

of the mutual fund industry, a United States senator introduced a "portfolio" he had selected by throwing darts at a page of stock listings from the *Wall Street Journal.* The portfolio selected by the darts outperformed nearly all the funds being investigated by the subcommittee. This example of random stock selection was a dramatic and humorous way of saying something about the investment performance of institutional investors such as mutual funds and banks. The evidence shows conclusively that randomly selected portfolios will often do as well as carefully selected ones.

Investors in some mutual funds pay a management fee for the privilege of having their money invested by professionals who sometimes cannot seem to do as well as somebody throwing darts at a page from the *Wall Street Journal.* The fee ranges from 1/2 of 1 percent to 2 percent of the value of the fund. Regardless of whether or not the fund performs well, the manager still collects. Despite these negative aspects, total assets of the mutual fund industry now exceed $284 billion, with over 21.4 million accounts owning shares in mutual funds.

In precise terms, a mutual fund is an investment company, and the terms "mutual fund" and "investment company" are sometimes used interchangeably. In this chapter, we will use the more commonly accepted term *mutual fund.*

WHAT ARE MUTUAL FUNDS?

All the investments we have discussed up to this point require that you buy them directly. Thus, lending investments, such as money market accounts, CDs, Treasury securities, corporate bonds, and municipal bonds, are bought directly from the borrower. **Mutual funds** provide a means through which you can invest in many of these same instruments, but you do so indirectly —through the mutual fund.

Let us illustrate this investment process using Exhibit 20-1. Alice Average decides to invest $500 in the XQ Mutual Fund. The $500 that Alice sends to XQ buys shares in this fund. The price she pays for those shares is based on the current value of XQ's investment holdings. (We will discuss this concept later in the section.) For its part, the XQ Mutual Fund puts together the small investments of a large number of individuals like Alice, and invests that money in such things as common stocks, corporate bonds, large CDs, and Treasury securities. The managers of XQ decide what investments to make and when to make them. Any interest and dividends earned on the investments are paid to XQ. At some point in the future, XQ may decide to sell one or more of the investments it holds; again, the managers of XQ make that decision. In addition to the money raised from this sale, there will also be money from investments that mature. All this money will be reinvested as the managers of XQ see fit. For managing and operating the mutual fund, the managers receive a fee (more on this later).

While Exhibit 20-1 illustrates an investor sending money to the XQ Mutual Fund, it could just as well be the reverse: Money could be withdrawn from the fund. Suppose that, at a later date, Alice Average decides, for whatever reason, to withdraw $500 from the XQ Mutual Fund. To do that, she will sell (redeem) some of her XQ Mutual Fund shares. The price she receives from those shares depends on what XQ's total investment holdings are worth the day she redeems her shares. (We will discuss this further in the next section.) Now the flows shown in Exhibit 20-1 will be exactly reversed. Where does XQ obtain the money to send to Alice? Most mutual funds retain a certain balance of cash to cover just such redemptions. But should that amount be insufficient, the fund sells enough investments to raise the cash it needs for redemptions.

Net Asset Value per Share

A mutual fund computes the **net asset value** (NAV) of its shares using the following steps:

It **computes** the total current market value of all the fund's present investments.

It **deducts** the total of the fund's liabilities (the amounts it owes to someone else).

It **divides** the net value of the mutual fund's holdings from steps 1 and 2 (total investment holdings minus total liabilities) by the total number of shares the mutual fund has sold.

The XQ Mutual Fund will be used to illustrate these steps. Assume that on Friday, the 13th, XQ has a total of 100,000 shares that are held by various investors. As of the close of business on the 13th, XQ values all its investments at their current price and finds they are worth $1,020,000. On the same day, XQ's liabilities total $20,000. The NAV of an XQ share is:

EXHIBIT 20-1

Investing indirectly through a mutual fund.

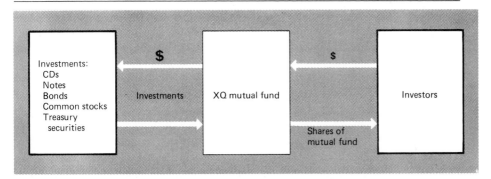

$$\$10 = (\$1,020,000 - \$20,000) \div 100,000 \text{ shares}$$

$$\text{NAV of} = \text{Current market} - \text{Total} \div \text{Total shares}$$
$$\text{XQ share} \quad \text{value of} \quad \text{liabilities} \quad \text{outstanding}$$
$$\text{investment}$$

Typically, mutual funds revalue their investment holdings at the close of every business day. That total is then used to compute the NAV of its shares for that day.

How do mutual funds use that NAV per share? First, whenever investors want to redeem their shares, the amount paid per share is the NAV. So, if Alice Average decided to sell 30 of her XQ Mutual Fund shares on Friday the 13th (the date of our NAV computation), she would receive $10 per share, or $300. After Alice's shares are redeemed, the NAV of XQ's remaining shares will be:

$$\$10 = (\$1,020,000 - \$300 - \$20,000) \div (100,000 - 30)$$

$$\text{NAV} = \text{Total} - \text{Redemption} - \text{Total} \div \text{Total} - \text{Redeemed}$$
$$\text{per share} \quad \text{investments} \quad \text{of shares} \quad \text{liabilities} \quad \text{shares} \quad \text{shares}$$

An immediate question is: Were those investors who did not redeem their shares treated fairly? Yes. Each of their shares is still worth $10; that is precisely what it was worth before Alice's redemption. Was Alice treated fairly? Yes. She received exactly what those shares were worth on Friday the 13th.

A second use of NAV is to set the price at which the fund will sell additional shares. Let us assume that, instead of selling her shares, Alice decides to invest an additional $1000 in the XQ Mutual Fund on the 13th. For her $1000, she receives 100 shares because the NAV is $10 per share. After her purchase, the NAV of XQ total shares will be:

$$\$10 = (\$1,020,000 + \$1000 - \$20,000) \div (100,000 + 100)$$

$$\text{NAV} = \text{Total} + \text{Added} - \text{Total} \div \text{Original} + \text{New}$$
$$\text{per share} \quad \text{investments} \quad \text{purchase} \quad \text{liabilities} \quad \text{shares} \quad \text{shares}$$

Have the original shareholders been treated fairly? Yes. Each of their shares is still worth the same $10 it was before Alice's purchase. And how about Alice? She now owns 100 shares that are worth $10 each, so she has received fair value.

As these two examples demonstrate, NAV per share is an integral part of operating a mutual fund. It determines what you receive when you redeem your shares. At the same time, it is the price that determines how many shares you receive when you invest in a mutual fund.

Management Fee and Operating Expenses As you might expect, managing and operating a mutual fund costs money. Part of the cost stems from the **management fee** that is paid to the service organization that manages the fund's investments. That firm decides what investments the fund should purchase, when to purchase them, and when to sell them. There are also the **operating expenses** of administering the fund on a day-to-day basis: keeping records on investors' accounts, advertising, preparing financial reports, mailing, and other administrative expenses.

All these management and operating expenses are passed on to the individuals who invest in the mutual fund. The net effect is to lower your return on your mutual fund investment. Thus, even if a mutual fund earns a 12 percent return on the investments it has made, investors in that mutual fund will receive less than 12 percent. Part of those returns will be used to pay the fund's management and operating costs. How much less? You can typically expect that between 1/2 percent and 2 percent of the fund's return will go for expenses. Why the sizable spread in costs of the different funds? In part, it can be due to the size of fund. Some small funds have higher fees. Also, the nature of the fund and its underlying investments can impact on the total cost: An aggressive mutual fund that actively turns over its holdings through frequent investment sales and purchases other investments may well have higher operating costs. Frequently, the organizations that manage mutual funds also charge different fees. Combine these and other factors and we have large variations in total costs.

While we think total costs are important, you should not be unduly concerned with them. We believe the essential thing is what remains after paying the fee. Thus, if High Dollar Mutual Fund earned an overall return of 17 percent before deducting its expenses of 2 percent, it will still have 15 percent for its investors. Old Mediocre Mutual Fund may well hold its expenses to 1 percent, but if it earns only a 13 percent return, its investors will receive only 12 percent. Assuming the two funds are comparable in other respects, we clearly favor High Dollar even with its higher expenses.

No-Load versus Load Mutual Funds

One major distinction among open-end mutual funds is how they are sold to investors. Funds that sell shares directly to the public are called **no-load mutual funds.** Those that sell their shares through a broker or salesperson are called **load mutual funds.** Exhibit 20-2 demonstrates how the two types of funds differ. Let's say Earl Swift plans to invest $1000 in a mutual fund. His two choices include Best Bet, a no-load fund (left side of Exhibit 20-2), and Sure Thing, a load fund (right side of Exhibit 20-2). We assume that the NAV per share for each fund is $10.

If Earl invests in Best Bet, he will purchase his shares directly from the fund. Because there is no commission on his purchase, he will receive 100 shares of Best Bet for his $1000. Of course, since no salesperson is involved, Earl must locate the fund and then decide whether it is appropriate for him. Since many no-load funds have toll-free telephone numbers, it may be easy for Earl to obtain information on them. Funds without the toll-free number may be reached either by mail or by a long-distance call to the fund's office.

If Earl decides to invest in the load mutual fund instead (Sure Thing), a salesperson will be involved. That salesperson may be working in a stock brokerage firm, as an insurance agent, as an independent sales representative, or possibly as a financial planner. Because that salesperson will have singled out Sure Thing, Earl avoids having to search out the fund. And if he is willing to rely on the salesperson's advice, he can even skip the analysis of whether the fund is appropriate for him. But that convenience comes at a price. The salesperson will charge a commission that ranges from 3 percent to 8.5 percent of each dollar invested. We will assume that Sure Thing's commission is 8.5 percent. (That is typical for mutual funds that concentrate on common stocks.) The commission on the purchase will be:

$$\$85 = \$1000 \times 8.5\%$$

$$\begin{array}{ccc}\Updownarrow & \Updownarrow & \Updownarrow\end{array}$$

$$\begin{array}{ll}\text{Commission} = & \text{Amount} \times \text{Commission}\\\text{on purchase} & \text{invested} \quad \text{rate}\end{array}$$

After the salesperson deducts the $85 commission, only $915 of Earl's $1000 remain to purchase shares in Sure Thing. At a NAV of $10 per share, Earl will buy 91.5 shares. When he decides to sell those shares, he will receive the NAV on the day of the sale. No commissions are charged on the sale. But every time Earl decides to invest additional money in Sure Thing, he will pay an 8.5 percent commission on his investment.

Price Quotes on Mutual Funds Most major newspapers, as well as business papers such as the *Wall Street Journal* and *Barron's*, report the prices of most mutual funds daily. Exhibit 20-3 shows how one of those price listings might look. Many listings parallel Exhibit 20-3, presenting three prices:

NAV per share: The price at which shares of a no-load fund are bought and redeemed. It is also the price at which load fund shares are redeemed.

EXHIBIT 20-2

Comparison of no-load and load mutual funds.

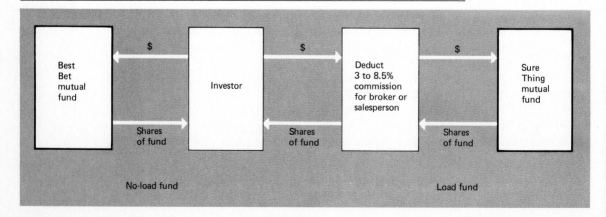

EXCUSE ME, MR. HARRIS...
COULD I ASK YOU A QUESTION
ABOUT THE AMOUNT OF COMMISSION
YOU GET FROM MY MUTUAL FUND?

Offering price per share: The price at which shares of a load fund can be purchased. It exceeds the fund's NAV because the salesperson's commission, or load, has been added to the NAV.

Change in NAV: The change in the fund's NAV from the previous day's, or prior week's, NAV.

A quick review of Exhibit 20-3 shows that Allied Growth, Bet-a-Buck, and Shoo-In must be no-load funds; both American Income and Go for Broke are load funds. The change in NAV, shown in Exhibit 20-3, says that Allied Growth's NAV rose $0.08 from the previous day. Yesterday's price listing must have shown a NAV of $10.12 for Allied Growth.

Open-End Funds   All the mutual funds we have discussed up to this point have been **open-end mutual funds.** "Open-end" means the mutual fund stands ready to sell additional shares to new or existing shareholders. At the same time, the fund is ready to redeem, or repurchase, any of its shares from

EXHIBIT 20-3

Typical newspaper price quotations on mutual funds.

	NAV	OFFER PRICE	NAV CHANGE
Allied Growth	10.20	NL*	+ .08
American Income	30.00	31.25	− .02
Bet-a-Buck	5.20	NL*	+ .09
Go for Broke	18.30	20.00	+ .11
Shoo-In	6.35	NL*	− .01

*NL = no-load fund.

current investors who want to sell. If the number of people who want to buy shares in a particular fund is high, that fund will grow quite large. At the opposite extreme, if many investors want to redeem their shares, the fund may shrink to a small size.

Returns to a Mutual Fund Investor

The return on your investment in a mutual fund can come from three possible sources. First, part of the return may consist of the dividend the mutual fund pays. Second, part of the return may come from a capital gain that the mutual fund distributes. Last, part of the return may be from a change in market price of the mutual fund's shares. To illustrate the first two kinds of return, we will use the diagram in Exhibit 20-4.

Dividend Distributions A mutual fund distributes the interest and dividends it receives on its investment to individuals who have invested in the fund. Flow (1) on the right side of Exhibit 20-4 illustrates the fund's **dividend distributions** to the fund's investors. By complying with the requirements that are stated in the tax regulations, the mutual fund is considered an intermediary. It pays no income taxes on the interest and dividends it receives. Instead, that income is passed to the investors, where it must be included on their respective tax returns. Any part of the mutual fund's dividend that is from dividends on common stocks qualifies for the dividend exclusion that we noted back in Exhibit 6-2 in Chapter 6.

Some mutual funds elect to distribute their dividends monthly; others choose to make quarterly distributions, while the balance distribute only once each year. Regardless of the frequency, all dividend payments are based on a set dollar amount per share. The more mutual fund shares you have, the larger your dividend payment.

Distribution of Capital Gains Whenever a mutual fund sells an investment for more than it paid for it, it generates a capital gain. If the fund has owned that investment for 1 year or less, it is a short-term gain; when it has held the investment more than 1 year, it is long-term. Of course, had the sale price been less than the fund's purchase price, it would generate a loss. Depending on the period the investment was owned, that loss may be either short- or long-term. By distributing most of its gains and losses to its investors, the fund avoids having to pay any income taxes.

Flow (2) on the right side of Exhibit 20-4 illustrates such a **capital gain distribution.** Each investor includes the gains and losses distributed by the mutual fund on his or her tax return. A long-term gain or loss from a mutual fund is treated the same as though the gain or loss were from a direct investment: only 40 percent of the gain is included in income, and only 50 percent of the loss can be deducted from income. Clearly, a long-term capital gain from a mutual fund receives the same favorable tax treatment as that of the individual who has held the investment directly. Likewise, any short-term gains and losses distributed by a mutual fund must be included in their entirety on the investor's tax return.

Most mutual funds distribute their capital gains and losses once each

EXHIBIT 20-4

CHAPTER 20

645

MUTUAL FUNDS

Dividends and capital gains distributed by a
mutual fund.

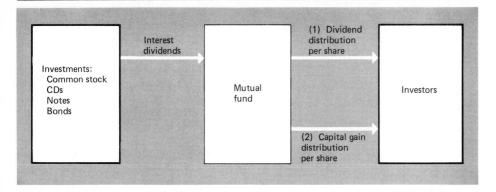

year. Again, the distribution is based on a set amount per share; consequently, the more shares an investor owns, the larger the payment.

Change in Market Price   You will recall from our earlier discussion that a mutual fund's NAV per share will vary as the market value of the fund's investment changes. Those funds which concentrate on investments showing wide swings in price will have a volatile NAV per share. At the opposite extreme, funds that hold investments with highly stable market prices will have only limited changes in their NAV per share. Changes in a mutual fund's NAV per share directly affect your return from an investment in that mutual fund. Your return improves if the fund's NAV rises above the amount you paid for your shares. Of course, there is no reason why the fund's NAV must necessarily rise. It can drop below your purchase price, thereby reducing your return.

Until you decide to sell your mutual fund shares, all the gains and losses from changes in the fund's NAV are unrealized. It is only when you redeem those shares that you actually have a gain (when redemption price exceeds purchase price) or loss (when redemption price is less than purchase price). If you have owned those shares more than 1 year, the gain or loss is long-term. Because it is long-term, only 40 percent of the gain is taxed in your reported income and only 50 percent of a loss can be deducted from your income. Shares owned a year or less are considered short-term holdings. The entire gain must be included and all the loss can, typically, be deducted.

Investor Returns on a Mutual Fund   To illustrate how all three returns can impact on the investor's rate of return, let's use an example. Assume that Ralph Risktaker invests $1000 on January 2 in Best Bet, a no-load mutual fund. On that day, the NAV of Best Bet's shares is $10. Because it is a no-load fund, Ralph's money purchases 100 shares. During the next year, Best Bet distributes $0.50 cents per share in dividends. The fund also distributes $0.40 cents per share as a long-term capital gain. On this year's tax return, Ralph includes $50 of dividends (100 shares at 50 cents) and $40 of long-term capital gains (100 shares at 40 cents). Assume that he has now owned the shares 1 year and wants to know how well the investment has done. From a newspaper quote, he finds that Best Bet's NAV per share is $10.20. For the entire year, Ralph's rate of return is:

$$11\% = \{\$50 + \$40 + (\$1020 - \$1000)\} \div \$1000$$

$$\begin{array}{l}\text{Rate of} \\ \text{return}\end{array} = \left[\begin{array}{l}\text{Dividend} \\ \text{return}\end{array} + \begin{array}{l}\text{Capital} \\ \text{gains}\end{array} + \begin{array}{l}\text{Price appreciation:} \\ \text{Current} - \text{Original} \\ \text{value} \quad \text{investment}\end{array}\right] \div \begin{array}{l}\text{Original} \\ \text{investment}\end{array}$$

Ralph's total return for the year is a very respectable 11 percent. Unless he decides to redeem the shares at this point, he does not include the $20 of price appreciation (the rise in the NAV from $10.00 to $10.20 on 100 shares) on his tax return, since it is an unrecognized gain.

TYPES OF MUTUAL FUNDS: INVESTMENT OBJECTIVE

All mutual funds must provide every prospective investor with a detailed statement, called a **prospectus,** that outlines the fund's **investment objective.** The variations in these objectives differentiate among the large number of mutual funds. The principal investment objective of some funds is current income. Another fund's investment objective may be long-term growth of capital. Still other funds will combine these two objectives in some way as their investment objective. A fund's prospectus must also disclose what investments it expects to purchase to achieve its investment objective. These investments can cover the entire spectrum from low-risk lending through high-risk ownership. We will group mutual funds here into three broad categories, based on their major investments:

Money market funds

Bond funds

Common stock funds

Exhibit 20-5 summarizes the major types of mutual funds that will be discussed in the next sections.

Money Market Funds

Money market funds concentrate on low-risk investments that have a very short maturity. With this focus, the risk is very low: Owing to the short maturity, fluctuations in the market value of the fund's investments are very limited. Interest earned on these investments is the sole source of your return on this type of mutual fund. Furthermore, the short maturity of the investments means that the fund will be continually reinvesting its funds. The rate of return can change quite dramatically if those new investments provide a significantly higher or lower return than did the fund's previous investments.

EXHIBIT 20-5

Chief types of mutual funds, with their investment objectives and their major investments.

MUTUAL FUND	INVESTMENT OBJECTIVE	MAJOR INVESTMENTS
Money market fund:		
General money market	Income, low risk	Commercial paper, large CDs, bankers' acceptances
Government	Income, very low risk	Treasury and federal agency securities
Tax-exempt	Tax-free income, low risk	Short-term municipal securities
Bond funds:		
Investment-grade	Income, low risk	Corporate notes and bonds
Aggressive bond	Income, moderate risk	Lower-quality corporate notes and bonds
Government	Income, very low risk	Treasury and federal agency securities
Municipal	Tax-free income, low risk	Municipal notes and bonds
Common stock funds:		
Aggressive growth	Maximum capital growth	Common stocks with above-average potential for growth
Growth	Long-term growth; income is secondary	Common stocks with good potential for growth
Growth and income	Long-term growth and income	Common stocks that pay dividends and have some growth potential
Income	Income with some potential for growth	Common stock and fixed-return investments that provide high current income
Specialized	Growth, income, or some combination	Common stocks that are heavily concentrated in one or two industries

General-Purpose Money Market Funds General-purpose money market funds pioneered the money market mutual fund concept during the mid-1970s. They continue to be the largest group within the money market category. These funds invest in money market investments such as commercial paper, large CDs, and bankers' acceptances. We will not explain in detail these investments except to note that they are considered low risk, have very short maturities, and typically require such large dollar investments that most individuals cannot purchase them directly. But, by consolidating money from a large number of small investors, a mutual fund can readily purchase those investments.

Government Money Market Funds Government money market funds are not associated with the government in any way, nor are the deposits in these funds insured. But they offer less risk than do general-purpose funds, since they invest in very short-term Treasury securities, and some funds choose securities issued by agencies of the federal government. While such purchases lower the fund's risk, they also lower its return. In general, the return is 1/2 to 1 1/4 percent less than what the general-purpose funds provide.

Tax-Exempt Money Market Funds Tax-exempt money market funds are the most specialized of the three in this group. They concentrate on municipal securities whose return is exempt from federal income taxes. Yet, by keeping the time to maturity on those investments very short, fluctuations in the fund's NAV per share are minimized. While the return on these funds is tax-exempt, it is also substantially lower than either general-purpose or government money market funds. For that reason, they are suitable only for investors who have a high maginal tax rate; typically, that marginal tax rate should be 40 percent or more for a tax-exempt fund to be the best choice. Investors with a lower tax rate would do better to invest in either a general-purpose or a government fund where, even after paying taxes, their return will remain higher.

Bond Funds

Bond funds concentrate on fixed-income lending investments such as corporate notes and bonds. Their investment objective is to provide a high, reasonably steady income over an extended period. Most of the return on a bond fund is from the dividends it distributes. Capital gains distributions on the shares of a bond fund will be limited because the fund's investments are made primarily for their interest-paying ability, not their future price appreciation. As long as interest rates remained reasonably stable, there was little need to consider the potential return from changes in the fund's NAV per share. But the highly volatile interest rates of the past several years have shown the necessity of considering changes in the fund's NAV.

In Chapter 17 we demonstrated that the market price of fixed-income investments moves inversely with market interest rates. The price rises as market rates decline and it declines when market rates rise. Furthermore, the longer the maturity of the fixed-income investment, the larger its change in market price. An example will illustrate how those price movements affect bond mutual funds. Assume that Tricia Timid invested in Steady Rock, a no-load bond mutual fund. When she made the investment, Steady Rock's NAV per share was $10. Shortly after she invested her money, market interest rates rose sharply. Now, as those rates rise, the market price of Steady Rock's fixed-income investments will do the exact opposite: they will plunge. Steady Rock's new NAV will drop below $10. If Tricia decides to redeem, or must redeem, her shares, she will have a capital loss. Of course, had interest rates declined, then Steady Rock's NAV would have risen. In this situation, Tricia would have generated a capital gain when redeeming her shares.

STRATEGY

When investing in a bond mutual fund, it is essential that you consider the potential gain or loss from a change in the fund's NAV caused by a decline or rise in interest rates, respectively.

Investment-Grade Bond Funds Investment-grade bond funds invest exclusively in corporate notes and bonds. Typically, they only purchase notes and bonds that are rated at least BBB or better by Standard & Poor's or Baa or higher by Moody's. By concentrating on high-rated notes and bonds, these funds keep the risk reasonably low. High current income is the typical investment objective for investment-grade bond funds.

Aggressive Bond Funds Aggressive bond funds concentrate on lower-rated corporate notes and bonds. Many of the fund's investments will be rated BB and lower by Standard & Poor's, or Ba and lower if rated by Moody's. By accepting the higher risk of these lower-rated investments, the fund obtains a higher return than it would from investment-grade notes and bonds. These funds usually provide an additional 1 or 2 percent return over those for investment-grade bond funds. The investment objective of these funds is to generate very high income, which is achieved by accepting moderate risk.

Government Bond Funds Government bond funds invest primarily in long-term U.S. Treasury securities and sometimes in securities issued by federal agencies. Those investments should hold the fund's risk to a low level. It is highly unlikely that the fund would have difficulty collecting the interest or face value on these investments. The investment objective of these funds is current income with very low risk. Some funds are organized in such a way that the interest from their Treasury and federal agency securities can be passed through to their investors free from state income taxes. But, before investing, review the fund's prospectus to see whether it provides this added benefit.

Municipal Bond Funds Municipal bond funds invest in municipal securities whose interest is exempt from federal income taxes. The fund, in turn, is able to pass this tax-exempt advantage on to its investors. In some states, interest on selected municipal securities is also exempt from state income taxes. Investors in those states receive the dual benefit of both a federal and a state income tax exemption. The investment objective of municipal funds is tax-free current income. Depending on whether the fund concentrates on investment-grade securities (rated BBB or Baa and better) or more speculative securities (rated below BBB or Baa), the risk can range from low to moderate.

The principal attraction of a municipal bond fund is its tax-free income. And that tax-free feature is most important to taxpayers with high marginal tax rates. Assume that Bernie Bigbuck (whose marginal income tax rate is 45 percent) is considering either an investment-grade bond fund that currently offers 14 percent return or a municipal bond fund of similar risk that currently offers an 11 percent return. With the investment-grade bond fund, Bernie's after-tax return is:

$$7.7\% \qquad = 14\% \qquad - (14\% \qquad \times 45\%)$$
$$\Uparrow \qquad\qquad \Uparrow \qquad\qquad \Uparrow \qquad\qquad \Uparrow$$

After-tax return = Total return − (Total return × Marginal tax rate)

The after-tax return on the municipal bond fund is 11 percent because it is not subject to income taxes—so he should select the municipal bond fund.

Common Stock Funds

Common stock funds invest primarily in the common stocks of corporations. The investment objectives of these funds are the most varied of the three categories of funds. At one end of the spectrum, there are funds whose objective is primarily current income, with only limited emphasis on attaining capital growth. At the other extreme, there are funds whose objective is almost exclusively maximum capital growth, with only limited concern for current income. Individuals who purchase shares in a common stock mutual fund can expect to receive part of their return from all three previously discussed sources: dividends distributed by the fund, capital gains distributed by the fund, and changes in the fund's NAV per share. A fund that emphasizes current income will generate most of its return through the dividends it earns on its common stock holdings. Returns from capital gains distributions and changes in the fund's NAV per share will be much less important. Those funds that stress maximum capital growth will likely generate little of their return from dividends on their common stock holdings. Instead, a large part of an investor's return on these funds will be some combination of capital gains distributed by the fund and appreciation in the fund's NAV per share.

As Chapter 19 amply demonstrated, the market price on common stocks in general can go through sizable price fluctuations. Furthermore, the price of selected common stocks can suffer even wider price swings. Changes in the market price of a fund's common stock holdings are directly translated as changes in a fund's NAV per share. Consequently, mutual funds that concentrate on common stocks with highly volatile market prices will likewise have a highly volatile NAV per share. On the other hand, mutual funds that concentrate on staid, blue-chip common stocks that have much smaller swings in market price will show more limited swings in the fund's NAV per share.

Individuals who invest in a common stock mutual fund must be prepared for wide swings in the NAV of their mutual fund shares. When the market prices of common stocks are depressed, the NAV of most common stock mutual fund's shares will also be depressed. Should Ron Risktaker (our common stock mutual fund investor) have to sell his shares when the market is low, he could suffer a sizable loss. In the long run, the market price of those common stocks may well recover, pushing up the NAV of Ron's mutual fund's shares. But that prospect offers little solace or hope for Ron if he must redeem those shares today.

STRATEGY

An investment in a common stock mutual fund should not be considered a short-term commitment; if common stock prices should decline sharply during the short period you planned to hold it, you could suffer a substantial loss.

Aggressive Growth Funds   The investment objective of **agressive growth common stock mutual funds** is maximum capital growth, with limited concern for current income. To meet that objective, they use investment techniques that typically entail considerable risk. Frequently, the funds invest in the common stocks of companies whose products and services are in emerging growth areas, that are recovering from previous serious financial reversals, or that are small and less well known. Pursuing one of these investment strategies can make the NAV per share of these funds highly unstable. For that reason, they can be very risky.

But aggressive growth mutual funds attempt to provide a tax advantage to their investors by concentrating on long-term capital gains. Because only 40 percent of a long-term capital gain is subject to income taxes, this focus can be highly attractive to investors with high marginal tax rates. And the higher the proportion of capital gains in the fund's return, the greater the tax advantage.

Growth Funds   The investment objective of **growth common stock mutual funds** is long-term growth of capital, with current income a secondary consideration. The funds typically invest in common stocks of companies that they believe have strong future growth potential. By emphasizing growth of capital, a large fraction of the investor's return is either through capital gains distributed by the fund or through appreciation in the NAV of the fund's shares. Assuming the investor has held the shares for more than 1 year, any appreciation in the share's NAV will qualify as a long-term gain. Since a great portion of the fund's return will likely be tax-advantaged, long-term capital gains (with only 40 percent subject to federal income taxes), the return remaining after paying taxes can be very attractive. This is especially true if you have a high marginal income tax rate.

The disadvantage is, however, that these funds carry considerable risk.

First, the fund's performance depends heavily on an increase in the market value of its common stock investments. If those increases do not materialize (and they can at times be very elusive), the fund's return will be disappointingly low. Second, the funds frequently concentrate on common stocks whose price can be rather volatile. During a period when stock prices in general are declining, the value of a growth fund's investments may be dropping even more sharply. That decline can make your investment return decidely negative. In summary, growth stock funds demonstrate the risk return trade-off we discussed in Chapter 17: A growth fund can provide an attractively high return but with considerable risk.

Growth and Income Funds Growth and income common stock funds have a dual investment objective: current income and long-term growth of capital. To do that the funds invest primarily in common stocks that pay a reasonable current dividend, yet have some prospect of future price appreciation. Investors in these funds will likely receive their return as a combination of all three return sources:

Dividend distributions from the income earned on the fund's common stock holdings

Capital gains distributions from the sale of common stock investments that have appreciated in price

Increases in the fund's NAV per share

While the latter two sources may qualify for the favorable tax treatment of long-term capital gains, they probably will be a smaller proportion of the fund's total return than they will be in either an aggressive growth or a growth fund.

Growth and income funds usually offer the investor less risk than either an aggressive growth or a growth fund. Typically, the funds invest in common stocks that provide relatively stable dividend payments. From those, the funds can distribute a reasonably stable dividend return to their investors. Also, the market price of these common stocks is frequently more stable, so the fund's NAV per share is likewise more stable. Nevertheless, during a period of declining stock prices, the fund's shares will also lose value. During such periods, the overall return on growth and income funds can still be relatively volatile.

Income Funds Income funds stress current income as their primary investment objective. In general, the funds invest not only in common stocks but also in fixed-return investments such as corporate bonds. When selecting investments, the funds concentrate on those that provide high current income either through regular, stable dividend payments or through interest payments. Returns to investors in these funds are chiefly from the fund's dividend distribution. All that return is to be included as part of the investor's income for tax purposes.

Because income funds concentrate on investments that offer a steady income and more limited price fluctuations, their return is the least volatile of the common stock mutual funds. For that reason, their risk is also the lowest. These funds are a compromise between mutual funds that invest exclusively in bonds and those that invest exclusively in common stocks.

Specialized Funds   Rather than hold a diversified portfolio of common stocks, **specialized funds** concentrate their investments in only one or two industries. For example, there are specialized funds that invest largely in the common stocks of companies that mine gold and other precious metals, companies that provide health care, companies that offer financial services, and companies that operate public utilities. As an investor in one of these funds, you will receive returns that parallel the fortunes of the industry in which the fund concentrates its investments. At times, those returns have been excellent. However, they have also been dismal when the industry has not done well.

We consider the investor's risk in specialized funds to be very high. First, by concentrating on a single industry, the funds violate the basic investment objective of diversification. The return on these funds can be highly volatile, especially if the fund concentrates on an industry that is subject to wide swings in its performance. Clearly, these funds are best suited to investors who want to single out an industry for investment and who can accept the sizable risk that this kind of holding entails.

ADVANTAGE OF MUTUAL FUNDS

Mutual funds provide a range of investment and record-keeping services that can be quite valuable for many investors. Some of the services are provided by all three major categories of funds: money market funds, bond funds, and common stock funds. Those services that are offered by only one or two of the categories are so noted. Exhibit 20-6 summarizes the major advantages that we will discuss in the next section.

Diversification of Investments   A major reason for buying bond and common stock mutual funds is to obtain diversification. Adequate diversification is nothing more than an application of the adage, "Don't put all your eggs in one basket." Diversification is critical to protecting your investment dollars. The person with limited resources, if buying directly, will find such diversification virtually impossible to achieve. Since between 10 and 15 different stocks are needed to obtain reasonable diversification, a small investor would have to purchase fewer shares of stocks, in lots of less than 100 shares. The commission on a small purchase is much higher as a percentage of the purchase price than is the commission on a larger purchase. Consequently, small investors attempting to diversify would pay so much in commissions that their returns would be reduced sharply.

Mutual funds achieve diversification by holding 30 to 50 or more different stocks or bonds. Unless the fund concentrates on volatile, risky securities, its investment performance should not differ too much from a randomly selected portfolio of stocks or bonds. It is important for you to be aware of the type of fund that you purchase because the more aggressive

EXHIBIT 20-6

Summary of mutual fund advantages.

ADVANTAGE	ACCOMPLISHMENTS	INVESTORS WHO WOULD BENEFIT
Diversification of investment	They spread the risk	Investors with less than $50,000
Access to investments	They allow investment in large denomination instruments paying market interest rates	All individuals
Professional management	They remove the burden of watching individual investments	Investors who do not want to manage investments
Dollar-cost averaging	They allow systematic, recurring investments at low cost	Individuals accumulating capital
Record keeping	They provide periodic, up-to-date reports to the fundholder	All individuals
Automatic reinvestment	They reinvest dividends and/or capital gains at no cost	Individuals accumulating capital
Systematic withdrawal	They provide set monthly payment from dividends, capital gains, and principal	Individuals who need steady income
Check writing	They permit immediate access to money in interest-earning account	People with $1000 or more to open account
Telephone exchange	They allow shift of money to another fund within that mutual fund group	People who want a flexible investment

funds will tend to perform better than the market when all stock prices are increasing, called an "up market," and worse than average in "down markets."

Access to Select Investments Money market mutual funds allow an individual with limited resources to invest in money market instruments that can be purchased only in very large dollar denominations. For example, the minimum investment in a large CD is $100,000 (larger amounts are readily accepted). For commercial paper the minimum can be $250,000 or more (amounts of $1 million or more are gladly accepted). Money market mutual funds provide a vehicle whereby a small investor can earn the interest rate that these money market investments pay without holding

them directly. Prior to the recent introduction of money market accounts by financial institutions, money market mutual funds were the only way small investors could earn market-determined-interest rates on highly flexible investments.

Professional Management   Despite the poor performance of some common stock mutual funds, there are mutual funds that can make a strong argument that the professional management an investor receives is worthwhile. A conservatively managed mutual fund will never make you rich, but most likely it will do a reasonably good job of preserving your capital. The fund managers usually avoid the major mistakes that investors make, such as overconcentration in a few stocks or bonds.

Investing in a mutual fund frees investors of the daily worry of managing their own portfolios. The money can simply be turned over to the fund and then ignored for most of the time. For many people, this aspect of mutual funds is well worth the management fee they must pay. It relieves them of having to make investment decisions and of worrying about possible disastrous losses.

Dollar-Cost Averaging   Regularly investing a fixed amount in a mutual fund will give the investor the benefits of dollar-cost averaging. **Dollar-cost averaging** means that each dollar you invest will buy more shares when the price is low, thus effectively lowering the average cost of each share you hold. Dollar-cost averaging is advantageous, no matter whether the market is falling or rising. Exhibit 20-7 shows the results of hypothetical investments made in a falling and a rising market respectively. The secret of dollar-cost averaging is investing the same dollar amount at regular intervals, not buying the same number of shares at regular intervals.

EXHIBIT 20-7

Examples of dollar-cost averaging in declining
and rising stock markets.

	Declining Market			Rising Market	
AMOUNT INVESTED	PRICE PER SHARE	NUMBER OF SHARES PURCHASED	PRICE PER SHARE	NUMBER OF SHARES PURCHASED
$120	$10	12	$ 8	15
120	8	15	10	12
120	5	24	12	10
120	4	30	15	8
$480 (Total)	$ 6.75 (Average Price)	81 (Total)	$11 (Average Price)	45 (Total)

Average cost ($5.93) = amount invested
($480) ÷ number of shares (81)

Average cost ($10.67) =
amount invested ($480) ÷
number of shares (45)

Continuing a dollar-cost averaging program requires self-discipline. Most people tend to be enthusiastic when the stock market is rising (a bull market), but lose the courage of their convictions in a declining market (a bear market). Actually, they should be more enthusiastic in a declining market because the investments made near the bottom of the market are the ones that ultimately produce the most satisfactory returns.

Reduction in Record Keeping Buying a mutual fund instead of a diversified list of common stocks substantially reduces an investor's record-keeping chores. Rather than having to record information for 10 to 15 different securities, you need to keep records for only one fund. Moreover, the mutual fund performs the record keeping for you. A typical mutual fund statement, like the monthly one shown in Exhibit 20-8, indicates total shares held, the price paid for each share, and the date on which the shares were acquired. Annually, the statement reports the amounts paid as dividends and capital gains distributions. All the investor must do is keep the statements filed chronologically, in order to have all the information needed for federal and state tax returns.

Automatic Reinvestment Investors in a mutual fund generally have three payment choices for their dividend and capital gain distributions. They can ask the funds to:

Reinvest both the dividends and capital gains distributions in additional shares of the fund

Pay the dividends to the investor but reinvest the capital gains distribution in additional shares

Pay both the dividends and capital gains to the investor

The **automatic reinvestment** option can provide several advantages. First, even if you already own shares of a mutual fund, some funds require that any additional investment must be at least $100 to $250; that restricts your option of investing small amounts. But funds waive this minimum for the automatic reinvestment of dividends and capital gains. Also, many load funds do not assess their typical load fee on the automatic reinvestment of dividends and capital gains. Last, automatic reinvestment provides yet one more opportunity for the investor to use dollar-cost averaging. With reinvestment, the money from the dividend and capital gains distributions purchases additional shares at the then-prevailing NAV per share.

EXHIBIT 20-8

Monthly statement from a mutual fund.

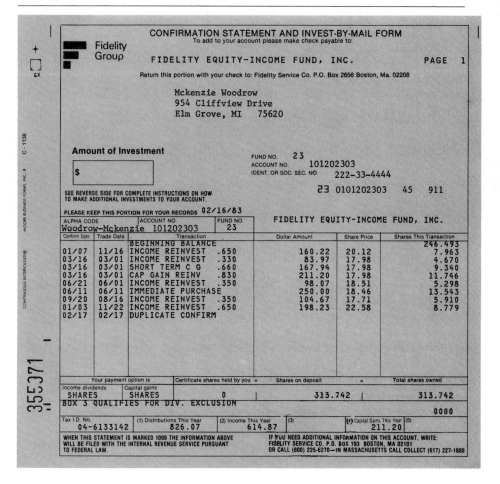

STRATEGY

Automatic reinvestment can help you invest additional amounts in a mutual fund. It would be inappropriate for some individuals, such as retired persons, who rely on the dividend or capital gains distribution as part of their regular income.

Systematic Withdrawal Plan With a **systematic withdrawal** plan, the mutual fund pays the investor a specified amount each month. As its first source, the mutual fund will use the investor's dividend and capital gains distributions to cover that monthly payment. If that source is insufficient, the shortfall is drawn from the investor's balance, or principal, in the fund. Depending on the size of the investor's monthly withdrawal, the fund balance will continue to grow, remain unchanged, or decrease. One consequence of having the withdrawal exceed the investor's dividend and capital gain distribution, of course, is that the fund balance continues to decline. Furthermore, as the fund balance drops, the investor owns fewer shares that earn dividends and capital gains distributions. As those distributions decrease, an increasingly larger share of the monthly withdrawal must come from liquidating the fund balance. An additional complication with a common stock fund is that the fund's NAV per share will be depressed when prices in the overall stock market are depressed. To raise a fixed dollar amount, far more shares of a common stock fund will have to be redeemed when the NAV is low.

Just because you begin with a particular withdrawal plan, you need not continue at that level. Most funds allow you to raise, lower, or terminate a withdrawal plan at any time. But you should carefully review your investment plans and objectives before beginning any withdrawal plan. If, for example, you don't want to draw down your investment in the mutual fund, your withdrawal must not exceed your dividend and capital gains distributions. This option is most appropriate if you need an income from the investment, yet want to maintain the investment intact. On the other hand, investors who plan to use both the income and a part of the investment itself to cover their monthly withdrawals can draw considerably more from their fund. An immediate question is: How large a periodic withdrawal can an investor make and still continue to make similar withdrawals for a specified number of years? The size of the permitted withdrawal depends jointly on what rate of return the investment earns during the withdrawal period and on how long the withdrawal period is to continue. Chapter 21 will demonstrate how you can make such a computation.

STRATEGY

Investors who elect a systematic withdrawal plan should carefully consider the impact of those withdrawals on their mutual fund investments. Too large a withdrawal may erode the investment to the point where it cannot continue to sustain the desired monthly withdrawal.

Check Writing Money market mutual funds permit **check writing;** that is, fund holders can write checks drawn on their accounts. The checks are readily accepted by most business and financial institutions. One factor that limits their usefulness, however, is that most funds require that each check be for $500 or more. You are not likely to use one for your phone bill. But there is no reason why you cannot draw a check on your money market fund and use it to replenish your checking, NOW, or share draft account; you can then use that account to pay your small bills.

Telephone Exchange   A number of large mutual fund organizations offer a group of various mutual funds ranging from money market funds right on through bond and common stock funds. And within each of these three categories, they may have several funds with different investment objectives. By having a fairly diverse range of mutual funds, you may be able to find one or more funds that meet your assorted needs, all within the same organization. To further enhance your investment flexibility, many mutual fund groups permit investors to switch their money among the funds within the mutual fund group. The transfer can be through a mail request, or some fund groups will accept **telephone exchanges.** Of the two, fund groups that provide a toll-free 800 phone number provide the quickest and most convenient service.

We will use several examples to illustrate the potential advantage of having the exchange privilege. Suppose that Stanley Steady, who currently has $3000 invested in a growth common stock fund, decides he wants to switch to a bond fund. The group of mutual funds where Stanley has his common stock fund has a bond fund that meets his needs and the group accepts telephone transfers. Stanley can transfer part or all of his money to the bond fund with just a phone call. To prevent a series of transfers within a short period, some funds limit the number of transfers you can make in a year's time: 4 to 6 transfers a year is frequently their limit. No-load funds rarely have a fee for making a transfer and, of course, do not charge a commission on the transaction. Some load funds will waive the commission but charge a nominal fee ($5 to $25 is typical) on each transfer.

As our second example, assume Linda Liquid has a money market fund and a common stock fund. They are with the same group of mutual funds and the group accepts telephone transfers. Thanks to several large, unexpected payments, Linda finds she needs to tap her common stock fund for $1000. With a simple telephone call, she can transfer the needed $1000 from her common stock fund to her money market fund. Once the money is in that fund, she can write checks against the $1000. These two examples give you an idea of how transfers can provide added flexibility to your mutual fund investments.

SPECIAL USES FOR FUNDS

Mutual funds may be used for two special-purpose investments, both of which provide unique tax advantages. These are investment accounts for children and tax-deferred retirement accounts.

Accounts for Children   Shares may be purchased for children under the Uniform Gifts to Minors Act. Since the child owns the fund (the child's Social Security number is on the account), any dividend or capital gain distributions are income to the child. Most children do not have to pay income taxes because their total income, even including the mutual fund, is not sufficiently large to be taxable. By having the child own the fund, the parents divert the income, which would probably be heavily taxed if held by an adult, to the child, where it may not be taxed at all. Parents whose marginal tax rate is 40 percent can save $40 of taxes on each $100 of mutual fund income. By avoiding that tax burden, the parent will accumulate money in the mutual fund more rapidly for a child's education fund or a similar purpose.

Recognize, however, that the money in the mutual fund is the child's. And as soon as the fund's owner becomes of age, usually at 18, the child can do with the money what he or she pleases. That privilege may be a decided disadvantage in some cases.

Retirement Accounts: Keogh and IRA When we discussed income taxes back in Chapter 6, we noted that any employed individual can establish an **Individual Retirement Account** (IRA). People who are self-employed can also establish a **Keogh account.** Either type of account can provide substantial tax advantages for a person accumulating a retirement fund. We will review those tax consequences in Chapter 21, which covers retirement plans. For now, we merely point out that a mutual fund account can be an ideal investment vehicle for both IRA and Keogh accounts. Because the mutual fund imposes restrictions on withdrawals from accounts designated as IRA or Keogh accounts, dividend and capital gains distributions on your IRA or Keogh are not subject to federal and most state income taxes. Because mutual funds cover most types of fixed-return and variable-return investments, you should be able to find a fund that meets your needs. Furthermore, by opening your IRA or Keogh account with a mutual fund group that permits telephone transfers, you can readily shift your money among the group's different funds. All earnings on your account remain exempt from income taxes as long as they remain in a restrictive IRA or Keogh account. Should you be unhappy with your present mutual fund group, most funds will readily transfer the money to whatever new mutual fund or other investment you request. Typically, there will be no income taxes on such a transfer.

INFORMATION ON MUTUAL FUNDS

A number of publications compile information on mutual funds that can greatly assist you in your search for a suitable mutual fund. Some publications provide detailed background information on individual mutual funds: (1) a fund's investment objective, (2) the minimum initial investment to open an account, (3) dollar limits on subsequent investments, (4) the length of time the fund has been operating, and (5) the current total dollar amount in the fund. Other publications stress investment performance data on individual funds: (1) the fund's rate of return during the past several months or the past year, (2) the fund's average return earned over periods ranging from 2 to 20 years, (3) the dividend and capital gains distributions paid by the fund during the past 12 months, and (4) dollar estimates to show what the current value would be if $1000 had been invested in the fund from 2 to 10 years ago. Exhibit 20-9 summarizes the major information sources, together with the types of information each one furnishes. You will likely find one or more of these sources at your local library.

A good way to begin your mutual fund search is to compare the past performance of various funds. While past performance can be a reasonable guide, it certainly is not an infallible basis for selecting a mutual fund. There are funds that perform extremely well for 1 or 2 years, only to follow that success with disastrous losses for the next several years. Rather than just

EXHIBIT 20-9

Major publications that provide information on mutual funds.

PUBLICATION	FREQUENCY	INFORMATION PROVIDED
No-Load Mutual Fund Directory	Annually	1, 2, 3, 5, 6, and 7
Wiesenberger Investment Companies Service	Monthly and annual summary	1, 2, 3, 4, 5, 6, 7, 8, 10, 11, 12, 13, 14, 15, and 16
Forbes	Mid-August issue each year	4, 6, 8, 9, 13, 14, 15, and 16
Barron's	Early to mid-month issue: Feb., May, Aug., Nov.	2, 6, 11, and 15
United Mutual Fund Selector, United Business Services	Biweekly	1, 2, 3, 4, 5, 6, 8, 10, 12, 14, and 15

Key to type of information:
1 Address and telephone number of fund
2 Investment objective
3 Minimum initial deposit and limits on subsequent investments
4 Sales charge or commission to purchase fund shares
5 Date fund was established
6 Current dollar size of fund
7 Special investor services fund provides
8 Fund's performance during prior 6 months, and/or 12 months
9 Fund's average rate of return for past 12 years.
10 Fund's rate of return averaged for a series of past periods ranging from 2 to 10 years
11 How a hypothetical $10,000 investment would have done had it been invested for 1 year, 5 years, and/or 10 years
12 Breakdown of fund's current investments
13 Comparative average performance results for similar mutual funds, and representative stock market indexes
14 Details on fund's annual expense charges
15 Dividend and capital gains distributions fund has paid during previous 12 months
16 Management fees and operating costs charged by fund

stress a mutual fund's performance over the most recent year or two, you should, instead, review its performance record over a period of 4 to 8 years. What you want is a fund that has a consistently good performance over an extended period. Certainly, there may be several years during that extended period when the investors received a negative return on a mutual fund. But if the fund can counter those negative years with years of solidly positive returns, it may still be able to provide its investors with an overall positive return for the period that adequately compensates them for the risk they accepted. Of course, just because a mutual fund performed well in the past does not guarantee it will continue to do so in the future. But we certainly prefer a mutual fund with a consistently good past record to one that has consistently snatched defeat from the jaws of success in order to compile a solid string of losses. All too often, the latter mutual funds seem to replicate their past record: they remain losers.

ARE COMMON STOCK OR BOND MUTUAL FUNDS FOR YOU?

Suppose you are at the point where you have decided to invest some money. How do you decide whether to invest it directly or through a mutual fund? The decision depends on your answers to three questions:

What amount of money can you invest?

What length of time can you devote to your investments?

What special services do you require?

We intentionally limit this section to common stock and bond mutual funds. Money market mutual funds purchase investments whose minimum dollar denominations are so large that direct purchase by an individual is out of the question.

Exhibit 20-10 is a checklist of questions that can help you decide whether to buy a mutual fund or, instead, to buy the investment directly. If

EXHIBIT 20-10

CHAPTER 20

663

MUTUAL FUNDS

Checklist on whether to invest in a mutual fund
or directly purchase the investment.

	YES	NO
1 Do you have enough money to diversify your investment adequately?	___	___
2 If you lack sufficient money for diversification, are you willing to accept the added risk from concentrating on a few investments?	___	___
3 Will you be able to invest $1000 or more each time you want to make an investment?	___	___
4 Do you have adequate training in economics, finance, and accounting to understand individual investments?	___	___
5 Can you spend the time needed to analyze individual investments adequately?	___	___
6 Will you devote the required time to monitor an investment once you have made it?	___	___
7 Will you enjoy spending the necessary time to manage your individual investments?	___	___
8 Will you be willing to keep the detailed records necessary to track your individual investments?	___	___

your answers to those nine questions are predominantly *no*, you should seriously consider a mutual fund. If, however, many of your answers are *yes*, buying the investment directly may be your best choice.

BUYING MONEY MARKET FUNDS

Buying a money market fund is reasonably straightforward. First, there are many funds from which to choose, so you are likely to find several that match your needs. Second, because the funds compete with one another nationally, the minimums and services are comparatively similar among funds. Therefore, you can easily compare competing funds. Last, because of the highly competitive environment, a new service or feature offered by several funds is likely to spread to others. So, even if a particular fund is not an innovator, it frequently has to match what the other funds are doing to remain competitive.

Match the Type of Fund to Your Risk-Return Preference

When selecting a money market mutual fund, you should match the fund with your personal risk-return preference. If you want to minimize risk, a fund that concentrates on government securities would be your first choice.

Recognize, however, that lowering the risk also lowers the return. Sacrificing that return would be unnecessary if you were willing to accept the higher risk of a general-purpose money market fund. Typically, you would receive an additional 1/2 to 1 percent added return to compensate for the higher risk.

Buy A Tax-Exempt Fund Only If Justified by Your Tax Bracket While the idea of tax-free income is appealing, tax-exempt money market funds are appropriate only for investors with a 40 to 50 percent marginal tax rate. To decide whether a tax-exempt fund is suitable for you, you need to compare its return with what you would earn on a general-purpose fund after paying taxes. A tax-exempt fund is the best choice if its return exceeds the general-purpose fund's after-tax return.

Buy a Fund Whose Total Assets Are Large Money market funds need to diversify among a number of investments and to manage those investments professionally. Most of the larger funds can achieve the needed diversification and provide qualified professional management at the lowest cost.

Insist on Check Writing The check-writing privilege is one of the attractive features of money market mutual funds. Make certain that a prospective fund offers it. If possible, try to find a fund that will allow checks to be written for amounts less than $500 (in 1983, $500 was the usual minimum).

Look for Telephone Exchange Services Select a fund from one of the large mutual fund groups that offer telephone exchange. This service gives you the added flexibility of being able to move your money among a number of mutual funds. Not only can you make additional investments in a common stock or bond fund; you can also readily liquidate your investment in those funds by transferring the money to your money market mutual fund. Completing those transfers through a phone call is simple and convenient.

BUYING BOND MUTUAL FUNDS

The range of mutual funds that concentrate on fixed-return notes and bonds has expanded during the past several years and will probably continue to do so. This expansion has meant that investors now have a wider range of alternatives. Among those alternatives, you are far more likely to find a bond fund that matches your investment objective. But that proliferation has also placed a greater burden on the investor to precisely define his or her investment objective for purchasing the bond fund. Once you define your objective, you will need to make a more detailed search to locate the fund or funds that will best match your objective.

Concentrate on No-Load Funds There is no solid evidence that load bond funds perform better on average than do no-load funds. And once the load (commission) is deducted, their overall performance is lower. The sizable commission on a load fund will practically wipe out your first year's return.

Buy Funds Whose Total Assets Are Large Bond funds can significantly reduce the investor's risk by diversifying their investments among several different notes and bonds. The larger the bond fund, the more easily it can achieve the necessary diversification. Moreover, large bond funds will likely buy and sell larger blocks of notes and bonds, and thus offer some economies in transaction costs when compared with smaller funds. The lower the fund's operating costs, the more income it can pass through to its investors.

Match the Bond Fund's Investment Objective to Your Risk-Return Preference When selecting a bond mutual fund, it is important to make sure its investment objective matches your personal risk-return preference. Selecting a fund with very low risk requires that you sacrifice some return. That is an unnecessary sacrifice for investors who can accept higher risk. At the opposite extreme, concentrating on obtaining the highest return may lead to purchasing a fund whose higher risk would be unacceptable to some investors.

Investors who prefer low risk should consider bond funds that invest in U.S. Treasury, as well as federal agency, notes and bonds. Investors who are willing to accept somewhat more risk should consider bond funds that

ONE IMPORTANT ASPECT OF MUNICIPAL BONDS IS THAT ALL INTEREST EARNED IS NON-TAXABLE, MR. EVERS... MR. EVERS?

concentrate on investment-grade corporate notes and bonds. To compensate for that higher risk, the investor receives a higher return. Investors who can accept even more risk should consider aggressive bond funds. They concentrate on lower-quality corporate notes and bonds, but because of their risk, they also provide the highest rates of return.

Consider Bond Funds with Short To Intermediate Maturities   Recent bouts of highly volatile interest rates have made many investors reluctant to commit money to investments with long maturities. In large part, this hesitation stems from the wide swing in market prices for these investments when interest rates rise and decline. In response, bond mutual funds have been developed that concentrate on investments with short (typically 1 to 3 years) or intermediate-term maturities (typically from 3 to 8 years). Investments with a shorter maturity, as Chapter 17 demonstrated, experience a smaller change in price for a given change in interest rates. The NAV per share of bond funds that focus on these investments should likewise experience smaller swings in value.

Consider Tax-Exempt Bond Funds   Carefully consider whether the return on a tax-exempt bond fund would exceed what you could earn on a corporate bond fund after paying income taxes. If it would, then a tax-exempt fund is what you should invest in. But make a detailed after-tax comparison rather than be unduly influenced by the prospect of tax-free income.

SELECTING THE RIGHT COMMON STOCK FUND

Even if you have decided that you want to purchase a common stock mutual fund, you still face the heavy task of deciding which fund to choose. With over 500 funds currently available, it is a challenge. The following guidelines can help you in that selection.

Match the Mutual Fund's Investment Objective to Your Investment Needs   Make sure that the mutual fund's investment objective matches your investment goals. For example, investors who are averse to risk will want to avoid aggressive growth funds and growth funds as well. Investors who are interested in long-term capital gains, and the tax advantage those gains can provide, will do well to avoid income common stock funds. On the other hand, someone interested in regular income payments will not be well served by funds that stress capital growth as their primary goal.

The first step in the process is to specify precisely what your investment goals are for the common stock mutual fund. Having done this, you will find that the field of qualifying mutual funds is significantly narrowed. Moreover, you will avoid selecting a fund whose risk is unacceptably high or one whose return does not parallel your needs.

Concentrate on No-Load Funds   There is solid evidence that load mutual funds do not, on average, outperform no-load funds. And if we deduct the commissions a load fund entails, that group's overall return is lower. Consequently, we think there is little justification for paying a commission to buy a load fund. There are many well-managed no-load funds that will likely better serve your investment needs. An added benefit is that concentrating on just no-load funds reduces the list of available funds by more than one-half.

Consider Smaller Mutual Funds When we say "moderate size," we generally mean funds that have assets of less than $100 million. Smaller mutual funds often perform very well when stock prices are rising. But the fluctuation in the fund's NAV per share along the way can cause all but the hardiest investors an occasional sleepless night. If your goal is a stable income with limited fluctuation in your fund's NAV per share, you may want to avoid smaller funds. But if you are willing to place part of your investment at risk, you may wish to consider some of the smaller mutual funds.

Use Mutual Funds Only for Long-Term Investments Since investing in common stock mutual funds involves considerable risk, you should expect to hold your mutual fund investment for a rather long time. As a general guide, you should plan to hold a fund for at least 2 and possibly 3 to 4 years. If you will need the money in a few months, a mutual fund is not the place for it. Your short-term emergency cash reserve does not belong in a common stock mutual fund. You want to avoid being forced to redeem your fund shares during a period when common stock prices are heavily depressed.

Invest Regularly Investor enthusiasm seems to peak at the same time the stock market is about to drop through the floor. Yet, when the market is poised for a solid advance, the same group of investors often are deserting it in droves. You can avoid all this turmoil by investing in your mutual funds on a regular recurring basis. When prices are depressed, you gain the advantages of dollar-cost averaging.

Buy More than One Fund Buy shares of two or three funds. It may seem strange to diversify among funds, since diversifying is precisely what the funds are trying to do. Nevertheless, from the historical performance results summarized in the publications shown in Exhibit 20-9, it is clear that returns can vary markedly from fund to fund. There is no guarantee that every fund you pick will be a winner. But, by purchasing several funds, you avoid basing your entire investment performance on one fund. And by having two or three funds, you should be able to pick at least one that will do reasonably well.

SUMMARY

1   Mutual funds consolidate the money received from a large number of small investors and invest it in such things as money market investments, U.S. Treasury securities, corporate bonds, municipal bonds, and common stocks. They allow individuals to invest indirectly in these different instruments.

2   Your ownership in a mutual fund is evidenced by the shares in that mutual fund that you own.

3   At the close of each business day, most mutual funds compute the net asset value (NAV) of their shares. The computation is:

$$\text{NAV} = \frac{\text{Current market value of mutual funds' investments} - \text{Liabilities of mutual fund}}{\text{Number of shares in mutual fund}}$$

4   Load mutual funds are sold to investors by representatives who collect commissions on those sales. No-load mutual funds are sold directly to investors without any commission.

5   Most large metropolitan newspapers, and financial publications such as the *Wall Street Journal* and *Barron's*, regularly quote the NAV per share on major mutual funds.

6   Investors in a mutual fund receive their investment returns through some combination of:

Dividend distributions from the fund

Capital gain distributions from the fund

Appreciation in the mutual fund's NAV per share

7   Every mutual fund must provide each prospective investor with a prospectus that explains the fund's investment objective and the investments it expects to hold.

8   The three broad categories of mutual funds include *(a)* money market funds, *(b)* bond funds, and *(c)* common stock funds. Within each category there is a range of funds with distinctly different investment objectives.

9   Advantages that a mutual fund can provide for small investors include *(a)* diversification of investments, *(b)* access to investments, *(c)* professional management, *(d)* investing for dollar-cost averaging, *(e)* record keeping, *(f)* automatic dividend and/or capital gains reinvestment, *(g)* systematic withdrawal plan, *(h)* check writing (on investor's money market fund shares), and *(i)* telephone exchange.

10   Mutual funds can be established as investments for minor children under the Uniform Gifts to Minors Act.

11   Individuals can establish a mutual fund to accumulate money for an Individual Retirement Account (IRA) or a Keogh account.

12   When searching for an appropriate money market mutual fund, investors should:

Match the fund's investment objective to their own risk-return preference.

Select a tax-exempt fund only if they have a high marginal tax rate.

Concentrate on funds with a large amount of assets.

Consider funds from large mutual fund groups that provide telephone exchange.

13   When picking a bond mutual fund, investors should:

Concentrate on no-load funds.

Buy funds that have large total assets.

Match the fund's investment objective to their own risk-return preference.

Consider funds that limit their investment maturities to the short to intermediate range.

Consider tax-exempt bond funds only if they provide a higher after-tax return.

14   When selecting a common stock mutual fund, investors should:

Match the fund's investment objective to their own risk-return preference.

Concentrate on no-load funds.

Consider smaller mutual funds.

Consider a mutual fund investment to be a long-term commitment.

Plan to invest regularly.

Buy more than one fund.

REVIEW YOUR UNDERSTANDING OF

Mutual fund	Aggressive bond
Management fee	Government
Operating expenses	Municipal
Net asset value (NAV)	Common stock fund
No-load fund	Aggressive growth
Load fund	Growth
Open-end mutual fund	Growth and income
Dividend distribution	Income
Capital gain distribution	Specialized
Prospectus	Dollar-cost averaging
Investment objective	Automatic reinvestment
Money market fund	Systematic withdrawal
General purpose	Check writing
Government	Telephone exchange
Tax-exempt	Individual Retirement Account (IRA)
Bond fund	Keogh account
Investment-grade	

DISCUSSION QUESTIONS

1   From an investor's standpoint, how does investing in a common stock or bond mutual fund differ from investing in those securities directly? What type of investor might be well served by a mutual fund investment?

2   How does a mutual fund compute its net asset value (NAV) per share? How often does it make this computation? For what purposes does it use that NAV?

3   Connie Concerned has just noted that the two similar common stock mutual funds she is considering have widely different management and operating costs. Low Cost Fund's total expenses per $100 invested were $0.95. Big Cost Fund's total expenses were

$2.01. Should Connie be concerned about Big Cost's seemingly higher expenses? Why?

4   Sidney Smidley noted the following price quotes in his local daily newspaper:

FUND	NAV	OFFER PRICE	NAV CHANGE
Low Cost	6.50	6.50	+.06
Sure Thing	8.00	8.75	+.09
Zero Sum	24.32	24.32	−.03

a Which are no-load and which are load funds?

b What does the change in the NAV column show for the various funds?

5   If you asked a brokerage firm about mutual funds, would you receive information on a broad cross section of different funds? Why or why not?

6   When an individual invests in a mutual fund, what are the potential sources of return on that investment? How are the different sources included on the investor's tax return?

7   What are the three major categories of mutual funds? Name the principal investment areas for each fund category.

8   If an investor wants to obtain some information on a particular fund's investment goals, what is a potential source? What types of information might your suggested source contain?

9   What are the similarities and differences among the following mutual funds:

Investment-grade bond fund

Aggressive bond fund

Tax-exempt bond fund

10   Borris Befuddled has only a small amount to invest, does not want to manage his investments, and has trouble reconciling his checkbook. What advantages of a mutual fund might interest Borris?

11   What important points should you consider when reviewing the historical performance of a mutual fund? Are there shortcomings you should evaluate when relying on that record?

12   What are the major differences among the three chief types of money market mutual funds? What purposes would likely be well served by one of these funds? How do money market mutual funds compare with money market deposit accounts (Chapter 18)?

13   What potential tax advantage can an investor obtain on the returns from an aggressive growth or growth common stock mutual fund? What investors would benefit most from this advantage?

14   What is the advantage of buying two or more common stock mutual funds? What may limit the number of funds an investor purchases?

PROBLEMS

20-1   Big Growth Mutual Fund wants to compute the net asset value (NAV) of its shares on April 1. Calculate the NAV of Big Growth's shares using the following information which the fund has summarized:

Market value of fund's investments on April 1: $50,100,000

Original purchase price of fund's investment: $50,200,000

Fund's total liabilities on April 1: $20,000

Number of current Big Growth shares: 1,000,000

Number of Big Growth shares when fund was established 10 years ago: 100,000

Calculate the NAV of Big Growth's shares.

20-2   Howard Hopeful plans to invest $1000 in a common stock mutual fund. One alternative is Technology Fund, a no-load fund whose NAV per share is currently $10. Worldwide Fund is Howard's second alternative. It is a load fund (8.5 percent commission on each purchase) whose NAV per share is also $10.

a How many Technology Mutual Fund shares will Howard's $1000 buy?

b How many Worldwide Fund shares will Howard's $1000 buy?

c Assume that neither fund is expected to distribute a dividend or capital gain for the next year. To earn a 10 percent rate of return on the original $1000 investment over the next year, what will Technology Fund's NAV per share have to be? What must Worldwide Fund's NAV per share be?

d Based on your answer to **c**, which mutual fund must have the superior performance?

20-3   Rhonda Regular has invested $400 in New High Fund (a no-load fund) every 3 months this past year. Details of her investments include:

AMOUNT INVESTED	DATE INVESTED	FUND'S NAV ON DATE INVESTED	SHARES PURCHASED
$240	March	$12	_____
240	June	8	_____
240	September	6	_____
240	December	4	_____

As this table vividly depicts, a stellar performer New High Fund has not been.

a How many shares did Rhonda buy during the year?

b What average price did she pay?

c Assume that rather than invest $240 each quarter, Rhonda, instead, chose to buy 32 shares each quarter. In total, how much would Rhonda invest under that plan? What would be her average price per share?

d If New High's present NAV per share is $5, what is Rhonda's profit or loss under the $240-per-month investment plan? What is it under the 32-shares-per-quarter plan?

20-4   During the past 12 months, Steady Return Mutual Fund has earned the following returns on its investments:

The total dividend and interest the fund earned was $250,000.

Long-term capital gains earned on investments Steady Return Mutual Fund sold during the year totaled $100,000.

Steady Return expects to deduct $50,000 in management and operating expenses from the dividend and interest amounts. The balance will be distributed across the 400,000 shares that Steady Return currently has outstanding.

a What dividend distribution will Steady Return make on each of its shares?

b How large a capital gain distribution will Steady Return make on each of its shares?

c Assume Sam Smalldollar owns 100 Steady Return Mutual Fund shares. What dollar distribution will Sam receive? How should Sam treat these distributions on his tax return?

20-5 Ron and Linda Swartz are considering establishing a mutual fund for their daughter, Ann, through the Uniform Gift to Minors Act. The Swartzes plan to purchase 50 shares of Winner Mutual Fund for Ann's account. Basing their estimate on the prior year's performance, the Swartzes expect Winner will distribute $1.70 per share as dividends and $1.40 per share as long-term capital gains this year. Ann currently has no other sources of income.

a What returns will Ann's account likely pay?

b Assuming that the returns you estimated in **a** were paid, how would those items appear on Ann's tax return? Will she likely have any income taxes? (*Hint:* Chapter 6 will help you answer this question.)

c If Ron and Linda's marginal tax rate is 40 percent, how much will they save in taxes by placing the account in Ann's name?

CASE PROBLEM

Carl and Karen Wills are currently outlining a detailed personal financial plan. Both Carl and Karen graduated from college 2 years ago and now they have repaid most of the loans they used to complete their education. At this time, they believe they can invest approximately $400 per month from their combined income. Of course, with each of them earning an excellent salary, their current marginal tax rate is a high 40 percent. When designing their financial plan, the Wills want to shelter part of their investment returns, if possible, from that sizable tax bite. Both Carl and Karen are quite busy with their careers and the care of their young son; neither one of them has much time to devote to investments. They have decided that they will rely heavily on mutual funds as their principal investment vehicle. At this time, Carl and Karen have only one investment: $3000 in a traditional savings account. They have just begun their search for mutual funds, so they have not singled out any specific funds.

Carl and Karen have outlined the following financial goals that require some investment vehicle:

To accumulate approximately $100 each month in two IRA accounts to provide a retirement plan. One motive for starting such a plan is to gain the tax-deferral benefit an IRA provides. Second, they each expect to change positions several times during their working career, making it essential for each of them to provide a separate retirement fund.

To accumulate a total of $8000 over the next 4 years to provide the down payment to purchase a condominium.

To start an education fund to cover the cost of their son's college expenses. They expect to contribute $50 each month to this fund.

To place their present $3000 emergency fund in an investment that provides a higher return than their present savings account.

a What one or more types of mutual funds might you recommend for their IRA accounts? Provide a brief statement supporting your choice or choices.

b What tax advantages can the IRA account provide? From a tax viewpoint, should the Wills be concerned whether their IRA mutual fund accounts provide returns from dividends, capital gains, or appreciation in each fund's NAV?

c To achieve their down payment goal of $8000, what monthly amount will they need to contribute if they can earn 8 percent annually? (*Hint:* Chapter 1 may be of interest.)

d What one or more types of mutual funds would you suggest for their down payment goal? Why?

e What should the Wills do with any dividends and capital gains distributions on the mutual fund(s) you suggested in **d**?

f What mutual fund investment plan should the Wills use to accumulate the desired education fund? What type of mutual fund might they use for this goal?

g What mutual fund would you recommend for their emergency fund? How should they select a particular fund from your recommendations?

h Would you suggest that Carl and Karen concentrate on load or no-load funds? Why? Where can the Wills find information on the funds you have suggested?

CHAPTER
21
RETIREMENT AND ESTATE PLANNING

**AFTER COMPLETING THIS CHAPTER
YOU WILL HAVE LEARNED**

What the *four major sources* of *retirement income* are

What *private pension plans* are all about

How *tax-deferred retirement accounts* provide sizable tax advantages

How to *estimate your retirement income needs*

How to *compute the amount of retirement income* each source must provide

What the *strengths and weaknesses of annuities* are

Why and how to design a *payout plan for a retirement account*

What a will is all about and why most people should have one

Who can serve as *your estate executor* and what the duties are

What *joint ownership* is and how it affects estate planning

What *probate* is, and why and how you should try to avoid it

RETIREMENT planning and estate planning

may seem very remote to young people just starting their working careers. Granted, it will actually be implemented at some fairly distant date in their lives. Yet, without planning, retirement can turn out to be a long period of doing without or scraping by. Without estate planning, the transfers of your worldly goods may, or may not, be what you really had in mind. The first section of the chapter discusses retirement planning. The second section turns to estate planning.

RETIREMENT PLANNING: IS IT NEEDED?

The time for retirement planning is when you are between the ages of twenty-five and fifty-five, and the earlier the better. By the time you reach sixty or sixty-five, it is too late for retirement planning to have a significant impact on the amount of money you will have to live on after you stop working. The key to success in retirement planning is making an early commitment to saving regularly. In Chapter 1, we showed you how savings grow at various interest rates. The more you save, the higher the rate of return you earn, and the longer the money is invested, the more you will have at the time you retire.

When you are planning for retirement, there are excellent ways to accumulate the capital to generate your retirement income. The potential tax savings from even the most basic planning are great. Tax shelters (ways of legitimately avoiding or deferring income taxes) are available to people of modest means as well as to those who are better off. Many people fail to accumulate as much retirement income as they might have because, before retirement, they did not take full advantage of what the tax laws allow.

To plan properly and sufficiently for your retirement, you not only have to think about retirement income; you must also consider other matters, such as insurance, housing, and related expenses.

BUILDING RETIREMENT INCOME

The major sources of retirement income include (1) Social Security benefits, (2) private pension plans, (3) payments from tax-deferred retirement accounts, and (4) returns from general investments. The first three sources relate to money you earn by working for an employer or through self-employment. You share in building your retirement income from one or more of these sources by making payments out of the money you earn.

Social Security Benefits

Social Security's original purpose was to supplement an individual's retirement income. And that purpose continues to be a major part of the Social Security system. We stress the word "supplement." Social Security retirement benefits were never intended to be anyone's sole source of retirement income. Retired persons were expected to provide some income either through a private pension plan or investments made during their working careers. The percentage of your preretirement income that Social Security payments will replace depends on your income. Generally, the higher your income, the lower Social Security's replacement percentage. Higher-income individuals must rely proportionally more on pension plans, tax-sheltered retirement accounts, and general investments for their retirement. We will return to the topic of replacement percentages later in the chapter.

One important feature of Social Security benefits is that they move with you. That is, no matter how many employers you have worked for, all your earnings count when your retirement benefits are estimated.

Private Pension Plans

Many people working in either private industry or the public sector are covered by their employer's pension plan. The **Employee Retirement Income Security Act (ERISA),** enacted in 1974, established certain minimum standards for private pension plans. The major thrust of that act was to spell out the rights of a pension-plan participant. It does not require that employers provide a pension. Nor, when an employer provides a pension plan, does it specify what form that plan must take. It does, however, establish minimum requirements for such things as when you are entitled to (or have a vested interest in) your pension rights, who must qualify for the pension, and how the pension benefits are accumulated.

When you switch jobs, you may or may not retain your pension rights from your previous job; that depends on whether your pension rights have been vested (we'll define that term in detail shortly). Your new employer will compute your retirement benefits based solely on your earnings at your new job—again, after you have fulfilled that company's vesting requirements. Pension plans, therefore, are less universal than Social Security benefits.

Defined-Benefit or Defined-Contribution Plan   Pension plans are either defined-benefit or defined-contribution plans. A **defined-benefit pension** plan uses a formula to specify what your benefits will be when you retire. Its formula is usually based on the years you have worked for the organization, coupled with the wages you have earned. It is the employer's responsibility to contribute sufficient money during your working career to provide the benefits called for in the plan. Defined-benefit plans are the most popular of the two plans.

Defined-contribution pension plans have a specified amount of money invested in your name. Thus, your employer might pay a set percentage of your annual salary into a retirement account. That amount would be invested in your name. Your pension benefits depend entirely upon the amount accumulated in your account. If the annual earnings on your pension account were sizable when combined with adequate annual contributions to the plan, you would likely receive a reasonable retirement benefit.

Vesting   Vesting is the technical term that designates the time when the pension benefits you have accumulated, or accrued, under a pension plan become yours. Even though your employer may have a pension plan, you are not guaranteed that you immediately earn rights to the money under that plan. First, some plans do not cover employees until they are 25 years old. Second, even when you are covered and begin to accumulate pension benefits, those benefits may not be your property. Some plans require you to work a set period of time before those benefits are vested in your name. Once vested, those benefits are legally yours. Should you leave the employer at that point, you retain those pension rights. You may not be able to collect your pension benefits immediately, however; many plans require that you wait until you have actually retired.

The vesting of your benefits in a pension plan typically follows one of three schedules:

Immediate: You are vested with your first salary payment. No waiting period is required.

Graduated: You vest, or earn, a fraction of your pension plan each year you work. After working 5 years, you may have vested 25 percent of your pension benefits. (Should you leave the company at this point, you would be entitled to 25 percent of your accrued pension benefits.) For the next 5 years, your vested portion may rise 5 percent each year. (After 10 years, you will be 50 percent vested.) For the next 5 years, your vesting may rise 10 percent per year. After 15 years, you will be 100 percent vested.

All or nothing: During the first 9-plus years with the employer, your vesting is zero. Then, at 10 years, you become 100 percent vested. Departing such a plan before that magic 10-year cutoff would leave you with nothing.

The above vesting schedules are the ERISA minimums; an employer can always have more liberal rules.

When considering a job, make certain that you understand how the vesting schedule for the firm's pension plan operates. It determines how rapidly your pension benefits will be vested, enabling you to take them with you should you change jobs. That schedule can be critical if you want to switch to a new employer. Many individuals have accepted a new job only to find that they left the old one several years too early to become fully, or substantially, vested in the pension plan. Therefore they have sacrificed benefits that might have totaled thousands of dollars. The new job would have to be irresistibly attractive to justify leaving behind those prior pension benefits.

Other Important Pension Features   In addition to the type of pension plan and the vesting schedule, you should investigate other provisions, such as (1) when you are covered, (2) who pays the plan's contributions, (3) whether the plan's benefits are integrated with Social Security provisions, (4) whether future benefits will be adjusted for inflation, (5) when you can collect benefits, (6) what happens if you die, and (7) what benefit payment options are offered. Exhibit 21-1 outlines a series of questions that address these points.

EXHIBIT 21-1

Questions and answers for evaluating a pension plan.

1 *Does eligibility for the plan begin at the start of employment, or is there a waiting period?*
The best plans do not have a waiting period. Less satisfactory plans may stipulate age and years of service for eligibility.

2 *Does the plan require employee contributions, or is it fully paid by the employer?*
Noncontributing plans are the best. However, a contributing plan may be satisfactory if the employee's share is low and the plan's provisions are adequate in all other categories.

3 *Will your retirement income from the pension be reduced by Social Security payments?*
A good pension plan does not reduce its payments because of Social Security payments.

4 *Are payments after retirement adjusted for inflation?*
The good plans are starting to include automatic adjustment provisions.

5 *Is early retirement available?*
Early retirement should be available at age 55 or 60 if the employee has a sufficient number of years vested.

6 *Does the plan have a death benefit that pays your beneficiaries if you die before retirement?*
Failure of the plan to include a death benefit is a severe weakness.

7 *Is there a variety of settlement options?*
A good plan permits a range of payment options similar to those provided by life insurance policies.

Tax-Deferred Retirement Accounts

Tax-deferred retirement accounts are one of the most effective ways to accumulate money for retirement. Income taxes on these accounts are merely postponed, or deferred, not eliminated. But by postponing those taxes, you gain several advantages. To begin, you can invest a portion of your current income without having to pay taxes on that money. Next, during the accumulation period (when you are adding money to your account), all returns on the account can be reinvested because you do not have to pay taxes as that income is earned. Furthermore, during the payout period (when you are collecting benefits and drawing down the account), your marginal tax rate will likely be lower, so the tax burden on those withdrawn dollars will be lower.

To illustrate, assume that Sidney Secure wonders whether he should invest $1000 of his current income in an **Individual Retirement Account** (IRA). (IRAs were first discussed back in Chapter 6.) His marginal tax rate is 40 percent and he expects he can earn a 10 percent return on the IRA account. Exhibit 21-2 summarizes Sidney's two investment options:

He can invest the $1000 in an IRA (middle column).

He can invest that $1000 in a general investment that earns a 10 percent return (far right column).

Clearly, the combination of deferring taxes on both the IRA's initial deposit and its earnings accelerates the account balance's growth. If Sidney continues to make annual deposits to his IRA for several years, that account will be much larger than if he follows the general investment option. Of course, when Sidney withdraws money from the IRA, every dollar he takes out is subject to income taxes. Sidney will never have paid any tax on the initial deposit or on the account's earnings. Presumably, at retirement his marginal tax rate will be less than his present 40 percent, since he will no longer be receiving a salary. Even if it is not, he should still consider a tax-deferred retirement account. All during the accumulation period, Sidney will earn a return on the entire initial deposit, and all the account's earnings will be reinvested to earn additional amounts.

Available Tax-Deferred Retirement Accounts There are four broad groups of tax-deferred accounts: (1) Keogh plans, (2) IRA plans, (3) salary-reduction plans for educators and employees of selected nonprofit organizations, and (4) salary-reduction plans for employees of some companies. Exhibit 21-3 summarizes the chief points of each alternative. We should add that the technical points shown here are the ones that prevailed in 1983

EXHIBIT 21-2

Comparison of a tax-deferred retirement
account and general investment, each earning
10 percent.

		Investment Accounts	
		IRA RETIREMENT	GENERAL INVESTMENT
Initial Deposit		$1000	$1000
Less: Taxes on initial deposit: 40% marginal tax rate		0	400
Net investment		$1000	$ 600
Return for first year: 10%	$100		$60
Less: Taxes on return: 40% tax rate	0		24
Net after-tax earnings		100	36
Balance after 1 year		$1100	$ 636

when this book was written. But this is a complex area and one where the Internal Revenue Service has made major changes during the past several years. Before you select one of these accounts, do check a tax reference manual, or your employer if you are considering an employer plan, for current regulations. The next section explains each option further.

Keogh Plan   Self-employed individuals can establish a **Keogh plan.** And self-employment need not be their sole source of income. To illustrate, suppose Phil Fast works for an accounting firm full-time and also prepares income tax returns for his own outside clients. Can he establish a Keogh plan? Yes. If Phil has earned $2000 from his tax-preparation business, his maximum contribution is $500 (25 percent of $2000). His regular salary cannot be used to compute his Keogh contribution.

All Keogh contributions are deducted as an adjustment to gross income. So you *do not* pay income taxes on deposits to your Keogh account.

IRA Plan   Everyone who earns money by working can establish an **IRA** account. The most you can contribute is the lesser of what you earn or $2000. If you are married and your spouse does not earn any income from working the maximum rises to $2250.

Contributions to an IRA are considered an adjustment to gross income. That adjustment reduces your income, so you pay no income tax on that amount.

EXHIBIT 21-3

Summary of currently available tax-deferred retirement accounts.

SPECIFICS	Tax-Deferred Retirement Options			
	KEOGH PLAN	IRA PLAN	SALARY REDUCTION	SALARY REDUCTION
Formal name of account	HR-10	IRA	403(b)	401(k)
Persons qualifying	Self-employed individuals	All paid workers	Educators and employees of some nonprofit groups	Employees of companies that offer such a plan
Maximum annual contribution	25% of self-employment income; $30,000 max.	Lower of $2,000 or earned income	Generally 20% of income, but pension can lower percentage	Generally 15% of income, but company may set lower maximum
Earliest age to receive benefits	59½	59½	59½	59½
Preretirement withdrawals allowed	On death, disability	On death, disability	On death, disability, or "serious" financial need	On death, disability, or "serious" financial need
Who decides the investment options	Individual	Individual	Range offered by employer	Range offered by employer

You must begin withdrawals from your IRA plan during the year you reach 70½ years of age. Since most people will be retired at that point, this is not a serious time limitation for them. Finally, you cannot continue annual contributions to your plan once you are 70½ years old.

Salary Reduction: Educators and Some Nonprofit Organizations Educators and employees of some nonprofit organizations may establish a **salary-reduction plan** (called a 403 (b) plan) if their employer provides this option. Under such a plan, a portion of the employee's salary is not paid to the individual; instead, it is invested in a qualifying tax-deferred investment program. Qualifying programs are offered by many mutual funds and insurance companies. To obtain the tax deferral, your employer must deduct your contribution from your salary before paying that salary. You are not permitted to deposit money in the plan yourself. So it is, literally, salary reduction, and it is essential that your employer be willing to make the reductions. Since you were not paid the money in your salary, it is not included in gross income on your annual W-2 statement. You do not pay income taxes on the reduction.

Your range of investment choices for a salary-reduction plan is limited to what your employer offers. Frequently, the choices include plans from insurance companies (the most numerous) and mutual funds (less frequent). Often the plans offered by insurance companies entail an annuity (we will discuss annuities later in the chapter). As an annuity, the tax regulations allow you to withdraw money prior to retirement for a wider range of reasons. Mutual funds, on the other hand, typically allow withdrawals prior to retirement for only three reasons: death, disability, or "serious" financial need. (Typically, serious needs include the purchase of a home, major medical expenses, and a child's education.) Of course, whenever the money is withdrawn, you must pay income taxes on it. The maximum amount you can contribute is usually 20 percent of your salary. But your employer's pension plan can reduce that maximum. So check your employer for your maximum.

Salary Reduction: Employees of For-Profit Organizations A number of for-profit organizations have begun offering a **salary-reduction plan** (called a 401(k) plan) which allows their employees to direct a portion of their salaries directly into tax-deferred investment plan. These newer plans differ from earlier company "thrift," or savings, plans in that you invest before-tax dollars. That means any dollars you invest in the plan are *not* part of your income and therefore you need pay no income taxes on them. In the past, dollars invested in thrift, or savings, plans were always included in your income. Consequently, you were investing after-tax dollars because you paid taxes on that money. And, as Exhibit 21-2 graphically illustrated, taxes can decimate those dollars before you get them invested.

Like the previously discussed salary-reduction plan, your contribution must be deducted from your salary before you receive it. You cannot make direct deposits. Since these plans were first offered only in 1982, they are not universal among employers. But indications are that an increasing number of employers will probably start offering salary-reduction plans.

Investment options that are open to you under a salary-reduction plan

I DON'T MEAN TO DISCOURAGE YOU
ABOUT SETTING UP A RETIREMENT
PLAN, MR. MARTIN. HOWEVER...

are limited to those provided by your employer. If present plans are any sign, investment options are likely to include one or more of the following: the common stock of your employer, a group of fixed-return investments, and a group of variable-return investments. (A mutual fund could be used for either investment option.) Most salary-reduction plans permit withdrawals prior to retirement for three causes: death, disability, and "serious" financial need.

Are Tax-Deferred Retirement Accounts a Good Choice? An unequivocal and emphatic *yes*. All the tax-deferred retirement accounts are excellent vehicles to accumulate money for retirement. By deferring taxes on the initial investments as well as on their earnings, your account will build rapidly. At the same time, your taxes will be reduced because you are shifting some income from your working years to your retirement period. This advice is especially appropriate if you must provide most of your retirement income. Those who qualify for several different plans might want to use more than one plan depending on their needs. For example, an educator with some self-employment income might establish:

A salary reduction plan with the employer

A Keogh plan for the self-employment income

An IRA plan

General Investments

All the **general investments** you accumulate during your working career can also provide retirement income. Those investments may be the mutual funds that you invested in during your working career. During retirement, you may well decide to cease further investment in those funds. In fact, you may decide to start drawing money from those accounts to provide retirement income. As another example, retirement income can come from the money you have accumulated in the cash-value component of your life insurance. At retirement, you may well decide that life insurance coverage is no longer necessary. By liquidating that cash value you can obtain retirement income.

General investments are usually not so effective as one of the tax-deferred options for accumulating retirement funds. First, you will be investing after-tax dollars. You must pay income taxes on the money *before* it is invested. Furthermore, the earnings on most general investments are also subject to income taxes. Not only do you start with fewer dollars, but you have a lower amount of the investment's earnings to reinvest after taxes.

STRATEGY

Given a choice between general investments and tax-deferred accounts, you should consider the latter as a much better way to accumulate retirement income.

ESTIMATING RETIREMENT INCOME NEEDS

One thing is certain: Planning is required to ensure having enough income to live comfortably during your 20 or more years of retirement. Social Security will not meet all your retirement needs. Even a pension plan coupled with Social Security benefits may not be adequate to meet your retirement goals. You may still have to supplement those two sources with your own accumulated funds.

The first step in planning your **retirement income needs** is to develop a detailed schedule of what those needs will likely be. Granted, the income projections may stretch some 20 to 40 years in the future for someone who has only recently entered the work force. Making those projections is a formidable task that requires some major assumptions. But we greatly prefer doing that chore to the other alternative: Doing nothing and hoping for the best! We suggest you plan for retirement as you would for any other long-term financial goal:

Clearly specify the future dollar cost of your goal.

Establish the time you expect to implement that goal.

Estimate how you will accumulate the dollars to achieve that goal.

During your working career, you will certainly need to revise certain parts of that goal. But even with those changes, you will have *planned* for comfortable retirement rather than just *hoped* for it.

Income Needed during Retirement

The first step is to estimate what income you will likely need when you retire. We assume that most people would like to maintain a standard of living in retirement similar to what they had while working. You need to know what percentage of your current working income you will need to maintain a similar life style in retirement. We would expect it to be less than 100 percent. After all, some expenditures (such as work-related expenses, savings, and Social Security taxes) may be eliminated. Other things, like income taxes, will be reduced. Exhibit 21-4 summarizes what percentage of various preretirement incomes must be replaced in retirement in order for both single people and married couples to maintain similar standards of living.

A review of Exhibit 21-4 shows that the percentage of preretirment income needed declines as income rises. Several factors account for that decline. First, higher-income individuals are assumed to save and invest a higher percentage of their income than do moderate-income persons during their working years. Since they will probably not be saving and investing after they retire, there is no need to replace that portion of income. Second, higher-income individuals pay sizable income and Social Security taxes during their working careers. Since the Social Security benefits that provide part of their retirement income are frequently tax-free, their tax burden declines. Less income is needed because less is lost to taxes.

Let us use several examples to demonstrate how Exhibit 21-4 can be used. Assume that Ted Elgin is single and is now earning $15,000. He needs $9,941 of retirement income, or 66 percent of his preretirement income, to maintain his current living standard. As a second example, assume that Earl and Jan Woo want to determine what part of their present combined $30,000 income they should plan to replace in retirement. Based on Exhibit 21-4, they will need roughly $18,062, or 60 percent, of their present income during retirement.

What if your income falls in between the levels shown in Exhibit 21-4? We would just interpolate, or average, the two replacement percentages that bracket your income. Thus, a single person earning $17,500 will need to replace approximately 63.5 percent. That is midway between the percentages for $15,000 and $20,000 incomes.

EXHIBIT 21-4

Retirement income required to maintain preretirement living standards

BEFORE-TAX RETIREMENT INCOME[†]	**Required Retirement Income***			
	SINGLE PERSON		MARRIED COUPLE	
$10,000	$ 7,272	73%[‡]	$ 7,786	78%[‡]
15,000	9,941	66	10,684	71
20,000	12,282	61	13,185	66
30,000	17,391	58	18,062	60
50,000	25,675	51	27,384	55

* Assumes retiring person qualifies for Social Security.
[†]Assumed income for individual or couple retiring in 1980.
[‡]Required retirement income as a percentage of preretirement income given in column 1.
Source: President's Commission on Pension Policy, November 1980.

The goal of Exhibit 21-4 is not to give a precise dollar estimate. Instead, it provides an estimate that can be used to plan retirement needs.

Inflation's Impact on Future Retirement Income Needs Clearly, as inflation pushes up prices in future periods, an individual's retirement income will also have to rise if present living standards are to be maintained. Doesn't that mean it's pointless to estimate your future income needs using today's income, as we did in Exhibit 21-4? We don't think so. Rather than attempt to inflate current retirement income needs to compensate for some future unknown inflation, we favor adjusting the sources of that income. That is, if you can adjust the sources of your retirement income in such a way that they will rise with inflation, your retirement income dollars should likewise rise. Despite higher prices, your higher income should permit a continuation of your present living standard.

Providing the Required Retirement Income

Once you estimate your retirement income needs, you should ask: Where will that income come from? We summarized earlier the four major sources:

Social Security retirement benefits

Employer pension plan

Tax-deferred retirement accounts

Regular investments

Of the four, we consider the first two as the primary sources of retirement income. We will first rely on the benefits from Social Security and pension plans to meet retirement needs. Only when they are inadequate will we look to tax-deferred retirement accounts and general investments to make up the difference.

The next step is to estimate what retirement income Social Security and employer pension plan(s) will provide. After that, we can estimate what retirement income must come from tax-deferred retirement accounts and general investments. On the basis of those needs, we can develop a financial goal to accumulate the money for that retirement income.

The easiest way to demonstrate the retirement income planning process is through an example. Assume that Ann Wells wants to plan her retirement income needs. Currently, she earns $20,000 annually and she is single. Exhibit 21-5 summarizes the various steps in Ann's retirement income plan. With her current $20,000 income, Ann estimates, based on Exhibit 21-4, that she will need approximately $12,282 a year after she retires; this is the starting point for the top of Exhibit 21-5.

Social Security Retirement Benefits Ideally, you should be able to ask the Social Security Administration to estimate what your likely future retirement benefit will be, based on your present income. Unfortunately, as this is written, the Social Security people provide such an estimate only 1 or

2 years before actual retirement. And that is much too late to do any meaningful retirement planning. Consequently, you must estimate your own benefits. One way to do that is through the income replacement table shown back in Exhibit 13-9. We readily admit that it provides only a rough approximation of what your benefits will likely be in a few years. But then, given a choice of no estimate or a rough approximation, we will gladly take the latter.

On the basis of Exhibit 13-9, Ann estimates that her Social Security payments will replace 34 percent of her current salary. That will give her a benefit of $6800, which is shown on line 2 of Exhibit 21-5. Clearly, Social Security will meet a significant portion of her total retirement needs.

We don't have to adjust Social Security benefits for inflation because the computation of benefits already contains an adjustment. If inflation averages 10 percent annually, Ann's benefit should rise by a similar amount. When she actually retires, her benefit will be considerably larger than the $6800 shown in Exhibit 21-5. Of course, prices will be much higher, so she will need that extra income to buy the same goods that $6800 of current dollars now buy.

Employer's Pension Plan Since defined-benefit pension plans are the most prevalent, we will concentrate on that type. Defined-benefit pension plans generally compute your monthly retirement pension using one of two techniques. Some pay a set dollar amount for each year you have worked for the employer. Thus, a pension plan might pay $7 monthly after you retire for each year of service. Had you worked for that employer 10 years, your monthly pension payment would be $70. With 30 years of service, your monthly pension payment would rise to $210.

Other pension plans pay a specified percentage of salary for each year you have worked for the employer. Thus, a pension plan might specify that an employee will receive 1 percent of the average salary received during the

EXHIBIT 21-5

CHAPTER 21

687

RETIREMENT AND
ESTATE PLANNING

Planning sources of retirement income.

1	Total retirement income needed*	= $12,282
2	Social Security retirement benefit:	

$20,000	× 34%	= $ 6,800
Preretirement income	Replacement precentage†	

3	Employer pension plan:

$15,000	× 30 years × 1.0%	= $ 4,500
Average income		

4	Retirement needs that remain:

Line 1 − (line 2 + line 3)	= $ 982

5	Required tax-deferred retirement account:

$982	× 25 years	= $24,550
Annual needs	Years of retirement	

6	Annual contribution to achieve retirement account:

$24,550	÷ 41.65	= $589.44
Total required amount (line 5)	Interest factor (Exhibit 1-6‡)	

*Based on details from Exhibit 21-4.
†Based on percentages shown in Exhibit 13-9.
‡Assumes 4% real interest rate and 25 years to accumulate money.

years of employment with the company. If you had worked for that company 10 years, your monthly pension payment would equal 10 percent of your average monthly salary. With 30 years of work credit, your payment would rise to 30 percent of your average salary. The "average salary" that a pension plan uses in its benefit computation typically takes one of two forms:

> The average salary earned during the most recent 3 to 5 years that the employee worked for the company

> The average salary the employee earned during the entire period of working for the company

The first technique has the decided advantage that it concentrates on your most recent work experience. For most people, those years will be the ones of their highest salary. A typical plan might average your highest annual salaries for 3 of the last 5 years you worked for the company. Or the plan might average the 5 highest years from your last 10 years with the company. The second averaging technique concentrates on your average salary during your entire working career. A major deficiency is that it includes your early years with the company, when your salary was likely much lower. Some companies use a higher percentage replacement for each year of work credit to offset this deficiency.

For our example, we will assume that the benefit under Ann Well's pension plan equals 1 percent of average salary for each year an employee works for the firm. The company computes average salary using all the employee's earnings since starting work with the firm. Ann expects she will have 30 years of work credit with the firm by the time she retires. Further, her average salary since joining the company is $15,000. Based on these two amounts, her estimated pension benefit will be:

$$\$4,500 = \$15,000 \times 1\% \times 30 \text{ years}$$

$$\underset{\substack{\text{Pension} \\ \text{benefit}}}{\triangle} = \underset{\substack{\text{Average} \\ \text{salary}}}{\triangle} \times \underset{\substack{\text{Replacement} \\ \text{percentage}}}{\triangle} \times \underset{\substack{\text{Years of service}}}{\triangle}$$

This amount is shown on line 3 of Exhibit 21-5.

Pension plans that base benefits on a percentage of your salary should adjust for inflation up to the time of your retirement. As inflation pushes up prices, your salary should also rise. Increases in your salary will raise your pension benefits. Plans that base average salary on the final 3 to 5 years with the company will provide a much better adjustment for inflation because they concentrate on your recent salary. Less effective are plans that use the individual's entire work history. Average salary in these plans is held down by the inclusion of early years when earnings are likely lower. How well a pension plan with fixed dollar benefits adjusts for inflation depends on whether that dollar benefit rises with inflation. To adjust fully, the pension benefit must rise at the same rate as inflation.

With most plans, the benefit stays fixed once you retire: It does not adjust for inflation. If inflation pushes up prices, the purchasing power of your benefit will decline. A few plans have raised current retiree benefits to offset some of the inflation since retirement. But any such adjustment is not guaranteed and most have not begun to match inflation. All these problems suggest that you may want to provide an income cushion in your needs computation. That may entail providing retirement income that starts out 10 to 20 percent above your initial needs. Later, you can use that extra income to offset the inflation-induced decline in the purchasing power of your fixed pension payment. We can use the example of Ann Wells's retirement plan from Exhibit 21-5 to illustrate. Since her pension benefit must provide a sizable portion of her retirement needs, she may want to add 10 to 20 percent to her retirement needs, shown in line 1. This adjustment would recognize that once Ann retires, her pension benefit remains fixed. By initially providing 10 to 20 percent extra income, she would offset some of the subsequent declines in the purchasing power of her pension benefit.

Information on Your Employer's Pension Plan   Many individuals do not even know how their employer's pension plan operates, let alone what their present standing is under the plan. There is no need to be uninformed. First, most employer's personnel departments have a brochure or summary sheet that outlines the details of the employer's pension plan. That should answer the first concern. Second, ERISA requires that, if you ask, your employer must provide an annual statement summarizing your benefits under the pension plan, but *only* if you request the statement. Typically, a statement shows your years of credited service with the employer as well as your vested benefits under the plan. Regrettably, all too many employers do not automatically provide annual statements.

STRATEGY

Unless your employer routinely provides an annual statement of your pension benefits, request one. If you are unclear about the plan and its operation, ask the employer for these details. This information is an essential basis for a personal financial plan.

Tax-Deferred Retirement Accounts So far, we have estimated what Social Security and pension benefits can contribute toward your retirement needs. Now let us estimate how large a tax-deferred retirement account you need to complete your retirement plan. Individuals whose Social Security and pension benefits are sizable will find their needs for additional income are modest. But if Social Security and your pension plan provide only a small fraction of your total retirement needs, you will want to have a substantial tax-deferred retirement account.

Estimating the required tax-deferred retirement account balance requires two pieces of information:

How many dollars are required each year of your retirement

How many years your retirement will likely continue

The annual required dollar amount is the amount that remains after deducting both Social Security and pension plan benefits from your total retirement needs. This figure is shown on line 4 of Exhibit 21-5. For Ann Wells (our example in Exhibit 21-5), that dollar amount is $982 per year.

Your life expectancy at the time you retire determines the length of your retirement period. One way to estimate life expectancy is to use a mortality table; we discussed this in Chapter 14. Such a table gives a rough estimate of how many years you will likely need a retirement income. For general guidance, we would plan a 20-year retirement period for a man retiring at age 65; for a woman, we would use 25 years. Actual life expectancy at age 65 is less than the suggested 20- and 25-year periods. But by adding several years, you provide a cushion that reduces the possibility of outliving your planned retirement income. Someone retiring at age 60 would just add 5 years to the above estimates.

Ann Wells's case will be used to demonstrate these two steps. Recall, from Exhibit 21-5, that she estimated her tax-deferred retirement account must provide approximately $982 each year of retirement. If she expects her retirement period will extend 25 years, her retirement account should total:

$24,550 = $982 × 25 years

⬆ ⬆ ⬆

$$\underset{\text{account}}{\underset{\text{retirement}}{\text{Required}}} = \underset{\text{income needed}}{\text{Annual}} \times \underset{\text{retirement}}{\text{Years of}}$$

Line 5 of Exhibit 21-5 shows this amount.

To implement this financial goal, the required retirement account balance must be converted to an annual amount. During the years you are accumulating the money, the tax-deferred retirement account will be earning interest; how *much* interest depends on how long the money remains in the account. You need to estimate how many dollars you must invest in the retirement account each year to achieve the required balance. Two pieces of information are required for the estimate:

The number of years until you will retire

What rate of return the account will earn while accumulating the money

The number of years depends on your current age and the date at which you plan to retire. For Ann Wells, we assume that she expects it will be 25 years before she retires.

For the rate of return, we suggest the expected *real rate of return* rather than the current nominal, or stated, return. While accumulating the money, part of the earnings on the account will be needed to offset inflation. Using the real return recognizes that fact by deducting inflation immediately. (Real return can be approximated by deducting the current inflation rate from the current interest rate.) For Ann Wells, we assume the real rate of return is 4 percent.

In Chapter 1 we demonstrated how you can use Exhibit 1-6 to estimate what annual investment is needed in order to accumulate a given future dollar amount. That is exactly what we need here. We already have the future amount needed: It equals the balance required in your tax-deferred retirement account. We have the accumulation period: It is the years you plan to work before you retire. Finally, we need the expected interest rate: It equals the real return you expect to earn on the account. For Ann Wells, the required annual contribution to her tax-deferred account equals:

$589.44 = $24,550 ÷ 41.65

⬆ ⬆ ⬆

$$\underset{\text{contribution}}{\text{Annual}} = \underset{\text{balance}}{\text{Total required}} \div \underset{\substack{\text{factor: 25 years} \\ \text{and 4\%}}}{\text{Interest}}$$

This amount is shown on line 6 of Exhibit 21-5.

Two inflation adjustments have been incorporated in the tax-deferred computations of the prior section. The estimate ignored any and all interest earnings the tax deferred account will earn during the retirement years while the payments are being made. Any balance remaining in the account continues to earn interest. Ignoring interest provides an allowance to offset inflation during those years.

During the accumulation period, the estimate was based on the potential real rate of return. That adds another inflation adjustment by recognizing that part of the account's earnings are needed to offset inflation. The combination of the two adjustments provides a conservative estimate of retirement needs.

General Investments Because of the highly favorable tax treatment given to tax-deferred investment accounts, most people should rely on such accounts to accumulate the money for their retirement needs. Consequently, in most cases, we consider general investments to be a secondary source of retirement income. However, under certain circumstances, general investments may be a significant part of a retirement plan.

One case might be where you expect to accumulate a sizable dollar balance in a general investment program during your working years. That money will likely be available at retirement time. Those general investments reduce any required balance in your tax-deferred retirement account. How do you incorporate this change? To start, you will need to estimate roughly how many dollars your general investment program will contain at retirement. Your dollar estimate should recognize both the deposits you will make and the interest you will earn up to your retirement. Again, we would favor using the expected real rate of return rather than the nominal, or stated, return, in order to provide an allowance for inflation.

It is possible that the money you will accumulate in general investments will replace all, or at least part, of your required tax-deferred retirement balance. To determine that possibility, go back to line 5 of Exhibit 21-5 to see what your tax-deferred retirement needs were. If your needs from line 5 are equal to, or less than, the balance you will likely have in general investments, you will not have to accumulate any additional money in a tax-deferred retirement account. Of course, if your needs on line 5 exceed what you will have in general investments, you will have to make up that difference. You can do this by accumulating that difference in a tax-deferred retirement account.

Another exception where general investments may be important is where your retirement needs are very large, especially where they exceed the amount you are permitted to contribute to a tax-deferred retirement account. Owing to limits on your maximum annual contribution, you may not be able to accumulate a sufficiently large balance in your tax-deferred plan. That restriction can force you to rely on general investments to complete your retirement plan. Computing the necessary annual deposit for a general investment plan parallels the method used for a tax-deferred retirement account:

Estimate what annual retirement income your general investment program must provide.

Given your expected retirement period, convert that annual amount into a total required dollar balance.

Estimate what annual deposit you need to make to accumulate the total required dollar balance.

Because the earnings on most general investments are subject to income taxes, your actual return after paying taxes will be considerably lower than the nominal, or stated, return. Consequently, you should use an after-tax interest rate when estimating the total dollar balance you will need.

PAYMENTS FROM YOUR RETIREMENT PLAN

Most people generally find that the dividends and interest from their tax-deferred retirement accounts and their general investment accounts just do not provide their desired retirement income. To supplement that return, they must also gradually liquidate part of the money held in these investment accounts. One concern in such a plan is to forgo drawing those investments down so rapidly that they are exhausted while the individual still needs an income. A perfect plan would have the balance in investments exhausted right at the point when the retired person dies. No one can plan that with certainty. But, through careful planning, you can design a withdrawal plan that will provide benefits extending across your retirement years. Two retirement payout plans are available. You can purchase an annuity. Then the insurance company that sold the annuity will set the monthly benefit payment. Or you can tailor your own payout plan to the amount of money you have available.

Annuities

Purchasing an annuity from an insurance company is the most conservative way of liquidating the value of your investments. With it you are certain that your income will continue for as long as you live. An **annuity** is a contract which guarantees that you will receive a set income every year for life. Through the process of risk sharing (much like that found in life insurance), people living "too long" continue to receive income at the expense of those who died "too early." The size of your payment is determined by three factors: (1) the dollar amount you invest in the annuity, (2) the interest rate that the insurance company pays on your investment, and (3) the payment option you select.

Your investment in an annuity can be either a single lump-sum payment—a **single premium**—or a series of annual payments—**annual premiums.** Obviously, the larger your payments into the annuity, the larger your payments from that annuity.

The interest rate the insurance company pays on the annuity also heavily influences your payments. And it is by no means uniform among different life insurance companies. Some rates exceed 10 percent, yet some are as low as 4 percent. Careful comparison shopping is essential.

The payment method you select determines how the benefits will be paid out under the annuity. We will discuss three of the most popular payment options here.

Straight-Life Annuity   Under a **straight-life** annuity, the benefits continue only as long as the annuitant (the person covered by the annuity) lives. When the annuitant dies, all payments cease. The payment period may therefore be as short as a few weeks or it may extend for quite a number of years. Because its sole purpose is providing benefits to the annuitant, a straight-life annuity offers the highest benefit for each premium dollar. But it does not guarantee any specific dollar payment. Should the annuitant die shortly after buying the annuity, very little of the premium payment would have been returned as benefits.

Guaranteed Minimum Payment   The annuitant who elects a **guaranteed minimum payment** option receives a guaranteed series of payments. That guarantee typically covers a set period, such as 5 years, 10 years, or 20 years. Should the annuitant die during that guarantee period, payments continue to the annuitant's estate or beneficiaries until the end of that period. Payments under the guaranteed minimum payment option are lower than under the straight-life option. And the longer the guarantee period, the larger the benefit reduction.

Joint and Survivor Payment   With the **joint and survivor payment** option, payments continue as long as either of the two persons named in the annuity survive. The benefit payment the survivor receives after the first person dies may equal the payment the two people received or it may be a portion of that payment. Under this option, the annuity must continue payments for two individuals' lifetimes, so the payments are lower than those offered by a straight-life annuity.

When Payments Begin: Immediate or Deferred   **Immediate annuities** are purchased with a single premium and the payments start immediately. An immediate annuity is most frequently purchased by someone who has just retired and who wants to convert a sum of money into a guaranteed stream of payments. The money can be from his or her tax-deferred retirement account, general investments, the sale of a house, or a lump-sum payment from an employer's pension plan.

Deferred annuities do not begin paying benefits until some specified period after the annuity's purchase. That purchase can be made through either a single lump-sum premium or a series of annual premiums. While these annuities ask you to set a starting date for payments at the time of purchase, most allow you to delay or accelerate that date later on.

A deferred annuity's principal advantage is that it postpones, or defers, any income taxes on its earnings. As long as those earnings remain invested in the annuity, you pay no income taxes. But once you begin drawing money from the annuity, you must pay income taxes on that money. Those payments are considered to be part of the annuity's earnings on which taxes have not been paid.

The premiums (lump-sum or recurring) to purchase the annuity receive no special tax treatment. When accumulating money for retirement, the previously discussed tax-deferred retirement accounts are the clear-choice over deferred annuities.

STRATEGY

Before considering a deferred annuity, you should exhaust all your tax-deferred retirement account alternatives. The latter not only provide a much better tax advantage; they also offer a wide range of investment options.

Advantages and Disadvantages of Annuities   The principal advantages and disadvantages of annuities are summarized in Exhibit 21-6. Two of them need some explanation. The fixed payments of annuities can be a serious disadvantage to someone whose retirement needs vary from one year to the next. The limited rate of return on some annuities is also a major shortcoming. Many alternative investments provide a higher return with similar risk. Our opinion is that, in most cases, the advantages of annuities do not offset their disadvantages.

STRATEGY

We believe annuities are appropriate in the following circumstances:

Immediate annuities are suitable in retirement situations where safety and guaranteed income for life are essential.

Deferred annuities are best used after you have exhausted your tax-deferred retirement options. Or, they can be used when you have a large single premium to invest and need the annuity's tax deferral.

Designing a Payout Plan for Your Retirement

If your total investments (tax-deferred retirement accounts plus general investments) are large enough, you will need to draw only the interest and

EXHIBIT 21-6

Advantages and disadvantages of annuities.

	Advantages		Disadvantages
1	Payments that you cannot outlive are guaranteed.	**1**	Dollars returned can be very limited if the annuitant dies shortly after benefits begin.
2	Income taxes on earnings from a deferred annuity are postponed.	**2**	A tax penalty is imposed on withdrawals from an annuity not held 10 years, unless annuitant is over 59½ years of age.
3	A retired person concerned with guaranteed income can have peace of mind.	**3**	Premiums to purchase the annuity receive no special tax advantage.
4	Risk is extremely low.	**4**	Returns on many annuities are disappointingly low.
		5	Payments are fixed: annuitant cannot alter them to fit needs.

dividends as retirement income. (We will call that a **nonliquidating payout plan**.) You are quite fortunate if that is the case. Because the investments remain intact, your heirs are also fortunate: They will inherit your holdings in the end. The top portion of Exhibit 21-7 illustrates just such a situation. Wanda Welloff has $100,000 in investments that are paying an 8 percent return. Because she has other retirement income, she draws only $8000, the earnings that the investment generates. If Wanda survives for 20 years, her investments will still total $100,000. So her heirs will receive that $100,000 on her death.

Not all retirees will find the interest and dividends from their investments are adequate. They must liquidate a small part of their investments each year to provide additional retirement income. (We will call this a **liquidating payout plan**.) Assume that Sam Shortfall, unlike Wanda, needs more income than just the $8000 of dividends and interest from his $100,000 of investments. Sam's other sources of retirement income are not large, so he must liquidate part of his investments to supplement his income. He wants to set the annual withdrawal just large enough so that the investments will provide payments for 20 years. At the end of those 20 years, the $100,000 will be completely liquidated. Consequently, his heirs will receive nothing.

Of course, Sam receives a larger income than the $8000 available if he had used just the investments' earnings. How much larger? The next section illustrates those computations, but for now, we will tell you Sam's annual payment is $10,185. We have illustrated his liquidating payout plan in the right half of Exhibit 21-7.

How large an annual payment a particular investment can provide depends on three things: (1) the size of the investment, (2) the annual rate of return that investment earns, and (3) how long the payments must continue. To design a good retirement payout plan, you need information on these three points. Your concern is to obtain as much income as possible, yet have that income continue for the whole time you are retired. Too large an

EXHIBIT 21-7

Two retirement payout plans, nonliquidating and liquidating, for a $100,000 investment earning an 8 percent return.

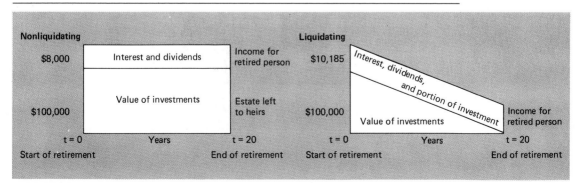

annual withdrawal means exhausting the investment before you, the retiree, die. Too small a withdrawal can force an individual to scrape by on a barely adequate income. Yet, at death, there still will be a sizable amount that could have been used for income.

Exhibit 21-8 shows how large an annual withdrawal you can make from a $1000 investment at different rates of return for different time periods. Suppose you want to know what annual withdrawal you can make from $1000 if you earn an 8 percent return and if your withdrawals have to continue for 20 years. As shown in Exhibit 21-8, you can withdraw $101.85 each year. Part of that $101.85 will be the interest or dividends earned on your $1000 investment. The balance will be drawn from the investment itself. Over the 20-year period, the entire $1000 investment will be consumed. When you draw your twentieth payment, the value of the investment will be zero. As you would expect, the longer the withdrawal period, the smaller those withdrawals can be. Also, the higher the investment's return, the larger the withdrawal can be. Since Exhibit 21-8 deals with $1000, it can readily be used for other amounts. Let us return to Sam Shortfall from the last section. Sam had $100,000 of investments and planned to make withdrawals over 20 years. During that time, he expected the investments to earn an 8 percent return. Sam's annual withdrawal is:

$$\$10,185 \quad = \$101.85 \quad \times (\$100,000 \quad \div \$1,000)$$

| Annual withdrawal | = Annual withdrawal: $1000 over 20 years at 8% | × Total investment | ÷ $1,000 |

That $10,185 is significantly more than the $8000 of interest and dividends which the $100,000 investment earns at 8 percent. The key is the fact that

EXHIBIT 21-8

Annual withdrawals from $1000 with different rates of return for various periods.

NUMBER OF YEARS	Rates of return						
	4%	6%	8%	10%	12%	14%	16%
4	$275.49	$288.59	$301.92	$315.47	$329.23	$343.20	$357.38
8	148.53	161.04	174.01	187.44	201.30	215.57	230.22
12	106.55	119.28	132.70	146.76	161.44	176.67	192.41
16	85.82	98.95	112.98	127.82	143.39	159.62	176.41
20	73.58	87.18	101.85	117.46	133.88	150.99	168.67
24	65.59	79.68	94.98	111.30	128.46	146.30	164.67
28	60.01	74.59	90.49	107.45	125.24	143.66	162.55
32	55.95	71.00	87.45	104.97	123.28	142.15	161.40
36	52.89	68.39	85.34	103.34	122.06	141.26	160.77

part of the $100,000 is being withdrawn each year to supplement interest and dividends: Sam is gradually liquidating his investment.

How Long a Retirement Period? Ideally, we would like the payout period for the withdrawals to equal the individual's remaining life span. But that ideal is not possible. A mortality table (introduced in Chapter 14) shows how many more years the *average* male or female of a certain age will continue to live. But the table is based on averages, which means some people live longer and some not so long. As a starting point for planning, you might use a mortality table. However, we favor adding a few years to your expected life span to provide a safety margin. As a rough guide, we suggest using 20-year payout period for males who are 65 years old and a 25-year period for women who are 65.

ESTATE PLANNING

Picture this scene in a lawyer's office. Sitting before the lawyer's desk for the reading of a will is the bereaved family of the deceased; all are potential heirs; all are mourning the departed but are expecting something. The lawyer begins to read the will: "Being of sound mind, I spent every damn cent before I died."

This represents a highly practical way to dispose of assets—to use and enjoy to the fullest all our material things and our money, exhausting them at the very time we expire, leaving nothing behind. But it is not possible to do so. We must plan and invest during our early working years to have

THE GOOD NEWS IS I INVESTED EVERYTHING IN 'ESTATE PLANNING'... THE BAD NEWS IS HE CAME IN LAST AT BELMONT....

investments that produce income regularly and for an indefinite period during our retirement years. And we should prepare to leave to our heirs in an orderly and efficient way what remains of our investments and material goods. The formal name for this is **estate planning.** It is simply the process of choosing the best way to dispose of everything a person owns. The disposition of an estate may take place prior to, at, or many years after the death of the person holding the assets.

WILLS

One thing is certain if you die without having made a **will:** You won't be aware of the unnecessary trouble and chaos you will have caused your family. All your worldly possessions, everything you own, which upon your death are called your **estate,** will be assigned to a court of law to decide who gets what. The process can be very complicated, time-consuming, costly (the expenses are paid out of your estate), and in the end, the heirs may not be the ones you would have preferred. In cases where the immediate survivors are minors, the court must appoint a guardian or trustee, who gets a fee that comes out of the estate. The estate will be placed in trust until the minors become legal adults. All these problems can be avoided or reduced if you have made a will.

Writing a will is a relatively straightforward and inexpensive procedure. Most lawyers are happy to draft wills, and the fee for a standard one may run from $50 to $200. Despite the ease of making a will and its modest cost, many people do not have one.

Do Not Do It Yourself Trying to avoid the legal fee by writing a will yourself can be a costly mistake. Even simple wills must comply with state laws regarding the details of execution, that is, how to go about doing what must be done to have a valid will. One of the common faults of do-it-yourself wills is improper witnessing. The cost of having an attorney prepare the document is a small price to pay for the assurance that it satisfies all the legal requirements. If you write the will yourself, even if your intent is clear and reasonable, failure to execute it properly may cause your family a great deal of expense and many legal complications. Why even take the chance when you can be sure everything is properly done by having a lawyer do it?

Intestate A person who dies without an executed will is said to have died **intestate.** The distribution of an estate that is intestate is determined by state laws, not by the wishes of the deceased. Even if that distribution conflicts with the desires of the deceased's survivors, nothing can be done to change it.

A typical state law may call for property to be distributed to both the surviving spouse and the children. The major problems occur when one or more of the children is a minor. In such cases, a trustee—not the surviving parent—must be appointed to oversee the child's money. Usually, the trustee will have to post a bond and file annual reports with the court under whose jurisdiction the trust was set up. These costs could easily have been

EXHIBIT 21-9

CHAPTER 21

699

RETIREMENT AND
ESTATE PLANNING

Distribution of property when no will exists.

STATUS OF DECEASED		PROPERTY TO
1	Married, one child	Spouse, 50% Child, 50%
2	Married, two or more children	Spouse, 33% Children, 67%
3	Married, no children, parent(s) surviving	Spouse, 75% Parent(s), 25%
4	Married, no children, parents deceased	Spouse, all
5	Unmarried, parent(s) surviving	Parent(s), all
6	Unmarried, parents deceased, surviving brother(s) and/or sister(s)	Brother(s) and/or sister(s) equally

avoided through a will. Exhibit 21-9 gives typical intestate distribution provisions for married and unmarried individuals.

Probate   When a person dies, his or her will is reviewed in a court hearing. The process is known as **probating** a will. All assets that pass to heirs through the will are subject to probate. And because probate means going through the courts, the services of an attorney will be necessary. Legal fees for probating a will are usually a percentage of the estate's value. Consequently, the greater the value of the property subject to probate, the higher the legal fee. Property can be distributed without probating if it is held in certain forms of joint ownership. Details of joint ownership will be discussed more fully in a later section.

Major Provisions of a Will   Wills may vary in length and the degree to which they specify the distribution of the individual's property. In general, however, standard wills have many or all of the following features:

1   *An introductory statement:* "I, Joan Swift, of Clare, Michigan, being of sound mind, do hereby make this my last will and testament. . . . "

2   *A statement calling for the prompt payment of all debts and funeral expenses.* This ensures that such expenses will be considered legitimate deductions from the estate.

3   *Specific instructions on funeral arrangements.* If you wish to be buried in a purple casket, you may include such an instruction in your will. This instruction should also be in the letter of last instructions.

4   *Appointment of a guardian for minor children.* Failure to include this provision means that the guardian will have to be appointed by the court. Although the surviving parent will usually be appointed, the court may require a guardianship bond (a sum of money to ensure that the guardian fulfills the obligation) and an annual report by the guardian on the management of the minor's money.

5 *Appointment of your executor.* You may appoint an individual, such as a friend or a relative, or you can name a bank trust department as your **executor.** Unless you designate the executor, the court will appoint the executor for you. In that case, the person will likely have to post a bond and pay its associated cost.

6 *A statement calling for guardians and executors to serve without bond.* This provision eliminates the expense of bonds for these functions. The savings can be substantial, about $1000 to $1500.

7 *A statement detailing the distribution of property.* Specific articles, such as jewelry or silver pieces, may be left to designated individuals. If a friend or relative is to be left an amount of money, this bequest can also be specified in the will.

Naming an Executor As we indicated earlier, the person selected as executor should be capable of settling an estate, that is, of making sure that all legal documents are filed, that tax returns are prepared, and that the things you own are distributed to the beneficiaries in the way you specified. The responsibilities include:

1 Locating the will and filing with the court to probate the will

2 Locating and inventorying safe-deposit boxes and bank accounts

3 Administering all assets of the estate

4 Determining whether adequate insurance is in force

5 Filing claims for insurance benefits

6 Filing state and federal income tax forms for the portion of the year the deceased person was alive

7 Filing state and federal fiduciary forms on the estate's income

8 Preparing federal estate and state inheritance tax forms

Updating Your Will You are, of course, free to change your will at any time. You should definitely reevaluate your will when any of the following events occur:

1 *Change in marital status.* If you get married or divorced, or if your spouse dies, changes are undoubtedly necessary.

2 *Birth of children.* Failure to change a will after children are born may create problems.

3 *Change in state residence.* Differences in state laws may necessitate changes. This is particularly true if you move to or from a so-called "community property" state, that is, a state that treats all assets of a husband and wife as belonging equally to each.

4   *Accumulation of capital.* The will you made when your estate totaled $10,000 may be inappropriate when it reaches $100,000.

5   *Loans to relatives.* Money lent to a family member cannot be forgiven unless the will contains a specific provision to that effect. Failure to make such stipulation will force the executor to collect the debt, even if your intent was that the obligation should be canceled on your death.

6   *Change in beneficiaries.* If you elect to change beneficiaries of your estate, the change you must make by writing a new will or updating your existing will with a **codicil** (the legal term for an addition to an existing will).

7   *Death of a guardian, trustee, or executor named in the will.* Should any of these parties to a will die, you must write a new will to appoint a new individual to the position.

Letter of Last Instructions

In the discussion of financial records back in Chapter 2, we stated that a **letter of instructions** should accompany a will. The letter simply provides information which will assist the executor of the estate. Updating a letter to reflect changed circumstances does not require legal assistance. The letter should include the location and identifying numbers for:

1   Bank accounts

2   Life insurance policies

3   Automobile title

4   Deeds to real estate

5   Prior income tax returns

6   Canceled checks

7   Stock brokerage accounts

8   Mutual fund accounts

9   Other insurance policies

10   Location and contents of safe-deposit box

When you have finished the letter, send copies of it to your attorney and your executor, and also place one in your safe deposit box. Attach another copy to a copy of your will and keep the original of the letter in a convenient place—perhaps a desk drawer or file cabinet at home. Having copies of the letter in several places will help to ensure that your instructions will be available when they are most needed.

One final point: The letter of instructions with supporting appraisals of your property may help to reduce your estate taxes. The value of the estate may be difficult to determine, particularly when it consists heavily of personal property which may be appraised quite differently by two individuals. When the Internal Revenue Service is setting the value of an estate, you can be sure that it will be very generous in appraising such items. If you have a personal inventory, with supporting appraisals, included with your letter of instructions, the IRS will most likely accept those values.

Property Ownership   The way in which property is owned can have a significant impact on both estate tax liability and the ease with which property is distributed to heirs. Property, of course, may be owned individually. In that event, it will be subject to estate taxes if the amount is large enough, and it will be subject to probate. The probate process can be avoided through some of the forms of joint ownership. Three types of joint ownership are discussed in the following paragraphs.

Tenants by the Entirety   **Tenants by the entirety** is restricted to a husband and wife and can be used only for real estate. The real estate may not be sold or transferred without the agreement of both the husband and the wife. Upon the death of one spouse, the property will pass to the surviving spouse. That transfer of ownership is completely unaffected by the will of the deceased spouse. The property does not pass through probate. However, the portion of the property owned by the deceased is subject to estate taxes if the estate's value is large enough.

Joint Tenancy   **Joint tenancy** is a broader form of joint ownership.

1   The owners do not have to be married to one another, and there can be more than two.

2   Any one of the owners may dispose of his or her share of the property without permission—even against the wishes of the other owners.

3   The property need not be real estate. Other common examples include bank accounts, stock and mutual funds shares, and bonds.

As with tenancy by the entirety, the ownership of the property passes to the surviving owners upon the death of one of them. The deceased owner's share of the property is not distributed by means of his or her will, and it is subject to estate taxes.

Tenancy in Common   Under this form of joint ownership, a deceased owner's share of the property is distributed according to his or her will. The owner's share must be probated. Except for this major difference, **tenancy in common** has the same features as those enumerated for joint tenancy. The limitations of tenancy in common make it appropriate in only a few circumstances.

Proof of Ownership   It is extremely important that jointly owned property have acceptable documentation of each owner's respective investments. The case of Nellie and Sam Farquard illustrates this point. Nellie had received an inheritance of $80,000 from her parents. She and Sam used the money to buy their dream house. Sam died shortly thereafter. Nellie was unable to prove that the entire $80,000 was hers. In the absence of acceptable proof, the IRS included part of the value of the property in Sam's estate. The house legitimately belonged to Nellie and should not have been included in Sam's holdings.

THE PURPOSE OF ESTATE PLANNING

The goal of estate planning is to convey the largest possible estate to your heirs while incurring the minimum tax liability and minimum legal and probate costs. Estate planning is very complex: Consideration should be given even to the future tax liability which may be imposed on your heirs when they die and leave the money they received from you to their heirs. However, recent changes in the tax regulations have greatly reduced the need to consider federal estate and gift taxes. First, the tax rates have been reduced from their previous top rate of 70 percent. Furthermore, they are scheduled to decline even more in future years so that, by 1985, the maximum tax will be 50 percent.

Even more important, today's regulations allow you a substantial tax credit. This permits you to pass on a very large estate with *no* tax. Currently, you can transfer an estate totalling $275,000 without paying any tax. Furthermore, a schedule included in the 1981 tax legislation raises the present tax credit up through 1987. Unless that legislation is revised, beginning in 1987 you can pass an estate totaling $600,000 without incurring any estate taxes. All these changes have the net effect of exempting most estates from federal estate taxes. In 1983, fewer than 2 percent of the estates in this country were subject to taxes. By 1987, if present legislation remains unchanged, fewer than 1 percent of all estates will be subject to taxes. Since estate taxes no longer apply to most estates, we will not discuss them. For those very few individuals who have estates so large that they need to be concerned with these taxes, there are numerous publications on the topic. And if your estate is that large, you will probably want to consult a tax professional about your tax problems.

SUMMARY

1   Retirement planning early in your work career is essential. The earlier you begin to plan, the easier it will be to achieve your goal.

2   The four major sources of retirement income include (1) Social Security retirement benefits, (2) private pension plans, (3) payment from tax-deferred retirement accounts, and (4) general investments.

3   When your pension plan benefits are vested, they become irrevocably yours. The time you must spend to become vested can vary from immediately to more than 10 years.

4   Major advantages to using a tax-deferred retirement account for accumulating money include the following:

Income taxes on the deposits to the accounts are deferred.

Income taxes on the earnings from the money in the account are deferred.

Taxes continue to be deferred until the money is withdrawn from the account.

5   Currently available tax-deferred retirement accounts include (*a*) Keogh plans, (*b*) Individual Retirement Account (IRA) plans, (*c*) salary reduction through 403(b) plans, and (*d*) salary reduction through 401(k) plans.

6   The combination of the number of dollars required in retirement, coupled with the expected length of retirement, determines how large a tax-deferred retirement account you will need.

7   An annuity guarantees that you will receive a fixed income for life. You cannot outlive that income payment.

8   Immediate annuities begin payments immediately, while deferred annuities postpone those payments for an agreed period.

9   When you are liquidating investments, the ideal is to plan the payments from those investments so that when you die, the investment is exhausted.

10   Having a will is essential for most people. Those who die without one are said to die intestate.

11   Probating a will means having a court review an individual's will after his or her death.

12   A letter of last instructions is an informal statement designed to assist the person who is the executor to settle the estate.

13   The three major types of joint ownership are (*a*) tenants by the entirety, (*b*) joint tenancy, and (*c*) tenancy in common.

14   Currently, individuals are allowed a very large credit against federal estate taxes; the net effect is that most estates pay no taxes.

REVIEW YOUR UNDERSTANDING OF

Employee Retirement Income
  Security Act (ERISA)
Employer's pension plan
  Defined-benefit pension
  Defined-contribution pension
  Vesting
Tax-deferred retirement accounts
  Keogh plan (HR-10)
  Individual Retirement Account (IRA)
  Salary-reduction plan (403(b))
  Salary-reduction plan (401(k))
General investments
Retirement income needs
Annuities
  Single premium
  Annual premium
  Straight-life

Guaranteed minimum payment
Joint and survivor payment
Immediate
Deferred
Nonliquidating payout plan
Liquidating payout plan
Estate planning
Estate
  Wills
  Intestate
  Probate
  Executor
  Codicil
Letter of last instructions
Tenants by the entirety
Joint tenancy
Tenancy in common

DISCUSSION QUESTIONS

1   What are the major sources of retirement income? Which of them are considered the primary source(s)? Which ones are secondary? Why is it important to begin accumulating those secondary sources early in your work career?

2 Consider the following pension plans:

The defined-contribution plan whereby the employer contributes 5 percent of an employee's salary each year

The defined-benefit plan whereby an employee receives 1 percent of average annual salary for each year of work for the employer.

How is an employee's retirement benefit determined under each of the two plans?

3 What does becoming vested in a pension plan mean? Do you become vested when you start work with an employer? What is the maximum number of years that are required to become fully vested?

4 What are the principal advantages of a tax-deferred retirement account? Why does money accumulate more rapidly in one of these accounts? When must you pay taxes on that accumulated money?

5 Sonya Brooks teaches business courses full-time in a local high school. On weekends and evenings, she does accounting work for several small business firms. Can she qualify for any tax-deferred retirement plans? If so, approximately how many dollars can she contribute each year?

6 What are the major similarities and differences between a 403(b) salary reduction plan and a 401(k) salary reduction plan? Who can qualify for each? Why must the employer offer these plans before you can use one?

7 The retirement benefit under Ajax Products' defined-benefit pension plan equals 1 percent of average salary multiplied by years of service with Ajax. Will the benefit levels adjust for inflation up to retirement? How? Once you retire, will the benefits continue to adjust for inflation?

8 If Ernie Unenlighten knows almost nothing about his employer's pension plan, how can he find out about it? Can he find out about his own benefits under the plan? How?

9 Borris Blum is considering purchasing a single-premium annuity when he retires in 6 months. How will that annuity operate? What are its major advantages?

10 Jane Leisure (now 65) has received two annuity proposals from an insurance salesperson. Both are for a $40,000 single-premium annuity with payments beginning when she retires in 3 months. She can chose between (a) a straight-life annuity that pays $330 monthly and (b) a 10-year guaranteed payment annuity that pays $320 monthly. What are the strengths of each alternative? Which would you suggest that Jane select?

11 What are the similarities in a nonliquidating retirement payout plan and a liquidating plan? What are their principal differences? What type of person would most likely choose each of the two plans?

12 Why should most people have a will? Why do you think many people do not have one?

13 What does dying intestate mean? Who decides how your financial affairs are to be closed? What are the problems associated with dying intestate?

14 What are the major duties of the person an individual names as executor? What qualities should he or she have?

15 What changes may require that a will be updated? List three situations that might necessitate updating a will and the reason(s) the change is needed.

16 What are the similarities and differences between the following three types of property ownership:

Tenants by the entirety

Joint tenancy

Tenancy in common

Can you describe a situation where each type might be appropriate?

17   Why are strategies for reducing federal estate taxes no longer a concern for many estates? Will this trend likely continue or abate over the next several years?

18   In 1983, when this book was written, how large an estate could you pass to your survivors without incurring federal estate taxes? How large is that estate scheduled to be by 1987? Will many estates be subject to estate taxes after 1987?

PROBLEMS

21-1   Brad Leftwich is about to retire after 20 years with Gray Service Company. The company's pension plan pays 1.3 percent of average salary for each year an employee has been with the firm. Average salary is based on the highest 3 years of earning during the employee's last 5 years with the firm. Brad's earnings record shows:

CURRENT YEAR	1 YEAR AGO	2 YEARS AGO	3 YEARS AGO	4 YEARS AGO	5 YEARS AGO
$14,990	$13,000	$14,600	$12,200	$14,400	$17,000

a   What is Brad's pension benefit?

21-2   Maude Mobile has accepted a position with Wonder Cookie Company. In the past, she switched jobs every 4 to 6 years. Wonder's pension plan has the following provisions for vesting:

Before 5 years' service, no vesting

After 5 years' service, 25 percent vested

Every year of service after 5, 5 percent additional vesting

After 10 years, every year of service, 10 percent additional vesting

100 percent vesting after 15 years of service

a   If Maude leaves after 4 years, what vesting will she receive? After 9 years? After 12 years?

b   Assume that she leaves after 9 years. Wonder's pension benefit will be:

$$\$1,386 = \$14,000 \times 1.1\% \times 9 \text{ years}$$

$$\frac{\text{Pension}}{\text{benefit}} = \frac{\text{Average}}{\text{salary}} \times \frac{\text{Percent}}{\text{replaced}} \times \frac{\text{Years of}}{\text{service}}$$

Will Maude receive that entire benefit? Why or why not?

21-3   Mel and Morris both started in similar positions in 1976 and have earned similar salaries since then. Their earnings have been:

	1983	1982	1981	1980	1979	1978	1977	1976
Mel	$15,400	$14,300	$13,200	$12,200	$11,300	$10,500	$9,700	$9,000
Morris	15,400	14,300	13,200	12,200	11,300	10,500	9,700	9,000

Mel's pension plan averages all the employee's earnings to compute average salary. It pays 1.3 percent of that average for each year of service. Morris's pension plan uses the highest 3 years from the final 5 years with the employer to compute average salary. It pays 1.2 percent of that average for each year of service.

a What is Mel's pension benefit? Morris's benefit? (Assume both individuals are 100 percent vested.)

b Mel argues that his pension plan is better because it uses 1.3 percent to compute the employee's benefit. Do you agree? Why?

c In a period of very high inflation and rapidly rising salaries, which plan would you favor? Why?

21-4 Zelda Prof (whose current marginal tax is 40 percent) is completing the details of her retirement plan. She estimates her 403(b) tax-deferred retirement account must provide $2000 each year of her projected 25-year retirement period. On the basis of her present age, she believes she will have approximately 20 years to accumulate money in the tax-deferred account. During that accumulation period, the account will earn 9 percent. She expects inflation to average 4 percent.

a What balance should she have in her tax-deferred account at retirement?

b What annual amount should she contribute to her tax-deferred account?

c Does the nominal interest rate or the real return call for the largest annual contribution? Why?

21-5 Conrad Confused (still single) needs help with his retirement plan. At this point:

His current preretirement income is $20,000.

Based on Conrad's earnings record, his employer's pension plan will provide an annual benefit of $2000.

a What part of Conrad's retirement needs must be provided by his tax-deferred retirement account? (*Hint:* Exhibit 13-9 will help with Social Security.)

b If he expects his retirement to extend 20 years, how large a balance will he need in his tax-deferred retirement account?

21-6 Fred Freedom plans to retire in several months. He wants to develop a retirement payout plan for the $40,000 he has in his tax-deferred account. He thinks he can earn an 8 percent return on his investment alternatives. Fred expects his retirement will likely continue for 20 years.

a If Fred establishes a nonliquidating payout plan, what annual payment will he receive?

b What annual payment will a liquidating payout plan provide?

c A friend, who is an insurance salesperson, has suggested a straight-life, single-premium ($40,000) annuity that pays $3860 annually. What are its advantages?

d Which option would you recommend? Why?

CASE PROBLEM

Len and Peg Latestart have begun to worry about where their income will come from when they retire in 20 years (when they will both be 65). They both have full-time careers with excellent salaries; each earns $25,000, giving them a combined income of $50,000. Because of that sizable income, they have never really done any retirement planning for several reasons. First, both have always been covered by Social Security. Since they have paid a large amount into that system over the years, they naturally expected they would each receive a "very large" retirement benefit. Second, they always considered retirement to be such a distant goal that probably planning just wasn't worthwhile. Consequently, retirement plans have always been "tomorrow's goal" in their financial plan. But, with retirement approaching in only 20 years, they have become increasingly concerned.

During their working careers, both Len and Peg have changed positions several times. Because of having done so, their only vested pension benefits are those under their current employers' plans. While each of them is covered by a pension plan, the respective details are quite different:

COVERED PERSON	LEN	PEG
Years of service	5 years	5 years
Current vesting	100%	100%
Benefit payment	$14 per month for each year of service	1% of "average salary" for each year of service
"Average salary"	Not applicable	$22,000
Reduction in benefit for early retirement	5% drop for each year before age 65	5% drop for each year before age 65

Len and Peg expect they will likely stay with their present employers until they retire. At that point, each of them will have accumulated 25 years of service.

With their substantial combined income, the Latestarts have always faced a considerable income tax burden. This year, their marginal tax rate is 40 percent. In part because of that high rate, Len and Peg have never saved for their retirement. They always said, "You lose so much of the investment's earnings to taxes, it probably is not worthwhile." Len's employer offers a salary-reduction plan (a 401(k) option) to all employees who want to participate. The plan allows employees to set aside up to 6 percent of their salaries each year under the plan. On the basis of his $25,000 salary, the personnel office told Len he could reduce his salary up to $1500 annually. But he never pursued the issue. The investment options offered under the salary-reduction plan currently provide a 9 percent rate of return.

Neither Len nor Peg has started an IRA, but they know that many financial institutions in their area offer them. Those accounts are now paying 9 percent rate of return. In designing a retirement plan, Len and Peg have established the following guidelines:

They want to maintain a standard of living in retirement similar to their present standard.

Their retirement period will likely extend for 25 years if they retire at age 65.

Currently, inflation is averaging 5 percent, and they expect it to continue at that level.

They want to consider the options of retiring at age 65 and at age 62.

1   At retirement, what income will Len and Peg need to maintain their present living standard?

2   Approximately how large a Social Security retirement benefit will Len and Peg each receive at age 65? At age 62? (*Hint:* Exhibit 13-9 may help.)

3   What pension benefits will Len and Peg receive if they retire at age 65? At age 62? (*Hint:* Reduce their years of service and the pension benefit for early retirement.)

4   How well does Peg's pension benefit adjust for inflation up to the time she retires? How well does Len's plan adjust for inflation? How will their pension plans adjust for inflation after retirement?

5   If they are to retire at age 65, what total balance will they need in their tax-deferred retirement account? What balance would they need at age 62?

6   To accumulate the balance you suggested in question **5**, would you suggest general investments or some tax-deferred retirement account? Why?

7   In order to retire at age 65, what annual contribution must Len and Peg make to their tax-deferred retirement account to accumulate the total balance you computed in question **5** if that account earns the current prevailing real rate of return? What annual contribution would be needed for them to retire at age 62? Had you used the nominal rate of return rather than the real return, would the required annual contribution increase or decrease? Why?

8   Are there any tax-deferred retirement options for which Len and Peg can qualify? Which one(s) would you recommend? Why?

INDEX